| | |
|---|---|
| NCD | negotiable certificate of deposit |
| NPV | net present value |
| $(OL|T)$ | coefficient of operating leverage, given $T$ (output) |
| $P$ | price per unit of output |
| $P$ | value of one payment of an annuity |
| $P_0$ | principal at Time zero |
| $P_i$ | probability of occurrence of $f_i$ |
| $P_n$ | net proceeds per share |
| $P_t$ | price at the end of Year $t$ |
| $P/E$ | price/earnings multiple (or ratio) |
| $R$ | dividend payout ratio (valuation models) |
| $r$ | holding period yield (actual, observed, or computed) |
| $R_i$ | expected rate of return from Asset $i$ |
| $R_f$ | rate of return on a risk-free asset |
| $R_m$ | expected rate of return on the market index |
| $R_p$ | expected rate of return on the portfolio |
| RANPV | risk adjusted net present value |
| ROI | return on investment |
| $S$ | subscription price per share (rights offering) |
| $S_n$ | compound amount, or sum, of an annuity consisting of $n$ payments |
| $\sigma$ | (lower case Greek sigma) standard deviation |
| $\sigma^2$ | variance |
| $\sigma_i$ | standard deviation of Security $i$ |
| $\sigma_{ij}$ | covariance between Securities $i$ and $j$ |
| $\sigma_{\text{NPV}}$ | NPV standard deviation |
| $\sigma_p$ | portfolio standard deviation |
| $\Sigma$ | (upper case Greek sigma) sum of |
| $T$ | number of units of output produced and sold |
| $t$ | corporate tax rate |
| $t$ | time span — number of years over which principal earns compound interest |
| TCS | target capital structure |
| TOTE | trading on the equity |
| $V$ | variable cost per unit |
| $V$ | theoretical or intrinsic value |
| $V_d$ | market value of firm's outstanding debt |
| $V_e$ | market value of firm's equity |
| $V_f$ | total market value of firm |
| $V_{i,n}$ | table value corresponding to interest rate ($i$) and number of annuity payments ($n$) |
| $V_l$ | market value of the levered firm's cash flows |
| $V_{\text{NPV}}$ | NPV coefficient of variation |
| $V_t$ | coefficient of variation |
| $V_u$ | market value of the unlevered firm's cash flows |
| $X_i$ | percentage of portfolio invested in Financial Asset $i$ |
| $Y$ | EBIT (earnings before interest and taxes) |
| YTM | yield to maturity |

Fundamentals of
MANAGERIAL
FINANCE

2d Edition

# Fundamentals of
# MANAGERIAL
# FINANCE

Raymond P. Neveu
Professor of Finance
University of Southern Maine

Published by
**F11** **SOUTH-WESTERN PUBLISHING CO.**

CINCINNATI    WEST CHICAGO, IL    DALLAS    PELHAM MANOR, NY    PALO ALTO, CA

# PREFACE

This book was designed and written for use in fundamental managerial finance courses. The first edition was used primarily in the first finance course taken by undergraduate business majors and in MBA programs that provide background courses for those students who have no prior exposure to managerial finance. In addition, portions of these materials have been used in executive development seminars. This second edition is intended for the same courses.

## The Teachability Goal

My goal in writing this book was to produce a managerial finance text that students would find both readable and understandable and that instructors would find teachable. Classroom use, student evaluations, and adopter comments have confirmed the attainment of this goal. Thus, when the time came to revise the manuscript, careful attention was paid to maintaining these desirable qualities in preparing chapter revisions; in addition, new chapters were designed, written, class tested, and revised with these qualities in mind.

## The Flexibility Goal

Flexibility became an additional goal for this second edition. This means giving the instructor a number of options in terms of deciding which chapters are to be assigned, the order of material coverage, the amount of financial theory to be introduced, and the mix of problems and/or cases to be assigned. A number of casebooks were used successfully in conjunction with the first edition. The book was also used without cases; the end-of-chapter materials were, and are, sufficient for this purpose. The flexible nature of this text is further described below. However, the lecture notes in the instructors' manual contain a chapter-by-chapter discussion of the options available in designing the course syllabus. By itself, this edition contains enough material for a one-semester or two-quarter course. The addition of a case book provides enough material for two semesters or three quarters.

**The Unifying Concept**

Maximizing shareholder wealth within a set of corporate risk-return characteristics is the unifying concept of this text. The opportunities and problems that confront financial managers and the decisions they must make are developed and explained within the framework of increasing shareholder returns and the accompanying risks that must be assumed. The concept of risk is itself examined repeatedly; traditional *total risk* as well as the modern portfolio concept of *systematic risk* are both explained. The implications of these alternative concepts of risk are identified and numerous applications of each are provided.

**The Role of Examples**

This text contains a large number of examples; they are intended to serve collectively as an important pedagogical tool both in and out of class. Some examples illustrate theoretical points, others explain computational procedures and techniques, and some examples describe current practices. The corporations that provided example data are identified wherever possible. In some cases, composite or typical practices are described, or the data are simplified for expository purposes. In these situations, corporate identity has been deleted.

**Student Preparation**

The materials in the text are fairly well self-contained. Students need to know some algebra. A course in accounting would help by providing some knowledge of financial statements. Some statistics is used, especially in Chapters 12, 16, and 17. However, all the needed statistical basics are explained in these chapters.

**Changes in the Second Edition**

The text has been expanded to 25 chapters organized into eight parts. The materials are intended to provide instructors with a large amount of flexibility in deciding the order and extent of material coverage. Additional end-of-chapter problems have been added to almost every chapter. The Glossary has been expanded. In addition, answers to selected end-of-chapter problems are included at the end of the book.

PART 1: INTRODUCTION. Chapter 1 contains added material on how risk affects the goal of corporate shareholder wealth maximization. The macroeconomic data used to explain the firm's operating environment in Chapter 2 have been updated; in addition, the section on depreciation and taxes has been rewritten and now includes some ACRS materials.

PART 2: FINANCIAL ANALYSIS AND PLANNING. The financial statements in Chapter 3 have been updated, and the funds statement is introduced earlier in the chapter. Additional explanations have been added to the budgeting techniques of Chapter 4. Some parts of Chapter 5 have been rewritten to improve clarity; the latter part of this chapter contains new materials that introduce the student to investment-financing decisions. Chapter 5 provides needed procedures for evaluating the expansion-financing problems contained in Chapter 15.

PART 3: WORKING CAPITAL MANAGEMENT. The examples in Chapter 6 have been updated and a discussion of the cash-to-cash cycle has been added. Chapter 7, Management of Current Assets, contains new sections dealing with money market mutual funds, money market strategies, and the implications for the management of corporate marketable securities. The section that deals with evaluating alternative credit terms has been rewritten. Chapter 8, Management of Current Liabilities, has been shortened with the deletion of some materials dealing with cash budgeting and revolving credit agreements. New materials deal with money market loans and the use of prime rates in pricing commercial and industrial loans. This Part can be covered immediately after Part 2; alternatively, Part 3 can be assigned after any of the subsequent sections have been covered.

PART 4: CAPITAL BUDGETING. Chapter 9, Mathematics of Finance, and Chapters 10 and 11, dealing with capital budgeting under conditions of certainty, have undergone some minor changes suggested by reviewers. Chapter 12, Capital Budgeting under Conditions of Risk, has been largely rewritten and now contains a Hiller type approach to risky capital budgeting. This group of chapters can be assigned any time after covering Part 1. Part 4 should be covered before assigning Part 5.

PART 5: VALUATION, COST OF CAPITAL, AND CAPITAL STRUCTURE. Chapter 13, Valuation, has undergone some changes intended to improve the students' understanding of the rationale behind the intrinsic value of financial assets. A number of new explanations have been added to Chapter 14, Cost of Capital. These additions provide links between the specific cost of capital measurements and the intrinsic value models of Chapter 13. Chapter 15, Capital Structure Planning Techniques, uses the additional materials added to Chapter 5 and presents a more extensive explanation of investment-financing decisions.

PART 6: CAPITAL ASSET PRICING AND MANAGERIAL FINANCE. The two chapters that constitute this part are new and contain an introduction to capital asset pricing theory and its applications to managerial finance. Chapter 16 develops the theory through security market lines; the needed statistics are explained as used. Chapter 17 begins with a summary of the Chapter 16 theory and then presents applications to capital budgeting, cost of capital, and capital structure planning. The chapter concludes by explaining the complications that are introduced in the presence of risky debt and bankruptcy costs. Taken together, these two chapters contain the most extensive development and explanation of capital asset pricing theory and applications found in any basic managerial finance textbook. The subsequent chapters in this text do not depend on Part 6 being covered. Thus,

Part 6 can be assigned after covering the desired sections of Parts 7 and 8. Part 6 should be preceded by a coverage of the major ideas found in Parts 4 and 5.

PART 7: LONG-TERM FINANCING. The five chapters in this section have had their data and examples updated. New developments in bond and preferred stock provisions are contained in Chapter 19. The leasing section of Chapter 21 has been updated to reflect developments in financial or capital leases.

PART 8: SPECIAL TOPICS IN MANAGERIAL FINANCE. Some new materials have been added to International Financial Management, Chapter 23. Some recent developments in merger activity have been added to the Chapter 24 discussion of mergers and acquisitions. Chapter 25, Failure and Bankruptcy, has been updated to reflect current legislative developments in this area.

**The Study Guide and Supplement**

The student supplement for this text has been greatly expanded. A large number of problems have been added. More important, however, the basic structure of the chapters has been modified, and each of the 25 chapters, corresponding to the textbook chapters, contains the following materials:

1. An introduction that identifies the major points of the chapter
2. A complete sentence outline of the chapter
3. Review questions
4. Primary and supplementary problems
5. Answers to review questions
6. Solutions to primary problems (Solutions to all supplementary problems are given at the end of the study guide.)

**The Instructor's Manual**

A number of important changes have occurred in this manual. There is a chapter corresponding to each textbook chapter. The format for these chapters is as follows:

1. Introductory notes on the chapter materials
2. A chapter outline
3. Teaching notes
4. Answers to end-of-chapter questions in the textbook
5. Solutions to end-of-chapter problems in the textbook

In addition, the instructor's manual contains an extensive test bank of objective questions. A set of transparency masters has also been added.

**Acknowledgments**

A large number of people contributed to the success of the first edition and to the improvements contained in this revision. Thanks must first be extended to the adopters who ultimately made this revised edition possible. Second, I would like to extend my appreciation to the many individuals who provided comments, reviews, and suggestions, on both the first edition and on the draft second edition. Realizing that some important contributors may be inadvertently omitted, I should like to thank the following individuals for their contributions:

Brian Belt, University of Missouri—Kansas City
Robert Brown, Penn State University—Capitol Campus
Philip Glasgo, Xavier University
George Hartman, University of Cincinnati
G. Bradlee Hodson, University of Southern Maine
John Houlihan, University of Southern Maine
James Johnson, Bentley College
Ruel Kahler, University of Cincinnati
Blair Lord, University of Rhode Island
James Owens, West Texas State University
Richard Sprinkle, University of Texas at El Paso
Howard Van Auken, Iowa State University
Jerry Viscione, Boston College

Thanks must also be extended to Carl Labbe and John Hebert for their editing and research help. In addition my appreciation for word processing of the various manuscripts is extended to Terry Devilin, Samantha George, and Margaret Noyes.

My greatest debt of gratitude, and the dedication of this text, goes to Dee Best whose encouragement and endless patience and understanding make all things possible.

*R. P. N.*

# TABLE OF CONTENTS

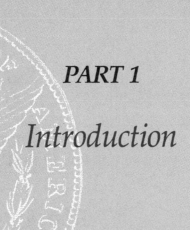

# PART 1

# Introduction

Part 1 contains an introduction to managerial finance. Chapter 1 defines managerial finance and explains the objectives of corporate financial management within the context of risk and return. This chapter also outlines the historical development of finance as a separate area of managerial specialization and summarizes the organization of the text.

Chapter 2 discusses the operating environment of corporate financial management and explains how the corporation is challenged by this environment in seeking to meet its goals. Special attention is focused on the importance of financial markets to financial managers.

# CHAPTER 1

## Scope and
## Methodology
## of
## Managerial Finance

*This text is about finance in general and managerial finance in particular. Most people use the word* finance *in the context of financing a purchase. A new home, for example, is financed with a mortgage. Or the federal government* finances *its expenditures with taxes and borrowed money. Finance as an area of study and managerial finance (or financial management) as a major business function, however, are much broader in scope than the financing activities described above.*

*As a consequence, the first sections of this chapter explain the meanings of finance and of financial management. These sections also discuss the overall objectives of profit-seeking corporations and relate these objectives to the goals of financial management. Other sections trace the evolution of financial management as a distinct area of study and present a brief overview of this text.*

## FINANCE AS AN AREA OF STUDY

What exactly is managerial finance, and what are the major responsibilities and duties of financial managers? The answers to these questions require an understanding of the role of capital in the world of business. Capital is essential to the operation of a business, and managerial finance is defined in terms of the relationships between capital and the firm.

**The Central
Role of Capital**

In order for a new firm to begin producing and selling its goods and services, it must obtain a certain amount of financing to meet the operating costs it expects to incur before sales revenues materialize. This initial financing consists of funds provided by the firm's owners and loans obtained from its creditors. Subsequent financing needs are met at least in part from the after-tax profits the firm earns. The financing provided to the firm, whether it is internally generated profits or externally generated from owners and creditors, constitutes the firm's capital sources and is recorded on the right-hand side of its balance sheet.

The capital thus acquired is used to hire personnel, to obtain office and manufacturing facilities, inventories, and other assets, and is spent on producing the goods and services to be offered for sale. The resulting assets constitute the firm's capital uses and are listed in the left-hand side of its balance sheet.

The balance sheet thus contains the firm's sources and uses of capital; the balance sheet records these values at a particular point in time. To complement the balance sheet, the firm records the results of its operations during a period of time, such as a year, in its income statement. This statement lists the firm's revenues generated, expenses realized, and profits earned over a span of time and provides a measure of the ability of the firm to manage its capital sources and uses. These two financial statements picture a firm as financing itself with capital sources and putting capital to various uses in generating revenues and profits.

**Managerial
Finance and
Capital**

Capital sources and uses must be carefully managed if the firm is to be profitable for its owners, and financial management is the specialized business function that deals with this problem. In general, **managerial finance** is defined as the management of capital sources and uses so as to attain a desired goal. **Capital** consists of items of value that are owned and used and items of value that are used but not owned. For example, office space that is leased and bank loans are items of value that a firm uses but does not own; similarly, inventories and fixed assets purchased by the firm are items of value that are owned and used by the firm. **Capital sources** are those items found on the right-hand side (or *Liabilities and Equity* section) of a balance sheet. Examples of capital sources are commercial bank loans, bond issues, and equity securities. **Capital uses** are those items found on the left-hand side (or *Assets* section) of a balance sheet. Examples of capital uses are receivables, inventories, and fixed assets.

As an area of study, finance is concerned with two distinct functions: (1) financing and (2) investing. **Financing** describes the management of capital sources. Thus, financing decisions concentrate on the type, size, and percentage composition of capital sources. **Investing,** on the other hand, describes the management of capital uses. Investing decisions, therefore, concentrate on the type, size, and percentage composition of capital uses. The specialized set of management duties and responsibilities that center around both of these functions is referred to as **financial management**.

One additional concept contained in the definition of finance is concerned with goal directed behavior, or the goal orientation, of financial management. Goal directed behavior is not unique to financial managers of profit-seeking corporations. The problems and opportunities faced by a financial manager and the decisions that are made depend a great deal on the purposes or goals of the organization. This text concentrates on the problems and opportunities faced by financial managers of profit-seeking corporations, as well as on the decisions that must be made in the pursuit of their goals.

## OBJECTIVES OF PROFIT-SEEKING FIRMS

A profit-seeking corporation should behave so as to maximize the wealth of its common stockholders. It is important to distinguish between wealth maximization and profit maximization. A person's **economic wealth** consists of money and material economic goods. Included among these economic goods are stocks of profit-seeking corporations. Since ownership of a corporation is vested in its common stock, the corporation is assumed to conduct its business in such a way as to increase the wealth of its common stockholders. (In this text the words *wealth* and *economic wealth* are used synonymously.)

**Stockholder Wealth Maximization**

There are two ways in which the ownership of common stocks can change a person's wealth: (1) dividends can be paid to the stockholder and (2) the market price of the stocks can change. During any period of time, the change in a person's wealth due to the ownership of common stock may be calculated as follows:

1.  Multiply the dividend per share paid during the period by the number of shares owned.

2.  Multiply the change in the stock's price during the period by the number of shares owned.

3.  Add the dividends and the change in market value computed in Steps 1 and 2 to obtain the change in the shareholder's wealth during the period.

In order to maximize the wealth of its owners, a corporation must seek to provide the *largest attainable combination of dividends per share and stock price appreciation*.

LIMITATIONS OF STOCKHOLDER WEALTH MAXIMIZATION. While a corporation may have considerable latitude in setting its dividend policy, it will have much less influence over its stock's price; that is, the corporation can adopt a dividend policy that sets the size and frequency of dividend payments, but the resale price of its common stock is set by the interaction of buyers and sellers in the securities markets. Stock prices will tend to reflect the market's perception of (1) the corporation's ability to earn profits and (2) the degree of risk it assumes in earning its reported and expected future profits.

CORPORATE AND INVESTOR RISK. The ultimate risk that continuously confronts a corporation is the probability or likelihood that it will fail and go through bankruptcy proceedings. In such an event, the owners of the corporation would see their investment become worthless, and the creditors would likely see at least some portion of their loans go unrepaid. The suppliers of the corporation's capital thus share this ultimate risk with the firm.

Short of failure, however, the corporation's owners and creditors face the risk that the corporation will not return to them their required rates of return. If a corporation defaults on a portion of a loan agreement, for example, the creditor may realize a rate of return that, while positive, is less than the agreed upon loan rate. Thus, if investors supply corporate financing when they predict that their actual rates of return will equal or exceed their required rates of return, they face the risk that their actual rates will fall below their required rates. Within this context business failure is an extreme outcome, and **risk** can be defined as the probability or likelihood that actual rates of return will deviate from required rates. When an investor provides capital to a corporation on the basis of the rate of return that the corporation is *expected* to earn, risk is defined in terms of the likelihood of the actual rate of return deviating from its expected value. Later chapters contain procedures for measuring risk in terms of required or expected rates of return.

The goals of profit-seeking corporations are thus stated in terms of shareholder wealth maximization subject to the degree of risk they must confront. In actual practice, corporations express these goals in various ways. In its 1977 annual report, General Cinema Corporation stated that its principal objective is "to create and maximize value for its equity shareholders." In its 1982 annual report, the firm reiterated its primary objective of creating value for its shareholders and stated:

> Management, therefore, has set as its objective for real growth, the expansion of General Cinema's earnings at an average annual rate of 5-10 percent in excess of the inflation rate.

Kollmorgen Corporation provides a different set of corporate goals. This firm has included the following statement in several of its annual reports:

> Our goal is to double sales and earnings every four years and exceed a 20 percent return on shareholders' average equity, while paying approximately 25 percent of the previous year's earnings in dividends.

Chapter 3 explains how to use financial statements in measuring shareholder rates of return. Parts 5, 6, and 7 provide some approaches to measuring both the value of shareholder wealth that a corporation provides for its owners and the risks that confront the corporation and its investors.

**Profit Maximization**

The microeconomic theory of the firm has historically assumed profit maximization as the corporate goal. Thus, when finance first developed as a separate area of study, it was natural to retain this profit maximization goal. As opposed to stockholder wealth maximization, which is a fairly new concept, profit maximization looks at *total corporate profits* rather than profit per share.

LIMITATIONS OF PROFIT MAXIMIZATION. Since profit maximization is measured by looking at total corporate profits rather than earnings per share (EPS), this means that the impact of corporate decisions on stock price behavior is not considered. Profit maximization typically does not take into account the amount of risk that has to be accepted by a firm in attempting to increase profits. Profit maximization does not speak to corporate dividends as either a return to stockholders or to the impact of dividend policy on stock prices.

PROFIT MAXIMIZATION VERSUS WEALTH MAXIMIZATION. Because of the limitations of profit maximization as a corporate goal, stockholder wealth maximization has replaced it as the prime corporate goal. This does not mean that stockholder wealth maximization is a perfect goal, in fact, some critics feel that it is an inappropriate goal for purposes of corporate decision making. Some argue that stockholder wealth maximization is normative, or prescriptive, since it states what corporations *should* be doing when in fact corporations behave quite differently. Others feel that stockholder wealth maximization is incompatible with national economic policy. While both these criticisms contain an element of truth, *stockholder wealth maximization* is by far the most useful corporate goal that has yet been formulated. Throughout the remainder of this text, therefore, this goal serves as a primary guide to financial decision making.

## OBJECTIVES OF FINANCIAL MANAGEMENT

Since the financial manager is first of all a corporate manager, he or she uses the overall corporate goal of stockholder wealth maximization in formulating financial policy and evaluating alternative courses of action. In order to do so, this overall goal is restated to take into account the following specific objectives of financial management:

1. To determine how large the corporation should be and how fast it should grow

2. To determine the best percentage composition of the firm's assets (capital uses)

3. To determine the best percentage composition of the firm's combined liabilities and equity (capital sources)

These three objectives are stated in normative terms; that is, the financial manager attempts to determine what the firm's size and growth rate *should* be, what assets the firm *should* invest in, and what sources of capital *should* be used in seeking the best return for the corporate stockholders.

**Determining Corporate Size and Growth Rate**

The size of a corporation is measured by the value of its total assets. If book values are used, then the firm's size is equal to the total assets listed in the balance sheet. When this approach is used, the firm's growth rate is measured by the yearly percentage change in the book value of its total assets.

The financial manager should recognize that being large and growing larger does not necessarily produce increasing earnings. For example, many corporations that entered the hand-held pocket calculator industry experienced large total asset growth rates for two or three years. However, their profits were drastically reduced, and a number of firms left the industry when price competition drove the wholesale price of calculators down by as much as 60 percent.

**Determining Asset Composition**

As stated earlier in this chapter, assets represent investments or uses of capital that the firm makes in seeking to earn a rate of return for its owners. The most common asset categories are cash, receivables, inventory, and fixed assets. However, financial institutions, such as commercial banks and insurance companies, have somewhat different asset categories. They may list loans and negotiable securities as assets, for example. The percentage composition of a firm's assets is measured by using balance sheet book values. It is computed as the ratio of the dollar value of each asset to the dollar value of total assets.

**EFFECTS OF CHANGES IN ASSET STRUCTURE.** Any change in the percentage composition of the firm's asset structure by altering the dollars committed to any given asset category affects the overall risk-return characteristics of the firm. This is true whether or not the change in the asset composition is intended. For example, the decision to increase accounts receivable by liberalizing credit terms as a way of increasing sales and profits may increase the firm's bad debt losses. This strategy may require a greater amount of risk exposure on the part of the firm, but the managers will presumably base their decisions on sufficiently large forecast profit increases to offset the accompanying increased risk.

Situations can occur where the percentage composition of the assets may change in ways that are neither planned nor desired by the firm. Unsold inventory produced in anticipation of demand that did not materialize, for example, becomes an unwanted investment of company funds. Consequently, this inventory may be sold at a loss in order to put funds into other assets.

The choice of asset structure also affects business risk. **Business risk** refers to that portion of a total risk that occurs as a result of asset structure and operating decisions. The asset structure decision relates to what products and services the firm should produce. Operating decisions (personnel staffing, pricing, and marketing decisions) seek to identify and implement those strategies that will generate profitable sales levels for the firm's products and services. Taken together, the decisions of *what areas of business to engage in* and *how to generate profitable sales* are said to contain business risk. The financial manager is directly involved in asset structure decisions but is not typically responsible for making operating decisions. What is being stressed here is the interaction of these decision-making areas within the concept of business risk.

**WEALTH-MAXIMIZING ASSET STRUCTURE.** The wealth-maximizing asset structure can be described in either of the following ways: (1) the asset structure that yields the largest return for a given risk exposure or (2) the asset structure that minimizes the risk exposure needed to produce a desired return. In either case the financial manager has to recognize that the firm's asset structure is a major determinant of its overall risk-return profile. Share prices and consequently shareholder wealth can be expected to change as the market perceives changes in the firm's risk-return characteristics.

**Determining Composition of Liabilities and Equity**

Liabilities and equity represent the capital sources, or financing sources, that the firm uses to make investments. The most common financing sources are accounts and notes payable, accruals for such items as taxes and wages, loans and debt securities of various maturities, common stock, preferred stock, and retained earnings. Here again, financial institutions might exhibit unique liabilities such as demand deposits, time deposits, and savings accounts. As is done for the percentage composition of assets, the firm's liability and equity percentage composition is measured by using balance sheet book values. It is computed by dividing the dollar value of each liability or equity account by the dollar value of total liabilities and equity. The mix of liability and equity capital is referred to as the firm's **capital structure.**

**EFFECTS OF USING DEBT CAPITAL TO FINANCE INVESTMENTS.** When a corporation finances its investments by using liabilities — including debt capital as opposed to equity capital — the firm and its stockholders face added risks along with the possibility of added returns. The added risk is the possibility that the firm will not be able to pay its liabilities and repay its debts as they mature. This type of risk is a major component of the firm's overall risk-return profile. Stock prices react to corporate financing decisions, as well as to the subsequent ability or inability of the firm to manage its capital sources. The added returns come from the firm's ability to earn a rate of return that exceeds the interest and related financing costs of using liabilities and debt capital. These added returns accrue to the stockholders and may be paid as dividends and/or reinvested by the firm to earn yet additional profits.

A great deal of financial management is devoted to obtaining needed investment capital. The phrase *aggressive liability management* is used to describe the practice of deliberately seeking debt rather than equity capital and consciously accepting the added default risk.

**WEALTH-MAXIMIZING CAPITAL STRUCTURE.** Corporate and stockholder risk which arises from the choice of capital structure is called **financial risk.** The most commonly used measure of financial risk is the ratio of debt to equity. Many financial managers and financial theorists feel that a unique wealth-maximizing percentage composition of liabilities and equity exists for each firm and that the debt-to-equity ratio is a good measure of this percentage composition. Determining this optimum percentage composition is a difficult and imperfectly understood task.

The need to formulate a dividend policy complicates the wealth-maximizing capital structure problem. Dividends are one way of increasing shareholder wealth. However, earnings not used to pay dividends become a financing source for the corporation. Although dividend policy is often identified as a separate finance function, dividend policy and capital-structure management are so interdependent that dividend policy is treated in this text as one aspect of capital-structure planning.

## EVOLUTION OF THE FINANCE FUNCTION

Finance first became a distinct area of study around 1900. Since then the duties and responsibilities of financial management have undergone constant change, and the future promises more of the same. The two major reasons why finance, as well as the other functional areas of business administration, are constantly evolving are (1) the continuing growth and increasing diversity of our national economy and (2) the gradual appearance of new analytical tools that have been adopted by financial managers.

**Finance before 1930: Mergers and Consolidations**

Up to 1900, finance was considered as a part of applied economics. The 1890s and early 1900s produced major corporate mergers and consolidations. In 1899, J. D. Rockefeller formed the Standard Oil Company of New Jersey in order to consolidate the Standard Oil group of companies. J. P. Morgan formed U.S. Steel in 1900 which then controlled 63 percent of the domestic steel industry's capacity and had a capital structure of $1.4 billion. Nothing that big had ever been seen before. Although the formation of U.S. Steel was the biggest merger of its day, there were over 300 other large mergers during this time. Of these mergers, 78 produced companies that controlled over half of the output in their respective industries.

This merger activity required unprecedented amounts of financing. Capital structure management became an important task, and finance emerged as a distinct functional area of business management. It is important to point out that the preparation of accounting statements and accompanying financial analysis was at an early stage of development. Financial analysis was prepared only for internal company use. Outsiders, such as potential investors, had very little published corporate data on which to base their buy-and-sell decisions.

Major technological innovations of the 1920s coupled with Henry Ford's successful introduction of mass production systems in 1913 created entirely new industries such as radio and broadcasting. These new industries produced not only output in large quantities but also earned high profit margins. Financial management began to consider problems of planning and control, especially with respect to liquidity. However, financing these new industries, as well as the capital structure problems of continuing merger activity, brought about the importance of investment banking as a financial industry. Investment banking syndicates helped solve corporate financing requirements by buying up entire security issues. These syndicates then faced the problem of finding ultimate investors for the corporate securities.

**Depression and Recovery: The 30s and 40s**

The stock market crash of 1929 and the subsequent depression produced the worst economic conditions to occur in this century. Between 1929 and 1932 the Dow Jones average of 30 industrial stocks fell 89 percent. The price of U.S. Steel common stock fell from $262 to $21 per share; General Motors, from $92 to $7; and RCA, from $115 to $3. The nation's unemployment rate rose from 3.2 percent in 1929 to a staggering 25 percent in 1933 and stayed above 10 percent until 1941 and the outbreak of World War II.

Bankruptcy, reorganization, and mere survival became major problems for many corporations. Capital structure decisions made years earlier that used debt as a major financing component aggravated corporate solvency and liquidity problems. Financial management took the additional function of planning the rehabilitation and survival of the firm.

These economic conditions brought about federal legislation that established governmental control over many financial practices and prohibited others outright. These same regulations also required the public disclosure of corporate financial data. In most cases it was the first time that corporations made their financial statements available to the public. This allowed outsiders to perform financial analyses of corporate performances, permitted industry and intercompany comparisons, and hastened the rise of security analysis as a major area of finance.

**Finance since 1950**

During the last three decades, our economy has experienced significant periods of real growth interrupted by recessions and occasionally stubborn inflation. One-half of all people employed today work in manufacturing and service industries that did not exist 30 years ago. Much of this rapid economic growth occurred because of the increased rate of technological development. Computer science is perhaps the most obvious example of the extent to which our economy has become dependent on new technologies. Yet the first electronic computer was not built until 1939.

As new industries have arisen and as older industries have sought ways to adapt to technological change, finance has become increasingly analytical and decision oriented. This evolution of the finance function has been marked by the addition of computer science, operations research, and econometrics as tools of financial management. Starting around 1950, techniques were developed for analyzing the risk-return characteristics of corporate investment alternatives. Large amounts of research and analysis went into determining the minimum rate of return on corporate investments that would be consistent with shareholder wealth maximization.

The 1950s also produced what has been called the *"modern" theory of portfolio management.* This theory uses statistical concepts to quantify the risk-return characteristics of holding a group, or portfolio, of securities. A fundamental premise of this approach is that the degree of risk faced by an investor should be measured by evaluating overall portfolio risk rather than concentrating exclusively on the riskiness of the individual securities contained in the portfolio. An entirely new theory of finance, still in various stages of development and refinement, traces its origins to this new approach to portfolio management.

To summarize this section, the evolution of the finance function contains three important points:

1. Finance is relatively new as a separate management function.

2. Financial management as practiced today is decision oriented and includes among its analytical tools quantitative and computerized techniques along with economics and managerial accounting.

3. The continuing rapid pace of economic development virtually guarantees that the finance function will not only continue to develop but also may even accelerate its developmental pace in order to keep up with the increasingly complex problems and opportunities faced by corporate managers.

## ORGANIZATION OF THIS TEXT

One difficult problem in writing a textbook is deciding on the sequence of topics. The choice of topics and how intensively to discuss each one is relatively easy, given that this text is meant for use in introductory finance courses. The problem is thus one of presenting the materials in a way that makes sense to the student. As a result, this text is organized into eight parts. Each part begins with an overview that introduces the central ideas contained in its set of chapters.

Part 1 defines managerial finance, elaborates on the functions and goals of financial management, and discusses the economic, institutional, and tax environments that corporations must consider in making both short-term and long-term decisions.

Part 2 contains a set of techniques that are useful in financial analysis and planning. Some of these techniques analyze the current financial strengths and weaknesses of the firm. Other techniques serve to forecast the financial impacts of alternative decisions.

The chapters in Part 3 deal with the need to meet the short-term liquidity needs of the corporation. They discuss the types of working capital the corporation invests in, the short-term financing sources used to meet these working capital requirements, and the policies used in making these investment and financing decisions.

Part 4 deals with the long-term investment decisions made by corporations. The emphasis is on profitability rather than liquidity. Techniques for evaluating alternative investment opportunities are explained and decision criteria for ranking and selecting long-term investments are presented.

Part 5 contains three interrelated topics. First, the valuation of assets and claims-to-income streams, such as stocks and bonds, is presented. Second, valuation techniques are used in estimating the minimum rate of return a corporation must earn on its invested capital if the goal of shareholder wealth maximization is to be pursued. Third, the impact of changes in a corporation's capital structure on its value is discussed.

Part 6 presents an introduction to the modern theory of finance. Portfolio concepts are used to develop a valuation technique that is then applied to corporate investment and financing decisions.

Part 7 discusses the techniques, strategies, and instruments of long-term financing. Included in this section is a discussion of the securities markets and financial intermediaries that make it possible for corporations to secure external financing. Corporate dividend policy is discussed as a source of returns to stockholders and as a source of internal financing through the retention of earnings.

Part 8 contains some special topics that, while important, do not fit easily into the other sections of this text. The topics it includes are international financial management, mergers, and business failure and bankruptcy.

# SUMMARY

This first chapter has provided an introduction to finance as an area of study and to managerial finance as an important business function. In order to provide clarity of discussion and to avoid subsequent confusion, a number of important terms were immediately defined. These include *managerial finance, capital sources, capital uses, financing, investing, financial management,* and *risk*.

The objective of a corporation was stated as that of shareholder wealth maximization. This goal attempts to take into account both risk and return and is superior in a number of important ways to the traditional economic goal of profit maximization. In seeking to contribute to overall shareholder wealth maximization, financial management uses specific objectives which center around determining the optimum corporate size, growth rate, asset composition, and capital structure.

Finance first appeared as a distinct area of study around 1900 and initially focused on capital structure composition. Short-term liquidity management became a second finance function during the 1920s. During the Great Depression, bankruptcy and reorganization became important considerations. Since 1950, finance has become decision oriented with respect to both asset and capital structure management and also has become increasingly analytical in nature. The tools of the financial manager now include accounting, economics, computer science, and quantitative analysis.

# QUESTIONS

**1-1.** Distinguish clearly between *finance* and *financing*.

**1-2.** Explain what is meant by the corporate goal of shareholder wealth maximization.

**1-3.** What is the meaning of *risk* within a corporate setting?

**1-4.** Why is wealth maximization superior to profit maximization as a corporate goal?

**1-5.** What are the objectives of financial management?

# SELECTED REFERENCES

Anderson, Leslie, Vergil Miller, and Donald Thompson. *The Finance Function*. Scranton, Pennsylvania: Intext Educational Publishers, 1971.

Anthony, Robert. "The Trouble with Profit Maximization." *Harvard Business Review* (November–December), 1960.

Davis, Lance, Jonathan Hughes, and Duncan McDougall. *American Economic History*. Rev. ed. Homewood, Illinois: Richard D. Irwin, Inc., 1965.

Hailstones, Thomas. *Basic Economics*. 6th ed. Cincinnati: South-Western Publishing Co., 1980.

Leffler, George, and Loring Farwell. *The Stock Market*. 3d ed. New York: The Ronald Press Company, 1963.

Weston, Fred. *The Scope and Methodology of Finance*. Englewood Cliffs, New Jersey: Prentice-Hall, Inc., 1966.

# CHAPTER 2

## Operating Environment
### of
## Financial Management

*In making financial decisions that seek to increase the wealth of a firm's owners, a number of important external factors provide essential inputs into the decision-making process. Among these factors, or variables, are (1) forms of business organizations, (2) the economic environment, (3) financial markets and intermediaries, and (4) corporate taxation.*

*This chapter stresses the importance of appreciating the impacts of the operating environment when dealing with specific functions of financial management. However, it is not possible to present all or even most of the details concerning the four variables of the operating environment mentioned above. Entire books have been written on each of these topics, so that an extended discussion is best left to more advanced and specialized financial management texts.*

## CHARACTERISTICS OF BUSINESS ORGANIZATIONAL FORMS

There are currently about 16.5 million business firms operating in the United States. While corporations account for only 16 percent of this total, they earned almost 80 percent of all business profits. Corporations are thus the dominant organizational business form in this country. This text, consequently, concentrates on the financial management of corporations.

**Sole Proprietorships**

A **sole proprietorship** is simply a business owned by one person which has no legal standing apart from its owner. The owner, or proprietor, assumes all the risks of running the business. In particular, the proprietor is faced with unlimited liability. This means that business creditors can look to the owner's personal assets in order to satisfy business claims. In return for assuming these risks, the owner realizes all the profits (or losses) generated by the business. These profits and losses are taxed at personal income tax rates.

Financing the growth of the business is difficult because the proprietorship does not issue debt or equity securities. The proprietor is responsible for meeting the terms of any business loan obtained, regardless of what happens to the business.

Transferring ownership of the proprietorship presents two problems. First, there is no transferable evidence of ownership even though certain licenses may be transferable. Second, measuring the value of the business in order to determine a selling price may be difficult. This is due to the uncertainty of future business income and to intangible factors such as the managerial skills of the current versus the prospective owner.

**Partnerships**

A **partnership** is a business owned by two or more persons. Partnership agreements, which can be filed in most states, have the effect of giving the partnership legal standing.

The owners of a partnership are classified as general or limited partners. General partners have unlimited liability and can enter into contractual obligations that are binding upon the partnership. The extent of liability of limited partners is described in the partnership agreement. Limited partners may not actively manage the business. Some limited partners simply provide capital in return for an agreed-upon share of the profits.

The presence of several partners in a firm allows all of them to specialize in their respective areas of interest and competence. However, management decisions can become more difficult to arrive at because of disagreements among the managing partners.

A major problem with the partnership form is that it is terminated upon the death of a partner and must be reorganized. Arriving at the value of the deceased partner's ownership of the firm can present further problems, especially when it is necessary to buy out the heirs of the deceased partner.

**Corporations**

A **corporation** is a state chartered entity that has a legal existence separate from its owners. As a legal entity, it can sue and be sued. Since the corporation legally exists apart from its owners, it has an indefinite lifetime.

Shares of common stock are authorized when a corporation is chartered by a state. These shares represent ownership of the firm, and transfer of ownership is accomplished by the sale of these shares. Such transfers become relatively easy, given that buyers can be found and a share price is agreed upon.

Corporate owners have limited liability. This means that creditors cannot look to the personal wealth of the owners to satisfy claims against the corporation. If a corporation becomes insolvent or suffers an adverse court judgment, the corporate owners stand to lose no more than the amount of their investment in the corporation.

Corporations can issue securities, such as stocks and bonds, in order to raise capital. Therefore, corporations that are financially sound have access to money and capital markets in order to finance their operations.

In 1983, the federal corporate income tax rate was 46 percent for taxable incomes in excess of $100,000. The tax is lower for taxable incomes of $100,000 or less. Dividends paid to stockholders by corporations are taxable to the owners at personal tax rates. Thus, taxing both corporate profits and dividends is sometimes referred to as **double taxation.** Furthermore, corporations are frequently taxed by the states and municipalities in which they operate.

One additional important characteristic of large corporations is that their managers do not own all or even most of the companies they manage. This separation of ownership and control became widespread at the beginning of the twentieth century. Although corporate managers presumably act in the best interest of the owners, it must be realized that managers have their own personal goals such as keeping their jobs and increasing their salaries or other benefits. Reconciling the goals of owners and managers can thus become a difficult task. For example, if a firm finds itself in a period of financial distress, the managers may concentrate on ensuring the firm's survival as a way of maintaining their employment status rather than seek to maintain or increase returns to owners.

Taking into account the comparative advantages and disadvantages of the three forms of business organization, it is obvious that there is no acceptable alternative to the corporate form for large businesses. Limited liability is vital to the owners since they have little or no control over the decisions made by the firm's managers. The existence of resale markets for corporate shares not only simplifies changes of ownership but also provides one measure of the value of the corporation. The indefinite lifetime of the corporation, coupled with its ability to finance itself by issuing securities, provides access to many sources of capital.

## ECONOMIC ENVIRONMENT

Business cycles, inflation, competition, and governmental regulation are several aspects of the general economic environment that affect the ability of a firm to operate profitably. Financial markets and intermediaries, as well as federal tax laws, are also parts of the firm's economic environment but are discussed separately as a way of indicating their added significance for financial decision making.

This section makes the following point: the economic environment can and does impact on the price of a corporation's common stock. Sometimes, economic events such as severe recessions can reduce a firm's share prices in spite of management's attempts at increasing shareholder wealth. The result is that the rates of return realized by shareholders deviate from their required or expected rates because of developments in the economic environment. In other words, some of the risk that corporations and their shareholders face is attributable to the impacts of the economic environment on the resale prices of corporate common stocks.

**Business Cycles**

The term **business cycle** refers to the recurring patterns of expansions and contractions experienced by the overall economy. Any one business cycle can have up to four phases: expansion, recession, depression, and recovery. **Expansion** is described as a period of rigorous business activity and low unemployment. A subsequent decrease in business activity that results in increased unemployment is referred to as a **recession**. A severe and sustained recession is called a **depression**. The subsequent upturn in business and decrease in unemployment is labeled as a period of **recovery**.

Economists have long argued as to when a recovery becomes an expansion and when a recession becomes a depression. Chapter 1 described the 1930s as a time of depression, and many people refer to that event as the *Great Depression*. Economic activity declined to the point that unemployment stayed above 10 percent until 1941. A popular way of distinguishing between a recession and a depression goes as follows:

When my neighbor is out of work
that's a recession.
When I'm out of work
that's a depression!

**ECONOMIC STABILIZERS.** Since the 1940s, a set of economic stabilizers has been incorporated into the economy. The stabilizers, which seek to prevent recessions from becoming depressions, are:

1. *Unemployment insurance,* which seeks to put a floor on personal income

2. *Fiscal policy* in the form of federal tax cuts and deficit spending, which seeks to increase corporate and personal income and to fight unemployment

3. *Monetary policy,* which seeks to lower interest rates in order to stimulate business activity by lowering borrowing costs

**TURNING POINTS.** Although economic stabilizers have been able to reduce the severity and duration of recessions, business cycles continue to occur. Therefore, economists have looked for ways of forecasting and measuring turning points in business cycles. One turning point occurs when the economy goes from a period of prosperity into a recession. A second occurs when a recession/depression gives way to a period of recovery. To date attempts at forecasting these turning points have not generally been successful. However, some progress has been made in defining a recession in quantitative terms, and from this the duration and severity of recessions can now be measured to some extent. As a result a number of business cycle indicators have come into use that allow business persons to judge the current status and general trend of the overall economy, as well as that of specific industries.

**BUSINESS CYCLE INDICATORS.** A **business cycle indicator** is a measure of the overall business cycle or some component of the business cycle. Some of the more commonly used indicators are the gross national product (GNP), corporate profits, and unemployment rates.

*Gross National Product.* The most widely used overall indicator of business cycles is the **Gross National Product,** which represents the dollar value of the economy's output of final goods and services. Economists generally look to changes in the GNP in identifying different phases of the business cycle.

Table 2-1 contains two sets of GNP figures for the first quarter of 1980 through the second quarter of 1983. The first GNP series, called **nominal GNP** (or *GNP in current dollars*), shows that the dollar value of the economy's output increased almost continuously throughout the period with a decline occuring during Q2, 1980. The second series adjusts GNP figures for price changes and expresses the GNP in 1972 dollars. This adjusted GNP is referred to as the **real GNP.** Economists look to the time series of the real GNP in seeking to identify business cycle turning points. When the real GNP declines for at least two consecutive quarters, the economy is said to be in a period of recession. Using this definition of recession, Table 2-1 shows that a recession began in the third quarter of 1981. The real GNP increased in Q2, 1982, then fell during the final two quarters of that year. The economy began recovering during Q4, 1982. By the second half of 1983, recovery had progressed to the point where the

National Bureau of Economic Research declared that the recession was over, that it had begun in Q3, 1981, and that it ended during Q4, 1982.

| Table 2-1. | **Gross National Product (In Billions of Dollars)** | |
| --- | --- | --- |
| | **GNP (In Current Dollars)** | **GNP (In Constant 1972 Dollars)** |
| **1980** | | |
| Q1 | $2,571.7 | $1,501.9 |
| Q2 | 2,564.8 | 1,463.3 |
| Q3 | 2,637.3 | 1,471.9 |
| Q4 | 2,730.6 | 1,485.6 |
| **1981** | | |
| Q1 | $2,853.0 | $1,515.4 |
| Q2 | 2,885.8 | 1,510.4 |
| Q3 | 2,965.0 | 1,515.8 |
| Q4 | 2,984.9 | 1,495.6 |
| **1982** | | |
| Q1 | $2,995.5 | $1,470.7 |
| Q2 | 3,045.2 | 1,489.3 |
| Q3 | 3,088.2 | 1,485.7 |
| Q4 | 3,108.2 | 1,480.7 |
| **1983** | | |
| Q1 | $3,171.5 | $1,490.1 |
| Q2 | 3,272.0 | 1,525.1 |

Seasonally adjusted annual rates
Source:  *Federal Reserve Bulletin.*

*Corporate Profits.* Table 2-2 contains before-tax and after-tax corporate profits from Q1, 1980, through Q2, 1983. Profits fell almost every quarter during the 1981-82 recession and did not increase until Q2, 1983, providing an indication of the recession's severity. By way of contrast, it is not uncommon for corporate profits to increase during the early stages of a recession and to decline only after a recession has progressed for several quarters.

*Unemployment Rates.* A third major business cycle indicator is the behavior of unemployment rates. During most recessions, unemployment rates do not reach their peak until the end of the recession. This reflects the common business practice of retaining employees when demand first begins to decrease and to defer rehiring until after demand has increased.

Table 2-3, which contains the unemployment rate figures for the same time span, shows that this is exactly what happened during the 1981-82 recession. At the beginning of the recession — Q3, 1981 — the unemployment rate was about 7.2 percent. This rate increased and reached its 10.8 percent maximum value in December, 1982 — the last month of the recession. This was the highest unemployment rate since before World War II and provided evidence of the recession's severity.

| Table 2-2. | Corporate Profits (In Billions of Dollars) | | |
|---|---|---|---|
| | | Corporate Profits (Before Taxes) | Corporate Profits (After Taxes) |
| **1980** | | | |
| | Q1 | $277.1 | $182.9 |
| | Q2 | 217.9 | 146.4 |
| | Q3 | 237.6 | 159.1 |
| | Q4 | 249.5 | 164.3 |
| **1981** | | | |
| | Q1 | $257.0 | $169.3 |
| | Q2 | 219.0 | 138.6 |
| | Q3 | 227.7 | 144.0 |
| | Q4 | 217.2 | 141.6 |
| **1982** | | | |
| | Q1 | $173.2 | $112.9 |
| | Q2 | 178.8 | 117.4 |
| | Q3 | 177.3 | 116.5 |
| | Q4 | 167.5 | 113.5 |
| **1983** | | | |
| | Q1 | $169.7 | $108.2 |
| | Q2 | 203.3 | 127.2 |

Seasonally adjusted rates

Source: *Federal Reserve Bulletin.*

BUSINESS CYCLES AND FINANCIAL MANAGEMENT. From the standpoint of financial management, business cycles are important because of their ability to influence shareholder wealth. A recession may reduce a corporation's earnings per share (EPS) and possibly dividends per share. Periods of expansion can produce opposite effects. Equally important is the tendency of corporate share prices to fluctuate directly with business cycles or to change in anticipation of developments in the economy. Since managers have no direct control over share prices, business cycles can produce situations where share prices and, consequently, shareholder wealth are both decreasing even though corporate profits and dividends

**Table 2-3.** **Unemployment Rates (Seasonally Adjusted Percentages of the Civilian Labor Force)**

| | Q1 | | | Q2 | | | Q3 | | | Q4 | | |
|---|---|---|---|---|---|---|---|---|---|---|---|---|
| | Jan. | Feb. | Mar. | Apr. | May | June | July | Aug. | Sept. | Oct. | Nov. | Dec. |
| 1980 | 6.3 | 6.2 | 6.3 | 6.9 | 7.5 | 7.5 | 7.8 | 7.7 | 7.5 | 7.5 | 7.5 | 7.3 |
| 1981 | 7.4 | 7.3 | 7.3 | 7.3 | 7.6 | 7.3 | 7.0 | 7.2 | 7.5 | 8.0 | 8.4 | 8.9 |
| 1982 | 8.5 | 8.8 | 9.0 | 9.4 | 9.5 | 9.5 | 9.8 | 9.8 | 10.2 | 10.5 | 10.7 | 10.8 |
| 1983 | 10.4 | 10.4 | 10.3 | 10.2 | 10.1 | 10.0 | | | | | | |

Source: *Federal Reserve Bulletin.*

are still increasing. The business cycle indicators of real GNP, corporate profits, and unemployment rates provide executives with a way of interpreting business cycle behavior. However, individual industries may react quite differently to business cycles. The following examples reinforce this point.

**Example:** Table 2-4 can be used to compare the index of automobile production against the total industrial production index during the 1981-82 recession. The first column of Table 2-4 shows that the total industrial production index declined steadily but modestly from Q3, 1981, until the recession ended in the last quarter of 1982. This index decreased 12.3 percent over this time span. However, the automobile production index decreased 24.7 percent from Q3, 1981, to Q4, 1982. These two indices indicate that the impact of the recession was much more pronounced on auto manufacturers than on the nation's total industrial production.

Financial managers in the auto industry were faced with a number of short-term cash management problems that were induced by the recession. The large employee layoffs did not reduce labor costs proportionately because of collective bargaining agreements. Inventories of raw materials and finished cars had to be financed. The substantial fixed costs of the auto industry had to be met. Long-term investment and financing decisions were postponed as the production and sale of new cars continued to decline, and manufacturers offered cash rebates as sales incentives.

**Table 2-4.**   Industrial Production
(In Percentages: 1967 = 100%)

| | Total Industrial Index | Automobile Production Index | Defense and Space Equipment Index |
|---|---|---|---|
| **1980** | | | |
| Q1 | 151.3 | 109.9 | 97.1 |
| Q2 | 145.5 | 93.7 | 97.2 |
| Q3 | 142.9 | 98.2 | 97.2 |
| Q4 | 148.5 | 110.1 | 100.0 |
| **1981** | | | |
| Q1 | 150.3 | 100.7 | 100.0 |
| Q2 | 153.5 | 118.5 | 101.7 |
| Q3 | 154.1 | 108.5 | 102.8 |
| Q4 | 146.1 | 83.9 | 104.9 |
| **1982** | | | |
| Q1 | 141.8 | 70.5 | 106.2 |
| Q2 | 139.4 | 95.1 | 107.5 |
| Q3 | 138.2 | 100.7 | 109.5 |
| Q4 | 135.3 | 81.7 | 113.5 |
| **1983** | | | |
| Q1 | 138.5 | 101.4 | 116.5 |
| Q2 | 144.5 | 109.5 | 117.9 |

Seasonally adjusted annual rates

Source: *Federal Reserve Bulletin.*

**Example:**   The third column of Table 2-4 contains the defense and space equipment production index for Q1, 1980, through Q2, 1983. The value of this index increased slowly throughout the time period; thus, defense and space industry production was not affected by this recession. The primary reason why this industry is insulated from recessions is the long-term nature of defense and space contracts. When the Defense Department or NASA orders a weapons system or a space exploration program into full production, the contractors can expect the production run to last five, seven, or even ten years.

In the defense and space industry financial managers worry much less about business cycles and much more about cost overruns and design changes which may require unanticipated commitments of working capital. Major contractors and subcontractors face long-term investment and financing decisions that shape the ultimate profitability of the contract. Cancellation of a major program may carry with it substantial financial consequences, but this is unrelated to business cycle fluctuations.

**Inflation**

Looking at the overall economy, **inflation** can be defined as the rate of increase in the price level over time. Price increases are inflationary when the price of a product or service increases without an accompanying increase in quality. Since quality and changes in quality are subjective and therefore hard to measure, commonly used inflation indices simply reflect price changes and contain no quality adjustments.

**CAUSES OF INFLATION.** Everyone seems to be an expert when it comes to identifying the causes of inflation. Two favorite targets are increases in the money supply and federal deficit spending. When talking about business and finance, however, more pragmatic causes are sought, and two frequently talked about causes are demand-pull and cost-push. Whatever the causes, individual corporations have little or no control over inflation and must adjust to the inflation rate that confronts them.

*Demand-Pull.* The term **demand-pull** describes a situation in which prices increase because demand for products and demand for inputs increase more rapidly than their supply. This type of inflation can have several causes. Increases in the money supply can lead to higher purchasing levels, and federal income tax reductions can have the same effect. Expectations of further price increases can generate additional demand, thus becoming a kind of self-fulfilling prophecy. To the extent that increases in demand generate additional production and increases in supply, price increases will be limited. Increasing demand will have the most inflationary effect when the economy is near full employment.

*Cost-Push.* The term **cost-push** refers to price increases mandated by increases in the cost of production (other than those arising solely from increases in demand for inputs). For example, increases in labor and material costs may be passed along to the purchaser in the form of higher prices. If the seller wishes to maintain its gross profit percentage on sales, then prices must be raised in proportion to the cost increases.

Attempts on the part of corporations at reversing, or at least minimizing, cost-push inflation have resulted in such things as increased automation—which substitutes capital for labor—and substitution of cheaper materials such as plastic for metal. In spite of these efforts, cost-push has been a major contributor to the overall inflation rate during the last several years.

**MEASURING INFLATION.** Several price indicators that are used to measure inflation are:

1.  A price deflator for the GNP that shows the extent to which nominal GNP increases are due to inflation

2.  The Producer Price Indexes which measure the average price changes received in primary markets by producers of commodities (formerly presented as the Wholesale Price Index)

3.  Consumer Price Index (CPI) which reflects the prices paid by ultimate consumers.

The CPI measures the rate of change of consumer prices in the categories of food, clothing and upkeep, health, recreation, and transportation. Table 2-5 contains the CPI values from January, 1980, through June, 1983. The CPI increased in value during the 1981-82 recession, but the rate of increase slowed considerably toward the end of the recession. This trend in the CPI generally confirmed expectations about continued increases in consumer prices.

**Table 2-5.**  Consumer Price Index (In Percentages: 1967 = 100%)

|  | Q1 | | | Q2 | | | Q3 | | | Q4 | | |
|---|---|---|---|---|---|---|---|---|---|---|---|---|
|  | Jan. | Feb. | Mar. | Apr. | May | June | July | Aug. | Sept. | Oct. | Nov. | Dec. |
| 1980 | 233.2 | 236.4 | 239.8 | 242.5 | 244.9 | 247.6 | 247.8 | 249.4 | 251.7 | 253.9 | 256.2 | 258.4 |
| 1981 | 260.5 | 263.3 | 265.1 | 266.8 | 269.0 | 271.3 | 274.4 | 276.5 | 279.3 | 279.9 | 280.7 | 281.5 |
| 1982 | 282.5 | 283.4 | 283.1 | 284.3 | 287.1 | 290.6 | 292.2 | 292.8 | 293.3 | 294.1 | 293.6 | 292.4 |
| 1983 | 293.1 | 293.2 | 293.4 | 295.5 | 297.1 | 298.1 | | | | | | |

Source: *Federal Reserve Bulletin.*

**INFLATION AND BUSINESS CYCLES.** Up until 1973, inflation and business cycles had a tendency to move together. Inflation would worsen towards the end of an expansionary period, and the subsequent recession /depression would see steady or falling prices. The 1974-1975 and 1981-1982 recessions, however, were exceptions to this behavior, and they may have established a new correlative pattern between inflation and business cycles. The real GNP figures in Table 2-1 defined the six-quarter recession, yet the CPI figures in Table 2-5 show that consumer prices continued to increase in spite of the economic downturn.

The inability of these recessions to dampen prices was apparently due to the cost-push component of overall inflation. Many costs of production had become fixed and could not be lowered. Examples include labor and benefit costs, lease payments for plant and equipment, long-term purchase

[1]Since 1978, the U.S. Dept. of Labor has been issuing two CPIs. The new CPI, which excludes only rural consumers, reflects the buying habits of 80 percent of our population. The first CPI reflects the spending patterns of only 40 percent of our population.

contracts for raw materials, and fixed financing costs of debt instruments. Business executives simply passed these costs along in the form of increased prices. In industries where sales and rebates did occur, such promotions were advertised as being temporary and the "regular" prices were always shown.

INFLATION AND FINANCIAL MANAGEMENT. Learning to deal with inflation is a task that confronts all business executives. Even though it may not be possible to insulate the corporation and its stockholders from the effects of rising costs and prices, there are some techniques that can help financial managers cope with inflation. One solution is to contract for the needed inputs in such a way that the prices paid by the corporation are fixed before the beginning of an inflationary period. Another solution is to use long-term financing, the strategies for which are discussed in later chapters.

INFLATION AND WEALTH MAXIMIZATION. The impact of inflation on wealth maximization is centered on corporate EPS, dividends per share, and share prices. *Nominal* EPS may increase because of inflated corporate sales even though *real* EPS may increase very little. Higher earnings may result in increased dividends. Thus, corporate management may appear to have done a very good job for the owners even though such dividend increases provide little or no increase in real shareholder wealth. At the very least, however, management can be credited with increasing nominal dividends so as to prevent shareholders from suffering a decrease in real dividends.

It was pointed out earlier in this chapter that business cycles can affect share prices. The same must be said of inflation and especially expectations about future inflation. The net result is that share prices may fluctuate adversely because of expectations about the economic environment over which financial managers have no control. Since investor expectations about inflation and recessions have not been consistently correct since 1945, corporations are faced with share price movements that contain an erratic, if not unstable, component. The best that financial managers can do in such situations is to use those strategies that protect the corporation against inflation and wait for a more stable price level to become established. At that time, presumably, share prices will once again react more directly to the earnings and dividends of the corporation.

**Competition**

Industrial concentration and imperfect competition are two general characteristics of the economic environment that can have substantial impacts on the functions and duties of corporate financial managers. **Industrial concentration** refers to the historical tendency of the overall competitive economy to be concentrated in a relatively small number of very large corporations. **Imperfect competition** refers to the competitive conditions that exist in any industry in which prices and outputs are determined principally by the few firms that together dominate that industry.

EXTENT OF INDUSTRIAL CONCENTRATION. Approximately 16 million firms were in business during 1980. The nominal GNP for that year was $2,632 billion, and corporations earned after-tax profits of $149.8 billion. The May, 1983, issue of *Fortune* magazine reported that the largest 500 industrial corporations had 1982 sales of $1,672 billion and after-tax profits of $61.4 billion. (The *Fortune* definition of industrial companies restricts the list to companies that derive at least 50 percent of their sales from manufacturing and/or mining.) Figure 2-1 illustrates the extent of industrial concentration in the manufacturing, life insurance, and commercial bank industries.

Concentration ratios can be computed for any industry. The figures reported here for the manufacturing, life insurance, and commercial banking industries tend to be typical of the economic environment as a whole. In addition, the continuing series of corporate mergers serves to increase the extent of industrial concentration.

EXTENT OF IMPERFECT COMPETITION. The degree of industrial concentration described above has produced a type of imperfect competition called an **oligopoly**. The market structure of an industry is said to be oligopolistic when: (1) a few sellers dominate the market, (2) the firms are interdependent or at least perceive that they are, and (3) the dominant firms have some control over the prices of their output. Examples of oligopolistic market structures are found in the aluminum, chemical, cigarette, computer, copper, motor vehicle, oil, steel, tin can, and tire industries.

Interdependence among competitive firms means that any one firm's decisions as to price, output, advertising, etc., are expected to have an impact on the sales and profits of its competitors, unless they are able to neutralize the decision in some way. Control over price is referred to as **administered pricing.** This means that companies set their price schedules and offer their product lines at the stated prices rather than let prices fluctuate according to supply and demand. One way for administered prices to change is for the industry price leader to announce new price schedules and for the competition to adjust its prices accordingly.

The firms in certain industries, such as aluminum and steel, sell fairly identical product lines. Because of this, there is a tendency for prices to be very close among competitors. In other industries, such as the automobile industry, a great deal of product design and marketing strategy is aimed at convincing the buyers that the competing product lines are differentiated or dissimilar. To the extent that such nonprice competition successfully creates the impression of product differentiation, the competing firms become less interdependent on one another; and each firm gains some independence in pricing its product lines.

COMPETITION AND FINANCIAL MANAGEMENT. The combination of industrial competition and oligopolistic markets has several implications for financial management. First, the desirability of many investment alternatives is directly affected by the competition because the profitability of the investments depends, among other things, on administered prices and a firm's ability to capture and retain the needed market share. When six or

Figure 2-1.  **Industrial Concentration in Manufacturing, Life Insurance, and Commercial Banking**

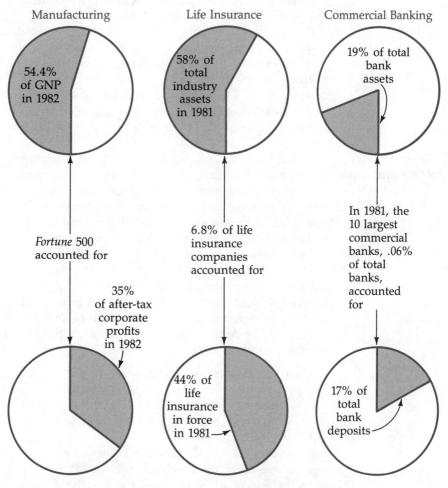

Sources: *Fortune* (May, 1983); *Life Insurance Fact Book* (1982); *Statistical Abstract of the United States* (1983).

seven firms account for 90 percent of total industry sales, capturing additional market share occurs at the expense of a few firms and some reaction from competitors must be expected.

Second, interdependence appears to be of somewhat less importance in corporate financing. The decisions of when to raise capital and how much is needed depend on investment decisions; hence, interdependence affects financing decisions in that respect. However, interdependence does not appear to greatly affect the percentage composition of a firm's capital structure. One firm's decision to raise debt capital, as opposed to equity capital, or vice versa, would appear to have little direct impact on the profitability or capital structure decisions of competing firms. This does not preclude the competing firms from exhibiting similar capital structures, however. When this does occur, the reasons are more likely to be the result of the cost structure pattern that is specific to that industry.

Third, the absence of great numbers of competitors does simplify the problem of judging a firm's performance relative to the industry. It is easy to make comparisons between any two firms; and the reactions of the competition to a new product line, a new advertising campaign, etc., can be evaluated on a firm-by-firm basis. The techniques needed for executing comparative financial analyses of this type are discussed in Chapter 3.

## Governmental Regulation

In a perfectly competitive market, the corporate goal of shareholder wealth maximization is consistent with the maximization of public welfare. The existence of imperfect competition coupled with the occurrence of so-called externalities create conflicts that make it difficult or impossible to maximize both shareholder wealth and public welfare. For example, a **negative externality** is said to occur when a producer acts in such a way as to harm some part of the economy without having to pay the costs of that harm. Firms have polluted rivers, streams, and the atmosphere for years without compensating the other parts of the economy for the poor quality of water and air. The advent of the environmentalist and consumer movements is a reaction to this externality. The result has been regulation, mostly by the federal government through the creation of the Environmental Protection Agency.

**THE REGULATORY ENVIRONMENT.** The regulatory environment includes those agencies that are concerned with externalities, as well as those that regulate the imperfect competition. An extreme case of regulation of imperfect competition concerns natural monopolies such as the natural gas and electric industries. Meaningful competition in these industries is not feasible. Hence, the Federal Power Commission and state and local agencies regulate these producers. In addition, a large number of other agencies affects all businesses. These include the Department of Justice (antitrust), the Department of Labor (equal job opportunities), and the Occupational Safety and Health Administration (employee safety).

REGULATION AND FINANCIAL MANAGEMENT. In addition to the regulatory agencies mentioned above, the financial manager comes in direct contact with several other regulatory bodies. The Securities & Exchange Commission regulates many financing activities of the firm, and the Internal Revenue Service establishes many of the rules used by corporations in recognizing profits and losses. Since commercial banks are a major source of corporate financing and make available many other financial services, financial managers must be familiar with the relevant directives of the Comptroller of the Currency, the Board of Governors of the Federal Reserve System, and the Federal Deposit Insurance Corporation. All of these bodies regulate the commercial banking industry.

Later chapters of this textbook deal with some of the specific regulations applicable to financial management. The important point here is that the regulatory environment affects the profitability and even the feasibility of both investment and financing decisions. As such, it imposes limits on what actions can be taken by financial managers in attempting to maximize shareholder wealth.

## Financial Markets and Intermediaries

Financial markets and the intermediaries that operate within those markets are the most important parts of the operating environment for the financial manager. This section presents an overview of these two topics and provides the student with the financial perspective needed for the rest of the book. Both financial markets and intermediaries are taken up in substantial detail in later chapters.

**Financial Assets**

A **financial asset** is a claim against the income and assets of its issuer. Note that these are assets to the holder of the claim but are liabilities or equity items to the issuer. It is important to realize that a financial asset is not the issuer's income or assets themselves but a claim against those items. A financial asset is given to the purchaser by the issuer in exchange for some valuable consideration, usually in the form of cash or another financial asset. Money, debt, and stock are regarded as financial assets. Money takes the form of cash and bank deposits. Examples of debt include mortgages, Treasury bills, and certificates of deposit. Almost all stock issues that appear as financial assets are either common stock or preferred stock. Individuals, corporations, and governments are all capable of issuing financial assets.

**Financial Markets**

**Financial markets** are said to occur wherever financial assets are bought, sold, or exchanged. Financial markets serve several vital functions for the overall economy as well as for individual corporations. Different segments of the financial markets meet the different needs of the participants. These markets are rather heavily regulated to keep them as competitive as possible and to prevent imperfect competition and market concentration from occurring.

**FUNCTIONS OF FINANCIAL MARKETS.** Financial markets serve three important functions for corporate financial management: (1) they provide a necessary step in the process of capital formation, (2) they help create a resale market for financial assets, and (3) they help set the prices of financial assets. Financial markets also serve similar functions for individuals and governments, but the emphasis here is on corporate activities.

*Capital Formation.* One part of the capital formation process involves corporations that look to financial markets to obtain their needed financing. In this context, capital refers to tangible assets such as plant, equipment, and inventory. Corporations use financial assets in exchange for the money needed to finance these tangible assets. Of course, there are situations where corporations have excess funds that can be used to purchase financial assets of other issuers. In these situations corporations hope to earn a return on their money capital until such time as the funds are needed to finance their own capital formation.

*Resale Market.* Financial markets provide resale markets for previously issued financial assets. This means that the purchaser of a financial asset can exchange it for another or simply sell it for cash rather than wait for it to mature. Since stocks issued by corporations have no maturity date, the purchaser looks to resale markets as a place to sell them whenever it becomes necessary or desirable to do so.

If resale markets did not exist, corporations simply would not be able to raise the billions of dollars needed to sustain the capital formation that goes on continuously in the economy. For example, a particular corporate bond that has a 20-year maturity may be a worthwhile investment, but relatively few purchasers are willing to "lock up" their funds for 20 years with no possibility of converting the bond into cash before the maturity date. There are two reasons for this reluctance. First, cash or another financial asset may simply become more desirable. Second, and perhaps more important, the bond may become less desirable because it has become too risky in the opinion of the bondholder.

*Price Setting of Financial Assets.* Price setting occurs by bringing the supply and demand of financial assets together either at designated physical locations or through the use of modern communications technology. For example, a corporation desiring to sell financial assets, such as a bond issue, finds that it is possible to use securities of similar characteristics that are already present in the resale market in order to set an initial selling price. The subsequent prices of the bond issue are determined by the buying and selling activities in the resale market.

The goal of shareholder wealth maximization requires that increases in shareholder wealth come from dividends and price appreciation of the common stock. The resale market within financial markets is where the price of common is determined. Hence, financial managers use financial markets to raise funds and look to the behavior of share prices in these same markets as a measure of the changes in shareholder wealth.

Finally, it must be pointed out once again that share prices react not only to the actions of individual corporations but also to business cycles, actual and anticipated inflation, imperfect markets, and externalities. Many other influences have been suggested. The net impact is to further weaken the link between corporate performance and share price. Financial managers must simply assume that, although certain components of the operating environment can distort the relationship between corporate performance and share price at any specific time, corporate performance is nevertheless the dominant, though not exclusive, determinant of share price.

**TYPES OF FINANCIAL MARKETS.** Financial markets can be characterized as to (1) whether the assets are being issued for the first time or have previously entered the market and (2) the maturity dates of the assets.

*Primary and Secondary Markets.* When a financial asset is first issued, it appears in that part of the financial markets called the **primary securities market.** The primary securities market is not a physical location. The public sale of a new security issue can be accomplished through a network of security brokers and dealers or through other means. The nationwide broker and dealer network is referred to as the over-the-counter (OTC) market.

When a previously issued security is offered for resale, it appears in the **secondary securities market.** The secondary securities markets consist of organized exchanges and the OTC markets. Organized exchanges are physical locations such as the New York Stock Exchange and the American Stock Exchange. Hence, organized exchanges are strictly resale markets; the OTC market handles both primary and secondary markets.

*Money and Capital Markets.* When a financial asset has a relatively short maturity, it is said to appear and be resold in the **money markets.** Most publicly traded money market assets have a maturity of 12 months or less. Examples of money market securities include Treasury bills and negotiable certificates of deposit.

Financial assets with longer or indefinite lifetimes are said to appear in the **capital markets.** This may be a somewhat unfortunate use of the word capital, but popular usage has prevailed in this instance. Capital market securities include bonds with maturities of greater than one year and common and preferred stocks.

**REGULATION OF FINANCIAL MARKETS.** The regulation of financial markets is due in part to past abuses which shook public confidence in these markets. The regulatory environment seeks to keep these markets as competitive as possible. This allows the prices of securities to reflect the values attached to financial assets by buyers and sellers.

A number of security laws were passed by Congress starting in 1933. These laws created the Securities & Exchange Commission (SEC) and gave it the power to regulate the public sale of securities in both the primary and secondary securities markets. As a result, the organized exchanges and the OTC markets are regulated by the SEC. In addition, the organized exchanges have developed their own regulations, and the National Association of Securities Dealers (NASD) provides self-regulation of the OTC markets.

The Board of Governors of the Federal Reserve System possesses a certain amount of authority over the financial markets because of its regulation of commercial banks and its ability to control the supply of credit available to meet corporate financing needs. Financial managers must be familiar with some of these regulations, especially when corporate financing requires the use of the primary securities markets. Later chapters discuss some of the specific regulations that must be followed.

## Financial Intermediaries

Corporations create a supply of financial assets that they issue in exchange for money capital. **Financial intermediaries** provide the demand for corporate financial assets and, in return, supply the desired money capital.

**INTERMEDIATION AND DISINTERMEDIATION.** The process of transferring funds from savers to ultimate users through a third party is called **intermediation**. This definition has two important concepts. First, the corporation that obtains the funds is referred to as the ultimate user in that the funds are intended for capital formation purposes. Second, the suppliers of funds do not provide them directly to the financing corporation but use a third party that is referred to as the financial intermediary.

When individuals consume less than their income, their savings can be simply buried, invested in capital goods for themselves, or invested by exchanging them for financial assets. Individuals can enter financial markets directly and transact in both the primary and secondary markets. Since transactions in the primary securities markets are one step in the capital formation process, individuals can meet corporate financing needs directly. However, most individual savings are exchanged for the financial assets of financial intermediaries. These intermediaries, in turn, exchange their funds for corporate financial assets. This is the basic idea behind intermediation.

There have been times in the past when certain financial assets, such as Treasury bills, carried very attractive rates of return and caused individuals to withdraw their savings from financial intermediaries and purchase Treasury bills directly. This is intermediation in reverse and is called **disintermediation**.

**FUNCTIONS OF FINANCIAL INTERMEDIARIES.** Financial intermediaries function so as to provide services that are vital to both the individual savers and the financing corporations. These functions are a consequence of their ability to pool funds, provide specialized services, diversify their investments, and achieve economies of scale.

*Pooling of Funds.* Intermediaries gather up, or pool, large amounts of individual savings. This means that corporations can look directly to intermediaries for their financing needs as opposed to seeking out individual savers.

*Specialized Services.* Intermediaries hire experts that specialize in dealing with financial markets and investing. As a consequence, they are able to make informed judgments about the desirability of alternative investment opportunities and recognize the distortive impacts of exogenous variables on the prices of financial assets.

*Diversification of Investments.* The large amounts of funds available to intermediaries allow them to make investment decisions that minimize the risk of loss to individual savers. Few individual investors possess sufficiently large amounts of funds to accomplish this task. Intermediaries can reduce the risk of loss to all individuals whose savings they pool, regardless of the amount of savings provided by each individual.

*Economies of Scale.* The large size of intermediaries, coupled with their specialized knowledge, allows them to perform their functions at a cost that is below what individual savers would incur if each saver performed these functions individually. Such economies of scale can produce higher returns to savers and lower costs to financing corporations.

**INTERMEDIARIES AND FINANCIAL INSTITUTIONS.** Financial intermediaries are often called financial institutions, although these two terms are not entirely synonymous. From the standpoint of corporate financial management, the most important intermediaries are commercial banks, insurance companies, pension and retirement funds, and mutual funds. Other intermediaries—such as savings and loans associations, savings banks, and credit unions—are important sources of financing for individuals rather than corporations.

A number of other organizations provide important services in the financial markets, but they are not intermediaries. For example, securities brokers form *investment banking syndicates* to market corporate financial assets in the primary securities markets. Brokers and dealers also provide the mechanisms for making transactions in the secondary securities markets. Organizations such as these are considered to be marketing institutions that operate within the financial markets. The term **financial institutions** is used to describe the set of firms that provide intermediary and/or marketing functions in the financial markets. Of course, intermediaries deal in the secondary securities markets on a fairly continuous basis. When they do so, they are acting not as intermediaries but as marketing institutions.

## CORPORATE TAXATION

The federal government and a number of states tax corporate profits. Local governments collect property taxes rather than tax corporate profits. The diversity of state and municipal tax laws precludes their discussion here, so attention is focused on selected areas of federal corporate taxation. However, there should be no doubt as to the extensive taxation that corporations face as part of the economic environment.

From the standpoint of financial management, certain aspects of the federal tax laws are of immediate concern while others are best left to tax specialists. For the most part, the portions of the tax laws relevant to financial managers are those that change the corporate tax liability as a result of investment or financing decisions. Therefore, the focus here is on understanding the computation of the incremental tax liability or credit that occurs as a result of making financial decisions. Capital budgeting and financial decisions typically have a tax component, and there are cases where the tax effect can be the critical factor in reaching a final decision.

The treatment of corporate taxes in this chapter is divided into three parts: (1) taxes on ordinary income, (2) taxes on depreciable assets, and (3) other tax situations. Simplifying assumptions are made in order to avoid computational and legal entanglements that would obscure the financial concepts being explained. The procedures presented here are used extensively in later chapters.

**Taxes on Ordinary Income**

Taxable corporate income represents that portion of total revenue that remains after the deduction of operating, administrative, interest, and depreciation expenses. The federal corporate income tax rates for ordinary income in effect in 1983 were as follows:

| Taxable Income | Tax Rate |
|---|---|
| $0 to $25,000 | 15% |
| over $25,000 to $50,000 | 18% |
| over $50,000 to $75,000 | 30% |
| over $75,000 to $100,000 | 40% |
| over $100,000 | 46% |

Note that these tax rates are progressive only until taxable income reaches $100,000. Beyond this income level, the tax rate is constant.

**Example:**   The federal corporate income tax on a taxable income of $106,000 equals $28,510 and is computed as follows:

$$
\begin{aligned}
(\$25,000)\,(.15) &= \$\ 3{,}750 \\
(\$25,000)\,(.18) &= \$\ 4{,}500 \\
(\$25,000)\,(.30) &= \$\ 7{,}500 \\
(\$25,000)\,(.40) &= \$10{,}000 \\
(\$\ \ 6{,}000)\,(.46) &= \underline{\$\ 2{,}760} \\
&\ \ \ \underline{\$28{,}510}
\end{aligned}
$$

As long as these tax rates are in effect, a corporation with a taxable income in excess of $100,000 pays $25,750 in taxes on its first $100,000 and is taxed at a rate of 46 percent on taxable income in excess of $100,000. In this situation, the average tax rate is 25.75 percent on the first $100,000 ($25,750/$100,000). All additional taxable income is taxed at a constant 46 percent. Throughout this text, the assumption is made that ordinary corporate income is taxed at the constant rate of 40 percent to simplify the arithmetic without violating the concept of a constant tax rate.

**Depreciation and Taxes**

Most fixed assets used by a corporation as part of its normal operations decrease in value with the passage of time. Depreciation expenses in the income statement allocate the assets' cost against income for each reporting period. Since depreciation is a noncash expense that reduces the corporate tax liability, depreciation is said to provide a tax shield. Factories, storage facilities, and machinery are examples of depreciable assets. *Land* is an asset that *does not depreciate.*

The Economic Recovery Tax Act of 1981 introduced some major changes in the depreciation methods that corporations (as well as partnerships and proprietorships) use to allocate their investments in depreciable assets against revenues for federal income tax purposes. Congress has amended the act a number of times and will likely do so again. Consequently, depreciation methods are introduced in this chapter only to the extent needed to provide an appreciation of how they affect the time series of the firm's tax liabilities. Later chapters explain how financial managers use these depreciation methods in evaluating the desirability of a firm's investment alternatives.

**ACRS.** The 1981 Tax Act introduced the accelerated cost recovery system (ACRS) for depreciable property placed into service after 1980. The schedules in this system depreciate an asset over a time period shorter than its expected economic lifetime. Under ACRS, assets are depreciated over 3, 5, 10, or 15 years, depending on the type of property involved. Most personal property is in the 5-year class. Some examples of the kinds of assets that fall within each class are as follows.

*Three-Year Property.* This class includes cars, light duty trucks, and special tools.

*Five-Year Property.* This class includes heavy duty trucks, lathes, productionlike machinery, office furniture, machinery and equipment, ships, aircraft, and all personal property not included in other classes.

*Ten-Year Property.* This class includes certain public utility property, railroad tank cars, some depreciable real property, and manufactured residential houses.

*Fifteen-Year Property.* This class contains long-lived public utility property.

The annual depreciation rates for each class are contained in Table 2-6. These rates are also used when a firm acquires used property. In addition, the value of property to be depreciated is not reduced by any expected salvage value.

**Example:** A corporation acquires some office furniture that costs $40,000, has a useful life of eight years, and has an expected trade-in value of $6,000. The furniture falls into the five-year class and the entire $40,000 is depreciated. Using the Table 2-6 rates, the annual depreciation expense, accumulated depreciation, and book value are calculated as follows:

| Year | Depreciation Expense | Accumulated Depreciation | Book Value |
|------|---------------------|--------------------------|------------|
| 0 | 0 | 0 | $40,000 |
| 1 | (.15) ($40,000) = $6,000 | $ 6,000 | 34,000 |
| 2 | (.22) ($40,000) = $8,800 | 14,800 | 25,200 |
| 3 | (.21) ($40,000) = $8,400 | 23.200 | 16,800 |
| 4 | (.21) ($40,000) = $8,400 | 31,600 | 8,400 |
| 5 | (.21) ($40,000) = $8,400 | 40,000 | 0 |

*Recapture.* When an asset that is being depreciated is sold, the firm may realize a gain or a loss depending on the asset's book value relative to its selling price. In computing the gain or loss, no depreciation is taken in the year of the asset's disposition.

*Gain on Disposal.* If the selling price of the asset exceeds its book value, the firm realizes a gain, treated and taxed as ordinary income up to the difference between the asset's original purchase price and its book value. Any additional gain is treated as a capital gain. In the above example, if the office furniture is sold during Year 2 for $38,000, the gain is computed on the basis of the Year 1 book value:

$$\$38,000 - \$34,000 = \$4,000$$

Assuming a 40 percent tax rate, the gain increases the firm's federal tax liability by:

$$(\$4,000)(.4) = \$1,600$$

*Loss on Disposal.* If the selling price of an asset is less than its book value, the difference is treated as an operating expense in the year of the asset's sale, and the firm's taxable income is reduced by the amount of the loss. In the above example, if the furniture is sold during Year 3 for $19,000, the selling price is less than book value and the loss equals:

$$\$25,200 - \$19,000 = \$6,200$$

The decrease in the firm's tax liability equals:

$$(\$6,200)(.4) = \$2,480$$

| Table 2-6. | ACRS Depreciation Rates | | | |
|---|---|---|---|---|
| Year | Three-Year Property | Five-Year Property | Ten-Year Property | Fifteen-Year Property |
| 1 | 25 | 15 | 8 | 5 |
| 2 | 38 | 22 | 14 | 10 |
| 3 | 37 | 21 | 12 | 9 |
| 4 | | 21 | 10 | 8 |
| 5 | | 21 | 10 | 7 |
| 6 | | | 10 | 7 |
| 7 | | | 9 | 6 |
| 8 | | | 9 | 6 |
| 9 | | | 9 | 6 |
| 10 | | | 9 | 6 |
| 11 | | | | 6 |
| 12 | | | | 6 |
| 13 | | | | 6 |
| 14 | | | | 6 |
| 15 | | | | 6 |

*No Gain or Loss.* If the selling price of an asset equals its book value, then there is no gain or loss as a result of the sale. Using the data in the above example, if the furniture is sold in Year 4 for $16,800, the selling price equals the book value and the firm realizes no gain or loss from selling the asset.

**STRAIGHT-LINE DEPRECIATION.** Although corporations calculate depreciation amounts using ACRS for federal income tax purposes, ACRS rules are not used in preparing financial statements intended for shareholders and the public at large. One alternative to ACRS is straight-line depreciation. This procedure reduces the asset's depreciable basis by the amount of expected salvage and divides the remainder into equal annual depreciation amounts over the economic life of the asset. The recapture rules are generally the same as those contained in ACRS; however, under straight-line rules, appropriate depreciation is taken in the year of an asset's disposal.

**Example:**

Some production line machinery is purchased for $1,200,000, has an 8-year economic life, and an estimated salvage value of $150,000. The amount to be depreciated on a straight-line basis is:

$$\$1,200,000 - \$150,000 = \$1,050,000$$

and the annual depreciation is:

$$\$1,050,000/8 = \$131,250$$

If the machinery is subsequently sold for $300,000 when its book value is $393,750, the loss on disposal is:

$$\$393,750 - \$300,000 = \$93,750$$

Assuming a 40 percent tax rate, the firm's tax liability decreases by

$$(\$93,750)(.4) = \$37,500$$

**INVESTMENT TAX CREDIT.** During the last several years, Congress has allowed business firms to realize an investment tax credit (ITC) when investing in certain types of property. The amount of the credit is computed on the value of the property purchased and reduces the firm's taxes payable. For example, a 10 percent ITC on a $90,000 investment would reduce the firm's taxes by

$$(.10)(\$90,000) = \$9,000$$

In addition, the tax credit does not reduce the amount of investment that the firm can depreciate. This allows the firm to write off more than 100 percent of the investment's cost against taxes and taxable income. ITC rates have been changed several times and have been withdrawn and later reinstated.

**OTHER TAX SITUATIONS.** The Internal Revenue Service (IRS) Code specifies the tax treatment for just about every situation. If a corporation's before-tax income is negative for the current tax year, for example, it has some options available that will let it offset the loss against prior years' taxes and obtain a tax refund. It may also be able to carry these losses forward against future taxes.

A second example deals with capital gains and losses incurred on the sale of assets not used by the corporation in its usual line of business. In this case the corporation can realize only limited tax benefits.

A somewhat different example concerns Subchapter S corporations with 25 or less stockholders. The owners of a Subchapter S corporation can elect to be taxed as if each owner were a sole proprietor. All owners declare their pro rata share of corporate profits on their individual income tax returns and pay taxes at personal rather than corporate tax rates. This results in a reduction in taxes because the firm itself pays little if any federal income taxes. In order to qualify for Subchapter S status, the firm must apply to the IRS and meet a number of requirements.

# SUMMARY

The corporation is the dominant organizational form for conducting business in our economy. The advantages that a corporation has over the proprietorship and partnership are (1) indefinite lifetime, (2) ease of transfer of ownership, (3) limited liability of stockholders, and (4) ability to finance itself by issuing securities. Double taxation of profits is a disadvantage of corporations but not of proprietorships or partnerships.

Business cycles, inflation, competition, and regulation are major factors of the economic environment that help determine the ability of a corporation to operate profitably and to maximize shareholder wealth. From the standpoint of financial management, probably the most important parts of the corporation's operating environment are financial markets, financial intermediaries, and financial institutions. Taken together, they provide essential inputs into the capital formation process. In addition, they help create resale markets for previously issued financial assets. As a result, they provide the mechanism for determining the prices of the securities that are traded in these markets. The regulation of financial markets is intended to keep these markets as competitive as possible.

Corporate profits are taxed primarily by the federal government. The tax rates are not a function of the levels of corporate profits. Hence, corporate tax rates are not progressive as are the rates on personal income.

# QUESTIONS

2-1.   What are the fundamental characteristics of (a) proprietorships, (b) partnerships, and (c) corporations?

2-2.   What are the reasons why corporations dominate other organizational forms in terms of business receipts and profits?

2-3.   What are the major phases of a business cycle? How are automatic stabilizers intended to affect business cycles?

**2-4.** What pattern of GNP figures indicates a recession?

**2-5.** What is meant by the terms *demand-pull inflation* and *cost-push inflation*?

**2-6.** What are the implications of industrial concentration and oligopolistic markets for financial management?

**2-7.** What are the major functions of financial markets?

**2-8.** What is the essential characteristic of the primary securities markets? The secondary securities markets? How are these two types of markets interrelated?

**2-9.** What is intermediation? disintermediation?

**2-10.** What are the functions of financial intermediaries? Why is this important to financial management?

**2-11.** What is the distinction between a financial intermediary and a financial institution?

# PROBLEMS

**2-1.** Using the nominal GNP and real GNP figures in Table 2-7 below, at what points of time do business cycle turning points occur? Which particular business cycle phases can be identified and over what intervals of time do they last?

Table 2-7.    Hypothetical Business Cycle Indicators

| | | Nominal GNP (Billions of $) | Real GNP (Billions of $) | CPI (%) | Unemployment Rate (%) |
|---|---|---|---|---|---|
| 19X1 | Q1 | 900 | 800 | 115 | 8.0 |
| | Q2 | 902 | 801 | 118 | 7.9 |
| | Q3 | 904 | 802 | 120 | 7.9 |
| | Q4 | 905 | 799 | 122 | 8.1 |
| 19X2 | Q1 | 906 | 794 | 124 | 8.4 |
| | Q2 | 906 | 787 | 125 | 8.7 |
| | Q3 | 905 | 785 | 124 | 8.9 |
| | Q4 | 904 | 780 | 123 | 9.0 |
| 19X3 | Q1 | 908 | 782 | 125 | 9.1 |
| | Q2 | 910 | 784 | 127 | 9.0 |
| | Q3 | 912 | 790 | 128 | 8.9 |
| | Q4 | 913 | 792 | 130 | 8.8 |

**2-2.** How does the behavior of the unemployment rate figures in Table 2-7 reinforce your answers to Problem 2-1?

**2-3.** Interpret the severity of inflation as contained in the CPI in Table 2-7.

**2-4.** Determine the type of inflation that is persistent by using both the real GNP and the CPI in Table 2-7.

2-5. Interpret the business cycle patterns contained in Table 2-7 using all 4 business cycle indicators.

2-6. Table 2-8 contains the values of the business cycle indicators from Q3, 1973, through Q3, 1975. Analyze the business cycle patterns contained in this data.

Table 2-8.       Business Cycle Indicators

|  | Nominal GNP* | Real GNP* | Corporate Profits* | Unemployment Rate (%) | CPI (%) |
|---|---|---|---|---|---|
| 1973 | | | | | |
| Q3 | $1,308.9 | $840.8 | $72.9 | 4.7 | 134.5 |
| Q4 | 1,344.0 | 845.7 | 73.2 | 4.7 | 137.6 |
| 1974 | | | | | |
| Q1 | 1,358.8 | 830.5 | 83.2 | 5.2 | 141.4 |
| Q2 | 1,383.8 | 827.1 | 83.1 | 5.1 | 145.6 |
| Q3 | 1,416.3 | 823.1 | 94.3 | 5.5 | 150.1 |
| Q4 | 1,430.9 | 804.0 | 79.5 | 6.6 | 154.3 |
| 1975 | | | | | |
| Q1 | 1,416.6 | 780.0 | 62.3 | 8.4 | 157.4 |
| Q2 | 1,440.9 | 783.6 | 70.3 | 8.6 | 159.5 |
| Q3 | 1,504.4 | 808.6 | 72.1 | 8.4 | 162.9 |

*In billions

Source: *Federal Reserve Bulletin.*

2-7. A fixed asset has an installed cost of $90,000, a 12-year life, and no expected salvage value. Assuming straight-line depreciation, what is the annual depreciation expense? What are the accumulated depreciation and book value figures after three years? after ten years?

2-8. The fixed asset in Problem 2-7 is sold for $10,000 after the asset has been depreciated for ten years. Assuming a 40% tax rate, compute the tax impact.

2-9. A corporation invests $4,000,000 in a production facility that is expected to be usable for 20 years and has no expected salvage. Assuming straight-line depreciation and a 40% tax rate, compute the tax impact that results from selling the facility for $3 million when it is seven years old.

2-10. Using the data in Problem 2-9, what selling price for the asset when it is ten years old would result in no tax impact for the firm?

2-11. A firm acquires a depreciable asset for a total of $120,000. The asset has a six-year economic life and a $20,000 estimated salvage. The asset is classified as three-year property for the purpose of ACRS depreciation. Calculate the depreciation expense for each year under ACRS.

2-12. An asset that costs $200,000 has a ten-year economic life and a $40,000 estimated salvage value. The asset is classified as five-year property under ACRS rules. Calculate the depreciation expense for each year under ACRS.

# SELECTED REFERENCES

Angle, E. A. *Keys for Business Forecasting*. 4th ed. Richmond, Virginia: The Federal Reserve Bank of Richmond, 1975.

Boyes, W. *Macroeconomics: The Dynamics of Theory and Policy*. Cincinnati: South-Western Publishing Co., 1984.

Gordon, R. A. *Business Fluctuations*. 2d ed. New York: Harper & Row, Publishers, 1961.

Mansfield, E. *Microeconomics: Theory and Applications*. 3d ed. New York: W. W. Norton & Company, Inc., 1979.

*Prentice-Hall Federal Taxes 1983*. Englewood Cliffs, New Jersey: Prentice-Hall Inc., 1983.

Robinson, R. I., and D. Wrightsman. *Financial Markets: The Accumulation and Allocation of Wealth*. 2d ed. New York: McGraw-Hill Book Company, 1980.

Wallace, W. H., and W. E. Cullison. *Measuring Price Changes: A Study of the Price Indices*. 3d ed. Richmond, Virginia: The Federal Reserve Bank of Richmond, 1976.

Welshans, M. and R. Melicher. *Finance: Introduction to Markets, Institutions, and Management*. 6th ed. Cincinnati: South-Western Publishing Co., 1983.

# PART 2

# Financial Analysis and Planning

The three chapters in Part 2 contain fundamental techniques of financial analysis, planning, and forecasting. These techniques are used repeatedly in the remainder of the text. The assumptions contained in each technique are spelled out, and the procedures, applications, advantages, and limitations of each technique are explained.

Ratio analysis and funds statements, explained in Chapter 3, are the standard tools for evaluating a corporation's financial performance. The cash-budgeting and pro forma techniques of Chapter 4 serve as tools of planning and control by forecasting a corporation's financial performance. The leverage concepts of Chapter 5 provide additional analytical tools for evaluating the current and future financial performance of the corporation.

# CHAPTER 3

## *Financial Statement Analysis*

The three fundamental accounting statements are the income statement, the balance sheet, and the statement of changes in financial position. The analysis of these statements combined with the preparation and analysis of related financial statements is called *financial statement analysis*. This type of analysis allows managers, investors, and creditors, as well as potential investors and creditors, to reach conclusions about the recent and current financial status of a corporation. What is perhaps more important, financial statement analysis is used in forming expectations about a corporation's future financial performance.

This chapter presents some fundamentals of financial statement analysis. The first section explains the purposes and contents of income statements, balance sheets, and statements of changes in financial position. These statements provide the analytical focus for the entire chapter. The next section explains how financial ratios are computed from income statement and balance sheet data and how these ratios are used to analyze and interpret a firm's financial condition. The third section explains the preparation and analysis of the statement of changes in financial position. The techniques presented in this chapter are some of the most basic and widely used tools in financial analysis. This chapter stresses the importance not only of *knowing how these tools are used but also stresses the importance of understanding their advantages and limitations.*

## BASIC FINANCIAL STATEMENTS

The data used in analyzing financial statements are contained in income statements, balance sheets, and funds statements. In explaining financial statement analysis, this chapter uses an existing corporation that operates in the computer hardware and software industry. It has been given the name *Braden Industries*, and its financial statements have been modified for explanatory purposes. The basic financial relationships, however, reflected in the income statements, balance sheets, and the funds statement used in this chapter remain a fairly accurate description of its recent financial condition.

**Income Statements**

An **income statement** measures the profitability of a firm over a period of time. Each of Braden Industries' income statements shown in Table 3-1, for example, covers a calendar year. For accounting purposes, however, many corporations have found it useful to adopt fiscal years that do not correspond to calendar years. In addition, income statements are frequently prepared on a quarterly basis and referred to as *interim* statements. Regardless of the starting and ending dates or the length of time, the essential point is that an income statement summarizes a corporation's operations over a given time interval. As illustrated by Figure 3-1, the firm's operations generate a flow of revenues, expenses, and profits or losses over time, and it is these flows that are reported in income statements.

Referring to Braden Industries' income statements for the years ending December 31, 1984 and 1985, in Table 3-1, note that *Net sales* appears at the top of the statement. The sum of cost of goods sold, administrative expenses, and other related expenses is subtracted from net sales to arrive at

*Earnings before interest and taxes* (EBIT). Interest expense on borrowed funds and federal income taxes are then subtracted to arrive at *Earnings after taxes,* or net income. When a corporation's income statements are to appear in its *Annual Report* to stockholders, common stock dividends and per share data are shown at the bottom of its income statements. Braden Industries' income statements in Table 3-1 show the total amount of dividends paid to stockholders, as well as per share earnings and dividends. The *Addition to retained earnings* represents the amount that is plowed back into the business for reinvestment purposes.

**Table 3-1.**   **Braden Industries' Income Statements**
                **(For the Years Ending December 31)**

|  | 1985 | | 1984 | |
| --- | --- | --- | --- | --- |
| Net sales | | $8,250,000 | | $8,000,000 |
| Less: Cost of goods sold | $5,100,000 | | $5,000,000 | |
| Administrative expenses | 1,750,000 | | 1,680,000 | |
| Other expenses | 420,000 | | 390,000 | |
| Total | | 7,270,000 | | 7,070,000 |
| Earnings before interest and taxes | | $ 980,000 | | $ 930,000 |
| Less: Interest expense | | 210,000 | | 210,000 |
| Earnings before taxes | | $ 770,000 | | $ 720,000 |
| Less: Federal income taxes | | 360,000 | | 325,000 |
| Earnings after taxes (net income) | | $ 410,000 | | $ 395,000 |
| Common stock cash dividends | | $ 90,000 | | $ 84,000 |
| Addition to retained earnings | | $ 320,000 | | $ 311,000 |
| Earnings per common share | | $ 3.940 | | $ 3.90 |
| Dividends per common share | | $ .865 | | $ .83 |

Notes to income statements:
1. No significant lease obligations
2. Depreciation expense: $80,000 in 1985; $75,000 in 1984

**Balance Sheets**   A **balance sheet** summarizes a firm's financial position at a particular point in time. It consists of two major sections: (1) assets and (2) liabilities and stockholders' equity. As shown in Figure 3-2, total assets equal total liabilities and stockholders' equity. This statement indicates the mix of liabilities and equity that finances the firm's assets. Braden Industries' balance sheets as of December 31, 1985 and 1984, are contained in Table 3-2.

**Figure 3-1.**          **The Income Statement**

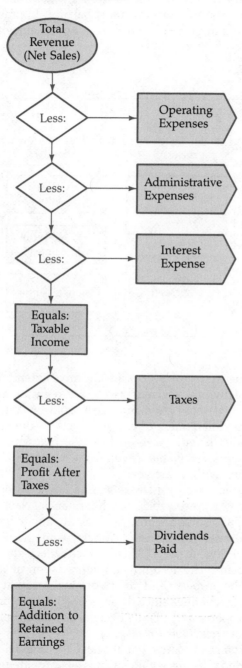

Referring to the assets section as the left-hand side and the liabilities and stockholders' equity section as the right-hand side is a convention emphasizing that the two sections must balance. In practice, in published statements, assets are often listed first, with liabilities and stockholders' equity below.

**Figure 3-2.**          **The Balance Sheet**

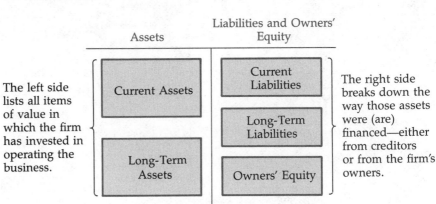

**ASSETS.** The **assets** of a firm are the investments it has made in its profit-seeking activities. **Current assets** are a firm's most liquid assets; that is, they can be converted into cash, sold or consumed within one year. Hence, the dollar value of current assets is sometimes referred to as **working capital**. Current assets include the following: cash, marketable securities, accounts receivable, inventories, and prepaid expenses which will be consumed within one year.

As contrasted to current assets, **fixed assets** consist of long-term (more than one year) receivables or other financial claims and investments in physical capital such as property, plant, and equipment. Referring to Table 3-2, Braden Industries' property and plant account shows a December 31, 1985 value of $2,037,000 which reflects the original cost of the property and plant. The accumulated depreciation of $862,000 represents the amount of the property and plant's original cost that has been allocated against corporate revenues since these assets were acquired. The difference between the property and plant's original cost and their accumulated depreciation is *Net property and plant*.

**Depreciation** is a process that allocates the original cost of fixed assets to the time periods during which such assets provide useful services. The depreciation expense for any given year may be included as part of the corporation's cost of goods sold and/or its administrative expenses in the income statement even though it may not appear as a separate entry.

**Table 3-2.** Braden Industries' Balance Sheets (As of December 31)

|  | 1985 | | 1984 | |
| --- | --- | --- | --- | --- |
| **Assets** | | | | |
| Current assets: | | | | |
| Cash | | $ 140,000 | | $ 115,000 |
| Accounts receivable | | 1,760,000 | | 1,440,000 |
| Inventory | | 2,175,000 | | 2,000,000 |
| Prepaid expenses | | 50,000 | | 63,000 |
| Total current assets | | $4,125,000 | | $3,618,000 |
| Fixed assets: | | | | |
| Long-term receivables | | $1,255,000 | | $1,090,000 |
| Property and plant | $2,037,000 | | $2,015,000 | |
| Less: Accumulated depreciation | 862,000 | | 860,000 | |
| Net property and plant | | 1,175,000 | | 1,155,000 |
| Other fixed assets | | 550,000 | | 530,000 |
| Total fixed assets — net | | $2,980,000 | | $2,775,000 |
| Total assets | | $7,105,000 | | $6,393,000 |
| **Liabilities and Stockholders' Equity** | | | | |
| Current liabilities: | | | | |
| Accounts payable | | $1,325,000 | | $1,225,000 |
| Bank loans payable | | 475,000 | | 550,000 |
| Accrued federal taxes | | 675,000 | | 425,000 |
| Current maturities (long-term debt) | | 17,500 | | 26,000 |
| Dividends payable | | 20,000 | | 16,250 |
| Total current liabilities | | $2,512,500 | | $2,242,250 |
| Long-term liabilities | | 1,350,000 | | 1,425,000 |
| Total liabilities | | $3,862,500 | | $3,667,250 |
| Stockholders' equity: | | | | |
| Common stock (104,046 shares outstanding in 1985; 101,204 shares outstanding in 1984) | | $ 44,500 | | $ 43,300 |
| Additional paid-in capital | | 568,000 | | 372,450 |
| Retained earnings | | 2,630,000 | | 2,310,000 |
| Total stockholders' equity | | $3,242,500 | | $2,725,750 |
| Total liabilities and stockholders' equity | | $7,105,000 | | $6,393,000 |

Depreciation is usually described as a *noncash* expense. This means that depreciation expense does not represent a cash outflow to the firm. It is important to note that neither the depreciation expense in an income statement nor the accumulated depreciation in a balance sheet attempts to measure the actual decrease in an asset's market value or its resale value.

**LIABILITIES AND STOCKHOLDERS' EQUITY.** The liabilities and stockholders' equity section of the balance sheet shows how a firm is financed. **Liabilities** are amounts owed to creditors. **Current liabilities** are payable in one year or less, and **long-term liabilities** are payable in later years. Table 3-2 shows that Braden Industries' current liabilities include amounts owed to creditors such as accounts payable, bank loans payable, and the current maturities of long-term debt. Accrued federal taxes are amounts payable to the federal government. Dividends payable represent dividend amounts that the corporation has declared and will shortly be paying to its stockholders.

The amount of funds provided directly by the stockholders of Braden Industries is represented by the *Common stock* and *Additional paid-in capital* portions of the stockholders' equity. Note that 2,842 (i.e., 104,046 − 101,204) additional shares of common stock were issued during 1985. This accounts for the increase in the common stock and additional paid-in capital accounts in 1985. **Retained earnings** are the accumulated profits earned by the corporation that were not paid out as dividends but were reinvested by the corporation. The increase in retained earnings represents the profits earned during 1985 that were not paid out as dividends.

The accounting procedures used to generate financial statements are not designed primarily to provide input data for financial statement analysis. As a consequence, financial statement data may not always yield the information that a financial analyst is seeking—an accurate picture of the firm's financial condition. For example, assets listed in the balance sheet at historic value may not reflect their current market values or their replacement costs. Inflation adjusted earnings may differ greatly from their reported values. In addition, some difficulties can be expected in interpreting financial statement accounts. An increase in the inventory accounts, for example, could mean that individual purchases cost more due to price increases and that the physical inventory levels have not increased, or it could mean that the firm is producing inventory in anticipation of sales, or it could mean that the firm is accumulating goods that it has been unable to sell. Other examples are contained in the subsequent sections of this chapter. Thus, the financial analyst must be aware that the shortcomings of accounting data limit the ability of statement analysis to produce useful interpretations concerning the financial condition of the firm.

**Other Related Statements**

The **statement of retained earnings** lists how much of the corporation's net income during a given year was paid out as dividends to the common stockholders and how much was reinvested by the corporation. Table 3-3 shows the statement of retained earnings for Braden Industries as of December 31, 1985.

**Table 3-3.**

**Braden Industries' Statement of Retained Earnings (As of December 31, 1985)**

| | |
|---|---:|
| Retained earnings as of December 31, 1984 | $2,310,000 |
| Add: Net income earned during 1985 | 410,000 |
| | $2,720,000 |
| Less: Dividends paid to common stockholders in 1985 | 90,000 |
| Retained earnings as of December 31, 1985 | $2,630,000 |

The statement of changes in financial position typically accompanies a corporation's income statements and balance sheets. This statement is discussed below.

Financial statements are normally documented by additional details and explanations of specific balance sheet and income statement items. This documentation is typically organized under the heading *Notes to Financial Statements*. These notes provide data that are useful or even critical in performing a corporate financial statement analysis. For example, one note might discuss the depreciation methods used by the corporation and list the depreciation expense that did not appear as a separate entry in the income statement. Another note might detail the lease payments that are required in the future. For purposes of this chapter, the financial statement notes are appended to Braden Industries' income statements (see Table 3-1). These notes indicate the absence of lease payments and identify the size of the depreciation expense contained in the income statement.

The statement of retained earnings illustrates one important relationship between the firm's operations, summarized in the income statement, and the firm's financial position, summarized in the balance sheet. Balance sheet retained earnings are increased by the amount that income statement net income exceeds dividends. There are many other ways in which these financial statements interact. The production and sale of the corporation's goods and services are reflected not only in the revenue and expense accounts of the income statement but are also reflected in the various balance sheet accounts. Purchases affect the inventory and accounts payable balance sheet accounts. When sold, inventories are expensed in the cost of goods sold section of the income statement. Cash and accounts receivable are reflected in the balance sheet accounts. In turn, cash is used to pay the accounts payable balance sheet liabilities and the related operating expenses listed in the income statement. Many other relationships between these statements exist, and some of these are explained in the next section.

**Statement
of Changes
in Financial
Position**

The third major financial statement of interest in this chapter is the **statement of changes in financial position**, also known as the **sources and uses of funds statement**, or simply, the **funds statement**. This statement measures the firm's net funds flows that occur between two points in time. Most of the data used in preparing this statement are taken from the two balance sheets that identify the time interval of interest. Additional data are obtained from the income statement that covers the same time interval. The importance of a funds statement as a source of financial information is evidenced by the fact that published annual reports include this statement along with balance sheets and income statements.

FUNDS AND FUNDS FLOWS. Chapter 1 provided a general definition of capital. In addition, a firm's capital sources and uses were said to be contained in its balance sheets. As general concepts, *funds* and *capital* are synonymous. Within the context of a single balance sheet, liability and equity accounts are a corporation's sources of funds, and its assets represent uses of funds.

PREPARATION ON A CASH BASIS. In preparing funds statements, analysts define **funds** more narrowly to mean net working capital (current assets minus current liabilities), or to mean cash. The content of the resulting funds statement depends in part on the choice of definition. This chapter explains how to prepare funds statements on a cash basis. There are two reasons for this choice. First, the resulting statement details the net changes in the individual current asset and current liability accounts, and this allows a closer examination of the firm's financial condition. Second, the cash basis provides a starting point for analysis that uses a broader definition of funds.

Figure 3-3 illustrates the concept of funds flow on a cash basis. Most of the transactions or events depicted in this figure are a source or use of cash. Some transactions, such as cash sales, generate immediate cash flows. Some transactions, such as purchases on open account, generate cash flows (in this case an outflow) at a time in the future. Some expenses, such as depreciation, are noncash expenses because recognizing the expense, even though it may reduce a firm's federal income tax liability, does not generate a cash flow. Figure 3-3 also illustrates that cash flows occur simultaneously and continuously. This makes it difficult if not impossible to analyze all the cash flows that occur during a period of time. Thus, as explained below, the funds statement measures the *net changes* in the various accounts.

**Figure 3-3.**          **Funds Flows within a Firm**

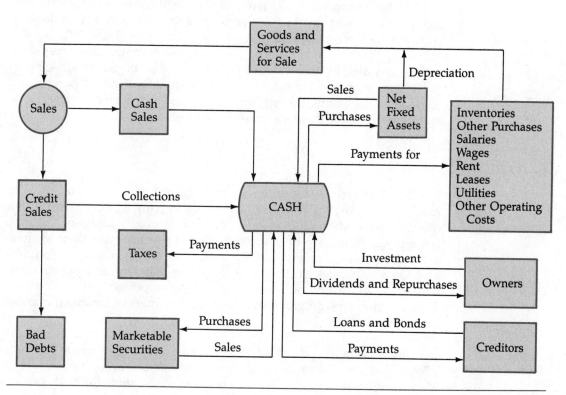

The funds statement for Braden Industries is given in the last section of this chapter, where the preparation of the funds statement is explained. As one of its names implies, the statement summarizes the firm's sources of funds or capital and the uses to which these funds are put. Total sources always equal total uses. One important property of this statement is that it provides a measure of the net dollar changes in each balance sheet account over a given time interval. Since funds are needed to acquire assets, any increase in an asset account represents a use of funds. Decreasing or paying off a liability account is also a use of funds. Similarly, decreasing assets or increasing liabilities are sources of funds.

For example, the cash account in the Braden balance sheet (Table 3-2) was $115,000 as of December 31, 1984, and $140,000 as of December 31, 1985. Several million dollars flowed through the cash account between those two dates, but the net change was a $25,000 increase in the balance sheet account amount; this increase in cash appears in the funds statement as a $25,000 use of funds. Subsequently decreasing this asset account will provide a source of funds for some other use, as, for example, when cash payments are made to acquire marketable securities or to decrease accounts payable.

The funds statement also requires the use of certain income statement accounts. For example, Braden's earnings after taxes and dividends paid, both of which are contained in its income statement (Table 3-1), are also contained in its funds statement. The $410,000 earnings after taxes are a source, and the $90,000 dividends paid are a use of funds. Thus, the funds statement, in making use of both income statement and balance sheet accounts in measuring the net funds flows during a period of time, helps to understand how these statements are interrelated.

# RATIO ANALYSIS

The first step in executing an analysis of financial statements is to carefully read the statements and their accompanying notes. This is frequently followed by ratio analysis. The use of ratio analysis has become widespread to the extent that computerized financial statement analysis programs prepare financial ratios as part of their overall analysis. Lenders and potential lenders, such as commercial banks and insurance companies, use similar automated programs in evaluating corporate loan applications. They use the same programs in measuring the financial condition of other borrowers.

**Basic Financial Ratios**

Financial ratios can be designed to measure almost any aspect of a corporation's performance. In general, analysts use ratios as one tool in identifying areas of strength or weakness in a corporation. Ratios, however, tend to identify symptoms rather than problems. A ratio whose value is judged to be "different" or unusually high or low may help identify a significant event but will seldom provide enough information, in and of itself, to identify the reasons for an event's occurrence.

**Liquidity ratios** measure a corporation's ability to pay its current liabilities as they mature. **Activity ratios** measure the degree of efficiency the corporation displays in using its resources. The extent to which a corporation finances itself with debt as opposed to equity sources is measured by **debt**, or **leverage**, **ratios**. Finally, the ability of a corporation to earn a positive rate of return for its stockholders is measured by **profitability ratios**. The computation and interpretation of some of the more widely used ratios that fall in these categories are explained in the balance of this section.

**LIQUIDITY RATIOS.** Liquidity ratios assume that current assets are the principal source of cash for meeting current liabilities. The two most widely used liquidity ratios are the current ratio and the quick ratio.

*Current Ratio.* The **current ratio** is computed by dividing current assets by current liabilities. Braden Industries' current ratios are:

$$\text{Current ratio} = \frac{\text{current assets}}{\text{current liabilities}}$$

$$= \frac{\$4,125,000}{\$2,512,500} = 1.64 \text{ times (for 1985)}$$

$$= \frac{\$3,618,000}{\$2,242,250} = 1.61 \text{ times (for 1984)}$$

The larger the current ratio, the less difficulty a corporation should encounter in paying its current liabilities. Lenders frequently require a corporation's current ratio to remain at or above 2.0 as a condition for granting or continuing commercial and industrial loans. This 2.0 standard is arbitrary although many security analysts feel that a corporation's liquidity can be questioned if its current ratio falls below 2.0. According to this criterion, Braden Industries' current ratios suggest that it might encounter some difficulties in paying its current liabilities.

*Quick Ratio.* The **quick ratio**, sometimes called the **acid-test ratio**, serves the same general purpose as the current ratio but excludes inventory from current assets. This is done because inventories are typically a firm's least liquid current assets. Thus, the quick ratio measures a corporation's ability to pay its current liabilities by converting its most liquid assets into cash.

The quick ratio is computed by subtracting inventories from current assets and dividing the remainder by current liabilities. For Braden Industries, the quick ratios are:

$$\text{Quick ratio} = \frac{\text{current assets} - \text{inventory}}{\text{current liabilities}}$$

$$= \frac{\$4,125,000 - \$2,175,000}{\$2,512,500} = .78 \text{ times (for 1985)}$$

$$= \frac{\$3,618,000 - \$2,000,000}{\$2,242,250} = .72 \text{ times (for 1984)}$$

If a company seeks to pay its current liabilities by using its **quick assets** (current assets minus inventories), then its quick assets must equal or exceed its current liabilities. Thus, its quick ratio must be 1.0 or more. This is the reasoning behind the quick ratio standard of 1.0 that many analysts use as the dividing line between sufficient and insufficient liquidity. Braden Industries' quick ratios of less than 1.0 for 1985 and 1984 suggest that it would not expect to be able to pay its current liabilities by using only its quick assets.

**ACTIVITY RATIOS.** As mentioned earlier, activity ratios measure how efficiently a corporation manages its assets. Efficiency is equated with rapid turnover; hence, these ratios are referred to collectively as *activity* ratios. Some activity ratios concentrate on individual assets such as inventory or accounts receivable. Others look at overall corporate activity. The three activity ratios discussed here measure inventory turnover, total asset turnover, and the average length of the accounts receivable collection period.

*Inventory Turnover.* The **inventory turnover** measures the number of times per year that a corporation sells, or turns over, its inventory. It is computed by dividing the dollar amount of cost of goods sold by the dollar value of the inventories. For Braden Industries, the inventory turnover ratios are:

$$\text{Inventory turnover} = \frac{\text{cost of goods sold}}{\text{inventory}}$$

$$= \frac{\$5,100,000}{\$2,175,000} = 2.34 \text{ times (for 1985)}$$

$$= \frac{\$5,000,000}{\$2,000,000} = 2.5 \text{ times (for 1984)}$$

In general, high turnover ratios are taken as a sign of efficient management. Other things being equal, a high inventory turnover ratio is seen as being more desirable than a low one.

Activity ratios, however, suffer from both conceptual and measurement problems. For example, a high inventory turnover could indicate that a firm's inventories are not adequate to meet customer demands and that lost sales are occurring as a result. On the other hand, a low turnover can be caused by the firm's addition of new product lines, each of which requires some minimum of inventory. In both of these examples, the inventory turnover—if used by itself—can lead to misleading conclusions.

A measurement problem is raised by the denominator used in calculating the turnover ratio. Since the purpose of this ratio is to measure the inventory turnover rate, the denominator should be a measure of the *average* amount of inventory that the corporation maintained during the year. However, in many cases—and Braden Industries' data are an example—the figure used for the denominator is the amount of inventory on hand *at a particular point in time*. If this figure is not representative of the average yearly inventory because of seasonal and/or cyclical production and selling patterns, for example, then the usefulness of this ratio becomes greatly limited.

*Total Asset Turnover.* The **total asset turnover** measures the relationship between a dollar of sales and a dollar of assets, usually on a yearly basis. This ratio is a measure of overall corporate activity. It is computed by dividing net sales by total assets. For Braden Industries, the total asset turnover ratios are:

$$\text{Total asset turnover} = \frac{\text{net sales}}{\text{total assets}}$$

$$= \frac{\$8,250,000}{\$7,105,000} = 1.16 \text{ times (for 1985)}$$

$$= \frac{\$8,000,000}{\$6,393,000} = 1.25 \text{ times (for 1984)}$$

✓The total asset turnover ratio can be used to measure the level of sales generated by a corporation against its production capacity. Given constant prices, presumably there is an upper limit for this ratio before a corporation reaches its production capacity. A decrease in this ratio might indicate decreased activity in one segment of the corporation. Thus, a decreasing total asset turnover could then be a signal to compute turnover ratios that focus on individual assets in order to isolate possible reasons for decreased corporate activity.

*Average Collection Period.* The **average collection period** seeks to measure the average number of days it takes for a firm to collect its accounts receivable. This ratio relates the firm's daily credit sales to its short-term accounts receivable. It is generally calculated in two steps: (1) Compute the average credit sales by dividing total credit sales by 360 days, and (2) compute the average collection period by dividing accounts receivable by the average credit sales per day. Assuming that Braden Industries' total credit sales are its net sales, its average collection periods are:

$$\text{Step 1. Average credit sales per day} = \frac{\text{total credit sales}}{360}$$

$$= \frac{\$8,250,000}{360} = \$22,916 \text{ (for 1985)}$$

$$= \frac{\$8,000,000}{360} = \$22,222 \text{ (for 1984)}$$

$$\text{Step 2. Average collection period} = \frac{\text{accounts receivable}}{\text{average credit sales per day}}$$

$$= \frac{\$1,760,000}{\$22,916} = 77 \text{ days (for 1985)}$$

$$= \frac{\$1,440,000}{\$22,222} = 65 \text{ days (for 1984)}$$

As with other activity ratios, the average collection period has measurement problems. For example, when sales are made substantially—but not entirely—on credit, total sales are used in place of credit sales. When allowing for seasonal fluctuations, the value used for accounts receivable should be a monthly average. Frequently, however, the accounts receivable value is simply the amount outstanding at a point in time. Braden Industries' average collection periods suffer from both of these measurement problems. Total sales were used in place of credit sales; and the accounts receivable value was not an average over time but the amount outstanding on December 31.

The average collection period requires careful interpretation even when these measurement problems are solved or at least recognized. An increasing or decreasing value should not, by itself, be used to evaluate the credit experience of the firm. For example, Braden Industries' collection period increased from 65 to 77 days during 1985. Is this desirable or not? If the firm has liberalized its credit terms from 60 to 90 days, the increase in the length of the collection period merely reflects that new policy. If Braden Industries is attempting to maintain a 60-day credit policy, then the ratio for 1985 indicates a worsening accounts receivable payment condition.

Credit granting and the structuring of credit terms have become major competitive tools used by marketing managers rather than financial managers. Many corporations find that their credit policies are being dictated by the dominant firms in their industry. This results in a situation where the ability to compete in such nonprice areas as credit terms may be the difference between making or not making a sale. The corporation's average collection period should always be interpreted in light of the credit terms available from the corporation's direct competitors.

DEBT (OR LEVERAGE) RATIOS. Two types of ratios are grouped under the heading of debt (or leverage) ratios. One type centers around the liabilities and stockholders' equity section of the balance sheet and measures the extent to which a corporation finances itself with debt as opposed to equity sources. Examples of this type are the long-term debt to equity ratio and the total debt to total assets ratio. The second type attempts to measure the corporation's ability to generate a level of income sufficient to meet its debt obligations. An example of this type is the times interest earned ratio. Other ratios that relate income to debt are developed in Chapter 5.

*Long-Term Debt to Equity.* The **long-term debt to equity** ratio measures the extent to which long-term financing sources are provided by creditors. It is computed by dividing long-term debt by stockholders' equity. For Braden Industries, the long-term debt to equity ratios are:

$$\text{Long-term debt to equity} = \frac{\text{long-term debt}}{\text{stockholders' equity}}$$

$$= \frac{\$1,350,000}{\$3,242,500} = .42 \text{ or } 42\% \text{ (for 1985)}$$

$$= \frac{\$1,425,000}{\$2,725,750} = .52 \text{ or } 52\% \text{ (for 1984)}$$

The decrease in this ratio from 0.52 to 0.42 occurred for several reasons: (1) some long-term debt matured, (2) Braden Industries increased the amount of stockholders' equity by selling additional shares of common stock, and (3) some amount was added to its retained earnings.

*Total Debt to Total Assets.* The **total debt to total assets** ratio measures the percentage of total funds provided by debt. Subtracting this percentage from 1.0 gives the percentage of total funds provided by equity sources. This ratio includes current liabilities. It is computed by dividing total liabilities by total assets. For Braden Industries, the total debt to total assets ratios are:

$$\text{Total debt to total assets} = \frac{\text{total liabilities}}{\text{total assets}}$$

$$= \frac{\$3,862,500}{\$7,105,000} = .54 \text{ or } 54\% \text{ (for 1985)}$$

$$= \frac{\$3,667,250}{\$6,393,000} = .57 \text{ or } 57\% \text{ (for 1984)}$$

At the end of 1985, 54 percent of Braden Industries' total assets was provided by debt funds and 46 percent (1.0 minus .54) was provided by equity sources.

Debt ratios of the type discussed above have several related applications. For example, many financial analysts are of the opinion that each corporation has its own optimal capital structure — measured by using debt ratios — that will make the greatest contribution to maximizing stockholder wealth. In addition, these ratios are often used as a measure of financial risk; that is, as debt becomes an increasing percentage of a corporation's financing sources, the probability of corporate insolvency increases due to its possible inability to meet debt obligations. Potential lenders use debt ratios in setting lending terms. If a lender feels that a borrowing corporation already has a heavy debt burden, the borrower may be asked to pay a higher interest rate and/or supply additional collateral because of the financial risk perceived by the lender. The measurement and consequences of financial risk are the subjects of several later chapters.

*Times Interest Earned.* The **times interest earned** ratio seeks to measure a corporation's ability to pay the interest on its debt. It is computed by dividing earnings before interest and taxes by interest expense. The times interest earned ratios for Braden Industries are:

$$\text{Times interest earned} = \frac{\text{earnings before interest and taxes}}{\text{interest expense}}$$

$$= \frac{\$980,000}{\$210,000} = 4.67 \text{ times (for 1985)}$$

$$= \frac{\$930,000}{\$210,000} = 4.43 \text{ times (for 1984)}$$

During 1985, Braden Industries' earnings before interest and taxes were 4.67 times larger than the interest payments required on its borrowed funds.

The times interest earned ratio implicitly assumes that remaining income (after subtracting production, operating, and administrative expenses from net sales) is available to meet interest expense. However, earnings before interest and taxes is an income concept and not a direct measure of cash. Consequently, this ratio provides only an *indirect* measure of the corporation's ability to meet its interest payments.

A decreasing value of the times interest earned ratio is sometimes used as an additional measure of financial risk. As is done with the current ratio, lenders will sometimes stipulate higher interest rates or other penalties should the times interest earned ratio fall below a specified value.

**PROFITABILITY RATIOS.** Profitability ratios provide an overall evaluation of the performance of a corporation and its management. These ratios measure the returns generated by the corporation from several different aspects: (1) on a per share basis, (2) on a per dollar-of-sales basis, (3) on a per dollar-of-assets basis, and (4) on a per dollar-of-stockholders'-equity basis. Several ratios falling in these categories are discussed below.

*Earnings per Share.* The **earnings per share** (EPS) ratio expresses the profits per common share earned by a corporation during a period of time. It is the single most frequently analyzed and quoted financial ratio. This ratio is computed by dividing earnings after taxes by the number of common shares authorized and outstanding. If the corporation also has preferred shares outstanding, preferred dividends are subtracted from earnings after taxes before converting to a per common share basis. Braden Industries' earnings per share are:

$$\text{Earnings per share} = \frac{\text{earnings after taxes} - \text{preferred stock dividends}}{\text{number of common shares outstanding}}$$

$$= \frac{\$410,000}{104,046} = \$3.94 \text{ (for 1985)}$$

$$= \frac{\$395,000}{101,204} = \$3.90 \text{ for (1984)}$$

Many of the reasons why attention is focused on EPS rather than total earnings (profits) revolve around the corporate goal of shareholder wealth maximization as opposed to profit maximization which was discussed in Chapter 1. In addition, dividends per share paid by the corporation are closely tied to its per share earnings. Finally, EPS is also used in computing the payout ratio.

*Dividends per Share.* The **dividends per share** ratio represents the dollar amount of cash dividends a corporation paid on each share of its common stock outstanding over a period of time. This ratio is calculated by dividing total common stock dividends by the number of common shares outstanding. Braden Industries' dividends per share are:

$$\text{Dividends per share} = \frac{\text{common stock cash dividends}}{\text{number of common shares outstanding}}$$

$$= \frac{\$90,000}{104,046} = \$0.865 \text{ (for 1985)}$$

$$= \frac{\$84,000}{101,204} = \$0.83 \text{ (for 1984)}$$

In computing earnings per share and dividends per share for Braden Industries, the denominator used represents the number of common shares outstanding as of December 31. This procedure implicitly assumes that these shares were outstanding for the entire 12 months. When the number of common shares outstanding changes significantly during the year, an average of the outstanding shares is used in computing per share financial ratios.

*Payout Ratio.* The **payout ratio** expresses the cash dividends paid per share as a percentage of EPS. This ratio is computed by dividing dividends per share by earnings per share. Braden Industries' payout ratios are:

$$\text{Payout ratio} = \frac{\text{dividends per share}}{\text{earnings per share}}$$

$$= \frac{\$0.865}{\$3.94} = .22 \text{ or } 22\% \text{ (for 1985)}$$

$$= \frac{\$0.83}{\$3.90} = .21 \text{ or } 21\% \text{ (for 1984)}$$

Some care must be exercised in interpreting the payout ratio since earnings per share are not in a corporation's checking accounts waiting to be reinvested or paid out in dividends. In the absence of legal impediments, the corporation could decide to pay dividends per share that exceed its per share earnings, in which case the resulting payout ratio would exceed 100 percent, or 1. For example, a corporation might adopt a dividend policy of paying dividends per share at 40 percent of EPS and state this policy in its reports to shareholders. Investors and potential investors can then decide if they want to own common shares whose returns are provided at least in part by this dividend stream.

Lenders sometimes refer to payout ratios when writing restrictive loan covenants. A lender might insist that a borrower's payout ratio *not* exceed a specified value while the loan is outstanding. The purpose of including restrictions, such as maximum allowable payout ratios and minimum required current ratios, is to force the corporation to maintain a degree of liquidity sufficient to meet its loan repayment schedule.

*Profit Margin.* The **profit margin** ratio, also called the **net profit margin**, measures corporate profitability on a per dollar-of-sales basis. It is computed by dividing earnings after taxes by net sales. The profit margins for Braden Industries are:

$$\text{Profit margin} = \frac{\text{earnings after taxes}}{\text{net sales}}$$

$$= \frac{\$410,000}{\$8,250,000} = .0497 \text{ or } 4.97\% \text{ (for 1985)}$$

$$= \frac{\$395,000}{\$8,000,000} = .0494 \text{ or } 4.94\% \text{ (for 1984)}$$

For 1985, Braden Industries earned 4.97 cents per dollar of sales. Its profit margin is essentially unchanged from the 4.94 cents earned per dollar of sales in 1984.

The profit margin ratio results from the interaction during the accounting period of three factors: (1) sales volume, (2) pricing strategy, and (3) cost structure. However, if a corporation decides that its profit margin is inadequate, this ratio will not, by itself, pinpoint which combination of these three factors produced the undesirable result.

*Return on Investment (ROI).* The **return on investment** ratio, commonly referred to as ROI, is also known as the **return on total assets**. This ratio measures corporate profitability per dollar of invested funds. ROI is calculated by dividing earnings after taxes by total assets. The ROIs for Braden Industries are:

$$\text{Return on investment (ROI)} = \frac{\text{earnings after taxes}}{\text{total assets}}$$

$$= \frac{\$410,000}{\$7,105,000} = .0577 \text{ or } 5.77\% \text{ (for 1985)}$$

$$= \frac{\$395,000}{\$6,393,000} = .0618 \text{ or } 6.18\% \text{ (for 1984)}$$

For 1985, Braden Industries earned 5.77 cents of profit for each dollar of assets. This value is down slightly from its 1984 ROI of 6.18 cents per sales dollar.

The ROI ratio essentially relates size to profits. If a corporation increases in size (as measured by total assets) but does not increase its earnings after taxes proportionally, then its ROI will decrease. Thus, increasing the corporation's size will not of itself advance the financial welfare of its shareholders.

It is possible to examine some of the components that produce a corporation's ROI by expressing this ratio as follows:

$$\text{ROI} = \frac{\text{earnings after taxes}}{\text{net sales}} \times \frac{\text{net sales}}{\text{total assets}}$$

or

$$\text{ROI} = \text{profit margin} \times \text{total asset turnover}$$

The profit margin measures profitability per sales dollar, and total asset turnover is an activity ratio also based on unit sales. Thus, corporate ROI can be understood as occurring from a combination of profit margin and activity.

Braden Industries' ROI can now be broken down as follows (the separate ratios were calculated earlier in this section):

$$\text{ROI} = .0497 \times 1.16 = .0577 \text{ or } 5.77\% \text{ (for 1985)}$$
$$= .0494 \times 1.25 = .0618 \text{ or } 6.18\% \text{ (for 1984)}$$

An analysis of these ratios indicates that the increase in Braden Industries' profit margin from 1984 to 1985 was more than offset by a decrease in total asset turnover. Thus, the decrease in ROI is a result of the decrease in total asset turnover but not profit margin.

The expanded form of the ROI ratio can also be used to point out that simply increasing net sales will not increase the ROI because net sales cancel out in the computation. What is needed is to increase either the rate of profitability or the rate of asset turnover, or both. This example demonstrates that the advantage of using the expanded ROI equation lies not only in the ability to separate profitability from activity, but also in the fact that the analytical focus is centered on the *rates* per dollar of sales as opposed to the *level* of sales.

*Return on Stockholders' Equity.* The **return on stockholders' equity**, also called **return on net worth**, measures corporate profitability per dollar of equity capital. It is computed by dividing earnings after taxes by stockholders' equity. Braden Industries' returns on stockholders' equity are:

$$\text{Return on stockholders' equity} = \frac{\text{earnings after taxes}}{\text{stockholders' equity}}$$

$$= \frac{\$410,000}{\$3,242,500} = .1264 \text{ or } 12.64\% \text{ (for 1985)}$$

$$= \frac{\$395,000}{\$2,725,750} = .1449 \text{ or } 14.49\% \text{ (for 1984)}$$

During 1985, Braden Industries' return on stockholders' equity was 12.64 percent, down from 14.49 percent during 1984.

The return on stockholders' equity ratio relates a corporation's profits to its equity sources. When a corporation such as Braden Industries has interest-bearing debt outstanding (including short-term and long-term debt), increases in shareholder wealth essentially require the corporation to earn a rate of return on the amount of debt financed that exceeds the effective cost of the debt. If the corporation meets this requirement, the rate of return over and above the cost of the debt accrues to the shareholders; and this will be reflected by an increase in return on stockholders' equity. Similarly, this ratio will decrease if the corporation is unable to earn a rate of return that exceeds its cost of debt financing.

**Common Size Statements**

Another type of ratio analysis involves the preparation of common size, or percentage, statements. A **common size statement** expresses each item in the income statement as a percentage of net sales and/or expresses each item in the balance sheet as a percentage of total assets. Since many balance sheet ratios are computed as part of the basic financial ratio analysis, attention is usually focused on the preparation and analysis of common size income statements.

Table 3-4 below contains the common size income statements of Braden Industries for 1981 through 1985. The percentages for 1985 and 1984 can be verified by taking the income statement items in Table 3-1 and expressing them as a percentage of net sales. The data in Table 3-4 were obtained from Braden Industries' annual reports. In generating its common size income statements, the percentages were rounded to the nearest one tenth of one percent.

During 1985, costs and expenses amounted to 88.1 percent of Braden Industries' net sales. Interest expense required 2.5 percent; and federal income tax, 4.4 percent. The 5 percent earnings after taxes represents the firm's profit margin. Comparing 1985 to 1984, there was little change in the expense items when expressed as percentages of net sales.

**Table 3-4.**          Braden Industries' Common Size Income Statements
                       (1981 through 1985)

|  | 1985 | 1984 | 1983 | 1982 | 1981 |
|---|---|---|---|---|---|
| Net sales | 100.0% | 100.0% | 100.0% | 100.0% | 100.0% |
| Cost and expenses: |  |  |  |  |  |
| Cost of goods sold | 61.8% | 62.5% | 63.3% | 62.5% | 64.3% |
| Administrative expenses | 21.2 | 21.0 | 20.5 | 21.3 | 21.1 |
| Other expenses | 5.1 | 4.9 | 5.7 | 5.4 | 5.0 |
| Total | 88.1% | 88.4% | 89.5% | 89.2% | 90.4% |
| Earnings before interest and taxes | 11.9% | 11.6% | 10.5% | 10.8% | 9.6% |
| Interest expense | 2.5 | 2.6 | 2.9 | 2.7 | 2.5 |
| Earnings before taxes | 9.3% | 9.0% | 7.6% | 8.1% | 7.1% |
| Federal income taxes | 4.4 | 4.1 | 3.5 | 3.8 | 3.3 |
| Earnings after taxes | 4.9% | 4.9% | 4.1% | 4.3% | 3.8% |

**Approaches to Using Financial Ratios in Statement Analysis**

There are two basic approaches in analyzing a set of financial statements through the use of financial ratios. One approach, called **cross-sectional analysis**, evaluates a corporation's financial condition at a point in time, compares its performance against that of the previous year, and compares its ratios against those of its competitors. The second approach, called **time series analysis**, evaluates the corporation's peformance over several years. These two approaches complement each other, and both should be included as part of a financial statement analysis.

**CROSS-SECTIONAL ANALYSIS.** The first step in a cross-sectional analysis of Braden Industries, for example, is to evaluate its financial position at the end of 1985. In order to do so, the firm's original financial statements (see Tables 3-1 and 3-2) and common size income statements (see Table 3-4) are needed. The second step is to compare its performance against that of the previous year by computing its basic financial ratios for 1985 and 1984 which are summarized in Table 3-5 below. This table also lists the formula for each ratio and illustrates the computations using the 1985 Braden Industries data. Finally, in order to compare Braden Industries' performance against that of its competitors, a number of industry average financial ratios are used. Dun & Bradstreet, Inc., for example, publishes financial ratios for each of 125 industries. Prentice-Hall, Inc., publishes industry averages for 170 separate major lines of business. Table 3-6 compares selected Braden Industries ratios with industry averages computed from that segment of the computer industry in which Braden Industries competes.

**Table 3-5.**          Braden Industries' Financial Ratios (1985 and 1984)

| Ratio | Formula | Calculation for 1985 | Ratios 1985 | 1984 |
|---|---|---|---|---|
| **Liquidity** | | | | |
| Current ratio | $\dfrac{\text{Current assets}}{\text{Current liabilities}}$ | $\dfrac{\$4,125,000}{\$2,512,500}$ | 1.64 | 1.61 |
| Quick ratio | $\dfrac{\text{Current assets} - \text{inventory}}{\text{Current liabilities}}$ | $\dfrac{\$4,125,000 - \$2,175,000}{\$2,512,500}$ | .78 | .72 |
| **Activity** | | | | |
| Inventory turnover | $\dfrac{\text{Cost of goods sold}}{\text{Inventory}}$ | $\dfrac{\$5,100,000}{\$2,175,000}$ | 2.34 | 2.50 |
| Total asset turnover | $\dfrac{\text{Net sales}}{\text{Total assets}}$ | $\dfrac{\$8,250,000}{\$7,105,000}$ | 1.16 | 1.25 |
| Average collection period | $\dfrac{\text{Total credit sales}}{360}$ | $\dfrac{\$8,250,000}{360}$ | $22,916 | $22,222 |
| | $\dfrac{\text{Accounts receivable}}{\text{Average credit sales/day}}$ | $\dfrac{\$1,760,000}{\$22,916}$ | 77 days | 65 days |
| **Debt** | | | | |
| Long term debt to equity | $\dfrac{\text{Long-term debt}}{\text{Stockholders' equity}}$ | $\dfrac{\$1,350,000}{\$3,242,500}$ | 42% | 52% |
| Total debt to total assets | $\dfrac{\text{Total liabilities}}{\text{Total assets}}$ | $\dfrac{\$3,862,500}{\$7,105,000}$ | 54% | 57% |
| Times interest earned | $\dfrac{\text{Earnings before interest and taxes}}{\text{Interest expense}}$ | $\dfrac{\$980,000}{\$210,000}$ | 4.67 | 4.43 |
| **Profitability** | | | | |
| Earnings per share | $\dfrac{\text{Earnings after taxes} - \text{perferred stock dividends}}{\text{Number of common shares outstanding}}$ | $\dfrac{\$410,000}{104,046}$ | $3.94 | $3.90 |
| Dividends per share | $\dfrac{\text{Common stock cash dividends}}{\text{Number of common shares outstanding}}$ | $\dfrac{\$90,000}{104,046}$ | $ .865 | $ .83 |
| Payout ratio | $\dfrac{\text{Dividends per share}}{\text{Earnings per share}}$ | $\dfrac{\$ .865}{\$3.94}$ | 22% | 21% |
| Profit margin | $\dfrac{\text{Earnings after taxes}}{\text{Net sales}}$ | $\dfrac{\$410,000}{\$8,250,000}$ | 4.97% | 4.94% |
| Return on investment | $\dfrac{\text{Earnings after taxes}}{\text{Total assets}}$ (Profit margin) (Total asset turnover) | $\dfrac{\$410,000}{\$7,105,000}$ (.0497) (1.16) | 5.77% | 6.18% |
| Return on stockholder equity | $\dfrac{\text{Earnings after taxes}}{\text{Stockholders' equity}}$ | $\dfrac{\$410,000}{\$3,242,500}$ | 12.64% | 14.49% |

*Evaluation of Financial Condition.* The data and associated ratios for Braden Industries reveal that the firm's net sales were slightly higher in 1985 as compared with 1984, and the profit margin changed very little. The 1985 EPS would have been higher if the corporation had not sold additional common shares during 1985. Dividends per share were increased by 3.5 cents over 1984.

| Table 3-6. | Selected 1985 Braden Industries Financial Ratios Compared with Industry Averages | | |
|---|---|---|---|
| | | **Braden Industries** | **Industry Average** |
| | Current ratio | 1.64 | 2.56 |
| | Inventory turnover | 2.34 | 4.50 |
| | Average collection period | 77 days | 59 days |
| | Long-term debt to equity | .42 | .44 |
| | Return on stockholders' equity | 12.64% | 14.26% |

*Comparison of Financial Ratios with Previous Year.* The firm's liquidity ratios changed very little. The activity ratios, especially the average collection period, point to a significant event in 1985. Why did the average collection period increase by 12 days? Was this the result of a management decision or does this ratio identify a previously unnoticed problem?

Two debt ratios (long-term debt to equity and total debt to total assets) were lower in 1985 than in 1984. This occurred because the long-term debt is gradually maturing and because the corporation sold additional shares of common stock in 1985. The times interest earned ratio increased because earnings before interest and taxes increased.

The decrease in return on investment has already been shown to be caused by a decrease in total asset turnover. The decrease in return on stockholder equity is the result of the corporation's floating additional shares of common stock. The other profitability ratios increased modestly.

*Comparison with Industry Averages.* Some questions arise when Braden Industries' ratios are compared with industry averages. The corporation's current ratio is substantially below the industry average. Does this reflect an inability of the firm to manage its working capital? Does the much lower inventory turnover of the firm indicate that it has accumulated obsolete inventory? Does the 18-day difference in the average collection period mean that Braden Industries has decided to offer more liberal credit terms as a competitive strategy, or does the firm face an accounts receivable collection problem?

It is important to note that per share profitability ratios are *not* used in making comparisons with industry averages. This is because per share profitability ratios are not comparable across firms due to the distorting effects produced by stock splits.

To summarize, a cross-sectional analysis raises some important questions that need to be answered before a definite opinion of a corporation's performance can be formed. By raising these questions, ratio analysis identifies for the corporate manager, as well as outside analysts, those aspects of corporate performance that need to be investigated. The fact that these ratios are able to identify potential problem areas is one of the principal reasons for performing a detailed ratio analysis on a set of financial statements.

**TIME SERIES ANALYSIS.** As stated earlier, the purpose of time series analysis is to evaluate corporate performance over a specified interval of time. This type of analysis looks for three factors: (1) important trends in the corporate data, (2), shifts in trends, and (3) **data outliers**, or values that deviate substantially from the other data points.

*Discovering Trends through Data Sets.* Braden Industries' common size income statements for 1981 through 1985 contained in Table 3-4 provide a good example of a data set that can be used for time-series analysis. This data set shows that the ratio of total costs and expenses to net sales decreased slowly but steadily from 90.4 percent in 1981 to 88.1 percent at the end of 1985. The trend of this ratio indicates sustained efficiency on the part of the firm. The same efficiency trend is seen in the behavior of the earnings before taxes and the profit margin. In effect, the steady increase in the firm's profit margin is the result of its ability to decrease total costs and expenses as a percentage of net sales. It is important to note, however, that the same results occur when a firm increases its prices faster than its increases in costs. In that case, it is not that the firm is so efficient as it is able to pass along the cost increases. It is up to the financial analyst to determine if this type of trend reflects efficiency or simply price increases.

Another data set that can be used to evaluate a corporation's performance over time consists of its quarterly earnings per share and dividends per share. Table 3-7 shows Braden Industries' quarterly figures for 1983, 1984, and 1985. Apparently this firm has some degree of seasonality in its earnings pattern because its largest quarterly EPS occurred in Quarter 4 in each of these three years. Allowing for this seasonality pattern, Braden's EPS is trending upward at a slow rate.

The dividend pattern of Braden Industries reinforces its earnings trend. Apparently the firm adopts a quarterly dividend rate and maintains it until a subsequent decision is made to once again increase the dividend. This is the firm's way of indicating to its shareholders that it expects to sustain the level of EPS and possibly increase it in the future.

**Table 3-7.**          Braden Industries' Quarterly Earnings and Dividends
                        (In Dollars per Share)

| Year | Quarter | Earnings | Dividends |
|------|---------|----------|-----------|
| 1983 | Q1 | $0.88 | $0.18 |
|      | Q2 | .97 | .18 |
|      | Q3 | .95 | .18 |
|      | Q4 | 1.02 | .2075 |
| 1984 | Q1 | .90 | .2075 |
|      | Q2 | .98 | .2075 |
|      | Q3 | .96 | .2075 |
|      | Q4 | 1.06 | .2075 |
| 1985 | Q1 | .90 | .2075 |
|      | Q2 | .95 | .2075 |
|      | Q3 | .93 | .2250 |
|      | Q4 | 1.16 | .2250 |

*Looking for Shifts in Trends and Isolating Data Outliers.* Quarterly EPS can also be used to illustrate shifts in trends and data outliers. Table 3-8 contains four years of EPS data for one of Braden Industries' competitors. These data are plotted in Figure 3-4.

Figure 3-4.          **Quarterly EPS Trends for Table 3-8 (In Dollars)**

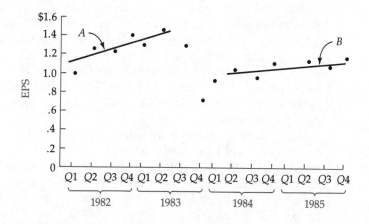

**Table 3-8.**          Quarterly EPS (In Dollars)

| Year | Quarterly | Earnings |
|------|-----------|----------|
| 1982 | Q1 | $1.00 |
|      | Q2 | 1.25 |
|      | Q3 | 1.22 |
|      | Q4 | 1.40 |
| 1983 | Q1 | 1.30 |
|      | Q2 | 1.45 |
|      | Q3 | 1.30 |
|      | Q4 | .74 |
| 1984 | Q1 | .95 |
|      | Q2 | 1.04 |
|      | Q3 | .99 |
|      | Q4 | 1.06 |
| 1985 | Q1 | 1.10 |
|      | Q2 | 1.12 |
|      | Q3 | 1.10 |
|      | Q4 | 1.15 |

The first six values in Table 3-8 shows that the EPS for Braden's competitor was growing at a fairly steady rate. Line *A* in Figure 3-4 is a freehand trend line drawn for these six values.

The $0.74 value for Quarter 4, 1983, is an example of a data outlier. The $0.74 is an extreme value when compared with the other 15 quarterly earnings. Presumably the competitor has an explanation for this sudden and sharp decrease in earnings. This corporation will want to consider the $0.74 as being irrelevant to future earnings estimates since the data outlier did not signal a change from increasing to decreasing EPS.

Note that a shift in the EPS trend occurred during the last three quarters of 1984 and became apparent in 1985. Over the last seven quarters, EPS increased very little. Line *B* in Figure 3-4 is a freehand trend line for these seven values. The shift in the time series trend is seen by comparing Lines *A* and *B* in Figure 3-4.

If a financial analyst were to forecast 1986 EPS for Braden's competitor, he or she would tend to discount or exclude completely both the 1982-83 trend and the $0.74 data outlier. The new trend established during the last six quarters is a much more relevant forecasting guide than the earlier 1982-83 trend. In addition, this corporation recovered from the sudden drop in EPS that occurred at the end of 1983. Hence, the data outlier is best left out of any data used to forecast its future EPS.

**Evaluation of Ratio Analysis**    The intelligent use of ratio analysis requires an understanding of the advantages and limitations of this technique. This section summarizes the strengths and weaknesses of ratio analysis that were identified in analyzing Braden Industries' financial statements.

**ADVANTAGES OF RATIO ANALYSIS.** The advantages of ratio analysis are:

1. Ratios are easy to compute.

2. Ratios provide a standard of comparison at a point in time and allow comparisons to be made with industry averages.

3. Ratios can be used to analyze a corporation's financial time series in order to discover trends, shifts in trends, and data outliers.

4. Ratios are useful in identifying problem areas of a firm.

5. When combined with other tools, ratio analysis makes an important contribution to the task of evaluating a corporation's financial performance.

**LIMITATIONS OF RATIO ANALYSIS.** The limitations of ratio analysis are:

1. Taken by itself, a ratio provides little useful information.

2. Ratios seldom provide the answers to the questions they raise because generally they do not identify the causes of a corporation's difficulties.

3. Ratios can be easily misinterpreted. For example, a decrease in the value of a ratio does not necessarily mean that something undesirable has happened.

4. Very few standards exist that can be used to judge the adequacy of a ratio or a set of ratios. Industry averages cannot be relied upon exclusively to evaluate a corporation's performance because, by definition, half the firms in the industry will perform worse than the industry average.

## THE FUNDS STATEMENT

This section explains the steps needed to prepare a funds statement and the end-of-chapter problems require you to generate these statements as part of financial statement analysis. The preparation of a funds statement helps to illustrate the interrelationship between income statements and balance sheets. In addition, the usefulness of a funds statement in financial statement analysis becomes clearer when the analyst understands how such a statement is prepared.

**Preparation of a Funds Statement**

The preparation of a funds statement typically requires three steps: (1) classifying the changes that occur in the individual accounts between two balance sheets as either sources or uses of funds, (2) making a number of adjustments to these changes, and (3) completing the funds statement from the data generated by the first two steps.

CLASSIFYING SOURCES AND USES. Changes in individual accounts between two balance sheets being compared are identified as either sources or uses of funds by using the following rules:

### Sources

1. An increase in a liability or equity account
2. A decrease in an asset account

### Uses

1. An increase in an asset account
2. A decrease in a liability or equity account

Increases in liability and equity accounts are sources of funds because they represent financing sources. Bank loans, for example, provide cash in the form of bank deposits. Accounts payable, the value of purchases that have not yet been paid, represent financing provided by vendors. Equity accounts increase when the firm sells stock and/or retains its earnings. In either case, funds are provided. Decreases in assets are sources of funds because they provide the assets that are sold and the cash that is used to make payments. Accounts receivable represent financing extended by the firm; when payment is received, the decrease in the receivable is seen to provide funds that were previously committed to the purchaser.

Increases in physical assets are uses of funds because they represent investments the company is making. Increases in accounts receivable means that the firm is financing its customers and is thus committing the value of the credit sales to them. An increase in cash indicates that funds are being used to accumulate the asset, cash. For example, when a check is received in payment of an account receivable, the decrease in the receivable is a source of funds; the corresponding increase in cash is the (perhaps temperorary) use of these funds. Decreases in liability and equity accounts are uses of funds because they represent repayments by the firm of previously obtained financing. Funds are used to repay bonds and loans, and to repurchase any of its own stock the firm may decide to acquire.

To illustrate the first step, refer to Braden Industries' balance sheets for 1985 and 1984 in Table 3-2. The changes in each account are computed as increases or decreases between December 31, 1985 and 1984. Each change is then classified as a source or a use of funds according to the above rules. Table 3-9 shows the mechanics of this step for Braden Industries' data. Note that *gross* property and plant and accumulated depreciation accounts are omitted in Table 3-9. These accounts are not included in a funds statement. However, the change in *net* property and plant is computed and appears in the funds statement.

**Table 3-9.**    **Braden Industries' Changes in Balance Sheet Accounts during 1985**

|  | 12-31-85 | 12-31-84 | Change | Source (S) or Use (U) |
|---|---|---|---|---|
| **Assets** | | | | |
| Current assets: | | | | |
| Cash | $ 140,000 | $ 115,000 | +$ 25,000 | U |
| Accounts receivable | 1,760,000 | 1,440,000 | + 320,000 | U |
| Inventory | 2,175,000 | 2,000,000 | + 175,000 | U |
| Prepaid expenses | 50,000 | 63,000 | − 13,000 | S |
| Total current assets | $4,125,000 | $3,618,000 | | |
| Fixed assets: | | | | |
| Long-term receivables | $1,255,000 | $1,090,000 | + 165,000 | U |
| Net property and plant | 1,175,000 | 1,155,000 | + 20,000 | U |
| Other fixed assets | 550,000 | 530,000 | + 20,000 | U |
| Total fixed assets | $2,980,000 | $2,775,000 | | |
| Total assets | $7,105,000 | $6,393,000 | | |
| **Liabilities and Stockholders' Equity** | | | | |
| Current liabilities: | | | | |
| Accounts payable | $1,325,000 | $1,225,000 | +$100,000 | S |
| Bank loans payable | 475,000 | 550,000 | − 75,000 | U |
| Accrued federal taxes | 675,000 | 425,000 | + 250,000 | S |
| Current maturities of long-term debt | 17,500 | 26,000 | − 8,500 | U |
| Dividends payable | 20,000 | 16,250 | + 3,750 | S |
| Total current liabilites | $2,512,500 | $2,242,250 | | |
| Long-term liabilities | 1,350,000 | 1,425,000 | − 75,000 | U |
| Total liabilities | $3,862,500 | $3,667,250 | | |
| Stockholders' equity: | | | | |
| Common stock | $ 44,500 | $ 43,300 | + 1,200 | S |
| Additional paid-in capital | 568,000 | 372,450 | + 195,550 | S |
| Retained earnings | 2,630,000 | 2,310,000 | + 320,000 | S |
| Total stockholders' equity | $3,242,500 | $2,725,750 | | |
| Total liabilities and stockholders' equity | $7,105,000 | $6,393,000 | | |

MAKING ADJUSTMENTS TO CHANGES.  A number of adjustments are necessary before the changes in the balance sheet accounts can be used to generate the complete funds statement. These adjustments help to provide a more accurate picture of a corporation's flow of funds.

*Change in Net Property and Plant.* Table 3-9 shows that net property and plant increased by $20,000 during 1985. This value can be misleading if partially depreciated assets were sold during 1985 for prices that differ from their book values or if partially depreciated assets were retired. A better, but not perfect, estimate of the change in net property and plant can be obtained by taking the following steps:

1.  Add the income statement depreciation expense incurred during the time period to the net property and plant recorded at the end of that period.

2.  Subtract from the sum obtained in Step 1 the net property and plant recorded at the end of the previous period.

For Braden Industries, the adjusted value of the change in net property and plant is computed as follows:

| | |
|---|---:|
| Net property and plant, 12-31-85 | $1,175,000 |
| Add: Depreciation expense for 1985 | 80,000 |
| | $1,255,000 |
| Less: Net property and plant, 12-31-84 | 1,155,000 |
| Change in net property and plant for 1985 | $  100,000 |

*Depreciation as a Source of Funds.* The two adjustments made to changes in net property and plant and in retained earnings require that the $80,000 depreciation expense for 1985 be added as a *source* of funds in the funds statement. Why is depreciation classified as a source of funds? Since depreciation is a noncash expense, this item did not require an outlay of funds during 1985. Consequently, the funds provided by operations (earnings after taxes of $410,000) are understated by the amount of the depreciation expense. In addition, depreciation expense was used in adjusting the change in net property and plant. Hence, depreciation expense is listed as a *source* in the funds statement.

*Change in Retained Earnings.* The $320,000 change in retained earnings shown in Table 3-9 is not shown directly in the funds statement. In preparing the funds statement, this change is replaced by the income statement earnings after taxes as a *source* of funds, and dividends paid during the year as a *use* of funds. For 1985, Braden Industries' earnings after taxes were $410,000; dividends paid were $90,000. The difference, $320,000, represents the increase in retained earnings. This adjustment explains how a corporation's earnings after taxes are sources of funds, while dividends paid are uses of funds.

COMPLETING THE FUNDS STATEMENT. Table 3-10 shows the completed 1985 funds statement for Braden Industries. The individual values in the funds statement consist of the balance sheet changes contained in Table 3-9 and the items generated by making the three adjustments described above. The accepted practice is to list earnings after taxes and depreciation as the first two *sources* in a funds statement, and dividends as the first *use* of funds.

| Table 3-10. | Braden Industries' Sources and Uses of Funds for 1985 | |
|---|---|---|
| | **Sources** | |
| | Earnings after taxes | $   410,000 |
| | Depreciation | 80,000 |
| | Prepaid expenses | 13,000 |
| | Accounts payable | 100,000 |
| | Accrued federal taxes | 250,000 |
| | Dividends payable | 3,750 |
| | Common stock | 1,200 |
| | Additional paid-in capital | 195,550 |
| | Total sources | $1,053,500 |
| | **Uses** | |
| | Dividends paid | $     90,000 |
| | Cash | 25,000 |
| | Accounts receivable | 320,000 |
| | Inventory | 175,000 |
| | Long-term receivables | 165,000 |
| | Net property and plant | 100,000 |
| | Other fixed assets | 20,000 |
| | Bank loans payable | 75,000 |
| | Current maturities of long-term debt | 8,500 |
| | Long-term liabilities | 75,000 |
| | Total uses | $1,053,500 |

**Interpretation of the Funds Statement**

Funds statements are no more difficult to interpret than are the income statements and balance sheets from which the funds statements are prepared. Braden Industries' 1985 funds statement, for example, lists total sources and uses of $1,053,500. This is the incremental amount of funds provided and used during the calendar year. Funds provided by operations accounted for $490,000 of the total sources ($410,000 + $80,000). Other major sources are the increase in accounts payable ($100,000) and the sale of common stock which provided $196,750 of new funds ($1,200 + $195,500). Presumably, the increase in accrued federal taxes payable reflects a tax liability that will be paid early in 1986.

The major uses of funds include increases in accounts receivable ($320,000), inventory ($175,000), and long-term receivables ($165,000). Net property and plant was increased by an estimated $100,000. Three liability accounts, all representing borrowed funds, were reduced: bank loans payable ($75,000), current maturities of long-term debt ($8,500), and long-term debt ($75,000).

**Using the Funds Statement in Statement Analysis**

The funds statement, like ratio analysis, is used to analyze a corporation's financial performance as reported in its income statements and balance sheets. Funds statements measure the *dollar changes* in balance sheet accounts that occur between two points in time. This is in contrast to the relative, or percentage, changes measured by financial ratios.

Braden Industries' funds statement in Table 3-10 can be used to formulate a number of questions that need to be answered. For example:

1. Do the increases in accounts payable and accrued federal income taxes mean that Braden has encountered some difficulties in generating the cash to pay these liabilities?

2. Does the increase in the level of accounts receivable signify (*a*) consistency with the extent to which sales increased in 1985 over 1984, (*b*) a change in Braden's credit policy, or (*c*) the result of external events over which Braden has no control?

3. Does the increase in inventories represent obsolete inventory, or was this increase planned by Braden?

4. What significance, if any, should be attached to the relatively large amount of increase in long-term receivables?

5. Was the repayment of the bank loan a scheduled repayment?

Some of the questions that have been formulated also occurred as a result of the earlier cross-sectional ratio analysis of Braden's financial performance. This demonstrates how financial ratios and funds statements work together to generate an analysis of financial statements.

**Evaluation of Funds Statements**

Understanding the advantages and limitations of using funds statements to analyze a corporation's income statements and balance sheets helps to insure that funds statements are not used or interpreted incorrectly.

**ADVANTAGES OF A FUNDS STATEMENT.** The advantages of a funds statement are:

1. It is not difficult to prepare as it follows a clearly defined set of steps.

2. Since it measures the dollar changes in balance sheet accounts, it is useful not only to the financial manager but also to the corporation's creditors and stockholders who need to know how the corporation finances itself and where the funds are committed.

3. It helps isolate existing and/or emerging problem areas within the corporation, thus focusing additional analysis where it will yield the most information.

**LIMITATIONS OF A FUNDS STATEMENT.** The limitations of a funds statement are:

1. By itself it cannot provide a complete analysis of a corporation's financial position.

2. When a funds statement is not used in conjunction with other analytical tools, it is easy to misinterpret changes in balance sheet accounts. For example, many current asset and current liability accounts vary as a function of a firm's sales, but these relationships are not evident in a funds statement.

3. The *change* in net property and plant cannot be measured exactly from the income statement and balance sheet; it must be estimated.

# SUMMARY

Financial analysis of the data contained in a corporation's income statements and balance sheets is aided by the use of two major techniques: (1) ratio analysis and (2) use of a funds statement.

Ratio analysis is used to obtain measures of corporate liquidity, activity, debt, and profitability. The cross-sectional approach to ratio analysis, supplemented with industry averages, can help evaluate the financial position of a corporation at a point in time. The time series approach, together with the preparation of common size income statements, can help isolate financial trends, shifts in trends, and outlier values.

The funds statement measures the dollar changes in balance sheet accounts that occur during a given time interval. This statement classifies these changes as sources or uses of funds. By identifying large dollar changes in balance sheet accounts, this statement helps isolate particular aspects of corporate performance for further study.

An in-depth evaluation of a corporation's performance — as reflected in its income statements and balance sheets — requires the preparation and analysis of both financial ratios and funds statements. However, neither technique, by itself, can do an adequate job of financial statement analysis. Even when financial ratios and funds statements are used together, they will not provide a complete understanding of a firm's activities. Rather, the use of these analytical techniques will raise questions that, when pursued, will provide the information needed to reach an informed judgment about a corporation's financial condition.

# QUESTIONS

**3-1.** What are the purposes of financial statement analysis?

3-2.  What type of information is contained in an income statement?
3-3.  What type of information is contained in a balance sheet?
3-4.  What major aspects of corporate performance can be evaluated by using ratio analysis?
3-5.  What does ratio analysis contribute to cross-sectional analysis?
3-6.  What does ratio analysis contribute to time series analysis?
3-7.  What are the advantages and limitations of ratio analysis?
3-8.  What type of information is contained in a funds statement?
3-9.  Identify each of the following as being a source or a use of funds:

   a.  Increase in cash
   b.  Decrease in cash
   c.  Decrease in accounts receivable
   d.  Increase in inventory
   e.  Decrease in net property and plant
   f.  Increase in accounts payable
   g.  Increase in loans payable
   h.  Decrease in long-term debt
   i.  Increase in retained earnings
   j.  Decrease in retained earnings

3-10.  What does the preparation and analysis of a funds statement contribute to financial statement analysis?
3-11.  What are the advantages and limitations of using funds statements as a part of financial statement analysis?

# PROBLEMS

*Note:* To solve Problems 3-1 through 3-7, refer to the income statements and balance sheets for G & F, Inc., in Tables 3-11 and 3-12.

Table 3-11.        G & F, Inc., Income Statements (For the Years Ending December 31)

|  | 1979 | | 1978 | |
|---|---|---|---|---|
| Net sales | | $11,730,000 | | $10,430,000 |
| Less: Cost of goods sold | $8,175,000 | | $7,600,000 | |
| Administrative expenses | 1,700,000 | | 1,470,000 | |
| R & D expenses | 500,000 | | 385,000 | |
| Interest expense | 105,000 | | 75,000 | |
| Total | | 10,480,000 | | 9,530,000 |
| Earnings before taxes | | $ 1,250,000 | | $  900,000 |
| Less: Income taxes | | 600,000 | | 432,000 |
| Earnings after taxes (net income) | | $  650,000 | | $  468,000 |
| Dividends paid | | $   70,000 | | $   50,000 |
| Addition to retained earnings | | $  580,000 | | $  418,000 |

*Notes to income statements:*
1. No significant lease obligations.
2. Depreciation expense: $110,000 in 1979; $95,000 in 1978.

**Table 3-12.**     G & F, Inc., Balance Sheets (As of December 31)

|  | 1979 | | 1978 | |
|---|---|---|---|---|
| **Assets** | | | | |
| Current assets: | | | | |
| Cash | | $ 330,000 | | $1,400,000 |
| Accounts receivable | | 2,725,000 | | 2,180,000 |
| Inventory | | 2,925,000 | | 2,060,000 |
| Total current assets | | $5,980,000 | | $5,640,000 |
| Fixed assets: | | | | |
| Plant and equipment | $3,040,000 | | $2,270,000 | |
| Less: Accumulated depreciation | 935,000 | | 910,000 | |
| Net plant and equipment | | 2,105,000 | | 1,360,000 |
| Other fixed assets | | 160,000 | | 130,000 |
| Total fixed assets | | $2,265,000 | | $1,490,000 |
| Total assets | | $8,245,000 | | $7,130,000 |
| **Liabilities and Stockholders' Equity** | | | | |
| Current liabilities: | | | | |
| Accounts payable | | $ 660,000 | | $ 455,000 |
| Short-term debt | | 52,000 | | 38,000 |
| Accrued liabilities | | 825,000 | | 800,000 |
| Other current liabilities | | 680,000 | | 630,000 |
| Total current liabilities | | $2,217,000 | | $1,923,000 |
| Long-term debt | | 1,580,000 | | 1,510,000 |
| Deferred taxes | | 283,000 | | 198,000 |
| Total liabilities | | $4,080,000 | | $3,631,000 |
| Stockholders' equity: | | | | |
| Common stock (190,000 shares outstanding in 1979; 184,000 shares outstanding in 1978) | | $ 190,000 | | $ 184,000 |
| Additional paid-in capital | | 1,755,000 | | 1,675,000 |
| Retained earnings | | 2,220,000 | | 1,640,000 |
| Total stockholders' equity | | $4,165,000 | | $3,499,000 |
| Total liabilities and stockholders' equity | | $8,245,000 | | $7,130,000 |

**3-1.** Compute the current ratios and quick ratios for G & F, Inc., for 1978 and 1979.

**3-2.** Compute the inventory turnover, total asset turnover, and average collection period for G & F, Inc., for 1978 and 1979.

**3-3.** Compute the long-term debt to equity, total debt to total assets, and times interest earned ratios for G & F, Inc., for 1978 and 1979.

**3-4.** Compute the earnings per share, dividends per share, payout ratio, profit margin, return on investment, and return on stockholders' equity for G & F, Inc., for 1978 and 1979.

**3-5.** Prepare the common size income statement for G & F, Inc., for 1978 and 1979.

**3-6.** Prepare the funds statement for G & F, Inc., for 1979.

3-7.   Combining the results of Problems 3-1 through 3-6, what information can be gathered concerning the financial status of G & F, Inc.?

3-8.   Table 3-13 contains four separate quarterly times series (A, B, C, and D). Discuss the pattern contained in each series. *Hint:* Your analysis may be improved if you plot each data set and examine each graph for trends and/or data outliers.

Table 3-13.          Financial Ratio Time Series

| Years by Quarters | Times Series A Earnings per Share | Time Series B Earnings per Share | Times Series C Profit Margin | Times Series D Profit Margin |
|---|---|---|---|---|
| 19X1 Q1 | $0.40 | $0.10 | 1.2% | 4.8% |
| Q2 | .40 | .30 | 1.4 | 5.0 |
| Q3 | .50 | .60 | 2.0 | 5.2 |
| Q4 | .60 | .85 | 2.6 | 5.4 |
| 19X2 Q1 | .30 | 1.10 | 3.4 | 5.5 |
| Q2 | .70 | 1.30 | 4.0 | 5.6 |
| Q3 | .75 | 1.35 | 5.0 | 5.7 |
| Q4 | .80 | 1.40 | 5.2 | 5.7 |
| 19X3 Q1 | 1.20 | 1.45 | 5.3 | 5.6 |
| Q2 | .90 | 1.45 | 5.4 | 5.5 |
| Q3 | 1.00 | 1.50 | 5.4 | 5.4 |
| Q4 | 1.05 | 1.52 | 5.5 | 5.2 |

*Note:* To solve Problems 3-9 through 3-15, refer to the income statements and balance sheets for Provitex, Inc., in Tables 3-14 and 3-15.

3-9.   Compute the current ratios and quick ratios for Provitex, Inc., for 1984 and 1985.

Table 3-14.          Provitex, Inc., Income Statements (For the Years Ending December 31)

| | 1985 | | 1984 | |
|---|---|---|---|---|
| | (In Thousands of Dollars) | | | |
| Net Sales | | $3,392,974 | | $3,235,640 |
| Less: Cost of goods sold | $2,525,689 | | $2,440,073 | |
| Administrative expenses | 484,345 | | 432,371 | |
| Depreciation expense | 64,125 | | 56,435 | |
| Interest expense | 37,221 | | 29,047 | |
| Total | | 3,111,380 | | 2,957,926 |
| Earnings before taxes | | $ 281,594 | | $ 277,714 |
| Less: Income taxes | | 132,800 | | 132,250 |
| Net income | | $ 148,794 | | $ 145,464 |
| Dividends paid | | $ 59,400 | | $ 52,800 |
| Addition to retained earnings | | $ 89,394 | | $ 92,664 |

*Notes to financial statements:* (1) No significant lease obligations and (2) 33 million common shares outstanding in both 1984 and 1985.

**Table 3-15.** Provitex, Inc., Balance Sheets (As of December 31)

|  | 1985 | 1984 |
|---|---|---|
|  | (In Thousands of Dollars) | |
| **Assets** | | |
| Current assets: | | |
| Cash | $ 22,952 | $ 16,500 |
| Short-term investments, at cost | | |
| (which approximates market) | 6,924 | 154,566 |
| Accounts receivable (less allowance | | |
| for losses of $16,180 and $13,811) | 546,504 | 539,319 |
| Inventories: | | |
| Finished goods | 266,480 | 233,993 |
| Work in process | 456,275 | 320,026 |
| Raw materials and supplies | 152,424 | 140,505 |
| Prepaid expenses | 13,424 | 14,084 |
| Total current assets | $1,464,983 | $1,418,993 |
| Fixed assets: | | |
| Land and buildings | $236,468 | $224,035 |
| Machinery and equipment | 745,801 | 664,365 |
| Less: Accumulated depreciation | 561,252 | 516,911 |
| Net plant, property and equipment | 421,017 | 371,489 |
| Other assets | 32,792 | 31,968 |
| Total Assets | $1,918,792 | $1,822,450 |
| **Liabilities and Stockholders' Equity** | | |
| Current liabilities: | | |
| Accounts payable | $ 176,446 | $ 185,437 |
| Short-term debt | 64,052 | 27,719 |
| Current maturities of long-term debt | 81,879 | 7,419 |
| Accrued liabilities | 193,278 | 178,070 |
| Federal income taxes | 42,755 | 59,011 |
| Other current liabilities | 40,869 | 62,682 |
| Dividends payable | 33,682 | 31,980 |
| Total current liabilities | $ 632,961 | $ 552,318 |
| Long-term debt | 222,864 | 290,426 |
| Other liabilities | 13,934 | 20,067 |
| Total liabilities | $ 869,759 | $ 862,811 |
| Stockholders' equity: | | |
| Common stock 25¢ par value | | |
| (authorized 75,000,000 shares) | $ 8,250 | $ 8,250 |
| Capital surplus | 105,214 | 105,214 |
| Retained earnings | 935,569 | 846,175 |
| Total stockholders' equity | $1,049,033 | $ 959,639 |
| Total liabilities and stockholders' equity | $1,918,792 | $1,822,450 |

3-10. Compute the inventory turnover, total asset turnover, and average collection period for Provitex, Inc., for 1984 and 1985.

3-11. Compute the long-term debt to equity, total debt to total assets, and times interest earned ratios for Provitex, Inc., for 1984 and 1985.

3-12. Compute the earnings per share, dividends per share, payout ratio, profit margin, return on investment, and return on stockholders' equity for Provitex, Inc., for 1984 and 1985.

3-13. Prepare the common size income statements for Provitex, Inc., for 1984 and 1985.

3-14. Prepare the funds statement for Provitex, Inc., for 1985.

3-15. Combining the results of Problems 3-9 through 3-14, what information can be gathered concerning the financial status of Provitex, Inc.?

*Note:* To solve Problems 3-16 through 3-22, refer to the income statements and balance sheets for Name, Inc., in Tables 3-16 and 3-17.

3-16. Compute the current ratios and quick ratios for Name, Inc., for 1984 and 1985.

3-17. Compute the inventory turnover, total asset turnover, and average collection period for Name, Inc., for 1984 and 1985.

3-18. Compute the long-term debt to equity, total debt to total assets, and times interest earned ratios for Name, Inc., for 1984 and 1985.

Table 3-16.        Name, Inc., Income Statements (For the Years Ending December 31)

| | 1985 | | 1984 | |
|---|---|---|---|---|
| | | (In Thousands of Dollars) | | |
| Net Sales | | $3,282,768 | | $2,868,379 |
| Less: Operating cost | $2,302,591 | | $2,008,068 | |
| Selling and general administrative expenses | 244,788 | | 220,880 | |
| Research and development expenses | 46,275 | | 30,326 | |
| Depreciation expense | 240,832 | | 195,261 | |
| Interest expense | 86,052 | | 65,699 | |
| Total | | 2,920,538 | | 2,520,234 |
| Earnings before income taxes | | $ 362,230 | | $ 348,145 |
| Less: Income taxes | | 131,000 | | 106,800 |
| Earnings after taxes (net income) | | $ 231,230 | | $ 241,345 |
| Retained earnings at beginning of year | | $1,539,610 | | $1,411,196 |
| | | $1,770,840 | | $1,652,541 |
| Dividends paid: | | | | |
| Common | | $ 101,904 | | $ 101,731 |
| Preferred | | $ 11,200 | | $ 11,200 |
| Retained earnings at end of year | | $1,657,736 | | $1,539,610 |

**Table 3-17.**   Name, Inc., Balance Sheet (As of December 31)

| Assets | 1985 | | 1984 | |
|---|---|---|---|---|
| | (In Thousands of Dollars) | | | |
| Current assets: | | | | |
| Cash, including interest bearing time deposits of $133,853 in 1985 and $79,932 in 1984 | | $ 117,897 | | $ 61,650 |
| Short-term investments at cost which approximates market | | 143,332 | | 231,588 |
| Receivables, less allowances of $6,151 in 1985 and $4,079 in 1984 | | 314,395 | | 258,472 |
| Inventories: | | | | |
| Product inventories | | 303,074 | | 308,234 |
| Materials and supplies | | 96,188 | | 88,800 |
| Prepaid expenses | | 34,632 | | 32,683 |
| Total current assets | | $1,009,518 | | $ 981,427 |
| Property, plant and equipment at cost: | | | | |
| Land | $ 598,599 | | $ 565,755 | |
| Buildings and improvements | 440,215 | | 420,230 | |
| Machinery and equipment | 2,635,337 | | 2,352,111 | |
| Rail and truck roads and other | 293,173 | | 256,970 | |
| | $3,967,324 | | $3,595,066 | |
| Less: allowance for depreciation and amortization | 1,382,889 | | 1,228,841 | |
| Net property, plant and equipment | | $2,584,435 | | $2,366,225 |
| Total assets | | $3,593,953 | | $3,347,652 |
| | | | | |
| **Liabilities and Stockholders' Interest** | | | | |
| Current liabilities: | | | | |
| Notes payables, principally to banks | | $ 1,800 | | $ 6,780 |
| Current maturities of long-term debt | | 24,338 | | 15,035 |
| Accounts payable | | 153,905 | | 131,897 |
| Accrued payroll | | 227,046 | | 177,815 |
| Accrued income taxes | | 72,090 | | 137,922 |
| Total current liabilities | | $ 479,179 | | $ 469,449 |
| Long-term debt | | 1,211,871 | | 1,093,426 |
| Total liabilities | | $1,691,050 | | $1,562,875 |
| | | | | |
| Stockholders' interest: | | | | |
| Preferred shares: authorized 7,000,000 shares; issued 4,000,000 shares, $2.80 convertible cumulative, first series, $1.00 par value | | $ 4,000 | | $ 4,000 |
| Common shares: authorized 140,000,000 shares: issued 128,622,462 shares, $1.875 par value | | $ 241,167 | | $ 241,167 |
| Retained earnings | | 1,657,736 | | 1,539,610 |
| Total stockholders' interest | | $1,902,903 | | $1,784,777 |
| Total liabilities stockholders' interest | | $3,593,953 | | $3,347,652 |

**3-19.** Compute the earnings per share, dividends per share, payout ratio, profit margin, return on investment, and return on stockholders' equity for Name, Inc., for 1984 and 1985.

**3-20.** Prepare the common size income statements for Name, Inc., for 1984 and 1985.

**3-21.** Prepare the funds statement for Name, Inc., for 1985.

**3-22.** Combining the results of Problems 3-16 through 3-21, what information can be gathered concerning the financial status of Name, Inc.?

**3-23.** Using the income statement and balance sheets contained in Tables 3-18 and 3-19, prepare the associated funds statement for 1985.

**Table 3-18.**        Income Statement (For Year Ending December 31, 1985)

| | | |
|---|---:|---:|
| Revenue: | | $150,000 |
| Less: Cost of goods sold | $50,000 | |
| Other expenses | 25,000 | |
| Depreciation | 15,000 | 90,000 |
| Taxable income | | 60,000 |
| Less: Income taxes | | 24,000 |
| Profit after taxes | | 36,000 |
| Dividends | | 16,000 |
| Transfer to retained earnings | | $ 20,000 |

**Table 3-19.**        Balance Sheets (As of December 31)

| | 1984 | 1985 |
|---|---:|---:|
| **Assets** | | |
| Current assets: | | |
| Cash | $ 10,000 | $ 15,000 |
| Accounts receivable | 50,000 | 60,000 |
| Inventory | 40,000 | 30,000 |
| Total current assets | $100,000 | $105,000 |
| Net fixed assets | 200,000 | 235,000 |
| Total assets | $300,000 | $340,000 |
| **Current Liabilities and Stockholders' Equity** | | |
| Current liabilities | $ 40,000 | $ 45,000 |
| Long term debt | 110,000 | 125,000 |
| Total liabilities | $150,000 | $170,000 |
| Stockholders' equity: | | |
| Common stock | $100,000 | $100,000 |
| Retained earnings | 50,000 | 70,000 |
| Total stockholders' equity | $150,000 | $170,000 |
| Total liabilities and stockholders' equity | $300,000 | $340,000 |

# SELECTED REFERENCES

Bernstein, L. A. *Financial Statement Analysis.* Rev. ed. Homewood, Illinois: Richard D. Irwin, 1978.

Foster, G. *Financial Statement Analysis.* Englewood Cliffs, New Jersey: Prentice-Hall, Inc., 1978.

Helfert, E. *Techniques of Financial Analysis.* 5th ed. Homewood, Illinois: Richard D. Irwin, Inc., 1982.

Moore, C., and R. Jaedicke. *Managerial Accounting.* 5th ed. Cincinnati, Ohio: South-Western Publishing Co., 1980.

Viscione, J. *Financial Analysis.* Boston; Houghton Mifflin Company, 1977.

# CHAPTER 4

# Budgeting
# and
# Forecasting Techniques

The decisions that corporate executives reach in seeking to increase shareholder wealth are based in part on their forecasts of future events. Short-run and long-run forecasts help to prepare the financial plans that a corporation develops, adopts, implements, and reevaluates as subsequent events unfold. Cash budgets and pro forma statements are examples of short-run financial forecasts. These techniques are useful in forecasting one year or less into the future, although pro forma statements are also useful in projecting a firm's financial position several years into the future.

Budgets and the budgeting process are used to identify the most efficient allocation of a corporation's resources and to provide planning and control mechanisms over funds flows. Corporate managers use several types of budgets in planning and executing the firm's operations. Production budgets detail the amount and timing of the funds required to produce a manufacturing corporation's product lines. This type of budget includes labor, materials, and other expenses incurred in the production process. The marketing and sales budgets contain the financial plan for advertising and selling the firm's products and services. The research and development budgets reflect the dollar commitments the firm makes for basic research and for developing future product lines. The administrative budgets *contain the other expenses incurred in overall managing of the corporation.*

*Financial managers combine these budgets in order to estimate the corporation's funds flows, profitability, and financial condition over a given planning period. Financial statement analysis, discussed in Chapter 3, provides useful data in generating these estimates and helps to construct the resulting cash budgets and pro forma statements. Cash budgets project cash inflows and outflows over time. Pro forma statements are projections or forecasts in the form of financial statements — they project how these statements will appear in the future. A pro forma income statement estimates the revenues, costs, and profitability of the firm for the planning period. A pro forma balance sheet estimates the financial condition of the corporation at the end of the planning period. Cash budgeting is the first topic of this chapter and is followed by a discussion of pro forma statements.*

## CASH BUDGETING

A **cash budget** is a forecast of a firm's cash inflows and outflows over a designated planning period. The cash budget helps identify periods of cash surpluses, as well as periods during which additional financing will be needed. Thus, a cash budget helps the financial manager to measure the amount and duration of cash shortages and to prepare repayment schedules if cash shortages are to be financed with borrowed funds. Cash budgeting is important because a firm's cash needs fluctuate during its course of operations. Typically a firm's most serious cash needs occur when sales are increasing; cash surpluses are more likely to occur after sales have leveled off or even declined. This is because a firm must increase its assets — notably inventory and accounts receivable — as its volume of sales increases. These increases in assets must be financed, and financial managers want to be prepared in advance to meet the need for external funds.

Assets that increase with sales are said to increase spontaneously. For example, accounts receivable increase spontaneously because a portion of the increased sales are sold on credit. Some liabilities also increase spontaneously, and this helps finance the spontaneous assets. Accounts payable are examples of liabilities that increase spontaneously. In addition to the source of funds provided by spontaneous liability increases, the increased sales may include an increase in cash. However, external funds are frequently needed; a firm may make arrangements with its bank for a line of credit to meet this short-term need.

After the cash budget is finalized and the planning period begun, deviations between actual and budgeted cash flows become important mechanisms of control. These deviations might require only modest changes in such items as loan arrangements or payment schedules of short-term liabilities. On the other hand, significant deviations might eliminate the need for short-term financing or might jeopardize the corporation's ability to meet its loan repayment schedule. Any major deviations — whether favorable or unfavorable to the corporation — should be investigated, and, if indicated, corrective action should be recommended. Such deviations may also require major revisions in the current and future cash budgets.

## Preparation of a Cash Budget

Cash budgets may be prepared on a monthly, weekly, or daily basis. When the budget period is longer than one or two months, the cash budget is partitioned into a set of shorter time intervals, or subintervals, and cash flows are estimated for each subinterval of time. For example, a four-month cash budget might be partitioned into 8 two-week or 16 one-week subintervals; cash flows are estimated for each of the 8 or 16 time segments. Some very large corporations estimate their cash flows on a daily basis and use planning periods that vary from one to three years in length.

The preparation of a cash budget is divided into four steps: (1) forecasting sales, (2) estimating cash inflows, (3) estimating cash outflows, and (4) estimating end-of-month cash and loan balances. For purposes of illustration, the cash budget for J & C, Inc., will be prepared on a ten-month planning period (March 1 to December 31). Cash flows are to be estimated on a monthly basis, and any needed financing is to be incorporated into the cash budget.

FORECASTING SALES. The first and perhaps the most important and difficult step in preparing a cash budget is to forecast monthly sales over the planning period. Monthly estimates of cash inflows and outflows are based primarily on sales forecasts. Since these forecasts are estimates of uncertain future values, errors in sales forecasts must be expected. The goal is to produce a sales forecast with only those errors that fall within an acceptable margin. An *acceptable margin of error* is determined by each corporation and corresponds roughly to the maximum error that can be managed with only minor revisions in its set of financial plans.

Some manufacturing corporations can forecast sales rather easily because of order backlogs. When products and/or services are ordered several months before delivery is anticipated, the resulting backlog of orders provides a good first estimate of planning period sales. On the other hand, retailers who specialize in the sale of consumer nondurables for which demand is seasonal and/or tied to current fashions have perhaps the most difficult sales forecasting problem. In the latter case, some help may be found by obtaining an estimate of industry sales and multiplying that figure by the firm's expected share of market. Sales during the most recent planning period can also be helpful. If all else fails, simply assume that sales during the next planning period will equal current planning period sales and factor in an adjustment for expected inflation.

Assume that J & C, Inc.'s sales are partly in cash and that credit sales are paid over several months. Sales forecasts for January and February are needed in order to estimate accurately the cash inflows during March and April. The 12-month sales forecast needed to prepare the 10-month, March through December cash budget is shown in the top line of Table 4-1. Some seasonality is evident in the firm's sales forecast. The dollar volume of sales is predicted to be at a minimum in May and June and is expected to peak in November and December.

COMPUTING CASH INFLOWS. The cash inflows portion of the cash budget includes two types of cash inflows: (1) receipts on cash and credit sales and (2) other cash inflows not tied directly to sales. Each type of cash inflow is computed separately.

*Cash and Credit Sales.* Cash sales occur when payment by check or currency is made at the time of purchase. These sales are recorded as cash inflows in the month when the sales are made. The accounts receivable generated from credit sales (including credit card transactions) are recorded as cash inflows in the months when the receivables are collected. For J & C, Inc., as for many businesses, a percentage of the accounts receivable is never collected and is written off as bad debts. The bad debt expense is estimated as a percentage of total monthly sales.

The following distribution of cash sales, accounts receivable collections, and bad debts are assumed for J & C, Inc.'s forecast sales. This distribution reflects the firm's historical experience.

**Table 4-1.**  J & C, Inc., Cash Inflows and Outflows (March through December)

| | Jan. | Feb. | March | April | May | June | July | Aug. | Sept. | Oct. | Nov. | Dec. |
|---|---|---|---|---|---|---|---|---|---|---|---|---|
| Sales | $50,000 | $40,000 | $30,000 | $26,000 | $25,000 | $23,000 | $28,000 | $30,000 | $32,000 | $49,000 | $63,000 | $64,000 |
| Cash and credit sales: | | | | | | | | | | | | |
| 15% of monthly sales | 7,500 | 6,000 | 4,500 | 3,900 | 3,750 | 3,450 | 4,200 | 4,500 | 4,800 | 7,350 | 9,450 | 9,600 |
| 60% of sales made in previous month | ----- | 30,000 | 24,000 | 18,000 | 15,600 | 15,000 | 13,800 | 16,800 | 18,000 | 19,200 | 29,400 | 37,800 |
| 20% of sales made two months previously | ----- | ----- | 10,000 | 8,000 | 6,000 | 5,200 | 5,000 | 4,600 | 5,600 | 6,000 | 6,400 | 9,800 |
| Other cash inflows: Sale of equipment | ----- | ----- | ----- | ----- | ----- | ----- | 9,000 | ----- | ----- | ----- | ----- | ----- |
| Total cash inflows | ----- | ----- | $38,500 | $29,900 | $25,350 | $23,650 | $32,000 | $25,900 | $28,400 | $32,550 | $45,250 | $57,200 |
| Purchases: | | | | | | | | | | | | |
| (.15)(.65) of monthly sales | $ 4,875 | $ 3,900 | $ 2,925 | $ 2,535 | $ 2,438 | $ 2,243 | $ 2,730 | $ 2,925 | $ 3,120 | $ 4,778 | $ 6,143 | $ 6,240 |
| (.85)(.65) of previous monthly sales | ----- | 27,625 | 22,100 | 16,575 | 14,365 | 13,813 | 12,708 | 15,470 | 16,575 | 17,680 | 27,073 | 34,808 |
| Salaries and wages: | 9,000 | 8,000 | 7,000 | 6,600 | 6,500 | 6,300 | 6,800 | 7,000 | 7,200 | 8,900 | 10,300 | 10,400 |
| Other operating costs: | 2,300 | 2,200 | 2,100 | 2,060 | 2,050 | 2,030 | 2,080 | 2,100 | 2,120 | 2,290 | 2,430 | 2,440 |
| Tax payments: | ----- | ----- | ----- | 5,000 | ----- | 5,000 | ----- | ----- | 5,000 | ----- | ----- | 5,000 |
| Other payments: Dividends | ----- | ----- | ----- | ----- | ----- | 2,000 | ----- | ----- | ----- | ----- | ----- | 2,000 |
| Equipment purchases | ----- | ----- | 5,000 | 5,000 | 5,000 | ----- | ----- | ----- | ----- | 5,000 | ----- | ----- |
| Total cash outflows | ----- | ----- | $34,125 | $37,770 | $30,353 | $31,386 | $24,318 | $27,495 | $34,015 | $38,648 | $45,946 | $60,888 |

|                                                              | **Percent of Monthly Sales Forecast** |
| ------------------------------------------------------------ | :-----------------------------------: |
| Cash sales                                                   | 15%                                   |
| Accounts receivable collected one month after the sale       | 60                                    |
| Accounts receivable collected two months after the sale      | 20                                    |
| Bad debts                                                    | 5                                     |
|                                                              | 100%                                  |

Since January sales are forecast to be $50,000, the resulting distribution of cash inflows is calculated as follows:

$$
\begin{array}{lll}
\text{January} & (.15)(\$50,000) = & \$\ 7,500 \\
\text{February} & (.60)(\$50,000) = & 30,000 \\
\text{March} & (.20)(\$50,000) = & \underline{10,000} \\
& & \$47,500 \\
\text{Bad debts} & (.05)(\$50,000) = & \underline{\ 2,500} \\
& & \underline{\$50,000}
\end{array}
$$

The cash inflows from cash and credit sales for the entire ten-month planning period of J & C, Inc., are shown in the upper portion of Table 4-1. The cash and credit sales portion of that table is calculated by using the percentages assumed above. Note that cash inflows for March are based in part on January and February sales. This why the sales forecast for January and February is needed.

*Other Cash Inflows.* In addition to the cash generated from sales, other cash inflows can occur during the planning period which should be included in the cash budget. Examples of cash inflows not directly related to sales include tax refunds, proceeds from the sale of marketable securities, and proceeds from the sale of other assets. Table 4-1 shows that J & C, Inc., expects to sell some equipment and forecasts that a $9,000 payment from this sale will be received in July.

**COMPUTING CASH OUTFLOWS.** The cash outflow portion of the cash budget includes five types of payments: (1) payments for purchases, (2) payments for salaries and wages, (3) payments for other operating costs, (4) tax payments, and (5) other payments. Each type of payment is estimated separately.

*Payments for Purchases.* Purchases are frequently made on a credit basis, thus creating accounts payable. Purchase payments are recorded as cash outflows in the months when payments are made by cash or check.

When estimating purchase payments on the basis of a sales forecast, it is necessary to estimate the percentage that purchases are contained in each dollar of sales. Previous income statements can provide a good first estimate of this. This is done by taking the purchases contained in the cost of goods sold and dividing by net sales. This percentage is then multiplied by the sales forecast in order to estimate the required purchase payments.

For J & C, Inc., the time series ratio of purchases as a percentage of sales has increased to 63 percent in recent years due to product line changes. Because further changes are planned, management estimates this ratio will be 65 percent during the next year.

Of the firm's purchases, 15 percent are obtained from vendors who require payment in 10 days; the remaining purchases are obtained from vendors that provide 30-day credit terms. On a monthly basis, the firm's schedule of purchase payments is thus estimated as follows:

|  | % of Monthly Sales Forecast |
|---|---|
| Accounts payable paid in the month purchase is made | 15% |
| Accounts payable paid one month after purchase | 85 |
|  | 100% |

Since January sales are forecast to be $50,000 and purchases represent 65 percent of these sales, the schedule of purchase payments is calculated as follows:

| Purchase payments for January purchases | (.65) ($50,000) = $32,500 |
|---|---|
| Purchase payments made in January | (.15) ($32,500) = 4,875 |
| Purchase payments made in February | (.85) ($32,500) = 27,625 |

The purchase payments for the ten-month planning period are shown in the lower portion of Table 4-1, using the percentages given above.

*Payments for Salaries and Wages.* Salaries and wages (including fringe benefits) are recognized as cash outflows in the month they are paid to employees. A firm typically incurs a minimum amount of payroll expense that is independent of sales volume. Once the sales volume exceeds some minimum amount, wages and salaries tend to increase proportionately with sales.

The monthly payments for salaries and wages for J & C, Inc., are assumed to equal $6,000 plus 10 percent of sales in excess of $20,000. Based on its sale forecast of $50,000 for January, the January payment for salaries and wages is calculated as follows:

$$\$6,000 + (.10)(\$50,000 - \$20,000) = \$9,000$$

The payments for wages and salaries for the ten-month planning period are contained in Table 4-1.

*Other Operating Costs.* Most of the remaining operating expenses for J & C, Inc., are fixed and are paid monthly. Utility and lease payments are estimated at $1,650 per month, and repairs and maintenance are expected to cost $150 per month. Miscellaneous purchases and other costs are estimated to be one percent of monthly sales. For January's forecast sales of $50,000, other operating costs equal:

$$\$1,650 + \$150 + .01\,(\$50,000) = \$2,300$$

The payments for other operating costs for the ten-month planning period are contained in Table 4-1.

*Tax Payments.* The rules that govern the payment of federal, state, and local taxes are simplified in order to keep the focus on the preparation of the cash budget. It is assumed that J & C, Inc., will make tax payments of $5,000 in April, June, September, and December. These payments are shown in Table 4-1.

*Other Payments.* There are several types of cash outflows that are not directly related to sales. These include dividend payments; payments for the purchase of real estate, property, plant and equipment; and the payments of principal and interest on long-term debt. All these payments are recorded as cash outflows in the months when the corporation makes the actual payments.

For J & C, Inc., the estimated schedule of payments not directly related to sales, as shown in Table 4-1, is as follows:

| | |
|---|---|
| Dividend payments: | $2,000 in June |
| | 2,000 in December |
| Payments for equipment purchases: | $5,000 in April |
| | 5,000 in May |
| | 5,000 in October |

**COMPUTING CASH AND LOAN BALANCES.** The final step in preparing a cash budget is to compute cash and loan balances. To compute cash balances, total cash inflows and outflows are combined with (1) the estimate of cash on hand at the start of the planning period and (2) the minimum cash balance desired at the end of each month. Setting a minimum cash balance is one way of allowing for the forecasting errors that occur in the cash budget estimates.

For J & C, Inc., the cash on hand at the beginning of the ten-month planning period is assumed to be $6,000. In addition, management sets the minimum cash balance for the end of each month at $1,000.

To compute loan balances, the loan and repayment schedule for each month must contain the following:

1. The amount borrowed

2. The interest cost

3. The maximum loan size — the maximum value of unpaid principal and interest that occurs in each month

4. The amount of the loan repaid during the month

5. The end-of-month loan size

For J & C, Inc., the rate of interest on borrowed funds is assumed to be .8 percent per month, computed on the end-of-month loan size and rounded to the next whole dollar. The interest is added to the loan during the following month.

**Completing the Cash Budget**

The completed cash budget for J & C, Inc.'s ten-month planning period is shown in Table 4-2. The cash inflows and outflows are taken from Table 4-1. An explanation of the other items in the cash budget is given below on a month-to-month basis:

1. J & C, Inc.'s opening cash balance in March is $6,000. Add to this amount the March cash inflows of $38,500 to arrive at the $44,500 cash available. Subtract the March cash outflows of $34,125 to arrive at net cash of $10,375.

   Since the net cash in March is greater than the $1,000 minimum cash balance requirement, no financing is needed. There is no unpaid loan carried over from earlier months since the maximum loan size and loan interest values are both zero in March. As a result, loan repayment and end-of-month loan size are also zero.

2. The opening cash balance for any given month is equal to the ending cash balance of the previous month. Thus, the May opening cash balance of $2,505 equals April's end-of-month cash. The −$2,498 net cash in May indicates that the firm needs this additional amount of cash in order to pay all of the May cash outflows. If the firm were to borrow $2,498, its end-of-month cash balance for May would be zero. Since the desired monthly minimum cash balance is $1,000, the firm borrows $3,498 in May.

   The zero loan interest in May indicates that no interest cost was paid in that month.

   The maximum loan size for any month is computed by adding the following items: (a) the amount borrowed during the month, (b) the loan interest, and (c) the end-of-month loan from the previous month. Thus, the maximum loan size in May is:

$$\$3,498 + 0 + 0 = \$3,498$$

   No portion of the loan is repaid in May. Thus, the end-of-month loan equals the $3,498 maximum loan size. At the end

**Table 4-2.**      J & C, Inc.'s Cash Budget (March through December)

| | March | April | May | June | July |
|---|---|---|---|---|---|
| Opening cash balance | $ 6,000 | $10,375 | $ 2,505 | $ 1,000 | $ 1,000 |
| Cash inflows | 38,500 | 29,900 | 25,350 | 23,650 | 32,000 |
| Cash available | 44,500 | 40,275 | 27,855 | 24,650 | 33,000 |
| Cash outflows | 34,125 | 37,770 | 30,353 | 31,386 | 24,318 |
| Net cash | 10,375 | 2,505 | −2,498 | −6,736 | 8,682 |
| Loan | 0 | 0 | 3,498 | 7,736 | 0 |
| Loan interest | 0 | 0 | 0 | 28 | 91 |
| Maximum loan size | 0 | 0 | 3,498 | 11,262 | 11,353 |
| Loan repayment | 0 | 0 | 0 | 0 | 7,682 |
| End-of-month loan | 0 | 0 | 3,498 | 11,262 | 3,671 |
| End-of-month cash | $10,375 | $ 2,505 | $ 1,000 | $ 1,000 | $ 1,000 |

| | Aug. | Sept. | Oct. | Nov. | Dec. |
|---|---|---|---|---|---|
| Opening cash balance | $ 1,000 | $ 1,000 | $ 1,000 | $ 1,000 | $ 1,000 |
| Cash inflows | 25,900 | 28,400 | 32,550 | 45,250 | 57,200 |
| Cash available | 26,900 | 29,400 | 33,550 | 46,250 | 58,200 |
| Cash outflows | 27,495 | 34,015 | 38,648 | 45,946 | 60,888 |
| Net cash | − 595 | −4,615 | −5,098 | 304 | −2,688 |
| Loan | 1,595 | 5,615 | 6,098 | 696 | 3,688 |
| Loan interest | 30 | 43 | 88 | 138 | 144 |
| Maximum loan size | 5,296 | 10,954 | 17,140 | 17,974 | 21,806 |
| Loan repayment | 0 | 0 | 0 | 0 | 0 |
| End-of-month loan | 5,296 | 10,954 | 17,140 | 17,974 | 21,806 |
| End-of-month cash | $ 1,000 | $ 1,000 | $ 1,000 | $ 1,000 | $ 1,000 |

of May the firm has both $1,000 in cash and a loan payable of $3,498.

3. To maintain the minimum cash balance of $1,000 for June, the firm borrows $6,736 + $1,000 = $7,736 to cover all its cash outflows. The loan interest on the amount borrowed in May is:

$$(.008)\,(\$3,498) = \$28$$

The maximum loan size in June is

$$\$7,736 + \$28 + \$3,498 = \$11,262$$

4. The $8,682 positive net cash in July allows some loan repayment to occur. The net cash is first reduced by $1,000 for the needed end-of-month cash balance. The remainder, $7,682, is used to repay part of the July maximum loan size of:

$$\$11,262 + \$91 = \$11,353$$

The end-of-month loan equals

$$\$11,353 - \$7,682 = \$3,671$$

5. The rest of the cash budget is prepared by repeating the above steps. As it turns out, the loan continues to increase and reaches a value of $21,806 at the end of December. J & C faces a seasonal sales pattern, however, and as sales decline in the early part of the following year, declining expenses and the collection of receivables are expected to generate sufficient cash inflow to reduce the loan balance.

**Evaluation
of Cash
Budgeting**

Cash budgets and cash-budgeting procedures make important contributions to corporate budgeting and short-term financial planning. The limitations of this technique are primarily the result of the explicit and implicit assumptions used in estimating the individual cash budget items.

**ADVANTAGES OF CASH BUDGETING.** The advantages of cash budgeting are:

1. It serves as an integrative analytical tool for the corporation. The individual components that produce cash inflows and outflows are brought together, and their overall impact on corporate cash flows can be estimated.

2. Cash budgeting forecasts the occurrence, amount, and duration of cash levels over and above the minimum desired end-of-month cash balances. This "excess" cash can be invested in various securities and earn additional profits for the firm.

3. Cash budgeting estimates the occurrence, amount, duration, cost, and repayment schedule for any needed financing. Such estimates are included as part of commercial and industrial loan applications submitted to commercial banks.

4. Cash budgeting is an important tool of planning and control because forecast errors can be traced to the individual components of the cash budget. If, for example, the needed financing exceeds the forecast amounts because actual production costs exceed their estimated values, the forecast errors in the accounts will identify these costs as the reason for the extra financing. These errors could be caused by faulty budgeting procedures and/or a change in the cost structure that took place after the beginning of the planning period. In either case, managers can concentrate their efforts on understanding the reasons why these costs exceeded their budgeted values.

**LIMITATIONS OF CASH BUDGETING.** The limitations of cash budgeting are:

1. The accuracy of a cash budget largely depends on the accuracy of the sales forecast. The more that the corporation has to accept large sales forecasting errors, that is, the greater the risk involved in these forecasts, the more the estimates in the cash budget will be subject to frequent revisions and the reliability of the cash budget will be reduced. In addition, some costs such as salaries are tied only in part to sales. Errors in these estimates will further reduce the cash budget's reliability.

2. Due to an assumption implied in the construction of the cash budget that all forecast cash inflows for a given month are available *before* cash outflows occur, both the monthly loan and the maximum loan size tend to be underestimated. For example, in Table 4-2 the entire $27,855 of cash available in May is assumed to be available to meet the cash outflows of $30,353. If only $21,855 is available until late in the month, both the loan and the maximum loan size would be increased by $6,000 to $9,498. There would then be a loan repayment of $6,000, and the end-of-month loan would be unchanged at $3,498. This limitation can be overcome somewhat by preparing semimonthly or weekly cash budgets. However, it is much more difficult to estimate cash flows on a weekly basis. In addition, a 12-month planning period using 52 weekly estimates can produce such a detailed document that it will become unwieldy unless computerized techniques are used.

## PRO FORMA STATEMENTS

Pro forma statements, like cash budgets, also serve important planning and control functions. The **pro forma income statement** is a forecast of a corporation's sales, expenses, and profits over the planning period. If the estimated profits are below corporate goals, then changes in various aspects of the firm's operations may be necessary in order to produce an acceptable level of profits. Once the planning period has passed and the actual income statement is prepared, comparisons between the actual and the pro forma income statements can be carried out as one way of evaluating the performance of the firm. This may produce changes in future operations. Such changes are then incorporated into the firm's subsequent financial plans.

The **pro forma balance sheet** forecasts the dollar amounts of a corporation's capital at the end of the planning period. One important contribution made by this statement is the estimate in the increased or decreased sources of funds required to meet the proposed financial plans.

For example, if short-term borrowing is planned as a source of funds, the pro forma balance sheet provides an estimate of the borrowing that will remain unrepaid at the end of the time period. Such estimates can be of use in tailoring the type of loan to be negotiated.

In explaining the preparation and analysis of pro forma statements as tools of financial planning and control, the 1984 financial statements of Rextex, Inc., shown in Tables 4-3 and 4-4, will be used.

**Preparation of the Pro Forma Income Statement**

The management of Rextex, Inc., wants to prepare a pro forma income statement for the 12-month planning period ending December 31, 1985. This statement will contain forecasts of each of the items in the firm's income statement, including sales, cost of goods sold, other expenses, and taxes. The bottom line is an estimate of the firm's earnings for the planning period, comprising dividends paid and additions to retained earnings.

**Table 4-3.**   Rextex, Inc.'s Income Statement
(For the Year Ending December 31, 1984)

|  | Dollars | % of Sales |
|---|---|---|
| Sales | 294,000 | 100 |
| Cost of goods sold | 214,500 | 73 |
| Gross profit | 79,500 | 27 |
| Operating expenses | 50,000 | 17 |
| Earnings before interest and taxes | 29,500 | 10 |
| Interest expense | 5,000 | 1.7 |
| Earnings before taxes | 24,500 | 8.3 |
| Taxes | 12,250 | 4.15 |
| Net income | 12,250 | 4.15 |
| Dividends paid | 3,500 | |
| Addition to retained earnings | 8,750 | |

When a cash budget is prepared that covers the same planning period as the pro forma income statement, some of the information needed to prepare the pro forma income statement can be found in the cash budget. Assume, for example, that a 12-month planning period is being used and that a quarterly cash budget is prepared that covers the 12 months. Then simply adding up the four sales figures contained in the cash budget will produce the pro forma income statement sales figure. Similar steps can be taken for operating expenses, interest payments, taxes, and dividends.

   If inventory levels are expected to be the same at the end of the period as at the beginning—that is, if the firm expects to sell the same amount of output that it produces during the period—then cost of goods sold will be equal to the cost of purchases plus labor and other expenses directly related to producing the output. However, cost of goods sold in an income statement reflects the cost of inventory that was sold, not payments for inventory that was acquired. If the firm anticipates increasing its inventory, then cost of goods sold will be less than total purchases and production costs by the amount of investment in inventory. Similarly, if the firm expects to sell more than it produces during the period, its cost of goods sold will be the cost of producing its output plus the value of inventory depletion. Thus, if beginning inventory is unusually high or low, adjustment should be made in estimating cost of goods sold from payments projected in the cash budget.

| Table 4-4. | Rextex, Inc.'s Balance Sheet (As of December 31, 1984) | |
|---|---|---|
| | **Assets** | |
| | Current assets: | |
| | Cash | $ 15,300 |
| | Accounts receivable | 17,726 |
| | Inventory | 24,000 |
| | Total current assets | $ 57,026 |
| | Net fixed assets | 80,000 |
| | Total assets | $137,026 |
| | **Liabilities and Equity** | |
| | Current liabilities: | |
| | Accounts payable | $  7,306 |
| | Other current liabilities | 7,000 |
| | Total current liabilities | $ 14,306 |
| | Long-term debt | 37,000 |
| | Common stock | 40,000 |
| | Retained earnings | 45,720 |
| | Total liabilities and equity | $137,026 |

   The cash budget will not provide a depreciation expense figure. In addition, not all cash flows contained in the cash budget are entered into the pro forma income statement. For example, payments for land and for assets that are to be capitalized and depreciated are excluded. Cash inflows that result from selling stocks and bonds that serve as financing sources are similarly excluded.

An alternative approach is to use financial ratios based on historical financial statements, especially common size income statements, to estimate those pro forma income statement accounts that vary directly with sales. These estimates can be adjusted to reflect new or emerging situations. Some expenses, such as operating expenses and cost of goods sold, may have a fixed component and a second component that varies with sales. For example, utility, rent, lease, and some maintenance expenses may be incurred regardless of sales and may increase once sales reach a specified level. These components can be estimated by examining historical income statements and using standard statistical techniques such as linear regression. Accounts that do not vary with sales, such as depreciation, interest expense, and dividends, have to be estimated separately.

A variation of this approach is the *percent of sales method*, which relies on previous common size income statements to identify items that vary proportionately with sales. Other items must still be estimated separately. This method can generate a pro forma income statement in very little time, so it is especially useful in forecasting the impact of alternative or what-if situations such as changes in sales, product lines, or operating costs.

To prepare a pro forma income statement using the percent of sales method, the following information is needed: (1) sales forecast for 1985, (2) identification of those income statement items that vary proportionately with sales, (3) estimates for those items that do not vary with sales, and (4) the dividend policy for 1985. For Rextex, Inc., the specific information needed to prepare this pro forma income statement is as follows:

1. 1985 sales are expected to increase by approximately 16 percent from 1984 sales. Management settles on a forecast of $341,000, a 15.98 percent increase.

2. For this firm, 1985 cost of goods sold and other expenses are expected to account for the same percentage of sales that they did in 1984.

3. 1985 interest expense will remain equal to the 1984 value of $5,000. Taxes will be estimated at 50 percent of taxable income.

4. The firm's dividend policy calls for it to pay $5,000 in common stock dividends during 1985.

The resulting pro forma income statement for Rextex is shown in Table 4-5. Based on the above information, the items in the pro forma income statement are calculated as follows:

Cost of goods sold = (.73)($341,000) = $248,930
Operating expenses = (.17)($341,000) = $57,970

Interest expense = $5,000 (unchanged from 1984)
Federal income tax = (.5) ($29,100) = $14,550
Addition to retained earnings = $14,550 − $5,000 = $9,550

| Table 4-5. | Rextex, Inc.'s Pro Forma Income Statement (For the Year Ending December 31, 1985) | |
|---|---|---|
| | Sales | $341,000 |
| | Cost of goods sold | 248,930 |
| | Gross profit | $ 92,070 |
| | Operating expenses | 57,970 |
| | Earnings before interest and taxes | $ 34,100 |
| | Interest | 5,000 |
| | Earnings before taxes | $ 29,100 |
| | Taxes | 14,550 |
| | Net income | $ 14,550 |
| | Dividends paid | 5,000 |
| | Addition to retained earnings | $  9,550 |

**Preparation of the Pro Forma Balance Sheet**

If a cash budget has been prepared, it may provide some of the data needed to prepare a pro forma balance sheet. End of year values for cash, accounts receivable, accounts payable, and bank loans payable can be estimated from the cash budget. Changes in long-term financing provided by debt and common stock may also be estimated from the cash budget cash flows. Although it is more difficult, it may also be possible to estimate the balance sheet inventory value by adding the inventory on hand at the beginning of the planning period to the purchases and production costs contained in the cash budget and subtracting the estimated cost of goods sold. Net fixed asset values cannot be estimated from a cash budget. The change in retained earnings is the addition to retained earnings found in the pro forma income statement.

An alternative approach is to identify those balance sheet accounts, the values of which are proportional to sales. Many current asset and current liability accounts fall into this category although there may be times when this relationship does not hold. Those balance sheet accounts, such as net fixed assets, with values that are not proportional to sales are estimated separately. In preparing a pro forma balance sheet, the long-term financing accounts are assumed constant; the exceptions are retained earnings and whatever changes, such as bond repayments, that are scheduled to occur. Holding these accounts constant allows the firm to estimate the amount, if any, of additional financing that is needed.

In addition to the 1984 balance sheet for Rextex, Inc., shown in Table 4-4, the following information is required to prepare its pro forma balance sheet: (1) sales forecast for 1985, (2) identification of those items that vary directly with sales, (3) estimates of those items that are independent of sales, and (4) an estimate of the change in retained earnings. For Rextex, Inc., the specific necessary information is as follows:

1. The 1985 sales forecast is $341,000.

2. Accounts receivable and accounts payable vary directly with sales. The firm estimates accounts receivable to be 70 percent of average monthly sales; the estimate is as follows:

$$\text{Average sales per month} = \$341,000/12 = \$28,417$$

$$\text{Accounts receivable} = (.7)(\$28,417) = \$19,892$$

Purchases, which generate accounts payable, are expected to equal 35 percent of sales and to be outstanding 30 days on the average. Thus, the estimate accounts payable is computed as follows:

$$\text{Purchases} = (.35)(\$341,000) = \$119,350$$

$$\text{Accounts payable} = \left(\frac{30}{360}\right)(\$119,350) = \$9,946$$

3. Balance sheet items that are independent of sales for this firm are cash, net fixed assets, other current liabilities, long-term debt, and common stock. The firm sets a minimum cash balance of $10,000. Inventories will increase slightly to $25,000 due to price increases. Other current liabilities, long-term debt, and the common stock accounts are expected to be unchanged from their 1984 balance sheet values. Net fixed assets are estimated to increase to $110,000.

4. Retained earnings are expected to increase by the $9,550 addition to retained earnings estimated in the pro forma income statement.

The resulting pro forma balance sheet for Rextex is contained in Table 4-6. After estimating the individual asset accounts, the value for total assets is computed as follows:

| | |
|---|---:|
| Cash | $ 10,000 |
| Accounts receivable | 19,892 |
| Inventory | 25,000 |
| Net fixed assets | 110,000 |
| Total assets | $164,892 |

Then the individual liability and equity accounts are estimated and added:

| Accounts payable | $ 9,946 |
| Other current liabilities | 7,000 |
| Long-term debt | 37,000 |
| Common stock | 40,000 |
| Retained earnings | 55,270 |
| Total liabilities and equity | $149,216 |

The value for total assets must equal the value for total liabilities and equity. If the value for total assets is *larger* than the sum of the forecast liabilities and equity, as is the case for Rextex, Inc., this means that additional financing is needed. Thus, the $15,676 difference between total assets of $164,892 and forecast liabilities and equity of $149,216 represents the

---

**Table 4-6.**     Rextex, Inc.'s Pro Forma Balance Sheet
(As of December 31, 1985)

**Assets**

| | |
|---|---|
| Current assets: | |
| Cash | $ 10,000 |
| Accounts receivable | 19,892 |
| Inventory | 25,000 |
| Total current assets | $ 54,892 |
| Net fixed assets | 110,000 |
| Total assets | $164,892 |

**Liabilities and Equity**

| | |
|---|---|
| Current liabilities: | |
| Accounts payable | $ 9,946 |
| Other current liabilities | 7,000 |
| Total current liabilities | $ 16,946 |
| Long-term debt | 37,000 |
| Common stock | 40,000 |
| Retained earnings | 55,270 |
| Additional financing needed | 15,676 |
| Total liabilities and equity | $164,892 |

---

added financing that will be outstanding at the end of 1985. This balance is shown as *additional financing needed* in the pro forma balance sheet. On the other hand, if the value for total assets is *smaller* than the sum of the forecast liabilities and equity, this means that surplus sources are forecast and that the firm will be able to reduce its liabilities by the amount by which sources exceed uses.

An interpretation of the items in the Rextex, Inc.'s pro forma balance sheet is as follows:

1. The increases in accounts receivable, inventory, and accounts payable reflect the increases in current accounts needed to support the $47,000 increase ($341,000 − $294,000) in sales.

2. The total uses of capital are forecast to increase by $164,892 − $137,026 = $27,866 which means sources must increase by the same amount. Of this increase, accounts payable will provide $2,640 and retained earnings will provide $9,550. The remaining $15,676 will have to be provided by an unspecified source. This source can be short-term loans, long-term debt, equity financing, or some combination of debt and equity.

**Evaluation of Pro Forma Statements**

The advantages and limitations of pro forma statements as tools of planning and control must be understood if they are to provide corporate managers with the ability to prepare useful planning period estimates.

**ADVANTAGES OF PRO FORMA STATEMENTS.** The advantages of pro forma statements are:

1. They make explicit forecasts of such items as profits, dividends, and financing needs.

2. By comparing the actual and the pro forma statements at the end of a planning period, corporate managers can evaluate the extent to which corporate goals were attained. They can also isolate those aspects of performance that deviated significantly from corporate plans.

**LIMITATIONS OF PRO FORMA STATEMENTS.** The following limitations of pro forma statements revolve around many assumptions used:

1. A sales forecast is needed to prepare the pro forma income statement. Many of the expense items are assumed to vary directly with sales, and historical relationships are often used in estimating the separate income statement accounts. If these relationships are expected to change during the planning period, the pro forma income statement will not produce useful results unless the new relationships are correctly forecast.

2. Similarly, many pro forma balance sheet accounts—especially current assets and current liabilities—are based on forecast sales. The balance account (negative or positive) that is estimated in the pro forma balance sheet is a forecast for the end of the planning period. However, the amount of financing

needed during the planning period, if any, can differ significantly from the end-of-period forecast.

# SUMMARY

Financial plans are management's way of preparing for the uncertain future. Financial plans in the form of cash budgets and pro forma statements contain the specific plans that the corporation intends to execute in seeking to advance the financial welfare of its owners. Cash budgets and pro forma statements also serve as tools of control when, at the end of a planning period, the actual financial results are compared with the plans. Major deviations are identified and analyzed.

# QUESTIONS

4-1. Explain some of the important uses of cash budgeting as a tool of corporate financial planning and control.

4-2. What are the major steps in preparing a cash budget?

4-3. Why is a sales forecast so important in cash budgeting?

4-4. What is the purpose of the end-of-month minimum cash balance in the cash budget?

4-5. How is the maximum loan size computed in the cash budget?

4-6. What are the most important limitations of a cash budget?

4-7. What corporate goals are contained in pro forma statements?

4-8. What major types of information are needed in order to prepare a pro forma income statement?

4-9. What major types of information are needed in order to prepare a pro forma balance sheet?

# PROBLEMS

4-1. A corporation is about to begin operations. The sales forecast for its first four months of business is as follows:

| | |
|---|---|
| January | $20,000 |
| February | 18,000 |
| March | 20,000 |
| April | 22,000 |

Assume the following distribution of cash sales, accounts receivable collections, and bad debt percentage; then compute the expected monthly cash inflows for January through April.

a.  Cash sales ............................................. 30%
b.  Accounts receivable collected one month after sale............. 60%
c.  Accounts receivable collected two months after sale........... 5%
d.  Bad debts............................................... 5%

**4-2.** Using the following data, compute the monthly cash outflows for January through April:

Sales Forecast

| | |
|---|---|
| January | $25,000 |
| February | 25,000 |
| March | 28,000 |
| April | 30,000 |

Assume the following schedule of purchase payments and other outflows:

a.  Purchases (accounts payable) ................. 70% of monthly sales
b.  Accounts payable paid in the month
    of the purchase............................. 40%
c.  Accounts payable paid one month
    after purchase .............................. 60%
d.  Monthly wages and salaries ................ $4,000 plus 12% of
    sales over $25,000
e.  Tax payment in April ........................ $6,000
f.  Payment in April of equipment purchase ...... $8,000

**4-3.** The sales forecast for the R.U. Reedy Corporation's July through December operations is:

| | | | |
|---|---|---|---|
| July | $16,000 | October | $22,000 |
| August | 25,000 | November | 20,000 |
| September | 25,000 | December | 20,000 |

Assume the following distribution of cash sales, accounts receivable collections, and bad debt percentage; then compute the expected monthly cash inflows for October through December.

a.  Cash sales as a percent of total sales ....................... 40%
b.  Accounts receivable, as a percent of monthly
    sales, collected one month after sale....................... 35%
c.  Accounts receivable, as a percent of monthly sales,
    collected two months after sale............................ 20%
d.  Bad debts, as a percent of monthly sales................... 5%
e.  Proceeds from sale of equipment, to be received
    in November ........................................... $15,000

**4-4.** Using the sales forecast in Problem 4-3 and the following assumptions, compute the monthly cash outflows for the R.U. Reedy Corporation for October through December.

a.  Purchases (accounts payable) ................ 60% of monthly sales
b.  Accounts payable paid in the month of
    the purchase .............................. 50% of purchases
c.  Accounts payable paid one month after
    purchase.................................. 40% of purchases
d.  Accounts payable paid two months after
    purchase.................................. 10% of purchases
e.  Monthly wages and salaries ................ $3,000 plus 10% of
                                                sales
f.  Tax payment in December.................... $1,500
g.  Quarterly lease payment in October .......... $2,000
h.  Equipment purchase payment due in
    November.................................. $20,000

**4-5.** Using the cash inflows and outflows computed in Problems 4-3 and 4-4, prepare the R.U. Reedy Corporation's cash budget for October through December. Assume the following additional information:

a.  The opening cash balance in October is $800.
b.  The desired end-of-month minimum cash balance is $1,500.
c.  The interest payment for any month is 0.9% multiplied by the end-of-month loan for the previous month, rounded to the nearest whole dollar.

**4-6.** Assuming the following information, compute the expected monthly cash inflows and outflows of the Big Guy Company for July through December:

### Sales Forecast

| | | | |
|---|---|---|---|
| April | $25,000 | September | $25,000 |
| May | 27,000 | October | 28,000 |
| June | 28,000 | November | 35,000 |
| July | 30,000 | December | 25,000 |
| August | 25,000 | | |

a.  All sales are for cash.
b.  There are no bad debts.
c.  In September, $10,000 will be received from the sale of equipment.
d.  Purchases (accounts payable) are expected to be 75% of monthly sales.
e.  Accounts payable paid in the month of the purchase are expected to be 60% of purchases.
f.  Accounts payable paid one month after the purchase are expected to be 40% of purchases.
g.  Monthly wages and salaries will be $2,000 plus 7% of sales.
h.  Other operating expenses will be $2,000 per month.
i.  Tax payments in September and December will be $1,500 each.

**4-7.** Using the following data, prepare the monthly cash budget for January through April:

|                | January  | February | March    | April   |
|----------------|----------|----------|----------|---------|
| Cash inflows   | $ 9,000  | $4,000   | $12,000  | $9,000  |
| Cash outflows  | 10,000   | 4,000    | 11,500   | 8,000   |

Assume the following additional information:

a.  The opening cash balance in January is $650.
b.  The desired end-of-month minimum cash balance is $1,000.
c.  The interest on any loans outstanding is 0.9% per month, computed on the end-of-month loan size and rounded up to the next whole dollar.

**4-8.** Using the following data, prepare a five-month April through August cash budget for the Den Company.

### Sales Forecast

| January  | $ 60,000 | May    | $140,000 |
|----------|----------|--------|----------|
| February | 100,000  | June   | 160,000  |
| March    | 110,000  | July   | 190,000  |
| April    | 90,000   | August | 180,000  |

Assume the following schedule of purchase payments and other outflows:

a.  Purchases (accounts payable) ................. 70% of monthly sales
b.  Accounts payable paid one month after purchase.................................... 100%
c.  Monthly wages and salaries................... $5,000 plus 10% of sales
d.  Tax payments in April and August ............ $10,000 each payment
e.  Dividends payable in June.................... $4,000
f.  Administrative cost (monthly)................. $5,000
g.  Rent (monthly) ............................. $2,500
h.  Construction payments due in April and August ............................... $20,000 each payment

Assume the following distribution of cash and accounts receivable collections:

a.  Cash sales............................................... 35%
b.  Accounts receivable, as a percentage of monthly sales collected one month after the sale ........................... 39%
c.  Accounts receivable, as a percentage of monthly sales collected two months after the sale ......................... 26%
d.  No bad debts

Other information:

a.  The opening cash balance on April 1 is $2,000.
b.  The desired end-of-month minimum cash balance is $5,000.
c.  The interest payment for any month is 0.9% of the end-of-month loan for the previous month, rounded up to the nearest whole dollar.

**4-9.** Using the following data, prepare the 12-month cash budget for January through December, 1986.

<u>Sales Forecast</u>

| | | | | | |
|---|---|---|---|---|---|
| 1985 | November | $12,000 | | | |
| | December | 8,000 | | | |
| 1986 | January | 8,000 | July | 24,000 |
| | February | 14,000 | August | 20,000 |
| | March | 16,000 | September | 20,000 |
| | April | 20,000 | October | 16,000 |
| | May | 24,000 | November | 15,000 |
| | June | 24,000 | December | 11,000 |

Assume the following additional information:

a. Cash and credit card sales ......................... 10%
b. Accounts receivable collected one month
after the sale ..................................... 70%
c. Accounts receivable collected two months
after the sale ..................................... 17%
d. Bad debts ........................................ 3%
e. Other cash inflows:
   March ............................................ $2,500
   September ........................................ $2,500
   December ......................................... $12,000
f. Purchases (accounts payable) ...................... 70% of
   monthly sales
g. Accounts payable paid in the month of the purchase.. 20%
h. Accounts payable paid one month after the purchase . 80%
i. Monthly wages and salaries ....................... $1,000 plus 8%
   of sales over
   $15,000
j. Other operating expenses (rents, leases, utilities,
   and miscellaneous purchases — monthly)............ $800 plus 2%
   of sales
k. Tax payments:
   April ............................................ $2,000
   June ............................................. $2,000
   September ........................................ $2,000
   December ......................................... $2,000
l. Payments for equipment purchases:
   July.............................................. $10,000
   November.......................................... $25,000
m. Other cash outflows:
   March ............................................ $5,000
   August ........................................... $1,000
n. Cash on hand, January 1 .......................... $300
o. Minimum desired end-of-month cash balance ........ $1,000

    *p.*  Interest per month, computed on the end-of-month
        loan size and rounded up to the next whole dollar. . . .  .8%

**4-10.**  The 1984 balance sheet for the 66 Granite Street Company is contained in Table 4-7. Using this statement and the following information, prepare the 1985 pro forma balance sheet:

    *a.*  Sales for 1985 are forecast at $3,200,000.
    *b.*  Accounts receivable are expected to be 70% of average monthly sales.
    *c.*  Inventory will increase to $220,000.
    *d.*  Other current assets and other current liabilities will remain unchanged.
    *e.*  Net fixed assets will increase to $1,860,000.
    *f.*  Purchases (accounts payable) are estimated at 48.6% of annual sales. The average length of accounts payable is 45 days.
    *g.*  Notes payable, long-term debt, and common stock will be unchanged. The installment purchase obligation will be paid off during 1985.
    *h.*  Assume 12-31-85 cash of $50,000.
    *i.*  Profits after taxes are estimated at 4% of sales, and dividend payments will equal 40% of profits after taxes.

**Table 4-7.**    66 Granite Street Company Balance Sheet
(As of December 31, 1984)

### Assets

| | |
|---|---:|
| Current assets: | |
|   Cash | $ 49,600 |
|   Accounts receivable | 147,700 |
|   Inventory | 212,000 |
|   Other current assets | 39,600 |
| Total current assets | $ 448,900 |
| Net fixed assets | 1,370,200 |
| Total assets | $1,819,100 |

### Liabilities and Equity

| | |
|---|---:|
| Current liabilities | |
|   Accounts payable | $ 209,800 |
|   Installment purchase obligation | 40,000 |
|   Notes payable | 29,500 |
|   Other current liabilities | 13,700 |
| Total current liabilities | $ 293,000 |
| Long-term debt | 656,400 |
| Common stock | 597,880 |
| Retained earnings | 271,820 |
| Total liabilities and equity | $1,819,100 |

**4-11.** The 1984 balance sheet for the Beta Best Company is contained in Table 4-8. Using this statement and the following information, prepare the 1985 pro forma balance sheet:

a. Sales for 1985 are forecast at $600,000.
b. Accounts receivable are expected to be 60% of average monthly sales.
c. Purchases (accounts payable) are estimated at 17.8% of annual sales. The average length of accounts payable is 45 days.
d. The 12-31-85 cash balance is $15,000.
e. Other current liabilities, other current assets, long-term debt, and the common stock account will remain unchanged from the 1984 balance sheet values.
f. Net fixed assets will increase slightly to $60,000.
g. Inventory will increase to $70,000.
h. Retained earnings will increase by $5,000.
i. Notes and bank loans payable will remain unchanged.

Table 4-8.

Beta Best Company Balance Sheet
(As of December 31, 1984)

Assets

Current assets:

| | |
|---|---:|
| Cash | $ 18,000 |
| Accounts receivable | 30,000 |
| Inventory | 64,750 |
| Other current assets | 16,300 |
| Total current assets | $129,050 |
| Net fixed assets | 55,220 |
| Total assets | $184,270 |

Liabilities and Equity

Current liabilities:

| | |
|---|---:|
| Accounts payable | $ 12,535 |
| Notes and bank loans payable | 37,606 |
| Other current liabilities | 3,560 |
| Total current liabilities | $ 53,701 |
| Long-term debt | 35,099 |
| Common stock | 15,594 |
| Retained earnings | 79,876 |
| Total liabilities and equity | $184,270 |

**4-12.** The 1985 income statement and balance sheet for the Dixie Mills Company are contained in Tables 4-9 and 4-10. Using these statements and the following information, prepare the 1986 pro forma statements:

*a.* Sales for 1986 are forecast at $24,000,000.
*b.* Cost of goods sold and operating expenses are proportional to sales levels.
*c.* Interest expense will be unchanged from the 1985 value.
*d.* Taxes are 50% of taxable income.
*e.* Dividend payments projected for 1986 are $160,000.
*f.* The minimum desired end-of-month cash balance is $1,000,000.
*g.* Accounts receivable are expected to be 71% of monthly sales.
*h.* Inventory will increase by 10%.
*i.* Other current liabilities and other current assets will remain unchanged.
*j.* Net fixed assets will decrease to a value of $2,220,000.
*k.* Purchases (accounts payable) are estimated at 19.7% of annual sales. The average length of accounts payable is 45 days.
*l.* Notes payable and bank loans payable, long-term debt, and common stock will be unchanged.

| Table 4-9. | Dixie Mills Company's Income Statement (For the Year Ending December 31, 1985) | |
|---|---|---|
| | Sales | $20,300,000 |
| | Cost of goods sold | 13,650,000 |
| | Gross profit | $ 6,650,000 |
| | Operating expenses | 5,200,000 |
| | Earnings before interest and taxes | $ 1,450,000 |
| | Interest | 500,000 |
| | Earnings before taxes | $ 950,000 |
| | Taxes | 475,000 |
| | Net income | $ 475,000 |
| | Dividends paid | 160,000 |
| | Addition to retained earnings | $ 315,000 |

Table 4-10.    Dixie Mills Company's Balance Sheet
(As of December 31, 1985)

### Assets

Current assets:
| | |
|---|---:|
| Cash | $ 700,000 |
| Accounts receivable | 1,200,000 |
| Inventory | 2,590,000 |
| Other current assets | 480,000 |
| | |
| Total current assets | $4,970,000 |
| Net fixed assets | 2,380,000 |
| | |
| Total assets | $7,350,000 |

### Liabilities and Equity

Current liabilities:
| | |
|---|---:|
| Accounts payable | $ 500,000 |
| Notes payable and bank loans payable | 1,500,000 |
| Other current liabilities | 142,000 |
| | |
| Total current liabilities | $2,142,000 |
| Long-term debt | 1,400,000 |
| Common stock | 622,000 |
| Retained earnings | 3,186,000 |
| | |
| Total liabilities and equity | $7,350,000 |

4-13.  The 1984 income statement and balance sheet for the Hebert Company are contained in Tables 4-11 and 4-12. Using these statements and the following information, prepare the 1985 pro forma statements:

a.  Sales for 1984 are forecast at $250,000.
b.  Cost of goods sold and operating expenses are proportional to sales levels.
c.  Interest expense will be unchanged from the 1984 value.
d.  Taxes are 48% of taxable income.
e.  Dividend payments projected for 1985 are $6,000.
f.  The 12-31-85 cash balance is $10,000.
g.  Accounts receivable are expected to be 85% of average monthly sales.
h.  Inventory will increase by 15%.
i.  Other current liabilities and other current assets will remain unchanged.
j.  Net fixed assets will be $45,000.
k.  Purchases (accounts payable) are estimated at 25% of annual sales. The average turnover of accounts payable is 45 days.
l.  Notes payable, long-term debt, and common stock will be unchanged.

Table 4-11.          Hebert Company's Income Statement
                     (For the Year Ending December 31, 1984)

| | |
|---|---:|
| Sales | $210,000 |
| Cost of goods sold | 150,450 |
| Gross profit | $ 59,550 |
| Operating expenses | 33,900 |
| Earnings before interest and taxes | $ 25,650 |
| Interest | 2,000 |
| Earnings before taxes | $ 23,650 |
| Taxes | 11,352 |
| Net income | $ 12,298 |
| Dividends paid | 6,000 |
| Addition to retained earnings | $  6,298 |

Table 4-12.          Hebert Company's Balance Sheet
                     (As of December 31, 1984)

### Assets

| | |
|---|---:|
| Current Assets: | |
| Cash | $ 12,100 |
| Accounts receivable | 17,670 |
| Inventory | 29,200 |
| Other current assets | 8,000 |
| Total current assets | $ 66,970 |
| Net fixed assets | 39,280 |
| Total assets | $106,250 |

### Liabilities and Equity

| | |
|---|---:|
| Current liabilities: | |
| Accounts payable | $  9,650 |
| Notes payable | 24,000 |
| Other current liabilities | 37,200 |
| Total current liabilities | $ 70,850 |
| Long-term debt | 10,000 |
| Common stock | 15,000 |
| Retained earnings | 10,400 |
| Total liabilities and equity | $106,250 |

# SELECTED REFERENCES

Bernstein, L. A. *Financial Statement Analysis.* Rev. ed. Homewood, Illinois: Richard D. Irwin, 1978.

Brigham, E. F. *Financial Management Theory and Practice.* 3d ed. New York: The Dryden Press, 1982.

Helfert, E. *Techniques of Financial Analysis.* 5th ed. Homewood, Illinois: Richard D. Irwin, Inc., 1982.

Moore, C., and R. Jaedicke. *Managerial Accounting.* 5th ed. Cincinnati, Ohio: South-Western Publishing Co., 1980.

Viscione, J. *Financial Analysis.* Boston: Houghton Mifflin Company, 1977.

# CHAPTER 5

## Leverage:
## Operating,
## Financial, and Combined

It is not at all uncommon for a corporation to report a substantial increase in profits coupled with only a moderate increase in revenue. Changes in profits that are disproportionate to changes in sales can occur as a consequence of managerial decisions or as a result of developments in the economic environment. The extent to which a profit measure, such as EPS, responds to a change in output or revenue is analyzed by computing the degree of leverage revealed in the corporate financial statements. This chapter explains how to measure, interpret, and apply three types of leverage: (1) operating leverage, (2) financial leverage, and (3) a combination of operating and financial leverage.

As a forecasting tool, leverage complements the other analytical techniques discussed in Chapters 3 and 4. Leverage is also used as a measure of risk. These two uses of leverage are especially important in analyzing the capital structure decisions that are discussed in later chapters.

## THE CONCEPT OF LEVERAGE

The leverage concept is very general. It is not unique to business or finance, and it can be used to analyze many different types of problems. For example, other disciplines, such as economics and engineering, use the same concept and refer to it as *elasticity*. When used in a financial setting, leverage measures the behavior of interrelated variables, such as output, revenue, earnings before interest and taxes (EBIT), and earnings per share (EPS).

The material in this chapter will be easier to understand if two points are kept in mind:

1. Leverage measures the relationship between two variables, as opposed to measuring variables independently, and the values that one variable assumes must depend on the values assumed by the second variable.

2. In order for leverage coefficients to have any useful applications, it must be possible to identify which variable is the dependent variable and which is the independent variable. In other words, the direction of causality must be known. When two variables are so related, the degree of leverage describes the responsiveness of the dependent variable to changes in the independent variable.

**Leverage Defined**

Let $y$ and $x$ represent two variables. When the values taken by $y$ are determined by the values taken by $x$, $y$ is said to be dependent on $x$. Accordingly, $y$ is called the *dependent* variable and $x$ is referred to as the *independent* variable. The algebraic statement of $y$'s dependence on $x$ is written as

$$y = f(x) \qquad (5\text{-}1)$$

and is read as: y *is a function of* x.

Suppose that the initial values of $y$ and $x$ are known. The independent variable $x$ now takes on a new value. The change in the value of $x$ and its percentage change are computed. The resulting change and percentage change in $y$ are also computed. **Leverage** is then defined as the percentage change in the dependent variable $y$ divided by the percentage change in the independent variable $x$. In algebraic terms, the definition of leverage is developed as follows:

Let $\Delta x$ = the change in the independent variable $x$

$\Delta y$ = the change in the dependent variable $y$

$\dfrac{\Delta x}{x}$ = the percentage change in $x = \% \Delta x$

$\dfrac{\Delta y}{y}$ = the percentage change in $y = \% \Delta y$

Then,

$$\frac{L(y)}{L(x)} = \frac{\Delta y / y}{\Delta x / x} \tag{5-2}$$

The left-hand side of Equation 5-2 is read as: *the leverage of* y *with respect to* x.

---

**Example:**

A company's sales depend, among other things, on the size of the company's advertising budget. Suppose a corporation spends $10,000 on advertising (independent variable) and sells 400 units of output (dependent variable). During the next time period, the advertising budget is increased to $11,000 and 500 units are sold.

The leverage of sales with respect to advertising, or the coefficient of leverage, can be computed by using Equation 5-2. The change in the advertising budget is $1,000, and the percentage change in this independent variable is $1,000/$10,000 = 10 percent. The change in units sold is 100 units and the percentage change in this dependent variable is 100/400 = 25 percent. By substituting into Equation 5-2, the coefficient of leverage is computed as:

$$\frac{L(y)}{L(x)} = \frac{100/400}{\$1,000/\$10,000} = \frac{.25}{.1} = 2.5$$

The leverage coefficient of 2.5 means that the resulting percentage change in sales is 2.5 times greater than the percentage change in the advertising budget.

---

**Leverage in a Financial Setting**

Income statements and balance sheets provide the variables and the functional relationships among these variables that financial managers need in order to use leverage as a tool of financial analysis. These functional relationships are made explicit by expressing the income statement in algebraic terms. Symbols are used to represent income statement accounts; the income statement relationships are then written in symbolic form.

The algebraic equivalent of an income statement can be quite complicated when a corporation markets several product lines. For purposes of simplicity, the following assumptions are made concerning the output, production costs, financing costs, and federal income taxes paid:

1. The corporation produces only one product and sells it for a constant price. (All output is sold, so output equals sales.)

2. Production and operation costs consist of a variable cost per unit of output and a fixed cost incurred over the accounting period.

3. The corporation pays the amount of interest required on any outstanding debt.

4. The corporation pays dividends on any preferred stock outstanding.

5. Corporate federal income taxes are 40 percent of taxable income.

Production and operating costs were introduced in Chapter 4. Some costs, such as rents, leases, utilities, and some salary and maintenance expenses, are essentially fixed over the accounting period. Other costs, such as costs of purchases and wages, tend to vary with the level of output. Some costs, called *semivariable costs,* have both a fixed and a variable component. For example, overtime payroll expenses and additional repair and maintenance costs may be incurred when the level of production approaches plant capacity. In this chapter, semivariable costs are not reported in a separate income statement account; rather, their fixed and variable components are separated and added to the fixed and variable cost accounts reported in the income statement.

Interest expense and preferred stock dividends are considered to be fixed financing costs in the income statement. Although interest must be paid when due, the firm is not legally required to pay preferred stock dividends. The assumption is made, however, that the firm would not have floated preferred stock unless it fully intended to pay the associated dividends.

INCOME STATEMENT NOTATION. Table 5–1 contains the symbols used to express the income statement relationships developed in this chapter. These symbols are defined so as to be consistent with the five assumptions that were stated above. The resulting income statement that uses these symbols is contained in Table 5-2.

INCOME STATEMENT FORMAT. Table 5-2 details the income statement format and relates the symbols contained in Table 5-1 to the income statement accounts. The algebraic expression of the income statement is developed as follows:

*Total revenue:*
      (units sold) (price per unit) = $TP$

*Total variable cost:*
(units sold) (variable cost per unit) = *TV*

*Earnings before interest and taxes:*
Total revenue − total variable cost − fixed cost

$$Y = TP - TV - F$$

or $Y = T(P - V) - F$                      (5-3)

---

**Table 5-1.**          **Income Statement Notation**

$T$ = number of units of output produced and sold
$P$ = price per unit of output
$V$ = variable cost per unit of output
$F$ = fixed costs
$Y$ = earnings before interest and taxes (EBIT)
$I$ = interest paid on debt
$t$ = federal corporate tax rate
$E$ = preferred stock dividends
$N$ = number of shares of common stock outstanding
EPS = earnings per share of common stock

---

*Profit before taxes:*
EBIT − interest on debt = $Y - I$

*Federal income taxes:*
(profit before taxes) (tax rate) = $(Y - I)\,(t)$

*Profit after taxes:*
profit before taxes − federal income taxes

$$(Y - I) - (Y - I)\,(t)$$

or $(Y - I)\,(1 - t)$

*Earnings available to common shareholders:*
profit after taxes − preferred stock dividends

$$(Y - I)\,(1 - t) - E$$

*Earnings per share of common stock:*

$$\frac{\text{earnings available to common shareholders}}{\text{number of common shares issued}}$$

$$\text{EPS} = \frac{(Y - I)\,(1 - t) - E}{N}$$                      (5-4)

Equation 5-3 expresses the operating portion of the income statement; Equation 5-4, the financial portion. The algebraic equivalent of the complete income statement is obtained by substituting the symbolic form of EBIT from Equation 5-3 into Equation 5-4 as follows:

$$\text{EPS} = \frac{[T(P - V) - F - I](1 - t) - E}{N} \tag{5-5}$$

| Table 5-2. | Income Statement Format |
| --- | --- |

Total revenue . . . . . . . . . . . . . . . . . . . . . . . . . . . . . . . . . . . . . . . . . . . . . . . . . . . . . . $TP$
   Less: Variable costs . . . . . . . . . . . . . . . . . . . . . . . . . . . . . . . . . . . . . . . . . . . . . $TV$
   Less: Fixed costs . . . . . . . . . . . . . . . . . . . . . . . . . . . . . . . . . . . . . . . . . . . . . . . . $F$
Equals: Earnings before interest and taxes . . . . . . . . . . . . . . . . $Y = T(P - V) - F$
   Less: Interest payments on debt. . . . . . . . . . . . . . . . . . . . . . . . . . . . . . . . . . . $I$
Equals: Profit before taxes . . . . . . . . . . . . . . . . . . . . . . . . . . . . . . . . . . . . . . . . $Y - I$
   Less: Federal income taxes. . . . . . . . . . . . . . . . . . . . . . . . . . . . . . . . . . . . . $(Y - I)(t)$
Equals: Profit after taxes . . . . . . . . . . . . . . . . . . . . . . . . . . . . . . . . . . . . $(Y - I)(1 - t)$
   Less: Preferred stock dividends . . . . . . . . . . . . . . . . . . . . . . . . . . . . . . . . . . . $E$
Equals: Earnings available to common shareholders . . . . . . . $(Y - I)(1 - t) - E$

Equations 5-3, -4, and -5 are used to develop the applications of leverage to managerial finance. The relevant variables and their functional relationships, as contained in these equations, are:

1.  Equation 5-3: $Y = f(T)$
    EBIT depends upon the number of units produced and sold.

2.  Equation 5-4: EPS = $f(Y)$
    EPS depends upon the level of EBIT.

3.  Equation 5-5: EPS = $f(T)$
    EPS depends upon the number of units produced and sold.

Note that EBIT is the dependent variable in Equation 5-3 but the independent variable in Equation 5-4.

## OPERATING LEVERAGE

Operating leverage measures the relationship between output and EBIT. Specifically, it measures the effect of changing levels of output on EBIT. The functional relationship between these two variables is:

$$Y = f(T)$$

and the income statement relationship is that of Equation 5-3:

$$Y = T(P - V) - F$$

When the level of output changes from its initial value, the initial value of EBIT also changes. Thus, **operating leverage** is defined as the resulting percentage change in EBIT divided by the percentage change in output. Symbolically, operating leverage is expressed as:

$$\frac{L(Y)}{L(T)} = \frac{\Delta Y/Y}{\Delta T/T} = \frac{\%\,\Delta \text{EBIT}}{\%\,\Delta \text{output}} \tag{5-6}$$

---

**Example:**

Assume that the price per unit of output $(P)$ is $10, the variable cost per unit of output $(V)$ is $4, the fixed cost $(F)$ is $30,000, and the level of output $(T)$ is 8,000 units. By using Equation 5-3, the EBIT at this level of output is computed as follows:

$$Y = T(P - V) - F$$
$$= 8,000\ (\$10 - \$4) - \$30,000$$
$$= \$48,000 - \$30,000 = \$18,000$$

Now assume that the level of output increases from 8,000 to 10,000 units. The resulting EBIT is computed as:

$$Y = T(P - V) - F$$
$$= 10,000\ (\$10 - \$4) - \$30,000$$
$$= \$60,000 - \$30,000 = \$30,000$$

By using Equation 5-6, the coefficient of operating leverage is computed as follows:

Percentage change in output = 2,000/8,000 = 25%
Percentage change in EBIT = $12,000/$18,000 = 66.7%

$$\frac{L(Y)}{L(T)} = \frac{\Delta Y/Y}{\Delta T/T}$$

$$\frac{L(Y)}{L(T)} = \frac{.667}{.25} = 2.67$$

The coefficient of operating leverage of 2.67 is interpreted as follows: A 1 percent change in output from an initial value of 8,000 units produces a 2.67 percent change in EBIT. Since output increased by 25 percent from its initial value of 8,000 units, EBIT increases by $(2.67)(.25) = .667$ or 66.7 percent.

---

**Measurement of Operating Leverage**

Equation 5-6 is the *definitional* equation for operating leverage. In practice, *measurement* equations equivalent to definitional equations are used to compute and to explain the properties of operating leverage. Equation 5-7 is the measurement equation used when the income statement relationship is described by Equation 5-3:

$$(OL \mid T) = \frac{T(P - V)}{T(P - V) - F} \qquad (5\text{-}7)$$

The left-hand side of Equation 5-7 is read as: *operating leverage, given the value of output.*

By putting the data of the previous example into Equation 5-7, the equivalence of Equations 5-7 and 5-6 can be illustrated as follows:

$$(OL \mid T = 8,000) = \frac{8,000\ (\$10 - \$4)}{8,000\ (\$10 - \$4) - \$30,000} = 2.67$$

Later discussions of operating leverage in this chapter center around Equation 5-7. One note of caution is in order: The definitional Equation 5-6 for operating leverage is quite general, but the measurement Equation 5-7 is correct *only* when the income statement relationship between output and EBIT is described by Equation 5-3. Very different measurement equations are needed, for example, when nonlinear costs and/or multiple product lines are involved.

**Properties of Operating Leverage**

The properties of operating leverage determine its use as a tool of financial analysis. These properties are best explained by using operating breakeven and EBIT. **Operating breakeven** is defined as the value of output that makes EBIT equal to zero. At this level of output, total revenue is just sufficient to pay operating variable and fixed costs, and no earnings are available to cover financial costs. When output exceeds operating breakeven, the total revenue that is generated provides a positive level of EBIT; below operating breakeven, the firm incurs an operating loss. For Equation 5-3, the operating breakeven is expressed as:

$$T(P - V) - F = 0$$

and solving for $T$ yields

$$T = \frac{F}{P - V} \qquad (5\text{-}8)$$

**Example:**

Assume that $P = \$25$, $V = \$10$, and $F = \$60,000$. Operating breakeven is calculated as follows:

$$T = \frac{\$60,000}{\$25 - \$10} = 4,000 \text{ units}$$

If operating leverage is calculated at operating breakeven, the coefficient of operating leverage computed by using Equation 5-7 is:

$$(OL \mid T) = 4,000) = \frac{4,000 \ (\$25 - \$10)}{4,000 \ (\$25 - \$10) - \$60,000}$$

$$= \frac{\$60,000}{0} = \text{undefined}$$

Note that the coefficient of operating leverage at operating breakeven has an *undefined* value, not a value of zero.

---

Using the same data in the above example, Equation 5-7 can now be used to compute the coefficients of operating leverage at the following different levels of output:

$$(OL \mid T = 1,000) = \frac{1,000 \ (\$25 - \$10)}{1,000 \ (\$25 - \$10) - \$60,000} = -.33$$

$$(OL \mid T = 3,000) = \frac{3,000 \ (\$25 - \$10)}{3,000 \ (\$25 - \$10) - \$60,000} = -3.0$$

$$(OL \mid T = 6,000) = \frac{6,000 \ (\$25 - \$10)}{6,000 \ (\$25 - \$10) - \$60,000} = 3.0$$

$$(OL \mid T = 10,000) = \frac{10,000 \ (\$25 - \$10)}{10,000 \ (\$25 - \$10) - \$60,000} = 1.67$$

$$(OL \mid T = 30,000) = \frac{30,000 \ (\$25 - \$10)}{30,000 \ (\$25 - \$10) - \$60,000} = 1.15$$

These values are plotted in Figure 5-1. The smooth curves that result from plotting these values demonstrate that there is a unique coefficient of operating leverage for each level of output. The vertical broken line is plotted at operating breakeven and indicates that operating leverage is *undefined* at that level of output. The horizontal broken line indicates the limiting value of operating leverage. For values of output greater than operating breakeven, the coefficient of operating leverage is greater than 1.0, decreases with increasing levels of output, and approaches 1.0 as a limit.

When the level of output is below operating breakeven, the coefficient of operating leverage has a negative value and approaches zero as output goes to zero. Thus, the algebraic sign of operating leverage indicates where the value of output is in relation to operating breakeven.

The values of coefficients of operating leverage at various levels of output depend on the relative mix of fixed and variable costs. Figure 5-1 illustrates the relationships between output and operating leverage when price, variable cost per unit, and fixed costs are held constant. If any or all of these change, operating breakeven changes and a new set of operating leverages occur over different levels of output. For the special case

Figure 5-1.          **Plot of Operating Leverage**

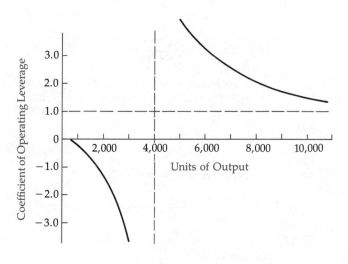

where fixed costs equal zero, the coefficient of operating leverage equals 1.0 for all levels of output greater than zero. This property of operating leverage is demonstrated by setting $F = 0$ in Equation 5-7. The result is:

$$(OL \,|\, T) = \frac{T(P - V)}{T(P - V)} = 1.0$$

In any situation where Equation 5-7 is the relevant equation for measuring operating leverage, the plot of operating leverage will be similar to that of Figure 5-1. The vertical broken line is placed at operating breakeven, and the horizontal broken line is plotted at 1.0. The curves that depict the set of output and operating leverage values will assume the same general shape shown in Figure 5-1.

**Interpretations of Operating Leverage**

There are fundamental and related interpretations of operating leverage. Although interpreting a coefficient of operating leverage is generally straightforward, there are instances where its algebraic sign and/or the value of output with respect to operating breakeven require added care in these interpretations.

FUNDAMENTAL INTERPRETATION. In general, any coefficient of operating leverage can be interpreted as follows: *The coefficient of operating leverage is the percentage change in EBIT that results from a 1 percent change in the level of output.*

**Example:**   Assume that $P = \$40$, $V = \$25$, and $F = \$105,000$. When the corporation sells 8,000 units of output, the values for EBIT and the coefficient of operating leverage are:

$$Y = 8,000 \ (\$40 - \$25) - \$105,000 = \$15,000$$

$$(OL \,|\, T = 8,000) = \frac{8,000 \ (\$40 - \$25)}{8,000 \ (\$40 - \$25) - \$105,000} = 8.0$$

If the level of output increases by 1 percent (from 8,000 units to 8,080 units) in the next accounting period, what happens to EBIT? The fundamental interpretation of operating leverage says that EBIT will increase by 8 percent. For $T = 8,080$, EBIT equals:

$$Y = 8,080 \ (\$40 - \$25) - \$105,000 = \$16,200$$

The percentage change in EBIT, therefore, is:

$$\frac{\$16,200 - \$15,000}{\$15,000} = .08 \text{ or } 8\%$$

This is the same percentage change obtained from the fundamental interpretation of operating leverage.·

The fundamental interpretation of operating leverage can be further generalized as follows: *The percentage change in EBIT that results from a given percentage change in output is equal to the value of operating leverage at the initial value of output multiplied by the percentage change in output.*

**Example:**   Using the data in the previous example, suppose that the initial output of 8,000 units decreases by 12 percent (from 8,000 to 7,040 units). The resulting percentage change in EBIT is $(8) \ (-.12) = -.96$ or $-96$ percent.

This percentage decrease can be verified by computing both the value of EBIT when $T = 7,040$ (12 percent below 8,000) and the resulting percentage change in EBIT:

$$Y = 7,040 \ (\$40 - \$25) - \$105,000 = \$600$$

$$\frac{\Delta Y}{Y} = \frac{\$600 - \$15,000}{\$15,000} = -.96 \text{ or } -96\%$$

**RELATED INTERPRETATIONS.** The following are related interpretations that are based on the properties of operating leverage:

1.   A *positive* coefficient of operating leverage indicates that leverage is being computed at a level of output *greater* than operating breakeven.

2.  A *negative* coefficient of operating leverage indicates that leverage is being computed at a level of output *below* operating breakeven.

3.  A *large absolute value* of operating leverage (the coefficient of operating leverage without regard to its algebraic sign) indicates that output is *close to* operating breakeven and that the absolute size of EBIT is *relatively small*.

4.  A *positive* coefficient of operating leverage *close to 1.0* indicates that output is relatively *far above* operating breakeven and that the amount of EBIT is *relatively large*.

**Applications of Operating Leverage**

The applications of operating leverage are a consequence of its properties and interpretations. The basic applications are discussed below. Additional applications are presented in the final section of this chapter which deals with combined leverage.

**EXPLAINING MAGNIFICATION OF PERCENTAGE CHANGES IN EBIT.** The fundamental application of operating leverage lies in explaining why changes in the level of output can produce disproportionate changes in EBIT. The explanation is found in Equation 5-7—the measurement equation used in the previous examples. This equation indicates that as long as fixed costs are greater than zero, a 1 percent change in output can produce a different percentage change in EBIT. In particular, for values of output greater than operating breakeven, the percentage change in EBIT which results from a 1 percent change in output is always greater than 1 percent. Figure 5-1 illustrates the extent to which changes in output produce magnified percentage changes in EBIT.

**EXPLAINING ERRORS IN EBIT FORECASTS.** A second application of operating leverage deals with the explanation of errors in EBIT forecasts. While there are many causes of such errors, the magnification of percentage changes in EBIT provides one reason why actual EBIT can deviate significantly from its forecast value.

When a corporation is forecasting its expected level of output for the coming accounting period, it must first determine the values for $P$, $V$, and $F$. The firm then forecasts its expected EBIT and computes the coefficient of operating leverage *at the forecast value of output*. For each 1 percent that actual output deviates from forecast output, the percentage deviation of actual from forecast EBIT is equal to the coefficient of operating leverage multiplied by the percentage error in forecast output. This explains why, for example, a 5 percent error in forecast output might be accompanied by a 30 percent deviation of actual from expected EBIT. Knowing the coefficient of operating leverage for the forecast output *before the accounting period begins* can help reduce any managerial anxieties that might be felt when an acceptable error in forecast output is accompanied by a much larger, unanticipated but predictable percentage error in forecast EBIT.

MEASURING BUSINESS RISK. In Chapter 1 *business risk* was defined as that component of overall corporate risk relating to asset composition and operating decisions. The results of these decisions, together with the impact of the operating environment, interact to produce corporate EBIT. Consequently, business risk is frequently described as the probability or likelihood that a corporation will go out of business because it is unable to earn a *positive* level of EBIT.

There are many approaches to measuring business risk. The use of operating leverage provides one such measure by combining the first two applications presented above. When output and EBIT are forecast for a given accounting period, the forecasts are said to be made under conditions of business risk whenever the actual levels of output and EBIT can deviate from their forecast values. The larger the possible deviation, the riskier the situation. The coefficient of operating leverage can be used to measure business risk since it indicates the extent to which an error in forecast output will produce a magnified percentage error in EBIT. The larger the coefficient of operating leverage, the greater the risk surrounding the forecast value of EBIT. Consequently, the greater the risk that the actual EBIT will turn out to be negative.

The degree of business risk also changes when a firm makes asset composition decisions that alter its fixed and variable production costs. If changing a firm's production costs changes its operating break-even point, a new set of operating leverage coefficients results and the firm's business risk changes. In general, increasing a firm's breakeven increases its degree of business risk; decreasing breakeven decreases the degree of business risk.

| | |
|---|---|
| **Example:** | A firm's production costs are as follows: |

$$F = \$4,800,000$$
$$V = \$26$$

With a selling price of $51 per unit, the operating breakeven is:

$$T = \$4,800,000/(\$51 - \$26)$$
$$= 192,000 \text{ units}$$

Coefficients of operating leverage for selected values of output are contained in the first two columns of the following table:

| $T$ | $(OL\mid T)$ before automation | $(OL\mid T)$ after automation |
|---|---|---|
| 225,000 | 6.82 | 13.00 |
| 250,000 | 4.31 | 5.91 |
| 275,000 | 3.31 | 4.09 |

The firm decides to automate a portion of its production process. As a result, fixed costs increase to $5,400,000, but the unit variable cost decreases to $25. The new operating breakeven is

$$T = \$5,400,000/(\$51 - \$25)$$
$$= 207,692 \text{ units}$$

The operating leverage coefficients that occur as a result of the automation are listed in the third column of the above table. Since the operating breakeven has now increased, the firm's operating risk, as measured using operating leverage coefficients, has also increased.

The output and operating leverage coefficients for the above example are plotted in Figure 5-2. The two lines that graph this data do not intersect, indicating that the expansion decision produces an increased level of operating risk over all values of output. Note, however, that the vertical distance between the two plotted lines decreases over increasing levels of output. This indicates that the *differential* business risk between the two alternatives gradually decreases over increasing output levels.

**Figure 5-2.**   **Operating Leverage Coefficients before and after Automation**

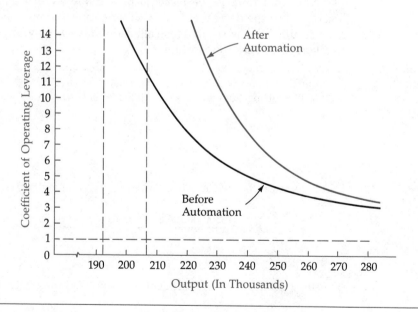

## FINANCIAL LEVERAGE

Operating leverage and financial leverage are applications of the same concept. As a result, the definition and properties of financial leverage are parallel to those of operating leverage.

Financial leverage measures the relationship between EBIT and EPS. Specifically, it reflects the effect of changing levels of EBIT on EPS. The functional relationship between these two variables is:

$$EPS = f(EBIT)$$

and the income statement relationship is that of Equation 5-4:

$$EPS = \frac{(Y - I)(1 - t) - E}{N}$$

When the level of EBIT changes from its initial value, the initial value of EPS also changes. **Financial leverage** is then defined as the resulting percentage change in EPS divided by the percentage change in EBIT. Symbolically, financial leverage is expressed as:

$$\frac{L(EPS)}{L(EBIT)} = \frac{\Delta EPS/EPS}{\Delta EBIT/EBIT} = \frac{\%\Delta EPS}{\%\Delta EBIT} \qquad (5\text{-}9)$$

Note that EBIT is the *independent* variable when measuring financial leverage, but the dependent variable when measuring operating leverage. As a result, EBIT is sometimes called the *linking pin* variable with respect to leverage applications in finance.

---

**Example:**

Assume that $I = \$100,000$, $t = .4$, $E = \$80,000$, $N = 60,000$, and that EBIT = $\$500,000$. By using Equation 5-4, the EPS at this level of EBIT is computed as:

$$EPS = \frac{(\$500,000 - \$100,000)(1 - .4) - \$80,000}{60,000}$$

$$= \$2.67$$

If EBIT increases from $500,000 to $600,000, the resulting EPS is:

$$EPS = \frac{(\$600,000 - \$100,000)(1 - .4) - \$80,000}{60,000}$$

$$= 3.67$$

By using Equation 5-9, the coefficient of financial leverage is computed as:

Percentage change in EBIT = $100,000/$500,000 = 20%
Percentage change in EPS  = $1.00/$2.67 = 37.45%

$$\frac{L(EPS)}{L(EBIT)} = \frac{.3745}{.20} = 1.87$$

The coefficient of financial leverage of 1.87 is interpreted as follows: a 1 percent change in EBIT from an initial value of $500,000 produces a 1.87 percent change in EPS. Since EBIT increased by 20 percent from its initial value, EPS increases by 1.87 (.20) = .374 or 37.4 percent.

---

**Measurement of Financial Leverage**

The measurement equation used to compute the coefficient of financial leverage when the income statement relationship is that of Equation 5-4 is:

$$(FL \mid Y) = \frac{Y}{Y - I - \dfrac{E}{1 - t}} \tag{5-10}$$

The left-hand side of Equation 5-10 is read as: *financial leverage, given the value of EBIT.*

By putting the data of the previous example into Equation 5-10, the equivalence of Equations 5-9 and 5-10 can be illustrated as:

$$(FL \mid Y = \$500,000) = \frac{\$500,000}{\$500,000 - \$100,000 - \dfrac{\$80,000}{1 - .4}} = 1.88$$

The use of Equation 5-10 to compute financial leverage values is correct whenever the income statement relationships between EBIT and EPS are described by Equation 5-4. When a firm has several issues of bonds and preferred stock outstanding, the values of $I$ and $E$ are the total amounts of bond interest and preferred stock dividends to be paid. The equations for defining (5-9) and measuring (5-10) financial leverage do *not* depend on any specific income statement relationships between output and EBIT as is true for operating leverage. These financial leverage equations are appropriate in situations where corporate EBIT involves multiple product lines and/or nonlinear production and operating costs. The term *financial leverage* is used because this type of leverage focuses on the EPS impacts resulting from the *financing* decisions of a corporation. Financial leverage is sometimes called **balance sheet leverage** or **capital structure leverage.**

---

**Example:**

A corporation produces and sells several different product lines. In financing these activities, the firm has floated two issues each of the following bonds and preferred stock, and has one million shares of common stock outstanding:

Bond issue A: $10,000,000 at 8% interest rate
Bond issue B: $20,000,000 at 10% interest rate
Preferred stock series A: 200,000 shares, $4.50 dividend per share
Preferred stock series B: 300,000 shares, $7 dividend per share

At the EBIT level of $10,000,000, the values of EPS and of financial leverage are:

$$I = .08\ (\$10,000,000) + .10\ (\$20,000,000) = \$2,800,000$$

$$E = \$4.5\,(200{,}000) + \$7\,(300{,}000) = \$3{,}000{,}000$$

$$EPS = \frac{(\$10{,}000{,}000 - \$2{,}800{,}000)\,(1 - .4) - \$3{,}000{,}000}{1{,}000{,}000} = \$1.32$$

$$(FL\,|\,Y = \$10{,}000{,}000) = \frac{\$10{,}000{,}000}{\$10{,}000{,}000 - \$2{,}800{,}000 - \$3{,}000{,}000/(1 - .4)}$$

$$= 4.55$$

## Properties of Financial Leverage

The properties of financial leverage can be explained by using the concept of financial breakeven. **Financial breakeven** is defined as the value of EBIT that makes EPS equal to zero. At financial breakeven, the firm's EBIT is just sufficient to cover its fixed financing costs (bond interest and preferred stock dividends) on a before-tax basis, leaving no earnings for common shareholders. Above this financial break-even amount of EBIT, the firm produces a positive level of earnings available to common shareholders and a positive EPS. Below this level, profit available to common shareholders and EPS are both negative. It is thus possible for a firm to earn a positive level of EBIT even though its EPS is negative. This will happen when the firm's EBIT is positive but less than its financial break-even level. Using Equation 5-4, financial breakeven is expressed as:

$$\frac{(Y - I)(1 - t) - E}{N} = 0$$

Solving this equation for $Y$, or EBIT, yields:

$$Y = I + \frac{E}{1 - t} \tag{5-11}$$

## Example:

Assume that $I = \$2{,}000{,}000$ and $E = \$1{,}300{,}000$. Financial breakeven is calculated as:

$$Y = \$2{,}000{,}000 + \$1{,}300{,}000/(1 - .4) = \$4{,}166{,}667$$

If financial leverage is calculated at financial breakeven, the resulting coefficient of financial leverage has an *undefined* value, computed by using Equation 5-10 as follows:

$$(FL\,|\,Y = \$4{,}166{,}667) = \frac{\$4{,}166{,}667}{\$4{,}166{,}667 - \$2{,}000{,}000 - \$1{,}300{,}000/(1 - .4)}$$

$$= \frac{\$4{,}166{,}667}{0} = \text{undefined}$$

Using the same data in the above example, Equation 5-10 can be used to compute the coefficients of financial leverage for different values of EBIT:

$$(FL \mid Y = \$2,000,000) = \frac{\$2,000,000}{\$2,000,000 - \$2,000,000 - \$1,300,000/(1 - .4)}$$

$$= -.92$$

$$(FL \mid Y = \$3,000,000) = \frac{\$3,000,000}{\$3,000,000 - \$2,000,000 - \$1,300,000/(1 - .4)}$$

$$= -2.57$$

$$(FL \mid Y = \$6,000,000) = \frac{\$6,000,000}{\$6,000,000 - \$2,000,000 - \$1,300,000/(1 - .4)}$$

$$= 3.27$$

$$(FL \mid Y = \$10,000,000) = \frac{\$10,000,000}{\$10,000,000 - \$2,000,000 - \$1,300,000/(1 - .4)}$$

$$= 1.71$$

These values are plotted in Figure 5-3. The smooth curves in Figure 5-3 indicate that there is a unique value of financial leverage for each value of EBIT. The vertical broken line is plotted at financial breakeven and indicates that financial leverge is *undefined* at financial breakeven. The horizontal broken line plotted at 1.0 indicates the limiting value of financial leverage; that is, for values of EBIT greater than financial breakeven, the coefficient of financial leverage is greater than 1.0, decreases with increasing values of EBIT, and approaches 1 as a limit.

When EBIT is below financial breakeven, the coefficient of financial leverage is negative and approaches zero as EBIT goes to zero.

Figure 5-3 illustrates the relationship between EBIT and financial leverage when bond interest, preferred stock dividends, and the income tax rate are held constant. If any or all of these change, financial breakeven changes and a new set of financial leverages occur over different levels of EBIT.

In the special case where $I + E = 0$ (where fixed financing costs are zero), the coefficient of financial leverage equals 1.0 for all values of EBIT greater than zero. This is shown by setting $I = E = 0$ in Equation 5-10; the resulting answer reduces the equation to $Y/Y = 1.0$.

In any situation where Equation 5-10 is the relevant measurement equation for financial leverage, its plot will be similar to that of Figure 5-3. A vertical broken line is placed at financial breakeven, and a horizontal broken line is plotted at 1.0. The curves that depict the paired values of EBIT and financial leverage will assume the same general shape as shown in Figure 5-3. This figure is also useful in understanding the interpretations of financial leverage that follow.

**Figure 5-3.**     **Plot of Financial Leverage When $I=\$2,000,000$ and $E=\$1,300,000$**

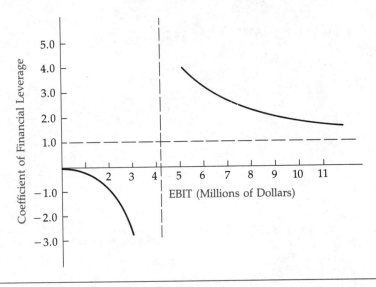

| Interpretations of Financial Leverage | As with operating leverage, there are fundamental and related interpretations of financial leverage. The size of the coefficient of financial leverage and the value of EBIT with respect to financial breakeven help interpret the coefficient in specific situations. |
|---|---|

**FUNDAMENTAL INTERPRETATION.** The fundamental interpretation of the coefficient of financial leverage is: *the coefficient of financial leverage is the percentage change in EPS that results from a 1 percent change in EBIT.*

**Example:**     Assume that $I = \$1,000,000$, $E = \$500,000$, $t = .4$, and $N = 100,000$. When the level of EBIT = $\$4,000,000$, the values for EPS and the coefficient financial leverage are:

$$\text{EPS} = \frac{(\$4,000,000 - \$1,000,000)(1 - .4) - \$500,000}{100,000} = \$13$$

$$(FL\,|\,Y = \$4,000,000) = \frac{\$4,000,000}{\$4,000,000 - \$1,000,000 - \$500,000/(1 - .4)} = 1.85$$

If EBIT decreases by 1 percent (from $\$4,000,000$ to $\$3,960,000$), the fundamental interpretation says that EPS will fall by 1.85 percent. To show the correctness of this interpretation, solve for EPS when EBIT decreases to $\$3,960,000$.

$$\text{EPS} = \frac{(\$3,960,000 - \$1,000,000)(1 - .4) - \$500,000}{100,000} = \$12.76$$

The percentage change in EPS is:

$$\frac{\$12.76 - \$13}{\$13} = -.0185 \quad \text{or} \quad -1.85\%$$

---

The fundamental interpretation of financial leverage can be further generalized as follows: *the percent change in EPS that results from a given percentage change in EBIT is equal to the value of financial leverage at the initial value of EBIT multiplied by the percentage change in EBIT.*

**Example:**   Using the data in the previous example, assume that the initial value of EBIT increases by 10 percent (from \$4,000,000 to \$4,400,000). The resulting percentage change in EPS is $(1.85)(.1) = .185$ or 18.5 percent.

This percentage increase can be verified by computing both the value of EPS when EBIT = \$4,400,000 (i.e., 10 percent above \$4,000,000) and the resulting percentage change in EPS:

$$\text{EPS} = \frac{(\$4,400,000 - \$1,000,000)(1 - .4) - \$500,000}{100,000} = \$15.40$$

$$\frac{\Delta \text{EPS}}{\text{EPS}} = \frac{\$15.4 - \$13}{\$13} = .185 \quad \text{or} \quad 18.5\%$$

---

**RELATED INTERPRETATIONS.** The following related interpretations are based on the properties of financial leverage:

1. A *positive* coefficient of financial leverage means that leverage is being computed for a value of EBIT that is *greater* than financial breakeven.

2. A *negative* coefficient of financial leverage indicates that leverage is being computed for a value of EBIT *below* financial breakeven.

3. A *large absolute value* of financial leverage indicates that leverage is being computed *close to* financial breakeven and that the absolute value of EPS is *relatively small*.

4. A *positive* coefficient of financial leverage *close to 1.0* indicates that leverage is being computed for a value of EBIT that is *relatively far above* financial breakeven and that the corresponding value of EPS is *relatively large*.

**Applications of Financial Leverage**   The applications, or uses, of financial leverage are based on its properties and on the fundamental interpretation of financial leverage. These applications occur repeatedly in managerial finance. Three applications are discussed below. A fourth application—as a component of combined leverage—is discussed in the final section of this chapter. A fifth application—as a tool in analyzing capital structure decisions—is discussed in Chapter 15.

**EXPLAINING MAGNIFICATION OF PERCENTAGE CHANGES IN EPS.** The fundamental application of financial leverage is to explain why changes in EBIT can produce magnified percentage changes in EPS. The explanation is found in Equation 5-10. This equation indicates that as long as fixed financing costs are greater than zero, a 1 percent change in EBIT can produce a very different percentage change in EPS.

**EXPLAINING ERRORS IN EPS FORECASTS.** A second application of financial leverage occurs in explaining errors in EPS forecasts. A corporation forecasts its expected EBIT and corresponding EPS for a particular sales period and computes the coefficient of financial leverage at the *forecast level of EBIT.* For each percent that actual EBIT deviates from its forecast value, the percentage deviation of actual from forecast EPS is equal to the coefficient of financial leverage multiplied by the percentage error in forecast EBIT.

---

**Example:**

A corporation forecasts its EBIT for the coming sales period at $30,000,000. The relevant values of its income statement items are: $I = \$4,000,000$, $E = \$1,500,000$, $N = 2,000,000$ common shares, and $t = .4$. The EPS and financial leverage for the forecast EBIT are:

$$EPS = \frac{(\$30,000,000 - \$4,000,000)(1 - .4) - \$1,500,000}{2,000,000} = \$7.05$$

$$(FL \mid Y = \$30,000,000) = \frac{\$30,000,000}{\$30,000,000 - \$4,000,000 - \$1,500,000/(1 - .4)}$$

$$= 1.28$$

If actual EBIT is 10 percent above its forecast value, actual EPS will be $(.10)(1.28) = .128$ or 12.8 percent above forecast EPS. Hence, an actual EBIT of $33,000,000 will yield an EPS value of $(\$7.05)(1.28) = \$9.02$.

---

This application of financial leverage suggests that it may be possible to anticipate EPS forecasting errors because one component in generating these errors is the coefficient of financial leverage at forecast EBIT. The larger the value of financial leverage the larger the range of possible EPS forecasting errors.

**MEASURING FINANCIAL RISK.** Financial risk is the probability or likelihood of serious fluctuations in EPS because of a firm's choice of capital structure. Financial leverage is only one of several approaches to measuring financial risk. Forecast values of EBIT and EPS are said to be risky whenever the actual EBIT and EPS values can deviate from their predicted values. The larger the possible deviation, the riskier the situation. Financial leverage can be used to measure financial risk because it indicates the size of the EPS forecasting error that a 1 percent EBIT forecasting error can produce. The larger the coefficient of financial leverage, the greater the degree of financial risk. This is because large values of financial leverage require relatively small EBIT forecasting errors in order to produce negative EPS values.

---

**Example:**

Two corporations forecast their EBIT values, and their corresponding coefficients of financial leverage are:

$$\text{Corporation \#1: } (FL \,|\, Y_1) = 8.0$$
$$\text{Corporation \#2: } (FL \,|\, Y_2) = 2.0$$

The EPS for Corporation #1 will be negative if actual $Y_1$ turns out to be more than 12.5 percent below its forecast value. However, actual $Y_2$ for Corporation #2 has to be more than 50 percent below its forecast value in order for its EPS to take a negative value. Therefore, the financial risk of Corporation #1 is greater than that of Corporation #2.

---

The firm's degree of financial risk changes whenever the firm alters its fixed financing costs. This typically happens because additional bonds or preferred stock are sold, thus increasing payments for interest and/or preferred stock dividends. Shifts in financial risk also occur when the firm substitutes one type of financing for another if new values for $I$ and/or $E$ emerge. Simply selling or retiring common shares does not alter the degree of financial risk as measured by financial leverage because common stock dividends are not contained in Equation 5-10, the measurement equation for financial leverage. Changes in the federal corporate income tax rate can also shift a firm's financial leverage; however, the tax rate is assumed to be constant in this discussion.

Changing the values of the fixed financing costs produces a new financial breakeven and a new set of financial leverage coefficients. Increasing the financial breakeven increases a firm's degree of financial risk; decreasing the financial breakeven decreases the degree of financial risk.

---

**Example:**

A corporation has a $4 million EBIT, $1.2 million in interest payments on debt, a 40 percent tax rate, and no other fixed financing costs. Financial breakeven is thus $1.2 million.

The firm has decided to expand and will finance the expansion by selling additional shares of common stock or by floating an initial issue of preferred stock that requires $600,000 in dividend payments.

If common stock is chosen as the financing alternative, financial breakeven and the degree of financial risk are not affected. Financial leverage coefficients for selected EBIT values are contained in the first two columns of the following table:

| EBIT | $(FL|Y)$ Common Stock | $(FL|Y)$ Preferred Stock |
|------|------------------------|---------------------------|
| $4.0 million | 1.43 | 2.22 |
| $4.5 million | 1.36 | 1.96 |
| $5.0 million | 1.32 | 1.79 |

If the firm decides to finance the expansion with preferred stock, financial breakeven increases to:

$$Y = \$1,200,000 + \$600,000/(1 - .4)$$
$$= \$2,200,000$$

The resulting financial leverage coefficients are listed in the third column of the above table. Since financial breakeven has now increased, the firm's financial risk, as measured by financial leverage coefficients, has also increased.

The financial leverage coefficients for the financing alternatives in the above example are plotted in Figure 5-4. The lines that represent the coefficients of financial leverage for alternative levels of EBIT do not intersect, indicating that the preferred stock financing alternative produces a higher level of financial leverage and thus of financial risk over all values of EBIT. Note however that the *differential* risk between these two alternatives decreases over increasing EBIT levels.

**Figure 5-4**       **Financial Leverage Coefficients for Two Expansion Financing Alternatives**

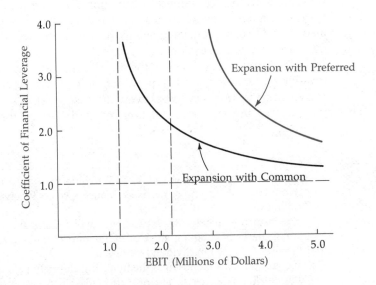

## COMBINED LEVERAGE

Combined leverage is not a distinct type of leverage. It is a combination of operating and financial leverage. Combined leverage measures the relationship between output and EPS. The functional relationship between these two variables is:

$$EPS = f(T)$$

and the income statement relationship is that of Equation 5-5:

$$EPS = \frac{[T(P - V) - F - I](1 - t) - E}{N}$$

Note that Equation 5-5 contains the definition of EBIT as specified in Equation 5-3:

$$Y = T(P - V) - F$$

In Equation 5-3, EBIT is the dependent variable. But if Equation 5-3 is substituted into Equation 5-5, EBIT becomes the independent variable. This is the linking pin function of EBIT: The sale of company output produces EBIT which, in turn, is translated into EPS. When the operating and financial portions of the income statement are combined as in Equation 5-5, EBIT disappears as a separate variable and is replaced by output as the independent variable.

When the level of output changes from its initial value, the initial value of EPS also changes. **Combined leverage** is defined as the resulting percentage change in EPS divided by the percentage change in output. The definitional equation of combined leverage is:

$$\frac{L(EPS)}{L(T)} = \frac{\Delta EPS/EPS}{\Delta T/T} \tag{5-12}$$

---

**Example:**

Assume that $P = \$50$, $V = \$30$, $F = \$150,000$, $I = \$40,000$, $E = \$20,000$, and $N = 10,000$ common shares. At an output of 15,000 units, EPS is computed by using Equation 5-5:

$$EPS = \frac{[15,000(\$50 - \$30) - \$150,000 - \$40,000](1 - .4) - \$20,000}{10,000}$$

$$= \$4.60$$

If output increases to 16,500 units, EPS increases to:

$$EPS = \frac{[16,500(\$50 - \$30) - \$150,000 - \$40,000](1 - .4) - \$20,000}{10,000}$$

$$= \$6.40$$

Using Equation 5-12, the coefficient of combined leverage is computed as:

Percentage change in output = 1,500/15,000 = 10%
Percentage change in EPS = $1.80/$4.60 = 39.1%

$$\frac{L(EPS)}{L(T)} = \frac{.391}{.1} = 3.91$$

The coefficient of combined leverage of 3.91 is interpreted as follows: a 1 percent change in output from a level of 15,000 units produces a 3.91 percent change in EPS. Since output increased by 10 percent, the resulting percentage increase in EPS is (.1)(3.91) = .391 or 39.1 percent.

**Measurement of Combined Leverage**

When the income statement relationships are those of Equation 5-5, the following two measurement equations can be used to compute the coefficient of combined leverage:

$$(CL\,|\,T) = \frac{T(P - V)}{T(P - V) - F - I - E/(1 - t)} \tag{5-13}$$

$$(CL\,|\,T) = (OL\,|\,T)(FL\,|\,Y) \tag{5-14}$$

The left-hand sides of these equations are read as: *combined leverage, given the value of output.*

Since Equation 5-5 can be used to compute EPS only in those cases where the firm's EBIT is earned from a single product (linear cost production function), this seems to limit the applications of Equations 5-13 and 5-14 as measurement equations of combined leverage. However, the definitional Equation 5-12 is independent of the income statement relationships in Equation 5-5. Thus, Equation 5-12 can be used in situations involving multiple product and/or nonlinear cost functions.

Equation 5-13 can be used to compute the coefficient of combined leverage directly from a set of data. Equation 5-14 is used when the separate coefficients of operating and financial leverage are also being computed. In addition, Equation 5-14 illustrates the specific way by which operating and financial leverage interact. Combined leverage is the *product* of operating and financial leverage.

The equivalence of the definitional and measurement equations for combined leverage can be demonstrated by using the data of the previous example as is shown in the following example:

**Example:**

At a level of output of 15,000 units, the values of EBIT, operating leverage, and financial leverage equal:

$$Y = T(P - V) - F$$

$$Y = 15,000(\$50 - \$30) - \$150,000 = \$150,000$$

$$(OL \mid T) = \frac{T(P - V)}{T(P - V) - F}$$

$$(OL \mid T = 15{,}000) = \frac{15{,}000(\$50 - \$30)}{15{,}000(\$50 - \$30) - \$150{,}000} = 2.0$$

$$(FL \mid Y) = \frac{Y}{Y - I - E/(1 - t)}$$

$$(FL \mid Y = \$150{,}000) = \frac{\$150{,}000}{\$150{,}000 - \$40{,}000 - \$20{,}000/(1 - .4)} = 1.957$$

By using Equation 5-14, the combined leverage is:

$$(CL \mid T) = (OL \mid T)(FL \mid Y)$$

$$(CL \mid T) = (2.0)(1.957) = 3.91$$

By using Equation 5-13, the combined leverage is:

$$(CL \mid T) = \frac{T(P - V)}{T(P - V) - F - I - E/(1 - t)}$$

$$(CL \mid T = 15{,}000) = \frac{15{,}000(\$50 - \$30)}{15{,}000(\$50 - \$30) - \$150{,}000 - \$40{,}000 - \$20{,}000/(1 - .4)}$$

$$= 3.91$$

Note that both measurement Equations 5-13 and 5-14 produce the same coefficient of combined leverage that was obtained from the definitional Equation 5-12.

---

**Properties of Combined Leverage**

The properties of combined leverage are similar to those of operating and financial leverage because combined leverage is a combination of the two distinct types of leverage. These properties can be explained by using the concept of overall breakeven. **Overall breakeven** is defined as the level of output that makes EPS equal to zero. Setting Equation 5-5 equal to zero and solving for $T$ yields the overall break-even value of output:

$$T = \frac{F + I + E/(1 - t)}{P - V} \tag{5-15}$$

Using the data set of the previous examples, overall breakeven is:

$$T = \frac{\$150{,}000 + \$40{,}000 + \$20{,}000/(1 - .4)}{\$50 - \$30} = 11{,}167 \text{ units}$$

Using this same data set, Equation 5-13 can be used to compute the coefficient of combined leverage at different levels of output, as follows:

$(CL \mid T = 5,000)$

$$= \frac{5,000(\$50 - \$30)}{5,000(\$50 - \$30) - \$150,000 - \$40,000 - \$20,000/(1 - .4)}$$

$$= -.811$$

$(CL \mid T = 10,000)$

$$= \frac{10,000(\$50 - \$30)}{10,000(\$50 - \$30) - \$150,000 - \$40,000 - \$20,000/(1 - .4)}$$

$$= -8.57$$

$(CL \mid T = 20,000)$

$$= \frac{20,000(\$50 - \$30)}{20,000(\$50 - \$30) - \$150,000 - \$40,000 - \$20,000/(1 - .4)}$$

$$= 2.26$$

$(CL \mid T = 25,000)$

$$= \frac{25,000(\$50 - \$30)}{25,000(\$50 - \$30) - \$150,000 - \$40,000 - \$20,000/(1 - .4)}$$

$$= 1.81$$

These values are plotted in Figure 5-5. The smooth curves in Figure 5-5 show that there is a unique value of combined leverage for each level of output. The vertical broken line is plotted at overall breakeven and indicates that combined leverage is *undefined* at this level of output. The horizontal broken line plotted at 1.0 indicates the limiting value of combined leverage; that is, for levels of output greater than overall breakeven, the coefficient of combined leverage is greater than 1.0, decreases with increasing levels of output, and approaches 1.0 as a limit.

When the level of output is below overall breakeven, the coefficient of combined leverage is negative and approaches zero as output goes to zero.

In the special case where fixed operating costs *and* fixed financing costs are *all* zero ($F = I = E = 0$), the coefficient of combined leverage is equal to 1.0 for all levels of output greater than zero.

**Interpretations of Combined Leverage**

Interpreting the coefficient of combined leverage rests on the properties that were just explained. The fundamental interpretation of the coefficient of combined leverage is: *the coefficient of combined leverage is the percentage change in EPS that results from a 1 percent change in output.* It is possible to generalize this interpretation as follows: *the percentage change in EPS that results from a given percentage change in output is equal to the value of combined leverage computed at the initial value of output multiplied by the percentage change in output.*

**Figure 5-5.**    **Plot of Combined Leverage (Where $P = \$50$, $V = \$30$, $F = \$150,000$, $I = \$40,000$, and $E = \$20,000$)**

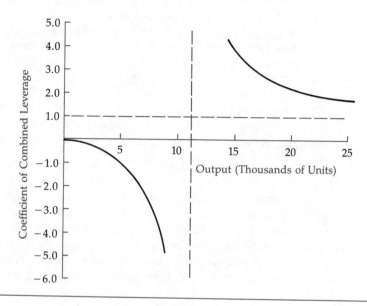

**Example:**    Assume the same data set used in the previous examples: $P = \$50$, $V = \$30$, $F = \$150,000$, $I = \$40,000$, and $E = \$20,000$. At the initial level of output of 15,000 units, EPS = $4.60 and CL = 3.91.

The fundamental interpretation states that if output increases by 15 percent (from 15,000 to 17,250 units), the percentage change in EPS will be $(3.91)(.15) = .587$ or 58.7 percent. Thus, EPS will increase by $(\$4.60)(.587) = \$2.70$. The resulting value of EPS is $4.60 + $2.70 = $7.30.

Similarly, if output decreases by 5 percent (from 15,000 units to 14,250), EPS would fall by $(3.91)(.05) = .196$ or 19.6 percent. The dollar decrease in EPS would be $(\$4.60)(.196) = \$.90$, and the resulting value of EPS would be $4.60 − $.90 = $3.70.

The following are related interpretations that are based on the properties of combined leverage:

1. A *positive* coefficient of combined leverage indicates that leverage is being computed for a level of output *greater* than overall breakeven.

2. A *negative* coefficient of combined leverage indicates that leverage is being computed at a level of output *below* overall breakeven.

3. A *large absolute value* of combined leverage indicates that output is *close to* overall breakeven, and the absolute value of EPS is

*minimal*. Consequently, a 1 percent change in output will produce a large percentage change in EPS since the initial value of EPS is, to begin with, very small.

4.  A *positive* coefficient of combined leverage *close* to 1.0 indicates that output is relatively *far above* overall breakeven and that the value of EPS is *sizable*. Therefore, a 1 percent increase in output will increase an already large value of EPS by a relatively small percentage.

**Applications of Combined Leverage**

Combined leverage can be used to: (1) explain why changes in the level of output produce magnified percentage changes in EPS, (2) explain EPS forecasting errors, and (3) provide a measure of overall corporate risk.

**EXPLAINING MAGNIFICATION OF PERCENTAGE CHANGES IN EPS.** The fundamental application of combined leverage explains why a 1 percent change in output produces a disproportionate percentage change in EPS as long as fixed operating costs and/or fixed financing costs are greater than zero. Increases in the fixed cost components used to measure operating leverage and/or financial leverage can produce greatly increased coefficients of combined leverage because combined leverage is the product of operating and financial leverage. The following example reinforces this point.

**Example:**

When $T = 20,000$, the following values occur for the data set used in previous examples where $P = \$50$, $V = \$30$, $F = \$150,000$, $I = \$40,000$, and $E = \$20,000$:

$$(Y \mid T = 20,000) = \$250,000$$

$$(OL \mid T = 20,000) = 1.6$$

$$(FL \mid Y = \$250,000) = 1.42$$

$$(CL \mid T = 20,000) = (1.6)(1.42) = 2.27$$

Now suppose an improved production method is introduced that has a higher production capacity, decreases the variable costs of production to $25 per unit, but increases fixed production costs to $250,000. In addition, the acquisition of this new technology is financed by selling additional preferred stock. This increases preferred stock dividends to a value of $60,000. The new leverage coefficients for $T = 20,000$ are:

$$(OL \mid T = 20,000) = 2.0$$

$$(FL \mid Y = \$250,000) = 2.27$$

$$(CL \mid T = 20,000) = (2.0)(2.27) = 4.54$$

Note that the coefficient of combined leverage has doubled in value even though only modest increases have occurred in the operating and financial leverages.

This example points out how easy it is to underestimate the contributions made by each of the two distinct types of leverage to combined leverage. The interaction of operating and financial leverage which produces combined leverage is the reason why corporate managers are sometimes cautioned against using debt and preferred stock issues to finance production and/or administrative facilities that result in substantially increasing fixed operating costs. The *acceptable range of combined leverage* is described as a function of the level and stability of EBIT because of its linking pin role in joining operating and financial leverage. The *level* of EBIT refers to the break-even requirements. The *stability* of EBIT refers to the magnification of changes in output on EPS. Stability, however, does not mean a constant or fixed value of EBIT. Stability implies a time series of EBIT that contains a predictable growth rate. When a corporation's EBIT meets these requirements of value and stability, it can act to increase its coefficient of combined leverage in order to further magnify increases in EPS. However, unanticipated decreases in EBIT will just as quickly produce magnified percentage decreases in EPS.

**EXPLAINING ERRORS IN EPS FORECASTS.** A corporation forecasts its expected level of output and corresponding EPS and computes the coefficient of combined leverage at the *forecast* level of output. Other things being equal, for each percent that actual output deviates from its forecast level, the percentage deviation of actual from forecast EPS is equal to the coefficient of combined leverage multiplied by the percentage error in forecast output.

---

**Example:**

Assume a forecast output of 20,000 units when $P = \$50$, $V = \$30$, $F = \$150,000$, $I = \$40,000$, $E = \$20,000$, and $N = 10,000$ common shares. The forecast EPS is computed as:

$$EPS = \frac{[20,000(\$50 - \$30) - \$150,000 - \$40,000][1 - .4] - \$20,000}{10,000} = \$10.60$$

Combined leverage when $T = 20,000$ has been computed above as:

$$(CL \mid T = 20,000) = 2.26$$

If actual output is 8 percent above its forecast level, then actual EPS will surpass forecast EPS by $(.08)(2.26) = .181$ or 18.1 percent. The dollar increase in actual EPS is $(\$10.60)(.181) = \$1.92$. Actual EPS will therefore be $\$10.60 + \$1.92 = \$12.52$.

---

**MEASURING OVERALL RISK.** The **overall risk,** or *ultimate risk*, that a corporation faces is the possibilty that it will go out of business and that its shareholders' investment will become worthless. In such an event, its share price will go to zero.

In previous sections of this chapter, operating leverage measured business risk and financial leverage measured financial risk. Since combined leverage contains both distinct types of leverage, it can be used as a measure of overall risk. When used in this manner, the larger the coefficient of combined leverage for a forecast level of output, the greater the overall risk faced by the corporation and its shareholders.

Another important consideration is the shift in overall risk that can occur when a corporation makes a combined investment-financing decision. If, for example a firm decides to increase its production capacity by replacing an aging facility with a new plant, or if it decides to produce a new product line that requires the construction of a new plant, a decision must also be made on how the new facilities are to be financed. The firm may also need to finance the increased inventory and receivables that are typically needed when a new product line is added.

If an investment-financing decision results in a change in the firm's overall breakeven, the degree of overall risk as measured by the coefficient of combined leverage also changes. A decrease in price, or increases in fixed production costs, unit variable production costs, or fixed financing costs increase overall breakeven and combined leverage. An increase in price or decreases in production or financing costs decrease overall breakeven and combined leverage. The overall impact of simultaneous changes in several of these components is evaluated by comparing the new overall breakeven against its value prior to the changes.

---

**Example:**

A corporation's production and financing costs are as follows: $V = \$24$, $F = \$4,500,000$, and $I = \$2,000,000$. In addition, 500,000 common shares are outstanding. With $P = \$46$, the firm's overall breakeven, using Equation 5-15, is:

$$T = \frac{\$4,500,000 + \$2,000,000}{\$46 - \$24}$$

$$= 295,455 \text{ units}$$

The firm's current output is 350,000 units. At this level, combined leverage, using Equation 5-13, is:

$$(CL|T = 350,000) = \frac{350,000 \, (\$46 - \$24)}{350,000 \, (\$46 - \$24) - \$4,500,000 - \$2,000,000}$$

$$= 6.42$$

Assuming a 40 percent federal corporate income tax rate, the firm's EPS at 350,000 units, using Equation 5-5, is:

$$EPS = \frac{[350,000 \, (\$46 - \$24) - \$4,500,000 - \$2,000,000](1 - .4)}{500,000}$$

$$= \$1.44$$

The firm decides to replace a portion of its production capacity and invests $3,000,000 into a line of automated equipment. As a result, fixed operating costs increase to $5,000,000, and unit variable production costs decrease to $22. The equipment purchase is financed by selling bonds that require annual interest payments of $360,000.

What is the impact of this investment-financing decision on the firm's overall risk? This question is answered by computing the new overall breakeven:

$$T = \frac{\$5,000,000 + \$2,000,000 + \$360,000}{\$46 - \$22}$$

$$= 306,667 \text{ units.}$$

Since overall breakeven has increased, so has the firm's overall risk. If output remains at 350,000 units, combined leverage increases to:

$$(CL|T = 350,000) = \frac{350,000\ (\$46 - \$22)}{350,000\ (\$46 - \$22) - \$5,000,000 - \$2,360,000}$$

$$= 8.08$$

Figure 5-6 plots the combined leverages before and after the replacement decision. Since the curves in this figure do not intersect, the replacement alternative has a higher degree of combined leverage and thus a higher degree of overall

Figure 5-6.

**Combined Leverage Coefficients before and after Replacement**

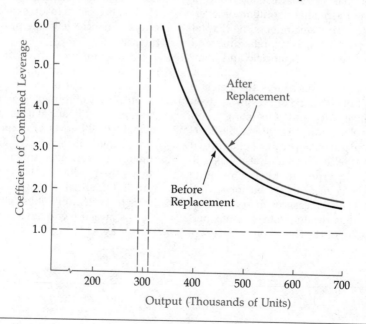

risk over all values of output. This figure also shows that the differential risk decreases over increasing levels of output. As a result of the replacement decision, the firm's EPS (when output is 350,000 units) decreases to:

$$EPS = \frac{[350,000 \, (\$46 - \$22) - \$5,000,000 - \$2,360,000](1 - .4)}{500,000}$$

$$= \$1.25$$

Thus, unless the firm increases its output, its price, or both, the net effect of the investment-financing replacement decision is to reduce its profitability, as measured by EPS, and to increase its overall risk, as measured by its degree of combined leverage.

The above example provides a first glimpse of the risk and return considerations that must be evaluated when a firm evaluates investment-financing alternatives. Subsequent chapters of this text consider this type of problem in greater detail. This section has focused primarily on the computation and interpretation of combined leverage as a measure of overall risk.

# SUMMARY

This chapter has introduced leverage as a tool of financial analysis. The leverage concept was discussed and a general definition of leverage was presented. The remainder of the chapter explained the properties, interpretations, and applications of operating, financial, and combined leverage.

Operating leverage measures the percentage change in EBIT that results from a given percentage change in output. Operating leverage helps to explain how changes in the level of corporate output can produce magnified changes in the level of EBIT and also helps to explain forecasting errors in EBIT. Operating leverage provides a measure of business risk.

Financial leverage measures the percentage change in EPS that results from a given percentage change in EBIT. This type of leverage helps to explain how changes in the level of EBIT can cause magnified changes in the level of EPS and also helps to explain EPS forecasting errors. Financial leverage provides a measure of financial risk.

Combined leverage, or overall leverage, measures the percentage change in EPS which occurs as a result of a given percentage change in output. Combined leverage explains how operating and financial leverage interact to make changes in the level of output produce magnified changes in level of EPS. Mathematically, combined leverage at any given level of output equals the product of the corresponding operating and financial leverages. Combined leverage helps to explain EPS forecasting errors and provides a measure of overall corporate risk.

# QUESTIONS

**5-1.** Explain the general concept of leverage.

**5-2.** Identify the dependent and independent variables in (a) operating leverage, (b) financial leverage, and (c) combined leverage.

**5-3.** Each type of leverage has an associated break-even point. Explain why the measurement equations for each leverage type are undefined at their respective break-even points.

**5-4.** What is the fundamental interpretation of the coefficient of operating leverage? Of financial leverage? Of combined leverage?

**5-5.** How are operating, financial, and combined leverages related algebraically?

**5-6.** Describe the type of risk measured by operating leverage, financial leverage, and combined leverage.

**5-7.** How does the operating leverage measurement equation explain the magnified percentage changes in EBIT that result from a given percentage change in output?

**5-8.** How does operating leverage explain EBIT forecasting errors?

**5-9.** How does the financial leverage measurement equation explain the magnified percentage changes in EPS that result from a given percentage change in EBIT?

**5-10.** How does financial leverage explain EPS forecasting errors?

**5-11.** Why is EBIT described as the *linking pin variable* in combined leverage?

**5-12.** How does the combined leverage measurement equation explain the magnified percentage changes in EPS that result from a given percentage change in output?

**5-13.** How does combined leverage explain EPS forecasting errors?

# PROBLEMS

**5-1.** Compute the value of EBIT for each of the following data sets:

a.. $P = \$10$; $V = \$3$; $F = \$16,000$; $T = 3,000$ units.
b.  $P = \$90$; $V = \$81$; $F = \$700,000$; $T = 82,500$ units.
c.  $P = \$22$; $V = \$18$; $F = \$43,000$; $T = 9,000$ units.

**5-2.** Assume that $P = \$10$, $V = \$4$, and $F = \$90,000$.

a.  Compute the operating breakeven in units.
b.  Compute EBIT and the coefficient of operating leverage for $T = 10,000$, $T = 15,000$, $T = 20,000$, and $T = 25,000$.

**5-3.** Assume that $(OL|T = 4,000) = 4.6$. If output subsequently changes by 8%, what is the resulting percentage change in EBIT?

**5-4.** A corporation forecasts $T = 10,000$ units and $Y = \$80,000$. Assume $(OL|T = 10,000) = 3.5$. If actual output turns out to be 11,000 units, compute the percentage forecasting error in EBIT and compute the actual EBIT.

**5-5.** A corporation forecasts $T = 10,000$ units and $Y = \$175,000$. Operating leverage is computed as 3.5 for $T = 10,000$. Management estimates that actual output could range from 5% below to 10% above its forecast value. Compute the range of possible percentage forecasting errors for EBIT and the corresponding EBIT values.

**5-6.** Assume that $(OL|T = 12,000) = 2.8$. If output subsequently changes by 12%, what is the resulting percentage change in EBIT?

**5-7.** A firm forecasts that it will produce and sell 22,000 units during the next marketing period and that EBIT will be $110,000. Operating leverage at 22,000 units is 2.9. Compute the percentage forecasting error in EBIT and the actual EBIT if the firm sells 27,000 units.

**5-8.** A corporation expects to produce and sell 66,000 units and to earn $262,000 before interest and taxes. Operating leverage at 66,000 units is computed as 2.2. Management estimates that actual sales can range from 8% below to 6% above forecast output. Compute the corresponding range of EBIT forecasting errors and the resulting EBIT values.

**5-9.** Fixed production costs for J. J. H. Inc. are currently $50,000 per year. Production engineers recommend the purchase of a new machine that will lower variable production costs per unit from $5 to $3 However, this new machine is expected to increase fixed production costs. If the unit selling price remains at its current value of $7, how much can the fixed production costs increase without changing the firm's current breakeven?

**5-10.** Kenney Payote Company is a manufacturer of motorcycle sprockets. For the coming production period, fixed costs are estimated to be $180,000; variable cost per unit is expected to be $4.75. Kenney Payote expects to sell 200,000 units at a unit price of $6.25. This level of production cannot be exceeded with its current plant.

The firm estimates that the machinery needed to increase production capacity by 20,000 units would increase fixed costs by $10,000 and decrease unit variable cost by 35 cents. However, the firm expects that 220,000 units can be sold only by reducing the unit price for all units to $6.00.

a. Compute operating breakeven assuming no expansion.

b. Assuming no expansion, compute EBIT and operating leverage when 200,000 units are produced and sold.

c. Compute the operating breakeven assuming expansion and the price decrease.

d. Compute EBIT and operating leverage assuming expansion, the price decrease, and sales of 220,000 units.

e. Suppose the firm expands, lowers its price, but sells only 200,000 units; compute EBIT and operating leverage at this level of output.

f. On the basis of these computations, evaluate the desirability of the expansion on the basis of risk and return.

**5-11.** Compute EPS for each of the following data sets, assuming $t = .4$.

| | EBIT | I | E | N |
|---|---|---|---|---|
| a. | $400,000 | 0 | 0 | 500,000 |
| b. | $350,000 | $200,000 | $125,000 | 80,000 |
| c. | $900,000 | 0 | $300,000 | 100,000 |

**5-12.** Assume that $I = \$50,000$, $E = \$75,000$, $N = 10,000$ common shares, and $t = .4$.

a. Compute the financial breakeven.

b.  Compute EPS and the coefficient of financial leverage when EBIT is $50,000; $100,000; $200,000; and $300,000.

5-13.  Assume that $(FL|Y = 100,000) = 6.0$. If EBIT subsequently decreases by 9%, what is the resulting percentage change in EPS?

5-14.  A corporation forecasts its EBIT at $100,000 and its EPS at 40 cents. Financial leverage is $(FL|Y = 100,000) = 3.0$. Actual EBIT is expected to be no more than 10% below and no more than 5% above forecast EBIT. Compute the range of possible percentage forecasting errors for EPS and the corresponding EPS values.

5-15.  For each of the data sets below, assume that $t = .4$ and compute:

a.  EBIT
b.  EPS
c.  operating breakeven
d.  financial breakeven
e.  overall breakeven
f.  coefficient of operating leverage $(OL|T)$
g.  coefficient of financial leverage $(FL|Y)$
h.  coefficient of combined leverage $(CL|T)$, using Equation 5-13
i.  coefficient of combined leverage $(CL|T)$, using Equation 5-14

|   | Data Set 1 | Data Set 2 | Data Set 3 | Data Set 4 |
|---|---|---|---|---|
| $T$ | 5,000 | 2,000 | 60,000 | 200,000 |
| $P$ | $10 | $40 | $4 | $17 |
| $V$ | $5 | $27 | $1.50 | $12 |
| $F$ | 0 | $10,000 | $100,000 | $375,000 |
| $I$ | 0 | 0 | $30,000 | $200,000 |
| $E$ | 0 | 0 | $30,000 | $140,000 |
| $N$ | 1,000 | 10,000 | 10,000 | 50,000 |

5-16.  A corporation estimates EPS = $2.00 with a forecast output of 400,000 units. Combined leverage is $(CL|T = 400,000) = 1.9$. Actual output is expected to be 6% either way of its forecast value. Compute the associated range of percentage forecasting errors for EPS and the corresponding EPS values.

5-17.  A firm's cost, output, and revenue structure for the coming planning period is as follows:

price/unit = $12
variable cost/unit = $4
fixed costs = $72,000
preferred stock dividends = $650,000
common stock: 800,000 shares outstanding
corporate tax rate = 40%

a.  Compute overall breakeven.
b.  Output is forecast to be 170,000 units. Compute EPS and combined leverage at this level of output.

The firm decides to expand its plant. Fixed costs increase to $90,000. Two financing alternatives for this expansion are as follows:

(1) Sell 100,000 shares of common stock.
(2) Sell bonds that require $120,000 in interest payments during each planning period.

Assuming the financing is accomplished by selling common stock:

c. Compute overall breakeven.
d. Compute EPS and combined leverage if forecast output remains unchanged.

Assuming the financing is accomplished by selling bonds:

e. Compute overall breakeven.
f. Compute EPS and combined leverage if forecast output remains unchanged.
g. On the basis of your answers to the above questions, evaluate the desirability of the expansion alternatives versus the desirability of not expanding from the standpoint of risk and return, assuming that forecast output remains unchanged.
h. If output increases to $T = 200,000$ units as a result of expansion, which financing alternative is preferable? Justify your answer in terms of risk and return.

# SELECTED REFERENCES

Ghandi, J. "On the Measurement of Leverage." *Journal of Finance*, Vol. 21 (December, 1966).

Hampton, J. *Handbook for Financial Decision Makers*. Reston, Va.: Reston Publishing, Company, Inc., 1979.

Hunt, P. "A Proposal for Precise Definitions of 'Trading on the Equity' and 'Leverage.'" *Journal of Finance*, Vol. 16 (September, 1961).

Helfert, E. *Techniques of Financial Analysis*. 5th ed. Homewood, Ill.: Richard D. Irwin, Inc., 1982.

Levy, B. "On the Association between Operating Leverage and Risk." *Journal of Financial and Quantitative Analysis*, Vol. 9 (September, 1974).

Levy, H. and M. Sarnat. *Capital Decisions and Financial Decisions*. 2d ed. Englewood Cliffs, N.J.: Prentice-Hall International, Inc., 1982.

Percival, J. "Operating Leverage and Risk." *Journal of Business Research*, Vol. 2 (April, 1974).

Shalit, S. "On the Mathematics of Financial Leverage." *Financial Management*, Vol. 4 (Spring, 1975).

# PART 3

# Working Capital Management

The three chapters in Part 3 concentrate on short-term financial management. Chapter 6 introduces the major components of working capital policy, discusses the concepts of conservative and aggressive working capital strategies, and explains the concept of an optimal working capital policy. The last section illustrates how the working capital policies of nonfinancial corporations have gradually become more aggressive.

The management of current assets is discussed in Chapter 7. Particular attention is paid to the management of cash and marketable securities. The management of credit, accounts receivable, and inventories is also contained in this chapter.

Chapter 8 discusses the management of current liabilities and explains how accounts receivable and inventories can be used as collateral in short-term financing. This chapter also explains how short-term liabilities, such as trade credit, commercial paper, and commercial bank lines of credit, frequently provide continuous financing. In addition, the importance of revolving credit agreements as corporate financing sources is explained in some detail.

# CHAPTER 6

# Working Capital Policy

*This chapter is an introduction to the financial management of working capital. The first section identifies the working capital accounts contained in a balance sheet, explains the relationship between working capital and sales, and summarizes the financial ratios used to analyze working capital problems. The second section explains the importance of working capital management and discusses the types of financial decisions involved in managing corporate working capital. The third section uses corporate data to illustrate actual working capital management policies.*

## THE NATURE OF WORKING CAPITAL

A corporation's *working capital* consists of its investment in current assets. **Net working capital** is the difference between a corporation's current assets and its current liabilities. **Working capital management** is the management of a corporation's sources and uses of working capital so as to advance the financial welfare of its stockholders.

**Sources and Uses of Working Capital**

A corporation's current assets consist of cash, marketable securities, accounts receivable, inventories, and other short-term assets. Much of a corporation's current assets are financed by its current liabilities — accounts payable, notes payable, short-term debt, and other short-term liabilities. It is not uncommon, however, for a corporation to finance a portion of its current assets with long-term debt or equity sources.

Some current assets, such as marketable securities, earn an explicit return in the form of interest payments. Other items, while they do not earn an explicit return, are essential to the firm's operation and thus contribute to its profitability. The working capital manager must continually balance the return on working capital against the cost of financing it.

**The
Cash-to-Cash
Cycle**

Producing an item of output requires the use of working capital—it ties up funds that could be used elsewhere—from the time materials are purchased for its production until payment is collected from its sale. This includes the time raw materials and the finished product are held in inventory, and the time after the sale before the payment is actually received. For a part of this time interval the use of working capital is financed by accounts payable and other accrued liabilities since payment is not made immediately for purchases and labor.

Firms operate more-or-less continuously with working capital committed to all stages of production. The generalized sequence from the initial outlay to the receipt of payment is called the *short-term operating cycle* or the **cash-to-cash cycle.** The length of this cycle comprises the average number of days in inventory plus the average collection period minus the average duration of accounts payable. Average days in inventory can be computed by dividing 360 by the inventory turnover ratio discussed in Chapter 3.

The length of the cash-to-cash cycle represents the time that cash is tied up in the corporation's operating process for each item of output. Shortening the cycle means that less cash is tied up for a given level of output—less net working capital is required and thus less financing costs are incurred. The cycle can be shortened by decreasing the average days in inventory or the average collection period, or by lengthening the accounts payable period. These options are discussed in the next two chapters.

The length of the cash-to-cash cycle is only one determinant of the amount of net working capital needed. Even if the length of the cycle and each of its components remains the same, the volume of production determines how much capital is committed to each stage of the cycle. This, in turn, depends on the volume of sales expected in the immediate future.

**Sales and
Working
Capital**

A corporation's actual and forecast sales have a major impact on the amount of working capital that the corporation uses and thus must finance. Actual and forecast sales cause what are called *spontaneous* increases in the firm's level of current assets and current liabilities. For example, purchases become inventories and payables. Sales generate cash and accounts receivable. Seasonal and/or unexpected demand may produce the need for additional short-term financing.

A corporation's ability to generate sales continuously results in a portion of its spontaneous current assets and current liabilities becoming permanent components of its balance sheet. This is illustrated in Figures 6-1 and 6-2. Figure 6-1 plots the major balance sheet asset categories over time. It assumes that sales are increasing and that a portion of total sales is seasonal. The permanent current assets shown in Figure 6-1 contain the spontaneous current assets needed to support the firm's expected level of sales. The fluctuating current assets are produced by that portion of total sales that is seasonal.

The capital structure that finances the assets shown in Figure 6-1 is illustrated in Figure 6-2. The permanent current liabilities in Figure 6-2

---

Figure 6-1.       **Asset Structure Composition over Time**

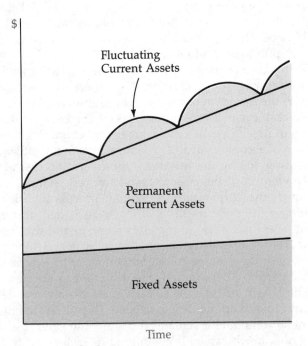

contain the spontaneous current liabilities needed to support the expected level of sales. The fluctuating current liabilities are the result of seasonal sales. The corporation's financial managers could choose to finance a portion of its permanent current liabilities with long-term debt or equity capital. The advantages and limitations of this financing strategy are discussed later in this chapter.

Figure 6-2.          **Capital Structure Composition over Time**

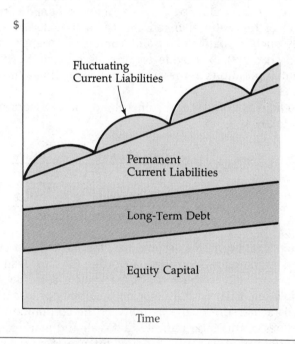

Working Capital Ratio Analysis

The analytical tools used in the management of working capital include some ratios discussed in Chapter 3 along with other ratios that deal specifically with working capital. The ratios drawn from Chapter 3 are the current ratio, current assets to total assets, and current liabilities to total assets.

The value of a corporation's current ratio is a direct function of its net working capital. In other words:

1. If current assets exceed current liabilities, net working capital is positive and the current ratio is greater than one.

2. If current assets equal current liabilities, net working capital is zero and the current ratio equals one.

3.  If current assets are less than current liabilities, net working capital is negative and the current ratio is less than one.

The current asset to total asset ratio is a useful way of summarizing the firm's investment in current assets relative to total assets. The value of this ratio depends in part on spontaneous changes in current assets in response to sales. However, the value of this ratio also depends on the amount of fixed assets needed to produce the goods and services sold by the firm.

The ratio of current liabilities to total assets measures the extent to which the firm uses short-term liabilities relative to total financing sources. The value of this ratio is affected by spontaneous liabilities and permanent sources of funds such as paid-in capital and retained earnings. However, the value of this ratio also reflects managerial decisions to use current liabilities such as bank loans and commercial paper (discussed in the next two chapters) to provide continuous financing. This ratio thus has important applications in measuring and evaluating a firm's working capital policies.

Two liquidity ratios used primarily to analyze working capital are defined as follows:

$$LR_1 = \frac{\text{Cash + Marketable securities}}{\text{Total current assets}}$$

$$LR_2 = \frac{\text{Cash + Marketable securities}}{\text{Total current liabilities}}$$

These two liquidity ratios assume that the most liquid current assets are cash and marketable securities. In order for this assumption to hold, current assets held in the form of marketable securities must be readily convertible into cash with little or no possibility of loss of principal.

$LR_1$ is a measure of the liquidity of the corporation's current assets. Large values of this ratio indicate that cash and marketable securities can provide substantial *sources* of funds to finance spontaneous current assets that occur with higher sales levels.

$LR_2$ measures the ability of a corporation to pay current liabilities without liquidating other assets or obtaining external sources of cash. The larger this ratio, the larger the amount of current liabilities that can be paid with cash or can be paid by converting marketable securities into cash.

## ALTERNATIVE STRATEGIES AND OPTIMAL POLICIES

The policies and procedures that constitute working capital management assume that the corporation has implemented some major decisions. These decisions include the choice of which product lines and/or services to produce and sell, as well as the choice of financing mix for the corporation's fixed assets. These decisions are a major determinant of a corporation's long-term profitability and have two important implications for working capital management. First, the products and/or services produced by the firm coupled with sales forecasts allow working capital managers to estimate the spontaneous levels of current assets and current liabilities. Second, working capital managers seek to advance the wealth of the corporation's common shareholders primarily by providing and maintaining corporate liquidity. Thus, working capital policies are not primarily designed to increase earnings per share; rather, they seek to provide the liquidity that will help the corporation attain its profitability goals.

**Importance of Working Capital Management**

The growing importance of working capital management has led to its establishment as a specialized area of financial management. In larger corporations it has produced executives who devote their time and efforts exclusively to the management of the firm's working capital. The following reasons account for this importance:

1. The actual and desired levels of current assets change constantly over time in response to changes in actual and forecast sales. This situation requires that decisions to bring current assets to their desired levels be made frequently, perhaps on a daily basis.

2. Previously made financing decisions may have to be revised in response to changing current asset levels. If, for example, substantial amounts of short-term debt are used to finance current assets, then securing additional loans when needed and replacing or renewing maturing debt will require additional management time and skills.

3. The extent to which a corporation's sources and uses of funds are committed to working capital must be determined. Current assets can represent as much as 75 percent of a corporation's total assets, and current liabilities can account for up to 60 percent of its capital structure. This means, for example, that a corporation with total assets of $500,000,000 can have as much as $375,000,000 in current assets and $300,000,000 in current liabilities.

4. Improper management of a corporation's working capital can result in lost sales and profits. It can even result in the corporation being unable to pay its liabilities as they come due.

**Working Capital Risk-Return Strategies**

Providing corporate liquidity through the management of current assets and current liabilities can be accomplished by using a number of different strategies. These strategies are identified by their risk-return characteristics and fall into two general classifications: conservative and aggressive. **Conservative strategies** provide liquidity in excess of expected needs.

They minimize the risks of not being able to finance spontaneous asset growth and of defaulting on maturing obligations. However, excess liquidity results in the corporation holding assets that earn little or no return. Hence, conservative strategies are called *low-risk, low-return* approaches to working capital management. **Aggressive strategies** seek to minimize excess liquidity while meeting short-term requirements. They accept the greater risk of illiquidity or even insolvency in order to earn a larger rate of return for the corporation. Thus, aggressive strategies are called *high-risk, high-return* approaches to working capital management. Separate strategies can be used for managing current assets and current liabilities. Optimal working capital policies are developed by combining separate strategies.

CURRENT ASSET STRATEGIES. Current asset strategies within working capital management involve setting and pursuing desired levels of individual current asset categories, as well as the level of total current assets, while holding corporate financing policies constant.

*Conservative Current Asset Strategy.* A conservative current asset strategy is one that seeks to maintain substantial amounts of liquid assets in the form of cash and marketable securities. It is low risk because excess liquid assets reduce the risk of lost sales by providing a financing source for unanticipated sales that generate spontaneous increases in inventory and accounts receivable. The inability to finance this needed increase in current assets could easily result in lost sales. Excess liquid assets also reduce the risk of illiquidity by providing a source of funds to pay maturing liabilities. The ordinary expectation is that customer payments on receivables provide a principal source of paying maturing current liabilities. In cases where such customer payments fall below expectations and/or where maturing obligations cannot be renewed or replaced, excess liquid assets can be used to help meet these debt payments.

A conservative strategy is low return because cash and marketable securities earn little or no return for the corporation. In addition, this strategy might set desired inventory levels substantially above expected sales levels in order to meet unanticipated demand. The funds needed to finance this extra inventory generate no profits for the corporation until the inventory is bought or until it is declared excess or unsalable and liquidated.

*Aggressive Current Asset Strategy.* An aggressive current asset strategy seeks to minimize the amount of funds invested in cash and marketable securities. A *very* aggressive strategy would also attempt to minimize the amount of funds invested in inventories. By minimizing the amount of cash and marketable securities in the corporation's current assets, the corporation increases the risk that it will be unable to pay its liabilities as they mature. It also increases the risk of lost sales because of its inability to finance unanticipated demand with liquid assets. By reducing its investment in inventories, the corporation also increases the risk of lost profits resulting from inventory stockouts. Offsetting these potential lost sales and profits, this strategy seeks to use cash and marketable securities as financing sources for the corporation's fixed assets. The implicit assumption in this strategy is that fixed assets earn a rate of return substantially larger than cash and marketable securities.

**CURRENT LIABILITY STRATEGIES.** Current liability strategies within working capital management set and pursue desired levels of financing sources while holding asset management policies constant. These strategies assume that interest rates on short-term loans are lower than those on long-term debt. However, experienced financial managers realize that occurrences in financial markets can cause this assumption to be violated. Under conditions of tight money, such as occurred in 1969–1970, 1973–1974, and in 1979–1981, short-term debt is more expensive than long-term debt. Furthermore, many corporations may find that short-term loans are not available at *any* price. Even in the absence of tight money, commercial and industrial short-term loans provided by commercial banks are frequently structured so as to make the effective cost of the funds to the corporation higher than the nominal interest rate on the loan. Chapter 8 contains a more extensive discussion of loans made by commercial banks to commercial and industrial borrowers. The current liability strategies discussed in the balance of this chapter implicitly assume that short-term debt is a cheaper financing source than long-term debt.

*Conservative Current Liability Strategy.* A conservative current liability strategy seeks to minimize the amount of short-term debt in the corporation's capital structure. This can be accomplished by floating long-term debt and using these funds to finance current assets. A *very* conservative strategy would seek to use equity capital in the place of nonspontaneous debt. If carried out, the desired capital structure for this very conservative strategy would consist almost entirely of accounts payable and equity capital. Maintaining a minimum amount of short-term loans in the capital structure reduces the probability or risk that the corporation will be unable to repay or replace its short-term debt as it matures. Using long-term debt and/or equity capital in place of short-term debt means choosing higher cost funds and thus reducing the rate of return earned by the corporation. (As explained in Chapter 14, the *cost* of equity funds to the corporation is greater than the cost of long-term debt.)

*Aggressive Current Liability Strategy.* An aggressive current liability strategy is designed to maximize the amount of short-term debt that is used to finance current assets. This strategy does not preclude the existence of long-term debt in the corporation's capital structure. The purpose of long-term debt in this strategy is to finance fixed assets, however.

By maximizing the amount of short-term debt in the corporate capital structure, the corporation increases the risk that it will be unable to service the debt as it matures. Tight money conditions can reduce the availability and increase the cost of short-term loans. Potential lenders might perceive the corporation to be a very risky borrower and thus deny loan applications or require high interest rates on loans. The high return from this strategy occurs as long as short-term loans cost the corporation less than long-term debt or equity capital. Given the choice of financing, the corporation will seek out the lowest cost source.

FINANCIAL RATIOS AND WORKING CAPITAL STRATEGIES. A successful conservative working capital strategy results in large values of $LR_1$, $LR_2$, the current ratio, and net working capital. An aggressive strategy would seek to reduce the values of these ratios and might even produce a negative value for net working capital. Two indicators of the type of strategy desired by individual corporations are (1) the time series trend of these ratios and of net working capital and (2) a comparison of the corporation's values for these ratios with those of its industry averages.

Table 6-1 contains some industry averages computed for 1982. A corporation pursuing a conservative current asset strategy would want its liquidity ratios and current ratio to exceed those of its industry averages contained in this table. An aggressive strategy would set desired ratio values lower than the relevant values in Table 6-1. For example, if an industrial chemicals manufacturer sets its desired values of $LR_1$ at 5 percent, $LR_2$ at 10 percent, and current ratio at 1.5, that firm would be pursuing an aggressive current asset strategy when compared with its industry averages. An automotive equipment wholesaler pursuing an aggressive current liability strategy would likely see its values of $LR_2$ and the current ratio fall below its industry averages.

| Table 6-1. | 1982 Industry Averages of Liquidity Ratios and Current Ratios | | |
|---|---|---|---|
| **Industry** | $LR_1$ | $LR_2$ | **Current Ratio** |
| Industrial chemicals (Manufacturing) | 8.93% | 13.57% | 1.52 |
| Automotive equipment (Wholesaling) | 7.04 | 12.50 | 1.74 |
| Department stores (Retailing) | 10.17 | 22.15 | 2.17 |
| Hotels, motels, and tourist courts (Services) | 43.36 | 27.67 | .64 |

*Source:* Computed from *Annual Statement Studies,* © Robert Morris Associates, 1983. Used with permission. RMA cautions that the Studies be regarded only as a general guideline and not as an absolute industry norm.

**Optimal Working Capital Policies**

The working capital policy adopted by a corporation can be stated in terms of the separate asset and liability strategies that have been discussed. A relatively conservative corporation could, for example, choose conservative strategies for both asset and liability management. Similarly, an aggressive corporation could choose to be aggressive in both areas. However, most companies adopt working capital policies that have *moderate* risk-return characteristics. A moderate working capital policy can be constructed to:

1. Structure the individual current account strategies so as to avoid assuming large degrees of risk in either strategy

2. Offset an aggressive strategy with a conservative one (For example, an aggressive current liability strategy combined with a conservative current asset strategy yields an overall policy that has moderate risk-return characteristics. Similar results occur when a conservative current liability strategy is combined with an aggressive current asset strategy.)

Figure 6-3 summarizes the concept of combining individual strategies into an overall working capital policy. Current asset strategies are plotted on the horizontal axis; current liability strategies, on the vertical axis. This

Figure 6-3.    **Risk-Return Characteristics of Working Capital Policies**

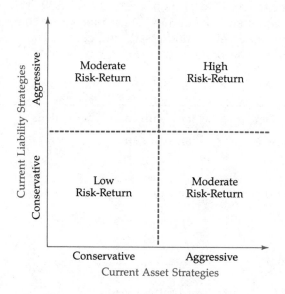

figure is constructed so as to indicate that conservative and aggressive strategies are the end points of a range of possibilities. Thus, a given strategy can be constructed so as to assume any desired risk-return characteristic within the range of possibilities.

Figure 6-3 also identifies the risk-return characteristics of the working capital policies that result from combining the individual working capital strategies. This figure is not intended to identify exactly at what point a given policy's risk-return characteristics go from low to moderate to high. Rather, this figure indicates that it is possible to combine individual strategies so as to produce the overall working capital policy desired.

**WORKING CAPITAL POLICIES AND SHAREHOLDER WEALTH.** What is the optimal working capital policy for a profit-seeking corporation? In general, this question can be answered very easily. The optimal working capital policy is the one that maximizes shareholder wealth. But translating this policy into desired liquidity ratios, current ratios, and net working capital is very difficult in practice. This is because of the many variables, including the operating environment of the corporation, that must be managed simultaneously. Thus, financial managers make subjective judgments in deciding which working capital policy to adopt and how best to structure the separate current asset and current liability strategies.

**WORKING CAPITAL POLICIES FOR NONFINANCIAL CORPORATIONS.** Some indications of the working capital policies followed by nonfinancial corporations can be obtained by analyzing Table 6-2 and Figure 6-4. Table 6-2 lists current ratios and liquidity ratios for nonfinancial corporations for selected years beginning with 1950. The time series of these ratios are plotted in Figure 6-4. These ratios were computed from data that listed current assets, liquid assets, and current liabilities summed over all nonfinancial corporations.

**Table 6-2.**   Working Capital Ratios for Nonfinancial Corporations

| Year | Current Ratio | $LR_1$ | $LR_2$ |
|------|---------------|--------|--------|
| 1950 | 2.14 | .30 | .64 |
| 1955 | 1.99 | .27 | .53 |
| 1960 | 1.92 | .20 | .39 |
| 1965 | 1.88 | .17 | .32 |
| 1970 | 1.61 | .12 | .19 |
| 1975 | 1.60 | .12 | .19 |
| 1980 | 1.50 | .11 | .16 |
| 1982 | 1.44 | .10 | .15 |

*Source: Federal Reserve Bulletin* (Various issues).

**Figure 6-4.**     **Working Capital Ratios for Nonfinancial Corporations**

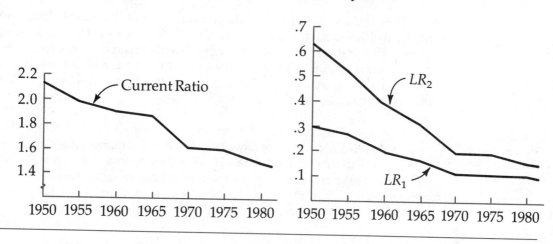

All three ratios contained in Table 6-2 declined steadily until 1970 but have fallen at a slower pace since that time. The data from which these ratios were computed show that both current assets and current liabilities of nonfinancial corporations increased throughout the time period. However, current liabilities increased at a faster rate than current assets even though they were smaller in dollar size than current assets. In addition, the amount of cash and marketable securities held by these corporations increased only at a modest rate. Therefore, the downward trends in the three ratios that are shown in Figure 6-4 were caused principally by the larger rate of increase in current liabilities relative to current assets and liquid assets. In addition, since the denominator of $LR_2$ is current liabilities, the much larger decrease in $LR_2$ relative to $LR_1$ is also explained by the increase in current liabilities relative to current assets.

To the extent that the time series behavior of the ratios in Figure 6-4 reflects the *desired* working capital policies of nonfinancial corporations, the conclusion drawn from these data is that working capital management became more aggressive over this time interval. There are at least two major reasons for this trend toward more aggressive working capital policies. First, credit became a major competitive weapon as total sales increased and larger percentages of sales were made by providing short-term financing to the purchasers. Second, the decrease in current ratios was made possible as managers began to use computerized and quantitative tools that enabled them to improve their sales and cash flow forecasts. These tools also provided managers with increasing amounts of timely information that improved their ability to make quick decisions.

## CURRENT WORKING CAPITAL PRACTICES

This section uses balance sheet data, income statement data, and financial ratios to illustrate recent working capital policies. Time series data of two corporations are used to show how asset and capital structure compositions change with increasing sales. An example of the risk-return characteristics of actual working capital policies is constructed by using financial ratios of several corporations.

**Sales and Balance Sheet Composition**

Raytheon Company and Carpenter Technology Corporation provide two contrasting examples of how balance sheet compositions change as sales levels increase over time. The Raytheon data are contained in Table 6-3. The trends in asset and capital structure composition for this company are shown in Figure 6-5. Similar data and trends for Carpenter Technology Corporation are contained in Table 6-4 and Figure 6-6.

**Table 6-3.**      **Raytheon Company Financial Data**

| Year | In Millions | | | | Current Assets to Total Assets | Current Liabilities to Total Assets | Current Ratio |
|------|-------------|---|---|---|--------------------------------|-------------------------------------|---------------|
|      | Total Sales | Total Assets | Current Assets | Current Liabilities | | | |
| 1975 | $2,245 | $1,031 | $ 752 | $ 476 | .73 | .46 | 1.58 |
| 1976 | 2,463 | 1,511 | 1,208 | 901 | .80 | .60 | 1.34 |
| 1977 | 2,818 | 1,813 | 1,417 | 1,108 | .78 | .61 | 1.28 |
| 1978 | 3,239 | 2,060 | 1,572 | 1,249 | .76 | .61 | 1.26 |
| 1979 | 4,354 | 2,297 | 1,632 | 1,335 | .71 | .58 | 1.22 |
| 1980 | 5,002 | 2,929 | 2,044 | 1,548 | .70 | .53 | 1.32 |
| 1981 | 5,636 | 3,364 | 2,339 | 1,752 | .70 | .52 | 1.34 |

*Note:* Dollar values are rounded.

*Sources:* Annual Reports of Raytheon Company.

Table 6-3 shows that Raytheon's sales more than doubled, and total assets increased by more than 300 percent from 1975 through 1981. Current assets and current liabilities both increased steadily through this period, but current liabilities as a percentage of total assets increased faster than the ratio of current assets to total assets. This increase in the use of short-term liabilities as a financing source explains the decrease in the company's current ratio from 1.58 to 1.34. These trends in balance sheet composition are illustrated in Figure 6-5. What stands out in this figure, as evidenced by

**Figure 6-5.**      **Raytheon Company Balance Sheet Composition**
**(In Millions of Dollars)**

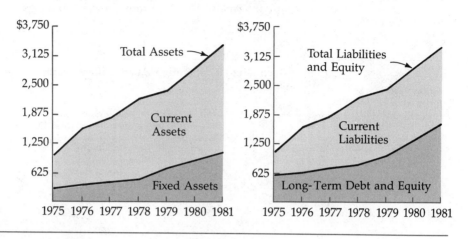

the growth in current liabilities in relation to the company's total capital structure, is the increasingly aggressive liability strategy pursued by the company.

Table 6-4 shows that Carpenter Technology Corporation's sales almost doubled between 1975 and 1981. Its ratio of current assets to total assets varied between 52 percent and 58 percent. The ratio of current liabilities to

**Table 6-4.**      **Carpenter Technology Corporation Financial Data**

| | In Millions | | | | Current Assets to Total Assets | Current Liabilities to Total Assets | Current Ratio |
|---|---|---|---|---|---|---|---|
| Year | Total Sales | Total Assets | Current Assets | Current Liabilities | | | |
| 1975 | $296 | $194 | $113 | $33 | .58 | .17 | 3.42 |
| 1976 | 266 | 210 | 123 | 42 | .59 | .20 | 2.92 |
| 1977 | 327 | 232 | 133 | 49 | .57 | .21 | 2.71 |
| 1978 | 384 | 264 | 144 | 53 | .55 | .20 | 2.72 |
| 1979 | 469 | 322 | 184 | 81 | .57 | .25 | 2.27 |
| 1980 | 559 | 353 | 204 | 83 | .58 | .24 | 2.46 |
| 1981 | 571 | 382 | 212 | 81 | .55 | .21 | 2.62 |

*Note:* Dollar values are rounded.

*Sources:* Annual Reports of Carpenter Technology Corporation.

total assets increased from 17 percent to 21 percent. The firm's large current ratio is the result of the low level of current liabilities in its capital structure. Although its current ratio has declined, its 1981 value of 2.62 shows that it is pursuing conservative liability management policies.

---

**Figure 6-6.**   **Carpenter Technology Corporation Balance Sheet Composition (In Millions of Dollars)**

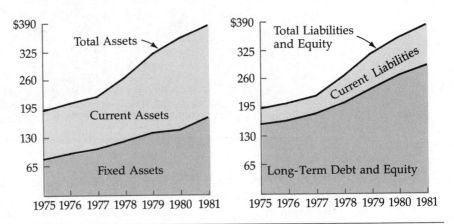

---

The balance sheet composition for Carpenter Technology is illustrated in Figure 6-6. The capital structure portion of Figure 6-6 illustrates the extent to which long-term debt and equity capital provide the bulk of the corporation's financing. It also shows the small amount of funds provided by current liabilities. This graph thus provides an example of a conservative current liability strategy.

The balance sheet compositions and underlying working capital policies of these two firms can be contrasted by examining Figures 6-5 and 6-6. Raytheon's current liability strategy appears to be much more aggressive than that of Carpenter's. However, Raytheon has committed proportionately more funds to current assets than Carpenter. Raytheon's overall working capital policy appears to be more aggressive than that of Carpenter. However, this conclusion must be tempered by two considerations. First, these companies do not compete in the same industries. Technological and managerial practices unique to each industry influence corporate balance sheet composition. Second, Raytheon is much bigger than Carpenter. Compare the sales and asset data in Tables 6-3 and 6-4. Because of its size, Raytheon may have access to short-term debt and other financing sources that are not available to smaller corporations like Carpenter.

Comparative
Working
Capital
Policies

It is possible to compare working capital policies among corporations by using financial ratios to construct a risk-return graph like that of Figure 6-3. The companies compared are listed in Table 6-5. The identification number given to each company in this table is used to plot their individual data values in Figure 6-7. For example, the point next to the 1 in Figure 6-7 represents the data values for Exxon Corporation.

**Table 6-5.**  Selected Corporate Financial Ratios for 1981

| Company | No. | In Millions | | | | $LR_1$ | $(1 - LR_1)$ | Current Liabilities to Total Assets |
| | | Liquid Assets | Current Assets | Total Assets | Current Liabilities | | | |
| --- | --- | --- | --- | --- | --- | --- | --- | --- |
| Exxon Corp. | 1 | $3,884. | $23,848. | $62,931. | $17,744. | .163 | .837 | .28 |
| ABC Inc. | 2 | 194. | 936. | 1,588. | 367. | .207 | .793 | .23 |
| Boise Cascade Inc. | 3 | 43. | 767. | 2,740. | 431. | .056 | .944 | .16 |
| Federal Express Corp. | 4 | 61. | 194. | 730. | 115. | .314 | .686 | .16 |
| Scientific Atlanta Inc. | 5 | 4. | 153. | 197. | 61. | .026 | .974 | .31 |
| ITT Inc. | 6 | 143. | 6,110. | 15,052. | 4,129. | .023 | .977 | .27 |
| Norton-Simon Inc. | 7 | 395. | 1,617. | 2,382. | 735. | .244 | .756 | .31 |

*Note:* Dollar amounts are rounded.

*Source: S&P 500 Stock Market Encyclopedia* (Spring, 1983).

Separate financial ratios measure the extent to which current asset and current liability strategies are conservative or aggressive. The ratio of current liabilities to total assets, plotted on the vertical axis of Figure 6-7, is used to measure current liability strategy. Larger values of this ratio indicate increasingly aggressive current liability strategies. $LR_1$ is used as a measure of current asset strategy. However, this ratio is not consistent with the horizontal axis of Figure 6-3 because small values of $LR_1$ indicate an aggressive rather than conservative strategy. This problem is remedied by computing $(1 - LR_1)$ for each company and plotting the resulting values on the horizontal axis of Figure 6-7. Thus, $(1 - LR_1)$ is used to measure the risk-return characteristics of current asset strategies. Increasing values of $(1 - LR_1)$ indicate a more aggressive current asset strategy because $(1 - LR_1)$ represents the percentage of current assets that are *not* committed to cash and marketable securities.

Figure 6-7 indicates that Boise Cascade, Scientific Atlanta, and ITT (Points 3, 5 and 6) follow similar working capital policies. These three corporations exhibit aggressive current asset and conservative current liability strategies. The most conservative current liability strategies are those of Boise Cascade and Federal Express (Points 3 and 4). Norton-Simon (Point 7) follows a current asset strategy similar to that of Federal Express (Point 4); however, Norton-Simon's current liability strategy is the most aggressive of the seven companies in this list.

Figure 6-7. **Working Capital Ratios for 1981**

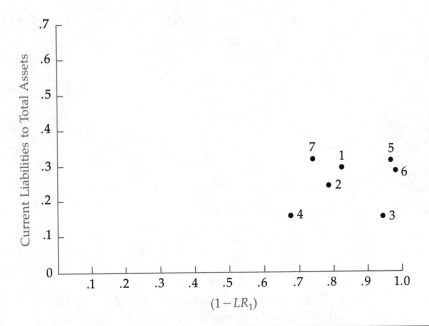

Comparing Figures 6-3 and 6-7 indicates that none of the seven companies used in this example pursued working capital policies that are clearly high risk-return or low risk-return. The working capital policies of these seven corporations can best be described as containing moderate risk-return characteristics. What values of these ratios would indicate a high risk-return, working capital policy? No precise answer to this question can be given. However, if a corporation pursues strategies to produce values in excess of .6 for both ratios, the working capital policies of that corporation would be labeled as moderate to aggressive by almost any type of analysis.

# SUMMARY

The management of a corporation's sources and uses of short-term funds is called working capital management. This area of managerial finance contributes to the overall goal of shareholder wealth maximization by meeting the liquidity needs of the corporation.

Spontaneous current assets and current liabilities are generated by actual and forecast sales. These spontaneous sources and uses of funds are a major component of a corporation's current assets and current liabilities. In addition, financial managers set the desired levels of investment in each current asset category and identify the types and amounts of financing needed to support current assets.

Working capital policies assume that the corporation has previously decided on its product lines and/or services and has obtained the capital needed to finance its fixed assets. Within this context, working capital management as a specialized area of managerial finance is important due to the repetitive decision making required to manage constantly changing current asset and current liability levels. These levels must be monitored in order to (1) bring actual working capital levels to their desired levels, (2) avoid lost sales, and (3) remain solvent.

Managing short-term assets and liabilities is accomplished by executing strategies with risk-return characteristics that identify them as being either conservative or aggressive. The desired risk-return characteristics contained in a corporation's overall working capital policy are obtained by combining separate strategies.

An optimal working capital policy is the one that maximizes shareholder wealth. The exact set of strategies that produce this optimal working capital policy is very difficult to estimate in practice. This is due to the large number of variables, not all of which are under managerial control, that must be managed simultaneously. Since 1950, working capital policies of nonfinancial corporations have become more aggressive, particularly in the area of short-term liability management.

# QUESTIONS

**6-1.** What types of current assets comprise a corporation's working capital?

**6-2.** What are the major financing sources of a corporation's working capital?

**6-3.** Explain the relationship between sales and spontaneous current assets and current liabilities.

**6-4.** What is the relationship between a corporation's net working capital and its current ratio?

**6-5.** How does working capital management contribute to shareholder wealth maximization?

**6-6.** Why is working capital management an important specialized area of managerial finance?

**6-7.** Describe conservative and aggressive strategies in terms of managing current assets.

**6-8.** Explain why conservative current asset strategies have low-risk, low-return characteristics.

**6-9.** Explain why aggressive current asset strategies have high-risk, high-return characteristics.

**6-10.** Describe conservative and aggressive strategies in terms of managing current liabilities.

**6-11.** Explain why conservative current liability strategies have low-risk, low-return characteristics.

**6-12.** Explain why aggressive current liability strategies have high-risk, high-return characteristics.

# PROBLEMS

*Note:* Problems 6-1, 6-2, and 6-3 use the financial data for FCI, Incorporated that are contained in Table 6-6.

**6-1.** For each of the six years of FCI's financial data, compute the following: net working capital, current ratio, $LR_1$, current liabilities to total assets, and current assets to total assets.

**6-2.** Using the values computed in Problem 6-1 and the data in Table 6-6, analyze the time series behavior of FCI's balance sheet composition.

**6-3.** Construct a risk-return graph for FCI similar to that shown in Figure 6-7. The graph is constructed by using the ratios computed from each year's data. Thus, the graph will contain six points. On the basis of your risk-return graph, is FCI's working capital policy aggressive or conservative? Explain. Does the firm's working capital policy show any trend toward becoming more aggressive or more conservative?

**Table 6-6.**          Selected Financial Data of FCI, Incorporated

| | | | In Millions | | |
|---|---|---|---|---|---|
| Year | Total Assets | Total Sales | Current Assets | Liquid Assets | Current Liabilities |
| 1975 | $150 | $230 | $ 97 | $30 | $40 |
| 1976 | 187 | 270 | 123 | 41 | 55 |
| 1977 | 219 | 338 | 150 | 52 | 70 |
| 1978 | 216 | 328 | 142 | 45 | 55 |
| 1979 | 246 | 376 | 170 | 55 | 74 |
| 1980 | 255 | 420 | 174 | 60 | 67 |

*Note:* Problems 6-4 and 6-5 use the financial data for Statewide Company, Inc. that are contained in Table 6-7.

**6-4.** Using the data in Table 6-7 and the ratios you consider relevant, analyze the time series behavior of Statewide Company, Inc.'s balance sheet composition.

**6-5.** Construct a risk-return graph for Statewide Company, Inc. Is its working capital policy aggressive or conservative? Explain. Does its working capital policy contain any trends?

Table 6-7.          Selected Financial Data of Statewide Company, Inc.

| | | In Thousands | | | |
|---|---|---|---|---|---|
| Year | Total Assets | Total Sales | Current Assets | Liquid Assets | Current Liabilities |
| 1975 | $1,400 | $1,300 | $510 | $163 | $395 |
| 1976 | 1,675 | 1,550 | 550 | 154 | 410 |
| 1977 | 1,975 | 1,981 | 595 | 149 | 415 |
| 1978 | 2,100 | 1,825 | 575 | 127 | 405 |
| 1979 | 2,400 | 1,950 | 580 | 121 | 425 |
| 1980 | 2,600 | 2,275 | 600 | 120 | 470 |

6-6.  Table 6-8 contains financial data for eight different corporations. Construct a risk-return graph that identifies the working capital policy risk-return characteristics for this data set. Which corporations have conservative working capital policies? moderate policies? aggressive policies?

Table 6-8.          Selected Financial Data for Eight Corporations

| | | In Thousands | | |
|---|---|---|---|---|
| Company Number | Total Assets | Current Assets | Liquid Assets | Current Liabilities |
| 1 | $   234 | $   128 | $   47 | $   103 |
| 2 | 306 | 140 | 85 | 49 |
| 3 | 857 | 279 | 76 | 301 |
| 4 | 6,044 | 3,152 | 895 | 3,720 |
| 5 | 1,368 | 470 | 110 | 575 |
| 6 | 14,729 | 7,935 | 809 | 8,200 |
| 7 | 28,380 | 16,400 | 3,274 | 9,015 |
| 8 | 912 | 467 | 75 | 213 |

*Note:* Problems 6-7 and 6-8 use the financial data for Lager Beer Company, Incorporated that are contained in Table 6-9.

6-7.  Using the data in Table 6-9 and the ratios you consider relevant, analyze the time series behavior of Lager Beer Company, Inc.'s balance sheet composition.

6-8.  Construct a risk-return graph for Lager Beer Company, Inc. Is its working capital policy aggressive or conservative? Explain. Does its working capital policy contain any trends?

Table 6-9.        Selected Financial Data of Lager Beer Company, Inc.

| | In Millions | | | | |
| Year | Total Assets | Total Sales | Current Assets | Liquid Assets | Current Liabilities |
| --- | --- | --- | --- | --- | --- |
| 1980 | $ 614 | $ 572 | $202 | $ 26 | $128 |
| 1981 | 694 | 653 | 242 | 61 | 118 |
| 1982 | 761 | 652 | 273 | 79 | 109 |
| 1983 | 827 | 688 | 298 | 98 | 119 |
| 1984 | 912 | 815 | 350 | 111 | 129 |
| 1985 | 983 | 977 | 363 | 88 | 128 |
| 1986 | 1,052 | 1,023 | 325 | 85 | 130 |

*Note:* Problems 6-9 and 6-10 use the financial data for R.I. Mane Company that are contained in Table 6-10.

6-9.   Using the data in Table 6-10 and the ratios you consider relevant, analyze the time series behavior of R.I. Mane Company's balance sheet composition.

6-10.  Construct a risk-return graph for R.I. Mane Company. Is its working capital policy aggressive or conservative? Explain. Does its working capital policy contain any trends?

Table 6-10.       Selected Financial Data of R.I. Mane Company, Inc.

| | In Millions | | | | |
| Year | Total Assets | Total Sales | Current Assets | Liquid Assets | Current Liabilities |
| --- | --- | --- | --- | --- | --- |
| 1980 | $ 444 | $ 661 | $329 | $137 | $132 |
| 1981 | 580 | 901 | 413 | 125 | 198 |
| 1982 | 676 | 1,100 | 459 | 109 | 239 |
| 1983 | 659 | 958 | 464 | 187 | 211 |
| 1984 | 790 | 1,161 | 548 | 206 | 293 |
| 1985 | 879 | 1,432 | 571 | 180 | 327 |
| 1986 | 1,063 | 1,785 | 641 | 81 | 446 |
| 1987 | 1,336 | 2,257 | 758 | 82 | 617 |
| 1988 | 1,690 | 2,853 | 909 | 98 | 680 |
| 1989 | 1,618 | 2,944 | 838 | 105 | 536 |

6-11.  Table 6-11 contains financial data for eight different corporations. Construct a risk-return graph that identifies the working capital policy risk-return characteristics for this data set. Which corporations have conservative working capital policies? moderate policies? aggressive policies?

Table 6-11.          Selected Financial Data for Eight Corporations

| Company Number | Total Assets | In Thousands Current Assets | Liquid Assets | Current Liabilities |
|---|---|---|---|---|
| 1 | $2,429 | $1,400 | $ 37 | $ 871 |
| 2 | 2,209 | 1,588 | 238 | 653 |
| 3 | 232 | 137 | 40 | 57 |
| 4 | 906 | 433 | 177 | 298 |
| 5 | 3,861 | 2,254 | 163 | 1,215 |
| 6 | 2,958 | 498 | 50 | 367 |
| 7 | 5,344 | 2,011 | 181 | 1,373 |
| 8 | 1,723 | 845 | 105 | 477 |

# SELECTED REFERENCES

Cascino, A. "How To Make More Productive Use of Working Capital." *Management Review,* Vol. 68, No. 5 (May, 1979).

Doggett, R. "Managing Working Capital." *Management Accounting,* Vol. 42, No. 6 (December, 1980).

Higgins R. *Financial Management: Theory and Application.* Chicago, Ill.: Science Research Associates, Inc., 1977.

Johnson J., D. Campbell, and J. Wittenbach. "Identifying and Resolving Problems in Corporate Liquidity." *Financial Executive,* Vol. 50, No. 5 (May, 1982).

Smith, K., and S. Sell. "Working Capital Management In Practice." In *Readings on the Management of Working Capital.* ed. Keith Smith. St. Paul, Minn.: West Publishing Co., 1980.

Smith, K. *Guide to Working Capital Management.* N.Y.: McGraw-Hill Book Company, 1979.

Smith, K. "State of the Art of Working Capital Management." *Financial Management,* Vol. 2, No. 3 (Autumn, 1973).

Van Horne, J. *Financial Management and Policy.* 6th ed. Englewood Cliffs, N.J.: Prentice-Hall, Inc., 1983.

Yardini, E. "A Portfolio-Balance Model of Corporate Working Capital." *Journal of Finance,* Vol. 33, No. 2 (May, 1978).

# CHAPTER 7

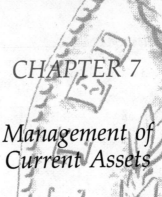

## Management of Current Assets

*In this chapter the management of current assets—cash, marketable securities, accounts receivable, and inventory—is discussed within the context of working capital policy. Financial managers are directly responsible for managing cash and marketable securities. The responsibility, however, for managing accounts receivable and inventory may be given to any of several functional areas of management. For example, the management of accounts receivable, also called* **credit management,** *may be a part of either the corporation's financial division or marketing division. Inventory management may fall within the realm of production or marketing managers. While financial managers do provide help in determining credit and inventory policies, the major contribution they make in these areas is to provide the financing needed to support the investment in accounts receivable and inventories.*

## CASH MANAGEMENT

Cash management strategies are built around two goals. These aim (1) to provide the cash needed to meet the firm's payments and (2) to minimize the amount of idle cash held by the firm. The second goal reflects the idea that unused assets earn no rate of return for the firm. Unfortunately these two goals can easily conflict with each other. Reducing the level of cash in order to eliminate idle balances can produce shortages in the amounts of cash available to make required payments. Cash management strategies, therefore, are needed to reconcile these two goals wherever possible. Meeting corporate payments, however, takes higher priority than minimizing idle cash balances.

**Cash Balance Requirements**

There are three major requirements that must be satisfied if the goal of meeting the corporation's cash needs is to be attained. These are transactions requirements, precautionary requirements, and compensating balance requirements. **Transactions requirements** are the amounts of cash needed to meet the forecast outflows contained in the firm's cash budget. **Precautionary requirements** are the amounts of cash needed to meet unanticipated cash payments. Cash balances held for precautionary requirements reflect the uncertainty of future cash flows. It is a common practice, however, to keep at least some of the firm's precautionary balances invested in marketable securities of the type discussed later in this chapter. **Compensating balance requirements** are the amounts of cash needed to meet certain lending terms of commercial bank loans. For example, a corporation applies to a commercial bank for a $100,000 loan. As a condition for receiving the loan, the borrowing firm agrees to keep an amount equal to 10 percent of the loan ($10,000) on deposit in a checking account of the lending bank until the entire loan is repaid. The $10,000 is called a compensating balance. Normal transaction and precautionary balances may be adequate to meet most or all of the required compensating balance.

**Desired Minimum Cash Balance**

The transactions, precautionary, and compensating balance cash requirements are managed simultaneously within the corporation's cash accounts because the levels of cash needed to meet each requirement are constantly changing. The interactions among these three requirements result in the need to identify the minimum cash balance that is desired at any given point in time. The **desired minimum cash balance** is the minimum amount of cash, after meeting transactions requirements, needed to satisfy precautionary and compensating balance requirements.

When cash budgets are prepared on a monthly basis, the desired minimum cash balance is estimated on an end-of-month basis. If the end-of-month cash is forecast to exceed the desired minimum cash balance, the difference between these two amounts is considered idle cash. If the desired minimum cash balance exceeds the forecast end-of-month cash, the corporation is faced with financing the difference and/or modifying its cash budget. The cash-budgeting format developed in Chapter 4 can be expanded to allow for these types of cash balance requirements. In addition, that format must allow for the special requirements imposed by commercial banks when they provide short-term financing. The cash-budgeting formats that allow for other types of cash balance requirements and for commercial bank financing requirements are contained in Chapter 8.

**Managing Cash Flows**

The preparation of cash budgets that accurately forecast cash flows is a major activity of current asset management. In addition, corporations have developed techniques that speed up the collection of cash inflows and slow the disbursements of cash outflows.

SPEEDING UP CASH INFLOWS. When a corporation sends an invoice to a customer, several days may elapse from the time the customer mails the payment to the time it becomes available for use by the corporation. To reduce this delay, commercial banks provide what is called *lock box* banking services which are especially valuable when long distances separate the corporation from its customers. The customer is asked to send the invoice payment to a post office box located in the customer's city. A local commercial bank empties the post office box several times each day, deposits the payments in a checking account maintained by the corporation, and notifies the corporation daily of the amount of funds deposited in its account. Thus, the corporation can arrange to write checks against those funds or transfer the funds by wire to its lead bank. Some banks charge a fee for providing lock box services. The more common arrangement, however, is for a corporation to maintain agreed upon compensating balances on deposit with banks that provide lock box services.

A lock box service does not, of itself, increase the total cash received by a corporation over the long range. However, the earlier receipt of cash does help to reduce the corporation's maximum loan size financing requirements and associated interest costs. It also allows the corporation to earn added profits from transactions in marketable securities. Still, the benefits of this service must be weighed against the cost of fees and/or compensating balances required for using it. In general, a relatively large volume of checks representing sizable dollar amounts is needed in order to justify the use of a lock box.

**SLOWING DOWN CASH OUTFLOWS.** Cash disbursements can be slowed by taking the maximum advantage of credit terms offered by vendors. For example, if a vendor offers credit terms of 3/15 net 60, the buyer is offered the choice of a 3 percent discount for paying the invoice within 15 days or of paying the full invoice price in 60 days. A cash discount of 2 or 3 percent for paying an invoice within 10 or 15 days of receipt represents a sizable savings over repeated purchases and should be taken whenever possible. Taking advantage of a cash discount, however, accelerates rather than slows the rate of cash outflows.

## MANAGEMENT OF MARKETABLE SECURITIES

Many types of securities are traded in this country's securities markets. Although any security that is bought and sold in the primary or secondary security markets can be called a marketable security, only those marketable securities known as *money market securities* are considered appropriate investment vehicles in the current asset management of nonfinancial corporations. Exactly what constitutes a money market security has never been defined. However, marketable securities that contain certain characteristics are labeled as money market securities. This section identifies the characteristics of money market securities and discusses the extent to which such instruments as Treasury bills, negotiable certificates of deposit, commercial paper, and money market mutual funds are suitable as short-term, or temporary, investment alternatives.

**General Characteristics of Money Market Securities**

Six general characteristics that can be used to identify money market securities and to evaluate their desirability as uses of temporarily idle corporate cash balances are discussed below.

**MINIMUM PURCHASE SIZE.** Federal regulations impose minimum purchase sizes on some money market securities. However, the minimums vary from one type of security to the next. The minimum purchase size of most money market securities is $10,000. Some require a minimum purchase size of $100,000.

**ORIGINAL MATURITY.** Some types of money market securities have a minimum original maturity that is set by federal law. If an investor needs a shorter maturity, the security must be sold before it matures, or the investor must buy a previously issued security the remaining lifetime of which equals the desired maturity. In the absence of regulations, maturities can be negotiated between investor and issuer.

**RATE OF RETURN.** The rate of return of most money market securities that corporations use as investment outlets for idle funds can be estimated within a very small range of error. This presumes only that the issuer will not default on payment at maturity.

Some money market securities are noninterest-bearing, are redeemed at face value (referred to as par value) at maturity, and are sold at a discount from par value. The rate of return earned by a purchaser is generated by the difference between the security's purchase price and par value. Other types of securities are interest-bearing, are sold initially at par value, and return par value plus interest at maturity. As explained below, money market mutual funds pay dividends rather than interest; as a consequence, the rate of return is not stated and must be forecast by the investor.

**DEFAULT RISK.** The probability that the issuer of a security will not pay it off at maturity is called **default risk.** Securities bought as temporary investments must have a minimum default risk because safety of principal is more important than rate of return. Money market securities with a minimum default risk earn rates of return lower than other securities where default risks are perceived as being larger.

**INTEREST RATE RISK.** The probability that an investor will incur a loss on the sale of a marketable security that is sold before its maturity due to an increase in the level of interest rates is called **interest rate risk.** This type of loss is incurred only when a security is sold before maturity.

Assume, for example, that a marketable security purchased to yield 8 percent must be sold at a time when rates of return for this type of security have risen to 10 percent. The resale price will have fallen in response to increasing interest rates, and the seller will be faced with the choice of accepting the lower price or holding the security until maturity. As a general rule, interest rate risk is greater among securities with longer maturities. A marketable security that matures six years from now has a larger interest rate risk than a comparable security that matures in 90 days. This type of risk is minimized by buying securities that have short maturities.

**MARKET RISK.** The probability that an active resale market will not exist for a given security when an investor desires to sell it is called **market risk.** An active market is one that allows a security to be bought and sold quickly, without causing volatile fluctuations in its price. This risk is minimized by dealing in those marketable securities that have large amounts outstanding, that are widely held, and that historically have been traded in well-developed markets.

**Treasury Bills**

Treasury bills, commonly referred to as T-bills, are direct obligations of the United States government. The minimum purchase size of a T-bill is $10,000. New issues of T-bills are sold by the U.S. Treasury and are available in three original maturities: 91 days, 182 days, and 52 weeks. Other maturities can be obtained by purchasing previously issued T-bills in the resale markets.

T-bills are sold at a discount from par value. They yield the smallest rates of return among short-term marketable securities because they have no default risk. The short-term maturities of T-bills serve to minimize interest rate risks. Active resale markets trade large amounts of T-bills daily and eliminate essentially all market risks.

Because T-bills contain no default risk and very little interest rate and market risks, they are often called risk-free securities. Securities that are perceived as being riskier than T-bills will have to yield returns larger than those of T-bills in order to compensate the investors for assuming greater amounts of risk.

**Negotiable Certificates of Deposit**

A negotiable certificate of deposit (NCD) is a receipt issued by a bank certifying that a specific sum of money has been deposited with it. NCDs are issued at par and are interest-bearing securities. At maturity the bank pays the owner of the NCD par plus accumulated interest. By law, the minimum size of NCDs is set at $100,000 and they must have an original maturity of at least 30 days. However, there are no other legal limitations on lengths of original maturity. Maturities of less than 30 days can be obtained by purchasing NCDs in the resale markets.

NCDs issued by commercial banks insured by the Federal Deposit Insurance Corporation (FDIC) are insured as to payment up to $100,000. NCDs with larger denominations thus have a slight default risk. In addition, NCDs with longer maturities are subject to interest rate risks. Active resale markets for these securities minimize market risks, however. Because NCDs contain some default and interest rate risks, their rates of return are higher than those of T-bills.

**Commercial Paper**

Commercial paper consists of unsecured short-term promissory notes issued by corporations. It is noninterest-bearing, is sold at a discount from par, and matures at par value. There are no legal restraints on minimum purchase size or minimum maturity. However, federal regulations effectively set maximum original maturities at 270 days.

Commercial paper that is purchased directly from an issuing corporation usually has a minimum size of $500,000. "Paper" that is purchased through a commercial paper dealer has a minimum purchase size of $50,000 or $100,000. Most paper matures in 60 days or less, but original maturities can be negotiated. For example, maturities as short as three days can be arranged.

There have been a few cases where a corporation has defaulted on the payment of its maturing paper. The most famous default occurred in 1970 when the Penn Central Transportation Company filed for bankruptcy while it had $82 million of commercial paper outstanding.

Resale markets for commercial paper exist only on a very limited basis. The default risk combined with the lack of general resale markets allows only the largest and financially strongest corporations to use commercial paper as a financing source. Less than 2,000 domestic corporations issue commercial paper.

Because of the default risk and the lack of resale markets, the rates of return on commercial paper are larger than those of T-bills but tend to be slightly lower than those of NCDs. There are many reasons why paper yields are lower than NCD yields. One important reason is that only those corporations that are perceived to be the most financially stable issue paper, while any commercial bank in the United States can issue NCDs.

**Money Market Mutual Funds**

Money market mutual funds, generally called *money market funds*, are a special type of investment company investing only in debt securities that generally have one year or less to maturity and have very low default risks. The average maturity of the portfolios owned by money market funds is usually less than 50 days. Money market fund assets tend to be concentrated in T-bills, NCDs, and commercial paper.

Investing in a money market fund is accomplished by purchasing its common shares. The minimum initial investment in most funds is $1,000 with subsequent investment minimums of $50. Because investors purchase the fund's common stock, they receive income in the form of dividends rather than interest. Dividends are computed daily and paid monthly. Investors have the choice of receiving the income or reinvesting it in the fund. Reinvested dividends purchase additional shares.

Investors are allowed to redeem their shares for cash on a daily basis. This amounts to the money market fund buying the shares from the investor. The fund simply redeems a number of shares equal to the dollar amount being withdrawn by the investor. If for example $975.43 is withdrawn, 975.43 shares are redeemed. Redemption is typically accomplished by writing a check against some or all of the amount invested in the fund. Most funds require checks to be $500 or larger, although at least one fund allows checks as small as $200. Redemption thus provides what amounts to daily maturity for investors.

Because of the very safe investments that make up money market fund portfolios, and because of the very short maturities of these portfolio assets, money market funds have minimum amounts of interest rate and default risk. There is no market risk as long as the fund redeems the shares on a demand basis, and the redemption option gives the shares daily maturity.

The rate of return obtained from investing in money market funds is not stated at the time the fund's shares are purchased and no minimum returns are promised by the fund. The fund's earnings are distributed each month to the investors as dividends, but these dividends could be zero for any given month. The actual rates of return compare very favorably to those of the other money market securities discussed in this chapter. Figure 7-1 shows the rates of return for these four types of money market securities from 1978 through 1982.

Figure 7-1.    **Money Market Rates (Annual Averages)**

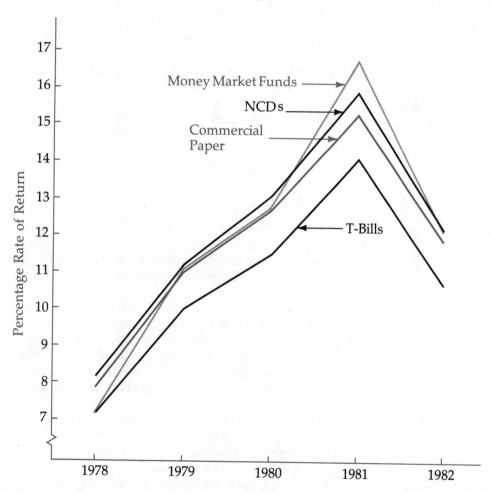

SOURCES: The Donoghue Organization (used with permission); *Federal Reserve Bulletin.*

**Money Market Strategies**

The risk-return characteristics of T-bills make them desirable money market instruments when a corporation is pursuing a conservative current asset strategy. Even though T-bills yield the lowest rates of return among the four types of money market securities under consideration, the small minimum purchase size allows the corporation to invest idle funds while still retaining precautionary cash balances. In addition, T-bills have no default risk and can be sold quickly in resale markets.

An aggressive working capital policy will seek to invest idle funds in the highest yielding money market securities, which means T-bills will be all but excluded. However, as shown in Figure 7-1, no one type of money market security always produces the highest rate of return, and an aggressive working capital policy may involve buying and selling as rates of return change relative to each other. An aggressive strategy must also realize that NCDs and commercial paper have default risks that are higher than T-bills and only limited resale markets exist for commercial paper. As long as market and default risks of money market funds remain as minimal as they currently are, they will offer aggressive strategies a desirable alternative to NCDs and commercial paper whenever the rates of return among these three money market securities are comparable.

## MANAGEMENT OF CREDIT AND ACCOUNTS RECEIVABLE

Accounts receivable are generated when a corporation sells its products and services on credit. Receivables are a component of a corporation's working capital and represent investments a firm makes in seeking to increase shareholder wealth.

The two major types of accounts receivable are retail credit and commercial credit. **Retail credit** is credit sales made by retailers to consumers. **Commercial credit** is credit sales made between corporations. The first part of this section deals with credit management policies and strategies. This is followed by separate discussions of retail and commercial credit. The financing of accounts receivable is discussed in Chapter 8.

**Credit and Credit Management**

Since World War II, the selling of goods and services on credit has become an essential characteristic of our economy. This is most noticeable in retailing, where credit cards are now more readily acceptable than checks as a means of payment. While some lines of business still settle transactions with cash or checks, most corporations realize they must extend or provide credit for their customers through third parties if they wish to remain in business. Corporate working capital management must therefore contain policies and strategies specifically formulated for credit management.

**ELEMENTS OF A CREDIT MANAGEMENT POLICY.** The goal of credit management is to establish policies and strategies that are consistent with the overall risk-return characteristics of the corporation. Returns are generated as customers abide by credit terms in paying for their credit purchases. The risk is the probability that any given account receivable will not be paid or that the corporation will have to incur extra expenses in collecting overdue balances. The only way a corporation can eliminate the risk of slow or uncollectible accounts is by refusing to make credit sales. This in turn may hurt profitability.

*Criteria for Extending Credit.* Two types of decisions are involved in extending credit. One type occurs when a customer seeks credit for the first time. The new customer may be required to submit financial and related data along with credit references. The services of a credit agency or credit bureau may be used to obtain additional information about the customer's financial condition and recent credit history.

The second type of decision occurs when an established credit customer submits a purchase order. Repeat orders from an established credit customer may be filled routinely unless the dollar value of the order increases significantly, the customer requests extended credit terms, or the customer becomes a slow-paying account.

Once a corporation decides to extend credit to a customer, the terms of credit must be decided upon. Credit terms include the length of time a customer has to pay for a credit purchase, the maximum amount of credit (line of credit) the customer is to be allowed, and whether or not interest is to be charged on unpaid balances. Credit terms tend to be uniform among competing firms.

Another aspect of the credit decision involves reviewing customer credit histories. The credit policies of the corporation may require that the desirability of each credit customer be evaluated once each year. As a result of the review, some customers may be granted extended credit terms while others may have their credit lines suspended. Customers themselves may also ask for their credit lines to be reviewed when they want to increase their credit purchases and/or need extended credit terms.

*Techniques to Protect Receivables.* Most accounts receivable represent sales made on open account. This means that the seller is an unsecured creditor of the customer. Should the customer default on the payment of an invoice, the seller would have to join other unsecured creditors in seeking payments of their invoices. However, their claims would be subordinated to those of secured creditors. The best way for a seller to protect its accounts receivable is to refuse credit to those potential customers that are seen as marginal credit risks. In some cases, particularly in the area of consumer durables, the merchandise that is sold on credit is used as collateral to secure the sale. The seller then becomes a secured creditor of the customer.

If the account receivable proves uncollectible and if the customer faces bankruptcy, the seller's claims will be senior to those of unsecured creditors.

*Collection Procedures.* The third major element in a corporate credit policy contains the procedures to be used in collecting slow-paying and delinquent accounts. The policy must spell out which steps the corporation is willing to take in collecting receivables and in what order these actions are to be taken. Since additional expenses are involved in these types of collection efforts, the credit policy must also attempt to identify the point at which collection efforts will not produce sufficient additional payments to be worthwhile. When this point is reached, the account receivable is written off as a bad debt expense and the customer's credit line is suspended or revoked.

When an account balance first becomes overdue, a common practice is to send the customer an overdue notice and to include a copy of the original invoice. The customer may also be notified that interest charges and/or extra service charges will be levied unless the payment is sent promptly, and that the customer's line of credit may be reduced or suspended if these balances remain overdue.

Some corporations use a series of short form letters that are sent sequentially. Each letter becomes more insistent and demanding; the final letter may threaten legal action and/or suspend credit facilities. Telephone calls requesting payment and an explanation as to why the account is overdue can be helpful to the seller in deciding how much additional effort should go into collecting a particular account. When the seller's efforts are unsuccessful, outside collecting agencies can be used. As a last resort, legal action can be taken against defaulted accounts.

**SUPPORTING CREDIT SALES.** One consequence of credit sales is that funds become invested in accounts receivable. The amount of funds needed for this purpose is a function of the credit sales extended by the seller. In addition, the desirability of changing credit terms — which usually means liberalizing the terms of credit — depends in part on any additional funds required to support the new credit policy. The following three steps estimate the funds needed to support credit sales:

1.  Compute the rate of receivables turnover.

2.  Compute the average accounts receivable.

3.  Multiply the average accounts receivable by the percentage that variable costs are of each sales dollar. The variable costs equal cost of goods sold plus other variable selling costs.

**Example:**   A corporation forecasts annual credit sales of $1,500,000. Its credit terms are net 60 days. Variable costs are 60 percent of each sales dollar. What is the average amount of funds needed to support its expected credit sales?

Step 1.   Find the accounts receivable turnover rate by dividing the credit terms in days into 360 days:

$$360 \div 60 = 6$$

Step 2.   Find the average accounts receivable by dividing annual credit sales by the accounts receivable turnover rate:

$$\$1,500,000 \div 6 = \$250,000$$

Step 3.   Multiply the average accounts receivable by the percentage that variable costs are of each sales dollar:

$$(\$250,000)\,(.6) = \$150,000$$

Thus, on the average, $150,000 committed to accounts receivable will support the expected credit sales of $1,500,000.

---

The above example shows that $150,000 can support ten times as much in credit sales ($1,500,000/$150,000). This large multiple is due in part to the credit terms which set the desired accounts receivable turnover rate. In general, increasing the receivables turnover rate increases the amount of credit sales that can be supported by a given amount of funds. Similarly, extended credit terms that result in a lower turnover rate of receivables require increased amounts of funds to support a given level of credit sales.

EVALUATING ALTERNATIVE CREDIT TERMS. Corporations design credit policies so as to identify those customers that are acceptable credit risks. However, circumstances can force corporations to evaluate the desirability of changing their credit terms. For example, competitors could introduce extended credit terms. A recession might force extended terms for all credit sales. Or a corporation might consider liberalizing credit terms as one way of increasing sales and profits. Whatever the reason, more liberal credit terms increase both bad debt losses and the amount of funds invested in accounts receivable. Increased sales have to be measured against both increased defaults on accounts receivable and the required rate of return the corporation sets on its added investment in accounts receivable. The desirability of alternative credit policies can be evaluated by using an incremental approach. The data in the following example are used to explain this procedure.

**Example:**   A corporation's annual credit sales are currently $1,200,000. Its credit terms are net 30 days. Only 2 percent of its accounts receivable becomes uncollectible. Variable costs are 65 percent of sales. It requires a 20 percent rate of return on its assets.

The corporation is considering the following three alternatives: (1) keeping credit terms at net 30 days, (2) changing credit terms to net 60 days, and (3) changing credit terms to net 90 days. It has estimated the credit sales level and bad debt percentage for each of these alternatives (see Table 7-1). Which alternative should the corporation select?

**Table 7-1.**   **Alternative Credit Terms**

|  | Net 30 Days | Net 60 Days | Net 90 Days |
|---|---|---|---|
| Receivable turnover rate per year | 12 times | 6 times | 4 times |
| Annual credit sales | $1,200,000 | $1,320,000 | $1,400,000 |
| Average accounts receivable | $100,000 | $220,000 | $350,000 |
| Investment in average accounts receivable | $65,000 | $143,000 | $227,500 |
| Bad debt percentage | 2% | 3% | 5% |
| Bad debt losses | $24,000 | $39,600 | $70,000 |
| Funds lost due to bad debts | $15,600 | $25,740 | $45,500 |

Step 1.   Compute the investment in average accounts receivable required for each alternative, using the procedure explained in the previous example. These values are shown in Table 7-1.

Step 2.   Compute the funds lost because of bad debts. For the first alternative, credit terms of 30 days produce 2 percent bad debts. Thus, for credit sales of $1,200,000, bad debt losses are:

$$(.02)\,(\$1,200,000) = \$24,000$$

Of this amount, 65 percent represents variable costs. Thus, the funds lost because of these bad debts are:

$$(.65)\,(\$24,000) = \$15,600$$

The corresponding figures for the other two alternatives are computed in a similar fashion.

Step 3.   Compute the following values for each alternative:

a.   Incremental investment in accounts receivable
b.   Required return on incremental accounts receivable investment
c.   Incremental credit sales

    *d.*  Gross profit on incremental credit sales
    *e.*  Funds lost due to incremental bad debts

The computations for all the above values are shown in Table 7-2 and are explained below.

Incremental values represent the dollar changes that occur between successively more liberal credit terms. Thus, one set of incremental values is computed by using the terms net 30 days and net 60 days. Another set is computed by using the

| **Table 7-2.** | **Incremental Analysis of Alternative Credit Terms** | |
|---|---|---|
| | **Net 30 Days to Net 60 Days** | **Net 60 Days to Net 90 Days** |
| Incremental investment in accounts receivable | $143,000 − $65,000 = $78,000 | $227,500 − $143,000 = $84,500 |
| Required return on incremental accounts receivable investment | (.2) ($78,000) = $15,600 | (.2) ($84,500) = $16,900 |
| Incremental sales | $1,320,000 − $1,200,000 = $120,000 | $1,400,000 − $1,320,000 = $80,000 |
| Gross profit on incremental sales | (.35) ($120,000) = $42,000 | (.35) ($80,000) = $28,000 |
| Funds lost due to incremental bad debts | $25,740 − $15,600 = $10,140 | $45,500 − $25,740 = $19,760 |

terms net 60 days and net 90 days. If the corporation's credit terms are changed from net 30 days to net 60 days, the accounts receivable investment increases from $65,000 to $143,000. Thus, the incremental investment is $143,000 − $65,000 = $78,000. If the credit terms are changed from net 60 days to net 90 days, the accounts receivable investment increases from $143,000 to $227,500. Thus, the incremental investment is $227,500 − $143,000 = $84,500.

The required returns (in dollars) that are needed to justify the incremental accounts receivable investment are computed by multiplying the corporation's 20% required rate of return on its assets by the incremental accounts receivable investment.

Incremental credit sales produce additional—or incremental—gross profits and bad debts. Because variable costs are 65 percent of each sales dollar, gross profit is $1.0 − .65 = .35$ of each sales dollar. The incremental bad debts are caused not only by incremental credit sales but also by higher bad debt percentages.

Step 4.   Compute the incremental profits associated with successively more liberal terms. Incremental profits are computed as follows:

Gross profit on incremental credit sales
   Less:     Funds lost due to incremental bad debts
   Less:     Required return on incremental accounts receivable investment
   _____
   Equals:   Incremental profit

The incremental profit computations are shown in Table 7-3.

The decision as to which set of credit terms to adopt is made on the basis of the computed incremental profits. The decision rule is: *Adopt the most liberal set of credit terms that yields a positive incremental profit.* Changing credit terms from net 30 days to net 60 days yields an incremental profit of $16,260. On the other hand, changing credit terms from net 60 days to net 90 days yields an incremental profit of −$8,660. Therefore, adopting the term of net 60 days is desirable and adopting the term of net 90 days is not desirable according to this decision rule. On the basis of this analysis and the decision rule, the corporation should change its credit terms from net 30 days to net 60 days.

**Table 7-3.**          **Incremental Profits for Alternative Credit Terms**

|  | Net 30 Days to Net 60 Days | Net 60 Days to Net 90 Days |
|---|---|---|
| Gross profit on incremental credit sales | $42,000 | $28,000 |
| Less:    Funds lost due to incremental bad debts | $10,140 | $19,760 |
| Less:    Required return on incremental accounts receivable investment | $15,600 | $16,900 |
| Equals:  Incremental profit | $16,260 | −$8,660 |

The procedure used to evaluate alternative credit terms is based on the microeconomic concept of expanding output until marginal cost equals marginal revenue. Changing credit terms from net 30 days to net 60 days is desirable if total profits increase. Similarly, credit terms will be expanded to net 90 days only if total profits are greater for 90-day terms than they would be for 60-day terms. However, in order for total profits to increase as credit terms are liberalized, incremental profits must be positive. Therefore, the corporation is choosing the most profitable alternative by liberalizing credit terms until incremental profits become zero or negative.

In deciding which items to include in calculating incremental profits, the general rule is to use those cost and profit items which have values that change when credit terms are changed. For example, if credit terms are changed from net 30 to net 60 days, the corporation realizes an increase of $42,000 in gross profits. However, there are two incremental costs with values that also change with changing credit terms. These costs are subtracted from the increased profits. One cost, $10,140, is due to incremental bad debts. The other cost, $15,600, represents the return the corporation requires on its incremental investment in accounts receivable. If incremental credit sales are not sufficiently profitable to justify the incremental investment in accounts receivable, then incremental profits as defined will be negative even though accounting profits increase. In this situation the increase in accounting profits would not be sufficient to earn the desired rate of return on the incremental investment in accounts receivable, and the corporation's desired rate of return on total assets will not be met.

This procedure assumes that the firm has the capacity to increase its sales without incurring added costs other than the variable costs included in the analysis. A further assumption is the ability of firms to estimate the future level of credit sales and the corresponding bad debt percentages. The firm's desired rate of return can be based in part on its historical ROI (return on investment) financial ratio that was introduced in Chapter 3. Decision making based on required rates of return is explained in greater detail in later chapters.

**Retail Credit**    The extension of retail credit in the purchase of both consumer durable and nondurable goods is an accepted practice in our economy. Historically, retail credit was available primarily in the form of secured credit and was used for the purchase of durable goods such as automobiles and furniture. The gradual introduction and acceptance of unsecured retail credit as a means of stimulating the sale of nondurable goods and certain types of durable goods have greatly changed the consumption and savings habits of consumers and have had major impacts on the ways in which corporations finance their sales and accounts receivables.

**TYPES OF RETAIL CREDIT.** Retailers often refer to their terms of credit as *credit plans*. While there are only a few major types of retail credit, many variations of each type are available. The particular credit plan offered by a retailer is often intended to produce a competitive advantage over other retailers. Three major types of retail credit are discussed below.

*Open Charge Credit.* The **open charge credit** plan offers unsecured, interest-free terms that allow customers as much as 90 days to pay for their purchases. Open charge terms are occasionally available through regional credit card plans. These credit terms are advertised as *90 days same as cash* and are used by independent retailers who sell such items as clothing and major appliances.

*Installment Credit.* The **installment credit** plan is a form of extended, secured credit that uses a written contract between buyer and seller. The contract is interest-bearing and requires the payment of specified amounts at specified times. A down payment may be required. The purchaser is given a payment book containing dated coupons, each of which is detached as it matures and is sent along with the specified payment. Installment credit contracts are offered by retailers who carry consumer durables in their product lines.

*Revolving Credit.* National credit cards are the most common form of **revolving credit,** or revolving charge. These cards provide a maximum line of credit and are used in making repeated purchases. Credit card sales are made on an unsecured basis. Customers receive monthly statements and usually can avoid interest charges by making prompt payments. Unpaid balances incur interest charges at the rate of, say, 1½ percent per month. Customers are required to make monthly payments at least equal to a minimum stated amount that varies with the size of the unpaid balance.

Credit cards are a very important marketing device in the sale of consumer nondurables. Those issued by large retailers, such as Sears Roebuck and J. C. Penney, and national bank credit cards, such as MasterCard and Visa, are used to finance consumer durable and nondurable purchases.

**RETAIL CREDIT STRATEGIES.** The credit strategies adopted by a retailer are influenced by the product lines it sells, the credit plans offered by its competitors, and its ability and willingness to operate a credit department. Many retailers prefer to use bank credit card services in order to avoid the need for creating and maintaining their own credit departments.

*Credit Risks.* When an application for retail credit is processed, the credit-granting seller faces the following two risks: (1) the risk of default by the purchaser if the application is accepted and (2) if the application is rejected, the risk that the purchaser might have complied with the credit terms. Which risk does the seller most want to avoid?

A conservative credit strategy seeks primarily to avoid uncollectible accounts receivable. In order to do so, a conservative strategy will accept the risk of rejecting desirable credit applicants so as to attain a very low percentage of bad debts. An aggressive credit strategy, on the other hand, seeks to extend credit to all desirable applicants. This is especially true in the case of revolving credit cards since interest charges on unpaid balances more than cover the cost of credit management. As a consequence, an aggressive credit strategy extends credit to applicants that are judged as being relatively high-default risks in order to minimize the percentage of desirable applicants that is rejected.

Most credit-evaluating systems will reject applicants who are unemployed or who have accumulated unsatisfactory credit ratings with other creditors. A common practice is to reject applicants who use only a post office box number for a return address. A conservative strategy might, for example, accept only those applicants who have established satisfactory credit experience elsewhere, who have both a checking and a savings account, and whose annual income is above a certain level. A more aggressive credit strategy might accept applicants who do not have savings accounts. Such a strategy also might lower the minimum acceptable income level for those applicants who have compiled satisfactory credit histories with other creditors.

*Credit Plans.* Some retailers offer a choice of credit plans to their customers. For example, a retailer pursuing an aggressive credit strategy might offer customers a choice of 90-day open charges on purchases of consumer durables as an alternative to the use of bank credit cards. Such a retailer assumes the risk of default, but revenue is increased by 2 to 5 percent since the discount charged by credit card firms is avoided.

Other retailers rely almost exclusively on revolving credit cards. When they turn in the bank credit card charges, they receive 95 percent to 98 percent of total credit charges. Such retailers are pursuing conservative credit strategies since they seek to shift the credit-granting and collection burdens away from themselves. Thus, the only credit plans offered as part of a conservative retail credit strategy may consist of accepting national bank credit cards.

**Commercial Credit**

The majority of sales made between corporations are done on a commercial credit basis and are called **open account sales,** or **trade credit sales.** This type of credit is generally unsecured, noninterest-bearing, and allows the customer up to 90 days to remit payment.

**CREDIT ANALYSIS.** The decision to extend credit to a new customer, to liberalize an existing customer's credit terms, or to refuse to sell on open account is reached after analyzing the customer's financial condition and trade history. The necessary information can be obtained directly from the customer, from the principal commercial banks used by the customer, and from credit bureaus.

For example, a financial statement analysis (see Chapter 3) can be performed on the customer's audited financial statements. The customer's commercial bank can supply an additional credit reference along with the loan and deposit information. Credit bureaus prepare and supply credit ratings, report payment histories, provide product line and operations data, prepare estimates of financial strength, and supply background information on a corporation and its principal executives.

The single most widely used credit-rating service is provided by Dun & Bradstreet, Inc. This company maintains files on approximately three million American and Canadian firms. Upon specific request, it can provide a detailed business information report on any of these firms. It also provides a summary credit rating on each of these firms in its *Dun & Bradstreet Reference Book,* which consists of four volumes and is published six times a year. This summary credit rating gives an estimate of each firm's financial strength and a composite credit appraisal. The estimated financial strength is an estimate of the firm's *tangible net worth,* which is defined as net worth minus the book value of intangible assets. The composite credit appraisal value is determined by Dun & Bradstreet as a result of its own analysis of the firm.

Table 7-4 lists and explains the Dun & Bradstreet ratings. For example, if a firm's Dun & Bradstreet rating is DC2, this means that its tangible net worth is between $50,000 and $74,999 and that it has a good record of paying its bills as they come due. Since a corporation does not receive a Dun & Bradstreet rating until information about it has been obtained from several sources, the fact that it has such a rating should be sufficient for a seller to conclude that it is a legitimate firm.

**COMMERCIAL CREDIT TERMS.** Once the decision has been made to allow the customer to make purchases on open account, the credit terms to be granted to that customer must be set. The length of the credit period may be determined by industry and competitive practices. However, maximum lines of credit are set for each customer.

New trade credit customers typically have their maximum line of credit set as a function of their financial position. A seller might set the maximum line of credit at 5 percent of the customer's working capital. A more common practice is to set the maximum line of credit at 10 percent of the customer's minimum financial strength as estimated by the Dun & Bradstreet ratings. For example, a new customer with a DD1 rating would have its maximum line of credit set at $(.1)($35,000) = $3,500$. Another practice is to set a maximum line of credit for all customers that cannot be exceeded without special review and approval. For example, a wholesaler might set the maximum line of credit available to any retail customer at 10 percent of the Dun & Bradstreet minimum estimated financial strength or $30,000, whichever is smaller. Any retailer requesting a line of credit greater than $30,000 would have to undergo a special credit investigation and explain the need for the higher credit line. Final approval might be needed from the seller's financial vice-president.

---

**Example:**    A small manufacturer sets the following maximum line of credit on trade credit sales: 10 percent of the Dun & Bradstreet minimum estimated financial strength or $20,000, whichever is lower. A new customer with a GG1 rating would have its maximum line of credit set at $(.1)($5,000) = $500$. A new customer with a credit rating of BB or higher, however, would have its maximum line of credit set at $20,000.

---

MONITORING RECEIVABLES. Accounts receivable are monitored in two distinct ways. First, they are reviewed individually on a scheduled basis

**Table 7-4.**    Dun & Bradstreet's Key to Ratings

### Key to Ratings

| Estimated Financial Strength | | | Composite Credit Appraisal | | | |
|---|---|---|---|---|---|---|
| | | | High | Good | Fair | Limited |
| 5A | $50,000,000 | and over | 1 | 2 | 3 | 4 |
| 4A | $10,000,000 to | 49,999,999 | 1 | 2 | 3 | 4 |
| 3A | 1,000,000 to | 9,999,999 | 1 | 2 | 3 | 4 |
| 2A | 750,000 to | 999,999 | 1 | 2 | 3 | 4 |
| 1A | 500,000 to | 749,999 | 1 | 2 | 3 | 4 |
| BA | 300,000 to | 499,999 | 1 | 2 | 3 | 4 |
| BB | 200,000 to | 299,999 | 1 | 2 | 3 | 4 |
| CB | 125,000 to | 199,999 | 1 | 2 | 3 | 4 |
| CC | 75,000 to | 124,999 | 1 | 2 | 3 | 4 |
| DC | 50,000 to | 74,999 | 1 | 2 | 3 | 4 |
| DD | 35,000 to | 49,999 | 1 | 2 | 3 | 4 |
| EE | 20,000 to | 34,999 | 1 | 2 | 3 | 4 |
| FF | 10,000 to | 19,999 | 1 | 2 | 3 | 4 |
| GG | 5,000 to | 9,999 | 1 | 2 | 3 | 4 |
| HH | Up to | 4,999 | 1 | 2 | 3 | 4 |

Classification Based on Both
Estimated Financial Strength and Composite Credit Appraisal

Financial Strength Bracket
1.  $125,000 and over
2.    20,000 to $124,999

When only the numeral (1 or 2) appears, it is an indication that the estimated financial strength, while not definitely classified, is presumed to be within the range of the ($) figures in the corresponding bracket and while the composite credit appraisal cannot be judged precisely, it is believed to be *High* or *Good*.

*INV.* shown in place of a rating indicates that the report was under investigation at the time of going to press. It has no other significance.

*FB* **(Foreign Branch).** Indicates that the headquarters of this company is located in a foreign country (including Canada). The written report contains the location and rating of the headquarters.

**ABSENCE OF RATING.** A blank(--) symbol should not be interpreted as indicating that credit should be denied. It simply means that the information available to Dun & Bradstreet does not permit us to classify the company within our rating key and that further inquiry should be made before reaching a credit decision.

Source: Dun & Bradstreet, Inc. Reproduced by permission.

in order to judge customer compliance with credit terms. In addition, a number of events can result in the seller's reevaluating on an unscheduled basis the credit terms available to a particular customer. Second, accounts receivable are reviewed in total in order to compare actual turnover rates with those set by the seller.

*Routine and Unscheduled Reviews of Credit Lines.* Most corporations routinely review customer credit lines once a year. An activity report may be prepared as part of the review. This report–

1. indicates how important the customer is to the seller in terms of yearly sales volume;

2. evaluates the customer's payment record;

3. indicates the customer's account balances;

4. contains any other information, such as a change in the customer's Dun & Bradstreet credit rating, that is pertinent in judging the desirability of the customer.

If the account experience is judged to be satisfactory, then no other action is required by the seller and the review is completed. If the account experience is satisfactory and the customer's Dun & Bradstreet credit rating has been *upgraded* since the last review, the customer might be encouraged to increase purchases by being informed that its maximum line of credit has been increased.

If the account experience is unsatisfactory, the seller may undertake any of several courses of action designed to improve the customer's compliance with credit terms or to revoke the customer's credit line. For example, the customer might receive a letter requesting the delinquent payments. As an alternative, the customer might be informed that new orders will not be accepted until the delinquent payments have been received. Subsequently the customer's maximum line of credit might be reduced.

Unscheduled reviews of customer accounts can be necessitated by a number of different events. For example, a review may be required when a customer exceeds its maximum line of credit or when its balances become overdue. A review might also be triggered when a customer's Dun & Bradstreet rating is lowered. Since this credit rating is based on information gathered by Dun & Bradstreet, a reduced rating may reflect a deteriorating financial condition.

There are cases where a customer requests a credit review in order to obtain more liberal credit terms. In this case the seller may require that the customer submit cash budgets and pro forma statements in order to justify the need for the more liberal credit and to explain when and how the cash will be generated to pay for the credit purchases.

The fact that an unscheduled credit review occurs does not automatically mean that the customer's credit line will be changed. Once the review has been completed, the options available to the seller are generally the same as those available at the end of a routine credit review. The credit terms available to the customer might be unchanged, liberalized, or reduced. In extreme cases, the line of credit might be suspended. If an account appears uncollectible, the seller will have to decide between simply writing off the account or taking legal action against the customer.

*Aging Schedules.* A seller can compute average collection periods and aging schedules in order to monitor total corporate receivables. As explained in Chapter 3, the average collection period is computed in two steps. (1) The average daily credit sales is computed by dividing credit sales by 360 days, and (2) the average collection period in days is computed by dividing accounts receivable by the average daily credit sales.

---

**Example:**

A corporation's yearly credit sales total $2,400,000, and its accounts receivable at the end of the year are $500,000. Average credit sales per day are:

$$\$2,400,000/360 \text{ days} = \$6,667 \text{ per day}$$

The average collection period is:

$$\$500,000/\$6,667 \text{ per day} = 75 \text{ days}$$

If the trade credit terms are net 60 days, the 75-day average collection period indicates that a sizable amount of trade credit is overdue. This may trigger individual credit reviews as some accounts past due may be uncollectible.

---

To compute an aging schedule, receivables are grouped by age, and the percentage of total receivables that falls in each age group is calculated.

---

**Example:**

A corporation with trade credit terms of net 60 days groups its receivables into four age groups and computes the following aging schedule:

| 0–30 Days | 31–60 Days | 61–90 Days | Over 90 Days |
|-----------|-----------|-----------|--------------|
| $350,000  | $100,000  | $30,000   | $20,000      |
| 70%       | 20%       | 6%        | 4%           |

This aging schedule shows that 10 percent of the dollar value of accounts receivable is overdue (assuming terms of net 60 days) and that $20,000 is more than 30 days overdue.

---

An aging schedule provides more information than the mere computation of the average collection period. Aging schedules are useful in identifying customer payment trends. Accounts more than 30 days overdue may be selected for immediate credit reviews. If a few customers account for the bulk of all the overdue accounts, the seller will have to decide if these customers have special credit needs or if they are likely to default on their payments. If the payments overdue less than 30 days are distributed among customers who make regular purchases, the seller may take no action or do no more than request that the overdue amounts be paid as quickly as possible.

**COMMERCIAL CREDIT STRATEGIES.** The commercial credit strategies available to a seller are constrained by the need to offer (1) trade credit in order to generate sales, and (2) credit terms that are generally similar to those offered by the competition. A conservative strategy might require new customers to pay for each purchase before a subsequent sale is made. Similarly, credit lines might be extended only to those firms that have established strong credit ratings with other sellers. Regular customers might not be able to obtain extended credit terms. The seller's accounts receivable monitoring system might be geared to identify all overdue balances on a weekly basis and automatically send out overdue notices.

The net impact of a conservative credit strategy is to minimize the probability of making uncollectible credit sales and to emphasize to all customers that violations of the seller's terms of credit invite suspension of their credit lines. However, this type of strategy can result not only in lost sales but also in established customers turning to other sellers whose credit policies are less stringent.

Aggressive commercial credit strategies extend credit to customers who appear to be marginal credit risks. When a new firm enters the industry and requests trade credit terms from suppliers, the suppliers are faced with the possibility that the new corporation will prosper and become an important customer. Refusing a line of credit initially may cost the suppliers substantial future sales and profits. An aggressive strategy will also attempt to meet the special credit needs of established customers in an attempt to capture additional profitable sales.

A logical extension of an aggressive strategy is to offer trade credit terms that are more liberal than those offered by the competition. If the seller is operating in an oligopolistic market, however, the competition may respond in kind, and the strategy will increase the risk of making uncollectible credit sales while not increasing sales and profits sufficiently to cover the added bad debt losses.

The net impact of an aggressive commercial credit strategy is to accept added credit risks in order to acquire additional profitable customers. Overdue accounts may not be pursued vigorously for a time in order to maintain customer goodwill. This type of strategy can result in a seller's profits not increasing in proportion to the increase in credit sales because of the funds lost due to uncollectible receivables.

# INVENTORY MANAGEMENT

Of the four types of current assets discussed in this chapter, inventory is the only one that is managed primarily in physical rather than monetary terms. Cash, marketable securities, and accounts receivable are managed in dollar terms, but inventories are managed in physical units. Inventory management seeks to advance stockholder wealth by designing and executing policies and strategies that minimize the costs of procuring and maintaining the types and quantities of inventories desired by the corporation.

Inventory policies usually are determined by production and marketing managers. Financial managers do not set major inventory policies; rather, they provide inputs as to the investment and financing implications of alternative strategies. Accordingly, the purpose of this section is to provide familiarity with some fundamentals of corporate inventory management. Chapter 8 contains some strategies that deal specifically with inventory financing.

Inventory management is based on recognizing the major types of inventories needed by a corporation and the functions that each type of inventory serves in the production-inventory-marketing system. The product lines and/or services offered for sale by a corporation determine the extent to which inventories constitute an important percentage of a firm's total assets.

**Types of Inventories**

The following are the four major types of inventories: (1) raw materials, (2) goods in process, (3) finished goods, and (4) spare parts. Manufacturing corporations process raw materials into the finished goods offered for sale. Raw materials that have entered a corporation's manufacturing process but have not yet emerged as finished goods are referred to as *goods in process*. Spare parts inventories consist of all the items used to repair and maintain machinery and equipment that fail because of worn-out parts.

Because manufacturing corporations have to provide for all four types of inventories, they find that total inventories constitute as much as 50 to 60 percent of their total assets. Wholesalers and retailers who are not involved in manufacturing the products they offer for sale focus their inventory decisions on finished goods. Their inventories average less than 50 percent of their total assets. Service corporations, such as management and tax consultants, do not typically face major inventory management problems. Thus, their inventories can be as low as 10 percent of their total assets.

**Functions of Inventories**

In a manufacturing corporation raw materials, goods in process, and spare parts inventories are essential in helping to produce finished goods at a minimum unit cost. When a shortage of one of these inventory types disrupts the production process, the time and effort needed to resume production results in added costs which are reflected in the cost of finished goods. Thus, inventory policies for raw materials, goods in process, and spare parts are set so as to minimize the probability of interrupting a scheduled production run. One implication of this policy is that raw materials and spare parts inventories are kept at levels higher than their expected usage rates.

The function of finished goods inventories is to meet actual or anticipated demand. In a marketing oriented society, finished goods inventories are managed on the basis of forecast sales. Setting desired inventory levels before actual demand is known involves balancing the risk of overstocks versus the risk of stockouts.

**Overstocking** occurs when actual demand is less than forecast demand, and the remaining inventory's market value falls. Overstocking results in an unintended and undesirable amount of funds tied up in the unsold inventory. If the inventory is stored for a longer period of time than was expected, additional storage costs, such as maintenance, utility, warehouse, and insurance costs, may be incurred. This can reduce asset turnover and decrease corporate profits. The remaining inventory may have to be sold at cost or less in order to recover some of the invested funds. Inventory liquidations of this type further decrease corporate profits.

A **stockout** is a demand for an item when its inventory level has fallen to zero. (If an item is sold out and is not futher demanded, there is no stockout—just a correct decision.) Stockouts result in back orders or lost sales. The seller may incur extra costs in placing back orders or other special orders for its customers. In either case, stockouts reduce corporate profits.

Which of these two risks do sellers most want to avoid? In general, sellers most want to avoid stockout risks. This has led to the development of safety stocks. **Safety stocks** represent inventoried items over and above forecast sales that are available in the event that actual demand exceeds forecast demand. To handle unsold inventories of items that have a seasonal demand, that have limited shelf lives, or that will not be restocked, sellers have developed various promotional techniques designed to clear away the remaining inventories and recover as much of the invested funds as possible. It is apparent, especially in retailing, that sellers would much rather face overstocks than stockouts.

**Inventory Policies**

In a manufacturing firm the desired levels of finished goods inventories determine the inventory policies for raw materials, goods in process, and spare parts inventories. Wholesalers and retailers deal mostly with finished goods. Consequently, this discussion of inventory policies is limited to finished goods.

Inventory policies are designed to provide the desired inventory levels while minimizing the costs of running the inventory system. Quite often, however, corporations face physical and/or financial constraints that restrict their ability not only to provide the desired amounts of inventory but also to minimize the costs of obtaining and maintaining inventoried items.

Separate inventory policies can be designed for individual products. Policies can also be structured for entire product lines. On the basis of estimated demand, each policy specifies the relevant costs, risks, constraints, and when and in what quantity the item or group of items is to be ordered.

**SINGLE PRODUCT POLICIES.** The process of establishing an inventory policy for individual products can be explained by using the following example.

---

**Example:**

One of the products sold by a retailer has the following characteristics:

1. Demand for the product is steady and is forecast to remain at the current rate.
2. The retailer incurs a cost of preparing and submitting a purchase order each time the item is ordered from a wholesaler.
3. The retailer incurs a cost of maintaining the inventoried goods. This is called the inventory-carrying cost.

The inventory policy for this product must answer the following questions:

1. How much inventory should be ordered each time in order to minimize the combined ordering and storage costs?
2. How often will orders have to be placed?
3. What is the total cost of this inventory system over a given period of time?

In order to answer the above questions, the retailer must forecast demand and estimate the ordering and carrying costs. The relevant time interval is set at one year. The retailer forecasts yearly demand to be 14,400 units. If the retailer is open for business 288 days per year, daily demand is thus 14,400 units/ 288 days = 50 units/day.

The ordering cost is estimated to be $8 per order. This $8 is incurred each time the order is prepared but does not depend on the quantity ordered. Total ordering cost over a period of time is $8 multiplied by the number of orders submitted.

The inventory-carrying cost includes labor, insurance, repairs, and related items. The retailer estimates the cost of carrying one unit in inventory for one year at $1.

The total cost, $C$, of ordering and carrying inventory for one year can be measured as follows:

Let $R$ = number of units demanded per year
  $S$ = cost of placing one order
  $I$ = inventory-carrying cost per unit
  $Q$ = number of units ordered at a time

Then

$$C = (R/Q)(S) + (Q/2)(I) \qquad\qquad \textbf{(7-1)}$$

$R/Q$ is the number of times per year that orders are placed. Multiplying that number by $S$ produces the total ordering cost. $Q/2$ is the average amount of inventory that is stored during the year. This is based on (1) $Q$ units arriving when the inventory is depleted and (2) a constant rate of sale from inventory. Multiplying $Q/2$ by the inventory-carrying cost, $I$, produces the total inventory carrying cost.

If the retailer orders 144 units at a time, then 100 orders (14,400/144) are placed during the year and the total ordering cost is (100)($8) = $800. The inventory-carrying cost is (144/2)($1) = $72. The total cost is $800 + $72 = $872. Alternatively, if the retailer orders 288 units at a time, the total cost is:

$$(14{,}400/288)(\$8) + (288/2)(\$1) = \$544$$

Increasing the quantity ordered from 144 to 288 units per order decreases total inventory system costs from $872 to $544. However, increasing $Q$ will eventually increase the total cost due to the inventory-carrying cost. If, for example, $Q$ is set at 1,440, then the total cost increases to:

$$(14{,}400/1{,}440)(\$8) + (1{,}440/2)(\$1) = \$800$$

Given the assumptions of this example, the order quantity that minimizes the total cost of the inventory system, called $Q^*$, is computed by using the following equation:

$$Q^* = \sqrt{(2)(R)(S)/I} \qquad\qquad \textbf{(7-2)}$$

In this retailer's example, $R = 14{,}400$, $S = \$8$, and $I = \$1$. Using Equation 7-2,

$$Q^* = \sqrt{(2)(14{,}400)(\$8)/\$1}$$

$$= 480 \text{ units}$$

The total cost of running the inventory system is computed from Equation 7-1 using $Q^*$ in the place of $Q$.

$$C = (14{,}400/480)(\$8) + (480/2)(\$1) = \$480$$

The optimum inventory policy for this product, which provides the inventory at a minimum cost, is thus:

1. Order 480 units at a time.
2. Place 14,400/480 = 30 orders a year.
3. Total system cost is $480.

The timing of each order is based on the daily demand rate of 50 units and the length of time required for inventory to arrive from the wholesaler. If inventory arrives four business days after the order is placed, then the order is placed each time the inventory level reaches (4)(50) = 200 units.

Equation 7-2 is called the *Economic Order Quantity model* or the *EOQ model*. This model does not allow for stockout or overstock risks, and no constraints are placed on the order size. In fact, Equation 7-2 assumes that the demand is constant and certain and that there are no constraints on $Q^*$. If a stockout risk does exist, the retailer can still use Equation 7-2 and establish a safety stock. If the desired safety stock were set at 100 units, $Q^*$ would still be 480 units, and an order would be placed each time the inventory level reached $(4)(50) + 100 = 300$ units. The net impact of safety stock is to increase the total inventory system cost because of the increase in the average amount of inventory that has to be maintained.

An example of a typical constraint is a limit on the amount of warehouse space available for storing the inventory. If in the above example 5 square feet are required to store each item and only 1,500 square feet of storage space are available for this product, what is the resulting impact on the inventory policy? Under this square-foot-storage constraint only $1,500/5 = 300$ units can be stored at any one time. Assuming that a safety stock is not needed, only 300 units can be ordered in each purchase unless the retailer finds extra storage space. The total cost that results from having to accept this constraint is found by using Equation 7-1:

$$C = (14,400/300)(\$8) + (300/2)(\$1) = \$534$$

The square-foot-storage constraint thus increases the inventory system cost by $\$534 - \$480 = \$54$ per year.

This example did not consider the purchase price paid by the retailer for the inventory. If the wholesaler does not discount the price for large purchases, then $Q^*$ is not affected by the unit price. If such discounts are available, Equations 7-1 and 7-2 are replaced with somewhat more complicated expressions. If the maximum amount of funds that can be invested in a given product inventory at one time is limited, then the unit purchase price is again relevant regardless of purchase discounts. Such constraints on inventory investment are handled in the same fashion as was the square-foot-storage constraint.

**MULTIPLE PRODUCT POLICIES.** In general, it is more difficult to develop multiple product inventory policies than it is to develop single product inventory policies. However, there are situations where an inventory policy must cover a group of products. For example, stockouts of some items in a product line may result in lost sales not only for the out-of-stock items but also for related items that are available for sale. Alternatively, the inventory policies of several products may share one or more common constraints. For example, a fixed amount of warehouse space may have to be shared by several products. Multiple product inventory policies are needed when individual products interact with one another so as to affect their individual $Q^*$s and their combined inventory system costs.

In the case of stockouts causing lost sales of related products, the inventory policy would set safety stocks for each item based in part on all the profits that can be lost due to a stockout in a given item. Introducing safety stocks and/or increasing their levels in order to avoid this type of lost sale will increase the total cost of running the inventory system. This is because the safety stock will increase the average inventory across the related products and thus increase total inventory-carrying costs.

When a group of products share one or more common constraints, the first step in formulating the inventory policy is to eliminate any constraints that do not affect the $Q^*$ of the individual products. Assume, for example, that four products must be stored in a common storage area *and* that only a limited amount of funds can be invested in the combined products. The $Q^*$ for each product is initially computed by disregarding the constraints. Each constraint is then tested to see if the combined $Q^*$ of the four products violates the constraint. Any constraint that is not exceeded is dropped from the inventory policy since it does not affect the individual $Q^*$. If this procedure results in dropping all the constraints, separate and much simpler inventory policies can be developed for each of the four products. Any constraints that are binding on the individual $Q^*$ are then integrated into the four-product inventory policy. The resulting multiple product policy specifies the $Q^*$ and ordering frequency for each item and calculates the total cost of running the four-product inventory system. The total cost is higher than it would be in the absence of binding constraints. Thus, the inventory policy provides a constrained cost-minimizing solution to the multiple product problem.

---

# SUMMARY

This chapter has presented working capital policies for managing cash, marketable securities, accounts receivable, and inventory. Transactions, precautionary, and compensating cash-balance requirements can be managed by using cash-budgeting techniques to estimate desired minimum cash balances.

Current assets held in the form of marketable securities by nonfinancial corporations are mostly in the form of money market securities. The suitability of Treasury bills, negotiable certificates of deposit, commercial paper, and money market mutual funds as investment vehicles for temporarily idle cash depends on the following six general characteristics: minimum purchase size, original maturity, rate of return, default risk, interest rate risk, and market risk.

Credit management policies contain the following three major elements: (1) the criteria for extending credit and the credit terms to be offered, (2) protection of the seller's investment

in credit sales, and (3) collection procedures. An incremental form of risk-return analysis can be used to evaluate alternative credit terms. The various types of retail credit and associated credit plans are designed to increase sales and profits. Commercial credit is extended as a normal part of intercompany sales and is not intended primarily as a sales incentive.

There are four major types of inventories. Raw materials, goods in process, spare parts, and finished goods. Inventory policies specify how much inventory should be ordered at a time and the ordering frequency that minimizes the cost of running the inventory system. Inventory policies can be designed for individual products and for product groups. Because of constraints and/or product interactions, a constrained cost-minimizing solution may have to be accepted as the best available inventory policy for a given product or group of products.

# QUESTIONS

**7-1.** Explain the goals of cash management strategies.

**7-2.** Explain the major types of corporate cash balance requirements.

**7-3.** Explain what is meant by the desired minimum cash balance contained in a cash budget.

**7-4.** Identify the six general characteristics that are used to evaluate the desirability of money market securities as uses of temporarily idle corporate cash balances.

**7-5.** Why are Treasury bills sometimes referred to as risk-free securities?

**7-6.** Explain what is meant by interest rate risk.

**7-7.** Explain what is meant by market risk.

**7-8.** Which of the four money market securities best fits a conservative current asset strategy? Why?

**7-9.** What are the three major elements of a corporation's credit policy?

**7-10.** What elements make up the terms of credit offered by a seller?

**7-11.** Identify and explain the three major types of retail credit.

**7-12.** Explain the risks involved in accepting or rejecting a credit application.

**7-13.** What are the major questions that a seller attempts to answer before accepting an application for commercial credit?

**7-14.** What are some of the reasons that necessitate unscheduled reviews of commercial credit customers?

**7-15.** Identify the four major types of inventories.

**7-16.** What are the risks involved in setting desired finished goods inventory levels before actual sales are known? Explain each risk.

**7-17.** What is the basic goal of finished goods inventory policies?

**7-18.** What are the major questions that must be answered by inventory policies?

# PROBLEMS

**7-1.** A firm's annual credit sales are $3 million and its credit terms are net 30 days. Variable costs are 65% of each sales dollar. What is the average amount of funds needed to support these credit sales?

**7-2.** A corporation's annual credit sales are $1.75 million, its credit terms are net 60 days, and variable costs are 40% of each sales dollar. What is the average amount of funds needed to support these credit sales?

**7-3.** A wholesaler sets the following maximum line of credit on trade credit sales: 15% of the Dun & Bradstreet minimum estimated financial strength or $30,000, whichever is lower. What is the maximum line of credit for a customer with a CB rating?

**7-4.** A manufacturer sets the following maximum line of credit on trade credit sales: 25% of the Dun & Bradstreet minimum estimated financial strength or $75,000, whichever is lower. What is the maximum line of credit for a customer with a 1A rating?

**7-5.** A small manufacturer's annual credit sales are currently $4,500,000, and it offers net 30 day credit terms to its wholesalers. Of its accounts receivable, 3% becomes uncollectible. It requires a 15% rate of return on its assets. Variable costs are 60% of sales.

The manufacturer is considering the following two alternatives relative to its credit policy: (1) keep terms at net 30 days or (2) change credit terms to net 60 days. Data for each alternative are shown below. Which alternative should the manufacturer select?

|  | Net 30 Days | Net 60 Days |
|---|---|---|
| Receivable turnover rate per year | 12 times | 6 times |
| Annual credit sales | $4,500,000 | $5,400,000 |
| Average accounts receivable | $ 375,000 | $ 900,000 |
| Bad debt percentage | 3% | 5% |

**7-6.** A wholesaler's annual credit sales are currently $14,400,000. The firm offers net 30 day credit terms to its retailers. Of its receivables, 3% becomes uncollectible. Variable costs are 70% of sales, and the firm requires a 20% rate of return on its assets.

The wholesaler is considering the following three alternative credit policies: (1) keep credit terms at net 30 days, (2) change credit terms to net 60 days, or (3) change credit terms to net 90 days. Data for each alternative are shown below. Which alternative should the wholesaler select?

|  | Net 30 Days | Net 60 Days | Net 90 Days |
|---|---|---|---|
| Receivable turnover rate per year | 12 times | 6 times | 4 times |
| Annual credit sales | $14,400,000 | $15,600,000 | $16,400,000 |
| Average accounts receivable | $ 1,200,000 | $ 2,600,000 | $ 4,100,000 |
| Bad debt percentage | 3% | 4% | 6% |

**7-7.** A wholesaler wants to evaluate alternative inventory policies for a special product. Annual demand is 4,000 units, ordering costs are $10 per order, and inventory-carrying costs are 50 cents per unit per year.

a. Using Equation 7-1, determine the ordering frequency, total ordering costs, total inventory-carrying costs, and the total cost of running the inventory system if the wholesaler orders 100 units at a time.

b. Repeat a if the wholesaler orders 800 units at a time.

c. Using Equations 7-1 and 7-2, determine the optimal inventory policy for this firm.

**7-8.** A product has the following characteristics: yearly demand is 6,400 units, ordering costs are $25 per order, and inventory-carrying costs are $2 per unit per year.

a. Using Equations 7-1 and 7-2, determine the optimal inventory policy for this product.

b. Assume that the purchase price for this product is $50 per unit and that no more than $15,000 can be invested in this product at any one time. Evaluate the impact of this constraint on the inventory policy for this product.

# SELECTED REFERENCES

Cole, R. *Consumer and Commercial Credit Management*. 5th ed. Homewood, Ill.: Richard D. Irwin, 1976.

The Conference Board. *Managing Trade Receivables*. New York: The Conference Board, 1972.

Federal Reserve Bank of New York. "Money Market Mutual Funds and Monetary Control." *Quarterly Review*, Vol. 6, No. 4 (Winter, 1981–82).

Gitman, L., and M. Goodwin. "An Assessment of Marketable Securities Management Practices." *Journal of Financial Research*, Vol. 2, No. 2 (Fall, 1979).

Grieves, R. *Cash Management*. Charlottesville, Va.: The Financial Analysts Research Federation, 1982.

Hadley, G., and T. Whitin. *Analysis of Inventory Systems*. Englewood Cliffs, N. J.: Prentice-Hall, Inc., 1963.

Kim, Y., and J. Atkins. "Evaluating Investments in Accounts Receivable: A Maximizing Framework." *Journal of Finance*, Vol. 33, No. 2 (May, 1978).

Metha, D. *Working Capital Management*. Englewood Cliffs, N. J.: Prentice-Hall, Inc., 1974.

Orgler, Y. *Cash Management*. Belmont, Calif.: Wadsworth Publishing Company, Inc., 1970.

Redinbaugh, L. *Retailing Management: A Planning Approach*. New York: McGraw-Hill Book Company, 1975.

# CHAPTER 8

# Management of Current Liabilities

This chapter discusses the management of current liabilities within the context of working capital policy. Separate sections are devoted to the management of trade credit, commercial paper, commercial bank loans, pledging and factoring of accounts receivable, and inventory financing.

While current liabilities have short maturities, some of these sources provide continuous financing and are considered by corporations to be permanent sources of funds. Trade credit, for example, is used extensively to finance purchases. In addition, some corporations issue commercial paper on a regular basis while others routinely factor their accounts receivable.

Most short-term financing sources are not close substitutes for each other because each source contains unique advantages and limitations. As a consequence, this chapter explains how the individual financing sources can be used in executing corporate financing strategies.

## TRADE CREDIT

The use of trade credit as part of a corporation's marketing effort was discussed in Chapter 7. When sales are made by extending commercial credit in the form of trade credit, the seller records the credit as part of its accounts receivable in the current asset section of its balance sheet. The liability that is created when purchases are made on a trade credit basis is recorded as part of the accounts payable in the current liability section of the purchaser's balance sheet.

In this chapter trade credit is examined as a financing source from the standpoint of current liability management. Trade credit can represent as much as 40 percent of the current liabilities and up to 10 percent of the total liabilities and equity of nonfinancial corporations.

## Terms of Credit

The terms of credit specify (1) the beginning of the credit period, (2) the length of time before the invoice must be paid, and (3) the amount of the cash discount and the length of the discount period if a cash discount for prompt payment is offered.

**BEGINNING OF THE CREDIT PERIOD.** The beginning of the credit period is frequently set as the date of the invoice. When several purchases are made during a month, the supplier may provide end-of-month (EOM) terms. This means that the credit period for *all* purchases made during a given month begins on the last day of the month.

**NET PERIOD.** The net period, stated in days, is the amount of time the purchaser has before the invoice must be paid in full. For example, *net 30* requires the purchaser to remit payment within 30 days after the beginning of the credit period. *Net 15 EOM* requires payment on purchases made during a given month by the 15th day of the following month.

*Seasonal dating* is a special type of net period. For items that have a seasonal demand, such as lawn and garden supplies, toys, and clothing, the manufacturers will often provide seasonal dating in order to encourage purchasers to place their orders prior to the selling season. For example, if a manufacturer of lawn mowers offers net 15 June 1 terms, the manufacturer requires that purchases made before June 1 be paid by June 15. If the manufacturer is selling directly to retailers, the manufacturer is, in effect, financing retailer inventories. Retailers are allowed to make purchases during March, April, and May in order to anticipate seasonal demand while not having to pay the invoices until June 15.

By offering seasonal dating terms, the manufacturer is able to avoid inventory-carrying costs associated with finished goods inventories and may be able to forecast demand accurately enough to minimize production costs and unsold inventory. The retailer can acquire the desired inventory and minimize the risk of stockouts during the seasonal selling period. In addition, the retailer hopes to be able to use the cash receipts from the sale of seasonal items to pay for the purchases made under seasonal dating terms.

**CASH DISCOUNTS.** A cash discount represents a reduction or discount in the dollar amount of an invoice in return for prompt payment. Cash discounts are quoted in percentages and also state the length of the discount period within the net period. For example, *2/10 net 30* means that a 2 percent cash discount is available only during the first 10 days of the 30-day credit period.

| | |
|---|---|
| **Example:** | A manufacturer offers terms of 1/10 net 30 on a \$4,000 purchase. The cash discount is 1 percent and represents (.01)(\$4,000) = \$40. If payment is made within 10 days, the purchaser remits only (1 − .01)(\$4,000) = \$3,960. If payment is made after the 10th day, the entire \$4,000 must be remitted. |

Cash discounts are sometimes available as part of EOM terms. For example, 2/10 EOM net 30 allows a 2 percent cash discount if purchases made during a given month are paid within the first 10 days of the following month. Cash discounts may also be offered as part of seasonal dating terms. For example, 3/10 net 30 January 1 allows a 3 percent cash discount on all purchases made prior to January 1 if payment is made by January 10.

**Cost of Credit**

Since trade credit is a source of funds, the terms of credit must be analyzed from the standpoint of the costs involved in using trade credit as a method of financing. There are two ways that trade credit can prove costly to the purchasing corporation. First, there is an implied financing cost when cash discounts are offered and forgone. Second, delaying payments beyond the net period can reduce the corporation's credit rating and make it more difficult and/or expensive to obtain financing.

**FORGOING CASH DISCOUNTS.** When cash discounts are not offered, there is no cost of using the credit because no interest is added to the invoice price so long as payment is made by the end of the net period. When cash discounts are offered and taken, there is no cost for using the credit during the discount period. If cash discounts are offered and not taken, however, a financing cost is incurred by having to remit payment after the expiration of the discount period.

The financing cost of not taking cash discounts can be expressed as an annualized interest rate. Let:

$$i = \text{cash discount (percentage)}$$
$$n = \text{net period in days}$$
$$d = \text{discount period in days}$$

Then

$$\text{annual interest rate} = \left(\frac{i}{1 - i}\right)\left(\frac{360}{n - d}\right) \qquad (8\text{-}1)$$

The first factor in this equation, $i/(1 - i)$, measures the interest rate per financing period. The second factor, $360/(n - d)$, measures the number of financing periods per year.

---

**Example:**

The annualized interest rate of not taking cash discounts when the credit terms are 2/10 net 30 is:

$$\left(\frac{.02}{1 - .02}\right)\left(\frac{360}{30 - 10}\right) = 36.7\%$$

If the invoice on a $1,000 purchase is paid within the 10-day discount period, only $(.98)($1,000) = $980$ is remitted. In order to delay payment an additional 20 days, the purchaser must forgo the cash discount and remit $1,000. The additional $20 payment is thus a financing cost.

In this example, the interest rate per financing period is $.02/(1 - .02) = .0204$ or 2.04 percent. The number of financing periods per year is $360/(30 - 10) = 18$. Multiplying the interest rate per period by the number of financing periods per year yields the implied financing cost expressed as an annualized interest rate.

---

Table 8-1 contains annualized interest rates for different cash discount rates and financing periods. For a given cash discount rate, this table shows that implied financing rates decrease as the length of the financing period increases. This table also illustrates the fact that even a modest discount rate of 3 percent can have an implied financing cost in excess of 100 percent per year.

Equation 8-1 and the sample values of Table 8-1 provide the following guidelines for a corporation that is offered credit terms that include a cash discount for prompt payment:

1. Cash discounts should be taken whenever possible. This is because of the high financing rates that are illustrated in Table

**Table 8-1.**   Annualized Interest Rates for Cash Discounts Not Taken

| Financing Period in Days | Annualized Interest Rates for Cash Discounts (Not Taken) of | | |
| --- | --- | --- | --- |
| | 1% | 2% | 3% |
| 10 | 36.36% | 73.44% | 112.24% |
| 20 | 18.18 | 36.72 | 55.62 |
| 30 | 12.12 | 24.48 | 37.08 |
| 40 | 9.09 | 18.36 | 27.81 |

8-1. However, payment should not be made until the end of the discount period. This provides cost-free credit for the maximum amount of time.

2. When a cash discount must be lost, payment should not be made until the end of the net period. Delaying payment in this manner will minimize the annual financing rates. This is shown in Table 8-1 where the annualized interest rate decreases as the length of the financing period increases.

**STRETCHING ACCOUNTS PAYABLE.** Stretching accounts payable refers to the practice of not paying for purchases until some time *after* the end of the net period. This has the impact of extending free credit if cash discounts are not offered and of reducing the financing rate if cash discounts are offered and forgone. On the other hand, this practice can result in the downgrading of a firm's credit rating. As a consequence, the firm may find it increasingly difficult to obtain trade credit terms and may be forced to accept COD (cash on delivery) terms.

The downgrading in the firm's credit rating (such as its Dun & Bradstreet rating) can occur as a result of the credit experience reported to Dun & Bradstreet by the firm's suppliers if the suppliers indicate that the firm consistently disregards the terms of credit. As a consequence, suppliers may reduce the firm's line of credit, decrease the length of the net period, or suspend altogether its credit lines. Some suppliers may not be willing to grant trade credit terms and may offer goods only on a COD basis. The firm may find it necessary to borrow funds in order to purchase raw materials and supplies. Stretching accounts payable in this manner can thus result in a corporation being denied the use of trade credit as a financing source.

**Trade Credit as a Financing Instrument**      As discussed in Chapter 6, trade credit is a spontaneous financing source and represents an important form of commercial credit. Trade credit is readily available once a supplier has approved a firm's application for a line of credit. Credit terms are managed informally and credit is extended on an unsecured basis. Trade credit is a short-term financing instrument, and seasonal dating can provide interest-free credit over a time span of several months.

## COMMERCIAL PAPER

Commercial paper can be a source or a use of funds for nonfinancial corporations. On balance, commercial paper is more important to nonfinancial corporations as a financing instrument than as an investing instrument. Commercial paper is issued by financial corporations, such as banks and finance companies, and by nonfinancial corporations such as manufacturers and retailers. However, the major investors or purchasers of commercial paper are financial corporations, especially insurance companies, money market mutual funds, and pension funds.

Chapter 7 explained the financial characteristics of commercial paper and evaluated its role as an investing medium. This section looks at commercial paper as an instrument of short-term financing used by nonfinancial corporations.

**Dealer Placed Paper**

Nonfinancial corporations market, or float, commercial paper by selling it to commercial paper dealers who in turn sell the paper to investors. The minimum size of a dealer purchase has a face value of $50,000 or $100,000. In return for making the purchase, the dealer charges the issuing corporation a fee that does not exceed one-eighth of 1 percent of the face value of the purchase. Most paper sold to dealers matures in three to six months. There are nine major paper dealers, and they are located mostly in New York City.

Although commercial paper is an unsecured debt of the issuing corporation, most corporations arrange forms of indirect assurance that the debt will be repaid at maturity. Examples would be lines of credit or letters of credit issued by commercial banks, or guarantees by the issuer's parent corporation. Commercial paper issued in these ways receives the rating of the commercial banks or of the guaranteeing firm. These practices have allowed lesser-known or less creditworthy firms to use commercial paper as a financing medium.

In order to sell its commercial paper to dealers, the issuing corporation must be favorably rated by one or more of the five commercial paper rating agencies. The three most widely known agencies are Moody's Investor Services, Standard & Poor's Corporation, and Fitch Investors Services. A corporation applies for the paper rating and pays a fee to these rating agencies for their services. The highest ratings provided by these agencies are as follows:

1. Moody's Investors Service—Prime-1 (P-1), Prime-2 (P-2), and Prime-3 (P-3)

2. Standard & Poor's Corporation — A-1, A-2, and A-3

3. Fitch Investors Service — F-1, F-2, and F-3

A 1 indicates the highest quality rating and a 3 is the lowest rating. In order to sell a commercial paper issue to a dealer, the corporation usually must have a rating of 1 or 2. As an example of a complete set of paper rating designations, Table 8-2 lists and explains the set of definitions used by Standard & Poor's.

When a corporation has a P-1, A-1, or F-1 rating, the backup line of credit provided by commercial banks may be smaller than the amount of paper outstanding. For example, a corporation with a P-1 rating and $8,000,000 of paper outstanding may have a $5,000,000 line of credit as a standby means of repayment. If the corporation's rating is lower than P-1, investors and dealers will insist that the line of credit be large enough to cover 100 percent of the outstanding paper and that the line of credit be contractually and exclusively pledged to repay the paper if the corporation does not have other cash sources available. In return for providing these backup lines of credit, commercial banks require the issuing corporation to maintain compensating balances that range between 10 percent and 20 percent of the maximum line of credit available to the corporation. In addition, corporations pay a fee to commercial banks that act as agents in collecting and paying maturing paper. The net effect of maintaining compensating balances and paying agency fees is to increase the cost of commercial paper as a financing source.

**Uses of Commercial Paper**

Nonfinancial corporations use dealer placed paper in order to meet any of the following different financing requirements:

1. Seasonal financing

2. Revolving credit in order to obtain a continuous source of funds

3. Delaying long-term financing when stock and bond markets do not provide what are considered to be desirable financing terms

4. Supplementing or substituting for commercial bank loans

The volume of paper handled by dealers now depends to some extent on the cost and availability of bank loans. When tight money conditions restrict the availability of bank loans, corporations that have the necessary paper ratings can float commercial paper as a substitute for bank financing because dealers sell the paper to nonbank investors who are not as affected by restrictive monetary policies.

Commercial bank interest rates on commercial and industrial loans are higher than commercial paper yields. Some banks base their lending rates for business loans on dealer quoted paper rates. Citibank, a very large bank in New York City, at one time set its minimum lending rate 1½ percent above commercial paper rates. During the first quarter of

1983, 90-day commercial-paper rates averaged 2 percent below the minimum average rates charged by commercial banks for commercial and industrial loans. Since both commercial paper and business loans for commercial banks typically require compensating balances, the effective interest rate on commercial paper is lower than the effective rate of commercial bank financing.

---

**Table 8-2.**  **Standard & Poor's Commercial Paper Rating Definitions**

A Standard & Poor's Commercial Paper Rating is a current assessment of the likelihood of timely payment of debt having an original maturity of no more than 365 days.

Ratings are graded into four categories, ranging from *A* for the highest quality obligations to *D* for the lowest. The four categories are as follows:

**A:** Issues assigned this highest rating are regarded as having the greatest capacity for timely payment. Issues in this category are delineated with the numbers *1, 2* and *3* to indicate the relative degree of safety.

**A-1:** This designation indicates that the degree of safety regarding timely payment is either overwhelming or very strong. Those issues determined to possess overwhelming safety characteristics will be denoted with a plus (+) sign designation.

**A-2:** Capacity for timely payment on issues with this designation is strong. However, the relative degree of safety is not as high as for issues designated *A-1*.

**A-3:** Issues carrying this designation have a satisfactory capacity for timely payment. They are, however, somewhat more vulnerable to the adverse effects of changes in circumstances than obligations carrying the higher designations.

**B:** Issues rated *B* are regarded as having only an adequate capacity for timely payment. However, such capacity may be damaged by changing conditions or short-term adversities.

**C:** This rating is assigned to short-term debt obligations with a doubtful capacity for payment.

**D:** This rating indicates that the issue is either in default or is expected to be in default upon maturity.

The commercial paper rating is not a recommendation to purchase or sell a security. The ratings are based on current information furnished to Standard & Poor's from other sources it considers reliable. The ratings may be changed, suspended, or withdrawn as a result of changes in or unavailability of such information.

Source: Standard & Poor's Corporation *Credit Directory*, (November, 1982). Reproduced with permission.

**Commercial Paper as a Financing Instrument**

Several factors account for the ability of commercial paper to meet diverse corporate financing needs. These are:

1. Commercial paper is sold on an unsecured basis and does not contain restrictive covenants that are found in other types of financing instruments.

2. Maturities of commercial paper can be tailored to fit the needs of the issuing corporation.

3. Maturing paper can be repaid by selling new paper, thus providing a continuous source of funds.

4. The cost of commercial paper to the issuing corporation is lower than that of commercial bank loans.

5. Commercial paper can be used as a source of funds when tight money conditions reduce the availability of bank loans.

In the light of these factors, it is unfortunate that less than 2,000 nonfinancial corporations have top quality paper ratings. Nonfinancial corporations that do not obtain paper ratings or have ratings that are neither P-1 nor P-2 are effectively prevented from having access to the commercial paper markets.

The stringent requirements for obtaining a P-1 rating seek to assure potential investors that commercial paper carries with it a very low default risk. However, the probability of default is not zero, as attested to by the Penn Central 1970 bankruptcy. When this corporation defaulted on its $82 million of commercial paper, investors questioned the safety of other corporate issues, and many corporations were unable to sell new paper. The problem was compounded because a number of firms relied on their ability to float new issues in order to repay the paper that was maturing. The inability to sell new paper was not due to financial weakness of the issuing corporations but was due to a sudden and severe drop in investor confidence. The Federal Reserve System (the "Fed") prevented a major financial crisis from developing by suspending some of its regulations and modifying others. The actions of the Fed allowed commercial banks to quickly advance loans to creditworthy corporations that had suddenly and unexpectedly lost access to commercial paper markets.

Most corporations that found themselves unable to sell commercial paper during the 1970 paper crisis were victims of a loss in investor confidence that affected the entire commercial paper market. However, a decrease in a corporation's financial strength can cause the rating services to downgrade its quality rating. As a result, the market for that particular corporation's commercial paper decreases or disappears entirely. This happened to Chrysler Corporation in 1974 when its rating was reduced from P-1 to P-2 as a result of substantial decreases in sales and earnings. Chrysler had about $1.5 billion in commercial paper outstanding but was unable to renew the $500 million portion that matured late in the year. The corporation used backup, commercial bank lines of credit to pay off the maturing paper. Chrysler had previously arranged for standby lines of credit sufficient to repay all of its commercial paper. However, the firm was able to maintain approximately $1 billion in commercial paper and did not have to use the remainder of its credit lines.

Chrysler's ability to sell commercial paper suffered another severe blow in 1979 when the company began reporting what eventually amounted to staggering losses. Standard & Poor's downgraded the company's credit rating, and Moody's withdrew its credit rating altogether. Chrysler had in excess of $1 billion of commercial paper outstanding but had previously secured commercial bank, backup lines of credit that could be used to repay its paper. As a result, the company was able to float only limited amounts of new paper and had to offer interest rates significantly higher than rates paid by other issuers.

# COMMERCIAL BANK LOANS

Commercial banks are second only to trade credit as important sources of short-term corporate financing. However, business firms depend on commercial banks for many financial services other than short-term loans.

**The Customer Relationship**

The historical distinction between commercial banks and other financial institutions has been the ability of commercial banks to accept demand deposits. Checks written against these deposits are the principal method of paying bills and otherwise transferring money in this country. Thus, a business firm establishes checking accounts at one or more commercial banks as one of its first orders of business.

Providing checking accounts and short-term loans to business firms is enough to make commercial banks very important in the business world. However, commercial banks and their subsidiaries also make available a large number of business services. These include:

1.  Preparing payrolls

2.  Clearing of accounts receivable

3.  Serving as agents in commercial paper issues

4.  Disbursing dividend and interest payments to a firm's owners and creditors

5.  Factoring accounts receivable

6.  Providing lock box payment collection systems

7.  Supplying credit information

8.  Making certain types of leases

Many of these services are provided on a fee basis. Others are provided in return for maintaining agreed upon compensating balances.

Commercial banks are interested in selling to each customer that package of loans and services that will return the greatest profit possible given the level of risk the banks are willing to accept. In order to do so, many of the larger and more aggressive commercial banks use what are known as *customer relationship managers*. Each customer relationship manager is assigned a number of clients. The manager is then responsible for selling as many services as possible to each client and for maintaining client satisfaction with the services used. The customer relationship manager is not typically a loan officer and thus neither approves nor disapproves loan applications. However, the manager is required to know the operating, financial, and managerial aspects of each client well enough so as to provide loan officers with the information they need in deciding on loan applications.

The term *customer relationship* is now generally used to describe the set of arrangements whereby a commercial bank provides loans and/or services to its business clients. As this customer relationship concept spread through the banking industry, commercial banks began looking less at the profit or loss earned on individual services used by a client and began to focus increasingly on the total return generated from each client. One consequence of this customer relationship is that a business firm might be able to negotiate more favorable loan terms because it uses—and pays for—several bank services. Commercial banks are motivated by the same concept to provide added help to those business clients with whom they have significant and long-standing customer relationships when such clients experience financial difficulties. In these circumstances, commercial banks have been known to renegotiate loan agreements, grant and/or arrange additional credit, and to provide significant amounts of advice to their clients on how best to solve their financial problems.

**Unsecured Short-Term Loans**

The two major types of unsecured short-term loans extended by commercial banks to their business clients are called *lines of credit* and *revolving credit agreements*. A third type of loan, called *money market loans*, has gained importance in recent years and is discussed briefly in this section.

A firm applying for short-term financing is usually requested to submit current and recent financial statements, cash budgets, and pro forma statements. The loan officer uses the financial statements to measure the risk-return characteristics of the firm. The type of financial statement analysis performed by the loan officer is quite similar to the techniques described in Chapter 3. The cash budgets and pro forma statements are intended to demonstrate the timing, amount, and duration of the requested financing and to explain how and when the firm proposes to repay the loan. The financial information and the results of the loan officer's analysis are integrated into the applicant's customer relationship profile in order to help the bank decide whether or not to grant the loan request and what terms of lending it will specify.

LINE OF CREDIT. A **line of credit** is an informal arrangement between a commercial bank and a business client stating the willingness of the bank to extend loans up to a stated dollar limit over a specified time interval. Subject to the terms of the lending agreement, the borrower can obtain line-of-credit loans as needed and can decide when to repay the loans. There are no fixed repayment schedules. Lines of credit are described as *informal* agreements because the bank does not legally obligate itself to extend loans requested as part of the line. The bank merely indicates its willingness to extend the loans. If the bank runs short of lending funds, for example, or if the financial condition of the borrower deteriorates, the bank can refuse to extend financing under line-of-credit terms.

Borrowing privileges under a line of credit normally extend for 12 months and are renewed on a year-to-year basis. Notification of the line renewal and the terms of lending are often conveyed to the borrower in letter form. Banks expect that funds borrowed under these arrangements are for seasonal or other very short-term needs. In order to stress this point, banks tend to require that the line be unused during some portion of its availability. For example, a line of credit effective for 12 months starting May 1 might require the borrower to have no line-of-credit loans outstanding for at least 30 consecutive days during the time of the line's availability. The particular 30 debt-free days are at the discretion of the borrower. The borrower who observes this requirement demonstrates ability to repay the loan.

REVOLVING CREDIT AGREEMENT. A **revolving credit agreement** is a legal commitment on the part of a commercial bank to extend loans to a business customer. Revolving credit agreements are often called *revolving lines of credit*, but loan officers refer to them as *revolvers*. Subject to the terms of the agreement, the borrower can request loans at any time and the bank is obligated to extend the financing. During periods of tight money, commercial banks may be forced to borrow funds in order to meet revolving credit borrowings.

Revolving credit agreement maturities vary between 12 and 40 months. When the maturities extend beyond 12 or 15 months, the loans may require that collateral be pledged as security. The revolving credit agreement specifies the maximum dollar amount of borrowing that can be outstanding at any one time. Subject to this limit and any other covenants in the agreement, a firm can, at its discretion, increase its borrowings as funds are needed and repay the loans as cash becomes available. There is no requirement that the line be unused during some portion of its availability. Thus, for example, a 24-month revolver can provide continuous financing until maturity.

Revolving credit agreements meet several types of corporate requirements. Revolvers can provide cash for seasonal financing or for nonseasonal, general working capital needs. Loans can be used to support the working capital needs of a new product line or to support expansion of an existing product line.

Revolving credit agreements are also used as a first step in long-term financing. For example, a corporation may use revolving credit loans to make progress payments on new plant construction. After the construction is completed, the corporation sells common stock or long-term bonds and uses the proceeds to pay off the revolving credit loans. Revolving credit arrangements that finance construction in this manner are called *bridge loans*. There are two advantages to bridge loan financing. First, the corporation borrows only as much money as is required. Second, the financing is not obtained until needed. This financing strategy thus allows the corporation to avoid raising too much or too little in the way of long-term funds.

**MONEY MARKET LOANS.** Financially strong corporations with access to the commercial paper market have gradually increased their use of paper as a way of meeting their short-term financing needs. Some of this commercial paper was used as a substitute for commercial bank loans. In response, commercial banks now offer what are called **money market loans.** These loans have very short maturities; most range from 5 to 30 days although a few have maturities as long as six months. Money market loans provide fixed rate financing and commercial banks use negotiable certificates of deposit (NCDs) rates as a basis for loan pricing. A 30-day money market loan, for example, might be priced at 1½ percent above the 30-day NCD rate. While most of the loans are for less than $25,000, most of the *money* lent goes into loans the principals of which exceed $1 million. Although money market loans compete against commercial paper as an alternative financing medium, the very short maturities of the loans result in a minimum of competition between money market loans and either line-of-credit or revolving credit loans (even though, as explained below, money market loans may carry lower interest rates). The remainder of this section focuses primarily on line-of-credit and revolving credit loans.

**Terms of Lending**

Informal lines of credit and formalized revolving credit arrangements contain specific lending terms, some of which are common to both forms of lending while others are specific to the type of financing provided. The terms of lending discussed here are (1) loans in note form, (2) interest rates, (3) compensating balance requirements, (4) commitment fees, and (5) loan repayment. Other lending terms become important when revolving credit arrangements allow conversion to term loans; these provisions are discussed in Chapter 21.

**LOANS IN NOTE FORM.** In order to make use of a line of credit or a revolving credit arrangement, borrowers execute notes with their lending banks. These notes usually have 90-day maturities. The banks are not legally obligated to renew notes written as part of a line of credit. However, notes that represent loans under revolving credit agreements must be renewed at the request of the borrower unless the borrower violates the conditions of the loan agreement. Each note states the annual interest rate, the interest payment date(s), and the date of the note's maturity.

Banks use notes in order to establish evidence of lending. Minimum sizes are set on the amount of each note. The loan created by the note is not given to the borrower in cash or check form. Rather, the lending bank credits the borrower's checking account for the amount loaned, and the borrower writes checks on the checking account. Generally a borrower may repay a note prior to maturity with no penalty.

**Example:**

A corporation is extended a $100,000 line of credit. The line is available for one year beginning March 1. The bank uses 90-day notes, sets a $10,000 minimum size on each note, and requires interest payments on the first day of each month. The borrower is charged an annual interest rate of 12 percent.

The monthly interest payment is .12/12 months = .01 of the loan amount outstanding during the previous month.

Assume that the corporation borrows $10,000 on April 1, $25,000 on May 1, and $30,000 on June 1. The April note is renewed on July 1. The other notes are paid at maturity.

Interest payments begin on May 1. The amounts on which interest is paid and the interest payments are as follows:

| Date Interest Is Paid | Amount on Which Interest Is Paid | Amount of Interest Paid |
|---|---|---|
| May 1 | $10,000 | $100 |
| June 1 | 35,000 | 350 |
| July 1 | 65,000 | 650 |
| August 1 | 65,000 | 650 |
| September 1 | 40,000 | 400 |
| October 1 | 10,000 | 100 |

**INTEREST RATES.** Although interest rates charged by commercial banks on commercial and industrial loans are determined by numerous factors, there is a well established practice of pricing line-of-credit and revolving credit loans on the prime rate. Historically, the **prime rate** has been described as the interest rate commercial banks charge their most creditworthy business customers. The prime rate became the minimum rate available on commercial and industrial loans.

A nationwide uniform prime rate was first established in 1933 when all banks began charging the same interest rate to their highest quality business borrowers. Until the 1960s the prime rate was administratively set by a few large New York City banks. The prime rate *posted* by these banks was simply adopted by the other banks in the commercial banking system. In 1965, major banks in Boston, Chicago, and San Francisco took the lead in announcing new prime rates.

Floating prime rates were introduced by New York City banks in 1971. This type is now in general use. A **floating prime rate** is a prime rate the value of which is set primarily by conditions in the money markets. At one time the floating prime was based on commercial paper rates. The floating prime is now frequently quoted as 1½ percent above 90-day NCD rates. Major banks located outside of New York City may quote a regional prime equal to the New York City prime plus ½ percent. Banks located in smaller cities tend to quote a local prime that is equal to the regional prime plus ½ percent. Thus, a 10½ percent New York City prime may produce an 11 percent prime in Boston and an 11½ percent prime in other parts of New England.

The prime rate, whether administratively set by commercial banks or determined by money market conditions, has had three major functions:

1. The prime rate has been the minimum bank rate on commercial and industrial loans, available only to the most creditworthy customers.

2. The prime is the base rate used to set loan rates for *nonprime* business customers.

3. Floating prime rates serve as the base rate in lending agreements that allow for variable interest rates during the life of the loan.

Most commercial and industrial loans now carry floating interest rates rather than fixed rate provisions. Only money market rate business loans have fixed interest rates.

Interest rates on money market rate loans, since they are set on the basis of NCD rates and not on prime rates, can often be lower than prime rates. This happens in part because prime rates tend to be somewhat *sticky*. This means that prime rates do not adjust instantly to changes in money market rates. Money market loan rates, however, change daily.

| | Average prime rate | 30-day NCD rates | 30-day NCD rates plus 1½% |
|---|---|---|---|
| January | 11.16% | 8.28% | 9.78% |
| February | 10.98% | 8.40% | 9.90% |
| March | 10.50% | 8.62% | 10.12% |
| April | 10.50% | 8.60% | 10.10% |

**Example:** The following 1983 average prime rates and 30-day NCD rates were taken from the *Federal Reserve Bulletin:*

Assuming that the money market loan rates were priced at 1½ percent above the 30-day NCD rate, money market loan rates were below the average prime rate for all four of these months.

Prime rates will continue to be used in pricing line-of-credit and revolving credit loans. However, very short-term money market rate loans available to corporations may be priced below the prime rate. Although money market rate loans are not effective substitutes for line-of-credit and revolving credit loans, their impact is to diminish the importance of the prime rate as the minimum commercial and industrial loan rate available from commercial banks.

**COMPENSATING BALANCE REQUIREMENTS.** The cash management section in Chapter 7 introduced the concept of compensating balances. Compensating balances are used as follows:

1.  In conjunction with lock box banking

2.  In floating commercial paper (The backup line of credit for commercial paper is actually a special type of revolving credit agreement.)

3.  In revolving credit agreements

4.  As a way of compensating commercial banks for providing check-clearing, collection, and other banking services.

Compensating balances are not a formal provision of line-of-credit financing. However, the borrowing corporation's deposit balance with the lending bank is usually considered in setting the other terms of lending.

The most important use of compensating balances occurs as part of revolving credit agreements. The compensating balances used with revolving credit agreements represent average deposit balances that the borrower must maintain in a noninterest-bearing account at the lending bank. Revolving credit agreements contain two general types of compensating balance requirements:

1.  *A percent of the line* — This type requires the borrower to deposit a stated percentage of the maximum borrowing available under the loan agreement. The stated percentage, or compensating balance, must be maintained during the entire life of the revolving credit agreement.

2.  *A percent of the use* — This type requires the borrower to deposit a stated percentage of the amounts borrowed during the time the loans are outstanding.

Some revolving credit agreements require only one type of compensating balance. Others require the borrower to maintain both types.

**Example:**   One major New England bank has developed five compensating balance alternatives:

1. 10% of the line
2. 15% of the line
3. 10% of the line plus 10% of the use
4. 10% of the line or 20% of the use, whichever is greater
5. 20% of borrowings.

Under the first alternative, a $100,000 revolver requires the borrower to maintain a $10,000 compensating balance with the bank as long as the loan agreement is in force. No added compensating balances are required to support the amounts actually borrowed.

Under the third alternative, compensating balances are required against both the availability and the use of the loan. A $100,000 revolver requires that $10,000 be kept on deposit as a compensating balance for the loan availability. If the borrower executes a $30,000, 90-day note, an additional $3,000 compensating balance is required during the 90-day life of the note.

Compensating balances increase the effective cost of borrowing when they are borrowed. There are times, however, when cash balances kept in a corporation's checking account to meet its normal transactions requirements are large enough to provide part or all of the needed compensating balances.

**Example:**   A corporation's checking account shows an average daily balance of $12,000. The corporation obtains a $200,000 revolving credit agreement and is required to maintain a 5 percent compensating balance against the line. This means that the corporation's checking account balance must average at least 5 percent of $200,000, or $10,000. As long as the checking account average balance meets or exceeds the $10,000 compensating balance requirement, the effective cost of the loan is not increased because the $10,000 compensating balance does not have to be borrowed.

The effective borrowing costs under revolving credit agreements are increased when loan proceeds are needed to meet some or all of the compensating balances. Under these conditions, the effective interest rate is the amount of interest paid on the entire loan as a percentage of the amount of the loan actually available for use by the borrower. Since some of the loan is held as a compensating balance and is unavailable to the borrower, the effective rate is higher than if the entire loan could be used.

The effective interest rate is a function of (1) the nominal interest rate, (2) the frequency of compounding, (3) the compensating balance requirement, (4) the amounts borrowed during the agreement, and (5) the percentage of the compensating balance requirement that must be met with borrowed funds. Table 8-3 contains the effective interest rates for selected compensating balance requirements assuming that all compensating balances are borrowed and that interest is compounded once a year. The *percent-of-line-used* values in Table 8-3 represent the average percentage of the revolving credit agreement actually used by the borrower and does not include the additional borrowed funds held as compensating balances.

The upper third of Table 8-3 lists effective interest rates when the only compensating balance requirement is 20 percent of the use and illustrates that the effective interest rate is constant for a given nominal interest rate regardless of the percentage of the line used. For example, a 10 percent nominal interest rate converts to a 12.5 percent effective rate for each

**Table 8-3.**   **Effective Interest Rates for Selected Compensating Balance Requirements**

| Percent of Line Used | At Nominal Interest Rates of | | | | |
|---|---|---|---|---|---|
| | 8% | 9% | 10% | 11% | 12% |
| | 0% of the Line and 20% of the Use | | | | |
| 30 | 10.00% | 11.25% | 12.50% | 13.75% | 15.00% |
| 40 | 10.00 | 11.25 | 12.50 | 13.75 | 15.00 |
| 50 | 10.00 | 11.25 | 12.50 | 13.75 | 15.00 |
| 60 | 10.00 | 11.25 | 12.50 | 13.75 | 15.00 |
| 70 | 10.00 | 11.25 | 12.50 | 13.75 | 15.00 |
| 80 | 10.00 | 11.25 | 12.50 | 13.75 | 15.00 |
| | 10% of the Line and 10% of the Use | | | | |
| 30 | 11.85% | 13.33% | 14.81% | 16.30% | 17.78% |
| 40 | 11.11 | 12.50 | 13.89 | 15.28 | 16.67 |
| 50 | 10.67 | 12.00 | 13.33 | 14.67 | 16.00 |
| 60 | 10.37 | 11.67 | 12.96 | 14.26 | 15.56 |
| 70 | 10.16 | 11.43 | 12.70 | 13.97 | 15.24 |
| 80 | 10.00 | 11.25 | 12.50 | 13.75 | 15.00 |
| | 15% of the Line and 5% of the Use | | | | |
| 30 | 12.63% | 14.21% | 15.79% | 17.37% | 18.95% |
| 40 | 11.58 | 13.03 | 14.47 | 15.92 | 17.37 |
| 50 | 10.95 | 12.32 | 13.68 | 15.05 | 16.42 |
| 60 | 10.53 | 11.84 | 13.16 | 14.47 | 15.79 |
| 70 | 10.23 | 11.50 | 12.78 | 14.06 | 15.34 |
| 80 | 10.00 | 11.25 | 12.50 | 13.75 | 15.00 |

*Source:* D. Thorndike, *The Thorndike Encyclopedia of Banking and Financial Tables* (Boston, Mass.: Warren, Gorham & Lamont, Inc. 1973). Reproduced with permission.

borrowed dollar available for use by the firm. The two lower portions of this table illustrate that the effective interest rate depends in part on the amounts actually borrowed when compensating balances are required on both the amount of the line and amount of the use. The effective interest rate decreases as the amount borrowed increases, however.

**Example:**

A corporation is negotiating a $300,000 revolving credit agreement that is to carry a 9 percent nominal interest rate. Two alternative compensating balance requirements are available: the firm can maintain either 20 percent of the use or 10 percent of the line and 10 percent of the use. Which alternative is preferable to the borrowing firm?

When the only compensating balance is 20 percent of the amount borrowed, the effective rate is 11.25 percent of the amount available to the firm, regardless of the size of the loan. If the firm needs $150,000 (or 50 percent of the line) to make a purchase, it must borrow $187,500. Of this amount it must keep 20 percent, or $37,500, on deposit as a compensating balance. The remaining $150,000 is available for its use. The firm pays 9 percent interest on the entire loan; 9 percent of $187,500 is $16,875. The effective interest rate is the actual interest paid as a percentage of the loan proceeds available, or:

$$\text{Effective interest rate} = \frac{\$16,875}{\$150,000}$$

$$= .1125 \text{ or } 11.25\%$$

When the compensating balance requirements are 10 percent of the line and 10 percent of the use, the effective interest rate is greater than 11.25 percent unless the entire line is being used. The firm must maintain a compensating balance of $30,000 plus 10 percent of the total amount borrowed. If it needs $150,000, it must borrow $200,000. It keeps 10 percent of this amount ($20,000), plus $30,000 as compensating balances; $150,000 is available to the firm. Interest paid is 9 percent of the entire loan, or $18,000. The effective interest rate is:

$$\text{Effective interest rate} = \frac{\$18,000}{\$150,000}$$

$$= .12 \text{ or } 12\%$$

Only if the firm borrows the entire $300,000 is the effective rate the same for the two alternatives. In this case $60,000 would be kept as compensating balances and $240,000 would be available to the firm.

COMMITMENT FEES. A **commitment fee** is a charge to the borrower by the lending bank that is based on the unused, or unborrowed, amount of the line. Commitment fees represent payments to the lender for committing funds in the form of a revolving credit agreement and are quoted as a percentage per month on the unused portion of the line.

A revolving credit agreement can contain both a compensating balance requirement and a commitment fee. For example, a revolver might require a 10 percent compensating balance against the amount of the line and a commitment fee of ¼ percent per year on the unused amount of the line. While compensating balances against the amount of the line are commonly used, there is a trend toward substituting commitment fees in place of compensating balances required on actual borrowings. Commitment fees increase the effective interest rate on loans as long as borrowings are less than the amount of the line. In addition, these fees provide income to the lending bank even when the line is available but not used.

| | |
|---|---|
| **Example:** | A corporation arranges a $200,000 revolving credit agreement that calls for a compensating balance of 10 percent of the line and a commitment fee of .6 percent per year or .05 percent per month. The bank uses 90-day notes to advance loans. The minimum note size is $5,000. The corporation expects to meet the compensating balance requirement with revolving credit loans.

The agreement goes into effect on April 1. The corporation borrows the $20,000 compensating balance requirement. Subsequent borrowings are $10,000 on May 1 and $10,000 on June 1.

The commitment fee is charged at the end of each month on the unused amount of the line. This fee is computed as follows:

| Month | Total Borrowings | Unused Line | Commitment Fee (.0005) (Unused Line) |
|-------|------------------|-------------|--------------------------------------|
| April | $20,000 | $180,000 | $90 |
| May | 30,000 | 170,000 | 85 |
| June | 40,000 | 160,000 | 80 |

The above example assumes that all borrowings are made at the beginning of the month. This assumption is made in order to simplify the commitment fee calculation for each month. In actual banking practice, loans are executed at various times during the month. The commitment fee is then imposed on the daily average of the amount of the line unused during the month.

**LOAN REPAYMENT.** Loans made under a line of credit or under a revolving credit agreement can be prepaid prior to maturity, or paid or renewed as the notes mature. When a line of credit is about to expire, the borrowing firm can apply for a new line in order to continue using this informal financing source. However, as discussed earlier, the borrowing firm may be required to demonstrate its ability to repay its line of credit by not using the line during some portion of its availability.

Revolving credit agreements may require that all borrowings be repaid by the time the agreement expires. Alternatively, revolving credit agreements with maturities of two years or longer may allow for a portion of the borrowings to be converted into a term loan. Term loans are an instrument of long-term financing and are discussed in Chapter 21.

**Commercial Bank Loans as Financing Instruments**

Commercial bank loans are a major source of commercial and industrial short-term corporate financing. There is nothing to indicate that this financing source will diminish in importance in the future. Although there are several major sources of corporate short-term financing, none of these is a complete substitute for commercial bank lines of credit and revolving credit agreements.

The customer relationship policies pursued by commercial banks are one important reason why business firms look to commercial banks for short-term borrowing. As part of developing this bank-business relationship, commercial banks became corporate financing specialists. Revolving credit agreements and their related lending terms were developed specifically to meet corporate borrowing needs. The revolving credit agreement is also a very flexible borrowing instrument because it—

1. allows the borrower to borrow when funds are needed;

2. does not require the borrower to borrow the entire amount of the line;

3. generally allows the borrower to repay notes before maturity without incurring early payment costs.

Revolving credit agreements are generally more expensive than commercial paper. In addition, compensating balance requirements increase the effective cost of borrowing, as was shown in Table 8-3. Commitment fees can be more expensive than a compensating balance on borrowings. However, as discussed earlier, commercial paper financing is available only to a small number of corporations. Even those firms floating commercial paper on a regular basis rely on commercial bank financing as an important source of funds because of the flexibility of revolving credit agreements and because of the other services available as part of the customer relationship.

## ACCOUNTS RECEIVABLE FINANCING

Trade credit, commercial paper, and revolving credit bank loans can provide substantial amounts of unsecured financing to a corporation. Additional short-term financing can be obtained by using certain corporate assets, such as inventories and accounts receivable, as collateral for obtaining secured loans. Alternatively, receivables can be sold to financial institutions that specialize in business financing. This section explains how corporations use accounts receivable in executing short-term financing strategies.

Pledging
Accounts
Receivable

Using accounts receivable as collateral for short-term loans is called **pledging**. The borrowing firm submits receivables to the lender for pledging. The lender decides which receivables are acceptable as collateral and lends the borrower a percentage of their value. The borrower repays the loan as the payment on the receivables is made. The loan must still be repaid in the event that the receivables become overdue or are defaulted. Loans secured with receivables are available from commercial banks or their business-financing subsidiaries. Receivables pledging is also available from commercial finance companies, nonbank financial institutions that make secured loans. Examples of such companies are General Electric Credit Corporation and Transamerica Financial Corporation. Some commercial finance companies specialize in financing commercial credit while others also engage in financing retail sales.

TERMS OF LENDING. Pledging terms extended by commercial banks and commercial finance corporations contain the following five characteristics:

1. Lenders assume no credit risk. If pledged receivables become uncollectible, the borrower absorbs the bad debts and must still repay the loans.

2. Lenders assume no collection risk. If pledged receivables are not paid by the end of the credit period, the borrowing firm is responsible for collecting the amounts due.

3. Pledging is available either on a notification or a nonnotification basis. Within the terminology of pledging, *notification* means that the customers whose accounts are pledged are notified of that fact and are instructed to send their payments directly to the lender. *Nonnotification* means that the borrower's customers are not notified of the fact that their accounts have been pledged. Most pledging is done on a nonnotification basis.

4. Lenders decide whether or not any particular receivable or group of receivables is acceptable as loan collateral. In addition, they set the maximum percentage of the receivables value against which loans can be made.

5. The effective annual rate on loans secured by pledging receivables is always greater than the prime rate. The minimum interest rate is usually 2 to 5 percent above the prime, and maximum rates are around 24 percent.

THE PLEDGING PROCESS. Before a pledging agreement is entered into, the lender must decide that the risk involved in making secured loans to the borrower does not exceed the degree of risk the lender is willing to accept. In reaching this decision, the lender investigates the financial, managerial, and operating characteristics of the potential borrower. This investigation includes a financial statement analysis and an analysis of the records and record-keeping system used by the borrower. In addition, credit histories are compared against the terms of sale in order to determine the extent to which accounts receivable are paid within the credit period, the percentage of receivables that becomes overdue, and the percentage of receivables that is charged to bad debt expense. If the potential borrower meets the requirements set by the lender, the terms of lending can then be discussed. A formal pledging agreement and related legal documents are signed after all terms have been agreed upon. This agreement sets forth the rights and obligations of each party and allows pledging on a continuous basis.

When the borrower submits a group of accounts receivable for pledging, the lender selects the receivables that are acceptable as loan collateral. Overdue receivables, for example, are not acceptable. Other receivables may be rejected because the purchaser's payment history is unsatisfactory. The dollar value of acceptable receivables is adjusted to allow for possible returns, as well as cash discounts and other allowances. The maximum loan size available to the borrower is determined by multiplying the adjusted receivables by the loan percentage the lender is willing to extend.

---

**Example:**

A corporation submits $140,000 of accounts receivable for pledging purposes. The lender rejects $50,000 of the receivables and reduces the dollar value of the acceptable accounts by 10 percent to allow for returns and cash discounts. The corporation is allowed to borrow up to 70 percent of the adjusted value.

The maximum loan size is:

$$(\$140,000 - \$50,000)(1 - .1)(.70) = \$56,700$$

---

**PLEDGING AS A FINANCING INSTRUMENT.** After a formal agreement has been signed, pledging can provide funds on a continuous basis. Alternatively, a corporation may decide that pledging is to be used only when other loan sources are unavailable or fully utilized. In either case, the biggest advantage of receivables pledging is that the loans are self-liquidating. Given that the lender accepts as collateral only those receivables that have a very low probability of being defaulted, the borrower's receivables will generate the cash needed to repay the loans.

The majority of firms pledging their receivables fall into one of the following categories:

1. New firms that need help in financing their initial working capital

2. Rapidly growing firms that need help in financing their sales growth

3. Firms facing what hopefully is a temporary shortage of working capital and that, for whatever reason, cannot obtain the needed funds through unsecured commercial bank loans

Loans extended under any of these three situations are viewed by lenders as containing extra elements of risk. As a result, borrowing rates are set to compensate lenders for the degree of risk contained in the loans.

Although interest rates associated with pledging exceed commercial bank rates, the dollar costs of using these two financing alternatives may not be so greatly different. This is because pledging agreements provide the exact loan amounts needed and do not contain compensating balance requirements, minimum borrowing size, and minimum loan maturities found in revolving credit agreements. As was discussed in the previous section, revolving credit lending terms can result in corporations borrowing funds in excess of their needs. Interest payments on such excess loans partially offset the higher costs of pledging.

Pledging and revolving credit loans are not close substitutes. Pledging is a form of secured borrowing, is designed to be self-liquidating, and provides very short-term credit. Continuous pledging is required in order to extend the financing period. Loans secured with accounts receivable are more expensive to the borrower than are revolving credit loans because, as described above, pledging occurs most frequently in those situations perceived by lenders as being riskier than typical short-term business financing. Taking all these factors into account, corporate managers generally prefer commercial bank financing and will pledge receivables only when short-term commercial bank financing is not available.

**Factoring Accounts Receivable**

**Factoring** is a second method of financing accounts receivable and consists of selling the receivables to financial institutions. The buying firms are called *factors* and are the same financial institutions that extend loans through receivables pledging. Factoring effectively transfers the accounts receivable credit and collection risks to the factor and allows a seller to minimize or avoid entirely the costs of running its own credit and collection department. Several types of factoring agreements are available. This section deals with standard, or conventional, factoring agreements.

FUNCTIONS OF FACTORS. Factors provide the following major functions when they enter into standard factoring agreements:

1. The factor evaluates the creditworthiness of its client's customers and indicates which receivables it is willing to buy. As a result, corporations that factor on a regular basis will not accept purchase orders until and unless the factor approves their customers' credit.

2. The factor assumes the collection risks for the receivables it purchases. If some receivables become overdue or uncollectible, the factor does not have recourse to the seller and must absorb any extra collection costs along with any bad debts that may result.

3. The factor is responsible for providing and maintaining the accounting system needed for factoring and collecting the receivables.

4. The factor will, for an added fee, allow its client to obtain the factoring proceeds before the end of the credit period.

**TERMS OF FACTORING.** Because factoring involves transferring assets and risks from the selling firm to the factor, standard factoring agreements tend to be long and involved documents. However, the factoring terms of importance to financial managers can be grouped into the following six categories:

1. The factor assumes credit and collection risks without recourse to the seller and agrees to make the funds available to the seller not later than the end of the credit period. For example, if a seller ships goods on net 60-day terms and factors the receivable the same day that the goods are shipped, the proceeds are available from the factor at the end of 60 days.

2. The factor does not assume responsibility for returns or allowances. For this reason, the factor creates what is called a *reserve* against the factored accounts. The reserve equals 5 to 10 percent of the value of the receivables and is used to meet any returns or cash discounts that reduce the value of the receivables. The reserve is made available at the end of the credit period unless claims remain outstanding.

3. Receivables are factored on a notification basis and payments are sent directly to the factor.

4. The price that is paid by the factor for the receivables is computed by subtracting the factoring commission from the value of the receivables.

5. The seller can obtain the factoring proceeds before the end of the credit period. Such early payments are called *advances*. The factor charges a fee for providing advances and deducts the fee from the amount available to the seller.

6. The factoring commission is at least 1½ percent of the value of the factored receivables. The fee for advances, stated as an annual interest rate, is usually 3 to 5 percent above the prime rate. However, the factor pays interest to its client on any amounts that are not withdrawn after the credit period has passed.

**THE FACTORING PROCESS.** Before entering into a factoring agreement, the factor evaluates the risk-return characteristics of the potential client by using techniques similar to those employed when a pledging agreement is being considered. In addition, the client's customer list is examined to determine how many customers are acceptable as credit and collection risks to the factor. This is especially important when the client intends to engage in continuous factoring, thus turning over the credit and collection problem entirely to the factor.

Once a factoring agreement has been signed, the client submits purchase orders to the factor for credit approval. In effect, the client does not accept the order until the factor agrees to purchase the resulting receivable. The factor notifies the client that either the order will qualify for factoring or the order will be accepted only at the client's risk.

When the client ships a factor approved order, the client prepares two copies of the invoice and sends both copies to the factor along with evidence of shipment. The factor mails an invoice to the client's customer. The invoice indicates that the receivable has been assigned to the factor and directs the customer to remit payment directly to the factor. All subsequent paper work related to the receivable is handled by the factor.

---

**Example:**

A factor buys a $10,000 invoice that carries commercial credit terms of net 60 days. The factoring commission is 2 percent, the reserve is 10 percent, and the fee for advances is 12 percent per year. If the client does not request an advance, the amount available at the end of 60 days is $10,000 − $200 = $9,800 — unless some claim has arisen. If the client requests an advance on the same day that the goods are shipped, the amount available is computed as follows:

| | |
|---|---:|
| Accounts receivable | $10,000 |
| Less: Factoring commission | 200 |
| Less: Reserve | 1,000 |
| Funds available for advance | 8,800 |
| Less: Fee on the advance | 176 |
| Funds available | $ 8,624 |

The 2 percent factoring commission and 10 percent reserve are computed on the $10,000 value of the receivables. The advance fee is based on the $8,800 available to be advanced. The $176 reflects two months of interest at 12 percent per year.

The client can draw up to $8,624 immediately. In addition, the client expects the $1,000 reserve to be available at the end of the credit period.

---

When a company routinely factors its receivables, the factor computes a weighted average credit period for all the accounts factored during each month. A reserve is established against the combined receivables, and advances can be drawn against the combined available funds. When the average credit period has passed, the reserve becomes available to the client and is added to whatever funds have not been withdrawn.

**FACTORING AS A FINANCING INSTRUMENT.** Factoring was historically concentrated in the textile industry but eventually spread to the apparel, shoe and furniture industries. Factoring is now an established practice in many areas of business including those that produce and sell sporting goods, toys, automotive accessories, plastics, building materials, frozen fish, and photographic and communication equipment.

The reason for the increasing popularity of factoring is contained in the functions provided by factors. Taken together, these functions allow a seller to avoid the costs of establishing and running its own credit and collection departments. The seller eliminates bad debts that would otherwise occur among its accounts receivable and knows in advance when and how much cash will be available as a result of factoring. The ability to obtain advances allows the seller to take advantage of favorable commercial credit terms it obtains from its own suppliers.

Factoring and commercial bank loans are not close substitutes. However, factoring may be seen as an alternative to pledging, and vice versa. The increasing use of factoring indicates that the associated costs are outweighed by the services provided. The specialized knowledge and experience available from factors is both difficult and expensive for a nonfinancial corporation to develop. The factoring commission is a relatively modest price to pay for transferring the firm's credit and collection risks on receivables. Although the interest rate for advances generally exceeds the rate on commercial bank loans, the client can obtain the exact amount of funds needed from the factor and does not have to meet the terms of lending contained in commercial bank revolving credit agreements.

## INVENTORY FINANCING

Inventories are second in importance to accounts receivable as collateral for obtaining secured short-term loans. Although inventories are considered liquid assets, only those types of inventories that possess certain characteristics are acceptable as collateral by lenders. Acceptable inventories are valued at cost, and borrowers can obtain loans of 70 to 90 percent of their value. Since inventories are physical rather than financial assets, special financing techniques are used for inventory backed loans. For example, floating liens and trust receipts allow the borrower to retain possession of the collateralized inventory, but warehousing techniques put the inventory in the possession of a third party. This section explains the characteristics of inventories that make them acceptable as loan collateral and explains the mechanics of inventory-collateralized short-term loans.

**Inventory Characteristics**

There are three general characteristics that lenders use to judge the acceptability of inventory as loan collateral. These are (1) type of inventory, (2) marketability, and (3) shelf life.

Chapter 7 classified inventories into these four types: raw materials, goods in process, finished goods, and spare parts. In general, only raw materials and finished goods inventories are acceptable as loan collateral.

However, floating lien loans sometimes include all the borrower's inventories. Marketability has the following two components: (1) the existence of a well-organized resale market for the inventory and (2) price stability in the resale market. Inventory must possess both components in order to be acceptable as loan collateral. Shelf life refers to the length of time that inventory remains marketable before it becomes unsalable. The expected shelf life of inventory must exceed the life of the loan in order to be acceptable.

Grains, oil, chemicals, basic metals, lumber, canned foods, and consumer durables such as cars and major appliances possess the desired inventory characteristics. By way of contrast, fashion clothing and ice cream are much less desirable as loan collateral.

The fact that a borrower's inventory contains desirable characteristics does not guarantee that a loan can be arranged. The lender's decision is still based primarily on the borrower's ability to meet the loan payment schedule. Lenders are not in the collateral liquidation business. They use these inventory characteristics to assure themselves that the collateral will be salable in the assumed unlikely event of loan default.

## Floating Liens

A **floating lien** is a claim on all the items that fall in a specified category. A floating lien on a borrower's inventories means that the lender has a claim on all the borrower's inventories. The borrower retains title and possession of the inventories, thus making it difficult for the lender to monitor the collateral.

A loan agreement that contains a floating inventory lien and requires the borrower to pledge accounts receivable with the lender can provide self-liquidating financing for the borrower. The loan finances the purchase of raw material inventories. These inventories provide the initial collateral for the loan. The finished goods inventories that emerge from the production process replace the raw materials as loan collateral. The receivables that result from the sale of the finished goods are pledged as part of the loan agreement. The loan is paid off as the receivables are collected. Thus, the entire production and selling cycle is financed in part by the loan agreement. Because the lender has no control over the inventory, the loan size will usually not exceed 50 percent of the cost of the raw material inventories. However, a loan agreement that contains both a floating inventory lien and the requirement that receivables be pledged gives the lender a claim on most of the borrower's current assets.

## Trust Receipt Loans

Trust receipt financing allows the borrower to retain possession of and to sell the inventory that serves as loan collateral. Unlike floating liens, however, all the items that make up the collateral are listed in the trust agreement and are identified by their serial numbers. The lender has a lien, or claim, on the specific inventory items listed in the trust receipt. Although the lender does not have direct control over the collateral, the borrower can be audited to see if the borrower has sold any of the collateral without remitting the proceeds as specified in the loan agreement.

One of the most common forms of trust receipt lending is called *floor planning*. This finances new car inventories bought by car dealers. The manufacturer ships cars directly to the dealer. The dealer prepares a security agreement that, when given to the lender, creates a lien on all the cars listed in the agreement. Each car is identified by year, make, model or motor number, and serial number. The lender pays the manufacturer for the cars listed in the security agreement. The lien is released as the cars are sold and payment, including interest, is made to the lender. Floor-planning loans made to car dealers can finance as much as 100 percent of the cost of the cars listed in the security agreement. These loans are provided primarily by large finance companies such as General Motors Acceptance Corporation. Commercial banks also provide this type of financing.

**Warehouse**
**Receipt Loans**

**Warehouse receipt loans** provide the lender with direct control over the inventory used as loan collateral. The borrower allows a public warehousing company to take possession of the inventory. The warehouse company issues a receipt for the inventory and will not release the goods unless the receipt is presented. The borrower secures a loan by giving the warehouse receipt to the lender.

There are two types of warehousing arrangements in common use— terminal or public warehousing, and field warehousing.

**TERMINAL WAREHOUSE RECEIPT LOANS.** Under a terminal warehousing arrangement, the borrower hires a public warehousing company to take possession of the inventory. The inventory is transported from the borrower's plant to the public warehouse. The receipt for the inventory issued by the warehousing company is given to the lender. The borrower thus loses possession of the collateral and requires the approval of the lender to regain its use.

Most terminal warehouse receipt loans involve the issuance of nonnegotiable warehouse receipts. However, negotiable receipts can be issued when basic commodities, such as vegetable oils, are stored. This allows the inventory to be sold and title transferred while the goods are still in storage. Other examples of inventory that is used as collateral to obtain terminal warehouse receipt loans, with either negotiable or nonnegotiable receipts, include lumber, basic metals, canned foods, and distilled spirits.

**FIELD WAREHOUSE RECEIPT LOANS.** As an alternative to storing loan collateral in a public warehouse, the borrower can hire a warehouse company to set up a *field warehouse* on the borrower's property. A field warehouse may consist of a fenced off section of the borrower's warehouse or a separate warehouse. In either case, the field warehouse is constructed by the public warehouse company, which issues receipts for the inventory stored in the field warehouse. Thus, as in terminal warehousing, the lender has control over the loan collateral. Field warehousing is desirable when the loan agreement allows the borrower access to the inventory as loan payments are made. In addition, field warehousing may be preferred over terminal warehousing if the inventory is difficult or expensive to transport from the borrower's property to the public warehouse.

**Inventories as a Financing Instrument**

Inventory financing is a specialized method of short-term borrowing that can be used only when the collateral possesses desirable characteristics that are required by the lender. In some areas of business, such as floor planning and food canning, inventory financing is a routinely used short-term financing technique. Alternatively, inventory financing can provide short-term loans when unsecured borrowings are not available or when lines of credit are fully utilized.

Interest rates on inventory loans are set several percentage points above the prime rate. In addition, the borrower must pay for the services provided by a public warehouse company when warehouse receipt loans are used. In many cases, therefore, the use of inventory as loan collateral is the most expensive technique of short-term financing.

---

# SUMMARY

This chapter has discussed the working capital aspects of current liability management. Trade credit, commercial bank loans, and commercial paper were identified as the most important unsecured financing sources to a corporation. The use of accounts receivable and inventories in obtaining secured short-term financing was also considered. Each alternative financing technique was explained and the desirability of each alternative was evaluated within the context of its advantages and limitations.

The two most important short-term corporate financing sources are trade credit and commercial bank loans. The importance of trade credit is due in part to its ease of availability. In addition, trade credit can represent as much as 40 percent of a corporation's short-term liabilities. The importance of commercial bank loans is due to the concept of the customer relationship. One of the lending areas that commercial banks specialize in is that of short-term corporate financing. Commercial banks have developed lines of credit and revolving credit agreements to meet the needs of their corporate customers.

Commercial paper is a third source of unsecured financing. The growing importance of this financing instrument is due to the absence of restrictions and covenants found in commercial bank loans. However, since most corporations cannot qualify for a P-1 rating, this source is currently restricted to less than 2,000 corporations.

Accounts receivable and inventories can provide collateral for obtaining secured short-term loans. Accounts receivable can be pledged or factored. Factoring, however, involves the outright sale of the receivables as opposed to collateralizing them as security for a loan. Pledging is a self-liquidating financing strategy. Continuous pledging can provide funds over an extended financing period. When a corporation decides to routinely factor its receivables, the factoring company assumes the responsibility and risks involved in extending credit and collecting the receivables. The use of inventory as loan collateral can be accomplished by using floating liens, trust receipts, or a public warehousing company. However, the lender must be willing to accept the inventory as loan collateral.

Lenders realize that collateralizing a loan with receivables or inventories does little to change the probability that the borrower will default on the loan. Financial assets, such as accounts receivable, are generally more desirable as collateral than are inventories of physical assets. In the event of loan default, lenders, if they have done an adequate job of selecting the accounts receivable to be pledged, can expect to recover all or most of the unpaid loan principal and interest. However, when inventories serve as loan collateral, lenders face the prospect of incurring the extra time and costs involved with selling the collateral. In addition, the dollar proceeds from selling the inventory are uncertain, further reducing the probability that defaulted loan and interest balances will be fully recovered.

# QUESTIONS

**8-1.** Explain each of the following terms of credit:
 *a.* 1/10 net 30
 *b.* net 10 EOM
 *c.* net 20 March 1

**8-2.** In what ways can the use of trade credit be costly to a corporation?

**8-3.** Identify some of the major uses of commercial paper.

**8-4.** When describing the multiple transactions between business firms and commercial banks, explain what is meant by the term *the customer relationship.*

**8-5.** What is the distinction between a prime rate and a floating prime rate? What is the common concept underlying these two rates?

**8-6.** Explain the two types of compensating balance requirements used with revolving credit agreements.

**8-7.** Explain the role of commitment fees in revolving credit agreements.

**8-8.** What is the major distinction between pledging and factoring of accounts receivable?

**8-9.** Identify the major terms of lending when accounts receivable are pledged as loan collateral.

**8-10.** Identify the major terms contained in standard factoring agreements.

**8-11.** Identify the general characteristics used by lenders in judging the acceptability of inventory as loan collateral.

**8-12.** What is the major difference between a floating lien and a trust receipt?

8-13. What is the major difference between terminal warehousing and field warehousing?

---

# PROBLEMS

8-1. If terms of credit are stated as 2/15 net 30, compute the annualized interest rate when cash discounts are not taken.

8-2. Compute the annualized interest rate on missed cash discounts when terms of credit are 3/10 net 60.

8-3. A corporation is granted a $130,000 line of credit. Borrowings under the line are available on February 1. The bank uses 90-day notes. The interest rate is 15% per year and is computed as 1.25% per month.

All borrowings and interest payments are made on the first business day of the month. Interest payments for each month are computed on the loan outstanding on the last business day of the previous month. Borrowings are as follows:

> February 1: $50,000
> March 1: $40,000
> April 1: $30,000

The February note is renewed in May and the March note is renewed in June.
For each month from March through September, compute the loan size on which interest is paid and the corresponding interest payment.

8-4. A $400,000 revolving credit agreement contains the following compensating balance requirements: 10% of the line and 5% of the use. Compute the compensating balance requirements when borrowings equal $50,000.

8-5. A $300,000 revolving credit agreement contains a commitment fee of ½% per month. EOM loan sizes are as follows:

| Last Day of | Loan Size |
|---|---|
| July | $240,000 |
| August | 220,000 |
| September | 200,000 |
| October | 200,000 |
| November | 170,000 |
| December | 140,000 |

The commitment fee is based on EOM loan sizes. Compute the commitment fee for each of these six months.

8-6. A factor buys a $165,000 invoice that carries credit terms of net 90 days. The factoring commission is 1½%, the reserve is 10%, and the fee for advances is 12% per year. The client requests an advance on the same day that the goods are shipped. Compute the advance received by the client.

# SELECTED REFERENCES

American Banker's Association. *A Banker's Guide to Commercial Loan Analysis*. Washington, D.C.: American Banker's Association, 1977.

The Conference Board. *Cash Management*. New York: The Conference Board, 1973.

Gendreau, B. "When is the Prime Rate Second Choice?" *Business Review* (May-June, 1983).

Hurley, E. "The Commercial Paper Market." *Federal Reserve Bulletin*, Vol. 63, No. 6 (June, 1977).

————. "The Commercial Paper Market since the Mid-Seventies." *Federal Reserve Bulletin*, Vol. 68 (June, 1982).

Merris, R. "The Prime Rate." *Business Conditions* (April, 1975).

————. "Prime Rate Updated." *Economic Perspectives*, Vol. 2, No. 3 (May-June, 1978).

————. "The Prime Rate Revisited." *Economic Perspectives*, Vol. 1, No. 4 (July-August, 1977).

Naitore, I. *Modern Factoring*. New York: American Management Association, 1969.

Trepeta, W. "Changes in Bank Lending Practices, 1979-81." *Federal Reserve Bulletin*, Vol. 67 (September, 1981).

Vancil, R., ed. *Financial Executive's Handbook*. Homewood, Ill.: Dow Jones-Irwin, Inc., 1970.

# PART 4

# Capital Budgeting

The remainder of this text emphasizes the long-term aspects of managerial finance, and the four chapters that make up Part 4 are an introduction to this topic.

Chapter 9 presents the mathematics of finance and explains how to adjust cash flows for the time value of money. This is a fundamental topic; the applications of financial mathematics go far beyond managerial finance.

Chapters 10, 11, and 12 explain the concepts, criteria, and decision rules of capital budgeting. Chapters 10 and 11 present some capital-budgeting techniques that can be used when future cash flows are known with certainty or can be accurately forecast. Chapter 12 introduces capital budgeting under risk and explains how the statistical properties of probability distributions can be used to analyze capital-budgeting alternatives when the values of future cash flows are uncertain.

# CHAPTER 9

## Mathematics
of
Finance

*A few years ago, a commercial bank in Pittsburgh, Pennsylvania, wanted to inform potential depositors of the high rate of interest it paid on savings accounts. The bank ran roadside billboard ads that read: "The XYZ Bank is the Most Interest-ing Place in Town." A subsequent informal poll among college students indicated that they had missed the message!*

*The first section of this chapter deals with explicit and implicit interest rates and the general assumptions that must be made in computing compound interest. Then the two fundamental procedures for computing interest—compounding and discounting—are explained in detail. The examples used to illustrate these procedures are intentional simplifications of actual situations. They are presented in this fashion in order to stress the importance of the underlying concepts. The last section presents a number of special applications of compounding and discounting techniques.*

## TIME VALUE OF MONEY

The concept of interest is one of the central ideas in finance. Individuals, as well as business organizations, frequently encounter situations that involve cash receipts or disbursements over several periods of time. When this happens, interest rates and interest payments become important and sometimes vital considerations.

Business firms deal with interest rates in both financing and investment decisions. Short-term commercial and industrial loans may be obtained at close-to-prime rates. Long-term financing through bond issues requires interest returns to the bondholders. Corporate investments in such things as real estate, machinery, and equipment are evaluated on the basis of expected profits. Since such investments require that funds be committed over several years, the expected profits are measured in terms of rates of return. Such rates are equivalent to receiving interest returns on the invested funds.

**Explicit and Implicit Interest Rates**

**Interest** is the price paid for the use of money over time. The rate of interest for a given transaction is frequently stated *explicitly*; that is, a savings and loan association may offer a 6.5 percent return for one year on savings deposits. Or a mortgage company may offer 20-year home mortgages at an interest rate of 12 percent.

Sometimes the interest rate is *implicit* in the transaction. For example, many commercial banks offer free checking accounts to customers who keep a $200 minimum balance in their account. Since the same $200 would earn interest if deposited in a savings account, there is an implicit interest cost to the bank customers of keeping a minimum checkbook balance.

**General Assumptions Needed in Computing Interest**

In order to focus on interest rates and to avoid complications that would tend to blur the essential concepts, this chapter makes use of three general assumptions: certainty, discrete time periods, and yearly interest computations.

FIRST ASSUMPTION: CERTAINTY. Certainty is the most restrictive assumption used throughout the chapters in this text. All current and future data values are assumed to be known with certainty, or a set of techniques exists for estimating the unknown values. Certainty also applies to the occurrence of future events. This means that future payments will be made or received as prescribed. There is no uncertainty as to whether or not the payments will materialize.

The reason for using this assumption is simple: The presence of uncertainty requires the introduction of techniques that cannot be appreciated or thoroughly understood unless the simpler case of certainty is used as a point of departure.

**SECOND ASSUMPTION: DISCRETE TIME PERIODS.** Time is divided into yearly intervals. The time that elapses between the last day of two consecutive years is measured as one year. For example, Year 6 is the time that elapses from the last day of Year 5 to the last day of Year 6. The immediate present is referred to as the end of *Year zero.*

| | |
|---|---|
| **Example:** | An investment that is described as producing a cash inflow two years from now in return for an immediate cash outflow is said to have an outflow at the end of Year zero and an inflow at the end of Year 2. For ease of reference, the *end of Year zero* is called *Time zero* or *Year zero;* the *end of Year 5* is simply called *Year 5.* |

This assumption does not require cash flows to occur at December 31 of each year. What is required is that cash flows be allowed to occur only at points of time that are separated by one-year intervals.

| | |
|---|---|
| **Example:** | If an investment is made on March 15, then that date becomes Time zero. A cash inflow from that investment occurring two years later on March 15 is said to occur at Year 2. |

This assumption thus allows us to abstract from specific calendar dates and to measure time from the point at which a particular investment or financing program begins.

It is frequently desirable to illustrate cash flows over a period of time. An outflow of $5,000 at Time zero that produces cash inflows of $1,000 in Year 2 and $6,000 in Year 4 can be depicted as follows:

| | End of Year | | | | |
|---|---|---|---|---|---|
| | 0 | 1 | 2 | 3 | 4 |
| Cash Flows | $5,000 | | $1,000 | | $6,000 |

**THIRD ASSUMPTION: YEARLY INTEREST COMPUTATIONS.** Interest is computed once a year and the computation is made at the end of the year. This assumption is thus consistent with the second assumption.

In reality, many situations involve monthly, daily, or even continuous interest computations. Monthly mortgage payments require monthly interest payments. Many commercial banks and savings and loan associations offer daily or continuous interest compounding on savings deposits. On the other hand, returns to corporate investments made in real capital, such as real estate and manufacturing plants, are measured on an annual basis even though cash flows may occur at several points of time within a given year. For this reason a brief discussion of intrayear interest computations is included at the end of this chapter. Although intrayear compounding has some interesting implications, this topic is considered to be a side issue in a textbook devoted to the fundamentals of finance.

## COMPOUNDING METHODS

There are two ways of depositing payments into an interest-bearing account. These are *single payments* and a *series of payments*. To simplify the procedures used in determining the amount of compounded money that results from either way of depositing payments, the use of interest rate tables is explained and a substantial number of examples are presented.

**Compounding Single Payments**

When a given amount of money is deposited in an interest-bearing account and is allowed to earn interest for a length of time, the resulting dollar value of the deposit account is called the **compound amount**. The original deposit is referred to as the **principal**. The process of adding interest and determining the resulting amount is called **compounding**. Each time compounding occurs interest is earned on all interest previously earned as well as on the principal. The **compounding frequency** is the number of times per year that interest is added to the deposit account. The third assumption of the previous section set the compounding frequency at once per year.

---

**Example:**

The amount of $5,000 is deposited into a savings account that pays 8 percent compounded once a year. The deposit is made at Year zero. At the end of Year 1, the compound amount available is:

$$\text{Compound amount} = \$5,000 + \$5,000(.08) \qquad \text{(9-1)}$$
$$= \$5,000(1 + .08) \qquad \text{(9-2)}$$
$$= \$5,400$$

If the $5,400 is left on deposit for a second year, the resulting compound amount is:

$$\text{Compound amount} = \$5,400 + \$5,400(.08)$$
$$= \$5,400(1 + .08)$$
$$= \$5,832$$

---

COMPOUND INTEREST DEFINED. In the above example the $5,000 principal grew to a compound amount of $5,832 over a two-year period. Since there was only one deposit, the $832 increase in principal was due entirely to interest. The amount of $400 was earned in Year 1, and $432 was earned in Year 2. Of the $432 earned in Year 2, $32 occurred because 8 percent was earned on the $400 of interest earned in Year 1 and kept on deposit in Year 2. The $32 is interest earned on interest, and this is what is meant by the term **compound interest.**

THE BASIC EQUATION. Four variables are involved when dealing with compound amount, single payment problems. These variables, along with their symbolic representations, are:

$$P_0 = \text{principal at Time zero}$$

$$i = \text{the annual rate of interest}$$

$$t = \text{the number of years over which the principal earns compound interest}$$

$$A_t = \text{the compound amount after } t \text{ years}$$

The compound amount available one year after the principal has been deposited is:

$$A_1 = P_0 + P_0(i) \tag{9-3}$$

$$\text{or} \quad A_1 = P_0(1 + i) \tag{9-4}$$

Note that Equations 9-3 and 9-4 are generalizations of Equations 9-1 and 9-2.

If $A_1$ is allowed to earn interest for one year, then:

$$A_2 = A_1 + A_1(i)$$

$$\text{or} \quad A_2 = A_1(1 + i) \tag{9-5}$$

Substituting the value of $A_1$ given in Equation 9-4 into Equation 9-5:

$$A_2 = P_0(1 + i)(1 + i)$$

$$\text{or} \quad A_2 = P_0(1 + i)^2 \tag{9-6}$$

Equation 9-6 can be illustrated with the use of the data in the previous example that illustrated Equation 9-1, as follows:

$$A_2 = \$5,000(1 + .08)^2$$

$$A_2 = \$5,000(1.1664)$$

$$A_2 = \$5,832$$

The advantage of Equation 9-6 is that the intermediate value of $A_1$ does not have to be computed. In addition, Equation 9-6 can be generalized as follows: the compound amount $A_t$ which results from depositing $P_0$ dollars in an account that earns $i$ percent over $t$ years is given as:

$$A_t = P_0(1 + i)^t \qquad (9\text{-}7)$$

Equation 9-7 is the basic form used to analyze single payment problems. However, for large values of $i$ or $t$, this equation is cumbersome to use, even when electronic calculators are available. Fortunately a special table is available that reduces the computational requirements to the point that hand calculations are possible.

THE COMPOUND AMOUNT, SINGLE PAYMENT TABLE. Appendix Table A-1 can be used to solve single payment problems. That table sets $P_0$ at \$1 and computes compound amounts for alternative combinations of $i$ and $t$. Hence, Appendix Table A-1 contains the values for $(1 + i)^t$ in Equation 9-7. A portion of that table is shown as Table 9-1.

**Table 9-1.**   Compound Amount of One Dollar

| Year | 6% | 7% | 8% | 9% | 10% |
|------|------|------|------|------|------|
| 1 | 1.060 | 1.070 | 1.080 | 1.090 | 1.100 |
| 2 | 1.124 | 1.145 | 1.166 | 1.188 | 1.210 |
| 3 | 1.191 | 1.225 | 1.260 | 1.295 | 1.331 |
| 4 | 1.262 | 1.311 | 1.360 | 1.412 | 1.464 |
| 5 | 1.338 | 1.403 | 1.469 | 1.539 | 1.611 |

**Example:**   A deposit of \$1,000 is made in a savings account that earns 7 percent compounded yearly. What is the compound amount available after 4 years?

Obtain the Table 9-1 value corresponding to 7 percent and 4 years. This is 1.311. Substitute the given data into Equation 9-7 and compute $A_4$.

$$A_4 = \$1,000(1.311) = \$1,311$$

OTHER COMPOUND AMOUNT, SINGLE PAYMENT APPLICATIONS. The basic single payment equation can also be used to find interest rates, as well as the number of years that will be needed for the compound amount to equal the desired value. In general, if the values of any three of the variables in Equation 9-7 are known, the value of the fourth variable can be found by solving the equation for the unknown variable and obtaining values for $(1 + i)^t$ from Appendix Table A-1.

*Finding the Interest Rate.* Estimating the rate of return on an investment is a recurring problem in corporate finance. A useful approach is to treat the rate of return as an implicit interest rate and to use the methods given in this chapter.

**Example:**

A company is offered a contract that has the following terms: an immediate cash outlay of $15,000 followed by a cash inflow of $17,900 three years from now. What is the company's rate of return on this contract?

Treat the $15,000 outflow as a principal which the company deposits into an account that pays an unknown rate of interest but returns a compound amount of $17,900 after three years. Substitute these values into Equation 9-7:

$$\$17,900 = \$15,000(1 + i)^3$$

$$\frac{\$17,900}{\$15,000} = (1 + i)^3$$

$$1.193 = (1 + i)^3$$

The compound amount, single payment table value corresponding to the interest rate on this three-year investment is 1.193. Hence, look up the three-year *row* in Table 9-1 and read *horizontally* until you find the table value closest to 1.193 — which is 1.191 and represents a 6 percent interest rate. Thus, the actual rate of return on the contract is slightly greater than 6 percent.

*Finding the Number of Years.* Equation 9-7 can be used to estimate the number of years that are required for an amount of money deposited at a specified interest rate to produce a desired compound amount.

**Example:**

A deposit of $1,000 is made in an interest-bearing account that pays 10 percent compounded yearly. The investor's goal is $1,500. How many years must the principal earn compound interest before the desired amount is realized?

Substitute the values into Equation 9-7:

$$\$1,500 = \$1,000(1 + .10)^t$$

$$\frac{\$1,500}{\$1,000} = (1 + .10)^t$$

$$1.5 = (1 + .10)^t$$

Now look up the 10 percent *column* in Table 9-1 and read *vertically* until you find a table value that equals or exceeds the computed value of 1.5 — this is 1.611, which corresponds to five years. If the $1,000 principal is left at 10 percent interest for five years, the resulting compound amount will be $1,611. This exceeds the desired $1,500. If the same principal was left at 10 percent interest for only four years, the compound amount available will be only $1,464. The need to leave the deposit for the entire fifth year is due to the assumption of compounding only at the end of each year.

**Compounding Annuities**

An **annuity** is a series of cash flows that are equal in size and occur over equally spaced points in time. Students may tend to recognize annuities only in the case of equal annual cash flows. It must be realized that monthly mortgage payment schedules and semiannual bond interest payments are also examples of annuities.

One basic annuity problem concerns finding the compound amount that results from making annuity payments into an interest-bearing account. Not surprisingly, this final amount is called the *compound amount of the annuity.*

**Example:**

Four equal annual payments of $1,000 are made into a deposit account that pays 6 percent per year. What is the compound amount of the annuity immediately after the last payment?

Assume that payments are made at Years 0, 1, 2, and 3. Using the compound amount, single payment table, compound each payment individually. Then add these compound amounts together. The compound amount of the annuity is $4,375.

The relationships between the annuity payments and their compound amounts are graphically illustrated in Figure 9-1.

**Figure 9-1.**      **Compound Amount Annuity, Four $1,000 Payments, 6 Percent Rate**

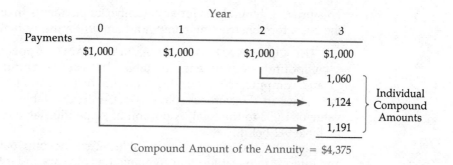

Compound Amount of the Annuity = $4,375

Note that the question called for computing the compound amount of the annuity at a time described as *immediately after the last payment*. This implies that the last payment earns no interest, as shown in Figure 9-1. In the Year 3 column of Figure 9-1, the compound amount of the $1,000 payment made at the end of Year 3 is exactly $1,000. Using Year 3 as a reference, Figure 9-1 shows that the Year 2 payment is compounded once. Similarly, the Year 1 payment is compounded twice; the Year zero payment is compounded three times. Measuring the compound amount of an annuity immediately after its last payment as opposed to some other time allows annuity interest tables to be derived directly from single payment tables. This approach also provides efficient solution techniques for problems that contain combinations of annuities and single payments.

**THE BASIC EQUATION.** The compound amount of the annuity shown in Figure 9-1 can be written in equation form. Let $S_n$ represent the compound amount (or sum) of an annuity consisting of $n$ payments. Then substitute the values given in the previous example:

$$S_4 = \$1,000(1.191) + \$1,000(1.124) + \$1,000(1.060) + \$1,000(1.0) \qquad \text{(9-8)}$$

Factoring the $1,000 constant from each term yields:

$$S_4 = \$1,000(1.191 + 1.124 + 1.060 + 1.0) \qquad \text{(9-9)}$$

$$= \$1,000(4.375) = \$4,375 \qquad \text{(9-10)}$$

The first three terms inside the parentheses of Equation 9-9 are table values taken from the compound amount, single payment table. Therefore, the compound amount of the four payment annuity can be obtained by—

1.  adding the first three compound amount, single payment table values for a given interest rate;

2.  adding a value of 1.000 to that total;

3.  multiplying by the value of *one* payment.

This process generalizes for any number of payments in an annuity and is the basis for constructing compound amount annuity tables.

**THE COMPOUND AMOUNT ANNUITY TABLE.** Appendix Table A-2 is a compound amount annuity table. It assumes annuity payments of $1 and computes compounded amounts of the annuity by summing up the values in the vertical columns of Appendix Table A-1 and adding a value of 1.000 to the total. A portion of Appendix Table A-2 is reproduced in Table 9-2 below.

Note that the values given in Table 9-2 are for combinations of *payments* and interest rates rather than combinations of years and interest rates. This

**Table 9-2.**   **Compound Amount of an Annuity**

| Number of Payments | 6% | 7% | 8% | 9% | 10% |
|---|---|---|---|---|---|
| 1 | 1.000 | 1.000 | 1.000 | 1.000 | 1.000 |
| 2 | 2.060 | 2.070 | 2.080 | 2.090 | 2.100 |
| 3 | 3.184 | 3.215 | 3.246 | 3.278 | 3.310 |
| 4 | 4.375 | 4.440 | 4.506 | 4.573 | 4.641 |
| 5 | 5.637 | 5.751 | 5.866 | 5.985 | 6.105 |

is done in order to point out the fact that the four payment annuity in Figure 9-1, for example, occurs over a period of only three years. When using annuity tables, the number of payments is counted rather than the number of years. Hence, an annuity whose first payment occurs in Year 4 and whose last payment occurs in Year 13 contains 10 payments within a nine-year interval. The correct compound amount annuity table value would be found in the ten payment row, and the compound amount of the annuity would occur right after the 10th payment. Measuring the compound amount of an annuity *immediately after the last payment* is an assumption unique to this table.

Appendix Table A-2 (and Table 9-2) are used as follows: Let:

$S_n$ = compound amount of an annuity of $n$ payments

$P$ = the value of *one* payment

$V_{i,n}$ = the table value corresponding to the annual rate of interest and the number of payments in the annuity

Then:

$$S_n = P(V_{i,n})\qquad\text{(9-11)}$$

Equation 9-11 illustrates the four variables that occur when annuities are compounded. These are:

1.  The value of one payment

2.  The interest rate

3.  The number of payments

4.  The compound amount of the annuity

When the values of any three variables are given, the value of the fourth variable can be determined by algebraic manipulation of Equation 9-11.

**Example:**   What is the compound amount that results when three equal yearly payments of $2,000 are deposited into an account that earns 7 percent compounded yearly?

The table value corresponding to three payments and 7 percent is 3.215. Substitute into Equation 9-11:

$$S_3 = \$2,000(3.215)$$

$$= \$6,430$$

**Example:**   A four payment annuity of $3,000 per year is deposited into an account that pays 9 percent compounded yearly. The annuity payments begin in Year 12. What is the compound amount of the annuity?

The compound amount of the annuity is:

$$S_4 = \$3,000(4.573)$$

$$= \$13,719$$

In the second example given above, the fact that the annuity begins in Year 12 and ends in Year 15 is irrelevant to computing its compound amount because the table only compounds over the time interval during which annuity payments are made. By way of further example, if the above annuity began in Year 50 rather than Year 12, its compound amount would still be $13,719 unless the other variables were changed.

**OTHER COMPOUND AMOUNT ANNUITY APPLICATIONS.** Equation 9-11 for the compound amount of an annuity can be manipulated to solve for the interest rate variable, as well as the number-of-payments variable, in a manner that is quite similar to that used in handling compound amount, single payment problems.

*Finding the Interest Rate.* Some financial contracts and certain types of corporate investments can be described as yielding a future sum in return for making a specific number of annuity payments. The rate of return is an important determinant in accepting or rejecting such opportunities, but it is rarely stated explicitly. The implied rate can be obtained by treating the future sums as the compound amount of the annuity payments and solving for the interest rate by using Equation 9-11.

**Example:**   Three equal yearly payments of $3,000 are offered in return for $9,800 to be received upon making the last annuity payment. What is the implied rate of return?

Let $9,800 be the compound amount of the annuity. Then substitute into Equation 9-11 and solve for the required table value:

$$\$9,800 = \$3,000(V_{i,n})$$

$$\frac{\$9,800}{\$3,000} = V_{i,n}$$

$$3.266 = V_{i,n}$$

Then look up the three payment *row* in Table 9-2 for the table values closest to 3.266. The 8 percent table value is 3.246, and the 9 percent table value is 3.278. Since the computed value of 3.266 lies between these two table values, the implied rate of return is greater than 8 percent and less than 9 percent.

**Example:**  In setting up an educational fund for a daughter's college expenses, the very proud and equally brand-new parents agree to make five yearly payments of $5,000 each into a "special college fund program." The first payment is to be made 12 years from now, and the special fund promises that upon making the last payment the amount available will have grown to $30,000. What is the rate of return on this special fund?

The final amount of $30,000 can be looked at as the compound amount of the annuity. Substitute these figures into Equation 9-11 and solve for the associated table value:

$$\$30,000 = \$5,000(V_{i,n})$$

$$6 = V_{i,n}$$

Then look at the five payment row in Table 9-2. The computed value of 6.000 falls between the table values of 5.985 and 6.105. Hence, the rate of return on this annuity is between 9 percent and 10 percent.

---

In the second example given above, the fact that the annuity does not begin until 12 years from now is irrelevant in computing the interest rate — or the rate of return the annuity earns — because the annuity table compounds only during the time interval over which the annuity payments are being made.

*Finding the Number of Payments.* Given the rate of return, the size of the desired final amount, and the value of each annuity payment, the number of payments required to attain the future sum of regular (annuity) deposits can be determined by using Equation 9-11.

---

**Example:**  How many annual deposits of $1,000 each must be made into an account paying 6 percent compounded per year in order to accumulate $5,500?

Let the compound amount of the annuity be $5,500. Substitute into Equation 9-11 and solve for the desired table value:

$$\$5,500 = \$1,000(V_{i,n})$$

$$\frac{\$5,500}{\$1,000} = V_{i,n}$$

$$5.5 = V_{i,n}$$

Then look at the 6 percent *column* in Table 9-2 and read *down* until a table value equals or exceeds the computed value of 5.5. The computed value falls between 4.375 and 5.637. Thus, the correct answer is 5.637 and corresponds to a value of five payments. Given that payments are made only once a year, four payments will yield only $4,375; hence, a fifth payment is necessary.

## Discounting Methods

Up to now, attention has centered on future values or compound amounts of single payments and annuities. Of equal importance to business and finance generally, and of specific importance in subsequent chapters, is the problem of determining the time value at *Year zero* of a future payment or series of payments. Implicit or explicit interest rates continue to reflect the time value of money. The three general assumptions introduced earlier are retained. If you have a basic understanding of the why's and how's of compounding, this section will increase your ability to handle time value problems and will present no additional conceptual difficulties.

**The Present Value Concept**

The **present value** of a future payment or series of payments is the dollar value at Year zero of the future payment or payments adjusted for the time value of money. **Discounting** is the term given to the set of techniques used to compute present values. Present values can be computed for future single payments or future annuities.

**Discounting Single Payments**

Four variables are used in present value, single payment problems. These are:

$A_t$ = the payment that occurs $t$ years from now

$i$   = the annual rate of interest

$t$   = the number of years over which the future payment is discounted

$P_0$ = the present value of the future payment, discounted at $i$ percent per year over $t$ years

**THE BASIC EQUATION.** The present value of a cash amount due one year from now can be discounted at a rate $i$ as follows:

$$P_0 = \frac{A_1}{(1 + i)} \qquad \text{(9-12)}$$

**Example:**

The present value of $1,000, due one year from now and discounted at 6 percent is:

$$P_0 = \frac{\$1,000}{(1 + .06)}$$

$$= \$943.39$$

This present value can be interpreted as follows: $943.39 invested at a 6 percent rate of return will grow to $1,000 in one year. Hence, the $943.39 is the value now, or the present value of $1,000 when the Time zero deposit earns 6 percent for one year.

Equation 9-12 and the accompanying example may appear to suggest that compounding and discounting are merely different sides of the same coin. Compare Equations 9-4 and 9-12. In general, this is true; the relationships between compounding and discounting are explored in some detail later in this chapter.

In general, the present value of a payment occurring $t$ years from now discounted at an annual rate of $i$ percent is computed by using the following basic equation:

$$P_0 = \frac{A_t}{(1 + i)^t} \qquad (9\text{-}13)$$

**THE PRESENT VALUE, SINGLE PAYMENT TABLE.** Appendix Table A-3 is used to solve present value, single payment problems. The body of that table contains the values of

$$\frac{1}{(1 + i)^t}$$

for different values of $i$ and $t$. When that table is used, the basic equation takes the following form:

$$P_0 = A_t \left[ \frac{1}{(1 + i)^t} \right] \qquad (9\text{-}14)$$

A portion of Appendix Table A-3 is reproduced in Table 9-3.

The table values in Table 9-3 (and Appendix Table A-3) correspond to the bracketed term in Equation 9-14. Hence, a given $A_t$ value is multiplied by the corresponding table value in order to arrive at the desired present value.

**Example:**

What is the present value of $10,000 due five years from now discounted at 10 percent?

The present value, single payment table value for five years and 10 percent is .621. The present value is thus computed as:

$$P_0 = \$10,000(.621)$$

$$= \$6,210$$

**Table 9-3.**        **Present Value of One Dollar**

| Year | 6% | 7% | 8% | 9% | 10% |
|------|------|------|------|------|------|
| 1 | .943 | .935 | .926 | .917 | .909 |
| 2 | .890 | .873 | .857 | .842 | .826 |
| 3 | .840 | .816 | .794 | .772 | .751 |
| 4 | .792 | .763 | .735 | .708 | .683 |
| 5 | .747 | .713 | .681 | .650 | .621 |

**OTHER PRESENT VALUE, SINGLE PAYMENT APPLICATIONS.** As with previous equations and tables, simple algebraic manipulations allow Equation 9-14 to be solved for any one variable when the other three variables are known. The desired answers are obtained with the help of Appendix Table A-3 (or Table 9-3).

*Finding the Interest Rate.* Although the terms of a contract may spell out all the relevant cash flows, the problem of determining the rate of return to the lender or investor may still remain. When single payments are involved, the implied interest rate approach used for compound amount problems can be readily adapted for use with present value tables.

**Example:**        A $1,200 loan is to be repaid as to principal and interest at the end of Year 3 by making a $1,500 payment. What is the rate of interest on the loan?

Let the present value of the loan be $1,200. Substitute into Equation 9-14 and solve for the table value:

$$\$1,200 = \$1,500 \left[ \frac{1}{(1 + i)^3} \right]$$

$$\frac{\$1,200}{\$1,500} = \left[ \frac{1}{(1 + i)^3} \right]$$

$$.8 = \left[ \frac{1}{(1 + i)^3} \right]$$

Look at the Year 3 *row* in Table 9-3 and locate the table values closest to .8. The resulting table values are .816 for 7 percent and .794 for 8 percent. Thus, the loan returns a compound rate of interest between 7 percent and 8 percent.

*Finding the Number of Years.* The following example demonstrates how Equation 9-14 can be used to determine the number of years required for a present value to equal its future value at a given rate of yearly compounding.

**Example:** How many years are required for a $1,000 deposit to grow to $1,200 when interest is compounded yearly at 6 percent?

Let the $1,000 be the present value of the future $1,200. Substitute into Equation 9-14 and solve for the desired table value.

$$\$1,000 = \$1,200 \left[ \frac{1}{(1 + .06)^t} \right]$$

$$\frac{\$1,000}{\$1,200} = \left[ \frac{1}{(1 + .06)^t} \right]$$

$$.833 = \left[ \frac{1}{(1 + .06)^t} \right]$$

Look at the 6 percent *column* in Table 9-3 and read *down* until a table value equals or falls below the computed table value of .833. The table value that meets this requirement is .792 and corresponds to four years. Therefore, the $1,000 will have to be left on deposit for four years (and compounded four times) before it grows to the desired value of $1,200.

**Discounting Annuities**    Some of the most frequent and important applications of the mathematics of finance involve computing present values of annuities. Determining loan repayment schedules, computing bond prices, and evaluating leasing alternatives are typical examples. The present value computations are greatly reduced through the use of a present value annuity table. However, as spelled out below, the table contains a special assumption that has to be allowed for whenever it is used to solve problems involving annuities and their present values.

**Example:** How much money has to be deposited now into a savings account that pays 6 percent compounded yearly in order to make four annual withdrawals of $1,000 each beginning one year from now?

The initial deposit is the present value of the four-year annuity. Let the deposit be made at Year zero; in that event, the withdrawals occur at the end of Years 1, 2,

3, and 4. One way of computing the desired present value is to discount each annuity payment separately, using Appendix Table A-3 (or Table 9-3), and to add up the individual present values. This procedure is graphically illustrated in Figure 9-2, where the sum of the present values is $3,465 and is the required deposit at Year zero.

**Figure 9-2.**  **Present Value Annuity, Four $1,000 Payments, 6 Percent Rate**

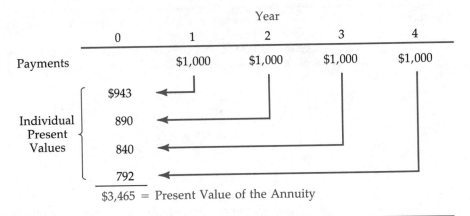

$3,465 = Present Value of the Annuity

It is useful to point out the time value mechanics of this problem. The amount of $3,465 is deposited at Year zero, and interest is added at the end of Year 1. The compound amount at that point of time is $3,672. The $1,000 withdrawal at Year 1 is made *after* interest is added; this leaves $2,672 to compound during the second year. At the end of Year 2, a compound amount of $2,833.27 is available after interest is added; $1,000 is withdrawn, leaving $1,833.27 to earn interest over Year 3. At the end of Year 3, the compound amount of $1,943.27 is on deposit; $1,000 is drawn down and $943.27 earns interest during Year 4. This produces a compound amount at the end of Year 4 of $999.86, which is just $0.14 short of the required $1,000 withdrawal. The missing $0.14 occurs because of rounding errors in Appendix Table A-3 and is not important for our purposes. What is important is to recognize that *the end-of-each-year interest is added before the withdrawal is made.*

**THE BASIC EQUATION.** The present value annuity problem contained in Figure 9-2 can be written in equation form. Let $S_0$ represent the present value of the annuity. Then:

$$S_0 = \$1,000(.943) + \$1,000(.890) + \$1,000(.840) + \$1,000(.792)$$

Factoring the $1,000 constant from each term yields:

$$S_0 = \$1,000(.943 + .890 + .840 + .792) \qquad \text{(9-15)}$$
$$= \$1,000(3.465) = \$3,465$$

The four numbers within the parentheses of Equation 9-15 are taken from the present value, single payment table. Thus, the present value of the four payment annuity can be computed by adding the first four values in Appendix Table A-3 and multiplying by the value of *one* payment. This approach can be followed for any number of payments and is the basis for constructing present value annuity tables.

THE PRESENT VALUE ANNUITY TABLE. Appendix Table A-4 is a present value annuity table. It assumes annuity payments of $1 and is constructed by summing the columns of Appendix Table A-3. A portion of Appendix Table A-4 is reproduced as Table 9-4.

**Table 9-4.** Present Value of an Annuity

| Number of Payments | 6% | 7% | 8% | 9% | 10% |
|---|---|---|---|---|---|
| 1 | .943 | .935 | .926 | .917 | .909 |
| 2 | 1.833 | 1.808 | 1.783 | 1.759 | 1.736 |
| 3 | 2.673 | 2.624 | 2.577 | 2.531 | 2.487 |
| 4 | 3.465 | 3.387 | 3.312 | 3.240 | 3.170 |
| 5 | 4.212 | 4.100 | 3.993 | 3.890 | 3.791 |

Appendix Table A-4 and Table 9-4 contain values for different combinations of payments and interest rates. The following special assumption is built into these tables: *The present value of any annuity is computed at a point of time that is one year before the first annuity payment.* Therefore, the present value of a five payment annuity when its first payment is made in Year 14 would be computed as of Year 13, one year before the first payment; the five payment row would be used in computing the present value of the annuity.

Appendix Table A-4 and Table 9-4 are used as follows: Let

$S_0$ = present value of an annuity

$P$ = the value of *one* payment

$V_{i,n}$ = table value corresponding to the annual interest rate and the number of payments in the annuity

Then:

$$S_0 = P(V_{i,n}) \qquad\qquad (9\text{-}16)$$

Equation 9-16 contains four relevant variables that are used in discounting annuities. These are:

1. The value of one payment

2. The interest rate

3. The number of payments

4. The present value of the annuity

---

**Example:**   What is the present value of a three payment, $5,000 annuity discounted at 7 percent?
  The table value corresponding to three payments and 7 percent is 2.624. Substitute into Equation 9-16:

$$S_0 = \$5,000(2.624)$$

$$= \$13,120$$

**Example:**   A five payment annuity of $10,000 each begins in Year 10. What is the present value of the annuity discounted at 9 percent?
  The table value for five payments and 9 percent is 3.890. The present value is computed as:

$$S_0 = \$10,000(3.890)$$

$$= \$38,900$$

---

In the second example, the present value of the annuity computed is set at Year 9. The present value computed from Equation 9-16 would still be $38,900 even if the annuity began in Year 20 because the present value annuity table considers the time value of money only over the interval beginning with the point of time at which the present value of the annuity occurs and ending with the last payment of the annuity. However, if the present value at *Year zero* of an annuity the payments of which begin in Year 10 was desired, then the final answer would depend in part on the fact that the present value of the annuity was set at Year 9. This situation is considered in the example on page 266. The point is this: The present value annuity table sets the computed present value at a point in time that is one year before the first annuity payment without regard to what specific years produce the annuity.

**OTHER PRESENT VALUE ANNUITY APPLICATIONS.** As with the other equations presented in this chapter, the present value annuity equation can be used to solve for any one of its four variables, given the values of the other three variables. The desired answers are obtained by utilizing Appendix Table A-4 or Table 9-4.

*Finding the Interest Rate.* Investment opportunities may promise annuity inflows in return for an initial amount of money. The rate of return on the investment, however, should be calculated as one step in evaluating the desirability of the investment.

---

**Example:**

A bank accepts an application for a $200,000 industrial loan and proposes the following payment schedule: four equal annual payments of $63,100. What rate of interest is the industrial borrower paying?

Let the $200,000 be the present value of the $63,100 yearly payments and assume that the payments begin one year after the loan is granted. Substitute these values into Equation 9-16 and obtain the associated table value:

$$\$200,000 = \$63,100(V_{i,n})$$

$$\frac{\$200,000}{\$63,100} = V_{i,n}$$

$$3.169 = V_{i,n}$$

Look at the four payment *row* in Table 9-4 and locate the closest table value to 3.169. It is 3.170, corresponding to a 10 percent interest rate.

---

*Finding the Number of Payments.* When a financial contract such as a loan is arranged, it is sometimes convenient to agree on the size of the equal payments. Once the rate of interest is known, the number of payments required to pay the loan can be determined. Such an approach has two problems, however:

1. The payment size has to be larger than the interest charged over the first year of the loan. If this requirement is not met, the loan can never be repaid.

2. The number of payments will seldom turn out to be an integer value. As a result, most loans negotiated in this manner will have a final payment that is larger than the other payments. The last payment is sometimes referred to as a *balloon payment.*

---

**Example:**

A $50,000 loan is to be repaid in equal yearly installments of $14,000. The loan carries a 6 percent interest rate. How many payments are required to repay this loan?

As a first step, you must be certain that the first year's interest is less than $14,000. Since 6 percent of $50,000 is only $3,000, the $14,000 payment at Year 1 will provide some payment to principal. Now substitute the data values into Equation 9-16:

$$\$50,000 = \$14,000(V_{i,n})$$

$$\frac{\$50,000}{\$14,000} = V_{i,n}$$

$$3.571 = V_{i,n}$$

Look at the 6 percent *column* in Table 9-4 and read *down* until a table value equals or exceeds the computed value of 3.571. The desired table value is 4.212, and this corresponds to a value of five payments. However, because the computed value of 3.571 is less than the table value of 4.212, the loan payment schedule does not require the fifth payment to be as large as $14,000. This is demonstrated in Table 9-5, which is the year-by-year payment schedule for this loan.

**Table 9-5.**          Payment Schedule of a $50,000 Loan, Five Payments at 6 Percent

| Year | Principal Owed | Interest on Principal | Total Amount Owed | Yearly Payment | Payment to Interest | Payment to Principal | New Principal |
|------|----------------|------------------------|-------------------|----------------|---------------------|----------------------|---------------|
| 1 | $50,000 | $3,000 | $53,000 | $14,000 | $3,000 | $11,000 | $39,000 |
| 2 | 39,000 | 2,340 | 41,340 | 14,000 | 2,340 | 11,660 | 27,340 |
| 3 | 27,340 | 1,640 | 28,980 | 14,000 | 1,640 | 12,360 | 14,980 |
| 4 | 14,980 | 899 | 15,879 | 14,000 | 899 | 13,101 | 1,879 |
| 5 | 1,879 | 113 | 1,992 | 1,992 | 113 | 1,879 | 0 |

The time value mechanics of the payment schedule in the preceding example are basically the same as those illustrated in a previous example (shown on page 261). The added complication revolves around dividing a loan payment into (1) payment to interest and (2) payment to principal.

Table 9-5 shows that $53,000 is owed at the end of Year 1. The $14,000 payment is used first to pay all the interest for that year. This leaves $11,000 which is used to reduce the unpaid principal to a value of $39,000. At the end of Year 2, 6 percent interest is computed on the $39,000 unpaid principal that was outstanding during the year. The amount of $2,340 out of the $14,000 payment is required to meet the Year 2 interest. The remaining $11,660 of the $14,000 payment is used to reduce the unpaid principal to a value of $27,340. All of this is repeated until Year 5; the unpaid principal for that year is only $1,879, and a payment of $1,992 pays off the entire loan.

The usual way of avoiding a final small payment is simply to pay off the entire loan in what would otherwise be the next-to-last payment. For the example demonstrated in Table 9-5, this would produce a balloon payment of $15,879 in Year 4, thus repaying the entire loan and saving $113 in interest charges for Year 5.

One additional note: Partitioning a payment schedule into payments to interest and to principal as is done in Table 9-5 is somewhat tedious but may be necessary in order to realize the federal income tax shield provided by the payments to interest. These tax shields play important roles in evaluating the desirability of many corporate investment-financing decisions.

## APPLICATIONS OF COMPOUNDING AND DISCOUNTING TECHNIQUES

This final section of the chapter presents a number of examples and special topics needed for use in later chapters. One important point to make is this: Investment and/or financing opportunities are typically described in terms of cash flows, but the cash flows themselves are seldom explicitly labeled as present values or compound amounts. Labeling cash flows properly, choosing the appropriate compounding and/or discounting techniques, and applying these techniques correctly are all necessary steps in reaching correct decisions when the time value of money is a consideration. Practice and experience both play important roles in assuring the proper execution of these steps.

**Problems Involving Unequal Cash Flows**

Whenever a series of cash flows or payments does not take an annuity form, it is described as an *unequal cash flow*, or a *mixed stream of cash flows*. This type of cash flow pattern also includes those situations where some years may be devoid of payments altogether. Compounding and/or discounting of unequal cash flow problems is accomplished by using single payment tables.

**Example:**

Assume that a deposit is to be made at Year zero into an account that will earn 8 percent compounded annually. It is desired to withdraw $5,000 three years from now and $7,000 six years from now. What is the size of the Year zero deposit that will produce these future payments?

Let the initial deposit be the sum of the present values of the two later withdrawals and compute the value of the initial deposit by using the present value, single payment table:

$$P_0 = \$5,000(.794) + \$7,000(.630)$$

$$= \$3,970 + \$4,410 = \$8,380$$

The $8,380 grows to a value of $10,559 in three years; $5,000 is withdrawn, leaving $5,559. This amount is left to compound for an additional three years and yields the desired $7,000.

**Choice of Interest Tables**

The choice of annuity table may not always be obvious when annuity-type problems must be solved. To avoid the use of an inappropriate table, answer the question, Which occurs first, the annuity payments or the corresponding "lump sum" dollar amount?

When the annuity payments occur first, the compound amount annuity table is used. For example, making an annuity of deposits into an interest-bearing account in order to realize a desired amount of money at a future specific time requires the use of a compound amount annuity table since the amount to be withdrawn occurs *after* the annuity payments are deposited.

When the lump sum occurs first, the present value annuity table is used. For example, converting a loan made at Year zero into an annuity of subsequent payments requires the use of a present value annuity table since the loan proceeds occur first.

Single payment problems, on the other hand, can be solved by using either the compound amount, single payment table or the present value, single payment table and their associated equations. These two tables are arithmetic reciprocals of each other: Appendix Table A-3 is obtained by dividing each table value of Appendix Table A-1 into 1.0. Thus, Equation 9-7,

$$A_t = P_0(1 + i)^t$$

can be algebraically rewritten as Equation 9-14,

$$P_0 = A_t \left[ \frac{1}{(1 + i)^t} \right]$$

The important point is that only one of these two tables is needed to solve single payment problems. It is equally important to remember that Equation 9-7 is a compound amount form requiring table values from Appendix Table A-1, and Equation 9-14 is a present value form that uses table values from Appendix Table A-3.

**Problems Involving Deferred Payments**

When a corporation finances an investment by obtaining a loan at Year zero, the repayments may not begin for several years, but the time value of the intervening years must be taken into account.

**Example:**

Assume that a $2,000,000 plant expansion is to be financed as follows: The corporation makes a 15 percent down payment and borrows the remainder at 9 percent interest rate. The loan is to be repaid in eight equal annual installments beginning four years from now. What is the size of the required annual loan payment?

The corporation borrows $1,700,000 (85 percent of the $2 million). Compound interest occurs over the entire 11 years of the life of the loan. The question may arise, Why does the loan not last 12 years? Because the eight payments are made over seven years beginning with the end of Year 4. In order to obtain the required annual loan payment, the following two additional points have to be remembered: (1) the loan repayment will be computed by using a present value annuity table and (2) the present value of an annuity, using Appendix Table A-4, is located one year before the first payment.

To compute the size of the annual payment, first compute the amount owed as of Year 3 (one year before the first payment). By compounding the $1.7 million for three years at 9 percent:

$$A_3 = \$1,700,000(1.295)$$

$$= \$2,201,500$$

Now $A_3$ becomes the present value of the eight payment annuity discounted at 9 percent. So, compute the equal yearly payment by using Equation 9-16 and Appendix Table A-4:

$$\$2,201,500 = P(5.535)$$

$$P = \$397,742$$

---

From the previous example, the corporation's plant expansion financing plan can be summarized as follows: Down payment at Year zero of $300,000; the balance borrowed at 9 percent interest. Eight yearly loan payments of $397,742 are to be made beginning at the end of Year 4.

**Bond-Pricing Problems**

Both the investor in bonds and the issuer of bonds face certain problems when considering the pricing of bonds.

---

**Example:**

A potential investor is considering the purchase of a bond that has the following characteristics: the bond pays 8 percent per year on its $1,000 principal, or face value; the bond will mature in 20 years; at maturity, the bondholder will receive interest for Year 20 plus the $1,000 face value. What is the maximum purchase price that should be paid for this bond if the investor requires a 10 percent rate of return?

Assume that if the bond is purchased now, the first interest payment will be received in one year and that the bond will mature 20 years from now. The yearly interest payment will be $80 (8 percent of $1,000). In Year 20 a payment of $1,080 will be received.

The maximum purchase price for this bond is the sum of the present values of the future inflows discounted at the 10 percent required rate of return. The interest payments are treated as an annuity; the $1,000 principal is discounted as a single payment. The present value of the interest payments is found by using Equation 9-16 and the Appendix Table A-4 value for 20 payments and 10 percent interest.

$$S_0 = \$80(8.514)$$

$$= \$681.12$$

The present value of the $1,000 bond is found by using Equation 9-14 and the Appendix Table A-3 value for 20 years and 10 percent interest.

$$P_0 = \$1,000(.149)$$

$$= \$149$$

The maximum purchase price is thus $681.12 + $149.00 = $830.12.

---

The issuing corporation faces the same type of pricing problem as does the investor. The bonds will provide an 8 percent return to investors if they are sold for their face value of $1,000. However, if the rate of return required by investors now increases to 10 percent, what price will have to be put on these bonds if the corporation hopes to sell the entire bond issue? The selling price will again have to be $830.12. The corporation will pay $80 per year interest and return a face value of $1,000 at maturity for each bond that is sold. Since the dollars of interest and bond principal are both fixed, the only way for this bond to offer a competitive rate of return is by adjusting its price. Setting the bond price that produces a required rate of return is accomplished by computing the sum of the present values of the future interest and principal payments discounted at the required rate of return.

**Problems Involving Savings/ Retirement Annuities**

Savings annuities are one way of accumulating funds to provide retirement annuities. Compounding and discounting techniques can be used to measure the savings needed to produce a desired annuity. The more common problem, however, is to measure the size of the retirement annuity that results from a given savings plan.

---

**Example:**

Assume that a ten-year savings annuity of $2,000 per year is begun at Year zero. The retirement annuity is to begin 15 years from now (the first payment is to be received in Year 15) and has to provide a 20-year annuity. If this plan is arranged through a savings bank that pays 7 percent per year on the deposited funds, what is the size of the yearly retirement annuity that will result?

The first step in solving this problem is to compute the compound amount of the annuity at Year 9. This value is then compounded forward as a single payment for five years. The question may arise, Why five years? The answer is that the compound amount at Year 14 becomes the present value of the 20 payment retirement annuity.

Obtain the compound amount of the ten payment savings annuity by using Equation 9-11 and the value in Appendix Table A-2 corresponding to ten payments and 7 percent.

$$S_{10} = \$2,000(13.816)$$

$$= \$27,632$$

The amount of $27,632 is available immediately after the last payment. Compound the $27,632 for five years as a single payment, using Equation 9-7 along with the value in Appendix Table A-1 corresponding to five years and 7 percent.

$$A_5 = \$27,632(1.403)$$

$$= \$38,768$$

Finally, obtain the size of the equal retirement annuity payment by using the $38,768 as the present value of the retirement annuity. Substitute into Equation 9-16 along with the Appendix Table A-4 value corresponding to 20 payments and 7 percent.

$$\$38,768 = P(10.594)$$

$$P = \$3,659$$

Thus, the savings annuity will produce a 20-year retirement annuity of $3,659 per year starting 15 years from now.

---

**Problems Involving Perpetuities**

A **perpetuity** can be defined as an annuity that has an indefinitely long life. A less formal approach is to describe a perpetuity as an annuity that won't quit. Any perpetuity can be discounted by dividing the value of *one* payment by the required rate of return.

---

**Example:**

If a $1,000 deposit is made into an 8 percent savings account, the $80 yearly interest payment is a perpetuity of returns that is available so long as the initial deposit and the rate of interest are unchanged.

Reversing the example, suppose you are offered a contract that will pay $80 per year indefinitely. If you require an 8 percent return on this contract, what is the maximum purchase price you would offer for the contract?

The purchase price is the present value of the $80 perpetuity and is obtained by dividing the value of one payment by the required rate of return. In this example, $80/.08 = $1,000.

---

Perpetuities occur in certain types of valuation problems. In addition, long-lived annuities can sometimes be treated as perpetuities in order to obtain good, first approximations of their present values. The advantage of using perpetuities as approximations to annuities is that present value tables are not required to discount perpetuities. Perpetuities can be used as approximations to annuities because the present value of an annuity approaches the present value of the corresponding perpetuity as the number of payments in the annuity increase. The present value annuity table, Appendix Table A-4, can be used to illustrate this point.

Note that the table values in the 10 percent column of Appendix Table A-4 approach the value of $1/.1 = 10$ over increasing numbers of payments. Similarly, the table values in the 20 percent column approach $1/.2 = 5$ as the number of payments increase. The present value of a

20 payment, $1,000 annuity discounted at 20 percent is $4,870; discounting this annuity as if it were a perpetuity produces a present value of $1,000/.2 = $5,000. The error is only $130, and this demonstrates how good an approximation can be obtained by using the perpetuity approach.

**Intrayear Compounding Problems**

Many commercial banks and most savings and loan associations have sought to attract savings depositors by compounding deposits several times per year. Intrayear compounding allows payment of an effective rate of return that is somewhat higher than the legal nominal rates.

**Example:**

If an 8 percent annual rate of interest is compounded quarterly, then interest is compounded quarterly at a rate of 2 percent. The amount of $1,000 deposited at a yearly 8 percent rate yields $1,080 after one year. The same $1,000 compounded quarterly yields $1,082 after one year. Thus, 8 percent compounded four times a year produces an effective interest rate of 8.2 percent.

In general, if $1 is deposited into an account that pays a nominal (yearly) interest rate of $i$ percent compounded $x$ times a year for $t$ years, the resulting compound amount is:

$$A_t = \$1.00 \left[ 1 + \frac{i}{x} \right]^{xt}$$

Intrayear compounding or discounting is no harder to perform than the yearly approach presented in this chapter. What is needed is a very extensive set of interest tables!

It should be pointed out that compounding a nominal rate more and more frequently will not produce an explosive rate of return. Daily or even continuous compounding of a nominal rate produces a maximum effective rate. Continuous compounding is accomplished by using an exponential equation that uses the base of natural logarithms. The references cited at the end of this chapter provide additional information on the mechanics of continuous compounding.

Some examples taken from savings and loan advertisements that offer continuous compounding are as follows:

| Nominal Rate | Effective Rate |
|---|---|
| 5.75% | 6.00% |
| 6.50% | 6.81% |
| 7.50% | 7.90% |
| 7.75% | 8.17% |

# SUMMARY

This chapter has presented the fundamentals of financial mathematics. The motivating concept is the time value of money. Interest is described as the price paid for the use of money over time. The large number of examples stress the importance of the mathematics of finance to individuals as well as to corporate managers. Later chapters use the techniques developed in this chapter to analyze corporate investment and financing decisions.

The time value of single payments or annuities is measured by compound amounts and present values. A compound amount is the sum of money that results when interest is added to a payment or series of payments and is sometimes referred to as a *future value*. The present value of a future payment or series of payments is the dollar value now of the future payment or payments adjusted for the time value of money. Compounding is the process of obtaining compound amounts or future values. Discounting is the process of obtaining present values.

In order to focus on essential ideas, three general assumptions are used throughout this chapter. In addition, the interest tables contain two specific assumptions. Thus, five assumptions result. First, data values are assumed to be known with certainty. Second, time is measured by discrete intervals that are one year in length. The point of time at which an investment or financing project begins is referred to as *Year zero*, or *the end of Year zero*. Third, interest computations are made once a year and on the last day of the year. Fourth, the compound amount annuity table (Appendix Table A-2) assumes that the compound amount occurs immediately after the last payment and measures the compound amount of the annuity at that time. Consequently, the last payment in an annuity does not earn interest when the compound amount is computed at that time. The fifth and last assumption is that the present value annuity table (Appendix Table A-4) assumes that the present value occurs one year before the first payment. It takes into account the interest that is earned during the year between the present value of the annuity and the first payment.

The appendix tables and corresponding equations for single payments and annuity compounding and discounting procedures are:

|  | Equation Number | Appendix Table |
|---|---|---|
| Compounding: | | |
| Single payment | 9-7 | A-1 |
| Annuity | 9-11 | A-2 |
| Discounting: | | |
| Single payment | 9-14 | A-3 |
| Annuity | 9-16 | A-4 |

When dealing with single payment problems, the four variables involved are (1) initial payment, (2) interest rate, (3) number of years, and (4) future value. Given any three of these variables, the fourth can be obtained by using Equation 9-7 or 9-14.

Compound amount annuity problems use the following variables: (1) number of payments in the annuity, (2) value of each payment, (3) rate of interest, and (4) compound amount of the annuity. Given the value of the other three variables, any one variable can be obtained by using Equation 9-11.

Present value annuity problems involve the following variables: (1) present value of the annuity, (2) size of each payment, (3) rate of interest, and (4) number of payments. Equation 9-16 is used to solve for any one of these variables, given the values of the other three.

Several applications of these time value techniques are made possible because of the ability to manipulate the basic equations and to combine unequal cash flows. These applications include (1) computation of implied rates of return, (2) loan repayment schedules, (3) deferred payment schedules, (4) bond pricing, and (5) savings/retirement annuity type problems.

Perpetuities are introduced as a special type of annuity. Perpetuities do not require present value tables in order to obtain their present values. Perpetuities have limited applications by themselves but can serve as good approximations to long-lived annuities. Intrayear compounding was discussed briefly.

# QUESTIONS

**9-1.** Explain in your own words why the time value of money plays such an important role in finance.

**9-2.** What three major assumptions were used to present the mathematics of finance in this chapter? Outline some examples of problems that would violate these assumptions.

**9-3.** Define *compound amount, compound interest, annuity,* and *present value.*

**9-4.** Explain the special assumption contained in the compound amount annuity table.

**9-5.** Explain the special assumption contained in the present value annuity table.

**9-6.** Why do the annuity tables deal with the number of payments rather than the number of years?

**9-7.** When dealing with annuity problems, what criterion is used to select the proper annuity table?

**9-8.** A corporation's purchase of some new equipment is financed through a bank loan. The loan is made at Year zero and is to be repaid in an annuity form. In determining the size of the repayments, which is the correct annuity table to use? Why?

**9-9.** The terms of a bank loan are negotiated so that the loan size, interest rate, and the amount of each equal payment are agreed upon. The last variable to be determined is the number of payments. What complications may occur in setting the number of payments? How can these complications be surmounted?

**9-10.** What technique would an investor use in setting his or her maximum purchase price for a particular bond? Why does this technique produce the maximum purchase price?

# PROBLEMS

**9-1.** A savings bank offers a 6% interest rate, compounded yearly, on its deposits. How many years will it take for a deposit to double in value? (Note: You should be able to solve this problem without performing any calculations.)

**9-2.** Compute the compound amount for each of the following single payment deposits:

| Amount Deposited | Interest Rate | Number of Years |
|---|---|---|
| $5,000 | 6% | 10 |
| 1,200 | 10 | 15 |
| 1 | 2 | 6 |
| 80 | 7 | 3 |
| 9,740 | 15 | 25 |

**9-3.** Compute the value of the missing variable for each of the following single payment problems:

| Deposit at Year Zero | Interest Rate | Number of Years | Final Amount |
|---|---|---|---|
| $10,000 | 8% | 12 | $   ? |
| 12,000 | ? | 4 | 14,000 |
| ? | 11 | 7 | 7,000 |
| 8,000 | 4 | ? | 9,000 |
| 900 | 5 | ? | 1,200 |
| ? | 12 | 10 | 35,000 |
| 70,000 | ? | 14 | 80,000 |
| 500 | ? | 13 | 1,000 |

9-4.   You borrow $2,000 from a bank today and agree to repay the loan by making one payment of $2,800 three years from now. What rate of interest is the bank charging you?

9-5.   Compute the value of the missing variable for each of the following compound amount annuity problems.

| Number of Payments | Amount of One Payment | Interest Rate | Compound Amount |
|---|---|---|---|
| 3 | $1,000 | 8% | ? |
| 7 | 8,000 | 6 | ? |
| 3 | 2,000 | ? | $  7,280 |
| 10 | ? | 13 | 80,000 |
| 5 | 500 | ? | 4,000 |
| ? | 6,540 | 2 | 104,470 |
| 20 | 4,000 | ? | 204,000 |
| ? | 4,750 | 11 | 79,429 |
| 8 | ? | 10 | 100,000 |

9-6.   Ten yearly payments of $2,000 each will be deposited into an account that pays 8% interest. The payments will begin five years from now. How much money will be available immediately after the last payment?

9-7.   Compute the value of the missing variable for each of the following present value annuity problems:

| Present Value | Number of Payments | Amount of One Payment | Interest Rate |
|---|---|---|---|
| ? | 8 | $ 2,000 | 9% |
| ? | 14 | 1,000 | 7 |
| ? | 9 | 5,000 | 14 |
| $ 96,000 | 12 | 8,000 | ? |
| 95,000 | 21 | ? | 8 |
| 100,000 | ? | 17,699 | 12 |
| 8,000 | ? | 1,498 | 16 |
| 88,000 | 10 | 11,000 | ? |
| 200,000 | 25 | 40,000 | ? |
| 300,000 | 16 | ? | 17 |

**9-8.** A contract costing $7,000 will produce a four-year annuity of $2,000 each year. The first payment is to be received one year from today. What is the implied rate of return for this contract?

**9-9.** A purchase of $50,000 is to be financed by making 25 equal payments beginning one year from now. Ninety percent of the purchase price is financed at an 11% interest rate; the other 10% is paid as a down payment. What is the size of the annual loan payment?

**9-10.** What is the present value at Year zero of a ten-payment annuity that pays $10,000 each year if the first payment is received six years from now and if the discount rate is 15%?

**9-11.** A $6 million industrial robot is to be purchased and financed as follows: down payment of $250,000; balance to be paid in nine equal payments beginning three years from now; interest rate of 14%. What is the size of the equal annual payment?

**9-12.** A sinking fund is to be established in order to accumulate a total of $3,450,000. Equal annual payments will be made starting June 1, 1984; the last payment is to be made June 1, 1991. If the fund earns 8% interest, what is the size of the annual payment that will produce the required $3,450,000 immediately after the last payment?

**9-13.** Determine the maximum purchase price you would pay for each of the following bonds if you require a 9% rate of return. The coupon rate is the rate of interest paid each year on the face value. At maturity you will receive the last interest payment plus an amount equal to the face value. The first payment is to be received one year from today.

| Face Value | Coupon Rate | Years to Maturity |
|---|---|---|
| $ 1,000 | 8.5% | 20 |
| 5,000 | 9.0 | 20 |
| 10,000 | 7.0 | 4 |
| 10,000 | 6.4 | 3 |
| 5,000 | 9.5 | 10 |
| 5,000 | 9.8 | 12 |

**9-14.** The following loans have been negotiated as to all terms except for the number of equal payments and the size of each payment. The payments begin one year after the loan is received. Compute the number of payments and the size of each payment for each loan. (Note: Balloon payments may be necessary.)

| Amount Borrowed | Interest Rate | Yearly Payment |
|---|---|---|
| $10,000 | 11% | $ 2,400 |
| 24,000 | 14 | 4,000 |
| 80,000 | 10 | 15,000 |
| 90,000 | 9 | 25,000 |

**9-15.** A savings annuity is to be used as a way of providing a retirement annuity. Ten equal yearly payments of $3,500 each are to be deposited into a savings account; the first deposit will be made four years from now. An 18-year retirement annuity (18 payments) is to begin 16 years from now. If the deposit account earns 10%, what is the size of the annual retirement annuity payment that can be withdrawn?

**9-16.** For each of the following investments, calculate the maximum purchase price at Year zero. Investments A, B, and C require a 12% return; D and E require a 15% return.

Investments — Cash Flows

| Year | A | B | C | D | E |
|------|-------|-------|--------|--------|--------|
| 1 | $5,000 | $3,000 | $20,000 | 0 | 0 |
| 2 | 5,000 | 4,000 | 10,000 | 0 | $1,000 |
| 3 | 5,000 | 5,000 | 0 | $2,000 | 1,000 |
| 4 | 5,000 | 6,000 | 0 | 3,000 | 1,000 |
| 5 | 5,000 | 6,000 | 10,000 | 4,000 | 0 |
| 6 | | 6,000 | | 5,000 | 2,000 |
| 7 | | | | 5,000 | 2,000 |
| 8 | | | | 5,000 | 2,000 |

**9-17.** Compute the present value of the following perpetuities using the given discount rates:

| Annual Payment | Discount Rate |
|------|------|
| $1,000 | 8% |
| 2,000 | 10 |
| 500 | 12 |
| 4,000 | 7 |

**9-18.** Thinking person's question: What is the present value at Year zero of a perpetuity that pays $500 per year if the first payment does not begin until Year 4 and if 10% is the relevant discount rate?

---

# SELECTED REFERENCES

Bierman, H., and S. Smidt. *The Capital Budgeting Decision*. 4th ed. New York: MacMillan Publishing Company, Inc., 1975.

Hampton, J. *Financial Decision Making: Concepts, Problems, and Cases*. 3d ed. Reston, Va.: Reston Publishing Company, Inc., 1983.

Mao, J. *Quantitative Analysis of Financial Decisions*. New York: MacMillan Publishing Company, Inc., 1969.

Van Horne, J. *Financial Management and Policy*. 6th ed. Englewood Cliffs, N.J.: Prentice-Hall, Inc., 1983.

# CHAPTER 10

## Capital Budgeting under Conditions of Certainty: The Criteria

*The time value of money concepts and techniques presented in the previous chapter are applied to capital-budgeting problems discussed in this and the next two chapters. This chapter first presents an overview of capital budgeting as a general corporate activity and then discusses the three capital-budgeting criteria that are of interest in this text. Emphasis is placed on understanding the conceptual and computational aspects of capital-budgeting criteria. The next two chapters deal with corporate decisions made as a result of applying these criteria to different types of capital-budgeting problems.*

## CORPORATE CAPITAL BUDGETING

Capital budgeting is a more or less continuous process carried out by the several functional areas of corporate management. Marketing, production, engineering, and financial managers all play vital parts in shaping the capital budgets that are decided upon by the corporation. In addition, other departmental staffs make important and at times critical contributions to the capital-budgeting process. While the emphasis here is on the financial aspects of capital budgeting, other line-and-staff contributions are not ignored and are illustrated at several points in these chapters.

**Role of Managerial Finance in Capital Budgeting**

The contributions that financial managers make to corporate capital budgeting occur primarily in evaluating profit-seeking investment alternatives. Attention is focused on the following two general types of investments: (1) those that seek to increase corporate profits directly and (2) those that seek to increase corporate profits by reducing costs. The long-term nature of these investments means that a corporate capital budget, once adopted, sets the tone for the profitability or nonprofitability of the corporation for several years. From the standpoint of financial management, the objective of capital budgeting is to select those long-term investment projects that promise to make the greatest contribution to shareholder wealth.

The criteria used to measure the profitability of investment alternatives omit nonfinancial considerations, such as the impacts on employee morale and on executive status, in accepting or rejecting specific investment alternatives. Because these considerations are recognized by the corporation and, as a consequence, affect the composition of the ultimate capital budget (as do the state and federal regulations discussed later), the capital-budgeting process will never be reduced to a set of mechanical rules that can be executed clearly and unambiguously.

**Capital Budget: Definition and Examples**

A **capital budget** is a set of investment alternatives that have one common characteristic: the set of returns associated with each alternative occurs over a period of *two or more years*. It is not uncommon, for example, for proposed investments to exhibit expected economic lifetimes of 10, 15, or even 20 years. Investments with this characteristic are called *long-term investments*.

Some long-term investments are relatively easy to identify. For example, what might be called *brick-and-mortar investments* refer to the construction of new manufacturing plants and distribution facilities. Increasing the capacity of existing plants and renovating production lines by replacing existing machinery are other examples of brick-and-mortar investments.

Other long-term investments may not be so obvious. For example, major advertising campaigns and research-and-development programs may entail the investment of funds over several years. Measuring the profitability of these investments can be very difficult. Corporate diversification through mergers and acquisitions also represents long-term investments. Some corporations have diversified to the point where they are called conglomerates. For example, one such conglomerate currently owns firms that produce everything from fountain pens to helicopters.

The commerical banking industry provides another interesting example of diversification. Some banking organizations have concentrated on acquiring other banks. Others have diversified into data processing, leasing, and factoring.

**Capital Budgeting: Definition and Procedures**

**Capital budgeting** is the process of generating the capital budget that is to be decided upon at a point in time. Essentially, a capital budget represents a set of corporate strategies that are revised over time as actual data replace forecast values, as new investment alternatives are identified, and as previously included alternatives are dropped or modified. Capital-budgeting procedures involve the following:

1. Identifying potential investment alternatives

2. Evaluating the desirability of individual investment alternatives

3. Choosing from among investment alternatives that are competing to do the same job

4. Constructing the final capital budget when available funds are insufficient to finance the entire set of desirable investments.

5. Analyzing the results of previous capital-budgeting decisions

Potential investment alternatives may be rejected during each of these first four procedures. The fifth procedure analyzes alternatives that have been adopted in order to determine if they should be continued, modified, or terminated. An investment is terminated when corporate managers decide that it no longer contributes to shareholder wealth, irrespective of the original figures that made the investment desirable. Reviewing past decisions should also improve management's ability to evaluate subsequent investment alternatives.

Capital budgeting is often described as a dynamic process because it is possible to identify potential alternatives almost continuously, and the firm's operating environment (as described in Chapter 2) may alter the desirability of actual or potential investments. For example, actions of competitors, market research studies, the impacts of business cycle phases, unanticipated inflation, regulatory decisions, and the development of new technologies all may alter—for better or for worse—the desirability of the firm's current or proposed investments. As a result, the capital-budgeting procedures listed above constitute an ongoing corporate activity. This chapter concentrates on the criteria used to evaluate the desirability of investment alternatives.

**Underlying Assumptions of Capital Budgeting**

A number of assumptions must be introduced in order to concentrate on the managerial aspects of capital budgeting. The effect of these assumptions is to exclude nonfinancial considerations and to remove some complications that would obscure the major points being presented. These assumptions constitute a general set of conditions within which the financial aspects of long-term alternatives can be evaluated. Using the capital-budgeting criteria and techniques presented in these chapters when these assumptions are violated may produce incorrect decisions.

**SHAREHOLDER WEALTH MAXIMIZATION IS THE BASIC MOTIVE.** All capital-budgeting alternatives considered here are accepted or rejected on the basis of their effect on shareholder wealth. No other corporate goals influence the investment selection decision.

**COSTS AND REVENUES ARE KNOWN WITH CERTAINTY.** The costs and revenues associated with each investment alternative are known with certainty, or there exists a forecasting technique that can generate the values with a very small error. It may be very difficult to estimate revenues and costs more than two or three years into the future. However, if a proposed investment has a ten-year economic life, accurate forecasts must be available for all ten years. (This assumption is relaxed in Chapter 12.)

**INFLOWS AND OUTFLOWS ARE BASED ON CASH.** The data required for evaluating investment proposals must be stated in cash as opposed to accounting income. This is because a corporation uses cash to pay its bills and to pay cash dividends on common and preferred stock. If the corporation does not generate cash returns from its investments, it will sooner or later become insolvent.

**INFLOWS AND OUTFLOWS OCCUR ONCE A YEAR.** The assumptions introduced in developing the financial mathematics of the previous chapter are needed here because capital-budgeting criteria use discounting techniques. Cash inflows or outflows occur only once a year—either at the end of a given year or at discrete yearly intervals. Compounding and/or discounting occur only once a year.

**CASH FLOWS EXHIBIT A CONVENTIONAL PATTERN.** The funds required to undertake an investment represent corporate outflows, and returns from the investment represent corporate inflows. If a minus sign represents an outflow and a plus sign represents an inflow, then a **conventional cash flow** is defined as a time series of cash flows that contains only *one change in sign.* For example, an investment that has one outflow followed by three inflows can be illustrated as:

$$-, +, +, +$$

and is considered to have a conventional cash flow pattern. A cash flow pattern such as:

$$-, -, +, +, +$$

is also a conventional pattern because a change in sign occurs only once even though there are two minus signs. A cash flow pattern like:

$$-, +, +, -$$

is not a conventional cash flow because the sign changes twice. Investment alternatives are assumed to exhibit conventional cash flows. Evaluating an investment alternative that violates this assumption can become very difficult and the criteria presented in this chapter may produce contradictory evaluations. Techniques for dealing with this problem are found in specialized capital-budgeting texts.

THE REQUIRED RATE OF RETURN IS KNOWN AND CONSTANT. The required rate of return is generally looked at as the minimum rate of return that the corporation must earn if shareholder wealth is not to decrease. (The required rate of return is usually referred to as the *cost of capital*, and some approaches at measuring this rate are discussed in Chapters 14 and 17.)

In these capital-budgeting chapters, the minimum required rate of return on investment alternatives is assumed to be known and constant over the life of the proposed investment. Arriving at the required rate of return is important for two reasons: (1) if the rate is set too high, the corporation will reject quite profitable projects and (2) if the rate is set too low, the corporation will accept projects that decrease shareholder wealth.

CAPITAL RATIONING DOES NOT EXIST. Whenever a corporation is not able to finance its entire capital budget, **capital rationing** is said to exist. In such a situation some investments will have to be given up. The capital-budgeting techniques in these chapters assume that the corporation is *not* faced with capital rationing. However, capital rationing does contain important implications for financial managers. Thus, one section of Chapter 11 contains an introduction to the solution of profit oriented, capital-rationing problems.

**Developing the Basic Data for Individual Investment Alternatives**

The procedure for evaluating the desirability of individual investment alternatives consists of several steps. The financial manager is responsible for executing three of the major steps:

1. Developing the net investment and cash flows for each investment alternative

2. Adjusting for the time value of money in determining the profitability of the project

3. Using capital-budgeting criteria to decide whether or not the investment alternative meets the corporation's profitability requirements

The first step is explained next. The remainder of this chapter, as well as Chapters 11 and 12, is devoted to Steps 2 and 3.

COMPUTING THE NET INVESTMENT. The net cash outflow that occurs when an investment project is accepted and funds are invested into it is called the **net investment**. The initial net investment is said to occur at time period zero, although net investment may occur at several points of time. The following equation provides a general format for computing net investment:

$$\text{Net investment} = \begin{aligned}&\text{project cost}\\ &+\text{ installation}\\ &-\text{ proceeds from asset disposal}\\ &\pm\text{ taxes on asset disposal}\end{aligned} \qquad \text{(10-1)}$$

*Project and Installation Costs.* **Project cost** is the outlay required to acquire or begin the investment proposal. When the project involves transporting and/or installing machinery and related equipment, or if the project requires a commitment of net working capital, such expenses are included as part of the net investment. Financing arrangements and ultimate salvage value for a new project are ignored in computing net investment.

---

**Example:**

A new production line is to be introduced. The cost of the needed machinery is $1,000,000. The machinery is expected to last for four years, after which time it will have a scrap value of $8,000. The corporation spends $19,000 in transporting the machinery from the manufacturer and in installing the machinery in its plant. The corporation pays for the machinery by making a down payment of $100,000 and finances the remainder with a bank loan.

The net investment is $1,019,000—the sum of the cost of the machinery and the transportation and installation expenses. Scrap value and financing arrangements are ignored.

---

*Disposal of Existing Assets.* An investment proposal sometimes involves replacing an existing asset with a new asset. The existing asset may have a market value or scrap value; it may or may not be fully depreciated. Any combination of these factors can produce an increase or a decrease in the federal income tax liability of the corporation. The tax impacts of such a disposal are *included* in computing the net investment of the project.

In this chapter corporations are assumed to pay an ordinary income tax rate of 40 percent and a capital gains tax rate of 20 percent. The rules presented in Chapter 2 to determine the tax impact of selling a depreciable asset are summarized below:

1.  If an asset is sold for less than its book value, the corporation realizes a decrease in its tax liability equal to 40 percent of the difference between the selling price and the book value of the asset.

2.  If the asset is sold for its book value, there is no impact on corporate taxes.

3.  If the asset is sold for more than its book value but for an amount equal to or less than its original cost, the corporation incurs an increase in its tax liability equal to 40 percent of the difference between the selling price and the book value of the asset.

4.  If the asset is sold for more than its original cost, the corporation incurs an increase in its tax liability equal to the tax on the capital gain plus the tax on the recaptured depreciation. The capital gains tax is 20 percent of the difference between the selling price and the original cost. The tax on the recaptured depreciation is 40 percent of the difference between the original cost and the book value.

Taking the above rules into account and using Equation 10-1, the computation of a project's net investment is demonstrated below.

**Example:**    A new line of machinery is purchased to replace an existing outmoded asset. The new machinery has an installed cost of $2,500,000 and an expected salvage value of $250,000 after ten years. The existing asset originally cost $800,000 and has a current book value of $100,000.

1.  Assume that the existing asset is sold for a scrap value of $10,000. The corporation realizes a tax savings of .40($100,000 − $10,000) = $36,000. The net investment of the project is:

| | |
|---|---:|
| Project and installation costs: | $2,500,000 |
| Proceeds from asset disposal: | − 10,000 |
| Tax savings on asset disposal: | − 36,000 |
| | $2,454,000 |

2.  Assume that the existing asset is sold for the amount of its book value. There is no tax impact from the sale. The net investment of the project is:

| | |
|---|---:|
| Project and installation costs: | $2,500,000 |
| Proceeds from asset disposal: | − 100,000 |
| | $2,400,000 |

3.  Assume that the existing asset is sold for $150,000. The corporation incurs an increase in its tax liability of .40($150,000 − $100,000) = $20,000. The net investment of the project is:

| | |
|---|---:|
| Project and installation costs: | $2,500,000 |
| Proceeds from asset disposal: | − 150,000 |
| Tax on recapture of depreciation: | + 20,000 |
| | $2,370,000 |

4.  Assume that the existing asset is sold for $1,000,000. The corporation incurs an increase in its tax liability of .20($1,000,000 − $800,000) + .40($800,000 − $100,000) = $320,000. The net investment of the project is:

| | |
|---|---|
| Project and installation costs: | $2,500,000 |
| Proceeds from asset disposal: | −1,000,000 |
| Taxes on asset disposal: | +   320,000 |
| | $1,820,000 |

COMPUTING THE CASH FLOW. The term **cash flow** is used to describe the cash oriented measure of return generated by an investment alternative. While it may not be possible to obtain exact cash measurements, it is possible to generate useful approximations by using accounting data. The yearly returns from any project are assumed to be estimates of the project's profit before depreciation and taxes. Cash flow is then defined by the following equation:

$$\text{Cash flow} = \text{profit before depreciation and taxes}$$
$$- \text{ depreciation}$$
$$- \text{ federal corporate income taxes}$$
$$+ \text{ depreciation} \qquad (10\text{-}2)$$

Cash flow can be equivalently defined as: *profit after taxes plus depreciation*. Since depreciation is a noncash expense, it creates a tax shield and lowers a corporation's tax liability. However, a project's yearly value of profit after taxes understates its cash flow by the amount of the depreciation expense. Thus, depreciation is added to profit after taxes in order to arrive at the project's estimate of cash flow. In computing cash flow in this chapter, straight-line depreciation is used and the federal corporate tax rate on ordinary income is assumed to be 40 percent.

**Example:**

A project's net investment is $600,000 of which $500,000 is the depreciable amount. The investment has a five-year economic life. Profit before depreciation and taxes is estimated at $175,000 per year.

Annual depreciation is $500,000/5 = $100,000. The yearly cash flows are obtained by using Equation 10-2 as follows:

| | |
|---|---|
| Profit before depreciation and taxes: | $175,000 |
| Depreciation: | −100,000 |
| Equals taxable profit | 75,000 |
| Federal corporate income taxes: | −  30,000 |
| Equals profit after taxes | $  45,000 |
| Depreciation: | +100,000 |
| Equals profit after taxes and before depreciation (cash flow) | $145,000 |

In the next example, both the net investment and the cash flow for an investment alternative are computed. This example demonstrates that where accrual accounting and managerial finance treat investment data differently, the distinctions have to be handled properly if the data for the investment alternative are to be transformed into their proper format for capital-budgeting purposes.

**Example:**

A corporation purchases several new metal-cutting machines. The relevant data regarding this purchase are:

| | |
|---|---|
| Purchase price: | $11,000,000 |
| Transportation and installation costs: | $34,000 |
| Economic lifetime: | 7 years |
| Estimated scrap value: | $300,000 |
| Yearly profit before depreciation and taxes: | $2,000,000 |

The net investment of the project is computed as follows:

| | |
|---|---|
| Project cost: | $11,000,000 |
| Transportation and installation costs: | +    34,000 |
| | $11,034,000 |

The depreciable amount is:

| | |
|---|---|
| Net investment: | $11,034,000 |
| Estimated scrap value: | −   300,000 |
| | $10,734,000 |

By using Equation 10-2, the yearly cash flow is computed as follows:

| | |
|---|---|
| Profit before depreciation and taxes: | $2,000,000 |
| Depreciation: | −1,533,429 |
| Equals taxable profit | 466,571 |
| Federal corporate income taxes: | −   186,628 |
| Equals profit after taxes | 279,943 |
| Depreciation: | +1,533,429 |
| Equals cash flow | $1,813,372 |

The cash flow is $1,813,372 in each of the first six years. In Year 7, cash flow will be increased by the estimated scrap value of $300,000. Thus, the Year 7 cash flow will be $1,813,372 + $300,000 = $2,113,372.

In the above metal-cutting machine example, the need to invest net working capital in order to produce the yearly cash flows would change the value of the Year zero net investment and the Year 7 cash flow. If $112,000 of net working capital were needed for this project, the net investment would increase by $112,000 to a value of $11,146,000. When the investment is terminated, in this case at the end of Year 7, the net working capital is presumed to be recovered and is treated as an addition to the firm's cash flow. The Year 7 cash flow thus increases by $112,000 to $2,225,372.

## CAPITAL-BUDGETING CRITERIA

This section defines, explains, interprets, and evaluates three capital-budgeting criteria: (1) payback, (2) net present value, and (3) internal rate of return. Attention is focused on the net present value criterion since it is frequently identified as the most useful capital-budgeting criterion.

**The Payback Criterion**

Of all the capital-budgeting criteria that are in use, payback is one of the easiest to understand and apply. **Payback** is defined as the number of years required for an investment's cumulative cash flows to equal its net investment. Thus, payback can be looked upon as the length of time required for a project to break even on its net investment.

**COMPUTATION OF PAYBACK.** When an investment's cash flows are in annuity form, payback can be computed by dividing the value of one annual cash flow into the project's net investment.

---

**Example:**

An investment has the following net investment and cash flows:

| Year | Net Investment | Yearly Cash Flows |
|------|----------------|-------------------|
| 0 | $12,000 | 0 |
| 1 | | $4,000 |
| 2 | | 4,000 |
| 3 | | 4,000 |
| 4 | | 4,000 |
| 5 | | 4,000 |

Payback = $12,000/$4,000 = 3 years.

---

When an investment's cash flows are *not* in annuity form, the cumulative cash flows are used in computing payback.

---

**Example:**

Compute the payback for the following cash flows, assuming a net investment of $20,000:

| Year | Net Investment | Yearly Cash Flows | Cumulative Cash Flows |
|------|----------------|-------------------|------------------------|
| 0 | $20,000 | 0 | 0 |
| 1 |  | $8,000 | $ 8,000 |
| 2 |  | 6,000 | 14,000 |
| 3 |  | 4,000 | 18,000 |
| 4 |  | 2,000 | 20,000 |
| 5 |  | 2,000 | 22,000 |

Payback = four years because four years are required before the cumulative cash flows equal the project's net investment.

---

A measurement problem occurs when the cumulative cash flows do not exactly equal a project's net investment. In such a situation, the problem is resolved by increasing the computed payback to the next integer.

---

**Example:**  Compute the payback for the following cash flows, assuming a net investment of $13,000:

| Year | Net Investment | Yearly Cash Flows | Cumulative Cash Flows |
|------|----------------|-------------------|------------------------|
| 0 | $13,000 | 0 | 0 |
| 1 |  | $5,000 | $ 5,000 |
| 2 |  | 5,000 | 10,000 |
| 3 |  | 5,000 | 15,000 |
| 4 |  | 5,000 | 20,000 |

Since the cash flows take an annuity form, payback is computed as $13,000/$5,000 = 2.6 years. However, cash flows occur only at the end of each year. Therefore, the project requires three years of cash flows before it earns its net investment. The computed payback period of 2.6 years is increased to the next integer, resulting in a payback of three years for this project.

---

**INTERPRETATION OF THE PAYBACK CRITERION.** The payback criterion measures the time required for a project to break even. It does not, however, measure the profitability of the investment because it ignores all cash flows that occur after the payback point. In addition, the computations that generate the payback value do not take into account the time value of money.

---

**Example:**  A project's net investment is $50,000, and it generates cash flows of $12,500 a year for seven years. Since the cash flows are in annuity form, payback is computed as $50,000/$12,500 = 4 years.

The amount of $37,500 generated by the project in Years 5, 6, and 7 constitutes the investment's profit but is not recognized by the payback criterion. The cash flows that occur throughout the years are added together without first discounting their yearly values. Hence, the time values of the cash flows are not recognized.

---

**EVALUATION OF THE PAYBACK CRITERION.** The payback method was among the first capital-budgeting criteria to be widely accepted. It continues to be in common use today for the following reasons:

1.  Payback is an easy concept to understand.

2.  Payback is easy to compute.

3.  Payback has a straightforward interpretation.

The two major limitations of the payback criterion are:

1.  Payback does not measure the profitability of investment alternatives.

2.  Payback does not take into account the time value of money.

The use of the payback criterion can produce incorrect decisions when investment alternatives are being accepted or rejected on the basis of their time adjusted profitability. Consequently, a decision to use the payback criterion has to balance its simplicity of concept and procedure against its inability to judge profit and time values. The capital-budgeting applications presented in Chapter 11 reinforce the advantages and disadvantages of this criterion.

**The Net Present Value Criterion**

When all factors are taken into account, the net present value (NPV) criterion is recognized as one of the best criteria available for capital-budgeting purposes. NPV techniques are also used in later chapters that deal with corporate valuation and financing strategies.

The **net present value** of an investment alternative is defined as the sum of the present values of the cash flows minus the sum of the present values of the net investments. That is, the NPV for any activity that involves inflows and outflows of funds over a period of time is the sum of the present values of the inflows minus the sum of the present values of the outflows. When the entire net investment occurs at Time zero, NPV is defined as the sum of the present values of the cash flows minus the net investment. NPV is measured in dollars.

**COMPUTATION OF NPV.** Since NPV can be positive, zero, or negative, attention must be paid to its algebraic sign.

---

**Example:**     An investment alternative has a net investment of $100,000 and produces a cash flow annuity of $14,000 for 16 years. Compute the NPV of the investment if the required rate of return for the investment is 10 percent.

The present value factor corresponding to a 16 payment annuity discounted at 10 percent is 7.824 (see Appendix Table A-4). NPV is calculated as follows:

$$NPV = \$14,000(7.824) - \$100,000 = \$9,536$$

If the cash flow annuity for this example were only $12,000, a negative NPV would result:

$$NPV = \$12,000(7.824) - \$100,000 = -\$6,112$$

---

**INTERPRETATION OF THE NPV CRITERION.** Net present value applications to capital budgeting use the corporation's minimum required rate of return as the discount rate in adjusting cash flows for their time values. In these applications NPV is interpreted as follows:

1. If NPV is positive and greater than zero, the project's rate of return exceeds the minimum required rate of return.

2. If NPV equals zero, the project's rate of return equals the minimum required rate of return.

3. If NPV is negative, the project's rate of return is less than the minimum required rate of return.

4. A positive NPV represents the amount by which time adjusted profits exceed the minimum required profits. A negative NPV represents the amount by which time adjusted profits fall short of the minimum required profits.

The following examples provide some techniques aimed at making it easy to interpret NPVs as they apply to capital-budgeting problems.

---

**Example:**   A project has a net investment of $10,000 and a cash flow annuity of $4,000 for three years. Compute and interpret the NPV if the required rate of return is 12 percent.

The present value factor for a three payment annuity discounted at 12 percent is 2.402. The NPV is computed as follows:

$$NPV = \$4,000(2.402) - \$10,000 = -\$392$$

The negative NPV indicates that the project's rate of return is less than the required 12 percent. Does this mean that the project is not profitable? To answer this question, add up all the *undiscounted* cash flows. If the total of undiscounted cash flows exceeds the net investment, the project is profitable. In this example, the sum of the undiscounted cash flows equals $12,000. Since this sum is greater than the net investment of $10,000, the project is profitable. However, the negative NPV indicates that the project fails to earn the required 12 percent rate of return by an amount of cash flows with present values amounting to $392.

**Example:**     A project has a net investment of $60,000 with the following cash flows and a required rate of return of 13 percent:

| Year | Yearly Cash Flows |
|------|-------------------|
| 1 | $20,000 |
| 2 | 20,000 |
| 3 | 20,000 |
| 4 | 15,000 |
| 5 | 15,000 |
| 6 | 15,000 |

The sum of the undiscounted cash flows is $105,000. Since this amount exceeds the project's net investment, the project is profitable.

The NPV is computed as follows:

$$NPV = \begin{aligned}&\$20,000(2.361)\\&+\$15,000(.613)\\&+\$15,000(.543)\\&+\$15,000(.480)\\&-\$60,000\end{aligned}$$     or     $$NPV = \begin{aligned}&\$20,000(2.361)\\&+\$15,000(1.636)\\&-\$60,000\end{aligned}$$

$$NPV = \$11,760$$          $$NPV = \$11,760$$

The positive NPV of $11,760 indicates that the project's rate of return is greater than the required 13 percent. But how much greater? The NPV criterion does not provide a direct answer. Rather, the positive NPV indicates that the profits over and above the cash flows needed to earn 13 percent have a present value of $11,760.

---

The next example is rather unusual, but it has proved very useful in demonstrating the interpretation of NPVs.

---

**Example:**     A financial manager is evaluating a project that has a net investment of $10,000 and cash flows as follows:

| Year | 1 | 2 | 3 | 4 |
|------|-----|-----|-----|-----|
| Cash Flow | $4,000 | $4,000 | $4,000 | $4,000 |

The financial manager first calculates the sum of the present values of the cash flows. The required rate of return is 10 percent.

$$\$4,000(3.170) = \$12,680$$

Thus, the NPV is:

$$NPV = \$12,680 - \$10,000 = \$2,680$$

On this basis the financial manager decides that the project is desirable. However, superiors say that the corporation has no funds to finance this project.

Now a friendly commercial bank loan officer appears and offers the needed funds at 10 percent interest as long as the loan principal and interest are paid from the investment's cash flows.

The financial manager does some quick calculations, borrows $12,680 from the bank, and invests $10,000 in the project. Note that the manager has borrowed the sum of the present values of the cash flows! Is this possible without violating the bank's terms? Can this strategy be profitable to the corporation? The answers to these questions are provided by the following analysis of the cash inflows and outflows:

1. The corporation realizes an immediate cash increase at Time zero equal to $2,680, calculated as follows:

|  | Year 0 |
| --- | --- |
| Amount borrowed: | $12,680 |
| Less net investment: | 10,000 |
| Corporation's cash gain | $ 2,680 |

The corporation's cash gain at Year zero is equal to the NPV of the project. This amount is now held by the corporation and can be invested in other projects or paid out as dividends.

2. The cash flows from the investment are just sufficient to repay the principal and interest on the loan, as shown next:

| Year | 1 | 2 | 3 | 4 |
| --- | --- | --- | --- | --- |
| Unpaid principal | $12,680 | $ 9,948 | $6,943 | $3,637 |
| Plus: Interest at 10% | 1,268 | 995 | 694 | 363 |
| Equals amount owed | $13,948 | $10,943 | $7,637 | $4,000 |
| Less: Loan payment | 4,000 | 4,000 | 4,000 | 4,000 |
| Equals new principal | $ 9,948 | $ 6,943 | $3,637 | 0 |

Since the yearly cash flows are used to make the loan payments, the bank's constraint is satisfied.

---

The above example demonstrates that the NPV is the present value of future cash profits over and above the required rate of return. The example was constructed so as to allow payments to the bank with the corporation's 10 percent required rate of return, with the remaining profits contained in the NPV. Thus, the NPV is the present value of the additional profits.

A slightly more realistic example occurs if the banker allowed the corporation to borrow only the net investment of $10,000 at an interest rate of 10 percent.

---

**Example:**        Using the same basic data for the project in the previous example, assume that the banker lends only $10,000 and that the loan is repaid in four equal payments. The annual payments are calculated as follows:

$$\$10,000/3.170 = \$3,154.57 \quad \text{or} \quad \$3,154.60 \text{ per year}$$

At Time zero the corporation borrows the net investment and initiates the project. The corporation incurs neither cash gain nor loss at Year zero. The loan repayments allow the corporation to receive the following cash flows:

| Year | 1 | 2 | 3 | 4 |
|---|---|---|---|---|
| Cash flow | $4,000.00 | $4,000.00 | $4,000.00 | $4,000.00 |
| Less: Loan payment | 3,154.60 | 3,154.60 | 3,154.60 | 3,154.60 |
| Equals "net" cash flow | $ 845.40 | $ 845.40 | $ 845.40 | $ 845.40 |

The yearly "net" cash flows of $845.40 are the corporation's profits. And the present value of this cash flow annuity is calculated as follows:

$$\$845.40(3.170) = \$2,680$$

Once again, note that the corporation pays the bank its required rate of return. In this case, however, only the net investment is borrowed; and the corporation receives "net" cash flows in each of the four subsequent years. The sum of the present values of the $845.40 annuity is the NPV of the project.

This modified example again demonstrates the "cash" interpretation of NPV: the NPV of $2,680 is the value at Time zero of the $845.40 annuity to be received by the corporation over four years.

If the corporation in the above example used internal funds to meet the net investment required, a zero NPV would result if the time adjusted profits produced a rate of return just equal to the required rate of return. Any additional profits would produce a positive NPV. Thus, the NPV is the present value of profits over and above the required rate of return.

The NPV also has an important interpretation from the standpoint of overall corporate performance. When the firm's total capital budget has a positive NPV, the value of the firm increases because its profits are projected to exceed its required rate of return. These extra profits can generate increased per share earnings and dividends. The higher EPS values can result in a higher resale value of the corporation's common stock. Thus, investments with a positive NPV can increase shareholder wealth.

**EVALUATION OF THE NPV CRITERION.** The NPV criterion is profit oriented and takes into account the time value of money. Consequently, it is capable of evaluating investment proposals that are profit seeking and that promise cash flows for several years into the future.

Since the NPV is measured in dollars, it provides a common denominator for:

1. Evaluating individual investments

2. Choosing from competing investment proposals

3. Measuring the impact on shareholder wealth produced by the set of investments that constitute the firm's capital budget

For these reasons, NPV is the preferred capital-budgeting criterion.

NPV is more difficult to compute than payback, and a careful interpretation is required because it does not provide a measure of a project's *actual* rate of return. If the rate of return used to discount the cash flows is not carefully chosen so as to reflect accurately the corporation's required rate, the NPV criterion may end up rejecting desirable projects or accepting those that generate relatively low rates of return.

Finally, NPV is the most conceptually difficult capital-budgeting criterion contained in this text. The applications discussed in Chapter 11, however, demonstrate that the NPV criterion is usable in situations that cannot be correctly handled by other capital-budgeting criteria.

**The Internal Rate of Return Criterion**

The **internal rate of return (IRR)** of an investment proposal is defined as the discount rate that produces a zero NPV. Thus, the IRR is the *actual* rate of return that a project earns when profits and the time value of money are taken into account. Note that it is stated as a percentage rate.

**COMPUTATION OF IRR.** As in the case of the payback criterion, different procedures are available for computing an investment's IRR depending on whether or not its cash flows are in annuity form.

*When Cash Flows Are in Annuity Form.* When the cash flows of an investment are in annuity form, its IRR can be computed very easily.

**Example:**

In the discussion of the NPV criterion on page 285, a project that required a net investment of $100,000 produced 16 annual cash flows of $14,000 each, required a 10 percent rate of return, and had an NPV of $9,536. Since the NPV is positive at a discount rate of 10 percent, this means that the project's actual rate of return exceeds 10 percent. The IRR for this project is found by dividing the value of one cash flow into the net investment and then locating the resulting quotient in the present value annuity table.

$$\$100,000/\$14,000 = 7.143$$

| Table Value | IRR |
| --- | --- |
| 7.379 | 11% |
| 6.974 | 12% |

Thus, the IRR for this project is between 11 percent and 12 percent. For many applications this is a sufficiently close approximation.

When a more exact IRR is needed, the following steps typically will produce an IRR that is correct to at least one decimal point:

1. Identify the closest rates of return, as was done above.
2. Compute the NPV for each of these two closest rates.

$$(\text{NPV} \mid 11\%) = \$14,000(7.379) - \$100,000 = \$3,306$$

$$(\text{NPV} \mid 12\%) = \$14,000(6.974) - \$100,000 = -\$2,364$$

The project's IRR occurs between the two discount rates that produce changes in the signs of the NPV coefficients. In this example the NPV is positive at 11 percent and negative at 12 percent. Therefore, the project's IRR is between these two rates.

3. Compute the sum of the *absolute* values of the NPVs obtained in Step 2:

$$\$3,306 + \$2,364 = \$5,670$$

4. Divide the sum obtained in Step 3 into the NPV of the smaller discount rate identified in Step 1. Then add the resulting quotient to the smaller discount rate:

$$\$3,306/\$5,670 = .58$$

$$\text{IRR} = 11\% + .58 = 11.58\%$$

---

*When Cash Flows Are Not in Annuity Form.* When the cash flows of an investment are not in annuity form, the computation of its IRR can become rather tedious even when calculators are used. In order to minimize the number of calculations, it is necessary to make a good first guess at the project's IRR. This can be accomplished by either of two ways:

1. If the cash flows at least approximate an annuity, *dominance techniques* can be applied.

2. If the cash flows display no general annuity pattern, a *weighted average* can be used.

---

**Example:**

(*Using the Dominance Technique*): A previous example (see page 287) contained a project with a net investment of $60,000, a required rate of return of 13 percent, and the following cash flows:

| Year | Yearly Cash Flows |
|------|-------------------|
| 1 | $20,000 |
| 2 | 20,000 |
| 3 | 20,000 |
| 4 | 15,000 |
| 5 | 15,000 |
| 6 | 15,000 |

This project was shown to have a positive NPV for a 13 percent discount rate. Thus, its IRR is greater than 13 percent—and this provides a good first guess.

Suppose the NPV at 13 percent had *not* been computed. A good first guess of the IRR can be obtained by using annuities that dominate or are dominated by the project's cash flows. To illustrate, a six-year annuity of $20,000 dominates the original set of cash flows because each $20,000 annual payment *equals or exceeds* its corresponding payment in the original set of cash flows. If the six-year, $20,000 annuity replaces the original set of cash flows, the IRR of this "modified" project is greater than the IRR of the original project because the $20,000 annuity dominates the original cash flows.

On the other hand, a six-year annuity of $15,000 is dominated by the original set of cash flows because each $15,000 annual payment is *equal to* or *less than* its corresponding payment in the original set of cash flows. Therefore, if the $15,000 annuity replaces the original set of cash flows, the IRR of the "modified" project is less than the IRR of the original project because the $15,000 annuity is dominated by the original set of cash flows.

The IRR for each of these replacement annuities is:

| Replacement Annuity | | Table Value | IRR |
|---|---|---|---|
| $20,000 | $60,000/$20,000 = | 3.0 | 24% |
| $15,000 | $60,000/$15,000 = | 4.0 | 12% |

Which of the two IRRs provides the better first guess? Chances are that the IRR based on the $20,000 annuity will provide a better first guess because it is based on the cash flows that occur in the *earliest years* of the original project. An alternative is to take the arithmetic average of the IRRs of the two annuities as follows:

$$\frac{.24 + .12}{2} = .18 \text{ or } 18\%$$

Now compute the NPV of the project, using an IRR of 18 percent for a first guess. (If the NPV is zero, the project's IRR is equal to the required rate of return, or 18 percent.)

$$
\begin{aligned}
NPV = \ & \$20,000\,(2.174) \\
+ \ & 15,000\,(.516) \\
+ \ & 15,000\,(.437) \\
+ \ & 15,000\,(.370) \\
- \ & 60,000 \\
\hline
NPV = \ & \$\ 3,325
\end{aligned}
$$

or

$$
\begin{aligned}
NPV = \ & \$20,000\,(2.174) \\
+ \ & 15,000\,(1.323) \\
- \ & 60,000 \\
\hline
NPV = \ & \$\ 3,325
\end{aligned}
$$

Since the NPV is positive, this means that the actual IRR exceeds 18 percent.

A second guess of the IRR at 21 percent is made, based on the size of the NPV. The NPV for the project discounted at 21 percent is:

$$
\begin{aligned}
NPV = \quad &\$20,000\,(2.074) \\
+ \quad &15,000\,(.467) \\
+ \quad &15,000\,(.386) \quad\text{or} \\
+ \quad &15,000\,(.319) \\
- \quad &60,000 \\
\hline
NPV = -\$ \quad &940
\end{aligned}
\qquad
\begin{aligned}
NPV = \quad &\$20,000\,(2.074) \\
+ \quad &15,000\,(1.172) \\
- \quad &60,000 \\
\hline
NPV = -\$ \quad &940
\end{aligned}
$$

Since the NPV is negative, this means that the actual IRR is less than 21 percent.

A third guess of the IRR at 20 percent is made, based on the preceding two guesses and their corresponding NPVs. The NPV for the project discounted at 20 percent is:

$$
\begin{aligned}
NPV = \quad &\$20,000\,(2.106) \\
+ \quad &15,000\,(.482) \\
+ \quad &15,000\,(.402) \quad\text{or} \\
+ \quad &15,000\,(.335) \\
- \quad &60,000 \\
\hline
NPV = \$ \quad &405
\end{aligned}
\qquad
\begin{aligned}
NPV = \quad &\$20,000\,(2.106) \\
+ \quad &15,000\,(1.219) \\
- \quad &60,000 \\
\hline
NPV = \$ \quad &405
\end{aligned}
$$

Thus, the actual IRR of the project is between 20 percent and 21 percent.

A more refined estimate is obtained by following the last two steps given earlier on page 291, as follows:

1. Compute the sum of the *absolute* values of the NPVs for the two closest rates:

$$\$940 + \$405 = \$1,345$$

2. Divide the sum obtained above into the NPV of the smaller discount rate, and then add the resulting quotient to the smaller discount rate:

$$\$405/\$1,345 = .30$$

$$IRR = 20\% + .30 = 20.3\%$$

Thus, the actual IRR of this project is 20.3 percent.

**Example:**   (*Using the Weighted Average Technique*):  A project requires a net investment of $16,000 and produces the following cash flows:

| Year | Yearly Cash Flows |
|------|-------------------|
| 1 | $4,000 |
| 2 | 6,000 |
| 3 | 5,000 |
| 4 | 5,000 |
| 5 | 4,000 |

Since this project has an irregular cash flow pattern, the techniques discussed for obtaining a first guess of the project's IRR are of little help. Therefore, the IRR of this project has to be estimated by calculating an average cash flow weighted by the number of years in the project's lifetime. The weighted average is computed as follows:

| Year | Cash Flow | Weight | Cash Flow × Weight |
|------|-----------|--------|--------------------|
| 1 | $4,000 | 5 | $20,000 |
| 2 | 6,000 | 4 | 24,000 |
| 3 | 5,000 | 3 | 15,000 |
| 4 | 5,000 | 2 | 10,000 |
| 5 | 4,000 | 1 | 4,000 |
| TOTALS | | 15 | $73,000 |

Note that the weights used in this procedure are the years listed in reverse order. This gives the greatest weight to the early cash flows. Each cash flow is multiplied by its corresponding weight. The sum of the weights is 15, and the sum of the weighted cash flows is $73,000. Divide the sum of the weighted cash flows by the sum of the weights to obtain the weighted average cash flow:

$$\text{Weighted average cash flow} = \$73,000/15 = \$4,867$$

The next step is to use the weighted average cash flow of $4,867 as an annuity that replaces the original set of cash flows. The value of one annuity payment is divided into the net investment:

$$\$16,000/\$4,867 = 3.288$$

By looking at a present value annuity table, the number 3.288 corresponds approximately to an IRR of 16 percent.

The NPV of the original project is now calculated by using a 16 percent discount rate:

$$
\begin{aligned}
\text{NPV} = \quad & \$\ 4,000(.862) \\
+ \quad & 6,000(.743) \\
+ \quad & 5,000(.641) \\
+ \quad & 5,000(.552) \\
+ \quad & 4,000(.476) \\
- \quad & 16,000 \\
\hline
\text{NPV} = & -\$225
\end{aligned}
$$

The negative NPV indicates that the actual IRR is less than 16 percent. The small NPV indicates that the IRR is close to 16 percent.

Thus, a second guess of IRR at 15 percent is made. The NPV of the project discounted at 15 percent is:

$$
\begin{aligned}
\text{NPV} = \quad & \$\ 4,000(.870) \\
+ \quad & 6,000(.756) \\
+ \quad & 5,000(.658) \\
+ \quad & 5,000(.572) \\
+ \quad & 4,000(.497) \\
- \quad & 16,000 \\
\hline
\text{NPV} = & \$\quad 154
\end{aligned}
$$

Since the NPV is positive, the IRR for the project is between 15 percent and 16 percent.

A more refined estimate can be obtained by using the techniques described earlier, as follows:

$$\$225 + \$154 = \$379$$

$$\$154/\$379 = .41$$

$$IRR = 15\% + .41 = 15.41\%$$

**INTERPRETATION OF THE IRR CRITERION.** Other things being equal, when two projects have the same net investment but different IRRs, the project with the higher IRR is preferred. When projects have different net investments, a problem arises in interpreting and using the IRR as a capital-budgeting criterion. This complication is developed more fully in Chapter 11, but the following simple example is presented to demonstrate the existence of the problem.

**Example:**

Two investment alternatives are to be evaluated by using IRR as the capital-budgeting criterion. The data for each alternative are as follows:

|                    | Project A | Project B  |
|--------------------|-----------|------------|
| Net investment     | $3,000    | $100,000   |
| Cash flow in Year 1| $6,000    | $110,000   |
| IRR                | 100%      | 10%        |

For purposes of simplicity, each project has only the one cash flow shown above. Note that the IRR for Project A is greater than the IRR for Project B. Does this mean that Project A is preferred to Project B? Not necessarily. Project A returns $3,000 over its net investment, but Project B returns $10,000 over its net investment. If these returns are seen as contributions to shareholder wealth, then Project B is preferred to Project A.

The difficulty is that the IRR criterion does not recognize, and consequently does not allow for, differences in the sizes of the net investments of each project. Therefore, ranking projects as to their desirability by using an IRR criterion does not guarantee that the resulting corporate capital budget will maximize its contribution to shareholder wealth.

**EVALUATION OF THE IRR CRITERION.** The IRR criterion takes into account the time value of money and is a profit oriented tool. This criterion measures the compound rate of return contained in investment alternatives the cash flows of which occur over several years into the future. Since the IRR is stated as a percentage, it has the added advantage of being a type of measure that is generally familiar to most managers. This makes it relatively easy to use IRRs when explaining the desirability of individual projects.

The IRR is the most computationally tedious of the three capital-budgeting criteria considered in this chapter. Repeated calculations may be needed when cash flows are not in annuity form. Although the dominance and weighted average techniques typically reduce the number of iterations, these techniques are not guaranteed to work in every situation. A more significant disadvantage of this criterion is its inability to allow for the size of a project's net investment. As a consequence, the IRR criterion is somewhat limited in the type of capital-budgeting application to which it can be applied.

# SUMMARY

A capital budget is a set of investment alternatives the returns of which occur over a period of two or more years. Capital budgeting is the process of generating the capital budget, and this process consists of several different types of procedures. The assumptions needed in order to concentrate on the managerial finance aspects of capital budgeting relate to (1) the wealth maximization motive, (2) certainty, (3) cash based income, (4) timing of cash flows, (5) conventional cash flow patterns, (6) a corporation's required rate of return, and (7) the absence of capital rationing. A major step in the procedure of evaluating the desirability of individual investments consists in computing both the net investment and the cash flows of these investments.

The three most widely used capital-budgeting criteria are (1) the payback, (2) the net present value, and (3) the internal rate of return. Each criterion has its advantages and disadvantages. Even though NPV is the most conceptually difficult of the three criteria, it is the preferred one because it takes into account the time value of money and it is measured in dollars.

# QUESTIONS

10-1. From the standpoint of managerial finance, what is the basic goal of capital budgeting?

10-2. What is the common characteristic shared by all projects contained in a corporation's capital budget?

10-3. What are the different types of procedures in the capital-budgeting process?

10-4. What are the major capital-budgeting assumptions made in this chapter? What are the reasons for making these assumptions?

10-5. What major steps in the procedure for evaluating the desirability of individual investment alternatives are the responsibility of the financial manager?

10-6. Why do net investment and cash flows concentrate on cash, rather than accounting, income?

10-7. What are the advantages and disadvantages of the payback criterion?

10-8. What are the advantages and disadvantages of the NPV criterion?

10-9. Why is the NPV identified as the preferred capital-budgeting criterion?

10-10. How is a negative NPV coefficient interpreted?

10-11. An investment alternative is discounted at 12% and yields an NPV of $14,500. Interpret this NPV.

10-12.   What are the advantages and disadvantages of the IRR criterion?

---

# PROBLEMS

*Note:* In these problems assume a 40% federal corporate income tax rate and a 20% capital gains tax rate.

10-1.   Compute the net investment and cash flows for the following investment alternative:

| | |
|---|---|
| Purchase price: | $2,700,000 |
| Transportation and installation: | $150,000 |
| Economic life: | 4 years |
| Scrap value at Year 4: | $50,000 |
| Profit before depreciation and taxes: | $900,000 each year |

10-2.   A corporation will replace an existing product with an improved and expanded product line. The needed machinery for the new product line costs $1,000,000; it will last for six years and has an estimated scrap value of $30,000.

The machinery for the existing product line cost $600,000 four years ago, and it is being depreciated over six years. This existing machinery is now obsolete and has a scrap value of $10,000.

Calculate the corporation's net investment.

10-3.   A capital-budgeting alternative has the following data set:

| | |
|---|---|
| Purchase price: | $3,670,000 |
| Installation cost: | $220,000 |
| Economic life: | 5 years |
| Salvage value at Year 5: | $40,000 |

The financing terms for this project are: 20% of the purchase price in cash, with the remainder to be paid in four equal yearly installments at an interest rate of 12%. The profit before depreciation and taxes for each of five years is as follows:

| Year | 1 | 2 | 3 | 4 | 5 |
|---|---|---|---|---|---|
| Amount | $900,000 | $1,200,000 | $1,200,000 | $900,000 | $800,000 |

Compute the net investment and cash flows of this project.

10-4.   A capital-budgeting alternative has the following data set:

| | |
|---|---|
| Purchase price: | $4,750,000 |
| Installation cost: | $ 165,000 |
| Economic life: | 5 years |
| Salvage value, Year 5: | $ 285,000 |

The firm estimates that net working capital equal to 10% of the asset's purchase price will have to be invested in the project at Year zero and will be recovered at the end of Year 5.

Profits before depreciation and taxes for each year are estimated to be $1,400,000. Compute the net investment and cash flows for this capital-budgeting project.

10-5. Compute the payback period for each of the following investment projects:

|  | Project A | Project B | Project C |
|---|---|---|---|
| Net investment: | $150,000 | $6,000 | $2,100,000 |
| Cash flows: | | | |
| Year 1 | 30,000 | 2,000 | 400,000 |
| Year 2 | 50,000 | 3,000 | 600,000 |
| Year 3 | 50,000 | 3,000 | 800,000 |
| Year 4 | 20,000 | 3,000 | 500,000 |
| Year 5 | 20,000 | 2,000 | 400,000 |

10-6. Compute the NPV for each of the following proposed investments, using the discount rate indicated for each:

|  | Project A | Project B | Project C |
|---|---|---|---|
| Net investment: | $250,000 | $400,000 | $160,000 |
| Discount rate: | 10% | 14% | 17% |
| Cash flows: | | | |
| Year 1 | $ 70,000 | $ 80,000 | $ 50,000 |
| Year 2 | 70,000 | 90,000 | 60,000 |
| Year 3 | 70,000 | 100,000 | 70,000 |
| Year 4 | 70,000 | 100,000 | 50,000 |
| Year 5 | 70,000 | 100,000 | 40,000 |
| Year 6 | 70,000 | 100,000 | 30,000 |

10-7. A proposal requires a net investment of $14,000,000. Cash flows are estimated to be $3,000,000 each year for 20 years. Compute the IRR for this project. (The cash flow annuity begins in Year 1.)

10-8. Compute the IRR for each of the following proposals, using the dominance technique:

|  | Project A | Project B | Project C |
|---|---|---|---|
| Net investment: | $24,000 | $100,000 | $40,000 |
| Cash flows: | | | |
| Year 1 | 8,000 | 40,000 | 10,000 |
| Year 2 | 8,000 | 40,000 | 10,000 |
| Year 3 | 8,000 | 25,000 | 12,000 |
| Year 4 | 6,000 | 25,000 | 12,000 |
| Year 5 | 4,000 | 25,000 | 10,000 |

10-9. Compute the IRR for each of the following proposals, using the weighted average technique:

|  | Project A | Project B |
|---|---|---|
| Net investment: | $35,000 | $250,000 |
| Cash flows: |  |  |
| Year 1 | 14,000 | 80,000 |
| Year 2 | 16,000 | 120,000 |
| Year 3 | 10,000 | 110,000 |
| Year 4 | 8,000 | 100,000 |

---

# SELECTED REFERENCES

*Note:* See the end of Chapter 11.

# CHAPTER 11

# Capital Budgeting under Conditions of Certainty: The Decisions

*This chapter applies the payback, net present value (NPV), and internal rate of return (IRR) criteria to five types of capital-budgeting decisions that confront financial managers. These five types of decisions are (1) accept/reject decisions, (2) replacement decisions, (3) mutually exclusive decisions, (4) lease/purchase decisions, and (5) capital-rationing decisions. The cash flows of the investment alternatives that fall within these five types of decisions are consistent with the capital-budgeting assumptions introduced in Chapter 10. Some additional assumptions are presented to deal with specific situations, and the capital-rationing section uses a slightly modified, but easily stated, assumption set. The chapter also continues the use of straight-line depreciation, a 40 percent corporate federal income tax rate, and a 20 percent capital gains tax rate.*

*This chapter devotes a separate section to each of the five types of capital-budgeting decisions. Each section explains a specific type of decision, states the decision rules in terms of the payback, NPV, and IRR criteria, and evaluates the ability of these criteria to help the decision maker reach correct conclusions. It will not be surprising to discover that the payback criterion can quite often produce an incorrect conclusion. The NPV and IRR criteria will also produce conflicting results in some cases involving mutually exclusive alternatives; in such situations, the NPV criterion is used in preference to the IRR criterion. In addition, the NPV criterion is the only one used in making decisions that involve capital rationing. As a result, the NPV criterion will emerge as the most desirable capital-budgeting criterion from among the three criteria that are used. It is important to remember that NPV is a measure of the contribution to shareholder wealth contained in an investment alternative.*

## ACCEPT/REJECT DECISIONS

An **accept/reject decision** occurs when an individual project is accepted or rejected without regard to any other investment alternative. This type of decision is made when projects are **economically independent**. A proposed investment is said to be economically independent when the following conditions exist:

1.  The proposal's net investment and cash flows do not affect and are unaffected by the net investments and cash flows of other projects.

2.  Accepting or rejecting the proposal has no impact on the desirability of other projects; that is, no other project is competing to do the same job.

**Decision Rules**      Decision rules for evaluating investment projects are formulated from the capital-budgeting criteria developed in the previous chapter. However, decision rules must be tailored for each type of investment decision. The following decision rules apply to accept/reject decisions:

1. *Payback Criterion.* Compute the project's payback. Accept the project if the computed payback is equal to or less than the maximum allowable payback set by the corporation. Otherwise, reject the project.

2. *NPV Criterion.* Compute the project's NPV, using the corporation's required rate of return as the discount rate. Accept the project if its NPV is greater than or equal to zero. Reject the project if its NPV is negative.

3. *IRR Criterion.* Compute the project's IRR. Accept the project if its IRR is greater than or equal to the corporation's required rate of return. Reject the project if its IRR is less than the required rate of return.

The application of these decision rules to accept/reject problems is shown in the following example.

---

**Example:**      A corporation is considering expanding the capacity of one of its production lines. The corporation's maximum payback is three years. Its required rate of return is 12 percent. The net investment required in order to achieve the desired extra capacity is $7,000,000. Cash flows over the expected life of the new production facilities are shown below, and salvage value at the end of Year 6 is expected to be zero.

| Year | Cash Flows |
|------|------------|
| 1 | $2,000,000 |
| 2 | 2,000,000 |
| 3 | 2,000,000 |
| 4 | 2,000,000 |
| 5 | 1,000,000 |
| 6 | 1,000,000 |

The proposal's payback is four years because it takes four years of accumulated cash flows to equal or surpass the net investment. Therefore, the project is *rejected* on the basis of the payback criterion.

The calculations for the project's NPV and IRR are shown in Table 11-1. Since the NPV discounted at 12 percent is a positive $148,000, the project is *accepted* on the basis of the NPV criterion.

Table 11-1 shows that the project's IRR is between 12 percent and 13 percent. A closer estimate of the IRR is found by adding the absolute values of the NPVs at 12 percent and 13 percent, dividing the sum into the NPV value at 12 percent, and adding the fraction to 12 percent, as follows:

$$\$148,000/(\$148,000 + \$29,000) = .836 \text{ or } .84$$

$$IRR = 12\% + .84 = 12.84\%$$

Therefore, the project is *accepted* on the basis of the IRR criterion.

**Evaluation of Decision Criteria**

When projects are evaluated on an accept/reject basis, the NPV and IRR criteria produce identical decisions. Since payback neither measures profitability nor takes into account the time value of money, it may yield decisions that are not consistent with the other two criteria.

**Table 11-1.**    Accept/Reject Example

| Year | Cash Flow | PV Factors 12% | Present Values | PV Factors 13% | Present Values |
|------|-----------|----------------|----------------|----------------|----------------|
| 1 | $2,000,000 | | | | |
| 2 | 2,000,000 | | | | |
| 3 | 2,000,000 | 3.037 | $6,074,000 | 2.974 | $5,948,000 |
| 4 | 2,000,000 | | | | |
| 5 | 1,000,000 | .567 | 567,000 | .543 | 543,000 |
| 6 | 1,000,000 | .507 | 507,000 | .480 | 480,000 |
| Total present values | | | $7,148,000 | | $6,971,000 |
| Less: Net investment | | | 7,000,000 | | 7,000,000 |
| Net present value | | | $+148,000 | | $ −29,000 |

The reason why the NPV and IRR criteria produce similar decisions for accept/reject problems can be explained by computing the NPV values at various discount rates and plotting what is called the NPV profile. For example, assume that an investment project requires a net investment of $1,000 and promises a four-year cash-flow annuity of $400 per year. The required rate of return is assumed to be 16 percent. The following results are produced when NPV is computed at various discount rates:

| Discount Rate | NPV |
|---------------|-----|
| 12% | $214.8 |
| 14 | 165.6 |
| 16 | 119.2 |
| 18 | 76.0 |
| 20 | 35.6 |
| 22 | −2.4 |
| 24 | −38.4 |

The NPV profile—the plot of NPVs for different discount rates—is contained in Figure 11-1. The curve intersects the horizontal axis at a discount

Figure 11-1.        A Net Present Value Profile

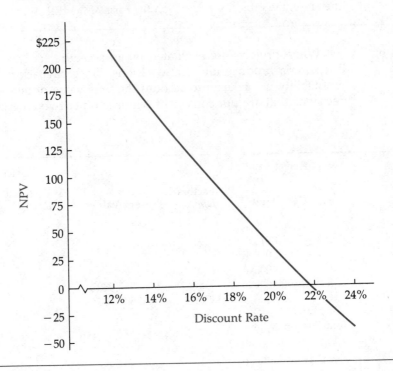

rate of between 21 percent and 22 percent, and this point corresponds to the project's  IRR. For any discount rate less than the IRR, Figure 11-1 shows that the resulting NPV is positive. Since the IRR is greater than the required rate of return of 16 percent, both the NPV and the IRR criteria accept this project. Similarly, if the required rate of return is greater than the project's IRR, the NPV will be negative, and both criteria will reject the project.

## REPLACEMENT DECISIONS

A **replacement decision** occurs when one productive asset is replaced with another in order to increase profits by decreasing costs and/or increasing output. This is a common type of capital-budgeting problem. An example of a replacement decision problem occurs when new machinery replaces existing machinery whose output has become inadequate. The same basic product is produced with the new machinery even though output may be increased and the quality of output may be changed. Another common replacement decision problem is that of replacing a firm's car and truck fleet to minimize the firm's transportation costs.

**Special Assumption**

The replacement decision problems discussed in this chapter make one special assumption: *the economic lifetime of a replacement asset is equal to the remaining economic lifetime of the asset being replaced.* For example, if an asset to be replaced had an original economic life of 12 years, is now 4 years old, and has a remaining economic life of 8 years, the special assumption made is that the replacement asset also has an economic life of 8 years.

**Incremental Cash Flow**

In order to evaluate a capital-budgeting problem that involves a replacement decision, it is necessary to compute both the net investment and the incremental cash flows that result from replacing the existing asset. **Incremental cash flow** is defined as the cash flow of the present asset subtracted from the cash flow of the replacement asset.

**Example:**

A set of machinery used in a production line is being considered for replacement. Given the following data, compute the net investment and the incremental cash flow:

| | Present Machinery | Proposed Machinery |
|---|---|---|
| Installed cost | $4,000,000 | $5,400,000 |
| Life/age | 10/4 | 6/0 |
| Depreciation per year | $400,000 | $900,000 |
| Accumulated depreciation | $1,600,000 | 0 |
| Book value | $2,400,000 | $5,400,000 |
| Current market value | $1,400,000 | —— |
| Profit before depreciation and taxes in: Year 1 | $800,000 | $1,500,000 |
| Year 2 | $800,000 | $1,500,000 |
| Year 3 | $800,000 | $1,500,000 |
| Year 4 | $500,000 | $1,500,000 |
| Year 5 | $500,000 | $1,500,000 |
| Year 6 | $500,000 | $1,500,000 |

Assuming that the present machinery is sold for its current market value, the corporation will suffer a loss in book value of $2,400,000 − $1,400,000 = $1,000,000. This would reduce its federal tax liability by ($1,000,000)(.4) = $400,000. The net investment for the proposed project is thus:

| | |
|---|---|
| Installed cost: | $5,400,000 |
| Proceeds from asset disposal: | −1,400,000 |
| Tax savings on asset disposal: | − 400,000 |
| Net investment | $3,600,000 |

The cash flows for each set of machinery are computed as follows:

| | Present Machinery | | Proposed Machinery |
| --- | --- | --- | --- |
| | Years 1-3 | Years 4-6 | Years 1-6 |
| Profit before depreciation and taxes: | $800,000 | $500,000 | $1,500,000 |
| Depreciation: | −400,000 | −400,000 | −900,000 |
| Equals taxable profit | $400,000 | $100,000 | $ 600,000 |
| Federal income taxes: | −160,000 | −40,000 | −240,000 |
| Equals profit after taxes | $240,000 | $ 60,000 | $ 360,000 |
| Depreciation: | +400,000 | +400,000 | +900,000 |
| Equals cash flow | $640,000 | $460,000 | $1,260,000 |

The incremental cash flows for each year are computed by subtracting the cash flows of the present machinery from those of the proposed machinery.

| Year | Cash Flow of Proposed Machinery | Cash Flow of Present Machinery | Incremental Cash Flow |
| --- | --- | --- | --- |
| 1 | $1,260,000 | $640,000 | $620,000 |
| 2 | 1,260,000 | 640,000 | 620,000 |
| 3 | 1,260,000 | 640,000 | 620,000 |
| 4 | 1,260,000 | 460,000 | 800,000 |
| 5 | 1,260,000 | 460,000 | 800,000 |
| 6 | 1,260,000 | 460,000 | 800,000 |

## Decision Rules

Decision rules for replacement problems are based on net investment and incremental cash flows. These rules are

1.  *Payback Criterion.* Compute the payback, using the incremental cash flows. If the computed payback is equal to or less than the maximum allowable payback set by the corporation, replace the present asset. Otherwise, keep the present asset and reject the proposed replacement asset.

2.  *NPV Criterion.* Compute the NPV, using the net investment and the incremental cash flows. Use a discount rate equal to the corporation's required rate of return. If the NPV is greater than or equal to zero, replace the present asset. Otherwise, keep the present asset and reject the proposed replacement asset.

3.  *IRR Criterion.* Compute the IRR, using the net investment and the incremental cash flows. If the IRR is greater than or equal to the corporation's required rate of return, replace the present asset. Otherwise, keep the present asset and reject the proposed replacement asset.

The application of these decision rules is shown in the example below.

| Example: | Using the data of the corporation in the previous example, assume that its maximum allowable payback is four years and that its required rate of return is 10 percent. |
|---|---|

Payback computed by using incremental cash flows is six years. Since the computed payback is greater than the corporation's maximum allowable payback, *reject* the replacement and keep the present asset.

The calculations for the proposed machinery's NPV and IRR are shown in Table 11-2. Since the NPV discounted at 10 percent is −$563,660, the replacement asset is rejected and the present machinery is retained.

Table 11-2 shows that IRR is between 4 percent and 5 percent. A closer estimate of the IRR, using the NPV coefficients for 4 percent and 5 percent, is computed as follows:

$$\$94,100/(\$94,100 + \$29,340) = .76$$

$$IRR = 4\% + .76 = 4.76\%$$

Therefore, on the basis of the IRR criterion, *reject* the replacement asset and keep the present asset.

**Table 11-2.**  Replacement Decision Example

| Year | Incremental Cash Flow | PV at 10% | Present Values | PV at 5% | Present Values | PV at 4% | Present Values |
|---|---|---|---|---|---|---|---|
| 1 | $620,000 | | | | | | |
| 2 | 620,000 | 2.487 | $1,541,940 | 2.723 | $1,688,260 | 2.775 | $1,720,500 |
| 3 | 620,000 | | | | | | |
| 4 | 800,000 | .683 | 546,400 | .823 | 658,400 | .855 | 684,000 |
| 5 | 800,000 | .621 | 496,800 | .784 | 627,200 | .822 | 657,600 |
| 6 | 800,000 | .564 | 451,200 | .746 | 596,800 | .790 | 632,000 |
| Total present values | | | $3,036,340 | | $3,570,660 | | $3,694,100 |
| Less: net investment | | | 3,600,000 | | 3,600,000 | | 3,600,000 |
| Net present value | | | $−563,660 | | $ −29,340 | | $   94,100 |

| Evaluation of Decision Criteria | As with accept/reject decisions, the NPV and IRR criteria produce identical decisions when replacement decisions are being evaluated. (In the above example, payback agreed with the other two criteria because the proposed machinery was only marginally profitable.) If an NPV profile were plotted for this replacement problem, it would resemble the one shown in Figure 11-1. As a result, a replacement decision will choose the proposed replacement asset whenever the required rate of return is equal to or less than the IRR of the net investment and the incremental cash flows. |
|---|---|

A replacement decision will choose to keep the present asset whenever the IRR of the net investment and incremental cash flows is less than the required rate of return.

## MUTUALLY EXCLUSIVE DECISIONS

Two or more investment alternatives are said to be **mutually exclusive** when accepting one of them excludes all others from being accepted. Mutually exclusive decisions occur whenever a corporation receives competitive bids for a given project. The bids are mutually exclusive because the winning bid excludes all other bids from being accepted. One example of mutually exclusive decision-making problems involves choosing the principal advertising medium that would receive the major portion of a firm's advertising budget. Another example is the selection of a firm's computer hardware and software configuration from among competing manufacturers, as well as from several models manufactured by the winning bidder.

**Special Assumption**

In applying capital-budgeting criteria to mutually exclusive problems, one special assumption is made: *all the alternatives are assumed to have the same economic lifetime.*

**Decision Rules**

Capital-budgeting criteria provide the following decision rules for making mutually exclusive decisions:

1. *Payback Criterion.* Compute the payback for each alternative. Choose the alternative with the smallest payback provided that the computed value is equal to or less than the maximum allowable payback set by the corporation. If this condition is violated, reject all alternatives.

2. *NPV Criterion.* Compute the NPV for each alternative, using the required rate of return as the discount rate. Choose the alternative with the highest NPV provided that the NPV is positive or zero. If this condition is violated, reject all alternatives.

3. *IRR Criterion.* Compute the IRR for each alternative. Choose the alternative with the highest IRR subject to two conditions:
   a. The IRR for the chosen alternative must be equal to or greater than the corporation's required rate of return.
   b. The selected alternative must be the same one chosen by the NPV decision rule.
   If the first condition is violated, reject all alternatives. If the second condition is violated, use the NPV decision rule.

The IRR decision rule thus indicates that it may produce incorrect results when evaluating mutually exclusive projects. The remainder of this section illustrates the use of these decision rules and demonstrates why the IRR and NPV criteria can produce conflicting rankings of alternatives. Techniques for modifying the IRR decision rule so as to make it yield rankings consistent with those of the NPV criterion are contained in more advanced finance texts.

**Consistent NPV and IRR Rankings**

Most mutually exclusive problems produce NPV and IRR rankings that are consistent with each other.

---

**Example:**

Two mutually exclusive investment alternatives have five-year economic lifetimes. Alternative *A* requires a net investment of $30,000 and produces cash flows of $10,000 per year. Alternative *B* requires a net investment of $20,000 and produces cash flows of $6,000 a year. Assume that the firm's maximum payback is three years and that its required rate of return is 10 percent. Which alternative is preferable? Using the three decision rules produces the following results:

| Alternative | NPV at 10% | IRR | Payback |
|:-----------:|:----------:|:------:|:-------:|
| A | $7,910 | 19.87% | 3 years |
| B | $2,746 | 15.24% | 4 years |

Thus, all three decision rules prefer Alternative *A* because (1) it has the smaller payback which is also equal to the maximum allowable payback, (2) its NPV is positive and greater than that of Alternative *B*, and (3) its IRR is greater than the required rate of return and is higher than that of Alternative *B*. It is thus the same alternative chosen by the NPV decision rule.

---

The NPV profiles of these two alternatives are contained in Figure 11-2. The profiles show that, at all discount rates equal to or less than the IRR of Alternative *A*, the NPV of Alternative *A* is greater than that of Alternative *B*. Thus, as long as the firm's required rate of return is equal to or less than the IRR of Alternative *A*, Alternative *A* will be chosen over Alternative *B*. If the required rate of return exceeds 19.87 percent, both alternatives will be rejected.

**Conflicting NPV and IRR Rankings**

The NPV and IRR capital-budgeting criteria can produce conflicting rankings among mutually exclusive investment alternatives for three major reasons. This section identifies and discusses these reasons.

**DOLLAR DIFFERENCES IN NET INVESTMENTS.** The dollar differences in net investments can cause conflicting rankings because the NPV criterion recognizes the dollar differences while the IRR criterion does not. Since the NPV is stated in present value dollars over and above the required net investment, the size of the net investment is explicitly recognized. The IRR, however, is not stated in dollars but as a percentage rate.

Figure 11-2.        **Net Present Value Profiles of Mutually Exclusive Alternatives A and B**

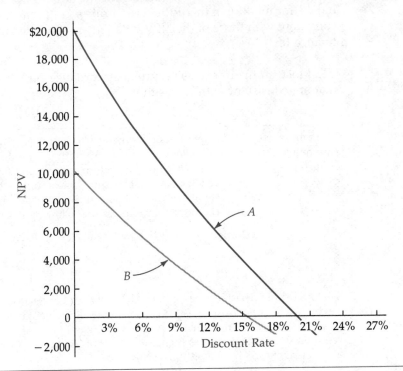

---

**Example:**        Assume that a corporation accepts two projects that are not mutually exclusive, with each having an IRR of 10 percent. Project C requires a net investment of $1,000. Project D requires $1,000,000. Since the projects have the same IRR, is the corporation indifferent about the two projects? Certainly not! Project C returns $100 a year, while Project D returns $100,000 a year. Thus, Project D makes a much greater contribution to increasing shareholder wealth than does Project C. However, the IRR criterion cannot make this distinction.

---

**DIFFERENT TIMINGS OF CASH FLOWS.** Conflicting rankings may occur when the largest cash flows from one investment occur early in its lifetime while the largest cash flows from a competing alternative occur toward the end of its economic lifetime.

---

**Example:**        A corporation wishes to evaluate Projects E and F, two mutually exclusive investment alternatives. The corporation's required rate of return is 8 percent, and the net investment and cash flows for each project are as follows:

|  | Project E | Project F |
|---|---|---|
| Net investment | $2,500 | $3,000 |
| Cash flow in: Year 1 | 2,000 | 500 |
| Year 2 | 1,000 | 1,000 |
| Year 3 | 500 | 3,000 |

The following values and rankings are obtained in computing the NPV and IRR of the two projects:

|  | NPV at 8% | IRR |
|---|---|---|
| Project E | $606 | 24.86% |
| Project F | $702 | 17.49% |

The decision rule for the NPV criterion chooses Project F over Project E; the IRR decision rule criterion chooses Project E over Project F.

The NPV profiles for each project are contained in Figure 11-3. This figure demonstrates why the conflict in rankings is due to the timing of the cash flows. The NPV profile for Project F has a much steeper slope than that of Project E because Project F's largest cash flow occurs in Year 3 while the largest cash flow for Project E occurs in Year 1. In addition, the NPV of Project F is greater than that of Project E at discount rates equal to or less than 10 percent. As a result, the two profiles intersect between 10 and 11 percent. For discount rates equal to or greater than 11 percent, Project E is preferable to Project F.

**DIFFERENCES IN REINVESTMENT RATE ASSUMPTIONS.** Given the conflict in rankings that has been demonstrated, the question still remains as to which capital-budgeting criterion is to be used. In the previous example there is nothing to suggest that the NPV criterion is superior to the IRR criterion, or vice versa. However, the IRR decision rule states that the NPV criterion is to be used when a conflict does occur. The answer to this problem is found in the different assumptions made by each criterion with regard to the reinvestment rates of all intermediate cash flows. **Intermediate cash flows** consist of all the cash flows earned by an investment other than the final one. The reinvestment rate assumptions are built into the compound amount and present value tables that are used by the NPV and IRR criteria in adjusting for the time value of money. The assumptions are

1.  The NPV criterion assumes that all intermediate cash flows are reinvested at a rate of return equal to the discount rate. The NPV decision rule for mutually exclusive alternatives assumes that the intermediate cash flows for any of the competing alternatives can be reinvested at the same rate, regardless of which alternative is selected.

2.  The IRR criterion assumes that all intermediate cash flows are reinvested at a rate of return equal to the project's IRR. The IRR

decision rule thus imposes different reinvestment rates for each competing alternative.

To illustrate, for Projects $E$ and $F$ in the previous example, the NPV criterion assumes that the intermediate cash flows from either project will be reinvested at the required rate of 8 percent. This criterion assumes only that the corporation will continue to find investments that return its minimum required rate. The IRR criterion, however, assumes that the intermediate cash flows from Project $E$ can be reinvested at a rate of 24.86 percent, and those of Project $F$ at a rate of 17.49 percent. Thus, the IRR criterion assumes that the firm will be able to find future investments that yield rates of return far greater than its minimum required rate. In addition, the magnitude of these future rates is based on the investment alternative accepted now. Since it may not be realistic to expect the firm to earn a rate

**Figure 11-3.**    **Net Present Value Profiles of Mutually Exclusive Projects $E$ and $F$**

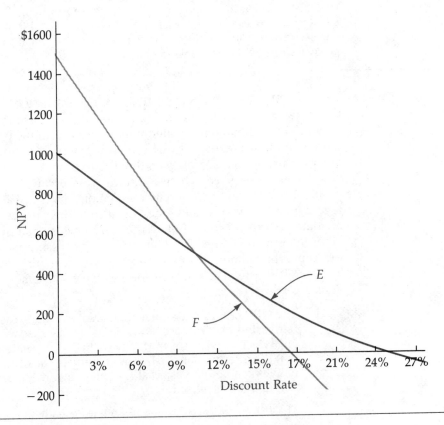

of return equal to the IRR's assumed reinvestment rate, the NPV criterion is used as the primary decision rule when conflicting rankings occur.

**Evaluation of Decision Criteria**

When mutually exclusive decisions are being evaluated, it is always possible that the NPV and IRR criteria will produce conflicting rankings. The most common reason for the occurrence of such conflicts lies in the implied reinvestment rates of these criteria. When conflicting rankings do occur, the NPV criterion should be used for two reasons.

1. The NPV's assumed reinvestment rates are consistent across the competing alternatives while the IRR's are not.

2. The NPV criterion assumes that the corporation will continue to accept projects the rates of return of which equal or exceed the current required rate while the IRR criterion assumes that the firm will accept only those projects the rates of return of which equal or exceed their implied reinvestment rates.

It has been pointed out several times that the payback criterion is not a very useful decision rule because it measures neither profitability nor the time value of money. Payback rankings can also be expected to differ from NPV rankings whenever the timings of cash flows differ significantly among competing alternatives. Thus, the NPV criterion provides a decision rule that is superior to both payback and IRR when mutually exclusive alternatives are to be evaluated.

# LEASE/PURCHASE DECISIONS

A **lease** is a contract under which the owner of an asset allows its use by another party in return for specified periodic payments. The party using the asset and making the lease payments is called the **lessee**. The owner of the asset is called the **lessor**.

Almost any asset that can be purchased can also be leased. A capital-budgeting decision arises when a corporation wishes to evaluate the desirability of leasing versus purchasing an asset that is to be used for longer than one year. This section deals only with a few of the capital-budgeting aspects of leasing (a more comprehensive treatment of leasing is found in Chapter 21).

The opportunity to lease or purchase an asset (or to do neither) is a special type of mutually exclusive capital-budgeting problem. For example, an investment alternative that would otherwise be evaluated on an accept/reject basis is transformed into a mutually exclusive set of alternatives when the investment can be leased or purchased. If a corporation already has two or more competing bids that would normally result in purchasing the selected alternative and it becomes aware that at least some of the other alternatives can also be leased, the situation becomes a complex, mutually exclusive decision problem.

**Net Investment and Cash Flow Computations**

For a purchase alternative, the net investment and cash flow computations use Equations 10-1 and 10-2 respectively. For a leasing alternative, the net investment is typically zero although a lease payment may be due at Time zero. The cash flow computations recognize the lease payments but do not include any adjustments for depreciation and salvage when the ownership of the asset remains with the lessor.

The cash flow for a leased asset is defined by the following equation:

$$\text{Cash flow} = \text{profit before lease payments and taxes}$$
$$- \text{ lease payments}$$
$$- \text{ federal corporate income taxes} \qquad (11\text{-}1)$$

The profit before depreciation and taxes for a purchase alternative may not be equal to the profit before lease payments and taxes for the leasing alternative. One reason for this divergence is due to the handling of maintenance costs. Under the purchase alternative, the buyer pays the costs of maintaining the asset. Many leasing companies, on the other hand, maintain their leased assets. Realistically, however, they expect to recover their maintenance expenses through lease payments.

**Example:**

A corporation can purchase an asset for $2,000,000. This asset has a ten-year economic life and little expected salvage value at the end of Year 10. Profit before depreciation and taxes is $800,000 for each of the first six years but decreases substantially in the last four years. The asset's expected resale value after six years is $500,000.

The corporation contacts a leasing company and negotiates a six-year lease for the asset. The yearly lease payments would be $350,000. Since the lessor would maintain the asset, the yearly profit before lease payments and taxes would be $850,000 over the six years of the lease.

The net investment and cash flow computations for each alternative are shown in Table 11-3. For the purchase alternative, yearly depreciation is computed as ($2,000,000 − $500,000)/6 = $250,000. At the end of Year 6, the cash flow under the purchase alternative is increased by the resale value of $500,000. For the lease alternative, the cash flow values are obtained by using Equation 11-1.

**Decision Rules**

Once the net investments and cash flows are computed, lease/purchase problems are treated as mutually exclusive decisions. Consequently, mutually exclusive decision rules and assumptions are used in measuring the desirability of each alternative.

The application of the NPV decision rule to the lease/purchase problem in the previous example is demonstrated below.

**Table 11-3.**          Net Investment and Cash Flow for a Lease/Purchase Example

### Purchase Alternative

| | |
|---|---:|
| Net investment | $2,000,000 |
| Yearly cash flows (excluding year 6 resale) | |
|   Profit before depreciation and taxes: | $ 800,000 |
|   Depreciation: | −250,000 |
|     Equals taxable profit | $ 550,000 |
|   Federal corporate income taxes: | −220,000 |
|     Equals profit after taxes | $ 330,000 |
|   Depreciation: | +250,000 |
|     Equals cash flow | $ 580,000 |
| | |
| Cash flow in year 6 | $ 580,000 |
| Resale value | +500,000 |
|   Equals net cash flow | $1,080,000 |

### Lease Alternative

| | |
|---|---:|
| Net investment | $      0 |
| Yearly cash flows | |
|   Profit before lease payment and taxes: | $ 850,000 |
|   Lease payment: | −350,000 |
|     Equals taxable profit | $ 500,000 |
|   Federal corporate income taxes: | −200,000 |
|     Equals cash flow | $ 300,000 |

**Example:**     Assume that the corporation in the previous example has a required rate of return of 10 percent. The NPV for each alternative is computed as follows:

$$\text{NPV (Purchase)} = (\$580,000)(4.355) + (\$500,000)(.564) - \$2,000,000$$
$$= \$807,900$$

$$\text{NPV (Lease)} \quad = (\$300,000)(4.355) = \$1,306,500$$

Thus, the lease alternative is more desirable than the purchase alternative when the time value of money is taken into account.

**Evaluation of Decision Criteria**          When evaluating lease/purchase alternatives by considering them to be mutually exclusive alternatives, the only useful decision rule is that based on the NPV criterion. This is because a lease alternative has a zero net investment. Payback and IRR coefficients cannot be computed for investment alternatives that have a zero net investment and only positive cash flows. The NPV criterion, however, produces correct rankings and can be relied upon when making lease/purchase decisions.

## CAPITAL-RATIONING DECISIONS

In the previous chapter capital rationing was defined as a situation in which a corporation is unable to finance its entire capital budget. Suppose a corporation desires to adopt all independent investment alternatives having NPVs that are at least zero. If the total net investment required at Year zero exceeds the corporation's available funds, the corporation is said to be operating under conditions of capital rationing. This section explains how the capital-budgeting process and mutually exclusive decision rules have to be modified in the presence of capital rationing.

The impacts of capital rationing on capital budgeting are best explained by using the following example.

**Example:**

Assume that a corporation is considering three independent capital-budgeting projects. The corporation advertises for competitive bids on each project. One bid is received on Project A, three bids are received on Project B, and two bids are received on Project C. The corporation's financial managers then calculate the following net investments and NPV coefficients on all the bids for each project:

|  | Net Investment | NPV |
|---|---|---|
| **Project A** | | |
| Bid A-1 | $3,000,000 | $250,000 |
| | | |
| **Project B** | | |
| Bid B-1 | 3,000,000 | 200,000 |
| Bid B-2 | 3,500,000 | 250,000 |
| Bid B-3 | 4,000,000 | 225,000 |
| | | |
| **Project C** | | |
| Bid C-1 | 5,000,000 | 300,000 |
| Bid C-2 | 6,000,000 | 325,000 |

Since only one bid is available for Project A, it is evaluated on an accept/reject basis. The bid is acceptable because its NPV is positive.

The three bids on Project B are mutually exclusive. B-2 is chosen over B-1 and B-3 because it shows the largest positive NPV.

The two bids on Project C are also mutually exclusive. C-2 is chosen over C-1 because of its larger NPV coefficient.

In the absence of capital rationing, the capital budget would consist of alternatives A-1, B-2, and C-2. The total net investment required in order to adopt this budget is $3,000,000 + $3,500,000 + $6,000,000 = $12,500,000. If $12,500,000 is available, the capital budget can be adopted. However, if only $12,000,000 is available, capital rationing exists because the funds needed for the capital budget exceed the amount of funds available.

Special
Assumption

The only special assumption made for capital-rationing decisions is that capital rationing can occur. The other assumptions made in the previous chapter remain unchanged.

Decision Rule

The decision rule for capital-rationing problems selects a capital budget from sets of feasible investment alternatives. A group of investment alternatives is called a **feasible set** when it meets the following conditions:

1. The set contains no mutually exclusive alternatives.

2. The total net investment required for the set does not exceed the net investment constraint, or capital constraint.

Feasible sets can be illustrated by using the data for Projects $A$, $B$, and $C$ in the previous example. The set composed of bids A-1, B-1, and C-1 is feasible because it contains no mutually exclusive alternatives, and its total net investment requirement of $11,000,000 is less than the $12,000,000 capital constraint. The following sets are *not* feasible because they contain mutually exclusive alternatives:

1. $B$-2 and $B$-3

2. $C$-1 and $C$-2

3. $A$-1, $B$-1, and $B$-2

Even though the set composed of $A$-1, $B$-3, and $C$-2 contains no mutually exclusive alternatives, it is *not* feasible because this set exceeds the capital constraint. Table 11-4 contains all the feasible sets for Projects $A$, $B$, and $C$.

When all the feasible sets have been identified, the following NPV decision rule is used: *choose the set of feasible investment alternatives that contains the largest total NPV.* Among the feasible sets contained in Table 11-4, the NPV decision rule would choose Set No. 20 because its NPV of $800,000 is the largest.

Now suppose that the capital constraint for the corporation is $10,000,000 for the same three projects discussed above. In this case only the first 17 sets contained in Table 11-4 would be feasible. The NPV decision rule would select Set No. 11 and Set No. 15 as being equally desirable because each of these sets contains the largest attainable NPV of $575,000. Corporate management might prefer Set No. 11 over Set No. 15 because it has a smaller required net investment.

Implications
of Capital
Rationing

The capital-budgeting implications of capital rationing can be illustrated by using the results obtained in the previous example. The capital budgets composed of competitive bids on Projects $A$, $B$, and $C$ were found to be as follows:

|  | Capital Constraint | Net Investment | NPV |
|---|---|---|---|
| Capital budget for A-1, B-2, and C-2 | None | $12,500,000 | $825,000 |
| Capital budget for A-1, B-2, and C-1 | $12,000,000 | 11,500,000 | 800,000 |
| Capital budget for A-1 and C-2 | 10,000,000 | 9,000,000 | 575,000 |
| Capital budget for B-2 and C-2 | 10,000,000 | 9,500,000 | 575,000 |

In the absence of a capital constraint, the corporation expects its capital budget to realize an NPV of $825,000 and to adopt all three projects.

With a $12,000,000 capital constraint, all three projects can still be adopted, but the capital budget's NPV is reduced to $800,000. The decrease in NPV occurs because C-1 replaces C-2 in the capital budget. This substitution is needed in order to produce a set of investment alternatives that meets the capital constraint. In the absence of capital rationing, the NPV decision rule could choose C-2 over C-1 since they are mutually exclusive alternatives. However, the capital constraint forces the choice of C-2 in order to maximize the NPV of the overall, constrained capital budget. This demonstrates that mutually exclusive decision rules may have to be

---

**Table 11-4.** Feasible Sets for Projects A, B, and C for a Capital-Rationing Example with a Capital Constraint of $12,000,000

| Feasible Set | | Net Investment | NPV |
|---|---|---|---|
| 1. | A-1 | $ 3,000,000 | $250,000 |
| 2. | B-1 | 3,000,000 | 200,000 |
| 3. | B-2 | 3,500,000 | 250,000 |
| 4. | B-3 | 4,000,000 | 225,000 |
| 5. | C-1 | 5,000,000 | 300,000 |
| 6. | C-2 | 6,000,000 | 325,000 |
| 7. | A-1 and B-1 | 6,000,000 | 450,000 |
| 8. | A-1 and B-2 | 6,500,000 | 500,000 |
| 9. | A-1 and B-3 | 7,000,000 | 475,000 |
| 10. | A-1 and C-1 | 8,000,000 | 550,000 |
| 11. | A-1 and C-2 | 9,000,000 | 575,000 |
| 12. | B-1 and C-1 | 8,000,000 | 500,000 |
| 13. | B-1 and C-2 | 9,000,000 | 525,000 |
| 14. | B-2 and C-1 | 8,500,000 | 550,000 |
| 15. | B-2 and C-2 | 9,500,000 | 575,000 |
| 16. | B-3 and C-1 | 9,000,000 | 525,000 |
| 17. | B-3 and C-2 | 10,000,000 | 550,000 |
| 18. | A-1, B-1, and C-1 | 11,000,000 | 750,000 |
| 19. | A-1, B-1, and C-2 | 12,000,000 | 775,000 |
| **20.** | **A-1, B-2, and C-1** | **11,500,000** | **800,000** |
| 21. | A-1, B-3, and C-1 | 12,000,000 | 775,000 |

put aside in the presence of capital rationing: any one project's best alternative may or may not be included in a capital budget that must satisfy a capital constraint.

When the more severe capital constraint of $10,000,000 is imposed, the resulting capital budget contains only two of the three projects. If the final capital budget consists of A-1 and C-2, Project B is dropped. If the final capital budget consists of B-2 and C-2, Project A is dropped.

Since all three projects display alternatives with positive NPVs, the corporation would want to include all three projects in its final capital budget in order to maximize shareholder wealth by maximizing the NPV generated by its capital budget. To the extent that the corporation cannot increase the funds available for net investment and thus must live with a capital constraint, the corporation is unable to make the greatest possible contribution to shareholder wealth. The firm may seek to reduce the impact of a capital constraint by adopting scaled down investment projects that require smaller net investments and generate proportionally lower net present values. This can result in greatly increasing the number of feasible sets, and mathematical programming techniques may be required to identify the NPV-maximizing capital budget.

# SUMMARY

The payback, NPV, and IRR capital-budgeting criteria can be used in making accept/reject, replacement, mutually exclusive, lease/purchase, and capital-rationing investment decisions. Each type of investment decision has specific decision rules. These decision rules have advantages and disadvantages.

The payback criterion is included as a basis for a decision rule because it continues to be used in making investment decisions. However, since payback does not measure profits or the time value of money, it cannot be relied upon to produce capital budgets that maximize the financial welfare of corporate owners.

NPV and IRR decision rules produce identical and correct results when making accept/reject and replacement decisions. If an investment alternative under consideration has an NPV that is zero or positive, its IRR will be equal to or greater than the corporation's required rate of return. Consequently, either decision rule can be relied upon to produce accept/reject and replacement decisions that are consistent with shareholder wealth maximization.

When investment alternatives are evaluated within a mutually exclusive framework, the NPV and IRR decision rules can produce conflicting rankings. Conflicting rankings can be caused by large differences among the net investments required by competing alternatives, differences in the timing of cash flows among competing alternatives, and by different reinvestment rate assumptions used by each capital-budgeting criterion. When conflicting rankings do occur, the NPV criterion provides the correct decision rule.

Lease/purchase investment alternatives are a special type of mutually exclusive decision. An NPV decision rule is used in evaluating lease/purchase decisions.

The presence of a capital constraint shifts the emphasis from alternatives within a given project to the contribution to shareholder wealth made by the entire capital budget. The decision rule used for capital-rationing situations selects the feasible set of investment alternatives that promises the largest total NPV subject to the capital constraint.

# QUESTIONS

**11-1.** What is meant by an accept/reject decision?

**11-2.** What are the decision rules for accept/reject decisions?

**11-3.** What are the basic reasons why the payback criterion may not agree with the NPV criterion when evaluating the desirability of investment alternatives?

**11-4.** Why do the NPV and IRR decision rules produce similar decisions in accept/reject problems?

**11-5.** What is meant by a replacement decision?

**11-6.** What are the decision rules for replacement decisions?

**11-7.** Do the NPV and IRR decision rules produce similar decisions in replacement problems? Explain.

**11-8.** What is meant by a mutually exclusive decision?

**11-9.** What is the NPV decision rule for mutually exclusive decisions?

**11-10.** What are the reasons why the NPV and IRR decision rules can produce conflicting rankings when evaluating mutually exclusive alternatives?

**11-11.** What is meant by a lease/purchase decision?

**11-12.** Why are lease/purchase decisions evaluated by using mutually exclusive decision rules?

**11-13.** Explain what is meant by capital rationing.

**11-14.** In terms of capital rationing, explain what is meant by a set of feasible investment alternatives.

**11-15.** What is the NPV decision rule for capital rationing?

**11-16.** What are the impacts of capital rationing on a corporation's overall capital budget?

---

# PROBLEMS

**11-1.** A financial manager is given the task of evaluating the desirability of the following independent projects on an accept/reject basis. The maximum allowable payback for each project is three years. The required rates of return are as follows: Project A, 10%; Project B, 11%; Project C, 8%.

|  | Project A | Project B | Project C |
|---|---|---|---|
| Net investment: | $10,000 | $21,000 | $2,000 |
| Cash flows in Year 1: | $ 3,000 | $ 5,000 | $ 400 |
| Year 2: | 3,000 | 5,000 | 600 |
| Year 3: | 3,000 | 5,000 | 800 |
| Year 4: | 3,000 | 5,000 | 500 |
| Year 5: | 3,000 | 5,000 | 500 |

a. Which projects are acceptable using the payback decision rule?

b. Which projects are acceptable using the NPV decision rule?

c. Which projects are acceptable using the IRR decision rule?

**11-2.** The Bowie Company has a metal stamping machine that is expected to yield ten more years of service. This machine is fully depreciated and has no market value. Bowie's engineers estimate that production costs can be decreased by $20,000 per year by replacing this stamping machine with a new model. The new machine has a $90,000 installed cost, a ten-year life, and no expected salvage value. Using a 12% required rate of return, should the present machine be replaced?

**11-3.** You have recently become aware of a new automated production system that could replace one of the production line systems your corporation presently uses. The present system is profitable and is expected to remain so for several more years. However, the proposed replacement system promises increased profits because its automated components will reduce unit production costs.

The present system was installed three years ago and has an estimated seven years of economic lifetime remaining. The system cost $1,000,000, has a zero expected salvage value, and has a current market value of $400,000.

The proposed system has an installed cost of $1,800,000, a seven-year economic lifetime, and an expected salvage value of $400,000.

Profits before depreciation and taxes for each alternative are as follows:

| Years | Present System | Proposed System |
|-------|----------------|-----------------|
| 1–4   | $300,000       | $400,000        |
| 5–7   | 200,000        | 400,000         |

a. Compute the net investment for this replacement decision.
b. Compute the cash flows for each alternative.
c. Compute the incremental cash flows.
d. If the corporation requires a 10% rate of return, which alternative is desirable according to the NPV decision rule?
e. Which alternative is preferable according to the IRR decision rule?

**11-4.** A corporation is contemplating the replacement of an existing piece of machinery with a new model. The data on the existing and the proposed machines are as follows:

|                                        | Existing Machine | Proposed Machine |
|----------------------------------------|------------------|------------------|
| Installed cost                         | $50,000          | $80,000          |
| Current market value                   | $12,000          | —                |
| Salvage value                          | 0                | 0                |
| Life/age                               | 25/15            | 10/0             |
| Profit before depreciation and taxes in: |                |                  |
| Years 1–5                              | $6,000           | $16,000          |
| Years 6–10                             | $4,000           | $16,000          |

a. If the corporation requires a 12% rate of return, which alternative is desirable according to the NPV decision rule?
b. Which alternative is preferred according to the IRR decision rule?

**11-5.** You have obtained the following data on three mutually exclusive investment alternatives:

|                        | Project A | Project B | Project C |
|------------------------|-----------|-----------|-----------|
| Net investment:        | $90,000   | $80,000   | $84,000   |
| Cash flow in Year 1:   | $30,000   | $30,000   | $40,000   |
| Year 2:                | 30,000    | 30,000    | 30,000    |
| Year 3:                | 30,000    | 30,000    | 20,000    |
| Year 4:                | 30,000    | 20,000    | 20,000    |

a. Using a 10% corporate required rate of return, rank these alternatives according to their NPVs. Which alternative, if any, is preferred according to the NPV decision rule?

b. Compute the IRR for each alternative. Rank the projects by their IRRs. Which alternative, if any, is preferred according to the IRR decision rule?

**11-6.** Two mutually exclusive alternatives, Project X and Project Y, have the following net investments and cash flows:

|                      | Project X | Project Y |
|----------------------|-----------|-----------|
| Net investment:      | $10,000   | $12,000   |
| Cash flow in Year 1: | $5,000    | $3,000    |
| Year 2:              | 5,000     | 7,000     |
| Year 3:              | 5,000     | 8,000     |

a. Using the following rates of return, compute the NPVs for Projects X and Y: 0%, 6%, 12%, and 18%.

b. Compute the IRR for each project.

c. Using the results from a and b, draw the NPV profiles for these alternatives. (*Note:* Draw both profiles on the same chart.)

d. Summarize the NPV and IRR rankings that are contained in your chart.

e. Using the mutually exclusive decision rules, which project is preferred at a required rate of return of 6%?

f. Using the mutually exclusive decision rules, which project is preferred at a required rate of return of 18%?

**11-7.** Northern Land Surveyors wants to evaluate two potential investment alternatives. Project NLX requires a net investment of $16,000 and is expected to generate a six-year cash flow annuity of $6,000. Project NLY requires a net investment of $16,000: the only cash flow for this project has a value of $55,695 and occurs at the end of Year 6.

a. Compute the NPV of each alternative using a 14% required rate of return.

b. Compute the IRR for each alternative.

c. On the basis of a and b, what should the company decide if the projects are economically independent?

d. On the basis of a and b, what should the company decide if the projects are mutually exclusive?

**11-8.** An investment alternative requires a net investment of $400,000. It has an eight-year life, with a Year eight salvage value of $40,000. Profit before depreciation and taxes is $125,000 per year for each of the first six years and $100,000 per year for the last two years.

This investment alternative can also be leased for eight years. Annual lease payments would be $75,000. Profit before lease payments and taxes would be $110,000 per year over the eight-year lease.

Assuming an 11% required rate of return, which alternative is preferred according to the NPV decision rule?

11-9.   A corporation advertises for bids on two investment projects. Three competitive bids are received for each project. The corporate financial managers compute the following net investment and NPVs for each bid:

|  | Net Investment | NPV |
|---|---|---|
| Project R |  |  |
| Bid R-1 | $700,000 | $100,000 |
| Bid R-2 | 650,000 | 80,000 |
| Bid R-3 | 725,000 | 85,000 |
| Project D |  |  |
| Bid D-1 | 500,000 | 60,000 |
| Bid D-2 | 525,000 | 62,500 |
| Bid D-3 | 550,000 | 67,000 |

Projects R and D are independent of each other. The competitive bids are mutually exclusive within each project.

a.   In the absence of capital rationing, which alternatives are preferred when using the NPV decision rule?

b.   Assume that the corporation has a capital constraint of $1,200,000. Identify all the feasible sets for Projects R and D and prepare a table of these feasible sets that is similar to Table 11-4.

c.   Which feasible set is preferred according to the NPV decision rule for capital rationing?

# SELECTED REFERENCES

Archer, S., G. Choate, and G. Racette. *Financial Management*. 2d ed. New York: John Wiley & Sons, 1983.

Bierman, H., and S. Smidt. *The Capital Budgeting Decision*. 4th ed. New York: Macmillan Publishing Co., 1975.

Clark, J., T. Hindelang, and R. Pritchard. *Capital Budgeting*. Englewood Cliffs, N.J.: Prentice-Hall, Inc., 1979.

Dorfman, R. "The Meaning of Internal Rates of Return." *Journal of Finance*, Vol. 36, No. 5 (December, 1981).

Levy, H., and M. Sarnat. *Capital Investment and Financial Decisions*. 2d ed. Englewood Cliffs, N.J.: Prentice-Hall International, Inc., 1982.

Osteryoung, J. *Capital Budgeting*. 2d ed. Columbus, Ohio: Grid Publishing Co., 1979.

Schall, L. "The Lease-or-Buy and Asset Acquisition Decisions." *Journal of Finance*, Vol. 29, No. 4 (September, 1974).

——, and C. Haley. *Introduction to Financial Management*. 3d ed. New York: McGraw-Hill Book Company, 1983.

Stephens, W. "The Lease-or-Buy Decision: Make the Right Choice." *Financial Executive*, Vol. 51, No. 5 (May, 1983).

# CHAPTER 12

## Capital Budgeting under Conditions of Risk

The previous two chapters developed several capital-budgeting criteria and explained how they can be used in reaching long-term investment decisions. The practical applications of these criteria are limited by the assumption that the cash flows of an investment alternative are known with certainty. This chapter is an introduction to capital-budgeting techniques that evaluate capital-budgeting alternatives when their net investments and cash flows can assume a range of possible values and thus are not known with certainty.

The first section of this chapter discusses the meaning of risk in a capital-budgeting framework and outlines the capital-budgeting and behavioral assumptions used throughout the chapter. Statistical techniques that are used in measuring the risk-return characteristics of risky capital-budgeting alternatives are explained in the second section. The third section presents the net present value (NPV) capital-budgeting criterion for evaluating risky projects. Finally, the chapter ends with a brief introduction to what is called the portfolio effect.

## RISK AND RETURN

When cash flows associated with a capital-budgeting alternative are known with certainty, a time adjusted profit measure, such as net present value, is used to evaluate the desirability of the project. When cash flows are not known with certainty, the measure of profit or return is supplemented with a measure of the project's risk. The resulting decision criterion evaluates the desirability of investment alternatives by considering both risk and return.

Uncertainty exists whenever future outcomes are not known with certainty. The risk of an uncertain alternative can be measured if probabilities can be assigned to all possible outcomes. The terms *risk* and *uncertainty* are used interchangeably in this text.

**Risk in a Capital-Budgeting Framework**

Chapter 1 defined overall corporate risk and partitioned it into business and financial risk. The type of risk encountered in capital budgeting is business risk because capital-budgeting procedures help determine the corporation's asset structure. An investment alternative is said to contain business risk when the set of possible net investment and cash flow values that can occur is known, but it is not possible to predict before the project is begun the specific values that will actually occur.

**Example:**

An investment alternative requires a net investment of $100,000 and produces a cash flow at the end of Year 1 of $125,000. If there is no question that the project requires a $100,000 net investment, and if the $125,000 is certain to be realized, the investment alternative is evaluated using capital-budgeting criteria under conditions of certainty. If either or both of these figures is not known with certainty the investment alternative is said to contain risk. Thus, the amount of the net investment might be certain because of a bid submitted by a vendor. If, however, the Year 1 cash flow could be $0, $50,000, $100,000, or $125,000 the investment alternative is risky.

The above example assumed that the financial manager can specify the set of possible future cash flows. The set of possible cash flows for each future period may consist of a list of discrete values, as in the example, or a continuous range of values. The techniques used in this chapter have the following four requirements:

1. The set of possible net investment values must be known.

2. The set of possible cash flows for each period must be known.

3. The values contained within each set must be *mutually exclusive*. This means that only one value can occur within each set.

4. The values contained within each set must be *collectively exhaustive*. This means that one value within each set *must* occur.

**Example:**    A capital-budgeting alternative requires a $90,000 net investment and has a three-year economic life. The sets of possible cash flows for each year are:

| Year | Cash Flow Sets |
|------|----------------|
| 1 | $40,000 |
| 2 | $30,000, $50,000, $70,000 |
| 3 | $20,000, $60,000 |

The cash flow for Year 1 is known with certainty. There are three possible cash flow values for Year 2: $30,000, $50,000, or $70,000. Only one of these values can occur, but one of these must occur. Similarly, the Year 3 cash flow will turn out to be either $20,000 or $60,000.

**Example:**    A capital-budgeting alternative consists of a materials handling system that will reduce processing costs. The initial investment, which includes costs incurred by interruption of the current process, will be between $25,000 and $33,000, depending on weather conditions and other factors during the installation period. Once in place, the system will result in cost reductions of $5,000 to $10,000 per year during its ten-year life.

The examples presented above illustrate what is meant by risky investments. The first is an investment alternative that has a set of discrete possible outcomes for each year. In the second example net investment and cash flow outcome sets are continuous; that is, the values may fall anywhere within specified ranges. Risky projects can be evaluated using risk adjusted decision criteria if probabilities can be assigned to all possible future outcomes.

**Capital- Budgeting Assumptions**

Capital budgeting under conditions of risk (or uncertainty) uses some of the assumptions introduced in Chapter 10, as well as other special assumptions. The assumptions that are the same under conditions of certainty and uncertainty are as follows:

1. The basic data used to describe an investment alternative are its net investment and its cash flows.

2. Cash flows occur at the end of each year.

3. Only conventional cash flow patterns are used.

4. The corporation is not faced with capital rationing.

Special assumptions that refer to risky cash flows and to the required rate of return are:

1. The set of possible net investment values for an investment alternative is known with certainty, is mutually exclusive, and is collectively exhaustive.

2. Each set of possible cash flows must be known with certainty and be mutually exclusive and collectively exhaustive.

3. The required rate of return is assumed to be a function of the risk-return characteristics of the investment alternative.

This chapter discusses only one approach that can be used to determine an investment alternative's required rate of return. A more extensive discussion of required rates of return is deferred until later chapters.

**Behavioral Assumptions**

Some assumptions are needed to describe the way in which a financial manager evaluates risky projects. In general, managers are assumed to be risk averse. This means that managers will not accept a risky project unless its expected profits compensate for the risk that must be accepted. Risk aversion also means that additional risk will be accepted only if coupled with an appropriate increase in expected return.

The upwardly sloping Line $R$ in Figure 12-1 can be used to demonstrate managerial risk aversion. Each point on Line $R$ represents the expected return that is required in order to accept the corresponding degree of risk. For example, assume that $A$ represents the corporation's overall risk and that $B$ represents the corporation's expected returns for accepting this degree of risk. In order for the corporation to increase its total risk exposure to $A'$, expected returns will have to increase to $B'$. The increase in risk, from $A$ to $A'$, requires a much greater increase in expected returns, from $B$ to $B'$. Thus, the steeper the slope, the greater the amount of risk aversion.

Managerial risk aversion provides two criteria that can be used to rank the desirability of risky projects.

1.  If two projects have the same expected return, the manager will prefer the project with the lesser amount of risk.

2.  If two projects have the same degree of risk, the manager will prefer the project with the higher expected return.

---

**Figure 12-1.**        **Managerial Risk Aversion**

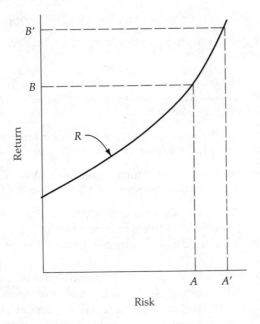

---

## STATISTICAL MEASURES OF RISK AND RETURN

Statistical methods can be used to evaluate the risk-return characteristics of investment alternatives. The data bases used in this analysis are the probability distributions of net investments and cash flows. From a probability distribution the following statistics are obtained:

1.  Expected value

2.  Variance

3.   Standard deviation

4.   Coefficient of variation

**Probability Distribution**

A **probability distribution** of cash values lists the set of possible cash values that can occur at a specific time and their associated probabilities of occurrence. Because the cash values are mutually exclusive and the set is collectively exhaustive, the probabilities sum to 1.0 or 100 percent. A probability distribution may be discrete or continuous, corresponding to a list of discrete possible outcomes or a continuous range of possible outcomes. For purposes of calculating the statistical measures of risk and return discussed in this section discrete distributions will be used.

---

**Example:**

The following is a probability distribution of cash flows at a point in time:

| Year 1 Cash Flow | Probability |
|---|---|
| $     0 | .2 |
| 400 | .3 |
| 800 | .4 |
| 1,200 | .1 |
| | 1.0 |

According to this probability distribution, there are four possible cash flows. The probabilities are interpreted as follows: There is a 20 percent chance that the cash flow will turn out to be $0, there is a 30 percent chance that the cash flow will turn out to be $400, etc. Because the cash flows are mutually exclusive, the probabilities can be added in the following manner: The probability that the cash flow will turn out to be *either* $800 *or* $1,200 is .4 + .1 = .5, or 50 percent.

---

Generating the data for a probability distribution is not an easy task. Estimates of possible net investments, cash flows, and their associated probabilities can be based on past corporate data, industry trends and ratios, and forecasts of gross national product and of industry sales. Probabilities can be subjectively estimated. Although it may be difficult to generate a probability distribution that accurately reflects possible future cash flows, in doing so the financial manager does not have to rely on certainty assumptions and can evaluate the investment alternative on the basis of both risk and return.

**Expected Value of a Probability Distribution**

Under conditions of risk, a separate probability distribution is used to summarize the possible net investments or cash flows for each year. The first step in evaluating the desirability of a risky project is to compute the **expected value** of each probability distribution. This is obtained by multiplying each possible cash value (of net investment or cash flow) by its probability of occurrence and adding the resulting products. The equation for computing the expected value for any year ($t$) can be stated as follows:

Let: $f_i$ = possible cash value $i$ for Year $t$

$P_i$ = probability of occurrence of $f_i$

$E_t$ = expected value of the probability distribution of cash values for Year $t$

$\Sigma$ = the Greek letter indicating summation

Then:

$$E_t = \sum_i (f_i)(P_i) \qquad \text{(12-1)}$$

**Example:**

A risky project has a two-year economic life. The probability distributions of its cash flows are shown in the first two columns of Table 12-1. Multiplying each cash flow by its probability of occurrence and adding the resulting products produces the expected values for each year. The expected values can also be computed by using Equation 12-1 directly, as follows:

Year 1: $E_1$ = $2,000(.3) + $4,000(.4) + $6,000(.3) = $4,000

Year 2: $E_2$ = $1,000(.1) + $3,000(.1) + $5,000(.4) + $7,000(.3) + $9,000(.1)
= $5,400

**Table 12-1.**      **Expected Values of Cash Flow Probability Distributions**

|        | Cash Flow $f_i$ | Probability $P_i$ | $(f_i)(P_i)$ |
|--------|-----------------|-------------------|--------------|
| Year 1 | $2,000          | .3                | $   600      |
|        | 4,000           | .4                | 1,600        |
|        | 6,000           | .3                | 1,800        |
|        |                 |                   | $E_1$ = $4,000 |
| Year 2 | $1,000          | .1                | $   100      |
|        | 3,000           | .1                | 300          |
|        | 5,000           | .4                | 2,000        |
|        | 7,000           | .3                | 2,100        |
|        | 9,000           | .1                | 900          |
|        |                 |                   | $E_2$ = $5,400 |

One assumption stated earlier in this chapter requires that probability distributions be known with certainty. An important implication of this assumption is that the probability distribution for the Year 2 cash flows in the preceding example does not change as a result of the actual cash flow that occurs in Year 1. The cash flows over successive years are independent and thus are not related to each other in any systematic way. If, for example, the actual cash flow at the end of Year 1 turns out to be $6,000, the probability distribution for Year 2 remains unchanged.

An expected value can be interpreted in two ways. First, an expected value can be considered to be a type of weighted average since each possible cash flow is weighted by its probability of occurrence. In this way all the information in the probability distribution is used in estimating the future cash flow. Second, an expected value may be considered to be a long-run average. For instance, in the preceding example $E_2$ is $5,400 but does not correspond to any of the possible cash flows in Year 2. However, if this probability distribution occurs in several different projects, the average of the *actual* cash flows generated from this probability distribution will approach $5,400.

**Variance and Standard Deviation of a Probability Distribution**

The second statistic that can be computed from a probability distribution is the **variance**, which measures the dispersion of the probability distribution around its expected value. In general, the greater the dispersion, the larger the variance. This is the basis for using the variance and related statistics as measures of risk.

The following steps are needed to compute the variance of a probability distribution:

1. Subtract each possible cash value from the expected value of the probability distribution.

2. Square the difference computed in Step 1.

3. Multiply the squared term obtained in Step 2 by the probability of occurrence of its corresponding cash value.

4. Add the products obtained in Step 3. The resulting sum is the variance.

These steps can be summarized in equation form as shown below:

$$\sigma_t^2 = \sum_i (E_t - f_i)^2 (P_i) \tag{12-2}$$

Where $\sigma_t^2$ = the variance for Year $t$.

---

**Example:** Using the probability distributions of the previous example and the expected values in Table 12-1, the variance of each probability distribution is computed by following the four steps, as shown in Table 12-2. These variances can also be computed directly from Equation 12-2 as follows:

$$\sigma_1^2 = (\$4{,}000 - \$2{,}000)^2(.3) + (\$4{,}000 - \$4{,}000)^2(.4) +$$
$$(\$4{,}000 - \$6{,}000)^2(.3)$$
$$= 2{,}400{,}000$$

$$\sigma_2^2 = (\$5{,}400 - \$1{,}000)^2(.1) + (\$5{,}400 - \$3{,}000)^2(.1) +$$
$$(\$5{,}400 - \$5{,}000)^2(.4) + (\$5{,}400 - \$7{,}000)^2(.3) +$$
$$(\$5{,}400 - \$9{,}000)^2(.1)$$
$$= 4{,}640{,}000$$

**Table 12-2.**   Variances of Cash Flow Probability Distributions

| | Cash Flow $f_i$ | $E_1 - f_i$ | $(E_1 - f_i)^2$ | Probability $P_i$ | $(E_1 - f_i)^2(P_i)$ |
|---|---|---|---|---|---|
| Year 1 | $2,000 | $2,000 | 4,000,000 | .3 | 1,200,000 |
| | 4,000 | 0 | 0 | .4 | 0 |
| | 6,000 | −2,000 | 4,000,000 | .3 | 1,200,000 |
| | | | | | $\sigma_1^2 = 2{,}400{,}000$ |

| | Cash Flow $f_i$ | $E_2 - f_i$ | $(E_2 - f_i)^2$ | Probability $P_i$ | $(E_2 - f_i)^2(P_i)$ |
|---|---|---|---|---|---|
| Year 2 | $1,000 | $4,400 | 19,360,000 | .1 | 1,936,000 |
| | 3,000 | 2,400 | 5,760,000 | .1 | 576,000 |
| | 5,000 | −400 | 160,000 | .4 | 64,000 |
| | 7,000 | −1,600 | 2,560,000 | .3 | 768,000 |
| | 9,000 | −3,600 | 12,960,000 | .1 | 1,296,000 |
| | | | | | $\sigma_2^2 = 4{,}640{,}000$ |

The variance is essentially a weighted average of the squared deviations from the expected value. The weights are the probabilities of occurrence of the cash values. The unit or dimension of the variance in this case is dollars squared, which has no meaningful interpretation, and is omitted.

The square root of the variance is called the **standard deviation.** Under conditions of risk, capital budgeting uses the standard deviation as a measure of risk. The equation for computing the standard deviation is stated as follows:

$$\sigma_t = \sqrt{\sigma_t^2} \qquad\qquad\qquad (12\text{-}3)$$

Where $\sigma_t$ = the standard deviation of a probability distribution.

**Example:**

The standard deviations of the variances contained in Table 12-2 are computed as follows:

$$\sigma_1 = \sqrt{\sigma_1^2} \qquad\qquad \sigma_2 = \sqrt{\sigma_2^2}$$
$$= \sqrt{2,400,000} \qquad = \sqrt{4,640,000}$$
$$= \$1,549 \qquad\qquad = \$2,154$$

Note that the standard deviation is stated in dollars.

---

All the deviations from the expected values are used in computing a standard deviation. This implies that managerial risk aversion extends to all deviations from an expected value, even when those deviations are caused by cash values *in excess* of the expected value. Because the standard deviation is computed from a variance, larger dispersions of cash values from their expected value will produce a larger standard deviation. Hence, larger standard deviations indicate riskier capital projects.

---

**Example:**

The following probability distributions have the same expected values one year from now but have different standard deviations. Probability Distribution B has a larger standard deviation. Therefore, B is riskier than A.

|  | Cash Flow | Probability |
|---|---|---|
| Probability Distribution A | $ 600 | .25 |
|  | 800 | .50 |
|  | 1,000 | .25 |
| Probability Distribution B | $ 400 | .10 |
|  | 600 | .20 |
|  | 800 | .40 |
|  | 1,000 | .20 |
|  | 1,200 | .10 |

The expected values, variances, and standard deviations of the two probability distributions are computed as follows:

**Distribution A**

$$E_1 = (\$600)(.25) + (\$800)(.5) + (\$1,000)(.25) = \$800$$

$$\sigma_1^2 = (\$800 - \$600)^2(.25) + (\$800 - \$800)^2(.50) + (\$800 - \$1,000)^2(.25)$$
$$= 20,000$$

$$\sigma_1 = \sqrt{20,000} = \$141$$

**Distribution B**

$$E_2 = (\$400)(.1) + (\$600)(.2) + (\$800)(.4) + (\$1,000)(.2) + (\$1,200)(.1)$$
$$= \$800$$

$$\sigma_1^2 = (\$800 - \$400)^2(.1) + (\$800 - \$600)^2(.2) + (\$800 - \$800)^2(.4)$$
$$+ (\$800 - \$1,000)^2(.2) + (\$800 - \$1,200)^2(.1)$$
$$= 48,000$$

$$\sigma_1 = \sqrt{48,000} = \$219$$

The relative riskiness of these two probability distributions can also be demonstrated by plotting the distributions in the form of histograms, or bar charts. Figure 12-2 contains the histograms for each distribution. The probabilities are shown on the vertical axis, and the possible cash flows are shown on the horizontal axis. Since both distributions have the same expected value of $800, any difference between them is caused by the dispersions of the cash flows around their expected values. Figure 12-2 reflects in two ways that the cash flows of Distribution $B$ are more dispersed than those of Distribution $A$. First, the histogram of Distribution $B$ covers

**Figure 12-2.**  **Histograms of Probability Distributions $A$ and $B$**

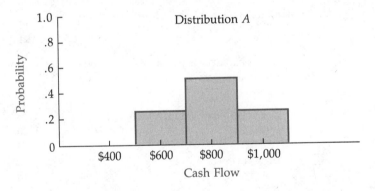

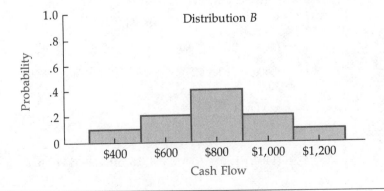

a wider range of possible cash flows than that of Distribution A. Second, the largest probability (.4) for any possible cash flow in Distribution B is smaller than the largest probability (.5) that occurs in any of the possible cash flows in Distribution A. Thus, the histogram of Distribution B has less vertical height than Distribution A.

Histograms were used in the above example to obtain a better understanding of the shapes of the two probability distributions. However, histograms can be used to compare the riskiness of two or more probability distributions only when the expected values of the probability distributions are equal.

**Coefficient of Variation of a Probability Distribution**

The fourth important statistic that can be computed from a probability distribution is the coefficient of variation. This statistic is another way of measuring project risk. The **coefficient of variation** is computed by dividing the standard deviation of a probability distribution by its expected value. For any given year ($t$) the equation for computing the coefficient of variation is stated as follows:

$$V_t = \frac{\sigma_t}{E_t} \qquad (12\text{-}4)$$

Where $V_t$ = the coefficient of variation.

---

**Example:**

The expected values and standard deviations of Probability Distributions A and B in the previous example were found to be as follows:

|  | Distribution A | Distribution B |
|---|---|---|
| $E_1$ | $800 | $800 |
| $\sigma_1$ | $141 | $219 |

Thus, the coefficients of variation for these two distributions in Year 1 are

| Distribution A | Distribution B |
|---|---|
| $V_1 = \dfrac{\$141}{\$800}$ | $V_1 = \dfrac{\$219}{\$800}$ |
| $= .176$ | $= .274$ |

Note that the coefficient of variation is a pure number and does not carry a dollar sign.

---

As with the variance and standard deviation, larger values of the coefficient of variation are indicative of larger risks. For example, Distribution B is riskier than Distribution A because Distribution B has a larger coefficient of variation.

The advantage of the coefficient of variation over the variance and the standard deviation is that it can be used to compare the riskiness of probability distributions even when their expected values are not equal. The coefficient of variation is also useful in helping to evaluate competing investment alternatives when their net investments and/or cash flow probability distributions differ substantially in dollar size.

**Net Present Value Statistics**

The previous section explained how various statistics are computed from individual probability distributions. When a capital-budgeting alternative involves investment and cash flows over several time periods, each with its own probability distribution, the risk and return characteristics of the project's net present value must be evaluated. The project's expected net present value and the variance, standard deviation, and coefficient of variation of its NPV can be computed if the expected value and variance of the probability distribution of each time period is known. Since the cash flow probability distributions occur at different times, the NPV statistics must include an adjustment for the time value of money. The discount rate used for this purpose is the rate of return an investor would require on a risk-free investment. A reasonable proxy for this is the rate of return on government securities.

The expected net present value of a capital-budgeting alternative, $E_{NPV}$, is computed as follows. Let $k^*$ represent the risk-free rate of return. Then:

$$E_{NPV} = \sum_{t=0} \frac{E_t}{(1 + k^*)^t} \tag{12-5}$$

The NPV variance, $\sigma^2_{NPV}$, is computed as

$$\sigma^2_{NPV} = \sum_{t=0} \frac{\sigma^2_t}{(1 + k^*)^{2t}} \tag{12-6}$$

Note that the exponent in the denominator of Equation 12-6 has a value of $2t$. This equation holds only if the probability distributions for each time period are independent, as was assumed.

The NPV standard deviation and coefficient of variation are computed as

$$\sigma_{NPV} = \sqrt{\sigma^2_{NPV}} \tag{12-7}$$

$$V_{NPV} = \frac{\sigma_{NPV}}{E_{NPV}} \tag{12-8}$$

Equations 12-5 and 12-6 adjust only for the time value of money, not for risk. The risk adjustment, explained in the next section, requires these equations as a first step. The values of $E_0$ and $\sigma_0^2$ in these equations represent the expected value and the variance of the project's net investment.

**Example:**

The data in Table 12-1 contain two years of cash flow probability distributions for a particular capital-budgeting alternative. Assume that the associated probability distribution of net investment is

| Possible Net Investment | Probability |
|---|---|
| −$4,000 | .3 |
| − 5,000 | .4 |
| − 6,000 | .3 |

As in previous capital-budgeting chapters, the negative values indicate that a net investment is a cash outflow.

This probability distribution has an expected value of −$5,000, a variance of 600,000, and a standard deviation of $775. (Take a moment and verify these statistics.) The statistics for this investment alternative's three probability distributions are thus:

| | $E_t$ | $\sigma_t^2$ |
|---|---|---|
| Year 0 | −$5,000 | 600,000 |
| Year 1 | 4,000 | 2,400,000 |
| Year 2 | 5,400 | 4,640,000 |

If the risk-free rate of return is 8 percent, the NPV statistics for this project are calculated as follows (all discounting calculations in this chapter use Appendix Table A-3). The expected NPV is computed using Equation 12-5.

$$E_{NPV} = \frac{-\$5,000}{(1 + .08)^0} + \frac{\$4,000}{(1 + .08)^1} + \frac{\$5,400}{(1 + .08)^2}$$

$$= \$3,332$$

The NPV variance is computed using Equation 12-6.

$$\sigma_{NPV}^2 = \frac{600,000}{(1 + .08)^0} + \frac{2,400,000}{(1 + .08)^2} + \frac{4,640,000}{(1 + .08)^4}$$

$$= 6,067,200$$

The NPV standard deviation is computed using Equation 12-7.

$$\sigma_{NPV} = \sqrt{6,067,200}$$

$$= \$2,463$$

The NPV coefficient of variation is computed using Equation 12-8.

$$V_{NPV} = \$2,463/\$3,332$$

$$= .739$$

In this example, the capital budgeting alternative has a positive expected NPV and thus might appear to be desirable from the standpoint of increasing shareholder wealth. This can be misleading, however, since the expected NPV statistic adjusts only for the time value of money, not for risk. The NPV coefficient of variation indicates that this project has a large standard deviation per dollar of expected value and thus is risky. This coefficient of variation provides the link that allows the computation of a project's NPV on a risk adjusted basis, thus permitting the correct use of the NPV criterion in evaluating risky projects.

## RISK, RETURN, AND NET PRESENT VALUE

This section uses statistics to develop a risk sensitive capital-budgeting criterion. The first step in doing so is to combine the concept of managerial risk aversion and the NPV coefficient of variation to estimate the rate of return that is required from a risky project. This rate of return is used to define a risk adjusted NPV criterion. This criterion is then applied to the accept/reject and mutually exclusive capital-budgeting decisions.

**Choice of a Required Rate of Return**

When a financial manager is considering a set of risky alternatives, one important consideration involves the choice of the required rate of return. Given managerial risk aversion, the required rate of return for each project is a function of its risk. The riskier the project, the higher its required rate of return.

Selecting the appropriate required rate of return involves subjective judgments. Given the general patterns of managerial risk aversion shown in Figure 12-1, some guidelines, nevertheless, can be established.

1.  The coefficient of variation can be used as a measure of risk per dollar of return. As such, it can be used to rank the riskiness of probability distributions of cash values.

2.  The required rate of return can be set to the sum of the risk-free rate plus some additional return to compensate for risk.

Figure 12-3 plots a hypothetical risk-return curve based on the concept of managerial risk aversion. The required rate of return $(k)$ is plotted on the vertical axis. The NPV coefficient of variation $(V_{NPV})$ is plotted on the horizontal axis. Note that the risk-return curve intersects the required-rate-of-return axis at the assumed risk-free rate of 8 percent. Thus, the required rate of return equals the risk-free rate when $V_{NPV} = 0$. If the risk-free rate rises or falls due to changing economic conditions, the curve shifts upward or downward and the required rate of return corresponding to any level of risk also rises or falls. The data in Table 12-3 approximate the Figure 12-3 curve. This table can be used to identify a project's required rate of return

**Figure 12-3.**   **Risk-Return Curve**

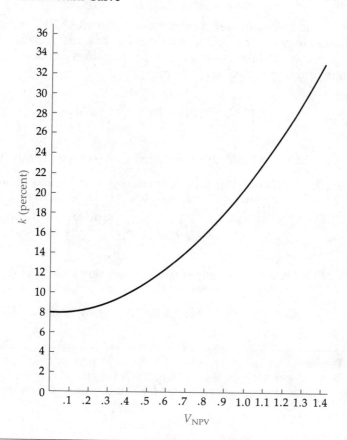

**Table 12-3.**   **Required Rates of Return for Risky Projects**

| At Least | But Less Than | k |
|---|---|---|
| | $V_{NPV}$ | |
| 0 | .1 | 8% |
| .1 | .3 | 9 |
| .3 | .5 | 11 |
| .5 | .7 | 14 |
| .7 | .9 | 18 |
| .9 | 1.1 | 23 |
| 1.1 | 1.4 | 30 |

based on its coefficient of variation when the risk-free rate is 8 percent and when Figure 12-3 is a useful representation of managerial risk aversion.

**The Risk Adjusted NPV Criterion**

The **risk adjusted net present value** (RANPV) serves as a capital-budgeting criterion under conditions of risk and is defined as the sum of the present values of the expected cash values discounted at the required rate of return. In equation form:

$$RANPV = \sum_{t=0} \frac{E_t}{(1 + k)^t} \qquad (12\text{-}9)$$

Obtaining the RANPV for a risky project requires the following steps:

1. Compute the expected value ($E_t$) and variance ($\sigma_t^2$) for each probability distribution using Equations 12-1 and 12-2.

2. Compute the project's expected NPV ($E_{NPV}$), standard deviation ($\sigma_{NPV}$), and coefficient of variation ($V_{NPV}$), using Equations 12-5, 12-7, and 12-8.

3. Obtain the required rate of return ($k$) by using a table of the type plotted in Figure 12-3 that relates $k$ and $V_{NPV}$.

4. Compute the project's RANPV using Equation 12-9.

---

**Example:**

The following data set, developed in earlier sections of this chapter, can be used to illustrate how a required rate of return is obtained and how a RANPV is computed. These statistics are computed for a risky capital-budgeting alternative:

$E_t$

| | | | |
|---|---|---|---|
| Year 0 | −$5,000 | $E_{NPV} =$ | $3,332 |
| Year 1 | 4,000 | $\sigma_{NPV} =$ | $2,463 |
| Year 2 | 5,400 | $V_{NPV} =$ | .739 |

Assuming that Table 12-3 adequately reflects managerial risk aversion in this case, the required rate of return that corresponds to $V_{NPV} = .739$ is 18 percent. Thus, using Equation 12-9:

$$RANPV = \frac{-\$5,000}{(1 + .18)^0} + \frac{\$4,000}{(1 + .18)^1} + \frac{\$5,400}{(1 + .18)^2}$$

$$= \$2,265$$

---

A RANPV coefficient that is positive or zero indicates that the project earns at least the risk adjusted required rate of return and that adopting such a project can increase the value of the firm and thus shareholder wealth.

**Accept/Reject Decisions**

When a risky investment alternative is to be evaluated on an accept/reject basis, the RANPV criterion provides the following decision rule: *Accept the project if the RANPV is positive or zero; reject it if the RANPV is negative.*

**Example:**

The data set used in this example provides a complete set of statistical computations. A risky capital-budgeting alternative's cash value probability distributions are contained in Table 12-4. Using Table 12-3 to estimate the required rate of return, evaluate the desirability of this project on an accept/reject basis.

**Table 12-4.**

**Probability Distributions for a Risky Investment Alternative with a Two-Year Life**

| | Net Investment | Probability |
|---|---|---|
| Year 0 | −$4,500 | .2 |
| | − 5,000 | .5 |
| | − 6,000 | .3 |
| | **Cash Flow** | **Probability** |
| Year 1 | $2,000 | .2 |
| | 3,000 | .6 |
| | 4,000 | .2 |
| Year 2 | $2,000 | .1 |
| | 3,000 | .2 |
| | 4,000 | .5 |
| | 5,000 | .2 |

The statistical computations for the individual probability distributions are contained in Table 12-5. Note that the only risk measure computed in this step is the variance.

The statistics for the project are computed as follows. An 8 percent risk-free rate is used because that value is consistent with the Table 12-3 data.

$$E_{NPV} = \frac{-\$5,200}{(1 + .08)^0} + \frac{\$3,000}{(1 + .08)^1} + \frac{\$3,800}{(1 + .08)^2}$$

$$= \$835$$

$$\sigma_{NPV}^2 = \frac{310,000}{(1 + .08)^0} + \frac{400,000}{(1 + .08)^2} + \frac{760,000}{(1 + .08)^4}$$

$$= 1,211,400$$

**Table 12-5.**    Statistics for the Probability Distributions Contained in Table 12-4

### Year 0

| Net Investment $f_i$ | Probability $P_i$ | $(f_i)(P_i)$ | $(E_0 - f_i)$ | $(E_0 - f_i)^2$ | $(E_0 - f_i)^2 P_i$ |
|---|---|---|---|---|---|
| −$4,500 | .2 | −$ 900 | $700 | 490,000 | 98,000 |
| − 5,000 | .5 | − 2,500 | 200 | 40,000 | 20,000 |
| − 6,000 | .3 | − 1,800 | − 800 | 640,000 | 192,000 |
| | | $E_0 = -\$5,200$ | | | $\sigma_0^2 = 310,000$ |

### Year 1

| Cash Flow $f_i$ | Probability $P_i$ | $(f_i)(P_i)$ | $(E_1 - f_i)$ | $(E_1 - f_i)^2$ | $(E_1 - f_i)^2 P_i$ |
|---|---|---|---|---|---|
| $2,000 | .2 | $ 400 | $1,000 | 1,000,000 | 200,000 |
| 3,000 | .6 | 1,800 | 0 | 0 | 0 |
| 4,000 | .2 | 800 | − 1,000 | 1,000,000 | 200,000 |
| | | $E_1 = \$3,000$ | | | $\sigma_1^2 = 400,000$ |

### Year 2

| Cash Flow $f_i$ | Probability $P_i$ | $(f_i)(P_i)$ | $(E_2 - f_i)$ | $(E_2 - f_i)^2$ | $(E_2 - f_i)^2 P_i$ |
|---|---|---|---|---|---|
| $2,000 | .1 | $ 200 | $1,800 | 3,240,000 | 324,000 |
| 3,000 | .2 | 600 | 800 | 640,000 | 128,000 |
| 4,000 | .5 | 2,000 | − 200 | 40,000 | 20,000 |
| 5,000 | .2 | 1,000 | − 1,200 | 1,440,000 | 288,000 |
| | | $E_2 = \$3,800$ | | | $\sigma_2^2 = 760,000$ |

$$\sigma_{\text{NPV}} = \sqrt{1,211,400}$$

$$= \$1,101$$

$$V_{\text{NPV}} = \frac{\$1,101}{\$835}$$

$$= 1.32$$

Using Table 12-3, the risk adjusted required rate of return equals 30 percent. RANPV is then computed as follows:

$$\text{RANPV} = \frac{-\$5,200}{(1 + .30)^0} + \frac{\$3,000}{(1 + .30)^1} + \frac{\$3,800}{(1 + .30)^2}$$

$$= -\$643$$

Because of the negative RANPV, the project is rejected.

In the above example, the project's NPV is positive when discounted at the risk-free rate, but its RANPV is negative when the risk adjusted required rate of return is used. This reinforces the importance of using a NPV criterion that adjusts for risk. The technique used to identify the risk adjusted discount rate is also important: Managerial judgement is required in specifying the relationship between a project's NPV coefficient of variation and its risk adjusted required rate of return. Chapter 17 contains some additional procedures that can be used to identify risk adjusted discount rates.

**Mutually Exclusive Decisions**

When two or more risky alternatives are to be evaluated on a mutually exclusive basis, the RANPV criterion provides the following decision rule: *Choose the alternative with the highest RANPV provided that it is positive or zero; reject all the alternatives if this condition is violated.*

This type of decision situation requires that the RANPV coefficient be computed for each alternative. However, as occurs in the following example, the same risk adjusted discount rate may not be applicable for all the alternatives in a given mutually exclusive application because of the alternatives' differing risk-return characteristics.

**Example:**

A corporation advertises for bids on a project that has an expected economic life of two years. Two bids, labeled *KA*-1 and *KA*-2 are received. The firm computes the following statistics for each bid:

|  | Bid *KA*-1 | Bid *KA*-2 |
|---|---|---|
| $E_0$ | $-\$10,000$ | $-\$11,000$ |
| $\sigma_0^2$ | 400,000 | 400,000 |
| $E_1$ | \$5,900 | \$7,000 |
| $\sigma_1^2$ | 490,000 | 600,000 |
| $E_2$ | \$7,500 | \$7,000 |
| $\sigma_2^2$ | 1,050,000 | 2,000,000 |

Bid *KA*-2 requires a larger net investment because of transportation costs. The differences in the expected net cash flows between the two bids are due to slightly different production capacities, maintenance costs, and differences in Year 1 start-up and training costs. Assuming that Table 12-3 provides an adequate description of managerial risk aversion for this firm, which bid, if either, should be accepted?

In order to arrive at a decision, the RANPV is computed for each bid.

**Bid *KA*-1:**

The expected NPV is computed by using the 8 percent risk-free rate assumed in Table 12-3:

$$E_{\mathrm{NPV}} = \frac{-\$10,000}{(1 + .08)^0} + \frac{\$5,900}{(1 + .08)^1} + \frac{\$7,500}{(1 + .08)^2} = \$1,891$$

$$\sigma^2_{\text{NPV}} = \frac{400{,}000}{(1 + .08)^0} + \frac{490{,}000}{(1 + .08)^2} + \frac{1{,}050{,}000}{(1 + .08)^4}$$

$$= 1{,}591{,}680$$

$$\sigma_{\text{NPV}} = \sqrt{1{,}591{,}680}$$

$$= \$1{,}262$$

$$V_{\text{NPV}} = \frac{\$1{,}262}{\$1{,}891}$$

$$= .667$$

The risk adjusted required rate of return for this alternative, using Table 12-3, is 14 percent. The RANPV equals

$$\text{RANPV} = \frac{-\$10{,}000}{(1 + .14)^0} + \frac{\$5{,}900}{(1 + .14)^1} + \frac{\$7{,}500}{(1 + .14)^2}$$

$$= \$946$$

### Bid KA-2:

$$E_{\text{NPV}} = \frac{-\$11{,}000}{(1 + .08)^0} + \frac{\$7{,}000}{(1 + .08)^1} + \frac{\$7{,}000}{(1 + .08)^2}$$

$$= \$1{,}481$$

$$\sigma^2_{\text{NPV}} = \frac{400{,}000}{(1 + .08)^0} + \frac{600{,}000}{(1 + .08)^2} + \frac{2{,}000{,}000}{(1 + .08)^4}$$

$$= 2{,}384{,}200$$

$$\sigma_{\text{NPV}} = \sqrt{2{,}384{,}200}$$

$$= \$1{,}544$$

$$V_{\text{NPV}} = \frac{\$1{,}544}{\$1{,}481}$$

$$= 1.04$$

The risk adjusted required rate of return for this alternative, using Table 12-3, is 23 percent. The RANPV equals

$$\text{RANPV} = \frac{-\$11{,}000}{(1 + .23)^0} + \frac{\$7{,}000}{(1 + .23)^1} + \frac{\$7{,}000}{(1 + .23)^2}$$

$$= -\$682$$

The RANPV thus rejects bid KA-2 and accepts bid KA-1.

In the above example, both bids have a positive NPV when adjusting for the time value of money and not for risk. However, when the RANPVs are computed, alternative KA-2 becomes undesirable due to its negative RANPV. This example thus reinforces two important points when dealing with risky, mutually exclusive projects. First, adjust for risk, not only for the time value of money. Second, use a NPV criterion that reflects the fact that competing alternatives may not be equally risky.

**Evaluation of the RANPV Criterion**

The RANPV criterion is profit oriented, takes into account the time value of money, and explicitly adjusts for project risk. As a consequence, the RANPV is interpreted as the amount by which the expected net present value of a risky capital-budgeting alternative exceeds the minimum return required to justify undertaking the risk involved. The RANPV criterion provides financial decision makers with a single figure on which to make capital-budgeting decisions.

The computation of the RANPV requires financial managers to generate probability distributions for a project's net investment and for its subsequent net cash flows and assumes that managerial risk aversion can be translated into appropriate discount rates. The rationale in using risk adjusted discount rates is that risky projects that have probability distributions with greater variability, and thus larger coefficients of variation, should have their cash values discounted at a higher rate than other risky projects that have net investments and net cash flows with less variability and thus are less risky. Using statistical techniques can make the computations of the RANPV somewhat tedious although the computations themselves are not difficult. The use of these techniques also forces financial managers to accept the assumption that the RANPV and the coefficient of variation are useful measures of risk and return. Despite the difficulties in making appropriate adjustments for risk, the results are generally preferred to those obtained by assuming that future cash flows are known with certainty.

# PORTFOLIO EFFECTS

The product lines and/or services offered by a corporation are essentially a set of risky investment alternatives that have been accepted by the corporation. Any set of investments is generally referred to as a **portfolio**.

When a corporation is deciding whether to accept or reject a risky capital-budgeting alternative, attention must be paid to two different risk-return considerations.

1. The risk-return characteristics of the proposed investment

2. The impact on the overall risk-return characteristics of the corporation's portfolio if the proposed alternative is accepted (This is called the *portfolio effect*.)

The RANPV criterion as presented in this chapter focuses entirely on individual investments. This final section presents a very general introduction to the portfolio effect. A formal development of portfolio concepts is contained in Part 6.

**Correlation between Projects**

One important determinant of a portfolio's risk-return characteristics is the **correlation** that exists between each pair of projects contained in the portfolio. Returns generated by risky projects are generally correlated to each other. When two or more projects are combined into a portfolio, the risk of the entire portfolio—measured by the standard deviation or the coefficient of variation of the portfolio—depends on the risk contained in each project and on the correlation between projects.

The concept behind correlation can be explained with the use of hypothetical Projects *A*, *B*, and *C*. Figure 12-4 plots the rates of return over time for these projects. It shows that the rates of return for Projects *A* and *B* move up and down together over time. As a consequence, these two projects are said to be *positively correlated*. Figure 12-4 also shows that the rates of return for Projects *B* and *C* move in opposite directions over time. Thus, these two projects are said to be *negatively correlated*.

When the correlation between two projects is computed, the resulting coefficient ranges from +1 to −1. A value of +1 means perfect positive correlation and indicates that the rates of return of the two projects always move in the same direction. A value of −1 means perfect negative correlation and indicates that the rates of return of the two projects always move in opposite directions. A correlation coefficient of zero indicates that the rates of return of the two projects are unrelated. In actual practice, the correlations between most projects are positive. Very few projects can be found with correlations that are zero or negative.

**Figure 12-4.**       **Rates of Return for Hypothetical Projects *A*, *B*, and *C***

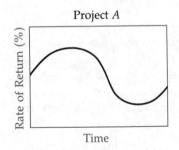
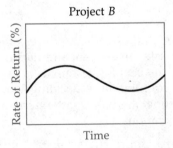
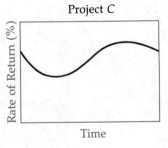

**Portfolio Risk and Return**

The three projects in Figure 12-4 are risky in that the rates of return earned at any time are not known with certainty. Each project's rate of return has an expected value and a coefficient of variation. Now assume that Projects A and C have identical net investments and probability distributions of rates of return. This means that, although the projects are negatively correlated, their rates of return have the same expected value and coefficient of variation. As a result, two hypothetical portfolios are now formed. One portfolio consists of Projects A and B; the other consists of Projects B and C. Two questions arise, (1) Which portfolio has the higher expected return and (2) Which portfolio has the greater amount of risk?

The answer to the first question is that both portfolios have the same expected rate of return. Since, by definition, Projects A and C are identical, adding the expected return of Project B to Project A and to Project C produces two portfolios with identical rates of return.

The second question can be answered by using the standard deviation or coefficient of variation of the portfolios as a measure of risk. The portfolio consisting of A and B is riskier than the portfolio consisting of B and C because the coefficient of correlation enters into the computation of portfolio risk. The portfolio's standard deviation and coefficient of variation increase with positive correlation and decrease with negative correlation. Since Projects B and C are negatively correlated while Projects A and B are positively correlated, the standard deviation and coefficient of variation for the portfolio consisting of Projects B and C will be smaller than those for the portfolio consisting of Projects A and B. Using the principle of risk aversion, the financial manager will prefer the portfolio consisting of Projects B and C. Why? Although both portfolios have the same expected return, the portfolio consisting of Projects B and C is less risky. Given two portfolios with the same rates of return, the financial manager will prefer the portfolio with the lesser amount of risk.

## Corporate Diversification

The impact of project correlation on portfolio risk provides an explanation for corporate diversification of product lines. The amount of risk contained in a corporation's portfolio is increased by the addition of a risky asset. However, the amount of increase is minimized if the correlations between the existing portfolio projects and the new project are zero or positive values close to zero. If a corporation identifies a risky project with a rate of return that is acceptable and negatively correlated to the corporate portfolio, accepting this project could decrease portfolio risk.

The impact of correlation on project risk also helps explain corporate diversification through mergers. In this case a corporation with desirable risk-return characteristics is bought by a second corporation. Given that the rate of return of the merger candidate is acceptable, the increase in the parent corporation's portfolio risk is minimized if the correlations between the merger candidate and the other corporations owned by the parent are close to zero.

# SUMMARY

Capital budgeting under conditions of risk is concerned with the evaluation of capital-budgeting alternatives when their net investments and subsequent net cash flows are known only to the extent of their probability distributions. Risky projects are evaluated by taking into account their risk and return characteristics. In order to develop capital-budgeting criteria for risky projects, financial managers are assumed to be risk averse.

Statistical measures of probability distributions are used to measure the desirability of a risky project. Project returns are measured by computing expected values; project risk is measured by computing variances, standard deviations, and coefficients of variation.

The RANPV criterion evaluates risky projects by using risk adjusted discount rates to compute the expected NPV of the project. As a first step the coefficient of variation of a project's NPV is computed using a risk-free discount rate. Financial managers then assign the risk adjusted required rate of return to the project on the basis of this NPV coefficient of variation. The resulting required rate of return is used to compute the project's RANPV.

When risky projects are combined into portfolios, the risk-return characteristics of the resulting portfolio must be considered. Adding a risky project to an existing portfolio changes the expected rate of return of the portfolio. The increased portfolio risk caused by the added project depends on the risk of the new project and on the correlations between the new project and the existing portfolio projects. The increase in the amount of portfolio risk can be minimized by adding a risky project that has correlations with the existing portfolio projects that are negative, zero, or, if positive, as close to zero as possible.

# QUESTIONS

**12-1.** What type of risk is contained in a risky capital-budgeting alternative?

**12-2.** Explain the meaning of *mutually exclusive* and *collectively exhaustive* when these terms are used to describe a set of possible cash flows.

**12-3.** Explain what is meant by managerial risk aversion.

**12-4.** What information is contained in a probability distribution of possible cash flows?

**12-5.** What characteristics of a risky project are measured by computing the expected values of cash flows and the standard deviations of future cash flows?

**12-6.** Why is the coefficient of variation preferred over the standard deviation as a measure of project risk?

**12-7.** How is project risk incorporated into the computation of a RANPV?

**12-8.** What are the advantages and limitations of the RANPV criterion?

**12-9.** What is the impact of project correlations on portfolio risk?

# PROBLEMS

**12-1.** Compute the expected value, variance, standard deviation, and coefficient of variation of the following probability distribution of possible cash flows:

| Cash Flow | Probability |
|-----------|-------------|
| $   0 | .1 |
| 100 | .2 |
| 300 | .3 |
| 500 | .3 |
| 700 | .1 |

12-2.   Compute the expected value, variance, standard deviation, and coefficient of variation of the following probability distribution of possible cash flows:

| Cash Flow | Probability |
|-----------|-------------|
| $  500 | .2 |
| 1,000 | .3 |
| 1,500 | .2 |
| 2,000 | .2 |
| 2,500 | .1 |

12-3.   A risky investment alternative has the following probability distribution of net investment:

| Net Investment | Probability |
|----------------|-------------|
| −$2,000 | .4 |
| −  2,500 | .4 |
| −  3,000 | .2 |

The project has a one-year life and has the following probability distribution of net cash flow:

| Net Cash Flow | Probability |
|---------------|-------------|
| $1,000 | .1 |
| 2,000 | .2 |
| 3,000 | .4 |
| 4,000 | .2 |
| 5,000 | .1 |

Using a 10% risk-free discount rate, compute the expected value and coefficient of variation of the project's NPV. How risky does this project appear? What is the probability that the net cash flows will exceed the expected net investment?

12-4.   A risky capital-budgeting alternative with a two-year economic lifetime is to be evaluated on an acept/reject basis. The following statistics are computed from the cash value probability distributions:

| | $E_t$ | $\sigma_t^2$ |
|-------|-------|-------------|
| Year 0 | −$10,000 | 1,600,000 |
| Year 1 | 6,000 | 1,600,000 |
| Year 2 | 6,000 | 2,200,000 |

Using the risk-return trade-off in Table 12-3, compute the RANPV for this project. Is the project desirable?

12-5.  Risky capital-budgeting alternatives $R$-1 and $R$-2 are mutually exclusive. Each has a two-year economic life. The following statistics are computed from the cash value probability distributions:

|  | Alternative $R$-1 | | Alternative $R$-2 | |
|---|---|---|---|---|
|  | $E_t$ | $\sigma_t^2$ | $E_t$ | $\sigma_t^2$ |
| Year 0 | −$16,000 | 200,000 | −$15,000 | 200,000 |
| Year 1 | 11,000 | 2,000,000 | 10,000 | 1,600,000 |
| Year 2 | 11,000 | 3,000,000 | 10,000 | 2,400,000 |

Using Table 12-3, evaluate these alternatives on the basis of their RANPVs.

# SELECTED REFERENCES

Bey, R. "Calculating Means and Variances of NPVs When the Life of the Project is Uncertain." *Journal of Financial Research*, Vol. 3, No. 2 (Summer, 1980).

Brigham, E. *Financial Management Theory and Practice.* 3d ed. Chicago: The Dryden Press, 1982.

Chen, S., and W. Moore. "Investment Decisions under Uncertainty: Application of Estimation Risk in the Hillier Approach." *Journal of Financial and Quantitative Analysis,* Vol. 17, No. 3 (September, 1982).

Clark, J., T. Hindelang, and R. Pritchard. *Capital Budgeting.* Englewood-Cliffs, N.J.: Prentice-Hall, Inc., 1979.

Hillier, F. "The Derivation of Probabilistic Information for the Evaluation of Risky Investments." *Management Science,* Vol. 9, No. 3 (April, 1963).

Levy, H., and M. Sarnat. *Capital Investment and Financial Decisions.* 2d ed. Englewood-Cliffs, N.J.: Prentice-Hall International, Inc., 1982.

# PART 5

# Valuation, Cost of Capital, and Capital Structure

The three chapters that make up Part 5 provide a first introduction to what is frequently called the traditional theory of finance.

Chapter 13 explains how to compute the intrinsic value of financial assets, such as stocks and bonds. Chapter 14 introduces the concept and measurement of cost of capital and develops, through the use of a simplified example, the interrelationships among cost of capital, value of the firm, and capital structure. Chapter 15 demonstrates how a corporation's capital structure affects its risk and return characteristics and provides some tools for evaluating the impacts of alternative capital structures on the value of the firm.

# CHAPTER 13

## Valuation

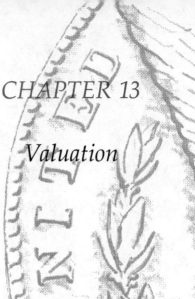

This chapter deals with measuring the worth, or value, of financial assets. The specific financial assets considered are corporate bonds, preferred stock, and common stock. The process of estimating the value of these financial assets is called **valuation**.

The first section of this chapter introduces several different concepts of value and explains the rationale for using intrinsic value methods in valuing financial assets. Later sections use intrinsic value procedures in valuing bonds, preferred stock, and common stock.

The point of view in this chapter is that of the individual investor interested in placing a value on corporate financial assets. This approach might appear to be inconsistent with the approach of previous chapters that concentrate on management decisions. However, it is investor buying and selling that determines the market value of a corporation's securities. If a corporation seeks to maximize shareholder wealth, corporate decisions must be aimed at making its securities more desirable to investors. The resulting demand will increase

*the resale price of its securities. As explained
in previous chapters, increases in the price of a
corporation's common stock is one way of
increasing shareholder wealth. Thus, it is
important for corporate managers to
understand what variables or factors investors
use in valuing securities. It is also important
to understand how a financial asset's value
emerges from the valuation process.*

## CONCEPTS OF VALUE

An asset, whether real or financial, has value to the extent that it can
satisfy desires, needs, or wants. Economists describe such an asset as one
that possesses utility. The value or utility of corporate assets is contained in
their ability to produce cash flows over a given time interval. A number of
different concepts are used to measure asset values. These concepts are
book value, market value, going concern value, liquidating value, and
intrinsic value. Each of these concepts has its own application, depending
in part on whether individual assets or the entire firm is being valued.

**Book Value**

**Book value** is an accounting concept that measures the value of individual assets based on historical data. Asset book values are the dollar
values of the assets as they appear in the corporation's balance sheet. Fixed

assets, for example, are listed net of depreciation. The book value of common stock is equal to the sum of all the items listed in the common stockholder equity section of the balance sheet. *Book value per share of common* is computed by dividing the total common stock book value by the number of shares of common that are outstanding.

**Market Value**

An asset's **market value** is the price that can be obtained from the sale of the asset. When a corporation's securities are traded on secondary security markets, their market values are generally equated with the prices at which the securities are bought and sold. Market values of real assets may be more difficult to measure. Although used computers, for example, have resale markets that can provide estimates of market value, land or obsolete buildings may not be readily marketable.

**Going Concern Value**

**Going concern value** refers to the value of a business as an operating entity. This concept does not attempt to value the firm with respect to its balance sheet assets but focuses instead on its ability to generate sales and profits. Suppose, for example, a person owns a small manufacturing firm that operates exclusively as a defense industry subcontractor. The owner wishes to sell the firm and retire from business. The selling price of the firm will be based primarily on estimates of its continuing ability to attract profitable contracts from defense contractors.

**Liquidating Value**

The **liquidating value** of a corporation is the amount of cash that would be realized if the firm's assets were sold and its liabilities paid off. The remaining cash would then be distributed to the firm's owners. If the firm's liabilities equal or exceed the cash obtained from the sale of its assets, the shareholders receive no payments, and the liquidating value is zero or negative. Liquidating value is an important concept primarily when a firm is failing or when, for whatever reason, the firm cannot be sold as a going concern.

**Intrinsic Value**

Intrinsic value concepts are used when measuring the desirability of corporate stocks and bonds as investment vehicles. Intrinsic value is often called *fair value, investment value,* or *capitalized value.* The **intrinsic value** of a financial asset can be defined as the sum of the present values of the cash flows returned by the asset when discounted at the investor's required rate of return.

**FINANCIAL ASSET VALUATION.** In measuring the desirability of financial assets as investment alternatives, intrinsic value provides the most useful concept of value. One reason is that financial assets represent claims on future cash flows. Bonds pay interest and return their principal amounts at maturity. Preferred and common stocks pay dividends and, when resale markets exist, exhibit prices that can be realized if the securities are sold.

Since these financial assets produce cash flows over a period of time, their valuation must also take into account the time value of money and the rates of return required by investors. Financial assets are thus valued by computing their present values. The mechanics of computing present values were explained in Chapter 9, and present value concepts were applied to capital-budgeting problems in Chapters 10, 11, and 12.

A second reason for using intrinsic value to judge the desirability of financial assets is that the valuation of real and financial assets is closely interrelated. Capital budgeting is essentially a set of techniques for valuing real assets by measuring their present values. As explained in Chapter 14, the discount rates used in capital budgeting are based on the rates of return required by investors in valuing financial assets. Thus, corporate financial managers use intrinsic value techniques in measuring the desirability of real asset investment alternatives, and investors use similar techniques in deciding whether or not the purchase of particular corporate securities will increase their personal wealth. These interrelationships are explained in greater detail in Chapters 14 and 15.

**RISK-RETURN ASSUMPTIONS.** Intrinsic value models contain a number of assumptions concerning how investors allow for the risk-return characteristics of financial assets. One assumption is that returns are estimated or forecast by using point estimates as opposed to probability distributions. This means that any particular future cash flow is represented by a single number. The forecast value is not an expected value in a statistical sense; it is meant to represent the value that is most likely to occur although no standard deviation is calculated to indicate the range of forecasting errors. How these forecast values are generated depends to some extent on the type of financial asset being evaluated. Each intrinsic value model incorporates a procedure for estimating future cash flows.

Another risk-return assumption is that investors recognize subjectively the various risks that accompany the purchase of financial assets by including these risks in the discount rate that is used to compute financial asset intrinsic values. The risks of primary concern are business and financial risk, interest rate risk, and inflation risk. Fixed payment securities contain the greatest amounts of interest rate and inflation risks. Variable payment equity securities contain the greatest amounts of business and financial risks.

## BOND VALUATION

Computing and interpreting intrinsic values of bonds is a direct application of financial mathematics and of present value concepts. There are two reasons why bond valuation is easily performed. First, bond interest payments are made in annuity form. Second, bonds mature at a specified future time and return the bond principal at maturity. This means that bondholders and potential bondholders know the amounts and timing of the payments promised by the issuing corporation. Although interest payments are typically made on a semiannual basis, annual payments are assumed in this text in order to simplify present value calculations. A related assumption is that a bond bought in a resale market produces its first interest payment one year after its purchase.

**Bond
Terminology**

In order to compute the intrinsic value of a bond, it is necessary to be familiar with some of the terminology used to describe the provisions of a bond issue. The terms introduced in this chapter center around bond prices, interest rates, and rates of return.

1.  *Bond*   A bond essentially is a long-term loan in the form of a promissory note.

2.  **Par value**   This is the principal amount, or face amount, of the bond. Bonds return their par values at maturity unless they are retired earlier by the issuer.

3.  *Bond quotations and prices*   The price of a bond is quoted in percentages of its par value. A $10,000 par value bond, for example, quoted at 100 — 100 percent of par value — has a price of $10,000. The same bond quoted at 102.5 would have a price of $10,250. A $5,000 par value bond quoted at 76 would cost $3,800.

4.  **Coupon rate**   The rate of interest paid on the bond's par value is the coupon rate. Unless otherwise stated, the coupon rate is fixed over the life of the bond.

5.  **Interest payment**   This equals the coupon rate multiplied by the par value. A $5,000 par value bond, for example, with an 11 percent coupon rate returns a yearly interest payment of $550. Since the coupon rate is fixed over the life of the bond unless otherwise stated, the interest payments must also be fixed over the life of the bond unless otherwise stated.

6.  **Current yield**   This is the ratio of a bond's interest payment to its current market price. For example, the current yield on a $5,000 par value bond with a 10 percent coupon quoted at 96 is $500/$4,800 = 10.42 percent.

7.  **Yield to maturity (YTM)**   A bond's YTM is its internal rate of return and is based on its purchase price, interest payments, and the par value that is received at maturity. The discount rate that produces a zero net present value — NPV — for this set of cash flows is the bond's YTM.

8.  *Selling at a discount*   Selling a bond below its par value is selling it at a discount. Because bond interest payments are fixed

amounts, a bond selling at a discount will have a c⌐
and a YTM that are larger than its coupon rate

9.  *Selling at a premium*   This is selling a bond above its p⌐
    when a bond sells at a premium, its current yield and YTM wₐ⌐
    be less than its coupon rate.

**Intrinsic Value of Bonds**

The intrinsic value of a bond is the sum of the present values of future interest payments plus the present value of the bond's par value that is paid at maturity. In order to compute a bond's intrinsic value, the required rate of return must be known. Given a required rate of return, the intrinsic value of a bond is computed in the following three steps:

1.  Compute the present value of the annuity of interest payments. Use Equation 9-16 on page 260 with the required rate of return as the discount rate.

2.  Compute the present value of the bond's par value that is received at maturity. Use Equation 9-14 on page 255 with the required rate of return as the discount rate.

3.  Add the two present values found in Steps 1 and 2. The sum is the bond's intrinsic value.

---

**Example:**

A $1,000 bond matures in 20 years and offers a 9 percent coupon rate. The required rate of return is 11 percent. Compute the bond's intrinsic value.

The annual interest payment is $90. At the end of Year 20, the bondholder receives the $90 interest payment and the $1,000 par value.

The present value of the interest payments is obtained by using the present value annuity factor for 11 percent and 20 payments.

$$\$90(7.963) = \$716.67$$

The present value of the $1,000 bond principal is obtained by using the present value, single payment factor for 11 percent and 20 years.

$$\$1,000(.124) = \$124$$

The intrinsic value is thus:

$$\$716.67 + \$124.00 = \$840.67$$

The discount rate exceeds the coupon rate. As a consequence, the bond's intrinsic value is less than its par value.

---

The intrinsic value of any financial asset can be interpreted as the maximum price that can be paid by an investor if the asset's rate of return is to equal or exceed the investor's rate of return. If the financial asset's intrinsic value exceeds its purchase price, then the asset's NPV is positive, and the asset is a desirable investment. A financial asset's intrinsic value that just equals its purchase price has a zero NPV; it is also a desirable investment. However, if a financial asset's intrinsic value is less than its purchase price, the asset's NPV is negative, and it is not a desirable investment. Thus, a bond's desirability as an investment alternative can be judged by computing its NPV and making an accept/reject decision. A bond's NPV is computed by subtracting its price from its intrinsic value.

**Example:**   A $5,000 bond with a 10 percent coupon rate matures in eight years and currently sells for 97. Is this bond a desirable investment for an investor whose required rate of return is 11 percent?

The intrinsic value of the bond is

$$\$500(5.146) + \$5,000(.434) = \$4,743$$

The bond's NPV is

$$\$4,743 - \$4,850 = -\$107$$

On an accept/reject basis, the bond is undesirable because its NPV is negative.

**Yield to Maturity**

A bond's YTM has been defined as its internal rate of return (IRR). Since bonds are bought and sold primarily to obtain a required rate of return for a given level of risk, investors and bond traders frequently use YTMs as the basis for reaching bond investment decisions. However, since a YTM is essentially a measure of the bond's IRR, the implicit assumption is made that all interest payments are reinvested at a rate of return equal to the bond's YTM.

Computing YTMs is not a difficult process because interest payments are in annuity form (the computational techniques were explained in Chapter 10). Furthermore, if the bond's price is not too far from its par value, a good first guess at the bond's YTM is obtained by using the coupon rate as the discount rate. The intrinsic value of a bond computed in this manner equals its par value, and the bond's NPV is found by subtracting its price from its par value. This approach to a first guess thus requires no calculations involving present value factors. As a rule of thumb, the coupon rate provides a good first YTM approximation when the bond's price is at least 90 and not more than 110.

**Example:**   A $10,000 bond matures in eight years, has a 12 percent coupon rate, and is selling for 106. Compute its YTM.

Because the price exceeds 100, the YTM is less than the 12 percent coupon rate. The price, however, is close to par. Thus, the first guess is to compute the bond's NPV using the 12 percent coupon rate. No discounting calculations are needed for this first NPV.

$$(NPV \mid 12\%) = \$10,000 - \$10,600 = -\$600$$

The second guess uses an 11 percent discount rate.

$$(NPV \mid 11\%) = \$1,200(5.146) + \$10,000(.434) - \$10,600$$
$$= -\$84.80$$

The third guess uses 10 percent discount rate.

$$(NPV \mid 10\%) = \$1,200(5.335) + \$10,000(.467) - \$10,600$$
$$= \$472$$

The bond's YTM is between 10 percent and 11 percent. Add the absolute values of these two NPVs.

$$\$84.80 + \$472 = \$556.80$$

and divide the NPV at 10 percent by $556.80.

$$\$472/\$556.80 = .85$$

Thus, the bond's YTM is approximately 10 percent + .85 = 10.85 percent.

---

There are occasions where a bond price deviates 20 to 30 percent or more from its par value. So-called deep discount bonds are one example. These bonds were issued 20 to 25 years ago and carry coupon rates as low as 3½ percent to 4 percent. In order for these bonds to earn YTMs that are competitive with current YTMs of 9 percent and higher, the bonds sell at a large — or deep — discount from par value. A good first guess at computing the YTM of a deep discount bond is to use a discount rate equal to the YTMs available on newly issued bonds. In the absence of such data, a first guess at a discount rate is to multiply the deep discount bond's coupon rate by 2.0.

---

**Example:**  A $10,000 bond issued 20 years ago has 10 years to maturity. The coupon rate is 5 percent and the bond is selling for 67.5. Compute the bond's YTM.

A first guess is a discount rate of 10 percent (coupon rate ×2).

$$(NPV \mid 10\%) = \$500(6.145) + \$10,000(.386) - \$6,750$$
$$= \$182.50$$

Since the NPV at 10 percent is positive, the second guess is to a discount rate of 11 percent.

$$(NPV \mid 11\%) = \$500(5.889) + \$10,000(.352) - \$6,750$$
$$= -\$285.50$$

The bond's YTM is between 10 percent and 11 percent. Add the absolute values of the two NPVs.

$$\$182.50 + \$285.50 = \$468$$

Then divide the sum into the NPV that occurs at 10 percent.

$$\$182.50/\$468 = .39$$

Thus, the bond's YTM is approximately 10 percent + .39 = 10.39 percent.

---

**Interest Rate Risk**

Previous chapters discussed the risks involved when investing in corporate securities. Bonds are subject to business and financial risks as are other types of financial assets. Thus, bond prices will fall if investors feel that the probability of the corporation defaulting on the bond has increased. Bondholders can sell their bonds if the firm's risk-return characteristics are no longer acceptable to them. Alternatively, bondholders can keep the bonds and accept the perceived higher level of risk.

In addition to business and financial risk, bonds are also subject to interest rate risk. As defined earlier, interest rate risk is the probability that bond prices will fall because of increases in the general level of interest rates. This type of risk is present in all bonds and is caused by business cycles and inflation.

The degree of interest rate risk contained in any bond is primarily a function of the number of years remaining before the bond matures. The longer a bond has until it matures, the greater the amount of interest rate risk. Thus, if a corporation has several issues of bonds outstanding and if each issue has a different maturity date, then each bond issue will have its own degree of interest rate risk.

---

**Example:**

A corporation has two bond issues outstanding. One issue matures in 5 years while the other matures in 20 years. The bonds in each issue are assumed to carry 8 percent coupon rates and have a $10,000 par value.

Table 13-1 contains the bond prices for each issue at different required rates of return. Figure 13-1 plots the values contained in that table. When required rates of return — often called simply *market rates* — are 8 percent, the bonds in each issue sell for 100. If interest rate levels increase to 9 percent, the 5-year bond prices fall to 96.1 while the 20-year bond prices fall to 90.8. The bond prices fall even further if the market rates increase to 10 percent. The bonds with a 20-year maturity, however, suffer a much steeper price decline than do the 5-year maturity bonds.

Accordingly, the 20-year maturity bonds are said to contain a greater degree of interest rate risk than do the bonds with a 5-year maturity.

On the other hand, if these bonds were purchased at 100 when market rates were 8 percent and market rates subsequently fell, the prices of both bonds would increase. The bonds with the longer maturity, however, would realize the larger price increases. If, for example, market rates fell from 8 percent to 6 percent, the 5-year maturity bond prices would increase to 108.4, but the 20-year maturity bond prices would increase much further and reach a value of 123.9. Thus, bondholders who choose longer bond maturities and accept greater amounts of interest rate risk also realize proportionately greater benefits if and when market interest rates fall.

**Table 13-1.**   **Prices at Different Required Rates of Return for 8 Percent Coupon Bonds**

| Required Rate of Return (%) | 5-Year Maturity | 20-Year Maturity |
|:---:|:---:|:---:|
| 6 | 108.4 | 123.9 |
| 7 | 104.1 | 110.6 |
| 8 | 100.0 | 100.0 |
| 9 | 96.1 | 90.8 |
| 10 | 92.4 | 83.0 |

**Figure 13-1.**   **Prices at Different Required Rates of Return for 8 Percent Coupon Bonds (Prices in Percent of Par Value)**

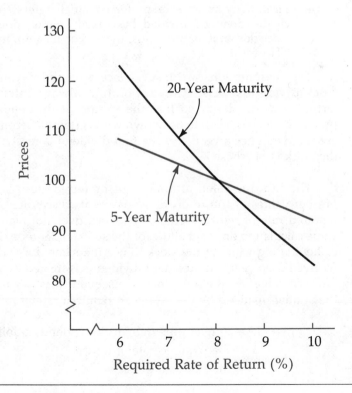

## PREFERRED STOCK VALUATION

Preferred stock is considered by many investors as a hybrid security because it possesses both debt and equity characteristics (see page 562-563) in Chapter 19). This mixture of characteristics affects the calculation of a preferred stock's intrinsic value.

Preferred Stock
Terminology

The terminology used in computing a preferred stock's intrinsic value is less involved than that of bonds. The terms introduced in this chapter are

1. *Par value/liquidating value*   Preferred stock may or may not have a face value, or par value. If it does not have a par value, it will contain a liquidating value. The par value or liquidating value is the dollars per share that the preferred stockholder is entitled to receive from the corporation in the event of liquidation. The total per share claim in the event of liquidation is the liquidating value plus unpaid dividends.

2. *Prices*   Preferred stock prices are quoted in dollars per share.

3. *Dividend rates*   Dividend rates are quoted as a percentage of par value or in dollars per share.

4. *Yield*   The yield of a preferred stock refers to its current yield — dividend divided by current market price. Preferred stock does not mature; thus, there is no meaningful measure of YTM for it.

Two assumptions are made concerning the payment of preferred stock dividends. First, the corporation always intends to pay preferred stock dividends so that the stream of dividends to be paid on preferred stock is taken to be known with certainty. Second, the dividends are received once a year, and the first dividend is received one year after the stock is purchased.

Intrinsic Value
of Preferred
Stock

The intrinsic value of a share of preferred stock is the sum of the present values of future dividend payments discounted at the investor's required rate of return. Because the stock does not mature, the intrinsic value calculation does not allow for the stockholder receiving the par value or liquidating value of the stock. Since the same dollar dividend is to be received each year, the stream of dividends is treated as a perpetuity. The intrinsic value of preferred stock, consequently, is calculated by dividing the annual dividend by the investor's required rate of return. Let

$$D = \text{annual preferred stock dividend in dollars}$$
$$k = \text{the required rate of return}$$
$$V = \text{the stock's intrinsic value}$$

$V$ is calculated by using the following equation:

$$V = D/k \qquad\qquad (13\text{-}1)$$

**Example:**   A share of preferred stock pays an $8 annual dividend. Calculate its intrinsic value to an investor whose required rate of return is 10 percent.

Using Equation 13-1:

$$V = \$8/.1$$
$$= \$80$$

In evaluating the desirability of a particular preferred stock, its intrinsic value can be compared with its purchase price, and an accept/reject decision can be made. If the stock's intrinsic value equals or exceeds its purchase price, the stock's rate of return will equal or exceed the investor's required rate of return. Otherwise, the stock should not be purchased. This decision rule is simply another application of the NPV criterion.

**Example:**   A preferred stock pays a $10 per share dividend and sells for $104 per share. Is this a desirable investment if a 10 percent rate of return is required?

Using Equation 13-1:

$$V = \$10/.1$$
$$= \$100$$

Since the purchase price exceeds the stock's intrinsic value, the purchase is not desirable.

The internal rate of return of preferred stock is computed by using Equation 13-2. Let

$$k = \text{IRR}$$
$$V = \text{the stock's purchase price}$$

Solving Equation 13-1 for $k$ yields

$$k = D/V \qquad\qquad (13\text{-}2)$$

**Example:**   A preferred stock sells for $110 and pays a yearly dividend of $9.50. Calculate the stock's IRR.

Using Equation 13-2:

$$k = \$9.50/\$110$$
$$= .0864 \text{ or } 8.64\%$$

**Investment Risks**

Preferred stocks contain interest rate risk because dividend payments are the same each year. When interest levels change, the resale prices of preferred issues react in the opposite direction. In addition, preferred issues contain substantial amounts of business and financial risk because dividend payments are not guaranteed by the corporation. Dividends will be reduced or eliminated if the corporation is unable to operate profitably.

## COMMON STOCK VALUATION

Of the three types of financial assets considered in this chapter, common stock is the most difficult to evaluate because of its residual ownership characteristic. Many different approaches for calculating intrinsic values of common stock have been developed, but no one approach appears to be superior under all circumstances. When the desirability of a corporation's common stock is being judged by calculating its intrinsic value, the particular valuation equation used depends on the assumptions the investor makes concerning the corporation's future earnings, the amounts and timing of its common stock dividends, and the behavior of the stock's price in secondary security markets. As a result, this section presents several valuation models and concentrates on explaining how different sets of assumptions produce different valuation models.

**Characteristics of Common Stock**

Common stock is an equity security and represents the residual ownership of a corporation. The word *residual* is used to describe the following characteristics of common stock:

1.  It has no date of maturity.

2.  It may or may not have a par value, but it has no stated liquidation value. In the event of liquidation, common shareholders share in whatever funds remain after all liabilities have been met and after preferred shareholders have received their par value or liquidating value payments.

3.  Dividends are never guaranteed, are not legally required, and are not fixed as in the case of preferred stock. Thus, common stock dividends can increase, remain constant, or decrease.

**Intrinsic Value of Common Stock**

The intrinsic value of a share of common stock is the sum of the present values of future cash flows to be received from owning it, discounted at the investor's required rate of return. Some valuation models include only dividends in calculating intrinsic value. Others include both dividends and an eventual resale price. In discussing alternative valuation models, the following assumptions are made: (1) that dividends are paid annually, (2) that the first dividend is received one year after a share is purchased, and (3) that any stock sale occurs at the end of a year.

The uncertainty as to the pattern of dividend payments and the difficulty of predicting a future market price is what makes the calculation of common stock intrinsic value a difficult task. The models contained in this section make different assumptions or forecasts about these future values. Thus, the model of choice in valuing any particular corporation's common stock is the one with underlying assumptions that best approximate the forecast or expected set of cash flows to be realized while owning the security.

NAIVE VALUATION. The simplest approach to common stock valuation is to assume that the stock's current dividend will be constant over time and that the stock, once purchased, will be held indefinitely. The dividend stream is thus a long-lived annuity and is treated as if it were a perpetuity. The intrinsic value of this dividend stream is computed by dividing one year's dividend by the investor's required rate of return. Equation 13-1 can be used for this purpose when $D$ stands for the constant dividend per share of common.

---

**Example:**

A corporation pays a dividend of $6 per year on each share of its common stock. Compute the intrinsic value of the stock if the investor's required rate of return is 12 percent.

Using Equation 13-1:

$$V = \$6/.12$$
$$= \$50$$

---

The advantage of this model is that no forecasting of future dividends or resale price is needed. On the basis that dividends will—in reality—be increased in the future, this naive model understates the stock's intrinsic value. The limitations of this model are the unrealistic dividend stream that is capitalized and the lack of an *explicit* resale price in calculating the stock's intrinsic value.

Under some restrictive assumptions this naive model does contain an *implicit* resale price. These assumptions are that the actual dividend stream turns out to be a perpetuity and that the rate of return demanded by investors in future years equals the rate of return earned from purchasing the stock at time period zero. Under these assumptions, the implied future selling price equals the current purchase price.

**Example:**  A stock pays a $2.25 annual dividend and is purchased by an investor for $15. Under the constant dividend assumption, the stock's IRR is computed by using Equation 13-2.

$$k = \text{IRR}$$
$$= \$2.25/\$15$$
$$= .15 \text{ or } 15\%$$

In order to have earned a 15 percent IRR, the selling price must be $15 if the investor sells this stock at some later date.

This implied rate can be verified by computing the NPV of the investment using a 15 percent discount rate. If the NPV is zero, the IRR is 15 percent. Assume, for example, that the stock is held for ten years and then sold. The investor receives the Year 10 dividend. The cash flows, discount factors, and NPV are as follows:

$15 purchase price at Year zero
$2.25 dividend per year for 10 years
$15 selling price at the end of Year 10
Discount rate = IRR = 15%

$$\text{NPV} = \$2.25(5.019) + \$15(.247) - \$15$$
$$= \$0$$

**CONSTANT DIVIDEND GROWTH RATE.** Most common stock valuation models are built around the assumption that dividends increase over time and that the rate of increase can be approximated by a compound growth rate. The most frequently used model of this type is based on the following assumptions: (1) dividends grow at a constant annual (compound) rate and (2) the dividend growth rate is *less* than the investor's required rate of return. On the basis of these assumptions, the intrinsic value is defined as the sum of the present values of the future dividends. No explicit resale price is included in the model. Since the dividend increases each year, it would appear—at least at first glance—that the stock's intrinsic value would increase without limit as more and more dividends are included. However, as long as the discount rate is greater than the dividend growth rate, the intrinsic value is a finite number.

The following symbols are used in developing this model:

$D_0$ = the most recent per share dividend

$D_t$ = the per share dividend paid at the end of Year $t$

$g$ = the dividend growth rate

$k$ = the discount rate which represents the investor's required rate of return

Using the compound amount concepts from Chapter 9, dividends paid in any future year are computed by using Equation 9-7 expressed in the following form:

$$D_t = D_0(1 + g)^t \tag{13-3}$$

Equation 13-3 is used as a forecasting equation. $D_0$ is supposedly known. The dividend growth rate is the investor's estimate of the future growth rate and is obtained by subjectively adjusting the historical growth rate.

---

**Example:**

For values of $D_0 = \$1$ and $g = 3$ percent, Equation 13-3 generates the following dividend payments. The values of $(1 + g)^t$ are taken from Appendix Table A-1.

$$D_1 = \$1.00(1 + .03)^1$$
$$= \$1.03$$

$$D_2 = \$1.00(1 + .03)^2$$
$$= \$1.06$$

$$D_5 = \$1.00(1 + .03)^5$$
$$= \$1.16$$

$$D_{20} = \$1.00(1 + .03)^{20}$$
$$= \$1.806$$

---

The intrinsic value of the dividend stream contained in Equation 13-3 is computed by discounting each future $D_t$ and adding the resulting present values. Since the right-hand side of Equation 13-3 provides the dividends in each year, dividing each dividend by $(1 + k)^t$ produces the required present values. Stated symbolically, the intrinsic value is

$$V = \frac{D_0(1 + g)^1}{(1 + k)^1} + \frac{D_0(1 + g)^2}{(1 + k)^2} + \cdots + \frac{D_0(1 + g)^t}{(1 + k)^t} + \cdots \tag{13-4}$$

Equation 13-4 can be written as

$$V = \sum_{t=1}^{\infty} \frac{D_0(1 + g)^t}{(1 + k)^t} \tag{13-5}$$

Equation 13-5 indicates an indefinite summation. However, as long as $k$ is greater than $g$, the value of each succeeding term becomes smaller and approaches zero as a limit. Algebraically, Equation 13-5 is a convergent geometric series and the indicated summation has a value of

$$\frac{D_0(1 + g)}{(k - g)} \tag{13-6}$$

However, $D_0(1 + g) = D_1$. When this substitution is made into Equation 13-6, the final intrinsic value equation becomes simply

$$V = \frac{D_1}{(k - g)} \tag{13-7}$$

**Example:**   This example demonstrates that the value of Equation 13-5 approaches that of Equation 13-7 as a limit, thus allowing the use of Equation 13-7 in computing the intrinsic value of common stocks when their dividend growth rate is constant and less than the discount rate.

Let $D_0 = \$2$, $k = .15$, $g = .02$. Table 13-2 contains $D_t$, the present values of each $D_t$, and the accumulative sum of the present values for ten years. Each $D_t$ is computed by using Equation 13-3.

**Table 13-2.**   **Calculations for Present Value and Intrinsic Value**
**($D_0 = \$2$, $k = .15$, and $g = .02$)**

| $t$ | $D_t$ | $D_t/(1 + k)^t$ | $\sum_t D_t/(1 + k)^t$ |
|----|-------|-----------------|------------------------|
| 1 | $2.04 | $1.77 | $ 1.77 |
| 2 | 2.08 | 1.57 | 3.34 |
| 3 | 2.12 | 1.39 | 4.73 |
| 4 | 2.16 | 1.23 | 5.96 |
| 5 | 2.21 | 1.10 | 7.06 |
| 6 | 2.25 | .97 | 8.03 |
| 7 | 2.30 | .86 | 8.99 |
| 8 | 2.34 | .76 | 9.75 |
| 9 | 2.39 | .68 | 10.43 |
| 10 | 2.44 | .60 | 11.03 |

Note that the present value of each $D_t$ becomes smaller with increasing values of $t$. As a result, the accumulative sum grows at a decreasing rate. Equation 13-7, the limit of this accumulative sum, is the intrinsic value and is equal to

$$V = \frac{\$2.04}{(.15 - .02)} = \$15.69$$

The $15.69 intrinsic value can be interpreted as the maximum purchase price that will earn the investor a 15 percent required rate of return.

The valuation model contained in Equation 13-7 is easy to compute and explicitly recognizes dividend growth. While the forecast $D_t$ cannot be expected to equal actual future dividends, the discounting process significantly reduces these forecasting errors. These advantages explain why Equation 13-7 is the most frequently used model when common stock is evaluated from an intrinsic value approach.

When an investor buys common stock at the current market price, Equation 13-7 can be used to indicate the rate of return actually earned by the investor. This is done by substituting the purchase price for the intrinsic value and solving for $k$. Let $P_0$ represent the purchase price. Then

$$P_0 = D_1/(k - g)$$

Solving for $k$ yields

$$k = \frac{D_1}{P_0} + g \tag{13-8}$$

If the investor wishes to sell the stock in a subsequent time period, the following equation can be used to identify the selling price that must be realized if the rate of return $(k)$ is to be realized. The investor buys the stock at Year zero and sells it at the end of Year $t$. The required selling price $(P_t)$ equals

$$P_t = \frac{D_0(1 + g)^{t+1}}{(k - g)} \tag{13-9}$$

The value of $P_t$ in this equation is the present value (*at Time* t) of the dividends that are forgone by the investor as a result of selling the stock. This forgone stream of dividends is assumed to grow at the rate $g$ and is discounted at the rate $k$. Thus, under the assumption that the investor's required rate of return is equal to the value of $k$ as computed in Equation 13-8, the implied selling price that allows the investor to earn the required rate of return is contained in Equation 13-9.

---

**Example:**

A stock currently sells for $7 per share. The current dividend is $1 per share and its estimated growth rate is 5 percent. If the stock is purchased, the IRR is computed by using Equation 13-8.

$$k = \text{IRR}$$

$$= \frac{\$1(1 + .05)}{\$7} + .05$$

$$= .2 \quad \text{or} \quad 20\%$$

If the investor wishes to sell the stock at the end of Year 2, the selling price that must be realized at the time of sale in order to have earned a 20 percent rate of return over the two-year period is found by using Equation 13-9.

$$P_2 = \frac{\$1(1 + .05)^3}{(.20 - .05)}$$

$$= \$7.72$$

This price represents the present value, *at the end of Year 2,* of the dividends that would have been received by the investor had the stock not been sold.

The cash flows realized from holding the stock for two years are the dividends received at the end of Years 1 and 2 and the selling price realized at the end of Year 2. The sum of the present values of these cash flows is the intrinsic value of this stock and is calculated as follows:

$$V = \frac{\$1(1 + .05)}{(1 + .2)} + \frac{\$1(1 + .05)^2}{(1 + .2)^2} + \frac{\$7.72}{(1 + .2)^2}$$

$$= \$7$$

Since this $7 intrinsic value equals the original purchase price, the NPV of the investment is zero when discounted at a 20 percent rate of return. Thus, the IRR is 20 percent as long as the stock can be sold for $7.72 at the end of Year 2.

**EXPLICIT RESALE PRICE.** A number of valuation models have been constructed that contain explicit resale prices. These models assume that common stock is purchased at Year zero, held for a certain number of years, and then sold. The intrinsic value equations for these models contain a separate term that represents the forecast selling price. The intrinsic value equals the sum of the present values of the dividends received while the stock is held plus the present value of the eventual selling price.

These models estimate dividends and resale price by forecasting earnings per share (EPS). The specific assumptions are

1.  EPS grows at a constant compound annual rate.

2.  At the end of each year, the corporation pays out a fraction of its EPS as dividends. This dividend payout ratio is constant.

3.  The stock's selling price is forecast by multiplying EPS at the time of sale by a price earnings multiple.

The intrinsic value equation that contains these assumptions can be stated as follows. Let

$E_0$ = EPS at Year zero

$g$ = growth rate of EPS

$R$ = dividend payout ratio

$M$ = price earnings multiple

$n$ = number of years that the stock is owned

$k$ = investor's required rate of return

Then

$$V = \left[ \sum_{t=1}^{n} \frac{R \cdot E_0(1 + g)^t}{(1 + k)^t} \right] + \frac{M \cdot E_0(1 + g)^n}{(1 + k)^n} \qquad (13\text{-}10)$$

The first term of Equation 13-10, the summation term, is the sum of the present values of the future dividends. EPS in each year is estimated as $E_0(1 + g)^t$. Multiplying each of these earnings by the payout ratio converts EPS to dividends per share. The second term in this equation is the present value of the forecast selling price at the end of Year $n$. EPS in Year $n$ is estimated as $E_0(1 + g)^n$. This value is multiplied by the price earnings multiple to produce the future selling price. In using Equation 13-10 to calculate the present value of the future dividends, this model does not require that $k$ be greater than $g$ as long as the stock is to be sold after a certain number of years.

**Example:**

A corporation's current EPS is $3. Its earnings growth rate is estimated to be 6 percent per year. The dividend payout ratio is 40 percent, and the stock sells for 12 times EPS. An investor requires a 15 percent rate of return and expects to sell the stock in three years. Compute the stock's intrinsic value.

Using Equation 13-10, the stock's intrinsic value is

$$V = \frac{(.4)\,(\$3)\,(1 + .06)}{(1 + .15)} + \frac{(.4)\,(\$3)\,(1 + .06)^2}{(1 + .15)^2}$$

$$+ \frac{(.4)\,(\$3)\,(1 + .06)^3}{(1 + .15)^3} + \frac{(12)\,(\$3)\,(1 + .06)^3}{(1 + .15)^3}$$

$$= \$1.10 + \$1.02 + \$0.94 + \$28.19$$

$$= \$31.25$$

The intrinsic value of $31.25 is the maximum purchase price that can be paid at Time zero if the investor is to earn a 15 percent rate of return. Thus, this investment can be evaluated by computing its NPV (intrinsic value less the purchase price at Time zero) and making an accept/reject decision.

This type of model has several advantages.

1. A finite horizon is stipulated and an eventual selling price is incorporated in the stock's intrinsic value.

2.  Growth in both earnings and dividends is allowed.

3.  The model recognizes that dividends and price are based on earnings.

Many security analysts feel that price earnings multiples for common stocks are fairly stable over time and that a stock's price can be forecast for up to five years in the future by estimating the future EPS and then multiplying forecast earnings by an historical price earnings multiple.

There are two major limitations to this model. First, the model assumes that the stock will be sold at a particular time in the future. Most investors do not make that sort of decision when evaluating common stock purchases. Second, using a price earnings multiple to forecast the stock's eventual selling price means that the stock's intrinsic value is composed primarily of the present value of the eventual price. Thus, the stock's intrinsic value is very sensitive to resale price forecasting errors. The discounting mechanism will not be able to reduce substantially the resale price forecasting errors and the resulting impact on the stock's intrinsic value if the stock is to be held for five years or less.

**INVESTMENT RISKS.** Because of their characteristics as residual ownership securities, common stocks contain the largest amounts of business and financial risk. However, their prices are generally less sensitive to changes in interest rate levels than bond prices.

Common stocks are often described as providing a hedge against inflation. This means that rates of return on common stocks presumably exceed inflation rates. A number of studies indeed have indicated that common stocks as a group have historically provided an inflation hedge. However, any particular stock's IRR may or may not exceed inflation rates.

---

# SUMMARY

This chapter has presented a series of intrinsic value models that can be used to measure the desirability of financial assets as investment alternatives. Several value concepts were identified; intrinsic value was chosen because of its ability to incorporate cash flows, the time value of money, and investor's required rate of return.

Separate intrinsic value models were constructed for valuing bonds, preferred stock, and common stock. Each model is based in part on the characteristics of the financial asset being evaluated.

Fixed payment securities are the least difficult to evaluate because cash flows are in annuity form and are relatively easy to forecast. The uncertainty surrounding both future dividend payments and the resale price of common stock make this type of financial asset the most difficult to evaluate. Accordingly, three common stock intrinsic value models were presented. One is essentially a naive model; the second is built around a constant dividend growth rate; and the third incorporates a finite investment horizon, dividend growth, and an explicit resale price.

# QUESTIONS

**13-1.** Explain why the market value of a financial asset may be easier to measure than the market value of a real asset.

**13-2.** Why is intrinsic value used to evaluate the desirability of financial assets?

**13-3.** What characteristics of bonds simplify the calculation of their intrinsic values?

**13-4.** Explain the relationships between a bond's par value, price, coupon rate, current yield, and yield to maturity.

**13-5.** A corporation has two bond issues outstanding. One issue matures in 5 years while the other matures in 15 years. Both issues currently have the same YTM. If an investor is convinced that interest rate levels will decline sharply within the next year, which bond issue would be the better investment? Why?

**13-6.** Explain why preferred stock is considered to be a hybrid security.

**13-7.** How is the intrinsic value of preferred stock calculated?

**13-8.** What factors make the calculation of common stock intrinsic value difficult?

**13-9.** What are the advantages and limitations of the common stock intrinsic value model that assumes a dividend growth rate that is constant and less than the discount rate?

**13-10.** What are the advantages and limitations of common stock intrinsic value models that contain an explicit resale price?

# PROBLEMS

**13-1.** A $10,000 bond carries a 7% coupon rate, matures in 12 years, and is currently quoted at 91.

   *a.* Compute the bond's current yield.
   *b.* Compute the bond's YTM.
   *c.* Compute the bond's intrinsic value and NPV if an investor's required rate of return is 9%.

**13-2.** A $1,000 bond matures in 19 years, carries an 11% coupon rate, and is currently quoted at 96. Compute its YTM.

**13-3.** A $5,000 bond has a 3% coupon, matures in 10 years, and is currently quoted at 65. Compute the bond's current yield and its YTM.

**13-4.** Hebert Incorporated sold a $100,000,000 bond issue in 1978 in order to obtain funds for expansion. The bonds were issued at face values of $1,000 with an original maturity of 20 years and a coupon rate of 9%. If an investor requires a 12% rate of return on these securities, what would be the value of one of these bonds to him in 1983? Assume the bond is to be purchased at the end of 1983 and that the first interest payment would be received at the end of 1984.

**13-5.** A dividend of $3.50 per share on its preferred stock is paid by 380 Incorporated. Assuming an investor requires a 10% rate of return, what is the value of 380 Incorporated's preferred stock to her?

**13-6.** Compute the intrinsic value of each of the following preferred stocks:

 a. A stock pays a $4.75 annual dividend and the investor's required rate of return is 11%.
 b. A stock pays an annual dividend of $6 and the investor's required rate of return is 8%.
 c. A stock pays a 9% dividend on its $50 par value and the investor's required rate of return is 10%.

**13-7.** Compute the internal rate of return for each of the following preferred stocks:

 a. Annual dividend is $9 and the current market price is $100.
 b. Annual dividend is $7.85 and the current market price is $48.75.
 c. Annual dividend is 8.75%, par value is $100, and the current price is $79.87.

**13-8.** In 1975, XYZ's common stock paid dividends of $2.00 per share; in 1983 they paid $3.70 per share. What was the dividends' compound annual growth rate over these eight years?

**13-9.** A corporation's common stock pays a current dividend of $6; the dividend is expected to grow at a rate of 2% per year indefinitely.

 a. Compute the dividends for each of the next three years.
 b. Compute the intrinsic value for this stock if the investor's required rate of return is 10%.
 c. Assume that the stock's current market price is $75. Compute the IRR if the stock is bought at this price.
 d. Assume that the stock is bought at Year zero for $75. What selling price must be realized at the end of Year 5 if the investor's IRR is to be unchanged?

**13-10.** A common stock pays a current dividend of $4 per share; the dividend growth rate is estimated at 4%.

 a. Compute the dividend payable eight years from now, nine years from now, and ten years from now.
 b. Assuming a 14% required rate of return, compute the stock's intrinsic value.
 c. Compute the IRR if the stock is bought for $35 per share.
 d. Assume that the stock is bought now for $35 per share. Compute the selling price that must be realized eight years from now if the investor's IRR is to be unchanged.

**13-11.** A corporation's current EPS is $6, and it has an expected EPS growth rate of 4% per year. The dividend payout ratio is 60% and the stock sells for ten times EPS. An investor requires a 14% rate of return and expects to sell the stock in five years. Given this information, compute the stock's intrinsic value to this investor.

**13-12.** A corporate common stock's current EPS is $5.50. The EPS growth rate is estimated to be 7%. The dividend payout ratio is a constant 30%. The stock's price earnings multiple is expected to remain at 15. An investor intends to buy the stock, hold it for four years, and sell out. If the investor's required rate of return is 13%, calculate the maximum price the investor should be willing to pay.

# SELECTED REFERENCES

Archer, S., G. Choate, and G. Racette. *Financial Management*. 2d ed. New York: John Wiley & Sons, 1983.

D'Ambrosio, C. *Principles of Modern Investments*. Chicago, Ill.: Science Research Associates, 1976.

Francis, J. *Investments: Analysis and Management*. 3d ed. New York: McGraw-Hill Book Company, 1980.

Gordon, M. *The Investment, Financing, and Valuation of the Corporation*. Homewood, Ill.: Richard D. Irwin, Inc., 1962.

Hayes, D., and W. Bawman. *Investments: Analysis and Management*. 3d ed. New York: Macmillan, Inc., 1976.

Hubbard, C., and C. Hawkins. *Theory of Valuation*. Scranton, Pa.: International Textbook Company, 1969.

# CHAPTER 14

## Cost of Capital

This chapter develops the concepts, measurement techniques, and implications of corporate cost of capital. The concepts contained in this chapter are a central topic in managerial finance because they provide a way of unifying the investment and financing decisions of a corporation.

The first section of this chapter defines cost of capital and spells out the implications of this concept for shareholder wealth maximization. The second and third sections explain ways of measuring cost of capital. The fourth section contains a simplified example that seeks to demonstrate the interrelationships among cost of capital, capital structure, and firm value. The final section introduces the concept of marginal cost of capital and explains how the investment and financing decisions of the firm are interrelated.

This chapter draws heavily from the materials contained in previous chapters. For example, the assumed goal of shareholder wealth maximization and the concepts of business and financial risk are taken from Chapter 1. The NPV capital-budgeting criterion introduced in Chapters 10 and 11 is used again. In addition, the techniques used to measure cost of capital are based on the valuation concepts and equations in Chapter 13. Bringing all these materials together means that *this chapter requires careful reading and may appear to be more difficult than previous chapters. However, the essential points may be more readily understood if these earlier materials are reviewed as needed and if the glossary is used to reinforce your understanding of the technical terms.*

## THE COST-OF-CAPITAL CONCEPT

The cost-of-capital concept is based on the assumption that the goal of profit-seeking corporations is to maximize shareholder wealth. This assumption makes it possible to formulate several equivalent definitions of cost of capital that identify some of the implications contained in the cost-of-capital concept.

**Cost of Capital Defined**

Every profit-seeking corporation has its own risk-return characteristics. Each group of investors in the corporation—bondholders, preferred stockholders, and common stockholders—requires a minimum rate of return commensurate with the risks it accepts by investing in the firm. From the standpoint of the corporation, these groups provide the capital needed to finance the firm's investments. *The minimum rate of return that the corporation must earn in order to satisfy the overall rate of return required by its investors is called the corporation's* **cost of capital.**

**Implications of the Cost-of-Capital Definition**

What is perhaps the most important implication of the cost-of-capital definition can be stated as follows: If a corporation's actual rate of return exceeds its cost of capital, and if this rate of return is earned without increasing the firm's risk characteristics, then shareholder wealth is increased, furthering the corporate goal of shareholder wealth maximization.

The reasoning behind this implication is that when the corporation's rate of return exceeds its cost of capital, the bondholders and preferred stockholders will receive their fixed rate of return. The remaining portion of the corporation's rate of return that is available to common stockholders will exceed their required rate of return. The excess earnings, then, may be treated in several ways:

1. The corporation may distribute these earnings to common stockholders through increased dividends.

2. The corporation may retain and reinvest these earnings to further increase its subsequent rate of return.

3. The corporation may divide these earnings between increased dividends and retained earnings.

As a consequence, the common shares will become more desirable to investors and the resulting demand for share ownership will increase their resale prices. In this way shareholder wealth will be increased, thus meeting the goal of the corporation.

Alternative definitions of cost of capital are possible when cost of capital is linked with the goal of shareholder wealth maximization. For example, the cost of capital can be defined as the minimum rate of return the firm must earn on its invested capital if the market value of the firm is to remain unchanged. This definition considers cost of capital as a "break-even" rate. If the cost of capital is not earned, the firm's market value will decrease. Conversely, if the firm's rate of return exceeds its cost of capital, the firm's market value will increase. Market value in this context equals the sum of the market values of the firm's security issues. This cost-of-capital definition is sometimes stated as the rate of return that is just sufficient to leave the price of the firm's common stock unchanged.

A second implication of the cost-of-capital definition links cost of capital with the firm's capital-budgeting process. The cost of capital serves as the discount rate used in evaluating capital-budgeting alternatives. Accepting projects with rates of return that exceed the firm's cost of capital will increase the value of the firm. Similarly, the firm's value is decreased when the rate of return on its investment projects falls below its cost of capital. Thus, using cost of capital to evaluate capital-budgeting alternatives is consistent with the goal of shareholder wealth maximization.

## MEASURING SPECIFIC COSTS OF CAPITAL

Each type of capital contained in a corporation's capital structure—bonds, preferred stock, common stock, and retained earnings—has its own minimum required rate of return and, consequently, its own cost of capital. The cost of capital for any particular capital source or security issue is called the **specific cost of capital.**

Measuring specific costs of capital is a difficult process, and the resulting costs must be looked upon as approximations. The difficulty arises primarily because the market value of the firm changes constantly, and a good deal of this fluctuation is caused by external factors, such as business cycles and inflation, over which the firm has no control. As a consequence, some relatively simple approximations are used.

The equations used to measure specific costs of capital are based on the valuation models presented in Chapter 13. These models assume that investors buy and sell financial assets on the basis of their intrinsic values. Consequently, using these models to measure specific costs of capital is consistent with the basic cost-of-capital concept.

**Cost of Debt**

Since most long-term corporate debt is in the form of bonds, computations for the specific cost of debt capital are based on the characteristics of bonds that were discussed in the previous chapter. Estimating this specific cost of capital requires computing the effective cost of the debt to the corporation and stating this effective cost as an annual compound rate. This is accomplished in part by using the yield to maturity (YTM) procedure explained in Chapter 13. The YTM required by purchasers of the bonds determines the effective before-tax cost to the firm. The firm's cost may be slightly higher than the investors' YTM because the firm may incur some costs in selling the bond issue.

Computing the specific cost of capital of bonds requires three steps:

1. Determine the net proceeds per bond to the corporation. The net proceeds per bond may be less than the bond's par value after the corporation's costs of selling the bonds are deducted. For example, the bonds in a particular bond issue may have a $1,000 par value. If they are sold at par and the corporation incurs a $20 selling cost per bond, the net proceeds per bond are $980.

2. Determine the effective before-tax cost of the bond. Use the net proceeds to the corporation as the Time zero cash inflow. Use the annuity-of-interest payments and the payment of the bond's par value at maturity as the cash outflows.

3. Because the interest payments are deductible for federal corporate income tax purposes, convert the computed cost to an after-tax cost. The resulting value is the specific cost of capital of the bonds.

Let:

$$k_m = \text{effective before-tax cost as an annual rate}$$

$$t = \text{corporate tax rate}$$

$$k_d = \text{after-tax specific cost of capital of the bond}$$

Then:

$$k_d = k_m(1 - t) \qquad\qquad (14\text{-}1)$$

---

**Example:**

A corporation sells a $20 million bond issue that is to mature in 25 years. Each bond has a $1,000 par value and carries a 12 percent coupon rate. The corporation nets $985 per bond. Assume a 40 percent tax rate. Compute the specific cost of capital of the bonds.

The effective before-tax cost is computed using the $985 proceeds per bond as the Time zero cash inflow. The computed cost is greater than 12 percent because the Time zero inflow is less than the bond's par value. Using the techniques explained in Chapter 13:

$$(\text{NPV} \mid 12\%) = -\$15$$

$$(\text{NPV} \mid 13\%) = -\$120(7.330) - \$1,000(.047) + \$985$$

$$= \$58.40$$

Adding the absolute value of the NPVs:

$$\$15 + \$58.40 = \$73.40$$

Then:

$$\$15/\$73.40 = .20$$

$$k_m = 12\% + .20 = .12.2\%$$

$$k_d = (12.2\%)(1 - .4) = 7.32\%$$

The specific cost of capital for the bond issue is 7.32 percent.

---

**Cost of Preferred Stock**

When a corporation sells preferred stock, it expects to pay dividends to investors in return for their money capital. The dividend payments are the cost to the firm of the preferred stock. In order to express this dividend cost as a yearly rate, the firm uses the net proceeds it receives after deducting whatever costs are incurred in selling the issue. If, for example, the firm sells the preferred stock for $40 per share and incurs a $2 per share selling cost, the firm uses the $38 net proceeds per share in computing the specific cost of the preferred stock.

The specific cost of capital of preferred stock is computed by dividing the value of one yearly dividend payment by the net proceeds per share to the corporation. Let:

$$D = \text{annual dividend per share}$$

$$P_n = \text{proceeds per share}$$

$$k_p = \text{specific cost of capital of preferred stock}$$

$$k_p = D/P_n \tag{14-2}$$

This measurement equation is based on Equation 13-2 which is used to compute the rate of return on a perpetuity of preferred stock dividends.

---

**Example:**

An issue of preferred stock is sold to investors for $78 per share. The corporation incurs a selling cost of $3 per share and pays an annual dividend of $8 per share. Compute the specific cost of capital of the preferred stock.

The net proceeds are $78 − $3 = $75 per share. Using Equation 14-2:

$$k_p = \$8/\$75 = .1067 \quad \text{or} \quad 10.67\%$$

The specific cost of capital of the preferred stock is 10.67 percent.

---

**Cost of Common Stock**

The specific cost of capital of common stock is the minimum rate of return that the corporation must earn for its common shareholders in order to maintain the market value of the firm's equity. When a firm sells a common stock issue and nets $P_n$ dollars per share, it can set the net proceeds equal to the stock's intrinsic value because investors have been willing to acquire the security at a price that nets the firm $P_n$ dollars. Equation 13-6 provides an estimate of the stock's intrinsic value:

$$V = \frac{D_0(1 + g)}{k - g} \tag{13-6}$$

Where:

$$D_0 = \text{current dividend per share}$$

$$g = \text{compound dividend growth rate}$$

$$k = \text{the rate of return required by investors}$$

As was explained in Chapter 13, this equation computes the intrinsic value of a share of common stock that returns an indefinite dividend stream. In addition, dividends are assumed to grow at a compound rate each year. The issuing corporation can use Equation 13-6 to estimate the specific cost of capital of common stock by setting

$$P_n = V$$

Then the market discount rate $(k)$ is a measure of the stock's specific cost and is given the symbol $k_e$:

$$k_e = \text{specific cost of capital of common stock}$$

Equation 13-6 can then be written:

$$P_n = \frac{D_0(1 + g)}{k_e - g}$$

Solving for $k_e$ yields the following measurement equation for the specific cost of capital of common stock:

$$k_e = \frac{D_0(1 + g)}{P_n} + g \qquad \text{(14-3)}$$

This is the equation most frequently used to measure the specific cost of capital of common stock. However, it is based on the assumption of a dividend stream that increases indefinitely at a compound rate. Therefore, the use of this equation is limited to those corporations whose expected future dividend stream at least approximates this assumption.

---

**Example:**

An issue of common stock is sold to investors for $20 per share. The issuing corporation incurs a selling expense of $1 per share. The current dividend is $1.50 per share and is expected to grow at a 6 percent annual rate. Compute the specific cost of capital of this common stock.

The net proceeds per share are $20 − $1 = $19.

$$D_0(1 + g) = (\$1.50)(1 + .06)$$
$$= \$1.59$$

$$k_e = \$1.59/\$19 + .06$$
$$= 14.37\%$$

The specific cost of capital of the common stock is 14.37 percent.

---

**Cost of Retained Earnings**

There are two difficulties with computing the specific cost of capital of retained earnings. Both difficulties arise because retained earnings are an internal, as opposed to an external, source of funds. First, retained earnings are not securities, such as stocks and bonds, and thus do not have market prices that can be used to compute costs of capital. Second, because retained earnings do not represent funds provided directly by investors, there may be a tendency to equate the specific cost of capital with zero.

The approach typically used to measure the specific cost of capital of retained earnings is to realize that retained earnings represent profits available to common shareholders that the corporation chooses to reinvest in itself rather than pay out as dividends. Thus, the shareholders are made to reinvest part of their earnings in the corporation. In return, they expect the corporation to earn a rate of return on these funds at least equal to the rate earned on the outstanding common stock. So, the specific cost of capital of retained earnings is equated with the specific cost of capital of common stock. However, since no selling costs are incurred, the current market price of the common stock is used in the computations. Let:

$P_0$ = current market price of the firm's common stock

$k_r$ = specific cost of capital of retained earnings

$$k_r = \frac{D_0(1 + g)}{P_0} + g \qquad (14\text{-}4)$$

**Example:**   In the previous example, the corporation's specific cost of capital of common stock was computed as 14.37 percent. The specific cost of capital of retained earnings for that data set, using Equation 14-4, is:

$$k_r = \frac{(\$1.50)\,(1 + .06)}{\$20.00} + .06$$

$$= 13.95\%$$

The specific cost of capital is 13.95 percent.

## MEASURING THE WEIGHTED AVERAGE COST OF CAPITAL

Once the specific cost of capital of each corporate long-term financing source has been measured, it is possible to measure the corporation's overall cost of capital. This has been defined as the rate of return that must be earned by the corporation in order to satisfy the requirements of the individual specific costs of capital. The overall cost of capital computed from the corporation's existing capital structure allows the firm to obtain a measure of the minimum rate of return that must be earned on its investments. As such, this overall cost of capital can be of help in identifying the discount rate to be used in evaluating capital-budgeting alternatives.

A first approximation of this overall cost of capital is obtained as follows:

1. Multiply the specific cost of capital of each source by its percentage composition in the capital structure.

2.   Add the products. The resulting sum is called the corporation's **weighted average cost of capital.**

The weights used in these computations can be either book value weights or market value weights. Each weighting system has advantages and limitations.

**Book Value Weights**

The first approach to measuring the firm's weighted average cost of capital is to use the balance sheet book values of the individual sources of long-term and permanent capital. These book values reflect the amount of capital the firm has raised by selling securities as well as the amount of capital that has been generated by reinvesting earnings that were not paid out as common stock dividends. Since each source of capital has its own specific cost, the three following steps are needed to compute the overall, or weighted average, cost of capital on the basis of book value weights:

1.   Find the percentage of long-term capital provided by each financing source. The dollar values for each capital source are taken from the corporation's balance sheet.

2.   Multiply each capital percentage by its specific cost of capital.

3.   Add the products.

**Example:**

Table 14-1 contains the capital structure and specific cost of capital of a hypothetical corporation. The specific costs of capital are assumed to have been computed by using the methods given in the previous section. The book value weights are

**Table 14-1.**   **Specific Costs of Capital for a Given Capital Structure**

| Source of Capital | Book Value | Specific Cost of Capital |
|---|---|---|
| 9% bonds, $1,000 par value | $15,000,000 | 5.4% |
| 50,000 shares $8 preferred stock | 5,000,000 | 8.0% |
| Common stock, 400,000 shares outstanding | 20,000,000 | 11.0% |
| Retained earnings | 10,000,000 | 10.5% |
| Total | $50,000,000 | |

obtained by dividing the dollar amounts of each financing source by total long-term capital. These weights are contained in Table 14-2. The book value weights are then multiplied by the specific costs of capital listed in Table 14-1. The products are

**Table 14-2.**   Weighted Average Cost of Capital Using Book Value Weights

| Source of Capital | Book Value Weights | Specific Cost | Weighted Cost |
|---|---|---|---|
| 9% bonds, $1,000 par value | .3 | .054 | .0162 |
| 50,000 shares $8 preferred stock | .1 | .080 | .0080 |
| Common stock, 400,000 shares outstanding | .4 | .110 | .0440 |
| Retained earnings | .2 | .105 | .0210 |
| | | Total | .0892 |

shown in Table 14-2 as weighted costs. The sum of these weighted costs equals 8.92 percent and is the corporation's weighted average cost of capital.

The advantages of using book value weights in computing a corporation's weighted average cost of capital are as follows:

1.  The weighted average cost of capital is easy to compute.

2.  The computed cost of capital is generally stable over time because book value weights are not dependent on market prices.

3.  When market prices of the corporation's securities are being influenced substantially because of external factors such as inflation and business cycles, book value weights may provide the only usable estimates of a firm's weighted average cost of capital.

There are two principal limitations in using book value weights:

1.  They provide an historical weighted average cost of capital that may not yield a cost-of-capital value that is useful for evaluating current strategies.

2.  Their use is not consistent with the concept contained in the definition of a corporation's overall cost of capital. That definition speaks of a minimum rate of return needed to maintain the firm's market value, but book value weights ignore market values. As a result, a corporation's weighted average cost of capital using book value weights can be used only to provide a quick first estimate of the rate of return that investors require from the corporation.

**Market Value Weights**

A second approach to measuring weighted average cost of capital is to use the market values of the firm's securities as the weights in the computational procedure. The resulting cost of capital reflects the rates of return currently required by investors rather than the historical rates embodied in the firm's balance sheet.

Computing a corporation's weighted average cost of capital using market value weights requires four steps:

1. Find the market value of each financing source, using current market prices.

2. Divide each of the market values by the total market value to obtain the market value weights.

3. Multiply the specific costs of capital by their corresponding market value weights.

4. Add the products.

---

**Example:**

Using the data contained in Table 14-1, the necessary market values for each financing source are assumed to be as follows: bond prices are 94 percent of par, preferred stock is $100 per share, and the common stock sells for $65 per share.

Assuming the corporation received $15,000,000 from the sale of the bonds, the market values of each financing source are:

$$(.94)\,(\$15,000,000) = \$14,100,000 \text{ for the bonds}$$

$$(\$100)\,(50,000 \text{ shares}) = \phantom{0}5,000,000 \text{ for the preferred stock}$$

$$(\$65)\,(400,000 \text{ shares}) = \underline{\phantom{0}26,000,000} \text{ for the common stock}$$

$$\$45,100,000 \text{ for total capital structure}$$

Retained earnings do not have a separate measurable market value. In order to compute the weighted average cost of capital, the common stock's market value of $26,000,000 is divided between common stock and retained earnings in proportion to the sum of their book values. Thus, ⅔ of the common stock's market value, or $17,333,333, is allocated to common stock; ⅓, or $8,666,667, is allocated to retained earnings. The resulting market values and the market value weights computed from the market values are contained in Table 14-3.

---

**Table 14-3.**     **Market Values and Market Value Weights for the Table 14-1 Capital Structure**

| Source of Capital | Market Value | Market Value Weights |
|---|---|---|
| 9% bonds, $1,000 par value | $14,100,000 | .313 |
| 50,000 shares $8 preferred stock | 5,000,000 | .111 |
| Common stock, 400,000 shares outstanding | 17,333,333 | .384 |
| Retained earnings | 8,666,667 | .192 |
| Total | $45,100,000 | |

The weighted average cost of capital computations are contained in Table 14-4. The specific costs of capital are taken from Table 14-1. The market value weights are multiplied by their corresponding specific costs of capital, and the resulting weighted costs are added. The sum is .0882, or 8.82 percent, which represents the corporation's weighted average cost of capital.

**Table 14-4.**   Weighted Average Cost of Capital Using Market Value Weights

| Source of Capital | Market Value Weights | Specific Cost | Weighted Cost |
|---|---|---|---|
| 9% bonds, $1,000 par value | .313 | .054 | .0169 |
| 50,000 shares $8 | | | |
|   preferred stock | .111 | .080 | .0089 |
| Common stock, 400,000 | | | |
|   shares outstanding | .384 | .110 | .0422 |
| Retained earnings | .192 | .105 | .0202 |
| | | Total | .0882 |

The advantages of using market value weights in computing a corporation's weighted average cost of capital are:

1. Their use is consistent with the concept of maintaining market values in the cost-of-capital definition.

2. They provide current estimates of investor required rates of return, which are more relevant than historical book value weights in evaluating current capital-budgeting alternatives.

3. To the extent that the corporation has attained its target or desired capital structure, market value weights will yield good estimates of the cost of capital that would be incurred should it require additional external financing.

The limitations of using market value weights in computing cost of capital are:

1. They are more difficult to use in computing cost of capital than book value weights. Not only do market prices have to be obtained, but also market values of common stock have to be allocated between common stock and retained earnings when their specific costs of capital differ.

2. Since market prices of a corporation's securities change daily, the market value of the firm and its corresponding cost of capital using market value weights also change daily.

3.  Market value weights can seriously distort a corporation's weighted average cost of capital when the prices of its securities are significantly influenced by external forces such as inflation and business cycles. For example, inflation can depress bond prices severely for a period of time. This increases the specific cost of capital of bonds beyond what would otherwise be justified by the corporation's risk-return characteristics. If market value weights are to be relied upon, the weighted average cost of capital may have to be adjusted subjectively for what are judged to be temporary distortions.

## INTERRELATIONSHIPS AMONG COST OF CAPITAL, CAPITAL STRUCTURE, AND FIRM VALUE: AN EXAMPLE

One way of summarizing the chapter up to this point is to say that corporations measure the costs of capital of their financing sources by using the same concepts investors employ in valuing securities. At the risk of oversimplifying, investor security valuation and corporate cost of capital are two sides of the same coin. This being the case, and given a set of specific costs of capital, financial managers can alter the firm's weighted average cost of capital simply by changing the firm's financing mix.

Using the Table 14-1 capital structure as an example, suppose the bonds mature and are paid off by selling $15 million of common stock. If the corporation incurs an 11 percent specific cost of capital for these new shares, the firm's weighted average cost of capital (using book value weights) increases from 8.92 percent to 10.6 percent. Is such a financing decision consistent with the goal of shareholder wealth maximization?

The Table 14-1 capital structure can be used to ask a more fundamental question. Suppose the bonds have not yet matured. The firm needs $12 million in *additional* financing but only $4 million is forthcoming from retained earnings. From the standpoint of shareholder wealth maximization, what financing sources should the corporation use to raise the remaining $8 million?

The need to replace maturing debt as well as the need to finance the growth of the corporation means that financial managers must evaluate the impacts of capital structure changes and the accompanying costs of capital on the value of the firm to its investors. These three concepts are interrelated, and this section demonstrates some of these relationships by using an example constructed as follows:

1.  A set of assumptions is introduced that holds constant all influences on corporate cost of capital and firm value other than capital structure.

2.  The income statement for the example corporation is developed.

3. A valuation equation is developed that is consistent with the assumptions given in this example. This valuation equation measures the value of the firm's debt and equity securities and thus measures overall firm value.

4. The impacts of capital structure changes on the example corporation's value and the weighted average cost of capital are analyzed by using both book value and market value weights.

This example provides an introduction to the concept of an optimal structure—the mix of long-term financing sources that makes the greatest contribution to shareholder wealth by making the value of the firm as large as possible. Chapter 17 contains a more extensive treatment of this topic.

**Assumptions of the Example**

Firm value and cost of capital are both influenced by a large number of factors. External factors include inflation, changes in corporate tax laws, federal and state regulations, business cycles, and actions taken by competitors. Internal factors include product demand, cost of production, marketing strategies, and managerial abilities. The assumptions given below hold constant the impacts of these factors on the corporation.

CONSTANT BUSINESS RISK. The degree of business risk contained in the corporation is held constant over time. This is accomplished by assuming that earnings before interest and taxes (EBIT) are constant. Under conditions of uncertainty, constant business risk means that the probability distribution of the firm's EBIT, and thus the expected value of EBIT, is constant over time. This assumption holds constant such internal corporate factors as marketing strategies and cost of production.

EXTERNAL INFLUENCES HELD CONSTANT. All external influences that affect the firm's market value and its cost of capital are held constant. Investors are assumed to react only to changes in the corporation's capital structure.

CONSTANT TOTAL FINANCING. The total amount of long-term capital in the corporation's capital structure is held constant. This assumption has two implications. First, in order to prevent increases in total capital through retained earnings, the corporation distributes all profits after taxes in the form of dividends. Second, changes in the corporation's capital structure are accomplished by selling securities, such as bonds, and using the proceeds to purchase common stock from the resale market.

INVESTOR BEHAVIOR. The rates of return that investors require from the corporation, expressed as specific costs of capital, are based on their perceptions of the corporation's risk-return characteristics. Since business risk is held constant, changes in specific costs of capital are based on how investors perceive changes in the corporation's financial risk. Specific costs of capital are assumed to increase once a corporation's degree of financial risk, as measured by the percentage that debt is of total financing, increases beyond some critical value.

**Earnings and Valuation Models of the Example**

The assumptions of constant business risk and constant total financing make it easy to specify the accounting relationships between EBIT and earnings after taxes. This accounting statement is used to calculate shareholder dividends and is also contained in the equation that measures total firm value.

**EBIT AND EARNINGS AFTER TAXES.** Earnings after taxes are computed by subtracting bond interest and federal corporate income taxes from EBIT. The symbols used to express these income statement relationships were introduced in Chapter 5. Let:

$$Y = \text{EBIT}$$

$$I = \text{bond interest in dollars}$$

$$t = \text{federal corporate tax rate (assumed to be 40\%)}$$

$$\text{EAT} = \text{earnings after taxes}$$

Then:   $\text{EAT} = (Y - I)(1 - t)$ (14-5)

Since constant total financing requires a 100 percent dividend payout ratio, dividends paid to shareholders equal earnings after taxes.

**FIRM VALUE.** The valuation principles in Chapter 13 indicate that the value of the firm equals the sum of the capitalized values of each of the firm's financing sources. The assumptions for this example restrict corporate financing to external debt and external equity sources. Let:

$$V_d = \text{value of the firm's bonds}$$

$$V_e = \text{value of the firm's equity}$$

$$V_f = \text{total value of the firm}$$

Then:   $V_f = V_d + V_e$ (14-6)

*Value of Bonds.* The value of a bond issue is the capitalized value that results when the bond cash flows are discounted at the investor's specific before-tax cost of capital. If a corporation sells a bond issue at par, then the intrinsic value of the issue equals its book value.

A somewhat more complicated valuation problem arises when bond issues are sold at different points in time. In general, the intrinsic value or market value of a corporation's bonds equals the sum of the present values of all the future bond payments discounted at the *current* before-tax specific cost of debt.

*Value of Equity.* The value of the firm's equity is the capitalized value of the future payments to shareholders discounted at the investors' specific cost of capital. The assumptions state that the payments to shareholders equal the firm's earnings after taxes. Given a constant expected value for the firm's EBIT, the resulting earnings after taxes also have a constant expected value. Thus, the dividend stream is in perpetuity form and is capitalized by dividing one yearly value by the relevant discount rate. The capitalized value of the firm's equity is:

$$V_e = EAT/k_e$$

Where $k_e$ is the specific cost of equity capital defined in Equation 14-3 when the growth rate (g) is set to zero. Using the accounting definition of earnings after taxes given in Equation 14-5:

$$V_e = (Y - I)(1 - t)/k_e \qquad \text{(14-7)}$$

Substituting Equation 14-7 into Equation 14-6, the value of the firm is stated as:

$$V_f = V_d + (Y - I)(1 - t)/k_e \qquad \text{(14-8)}$$

In using Equation 14-8 the restrictive assumption has been made that the value of the company's debt equals its book value.

**Changes in Capital Structure**

The assumptions and valuation models can now be combined with an example in order to analyze the changes in firm value that result from changes in capital structure. The data set values for the example are:

$$EBIT = \$50,000$$

$$t = .4$$

$$k_m = .10 \text{ (interest rate on debt)}$$

$$k_d = k_m(1 - t) = .06$$

Total financing is a constant $100,000, and $k_e$ is a function of the amount of debt in the firm's capital structure. The values of $k_e$ corresponding to corporate debt levels are:

| Debt | $k_e$ |
|---|---|
| $    0 | .10 |
| 10,000 | .10 |
| 15,000 | .10 |
| 20,000 | .10 |
| 25,000 | .12 |
| 30,000 | .15 |

The reason why the specific cost of equity capital is not constant over all capital structures is as follows. The stream of dividend payments received by shareholders consists of earnings after taxes. When the firm adds bonds to the capital structure (and retires an equal dollar amount of debt) the interest payments to bondholders come from the firm's expected EBIT. When the firm introduces small amounts of debt into its capital structure, the expected value of the dividend payments to the shareholders is reduced, but the decrease is not perceived by shareholders as causing their investment to become riskier. As the firm continues to add debt, more of its EBIT is paid as interest to bondholders, and shareholders eventually conclude that their dividend payments will be jeopardized if actual EBIT falls below expected EBIT. Shareholders thus increase the rate of return they require for investing in what they now perceive to be a riskier security. This increased required rate of return becomes a higher specific cost of equity capital to the corporation.

The weighted average cost of capital for the firm, using either book value weights or market value weights, is calculated below. Let:

$$D = \text{dollar value of debt}$$

$$E = \text{dollar value of equity}$$

$$k_w = \text{firm's weighted average cost of capital}$$

Then:
$$k_w = k_d\left(\frac{D}{D + E}\right) + k_e\left(\frac{E}{D + E}\right) \tag{14-9}$$

$V_f$ AND $k_w$ USING BOOK VALUE WEIGHTS. The firm's initial capital structure is assumed to consist of 100 percent equity. The value of the firm, using Equation 14-8 is:

$$V_f = 0 + (\$50,000 - 0)(1 - .4)/.1$$
$$= \$300,000$$

The firm's $k_w$, using book value weights, is computed by using Equation 14-9:

$$k_w = .06\left(\frac{0}{0 + \$100,000}\right) + .1\left(\frac{\$100,000}{0 + \$100,000}\right) = .1$$

The corporation now changes its capital structure as follows: $10,000 of debt is sold, and the proceeds are used to retire $10,000 of common stock. Interest payments on the debt are:

$$I = (.1)(\$10,000) = \$1,000$$

The capitalized value of the firm increases to:

$$V_f = \$10,000 + (\$50,000 - \$1,000)(1 - .4)/.1$$
$$= \$10,000 + \$294,000 = \$304,000$$

Then $k_w$ decreases to:

$$k_w = .06\left(\frac{\$10,000}{\$10,000 + \$90,000}\right) + .1\left(\frac{\$90,000}{\$10,000 + \$90,000}\right)$$
$$= .006 + .09 = .096$$

The decrease in the firm's weighted average cost of capital from 10 percent to 9.6 percent occurs because the specific cost of the debt that is being added is less than the specific cost of the equity that is being retired *and* the specific cost of equity remains constant. The increase in the value of the firm occurs because the $10,000 of new debt is greater than the $6,000 decrease in the market value of the stock. The decrease in the stock's market value is due to the decrease in the number of shares outstanding.

The corporation floats an additional $5,000 of debt and retires an equal amount of equity. The new values for $V_f$ and $k_w$ are computed below:

$$V_f = \$15,000 + (\$50,000 - \$1,500)(1 - .4)/.1$$
$$= \$15,000 + \$291,000 = \$306,000$$

$$k_w = .06\left(\frac{\$15,000}{\$15,000 + \$85,000}\right) + .1\left(\frac{\$85,000}{\$15,000 + \$85,000}\right)$$
$$= .009 + .085 = .094$$

Once again, the weighted average cost of capital falls because cheaper debt is being substituted for more expensive stock *and* its specific cost remains constant. The value of the firm increases because the $5,000 of added debt is larger than the $3,000 decrease in the value of the remaining common shares.

The firm's value and weighted average cost of capital for increasing amounts of debt up to $30,000 are contained in Table 14-5. $V_f$ increases and $k_w$ decreases until the firm's capital structure, using book value weights, consists of more than 20 percent debt. When the firm increases the amount of debt in its capital structure from $20,000 to $25,000 the common shareholders increase their required rate of return, and thus the specific cost of equity capital to the firm, because they perceive that the amount of debt in the capital structure has increased the amount of risk contained in the common stock. The weighted average cost of capital increases because of the increase in the specific cost of common. The value of the firm decreases

**Table 14-5.**     $V_f$ and $k_w$ Using Book Value Weights

| Debt | $V_e$ | $V_f$ | $k_w$ |
|---|---|---|---|
| $     0 | $300,000 | $300,000 | .1000 |
| 10,000 | 294,000 | 304,000 | .0960 |
| 15,000 | 291,000 | 306,000 | .0940 |
| 20,000 | 288,000 | 308,000 | .0920 |
| 25,000 | 237,500 | 262,500 | .1050 |
| 30,000 | 188,000 | 218,000 | .1230 |

from $308,000 to $262,500 because the $50,500 decrease in the value of the common (from $288,000 to $237,500) more than offsets the $5,000 increase in the amount of debt in the capital structure. Subsequent additions of debt to the firm's capital structure decrease the firm's value and increase the firm's weighted average cost of capital. Consequently, *the firm's value is maximized and its cost of capital is minimized when its capital structure contains 20 percent debt as measured by using book value weights.*

The relationship between firm value and cost of capital contained in Table 14-5 is shown graphically in Figure 14-1 where $k_w$ and $V_f$ are each plotted against capital structure composition. The curved plot of $k_w$ is referred to as a *U-shape* cost-of-capital curve. Figure 14-1 reinforces the conclusion that *the same capital structure that minimizes the firm's* $k_w$ *simultaneously maximizes firm value.*

**Figure 14-1.**     $V_f$ and $k_w$ Using Book Value Weights

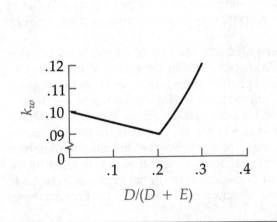
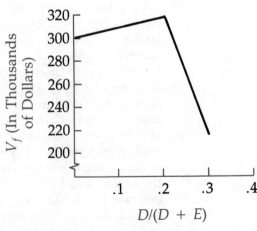

$V_f$ AND $k_w$ USING MARKET VALUE WEIGHTS. The procedure for measuring the firm's value and weighted average cost of capital using market value weights parallels the steps used to measure $k_w$ using book value weights. The firm's value computed for a given capital structure is independent of the method used to compute the firm's weighted average cost of capital. This is because Equation 14-8 that is used to compute $V_f$ contains none of the capital structure weights used to measure $k_w$. Thus, the values of $V_e$ and $V_f$ for alternative capital structures listed in Table 14-5 provide the market value weights for computing $k_w$.

The assumed initial capital structure is 100 percent equity, and the corresponding $V_f$ is $300,000. In computing $k_w$ using Equation 14-9, market values for debt and equity are used. Thus, for 100 percent equity financing:

$$k_w = .06\left(\frac{0}{0 + \$300,000}\right) + .1\left(\frac{\$300,000}{0 + \$300,000}\right)$$

$$= .1$$

The firm now floats $10,000 of debt and uses the proceeds to retire $10,000 of equity. $V_d = \$10,000$, and $V_e = \$294,000$. The firm's value thus increases to $304,000, and $k_w$ decreases to:

$$k_w = .06\left(\frac{\$10,000}{\$10,000 + \$294,000}\right) + .1\left(\frac{\$294,000}{\$10,000 + \$294,000}\right)$$

$$= .0020 + .0967 = .0987$$

The firm increases its total debt to $15,000. $V_e$ is computed as $291,000, $V_f$ increases to $306,000, and $k_w$ decreases to:

$$k_w = .06\left(\frac{\$15,000}{\$15,000 + \$291,000}\right) + .1\left(\frac{\$291,000}{\$15,000 + \$291,000}\right)$$

$$= .0029 + .0951$$

$$= .0980$$

The values for $V_f$ and $k_w$ using market value weights for alternative levels of debt financing are contained in Table 14-6. This table demonstrates that the firm's weighted average cost of capital decreases and reaches a minimum when the firm's capital structure contains $20,000 in debt. This capital structure also maximizes the firm's market value. Adding more debt to the capital structure increases the firm's weighted average cost of capital using market value weights and decreases the value of the firm. Consequently, the firm's value is maximized where the corporation's weighted average cost of capital using market value weights is minimized.

The cost-of-capital curve using market value weights has a U-shape with a minimum value of 9.74 percent. The plot of this curve is similar to

| **Table 14-6.** | $V_f$ and $k_w$ Using Market Value Weights | | |
|---|---|---|---|
| | **Debt** | $V_f$ | $k_w$ |
| | $     0 | $300,000 | .1000 |
| | 10,000 | 304,000 | .0987 |
| | 15,000 | 306,000 | .0980 |
| | 20,000 | 308,000 | .0974 |
| | 25,000 | 262,500 | .1143 |
| | 30,000 | 218,000 | .1376 |

that of $k_w$ using the book value weights contained in Figure 14-1. Market value weights yield higher $k_w$ values than book value weights; but, under the assumptions of this example, both curves are U-shaped and their minimum values occur where the value of the firm is a maximum.

**Optimal Capital Structure**

The two conclusions that this section seeks to demonstrate are illustrated in Tables 14-5 and 14-6. These conclusions are:

1. Changes in capital structure affect the firm's value and its cost of capital.

2. The capital structure that minimizes the firm's weighted average cost of capital is the same capital structure that maximizes firm value. This value-maximizing, cost-of-capital-minimizing capital structure is referred to as the firm's **optimal capital structure.**

These conclusions have some important implications; namely:

1. A firm that is able to reduce its cost of capital should realize an increase in its market value.

2. Since a firm has some control over its capital structure composition and thus its cost of capital, it is able to indirectly affect its market value by changing its capital structure.

3. Since the firm's optimal capital structure maximizes its value, the same capital structure maximizes shareholder wealth. Thus, the corporate goals of minimizing cost of capital and attaining an optimal capital structure are consistent with the goal of shareholder wealth maximization.

4. Either book value weights or market value weights can be used in computing the firm's $k_w$ when the purpose of this computation is to identify the firm's optimal capital structure. Book value and market value weights will produce different $k_w$ values, but the resulting U-shaped cost-of-capital curves will each realize their minimum values at the same maximum firm value.

Thus, the choice of book value weights versus market value weights in computing $k_w$ is important in certain applications such as capital budgeting, but not crucial when $k_w$ is to be used in identifying the firm's optimal capital structure.

## MARGINAL COST OF CAPITAL

The previous section analyzed cost of capital when the firm's total financing remained constant. In reality, the desire to finance new investments using internal and/or external funds requires that total capital increase. When this happens, the cost of capital of the additional funds is called the **marginal cost of capital (MCC).** If additional financing uses more than one type of funds, such as a combination of retained earnings and debt, the weighted average cost of capital of the new financing is referred to as the *weighted marginal cost of capital.* This section explains how a corporation's marginal cost of capital is computed and how a firm's MCC helps determine the size and composition of its capital budget.

**Calculating Marginal Cost of Capital**

The firm's marginal cost of capital is a function of several variables. Because of this, calculating the MCC is often a difficult process that yields only approximations of the true values. The four variables that impact on MCC do so by influencing the specific costs of capital of the new financing. These variables are:

1. Investors may perceive that the firm's business risk will increase as a result of its investment decisions.

2. If the new financing changes the firm's capital structure composition, its financial risk may increase. Increases in business and/or financial risk will be reflected in higher MCC.

3. The desirable investment alternatives available to the firm may require a large amount of financing relative to its existing total capital. In this case the size of the desired financing may increase the firm's MCC and thus may reduce the desirability of some of its investment alternatives.

4. External variables, such as inflation and business cycles, may increase the firm's MCC to the point where it delays raising long-term external capital and finances itself with retained earnings and short-term sources such as revolving credit agreements and term loans.

**FINANCING ASSUMPTIONS.** In this section the procedures for calculating MCC are based on the following assumptions:

1. The new financing has a *minimum* impact on the firm's existing capital structure composition. This implies that the percentage composition of the new financing is specified by the firm's financial managers.

2.  The firm accurately forecasts the specific costs of capital of the new financing. This implies some ability to estimate the impacts of added business risk and of external variables on the specific costs of capital.

3.  Market value weights are used. The choice of weights is based on the realizations that new capital is obtained by paying its market value and that market value weights produce MCC values that are more relevant in evaluating capital-budgeting alternatives than book value weights.

**FINANCING WITH RETAINED EARNINGS.** When a corporation is able to finance itself completely with retained earnings, its MCC equals the specific cost of capital of the retained earnings.

**Example:**

A corporation's existing capital structure composition and specific costs of capital are as follows:

| Source | Percentage Composition | Specific Cost of Capital |
|--------|:----------------------:|:------------------------:|
| Bonds | .3 | .06 |
| Common equity | .7 | .13 |

The weighted average cost of capital for this capital structure is:

$$(.3)(.06) + .7(.13) = .109 \text{ or } 10.9\%$$

Since all the new financing is to be provided by retained earnings, its 13 percent cost of capital is the firm's MCC rather than its 10.9 percent weighted average cost of capital.

**FINANCING WITH CONSTANT COSTS OF CAPITAL.** When a corporation is raising new capital, the MCC does not automatically have to exceed the firm's weighted average cost of capital. If the specific costs of capital in the new financing equal the specific costs of the corporation's existing capital structure, and if the new financing does not alter the firm's capital structure composition, then the firm's MCC equals its weighted average cost of capital.

**Example:**

A corporation's existing capital structure composition and specific costs of capital are as follows:

| Source | Percentage Composition | Specific Cost of Capital |
|--------|:----------------------:|:------------------------:|
| Bonds | .1 | .05 |
| Common stock | .5 | .10 |
| Retained earnings | .4 | .09 |

The weighted average cost of capital is 9.1 percent. The firm proposes to finance a $4 million capital budget by using retained earnings of $1.6 million generated during the current accounting period and by raising $400,000 in bonds and $2 million in common stock. It estimates the specific costs of capital of the new funds and finds that they equal the cost of capital for existing capital. Of the new financing, each source provides the following:

Retained earnings: $1.6 million/$4 million = 40%
Bonds:               $400,000/$4 million = 10%
Stocks:            $2 million/$4 million = 50%

The weighted MCC is thus:

$$(.4)(.09) + (.1)(.05) + (.5)(.1) = .091 \text{ or } 9.1\%$$

Thus, the weighted MCC equals the firm's $k_w$.

---

**FINANCING WITH CONSTANT SPECIFIC COSTS OF CAPITAL.** There are situations where the specific costs of capital will not be affected by the amount of funds raised. If the percentage composition of new financing remains constant (such as 20 percent debt and 80 percent equity), then the firm's weighted marginal cost of capital remains constant. When the weighted MCC exceeds the $k_w$ of its existing capital structure, raising the additional funds will increase the firm's weighted average cost of capital.

---

**Example:** A corporation's current capital structure contains $50 million and has the following characteristics:

| Source | Percentage Composition | Specific Cost of Capital |
|---|---|---|
| Bonds | .25 | .055 |
| Common stock | .50 | .110 |
| Retained earnings | .25 | .105 |

$$k_w = (.25)(.055) + (.50)(.110) + (.25)(.105) = .095$$

The firm expects to generate $2 million in retained earnings from current operations. Total expenditures in the firm's proposed capital budget run from $5 million to $10 million.

In order to keep its capital structure composition constant, realizing that $2 million will be provided by retained earnings, the firm would have to raise exactly $8 million in new capital as follows:

| | | |
|---|---|---|
| Bonds: | $2 million | (25%) |
| Common stock: | 4 million | (50%) |
| Retained earnings: | 2 million | (25%) |

The specific costs of capital of raising the $8 million are estimated as follows:

| Source | Specific Cost of Capital |
|---|---|
| Bonds | .06 |
| Common stock | .12 |
| Retained earnings | .105 |

The weighted MCC equals:

$$(.25)(.06) + (.5)(.12) + (.25)(.105) = .101 \text{ or } 10.1\%$$

Further research indicates that the additional $2 million needed to finance the entire $10 million capital budget could be raised by issuing additional common stock without changing any specific costs of capital. The weighted MCC of the $10 million would then be:

| Source | Dollar Amounts | Percentage Composition |
|---|---|---|
| Bonds | $ 2,000,000 | .2 |
| Common stock | 6,000,000 | .6 |
| Retained earnings | 2,000,000 | .2 |
| Total | $10,000,000 | |

The weighted MCC equals:

$$(.2)(.06) + (.6)(.12) + (.2)(.105) = .105 \text{ or } 10.5\%$$

If the firm raises the entire $10 million, the weighted average cost of capital of the new $60 million capital structure then becomes:

| Source | Dollar Amounts | Percentage Composition | Specific Cost of Capital | Weighted Cost |
|---|---|---|---|---|
| Bonds | $12,500,000 | .2083 | .055 | .0115 |
| Bonds | 2,000,000 | .0333 | .060 | .0020 |
| Common stock | 25,000,000 | .4167 | .110 | .0458 |
| Common stock | 6,000,000 | .1000 | .120 | .0120 |
| Retained earnings | 12,500,000 | .2083 | .105 | .0219 |
| Retained earnings | 2,000,000 | .0333 | .105 | .0035 |
| Total | $60,000,000 | 1.0000 | | $k_w = .0967$ |

The firm's $k_w$ increases from 9.5 to 9.67 percent as a result of its $10 million financing. The percentage composition of its capital structure also changes and is now:

| Source | Dollar Amounts | Percentage Composition |
|---|---|---|
| Bonds | $14,500,000 | .24 |
| Common stock | 31,000,000 | .52 |
| Retained earnings | 14,500,000 | .24 |
| Total | $60,000,000 | 1.00 |

In this example, the firm's weighted MCC is 10.1 percent for $8 million financing and 10.5 percent for $10 million financing even though the specific costs of capital remain constant. This increase in the weighted MCC occurs because the percentage composition of each financing "package" is different. This example implicitly assumed that the small changes in the firm's overall capital structure composition produced no changes in the specific costs of capital of its new financing. For an $8 million capital budget the discount rate is the MCC value of 10.1 percent. Similarly, the discount rate for evaluating the $10 million capital budget is the 10.5 percent MCC value.

**BREAKS IN SPECIFIC COSTS OF CAPITAL.** Specific costs of capital can be affected by the amount of financing that the corporation seeks to obtain. When this happens, the weighted MCC of the total financing package increases. For example, a corporation may want to float $5 million of bonds as part of a $20 million security offering. If $3 million of the bonds can be sold at a specific cost of capital of 6 percent, but the cost of raising $5 million of bonds is 7 percent, the firm's weighted MCC will depend on the total amount of funds raised and how much of the total is provided by the bond issue.

*Breaks* in the weighted MCC are said to occur when the specific cost of capital increases as a function of the amount of funds acquired. The corporation's problems are to estimate at what levels of *total new financing* the breaks in the weighted MCC occur and to measure the weighted MCC at each of the breakpoints. The following procedure can be used to measure the weighted MCC when the specific costs of capital depend on the amounts financed:

1. Determine the percentage composition of the new financing.

2. Prepare a schedule that lists, for each source of funds, the amounts of financing that can be obtained and the specific costs of capital associated with each amount raised.

3. Estimate the breakpoints in the weighted MCC by using the information contained in the first two steps. The breakpoints identify the levels of total new financing at which the weighted MCC increases.

4. Compute the weighted MCC at each breakpoint.

The first step is critical to the above procedure. If the corporation does not set the percentage composition of its additional financing, a large number of breakpoints will occur, and no usable estimates of the weighted MCC will be identifiable.

---

**Example:** A corporation wishes to raise up to $10 million of new financing but realizes that its MCC may depend on the amount of financing raised. In order to measure its weighted MCC, the corporation executes the four-step procedure described above.

*Step 1.* The percentage composition of the new financing is set as follows: debt, 25 percent; equity, 75 percent. Equity financing is a combination of retained earnings generated during the current accounting period and any new common stock that has to be floated.

*Step 2.* The following specific costs of capital are estimated for each source and for different levels of financing:

| Source | Amount Raised | Specific Cost of Capital |
|--------|--------------|--------------------------|
| Bonds | Up to $1 million | .05 |
| | $1 million up to $2 million | .06 |
| | $2 million up to $3 million | .08 |
| Equity | $1.5 million | .12 |
| | $1.5 million up to $6 million | .14 |
| | $6 million up to $9 million | .17 |

Exactly $1.5 million of equity will be provided by current retained earnings, and its specific cost of capital is estimated at 12 percent. Additional needed equity will be raised by selling common stock.

*Step 3.* To estimate the weighted MCC breakpoints, take each source of funds and divide the maximum amount of financing available at each specific cost of capital by the percentage composition of that source. The resulting values are the weighted MCC breakpoints for *total new financing.* The breakpoints for this example are calculated in Table 14-7. The computations in this table indicate that the firm's weighted MCC breaks or shifts at $2 million, $4 million, $8 million, and $12 million of new financing.

**Table 14-7.**   Weighted MCC Breakpoints

| Source of Capital | Breakpoint | Range of Total New Financing | Specific Cost of Capital |
|-------------------|-----------|------------------------------|--------------------------|
| Debt | $1 million/.25 = $4 million | Up to $4 million | .05 |
| | $2 million/.25 = $8 million | $4 million up to $8 million | .06 |
| | $3 million/.25 = $12 million | $8 million up to $12 million | .08 |
| Equity | $1.5 million/.75 = $2 million | $2 million | .12 |
| | $6 million/.75 = $8 million | $2 million up to $8 million | .14 |
| | $9 million/.75 = $12 million | $12 million | .17 |

*Step 4.* The last step calculates the weighted MCC for each range of financing. The calculations for this example are contained in Table 14-8. The data needed for the computations are contained in Table 14-7.

The calculating procedure in Table 14-8 slightly overestimates the weighted MCC for levels of new financing that include *both* retained earnings and common stock. For example, at $8 million of new financing the specific cost of capital of equity is given as 17 percent. However, $1.5 million of that source is retained earnings whose specific cost of capital is only 12 percent. This estimating error decreases over increasing amounts of new financing.

The weighted MCC for this corporation is thus:

| Level of Financing | Weighted MCC |
|---|---|
| Up to $2 million | 10.25% |
| $2 million up to $4 million | 11.75% |
| $4 million up to $8 million | 12.00% |
| $8 million up to $12 million | 14.75% |

These weighted MCC values can be used to evaluate the firm's capital budget. A proposed $7.5 million budget, for example, can be evaluated by using the 12 percent weighted MCC value as the discount rate in computing the capital budget's net present value. A $10 million budget would be evaluated using the 14.75 percent rate.

| Table 14-8. | Weighted MCC for Ranges of Total New Financing | | | | |
|---|---|---|---|---|---|
| | **Range of Total New Financing** | **Source of Capital** | **Percentage Composition** | **Specific Cost of Capital** | **Weighted Costs** |
| | $2 million | debt | .25 | .05 | .0125 |
| | | equity | .75 | .12 | .0900 |
| | | | | Weighted MCC = | .1025 |
| | $2 million up to $4 million | debt | .25 | .05 | .0125 |
| | | equity | .75 | .14 | .1050 |
| | | | | Weighted MCC = | .1175 |
| | $4 million up to $8 million | debt | .25 | .06 | .0150 |
| | | equity | .75 | .14 | .1050 |
| | | | | Weighted MCC = | .1200 |
| | $8 million up to $12 million | debt | .25 | .08 | .0200 |
| | | equity | .75 | .17 | .1275 |
| | | | | Weighted MCC = | .1475 |

Figure 14-2 plots the weighted MCC when the firm's MCC increases as a function of total new financing. The straight-line segments in this figure are the weighted MCC values calculated in Table 14-8. The smooth curved line is an approximation of the weighted MCC that would result if the MCC increased continuously rather than increased in discrete steps. This figure also illustrates the fact that breaks in the firm's weighted MCC do not necessarily occur at equally spaced intervals of new financing.

**Figure 14-2.**   **Weighted MCC as a Function of Total New Financing**

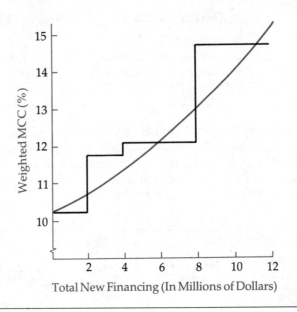

Total New Financing (In Millions of Dollars)

**MCC and Capital Budgeting**

The firm's MCC is the discount rate that is used in evaluating capital-budgeting alternatives. Based on the criteria in Chapters 10 and 11, a project is desirable when its NPV, discounted at the firm's MCC, is zero or positive.

**CONSTANT MCC.** When a firm's MCC is constant, evaluating a set of capital-budgeting alternatives is accomplished by computing the NPV of each project and accepting the set of projects that yields the highest (positive) total NPV. This process assumes that enough funds can be obtained at the specified costs of capital to finance all the accepted projects.

**INCREASING MCC.** When a firm's MCC contains breaks over increasing levels of new financing, identifying the optimal capital budget becomes a somewhat complex problem in capital rationing. Exact solutions to this problem are beyond the scope of this text; however, the following procedure provides an approximate solution:

1.  Find the set of projects that generates the largest total NPV for each level of financing that contains an MCC break.

2.  Select the level of financing and the corresponding set of projects that promise the largest total NPV.

---

**Example:**   Assume that breaks in a corporation's weighted MCC occur at the following levels of financing: $6 million, $9 million, $14 million, and $20 million. The corporation estimates the weighted MCC values to be as follows:

| Level of Financing (Millions of $) | Weighted MCC (%) |
|:---:|:---:|
| 6 | 10.5 |
| 9 | 12.2 |
| 14 | 16.6 |
| 20 | 21.0 |

The firm begins by assuming a capital constraint of $6 million and a discount rate of 10.5 percent. Using these values, the firm identifies the set of projects that returns the highest (positive) total NPV. The firm repeats the procedure using a $9 million capital constraint and a 12.2 percent discount rate, and so forth. The resulting NPVs are found to be:

| Level of Financing (Millions of $) | Total NPV (Millions of $) |
|:---:|:---:|
| 6 | 1.0 |
| 9 | 1.9 |
| 14 | 2.6 |
| 20 | 2.3 |

The largest, and positive, total NPV occurs when the firm raises $14 million at a cost of capital of 16.6 percent. From the standpoint of shareholder wealth maximization, the optimal capital budget consists of the set of opportunities that returns a total NPV of $2.6 million and requires $14 million of financing.

---

# SUMMARY

Cost of capital is a central concept in financial management because it provides a way of linking the investment and financing decisions of the firm. Several equivalent definitions of cost of capital are possible so long as each definition is consistent with the goal of shareholder wealth maximization. In general, a corporation's cost of capital is the minimum rate of return it must earn in order to satisfy the rate of return required by its investors.

The techniques used to measure specific costs of capital are based on valuation principles. Separate measurement equations are used for calculating the specific costs of capital of bonds, preferred stock, common stock, and retained earnings. These specific costs of capital are used to measure the corporation's weighted average cost of capital. The corporation's overall cost of capital can be computed by using book value or market value weights. Market value weights are consistent with the goal of shareholder wealth maximization; but book value weights, being more stable over time, are frequently used in practice.

The relationships among cost of capital, capital structure, and firm value are of vital importance to financial managers because capital structure composition can be used to exert some influence on a firm's value. A firm's optimal capital structure can be identified by using a set of assumptions that hold the influence of other factors constant and by specifying how investors are assumed to perceive and react to changes in its degree of financial risk. An optimal capital structure is the capital structure percentage composition that simultaneously maximizes the firm's market value and minimizes its weighted average cost of capital. Under assumptions made in this chapter, the value of the firm is maximized when its weighted average cost of capital, using either book value or market value weights, is minimized.

The cost of capital of new financing is called the firm's marginal cost of capital (MCC) and is the discount rate used in evaluating capital-budgeting alternatives. Calculating a firm's marginal cost of capital is a straightforward process when retained earnings provide all the new financing or when the specific costs of capital of the additional financing are constant. Breaks occur in the firm's weighted MCC when the specific costs of capital are a function of the size of the new financing. This requires that the firm measure its weighted MCC at each level of total new financing where weighted MCC breaks occur. Under these conditions, selecting the firm's optimal capital budget becomes a problem in capital rationing.

# QUESTIONS

**14-1.** In what sense is a firm's cost of capital considered to be a "break-even" rate of return?

**14-2.** What steps are needed to compute the specific cost of capital of bonds?

**14-3.** The specific cost of capital of common stock is most frequently measured by using Equation 14-3. What assumptions are contained in this equation?

**14-4.** Why is the specific cost of capital of retained earnings equated with the specific cost of capital of common stock?

**14-5.** What are the advantages and limitations of using book value weights in measuring a corporation's weighted average cost of capital?

**14-6.** What are the advantages and limitations of using market value weights in measuring a corporation's weighted average cost of capital?

14-7. State the basic relationships among cost of capital, capital structure, and a firm's value.

14-8. Explain what is meant by an optimal capital structure.

14-9. Identify the major types of variables that can affect the firm's MCC.

14-10. What are the implications for the corporation when breaks occur in its weighted MCC?

# PROBLEMS

14-1. Compute the specific cost of capital of each of the following bonds. Assume a 40% tax rate.

| Face Value | Net Proceeds | Coupon Rate | Years to Maturity |
|---|---|---|---|
| $ 1,000 | $ 1,000 | 11% | 10 |
| $ 5,000 | $ 4,985 | 8% | 20 |
| $10,000 | $10,200 | 13% | 30 |

14-2. Compute the specific cost of capital of each of the following preferred stocks:

| Price to Investor | Selling Cost | Annual Dividend |
|---|---|---|
| $104 | $2 | $10.00 |
| $ 50 | $3 | $ 5.50 |
| $ 80 | $2 | $ 7.00 |

14-3. Compute the specific cost of capital of each of the following common stocks:

| Price to Investor | Selling Cost | Current Dividend | Growth Rate |
|---|---|---|---|
| $20 | $2 | $0.60 | 4% |
| $52 | $2 | $5.00 | 0% |
| $70 | $3 | $8.00 | 2% |

14-4. Using the data in Problem 14-3 and assuming that prices to investors equal the current market prices, calculate the cost of capital of retained earnings for each of the three data sets.

14-5. Compute the weighted average cost of capital of the following capital structure by using book value weights:

| Source of Capital | Book Value | Specific Cost of Capital |
|---|---|---|
| 10% bonds, $1,000 par value | $ 6,000,000 | .05 |
| Common stock, 1,000,000 | | |
| shares outstanding | 10,000,000 | .12 |
| Retained earnings | 4,000,000 | .11 |

**14-6.** Compute the weighted average cost of capital of the capital structure given in Problem 14-5 by using market value weights. Assume that the bonds currently are quoted at 94 and that the common stocks currently sell for $18 per share.

**14-7.** A corporation's capital structure consists of $1,000,000 of equity capital. It wants to estimate its optimal capital structure while not changing its total amount of capital. The firm estimates its specific cost of equity capital for various levels of debt to be:

| Debt | $k_e$ |
|---|---|
| $      0 | .12 |
| $ 25,000 | .12 |
| $ 50,000 | .12 |
| $ 75,000 | .14 |
| $100,000 | .17 |

Debt can be floated at par and would carry a 10% coupon rate. The firm's $k_d = .06$. Its EBIT is forecast to be a constant $500,000. Assume a 40% corporate tax rate.

Compute the value of the firm and its weighted average cost of capital for each of the five alternative levels of debt, using book value weights. Use Equations 14-8 and 14-9. What is the optimal capital structure for this firm?

**14-8.** Using the data in Problem 14-7, compute $V_f$ and $k_w$ by using market value weights. What is the optimal capital structure under these conditions? Why?

**14-9.** A corporation seeks up to $10 million in new financing. Its desired percentage composition of this financing is debt, 40%; equity, 60%. Equity is a combination of retained earnings for the current period and of new common stock. The corporation expects to generate $1.5 million of retained earnings during the current accounting period.

The corporation estimates the following specific costs of capital as a function of the amount of new financing. Compute each of the MCC breakpoints and the weighted MCC at each breakpoint.

| Source | Amount Raised | Specific Cost of Capital |
|---|---|---|
| Bonds | Up to $2 million | .05 |
| | $2 million up to $4 million | .06 |
| Equity | $1.5 million | .13 |
| | $1.5 million up to $3 million | .14 |
| | $3 million up to $6 million | .17 |

# SELECTED REFERENCES

Haley, C., and L. Schall. *The Theory of Financial Decisions.* 2d ed. New York: McGraw-Hill Book Company, 1979.

Henderson, G. "In Defense of the Weighted Average Cost of Capital." *Financial Management,* Vol. 8, No. 3 (Autumn, 1979).

Lewellen, W. "A Conceptual Reappraisal of Cost of Capital." *Financial Management,* Vol. 3, No. 4 (Winter, 1974).

Nantell, T., and R. Carlson. "The Cost of Capital as a Weighted Average." *Journal of Finance,* Vol. 30, No. 5 (December, 1975).

Porterfield, J. *Investment Decisions and Capital Costs.* Englewood Cliffs, N.J.: Prentice-Hall, Inc., 1965.

Robichek, A., and S. Myers. *Optimal Financing Decisions.* Englewood Cliffs, N.J.: Prentice-Hall, Inc., 1966.

Van Horne, J. *Financial Management and Policy.* 6th ed. Englewood Cliffs, N.J.: Prentice-Hall, Inc., 1983.

# CHAPTER 15

## Capital Structure
## Planning Techniques

The previous chapter used a set of
restrictive assumptions to demonstrate the
impact of capital structure changes on firm
value. By holding business risk, total
financing, and external influences constant,
the analysis could focus exclusively on
explaining the relationships between these two
concepts. This chapter explains how to analyze
the impacts of alternative capital structures on
the risk and return characteristics of the firm
when these assumptions are relaxed.

Capital structure decisions have two
components. First, the firm must decide how
much capital is needed. Second, the financing
mix must be chosen. This chapter assumes that
the corporation has a good estimate of how
much capital is needed. The problem then
becomes one of determining the best mix of
debt and equity to be used in raising the
needed capital.

The process that leads to the final choice
of capital structure is referred to generally as
capital structure planning. This chapter focuses
on some capital structure planning techniques
that allow the firm to quantify the risk-return
characteristics of alternative capital structures.
Later chapters introduce other aspects of
capital structure planning that are not
easily quantifiable and are thus evaluated
subjectively.

*The first section of this chapter specifies the assumption set and the equations used to measure corporate risk-return characteristics and introduces the concept of trading on the equity. Then indifference point analysis is explained as a way of comparing the profitability of alternative capital structures. The materials developed in the first two sections are then used to compare the combined risk-return characteristics of alternative capital structures.*

## RISK AND RETURN MEASUREMENTS

The goal of capital structure planning is to identify and obtain the corporate financing mix that provides the greatest contribution to shareholder wealth. Although this can be done easily enough within the theoretical framework of Chapter 14, the task is much more difficult in actual practice. Why? Because, as first described in Chapter 2, share prices, a major component of shareholder wealth, are influenced by a large number of factors, or variables, and the firm's choice of capital structure is only one of these variables. However, as explained in Chapter 5, the firm's capital structure decisions affect its risk and return characteristics. When a firm sells additional debt, for example, its financial breakeven and degree of financial leverage both increase. In addition, earnings per share (EPS) will increase if the firm earns at least the specific cost of capital of the debt; otherwise EPS will fall. As a consequence, financial managers focus on the impact that alternative financing plans will have on the firm's risk and return characteristics as a way of estimating the resulting impact on shareholder wealth.

In this chapter, EPS is used as a measure of returns, and financial leverage is used to measure financial risk. EPS and financial leverage are used because both are a function of the corporation's earnings before interest and taxes (EBIT). Thus, the capital structure planning techniques contained in this chapter are based on a corporation's risk and return characteristics being a function of the level and stability of the firm's EBIT.

The conditions under which the corporation is assumed to make capital structure decisions are listed below. This set of assumptions holds constant certain internal factors but allows the corporation to change its degree of financial risk as a consequence of its financing decisions.

1. *Business Risk*   Corporate EBIT can vary over time as a result of both internal and external factors. Thus, business risk is not held constant.

2. *Needed financing*   The corporation is assumed to measure accurately the amount of financing it needs. The amount to be provided by retained earnings is subtracted from the required financing, and the remainder is obtained from external sources. The corporation's total liabilities and equity increase as a result of raising the needed funds.

3. *Capital structure composition*   The percentage composition of the corporation's capital structure can change as a result of the new financing. This allows the firm to evaluate any number of mutually exclusive financing alternatives and allows each alternative to raise the needed funds by using different combinations of external sources.

4. *Financial risk*   Each financing alternative that contains debt and/or preferred stock shifts the corporation's financial break-even and its degree of financial risk. Thus, the corporation's financial risk can change as a result of its capital structure decisions.

These conditions identify a situation in which a corporation has decided to increase total assets. This decision means that the firm has identified, through its capital-budgeting system, a set of desirable investment alternatives along with the amount of net investment needed to implement the capital budget. While these investments will contribute to increasing the firm's earnings and may alter its degree of business risk, the financing mix will also affect earnings and may change the firm's financial risk. Capital structure techniques help financial managers estimate, for any given financing plan, the level of EBIT that must be forthcoming from the firm's assets if EPS are not to decrease as a result of financing the asset expansion. These techniques also provide a measure of the financial risk contained in each financing plan. The firm must then identify which alternative, including the possibility of not expanding, contains the most desirable risk and return characteristics.

**Measuring Returns**

There are two equations that help to explain how a given capital structure determines the relationship between a corporation's EBIT and its EPS. The first, Equation 5-4, uses the income statement definition of EPS; the second, Equation 5-11, computes the firm's financial breakeven. While both equations are used to measure corporate profitability, the financial breakeven equation also provides a way of linking profitability and risk.

**EBIT AND EPS.** Equation 5-4 is used to measure corporate EPS as a function of EBIT. The symbols used in this equation are contained in Table 5-2 and summarized here for convenience. Let:

$Y$ = EBIT
$I$ = dollars of interest on debt
$t$ = federal corporate income tax rate, assumed to be 40%
$E$ = dollars of preferred stock dividends
$N$ = number of shares of common stock outstanding

Then:

$$\text{EPS} = \frac{(Y - I)(1 - t) - E}{N} \qquad (5\text{-}4)$$

The values of $I$, $E$, and/or $N$ are changed as a result of raising external funds, and these variables must reflect the increased totals.

---

**Example:**

A corporation's existing capital structure contains $10 million of 9 percent debt and 100,000 shares of common stock. Its EPS equation is as follows:

$$\text{EPS} = \frac{(Y - \$900,000)(1 - .4)}{100,000}$$

$$= \frac{.6Y - \$540,000}{100,000}$$

The firm then floats $5,000,000 of 10 percent debt, 100,000 shares of preferred stock that pays a dividend of $7.20 per share, and 25,000 shares of common stock. Its new EPS equation is:

$$\text{EPS} = \frac{(Y - \$900,000 - \$500,000)(1 - .4) - \$720,000}{100,000 + 25,000}$$

$$= \frac{.6Y - \$1,560,000}{125,000}$$

---

**FINANCIAL BREAKEVEN.** Equation 5-11, repeated below, measures the corporation's financial breakeven. This is the value of EBIT that yields a zero value of EPS. Let $Y_b$ represent financial breakeven. Then:

$$Y_b = I + \frac{E}{(1 - t)} \qquad (5\text{-}11)$$

| | |
|---|---|
| **Example:** | Using the capital structures contained in the previous example, $Y_b$ for the existing capital structure equals \$900,000. After the additional external capital is raised the following results: |

$$Y_b = \$900{,}000 + \$500{,}000 + \$720{,}000/(1 - .4)$$
$$= \$2{,}600{,}000$$

**Measuring Risk**

The financial leverage (FL) equation, Equation 5-10, is used to measure the degree of financial risk contained in a corporation's capital structure. Using the symbols defined above:

$$(FL \,|\, Y) = \frac{Y}{Y - I - E/(1 - t)} \qquad (5\text{-}10)$$

There are two reasons for using this equation. First, financial leverage provides a measure of financial risk. Second, Equation 5-10 uses the same independent variable — EBIT — that is used in the equation for measuring returns. As a consequence, it is possible to measure a capital structure's risk-return characteristics for any value of EBIT by using Equations 5-4 and 5-10.

**Trading on the Equity**

Bond interest and preferred stock dividends represent fixed financing costs to the issuing corporation. These payments are fixed in the sense that the issuing corporation states the interest and dividend rates carried by the securities. When floating rates are used, as in the case of floating rate bonds, the interest rate paid by the security can vary only within stated limits, and these types of securities are considered to impose fixed or stated financing costs on the issuing firm. The firm is legally obligated to pay bond interest but not preferred dividends. For reasons explained in Chapter 19, however, the assumption is made that preferred stock dividends will be paid unless the firm becomes insolvent.

A firm is said to engage in *trading on the equity* (TOTE) when it finances itself by selling securities on which it pays fixed or limited returns. A firm thus is using TOTE when it floats bonds and preferred stock. A firm is not using TOTE when it sells common stock or transfers earnings after taxes to retained earnings.

The importance of TOTE to capital structure planning is explained as follows. When a corporation finances itself by TOTE, its financial breakeven and degree of financial leverage both increase. TOTE thus increases a firm's financial risk. If a firm wishes to avoid increasing its financial risk as a result of financing an expansion, its financing plan must use a combination of common stock and retained earnings.

---

**Example:**   A corporation's capital structure consists of $8,000,000 of 8 percent debt and 500,000 shares of common stock. The financial breakeven for this capital structure is:

$$Y_b = (.08)(\$8,000,000)$$
$$= \$640,000$$

The degree of financial leverage when EBIT equals $1,600,000 is:

$$(FL \mid Y = \$1,600,000) = \frac{\$1,600,000}{\$1,600,000 - \$640,000}$$
$$= 1.67$$

The corporation engages in further TOTE by selling 50,000 preferred shares that carry a $6 per share dividend. The financial breakeven increases to:

$$Y_b = \$640,000 + \$300,000/(1 - .4)$$
$$= \$1,140,000$$

The degree of financial leverage for EBIT when it equals $1,600,000 increases to:

$$(FL \mid Y = \$1,600,000) = \frac{\$1,600,000}{\$1,600,000 - \$640,000 - \$300,000/(1 - .4)}$$
$$= 3.48$$

---

The financial risk measured in the financial leverage equation is not the probability or likelihood that a particular value of EBIT will be attained. Financial leverage measures the impact on EPS that results from a percentage change in a *given* level of EBIT. If EBIT is volatile in the sense that it is subject to large and unpredictable changes over time, then financing by TOTE increases the firm's financial leverage — and thus its financial risk — because TOTE further increases the volatility of EPS. If, on the other hand, EBIT is stable in the sense of following a regular and predictable increasing trend over time, the corporation can use TOTE to magnify its EPS growth. Thus, from the standpoint of financial risk, the decision to raise funds by TOTE depends on the stability of a corporation's EBIT, and the financial leverage coefficient measures the extent to which TOTE magnifies EPS growth or increases its volatility.

# INDIFFERENCE POINT ANALYSIS

The use of financial breakeven and return measurement equations to compare the profitability of alternative capital structures is called **indiffer-**

ence point analysis. When EBIT is used as the independent variable and EPS is used as the dependent variable, this technique is sometimes referred to as *EBIT-EPS indifference point analysis.* When a firm has several alternative ways of financing an expansion, each alternative can produce a different overall capital structure. The purpose of indifference point analysis is to identify, for each possible value of EBIT, the particular capital structure that produces the largest EPS. Indifference point analysis thus provides a way of evaluating the desirability of alternative capital structures on the basis of their profitability. There are three basic steps in indifference point analysis:

1. For each alternative capital structure, obtain the EBIT-EPS return equation (Equation 5-4).

2. Obtain the pairwise simultaneous solutions for these equations.

3. On the basis of the first two steps, identify the EPS-maximizing capital structure for each possible value of EBIT.

These steps become cumbersome when several capital structures are to be evaluated. For purposes of simplicity, the balance of this chapter assumes that the corporation seeks to evaluate only a limited number of capital structures.

**EBIT-EPS Equations**

The three steps in executing an indifference point analysis are explained by using the hypothetical data contained in Table 15-1. The corporation's current EBIT of $14,600,000 cannot be increased unless external funding is obtained. It has decided to raise $5 million of additional capital and has identified two mutually exclusive alternatives. From the standpoint of maximizing EPS, which alternative is more profitable?

**Table 15-1.**   **Hypothetical Data for an Indifference Point Analysis**

**Existing Capital Structure**

| | |
|---|---|
| Bonds: | $20 million, 10% interest rate |
| Common stock: | 3 million shares |
| Current EBIT: | $14,600,000 |
| Current EPS: | $2.52 |
| Current common stock price: | $25 per share |
| Financing Alternative *A*: | Bonds—$5,000,000 at 12% interest rate |
| Financing Alternative *B*: | Common stock—200,000 shares |

If Alternative *A* is accepted, the corporation's capital structure will consist of $20 million of 10 percent bonds, $5 million of 12 percent bonds, and 3 million shares of common stock. The financial breakeven for this structure is:

$$Y_b = (.1)(\$20,000,000) + (.12)(\$5,000,000)$$
$$= \$2,600,000$$

The EBIT-EPS equation for this structure, referred to as $EPS_A$, is:

$$EPS_A = \frac{(Y - \$2,000,000 - \$600,000)(1 - .4)}{3,000,000}$$

This equation can be simplified to:

$$EPS_A = \frac{.6Y - \$1,560,000}{3,000,000} \qquad \text{(15-1)}$$

If Alternative B is chosen, the resulting capital structure will consist of $20 million of 10 percent bonds and 3,200,000 common shares. The financial breakeven for this alternative is:

$$Y_b = (.1)(\$20,000,000)$$
$$= \$2,000,000$$

The EBIT-EPS equation for this alternative, $EPS_B$, equals:

$$EPS_B = \frac{(Y - \$2,000,000)(1 - .4)}{3,000,000 + 200,000}$$

This equation simplifies to:

$$EPS_B = \frac{.6Y - \$1,200,000}{3,200,000} \qquad \text{(15-2)}$$

**Obtaining the Indifference Point**

Equations 15-1 and 15-2 are plotted in Figure 15-1 and identify the value of EPS produced by each capital structure for different values of EBIT. The point at which the plotted lines intersect is called the **EBIT-EPS indifference point** and is defined as the value of EBIT that produces the same value of EPS for both capital structures. If the corporation expects to generate exactly the amount of EBIT at which the capital structure plots intersect, from the standpoint of profitability it will be *indifferent* as to the choice of capital structure because the same EPS would result from either alternative.

The indifference point values of EPS and EBIT are obtained as follows. At the indifference point:

Figure 15-1.        **EBIT-EPS Indifference Point**

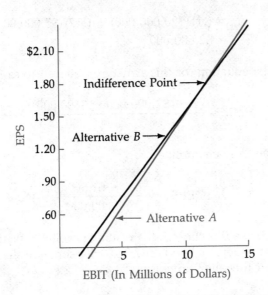

EBIT (In Millions of Dollars)

$$EPS_A = EPS_B \tag{15-3}$$

Substituting Equations 15-1 and 15-2 into 15-3 yields:

$$\frac{.6Y - \$1,560,000}{3,000,000} = \frac{.6Y - \$1,200,000}{3,200,000} \tag{15-4}$$

Equation 15-4 is a linear equation in one unknown. Solving this equation yields the indifference point value of EBIT.

As a first step, both sides of Equation 15-4 can be multiplied by 1,000,000, thus moving the decimal points in the denominators six places to the left. The resulting equation is:

$$\frac{.6Y - \$1,560,000}{3} = \frac{.6Y - \$1,200,000}{3.2} \tag{15-5}$$

Equation 15-5 is now cross multiplied by its denominators:

$$3.2(.6Y - \$1,560,000) = 3(.6Y - \$1,200,000)$$

Thus:

$$1.92Y - \$4,992,000 = 1.8Y - \$3,600,000$$
$$.12Y = \$1,392,000$$
$$Y = \$11,600,000$$

The value of EBIT at the indifference point is $11,600,000.

The corresponding indifference point value of EPS is obtained by substituting $Y = \$11,600,000$ into Equation 15-1:

$$EPS_A = \frac{(.6)\,(\$11,600,000) - \$1,560,000}{3,000,000}$$

Thus:

$$EPS_A = \$1.80$$

As a check of accuracy, $EPS_B$ also is calculated at the EBIT indifference point:

$$EPS_B = \frac{(.6)\,(\$11,600,000) - \$1,200,000}{3,200,000}$$
$$= \$1.80$$

For the two capital structure alternatives, the EBIT-EPS indifference point occurs where EBIT equals $11,600,000 and EPS equals $1.80. The EBIT-EPS indifference point provides important information concerning the relative profitability of the alternative structures. To the right of the indifference point, Figure 15-1 shows that Alternative $A$ is more profitable than $B$. Similarly, Alternative $B$ is more profitable than $A$ for values of EBIT below the indifference point. In addition, horizontal intercepts identify the break-even levels of EBIT for each alternative.

**Ranking the Capital Structures**

Once the EBIT-EPS indifference point has been obtained, the capital structure alternatives can be ranked according to their profitability. For the example contained in Table 15-1, the corporation has the following three alternatives:

1. Sell bonds.

2. Sell common stock.

3. Sell no securities and do not expand.

Alternative 3 results in no external financing. Why is this alternative included? Because the corporation should reject any expansion plan that reduces EPS below its current value of $2.52. At the current EBIT value of $14,600,000, Alternative $A$ (sell bonds) is more profitable in terms of EPS than Alternative $B$ (sell stocks) because the $14,600,000 EBIT is greater than the indifference point value of \$11,600,000. However, is Alternative $A$ more profitable than the *current* capital structure? To answer this question, $EPS_A$ is computed at EBIT = \$14,600,000 by using Equation 5-4:

$$EPS_A = \frac{(\$14,600,000 - \$2,000,000 - \$600,000)(1 - .4)}{3,000,000}$$

$$= \$2.40$$

Thus, Alternative $A$ is less profitable than the current capital structure when EBIT equals \$14,600,000.

The problem raised in this example is that the corporation requires external financing in order to increase EBIT. This implies that retained earnings are sufficient only to maintain the current EBIT-EPS values. If the needed external financing is provided by adopting Alternative $A$, what level of EBIT is needed in order to produce an EPS at least equal to the current value of \$2.52? Equation 15-6 is used to answer this type of question. Substitute the desired value of EPS along with the capital structure values into the right-hand side of this equation. The resulting number is the EBIT needed to earn the desired EPS value:

$$Y = \frac{(EPS)(N) + E}{(1 - t)} + I \qquad (15\text{-}6)$$

For Alternative $A$, the EBIT that yields EPS equal to \$2.52 is:

$$Y = \frac{(\$2.52)(3,000,000)}{(1 - .4)} + \$2,600,000$$

$$= \$15,200,000$$

Similarly, the value of EBIT that yields an EPS of \$2.52 for Alternative $B$ is:

$$Y = \frac{(\$2.52)(3,200,000)}{(1 - .4)} + \$2,000,000$$

$$= \$15,440,000$$

These relationships are plotted in Figure 15-2. The broken-line portion of the current capital structure plot indicates that the corporation cannot generate EBIT beyond \$14,600,000 by using only internal financing. The figure indicates that for EBIT values of \$14,600,000 or less the current capital structure produces higher EPS values than either alternative. Alternative $A$ produces the highest EPS values once EBIT exceeds \$15,200,000. Consequently, in the interval of \$14,600,000 to \$15,200,000 of EBIT, the corporation is better off rejecting both alternatives and not expanding.

**Figure 15-2.**        **EPS for Alternative Capital Structures**

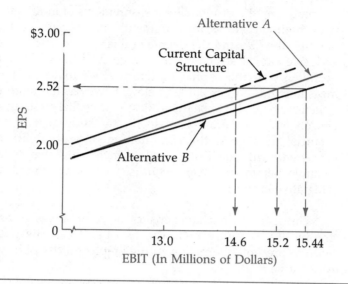

EBIT (In Millions of Dollars)

The EPS-maximizing capital structure alternatives are summarized as follows:

1.   For values of EBIT greater than $15,200,000, Alternative A is preferable.

2.   For values of EBIT equal to or less than $15,200,000, the current capital structure is preferred.

In terms of profitability, the final choice between these two alternatives is based on the likelihood that the $5 million raised by floating bonds (Alternative A) can be invested in capital-budgeting alternatives that will increase EBIT by at least $600,000. If the corporation accepts this financing alternative and is subsequently unable to increase EBIT by more than $600,000, the net result is a larger corporation in terms of total assets that is less profitable in terms of EPS. On the other hand, if the expansion increases EBIT by more than $600,000, Alternative A uses trading on the equity to increase EPS to a higher value than would occur if the expansion were financed by floating the common stock of Alternative B.

## RISK-RETURN ANALYSIS

Having explained how indifference point analysis measures the profitability of capital structure alternatives, and given that coefficients of financial leverage measure capital structure financial risk, the combined risk and return characteristics of a given capital structure can be evaluated by combining the profitability measurements of indifference point analysis with the financial risk measurements of financial leverage. The goal is to measure the EPS and the degree of financial leverage for a set of mutually exclusive capital structures at any given value of EBIT and to rank the desirability of the capital structure alternatives on the basis of these measurements. As explained below, however, the more profitable capital structures tend also to be the riskiest. The capital structure that is ultimately chosen must therefore contain, in the judgment of the corporation's financial managers, the combination of profitability and risk that is consistent with the firm's goal of increasing shareholder wealth. The example begun in the previous section is continued and provides an integrative example.

**Individual Capital Structures**

The risk-return characteristics of Alternatives *A* and *B* are shown graphically in Figure 15-3. The two graphs in the left portion of this figure represent Alternative *A*; the graphs on the right portion represent Alternative *B*.

For Alternative *A*, the top left graph contains values of financial leverage—as a measure of financial risk—computed by using Equation 5-10. The bottom left graph contains values of EPS—as a measure of return—computed by using Equation 5-4. Because EBIT appears on the horizontal axis of both graphs, it is possible to measure the risk-return characteristics of this alternative for any given value of EBIT. Since the coefficient of financial leverage is undefined at financial breakeven, the vertical broken line representing the financial break-even value of EBIT in the financial leverage graph corresponds to the horizontal intercept on the EBIT-EPS returns graph.

The risk-return coefficients for Alternative *A*, computed at different levels of EBIT, are as follows:

| EBIT | Financial Leverage | EPS |
|---|---|---|
| $ 4,000,000 | 2.85 | $0.28 |
| 8,000,000 | 1.48 | 1.08 |
| 12,000,000 | 1.28 | 1.88 |
| 16,000,000 | 1.19 | 2.68 |
| 18,000,000 | 1.17 | 3.08 |

As explained in Chapter 5, the coefficient of financial leverage decreases over increasing EBIT once the financial breakeven has been surpassed. The small coefficients of financial leverage for EBIT values of $12 million or more reflect the fact that financial breakeven occurs at the

**Figure 15-3.** **Individual Risk-Return Characteristics**

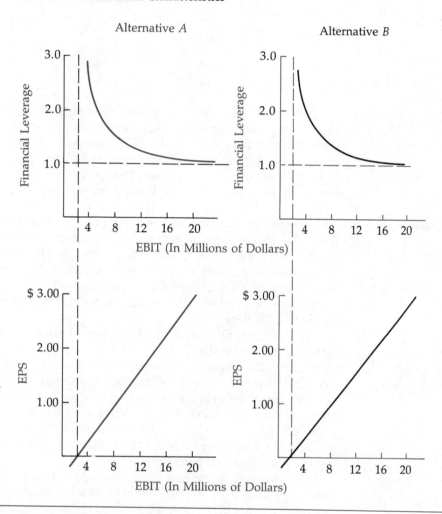

much smaller EBIT value of $2,600,000. Thus, once the corporation attains an EBIT level of $18 million, a 10 percent decrease from that value will decrease the $3.08 EPS by only 11.7 percent. The graphs for Alternative *A* thus indicate increasing profitability and decreasing financial risk over successively higher levels of EBIT.

The risk-return graphs for Alternative *B* are plotted in the same general manner as the graphs for Alternative *A*. Risk-return coefficients for selected values of EBIT for Alternative *B* are as follows:

| EBIT | Financial Leverage | EPS |
|---|---|---|
| $ 4,000,000 | 2.00 | $0.38 |
| 8,000,000 | 1.33 | 1.13 |
| 12,000,000 | 1.20 | 1.88 |
| 16,000,000 | 1.14 | 2.63 |
| 18,000,000 | 1.13 | 3.00 |

The small coefficients of financial leverage that occur when EBIT is equal to or greater than $12 million once again indicate that financial break-even occurs at the much smaller EBIT value of $2 million. If, for example, EBIT reaches $16 million, a 10 percent decrease from that level decreases the $2.63 EPS by only 11.4 percent. The graphs for Alternative B indicate increasing profitability and decreasing financial risk as EBIT increases.

**Comparing Capital Structures**

In order to compare the risk-return characteristics of the two alternatives, the four graphs of Figure 15-3 are combined into the two graphs contained in Figure 15-4. The top portion of Figure 15-4 contains the financial leverage plots for the two alternatives; the bottom portion contains the two EBIT-EPS plots. As in the previous figure, the vertical asymptotes of the financial leverages occur at the horizontal intercepts of the EBIT-EPS plots.

The comparative riskiness of the two alternatives can be evaluated by using the top portion of Figure 15-4. For all values of EBIT greater than $2,600,000, the larger of the two financial breakevens, Alternative A's financial leverage is always greater than that of Alternative B. In general, when the financial leverage coefficients of two alternative capital structures are compared, the alternative with the higher financial breakeven will always have larger coefficients for all levels of EBIT in excess of its financial breakeven. The plots of the two financial leverage coefficients do not intersect each other.

However, the *differential risk* between these two alternatives decreases with increasing EBIT because both graphs approach 1.0 as a limit. For example, when EBIT equals $4,000,000, the difference between the two financial leverage coefficients is 2.85 − 2.0 = .85. When EBIT equals $16 million, the difference is only 1.19 − 1.14 = .05. Thus, while Alternative A is riskier than Alternative B in terms of their financial leverage coefficients, these two alternatives become almost equally risky for values of EBIT equal to or greater than $16 million.

For values of EBIT less than $2,600,000, Alternative A's financial leverage is negative, indicating a negative EPS. Similarly, for values of EBIT less than $2 million, Alternative B's financial leverage and EPS are negative. Thus, the financial leverage graph rejects Alternative A for EBIT values less than $2,600,000 and rejects Alternative B for EBIT values less than $2,000,000.

The bottom portion of Figure 15-4 is used to compare the relative profitability of the two alternatives and is the same indifference point graph contained in Figure 15-1. Alternative *B* is preferable for EBIT values below the $11,600,000 indifference point; Alternative *A* is preferable for EBIT values in excess of the indifference point.

The comparative risk-return characteristics of the two alternatives can be summarized as follows:

1.  For values of EBIT greater than the $11,600,000 indifference point, Alternative *A* is more profitable but is also riskier than Alternative *B*.

2.  For values of EBIT from $2,000,000 to $11,600,000, Alternative *B* is more profitable and less risky than Alternative *A*.

3.  For values of EBIT less than $2,000,000, neither alternative is desirable.

**Figure 15-4.**      **Comparative Risk-Return Characteristics**

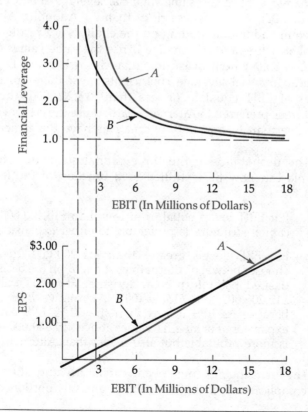

Given that the corporation has decided to expand by using either Alternative *A* or *B*, *the choice of capital structure thus depends on the level and stability of EBIT and the risk-return characteristics of the corporation.* If EBIT is forecast to remain below the $11,600,000 indifference point, Alternative *B* is superior to Alternative *A* in both risk and return. However, if EBIT is expected to be greater than the indifference point, Alternative *A* will be chosen if the financial managers conclude that the differential risk is more than offset by the higher EPS generated by Alternative *A*. If the corporation is substantially risk averse, Alternative *B* will be chosen on the basis of its lower financial risk and the differential EPS that would result from adopting Alternative *A* will be forgone.

**Ranking the Alternatives**

Under what conditions will the example corporation decide not to expand? From the standpoint of EPS, the existing capital structure is more profitable than either expansion alternative for values of EBIT equal to or less than $15,200,000. Above this value the corporation selects one of the expansion alternatives. From the standpoint of financial risk, is the current capital structure also more desirable for values of EBIT less than $15,200,000? The answer is yes because the current capital structure and Alternative *B* have the same financial leverage coefficients at any given level of EBIT, and *B* is less risky than *A*. Adopting Alternative *B* does not require additional trading on the equity. As a result, both the current capital structure and Alternative *B* use the same values of $I = \$2$ million and $E = \$0.0$ when measuring financial risk using Equation 5-10, and identical financial leverage coefficients must therefore result. Thus, for values of EBIT equal to or less than $15,200,000, the current capital structure is preferred to Alternative *B* because the current structure is more profitable than *B*, and both alternatives have the same degree of financial risk.

The desirability of the three capital structure alternatives in the example can now be identified as a function of the level and stability of EBIT:

1. For EBIT levels equal to or less than $15,200,000, the current capital structure is preferable to either expansion alternative.

2. For EBIT levels greater than $15,200,000, the corporation chooses between Alternatives *A* and *B* on the basis of the firm's desired risk-return characteristics. For EBIT values between $15,200,000 and $15,440,000, Alternative *B* is not desirable because its EPS is less than the $2.52 EPS earned without expansion. For all EBIT values above $15,440,000, Alternative *A* is more profitable but also riskier than Alternative *B*.

**Financing Mix Complications**

The financing mix contained in capital structure alternatives may cause two complications in the profitability analysis portion of the techniques explained above. First, if neither of two mutually exclusive financing alternatives involves floating common stock, then no EBIT-EPS indifference point will exist and the two alternatives will plot as parallel lines on an EBIT-EPS graph. Second, a given set of financing alternatives may combine to cause the EBIT-EPS indifference point to occur at a negative EPS value. In both of these situations, the capital structure alternative with the smaller financial breakeven is more profitable (or incurs a smaller loss) than the competing alternative over all values of EBIT. The financial risk portion of the analysis is unaffected.

**Example:**

A corporation's capital structure consists of 1 million shares of common stock. External capital of $10 million is to be raised. Alternative $C$ consists of floating 10 percent bonds, and Alternative $D$ involves floating 200,000 shares of preferred stock paying a $6 dividend per share. The EBIT-EPS indifference point is calculated by using Equation 15-3:

$$EPS_C = EPS_D$$

$$\frac{(Y - \$1,000,000)(1 - .4)}{1,000,000} = \frac{(Y)(1 - .4) - \$1,200,000}{1,000,000}$$

Multiplying both sides of this equation by 1,000,000 and simplifying yields:

$$.6Y - \$600,000 = .6Y - \$1,200,000$$

Or:

$$0 = -\$600,000$$

This inconsistent result indicates that no indifference point exists. The EBIT-EPS graphs for these two financing alternatives are contained in the left-hand portion of Figure 15-5. The two equations plot as parallel lines. Alternative $C$, having the lower financial breakeven, is more profitable or incurs a smaller loss than Alternative $D$ for each possible value of EBIT.

**Example:**

Assume that the same corporation rejects both Alternatives $C$ and $D$. Its capital structure still contains only 1 million shares of common stock, and it still requires $10 million of external financing. Two new financing alternatives are identified. Alternative $E$ sells 200,000 shares of common stock and $5 million of 9 percent bonds. Alternative $F$ sells 300,000 shares of common stock and 25,000 shares of preferred stock paying a $12 dividend per share. Using Equation 15-3, the EBIT-EPS indifference point occurs where:

$$EPS_E = EPS_F$$

$$\frac{(Y - \$450,000)(1 - .4)}{1,200,000} = \frac{(Y)(1 - .4) - \$300,000}{1,300,000}$$

Multiplying both sides of the equation by 1,000,000 and cross multiplying the resulting denominators:

$$(1.3)(Y - \$450,000)(1 - .4) = (1.2)(Y)(1 - .4) - (1.2)(\$300,000)$$
$$.78Y - \$351,000 = .72Y - \$360,000$$
$$.06Y = -\$9,000$$
$$Y = -\$150,000$$

The indifference point occurs at a negative value of EBIT. The EBIT-EPS graph of the two alternatives is contained in the right-hand portion of Figure 15-5. For all values of EBIT, Alternative $E$ with the lower financial breakeven is more profitable or incurs a smaller loss than Alternative $F$.

**Figure 15-5.**  **EBIT-EPS Graphs for Capital Structure Alternatives**

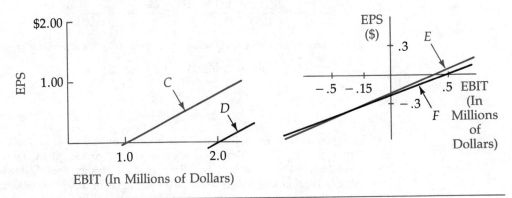

EPS

EBIT (In Millions of Dollars)

## ADVANTAGES AND LIMITATIONS
## OF CAPITAL STRUCTURE
## PLANNING TECHNIQUES

The advantages in using the capital structure planning techniques explained in this chapter are:

1.  They focus directly on corporate EBIT and EPS, the income statement variables directly involved in evaluating the impact of capital structure decisions.

2.  They allow for explicit risk-return measurements for each value of EBIT.

3.  The measure of returns — EPS — is the single most widely used corporate profitability ratio.

4.  Financial leverage provides a useful measure of financial risk because its coefficient is affected by both the choice of capital structure and the level of EBIT.

5.  Indifference point analysis allows for unambiguous profitability rankings between mutually exclusive alternatives.

The limitations of these techniques are as follows:

1.  The risk-return measurements do not relate capital structure decisions directly to the corporate goal of shareholder wealth maximization. The impact is traced only as far as EPS, but shareholder returns are realized from dividends and price appreciation of common stock.

2.  The financial leverage coefficient does not measure the probability that a particular level of EBIT will be attained.

3.  The techniques do not relate capital structure decisions directly to firm value as was done in Chapter 14. The best that can be said is that the risk-return measurements help determine the discount rates which, in turn, determine firm value.

# SUMMARY

This chapter has presented a set of capital structure planning techniques. The fundamental concept is that capital structure decisions are made on the basis of the risk-return characteristics contained in each financing alternative.

The capital structure planning techniques contained in this chapter use the following assumptions: business and financial risks are not held constant, external financing is needed, and the firm's capital structure is allowed to vary both in total value and in percentage composition. EPS is specified as a measure of returns, and financial leverage is specified as a measure of financial risk.

Indifference point analysis is used to rank mutually exclusive capital structure alternatives according to profitability. Financial leverage coefficients are used to compare the relative riskiness of competing alternatives. When combined, indifference point analysis and financial leverage coefficients allow a financial manager to rank the desirability of capital structure alternatives according to their risk-return characteristics and to do so over various levels of EBIT. In this type of analysis, the level and stability of EBIT become major determinants in identifying a desired external financing mix. There are major advantages and limitations in using these techniques as part of capital structure planning.

# QUESTIONS

**15-1.** Identify the two major components of capital structure decisions.

**15-2.** Why is the coefficient of financial leverage used as a measure of risk in evaluating financing alternatives?

**15-3.** Why is the sale of preferred stock and/or bonds considered to be a form of trading on the equity?

**15-4.** Under what conditions does external financing increase financial risk?

**15-5.** What is the purpose of indifference point analysis?

**15-6.** What are the three basic steps in performing an indifference point analysis?

**15-7.** Capital Structure $E$ has a financial breakeven of $3,000,000, and Capital Structure $F$ has a financial breakeven of $3,750,000. For an EBIT value of $4,000,000, which alternative has the smaller coefficient of financial leverage? Why?

**15-8.** Capital Structure $G$ has a financial breakeven of $1 million, and Capital Structure $H$ has a financial breakeven of $2 million. The EPS-EBIT indifference point occurs at $3,400,000. Compare the risk-return characteristics of these alternatives for an EBIT value of $3 million. Compare the same characteristics when EBIT equals $4 million.

**15-9.** Under what conditions will two capital structure alternatives not have an EBIT-EPS indifference point?

**15-10.** What are the advantages and limitations of using indifference point analysis as a capital structure planning technique?

**15-11.** What are the advantages and limitations of using financial leverage as a capital structure planning technique?

# PROBLEMS

*Note:* Assume a constant tax rate of 40% in these problems.

15-1.  A corporation's capital structure contains the following: $5 million of 8% bonds, $8 million of 10% bonds, 12,000 preferred shares paying a $7 per share dividend, and 425,000 shares of common stock. What is the EBIT-EPS equation for this corporation?

15-2.  Compute the financial breakeven for the data contained in Problem 15-1.

15-3.  A corporation's capital structure consists of 500,000 shares of common stock. It requires $10 million of external financing. Alternative A requires that 200,000 shares of common stock be sold. Alternative B requires that $10,000,000 of 12% bonds be sold.

a.  Compute the financial breakeven if Alternative A is adopted.
b.  What is the EPS-EBIT equation if Alternative A is chosen?
c.  Compute the financial breakeven if Alternative B is adopted.
d.  What is the EPS-EBIT equation if Alternative B is chosen?
e.  Compute the EBIT-EPS indifference point.
f.  Rank the alternatives according to EPS over varying levels of EBIT.

15-4.  A corporate capital structure contains the following external financing: $25,000,000 of 11% bonds, 100,000 shares of preferred stock paying an $11.22 per share dividend, and 900,000 shares of common stock. What value of EBIT is required in order to earn an EPS of $0.90?

15-5.  A corporation's current capital structure contains 800,000 shares of common stock and 120,000 shares of preferred stock paying a $4 per share dividend. The firm's current EBIT is $6,200,000 and the corresponding EPS equals $4.05. EBIT is not expected to increase unless $4 million of external financing is obtained. Two financing alternatives are identified. Alternative A consists of floating 100,000 shares of common stock. Alternative B sells $4 million of 10% debt.

a.  Compute the financial breakevens that result from adopting the alternative financing plans.
b.  Compute the EPS-EBIT indifference point.
c.  Identify the EPS-maximizing alternative for all levels of EBIT. *Remember*, there are three alternatives open to the corporation.
d.  Evaluate the financial risk contained in each of the three alternatives as measured by their coefficients of financial leverage.
e.  Evaluate the alternative capital structures on the basis of their combined risk-return characteristics over different values of EBIT.

15-6.  A corporation has decided to raise external capital. Two alternative financing plans have been proposed. The corporation's capital structure, if it accepts Alternative C, would consist of $15,000,000 of 11% debt and 5 million shares of common. If Alternative D is accepted, the resulting capital structure would consist of 300,000 shares of preferred stock paying $5 dividend per share and 5 million shares of common stock. Evaluate the risk-return characteristics of these two mutually exclusive capital structures.

# SELECTED REFERENCES

Ghandi, J. "On the Measurement of Leverage." *Journal of Finance*, Vol. 21, No. 5 (December, 1966).

Levy, H., and M. Sarnatt. *Capital Investment and Financial Decisions*. 2d ed. Englewood Cliffs, N.J.: Prentice-Hall International, 1982.

Masulis, R. "The Impact of Capital Structure Change on Firm Value: Some Estimates." *Journal of Finance*, Vol. 38, No. 1 (March, 1983).

Oswald, B., J. Martin, and D. Scott. *Guide to Financial Analysis*. New York: McGraw-Hill Book Company, 1980.

Peterson, P., and G. Benesh. "A Reexamination of the Empirical Relationship between Investment and Financing Decisions." *Journal of Financial and Quantitative Analysis*, Vol. 18, No. 4 (December, 1983).

Pinches, G. *Essentials of Financial Management*. New York: Harper & Row, Publishers, 1984.

Scott, D. "Evidence on the Importance of Financial Structure." *Financial Management*, Vol. 1, No. 2 (Summer, 1982).

Shalit, S. "On the Mathematics of Leverage." *Financial Management*, Vol. 4, No. 1 (Spring, 1975).

Viscione, J. *Financial Analysis: Principles and Procedures*. Boston, Mass.: Houghton Mifflin Company, 1977.

# PART 6

# Capital Asset Pricing
# and
# Managerial Finance

The two chapters that make up Part 6 of this text present an introduction to what is called the modern theory of finance. This theory is often referred to as capital asset pricing theory.

Chapter 16 contains a mix of statistical and investment theory that forms the underpinnings of capital asset pricing. A thorough appreciation of the applications to managerial finance, contained in Chapter 17, requires that the concepts of Chapter 16 be well understood. In particular, attention should be focused on the concepts, measurements, and implications of systematic risk and security market lines.

Chapter 17 contains some applications of capital asset pricing to managerial finance. The first section briefly reviews the implications of the model developed in Chapter 16 that will be used here. The second section explains how this theory can be used to estimate capital-budgeting discount rates and also explains the implications for corporate cost of capital. The third section explains the implications of this theory for the existence of an optimal capital structure and goes on to modify the conclusions when corporate debt becomes risky.

# CHAPTER 16

# Risk, Return,
# and
# Financial Asset Portfolios

This chapter presents a set of investor oriented techniques for evaluating the desirability of investing in financial assets under conditions of risk and taking into account the impact that the proposed investments will have on the investor's overall risk and return. It may appear at first glance that the focus on corporate financial management has been put aside, but this is not the case. As was explained in Chapter 13, the market value of a firm's debt and equity securities is affected by investor decisions to buy and sell these assets. The valuation procedures used by investors provide financial managers with guidelines with which to make capital-budgeting and capital structure decisions. The two chapters in this section thus provide a direct link between financial decision making and the resulting impact on firm value when investors take risk into account.

The first section of this chapter specifies the rules of investor behavior and explains the statistical surrogates that investors are assumed to use in measuring the risk and return properties of financial assets. This is followed by two sections that explain how to compute statistical risk and return measures for individual financial assets and for portfolios of financial assets. As defined in Chapter 12, a portfolio is simply a set of investments. The *fourth section illustrates similar concepts for stock indexes. The fifth section develops a fundamental market model that forms the basis for the managerial decision-making procedures contained in Chapter 17. The appendix to this chapter contains additional material in the area of portfolio construction and evaluation.*

## INVESTOR BEHAVIOR

Purchasing the debt and equity securities of a corporation forces investors to accept risk because the rates of return eventually realized from such investments are not known with certainty. This concept of risk and the statistical decision rules investors follow are extensions of the ideas first introduced in Chapter 12. Investors are assumed to use the following rules in making investment decisions:

1. Investors are interested only in the expected rate of return of an investment and its associated risk. No other factors are relevant.

2. The expected rate of return of a financial asset or of a portfolio is measured by computing its expected value using either historical rate of return data or probability distributions of rates of return. Risk is measured by computing the variance or standard deviation of the rate of return of the financial asset or portfolio using either historical or probability distribution rate of return data.

3. Investors are risk averse. For a given amount of risk, a higher rate of return is preferred to a lower one. For a given rate of return, an investor prefers less risk rather than more.

These rules use rates of return rather than dollars of net present value, and these rates are interpreted to mean the rate of return per dollar invested. These rules thus do not depend on the amounts of cash available to each investor. In addition, using rates of return simplifies the calculations needed to measure the risk and return characteristics of portfolios.

# RISK AND RETURN: INDIVIDUAL FINANCIAL ASSETS

In order to measure a financial asset's risk and return, it is first necessary to specify the investment time horizon and the types of payments the investment generates. Financial assets are assumed in this model to be purchased at a point in time, held for one year, and sold. The initial cash outlay consists of the purchase price. The cash payments received by the investor consist of the selling price and dividends or interest received while owning the financial asset. While dividend and interest payments can be received at any time, they are assumed to occur at the end of the year.

**Holding Period Yields**

The **holding period yield** (HPY) of a financial asset is defined as the rate of return realized from owning the asset for one year. A financial asset's HPY can be interpreted to be the discount rate that equates future payments with the purchase price and is thus the investment's internal rate of return.

Using the symbols from Chapter 13, the HPY for a stock can be expressed as follows. Let:

$$P_t = \text{purchase price at Time } t$$
$$P_{t+1} = \text{selling price at Time } t + 1$$
$$D = \text{dividends received while owning the stock}$$
$$r = \text{HPY}$$

The HPY discounts the future payments $(P_{t+1} + D)$ and makes them equal to the purchase price, $P_t$. Symbolically:

$$P_t = \frac{P_{t+1} + D}{1 + r} \tag{16-1}$$

Solving Equation 16-1 for $r$ provides the following measurement equation for a stock HPY.

$$r = \frac{P_{t+1} - P_t + D}{P_t} \tag{16-2}$$

A slightly different equation is used to measure bond HPYs. Let $I$ = interest received while owning the bond. Then bond HPYs are computed using:

$$r = \frac{P_{t+1} - P_t + I}{P_t}$$ (16-3)

HPYs are computed on a before-tax basis. The following examples show that HPYs can be positive, zero, or negative.

---

**Example:** An investor purchases common stock for $82 per share, receives a per share dividend payment of $3, and sells the stock for $87 per share after owning the securities for one year. The stock's HPY is computed using Equation 16-2:

$$r = \frac{\$87 - \$82 + \$3}{\$82}$$

$$r = .0976 \quad \text{or} \quad 9.76\%$$

If the selling price for this stock were $79 per share, its HPY would then be:

$$r = \frac{\$79 - \$82 + \$3}{\$82}$$

$$r = 0.0$$

**Example:** A $5,000 bond with a 7 percent coupon is bought for 102 and held for one year. The interest payment is received and the bond is sold for 91. What is the HPY for this investment? The dollar amounts that go into Equation 16-3 are computed as follows:

$$P_t = (1.02)\,(\$5,000)$$
$$= \$5,100$$

$$I = (.07)\,(\$5,000)$$
$$= \$350$$

$$P_{t+1} = (.91)\,(\$5,000)$$
$$= \$4,550$$

The bond HPY is then:

$$r = \frac{\$4,550 - \$5,100 + \$350}{\$5,100}$$

$$r = -.0392 \quad \text{or} \quad -3.92\%$$

---

**Forecasting Holding Period Yields**      Since future HPYs are not known with certainty, investors face the problem of forecasting or estimating the eventual yields of financial assets. The problem is one of estimating the **expected rate of return of a financial**

**asset** — the HPY that is expected to result from owning a financial asset for one year. One approach to this problem is to estimate the probability distribution of future HPYs. For example, the probability distribution of a particular financial asset might be estimated as follows:

| Possible HPY | Probability |
|:---:|:---:|
| −.1 | .1 |
| 0.0 | .2 |
| .1 | .4 |
| .2 | .3 |

The expected value and standard deviation of this probability distribution can be computed by using the techniques contained in Chapter 12. However, the investor is faced with the larger problem of generating the probability distribution. This requires that each possible future HPY be specified along with the probability of that HPY occurring.

A solution to the problem of generating HPY probability distributions is to use the historical time series of the financial asset's HPYs. In doing so, the assumption is made that historical HPYs are a useful guide to a financial asset's future HPY. Given that this assumption is reasonable, the mean and standard deviation of the historical HPYs are used as estimates of the expected value and standard deviation that would otherwise have to be computed from the financial asset's probability distribution.

**Calculating HPY Statistics**

Calculating the mean and standard deviation statistics from historical HPY data requires three equations. The variables used in these equations are:

$$HPY_t = \text{HPY for Year } t$$

$$\overline{HPY} = \text{mean HPY}$$

$$\sigma^2 = \text{HPY variance}$$

$$\sigma = \text{HPY standard deviation}$$

$$N = \text{number of HPYs}$$

Then:

$$\overline{HPY} = \frac{\sum_t HPY_t}{N} \tag{16-4}$$

$$\sigma^2 = \frac{\sum_t (HPY_t - \overline{HPY})^2}{N} \tag{16-5}$$

$$\sigma = \sqrt{\sigma^2} \tag{16-6}$$

**Example:**   Table 16-1 illustrates the statistical computations using time series data for a hypothetical financial asset. A stock is used in this example; bonds follow a similar format but use Equation 16-3 rather than Equation 16-2. The first three columns contain the time series data. End-of-year prices are used. The dividends are paid during the year. The HPYs for each year, listed in Column 4, are computed using Equation 16-2.

Note that the HPY computation for the first year, 1980, requires the 1979 end-of-year price. The sum of the HPYs is .4995. The mean HPY is calculated using Equation 16-4:

$$\overline{HPY} = .4995/5$$
$$= .0999 \quad \text{or} \quad 9.99\%$$

**Table 16-1.**   **Mean and Standard Deviation Calculations Using Historical HPY Data**

| End of Year | Price | Dividend | $HPY_t$ | $(HPY_t - \overline{HPY})$ | $(HPY_t - \overline{HPY})^2$ |
|---|---|---|---|---|---|
| 1979 | $21 | | | | |
| 1980 | 19 | $1.00 | −.0476 | −.1475 | .0218 |
| 1981 | 18 | 1.00 | .0 | −.0999 | .0099 |
| 1982 | 21 | 1.05 | .2250 | .1251 | .0157 |
| 1983 | 24 | 1.05 | .1929 | .0930 | .0086 |
| 1984 | 26 | 1.10 | .1292 | .0293 | .0009 |
| | | | .4995 | | .0569 |

Calculating the variance begins by subtracting the $\overline{HPY}$ from each $HPY_t$. These deviations are contained in Column 5. Each deviation is then squared (these values are in Column 6). The sum of the squared deviations is .0569. The variance is computed using Equation 16-5:

$$\sigma^2 = .0569/5$$
$$= .0114$$

The standard deviation is computed using Equation 16-6:

$$\sigma = \sqrt{.0114}$$
$$= .1067 \quad \text{or} \quad 10.67\%$$

For this hypothetical financial asset, the estimated mean HPY is .0999; its corresponding standard deviation is .1067

**Mutually
Exclusive
Financial
Assets**

Financial asset HPY statistics can often be used to rank the desirability of mutually exclusive investment alternatives. Such rankings must be consistent with the three rules of investor behavior described earlier. This consistency is obtained by restating the third rule as follows:

> If two financial assets have the same mean HPY, the asset with the lesser standard deviation will be preferred. If two financial assets have equal standard deviations, the asset with the greater mean HPY will be preferred.

Although this rule provides a very specific ranking procedure, the following examples demonstrate that it does not work in all situations.

---

**Example:**

Financial Assets $A$ and $B$ are mutually exclusive. Their statistics are computed as follows:

|  | $A$ | $B$ |
|---|---|---|
| Mean HPY | .14 | .14 |
| Standard deviation | .30 | .40 |

Alternative $A$ is preferred to $B$. They have equal HPYs, but $A$'s standard deviation is less than $B$'s.

**Example:**

Financial Assets $C$ and $D$ are mutually exclusive and have the following statistics:

|  | $C$ | $D$ |
|---|---|---|
| Mean HPY | .16 | .18 |
| Standard deviation | .50 | .50 |

Alternative $D$ is preferred to $C$. These assets have equal standard deviations, but $D$ has the larger $\overline{\text{HPY}}$.

**Example:**

Assume that an investor wants to rank alternatives $A$ and $D$ that were preferred in the previous examples. The statistics are:

|  | $A$ | $D$ |
|---|---|---|
| Mean HPY | .14 | .18 |
| Standard deviation | .30 | .50 |

The rules of investor behavior cannot rank these alternatives. $D$'s $\overline{\text{HPY}}$ and standard deviation are both higher than $A$'s. In other words, $D$ has a higher expected rate of return than $A$ but is also riskier. In this case, investors' rankings depend on the extent to which the investors considered themselves to be risk averse. Investors can be expected to differ in their rankings.

---

It might appear from this set of examples that the rules of investor behavior have a very limited usefulness. It turns out, however, that the statistical tools explained below greatly increase the applicability of these rules. This section has provided a necessary first step to what follows.

# RISK AND RETURN: FINANCIAL ASSET PORTFOLIOS

This chapter has so far focused on the risk-return characteristics of individual financial assets. In practice, however, investor portfolios contain more than one financial asset at any time. This practice raises the following two fundamental questions and the appropriate answer for each:

1. Why do investors prefer holding portfolios of financial assets rather than investing all their funds in one desirable financial asset? Because portfolios can be constructed so as to produce risk and return characteristics that are superior to those of individual financial assets.

2. How are portfolio statistical risk and return measurements obtained? By using extensions of the HPY mean and standard deviation statistics discussed above.

Demonstrating the superiority of portfolios over individual financial assets is accomplished by using the mean HPYs and standard deviations of portfolios. In order to compute these statistics, the historical HPYs of financial assets are again assumed to be useful guides to future HPYs.

**Portfolio Returns**

The **expected rate of return of a financial asset portfolio** is the HPY that is expected to result from owning the portfolio for one year. Computing this rate of return requires that the HPY of each financial asset be known along with the percentage of the portfolio invested in each financial asset. Let:

$X_i$ = percentage of the portfolio invested in Financial Asset $i$

$\overline{HPY}_i$ = mean HPY for Asset $i$

$R_p$ = expected rate of return of the portfolio

Then:

$$R_p = \sum_i (X_i)(\overline{HPY}_i) \qquad (16\text{-}7)$$

In using Equation 16-7, the sum of the $X_i$s must equal 1.0.

---

**Example:**   A portfolio is to be constructed by investing $100,000 in three financial assets. The dollar amount committed to each asset, the resulting $X_i$ values, and the assumed historical $\overline{HPY}_i$ are as follows:

| Financial Asset | Dollar Investment | $X_i$ | $\overline{HPY}_i$ |
|---|---|---|---|
| 1 | $20,000 | .2 | .09 |
| 2 | 30,000 | .3 | .11 |
| 3 | 50,000 | .5 | .14 |

Using Equation 16-7, the expected rate of return for the portfolio is:

$$R_p = (.2)(.09) + (.3)(.11) + (.5)(.14)$$

$$= .121 \text{ or } 12.1\%$$

---

**Portfolio Risk**      The risk contained in a portfolio is measured by computing its standard deviation. The following three types of data are needed in order to compute this statistic:

1. The values for each $X_i$

2. The HPY variance for each asset

3. The covariance for each pair of financial assets in the portfolio

This third item can be explained with the use of Figure 16-1 and the following data. The HPY time series for two financial assets are recorded over a period of five years. Let:

$$HPY_{it} = \text{the HPY that occurs in Year } t \text{ for Asset } i$$

The time series are:

| Year | $HPY_{1t}$ | $HPY_{2t}$ | $R_{pt}$ |
|---|---|---|---|
| 1 | .14 | .07 | .105 |
| 2 | .09 | .12 | .105 |
| 3 | .12 | .06 | .09 |
| 4 | .04 | .10 | .07 |
| 5 | .11 | .05 | .08 |
| $\overline{HPY}_i$ | .10 | .08 | |

A portfolio consisting of equal amounts of these securities ($X_1 = X_2 = .5$) would generate the yearly returns shown in the $R_{pt}$ column (the rate of return of the portfolio for Year $t$). These three time series are plotted in Figure 16-1.

When the graphs of Assets 1 and 2 are compared, there appears to be a tendency for the HPY of Asset 2 to decrease when Asset 1's HPY increases, and vice versa. This interaction between the two securities produces a stable $R_{pt}$ time series even though the individual asset HPYs undergo large year-to-year changes. This interaction also affects the portfolio standard deviation and must be explicitly measured; the statistic used for this purpose is called the covariance. In general, **covariance** is a measure of the degree to which two variables move together. In measuring portfolio risk the covariance between two financial assets measures the extent to which the two HPY time series move, interact, or "co-vary" together.

| Figure 16-1. | **HPY Time Series** |

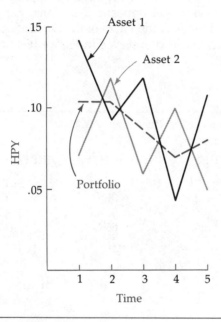

COMPUTING COVARIANCES. Let $\sigma_{ij}$ represent the covariance between Financial Assets $i$ and $j$, and let $N$ equal the number of paired observations of HPYs for the two assets. Then the covariance between these two securities using historical data is computed from:

$$\sigma_{ij} = \sum_t (\text{HPY}_{it} - \overline{\text{HPY}_i})(\text{HPY}_{jt} - \overline{\text{HPY}_j})/N \qquad \text{(16-8)}$$

| Example: | The top portion of Table 16-2 illustrates the use of Equation 16-8 in computing a covariance. The HPYs for these two financial assets are the same ones plotted in Figure 16-1. As a first step, the mean HPY is computed for each asset. Then in |

Column 4 the mean HPY for Asset 1 is subtracted from each of its historical HPYs. Column 5 contains similar calculations for Asset 2. The mean deviations in Columns 4 and 5 are multiplied, and the products are entered in Column 6.

The sum of the items in Column 6 is −.0027. This value is the numerator of Equation 16-8. Using this equation, $\sigma_{ij}$ equals:

$$\sigma_{ij} = -.0027/5$$

$$= -.0005$$

A positive covariance indicates that the values of two variables tend to increase and decrease together. A negative covariance indicates that the two variables tend to move in opposite directions. For the example discussed above, the tendency of the HPYs of the two financial assets to move in opposite directions that was observed in Figure 16-1 is confirmed by the negative covariance.

**Table 16-2.**   **Covariance Calculations Using Historical HPY Data**

| End of Year | $HPY_{1t}$ | $HPY_{2t}$ | $(HPY_{1t} - \overline{HPY_1})$ | $(HPY_{2t} - \overline{HPY_2})$ | Product |
|---|---|---|---|---|---|
| 1 | .14 | .07 | .04 | −.01 | −.0004 |
| 2 | .09 | .12 | −.01 | .04 | −.0004 |
| 3 | .12 | .06 | .02 | −.02 | −.0004 |
| 4 | .04 | .10 | −.06 | .02 | −.0012 |
| 5 | .11 | .05 | .01 | −.03 | −.0003 |
| $\overline{HPY_i}$ | .10 | .08 | | | $\Sigma = -.0027$ |

| | $(HPY_{1t} - \overline{HPY_1})^2$ | $(HPY_{2t} - \overline{HPY_2})^2$ |
|---|---|---|
| | .0016 | .0001 |
| | .0001 | .0016 |
| | .0004 | .0004 |
| | .0036 | .0004 |
| | .0001 | .0009 |
| | $\Sigma = .0058$ | $\Sigma = .0034$ |

**PORTFOLIO STANDARD DEVIATION.** Calculating the variance and standard deviation of a portfolio that consists of two financial assets proceeds as follows. Let:

$$\sigma_i^2 = \text{variance of Security } i$$
$$\sigma_p^2 = \text{portfolio variance}$$
$$\sigma_p = \sqrt{\sigma_p^2} \text{ the portfolio standard deviation}$$

Then:

$$\sigma_p^2 = X_1^2\sigma_1^2 + X_2^2\sigma_2^2 + 2X_1 X_2\sigma_{12} \qquad (16\text{-}9)$$

The chapter appendix explains how to compute $\sigma_p^2$ and $\sigma_p$ when more than two financial assets are involved.

---

**Example:**   Equation 16-9 is illustrated by using the data for the two financial assets contained in Table 16-2. Since the variance of each asset is required, these intermediate calculations are shown in the bottom portion of Table 16-2. The variance of each asset is calculated by using Equation 16-5:

$$\sigma_1^2 = .0058/5 \qquad\qquad \sigma_2^2 = .0034/5$$

$$= .0012 \qquad\qquad\qquad = .0007$$

Using Equation 16-9, the portfolio variance when $X_1$ equals .5 and $X_2$ equals .5 is:

$$\sigma_p^2 = .5^2(.0012) + .5^2(.0007) + 2(.5)(.5)(-.0005)$$

$$= .0002$$

The computed variance is .000225, but only four digits are kept to the right of the decimal point since four digits are used in the variance equation.
   The portfolio standard deviation is:

$$\sigma_p = \sqrt{.0002}$$

$$= .0141$$

---

Changing the portfolio composition can produce new values for the portfolio variance and standard deviation even though the covariance is unchanged.

---

**Example:**   Using the above data set, let $X_1$ equal .3 and $X_2$ equal .7. The resulting $\sigma_p^2$ and $\sigma_p$ values are:

$$\sigma_p^2 = .3^2(.0012) + .7^2(.0007) + 2(.3)(.7)(-.0005)$$

$$= .0002$$

$$\sigma_p = \sqrt{.0002}$$

$$= .0141$$

Similarly, if $X_1$ equals .7 and $X_2$ equals .3:

$$\sigma_p^2 = .7^2(.0012) + .3^2(.0007) + 2(.7)(.3)(-.0005)$$

$$= .0004$$

$$\sigma_p = \sqrt{.0004}$$

$$= .0210$$

**RANKING PORTFOLIOS.** The three rules of investor behavior stated earlier can be used to rank portfolios according to their risk-return characteristics.

**Example:**

Table 16-3 contains the rates of return and standard deviations of five portfolios. These values are based on the Table 16-2 data and the standard deviations computed in the previous section.

The $R_p$ values in Table 16-3 were computed using Equation 16-7. Take a moment and verify these values. Portfolios $A$ and $B$ contain only one financial asset. Their $\sigma_p$ values are the square roots of the individual $\sigma_i^2$ values.

In terms of comparative risk and return, Portfolio $A$ has the highest $R_p$ and the highest $\sigma_p$. Portfolios $D$ and $E$ have the lowest $\sigma_p$; $D$ is preferred to $E$ on the basis of its higher $R_p$. Portfolios $C$, $D$, and $E$ are preferred over $B$. Each of these portfolios has a higher $R_p$ and a lower $\sigma_p$ than does Portfolio $B$.

As a result of these rankings, Portfolios $B$ and $E$ are judged not desirable because better portfolios are available. Of the three remaining portfolios, $A$ displays the highest, and $D$ the lowest risk-return characteristics. In addition, Portfolio $C$ falls between $A$ and $D$ in terms of risk and return.

**Table 16-3.**   **Portfolio Rates of Return and Standard Deviations**

| Portfolio | $X_1$ | $X_2$ | $R_p$ | $\sigma_p$ |
|---|---|---|---|---|
| A | 1.0 | .0 | .100 | .0346 |
| B | .0 | 1.0 | .080 | .0265 |
| C | .7 | .3 | .094 | .0210 |
| D | .5 | .5 | .090 | .0141 |
| E | .3 | .7 | .086 | .0141 |

The above example identified Portfolios $A$, $C$, and $D$ as meeting the rules of investor behavior. Portfolio $A$ will be desirable to investors who wish to maximize their rates of return if the accompanying risk is acceptable. Portfolio $D$ is desirable when risk is to be minimized. Note, however, that the three portfolios that contain both financial assets (Portfolios $C$, $D$, and $E$) all have a portfolio standard deviation that is lower than the portfolios that contain only one financial asset (Portfolios $A$ and $B$). This happened because of the negative covariance ($\sigma_{12} = -.0005$). The ability to find financial assets with covariances that are negative, or close to zero when positive, produces portfolios with standard deviations that are lower than the standard deviations of the individual assets. *This is why owning a portfolio consisting of several financial assets is preferable to owning only one financial asset.*

**Covariance and Correlation**

Although covariances are used to compute portfolio standard deviations, the covariances themselves are difficult to interpret because they can assume an unlimited range of values. This complicates the task of evaluating the relative importance of financial asset interactions within a portfolio. Fortunately every covariance has a *coefficient of correlation* that does not contain these limitations. In addition, correlation coefficients can be computed directly from covariances. Let:

$C_{ij}$ = coefficient of correlation between Financial Assets $i$ and $j$

Then:

$$C_{ij} = \frac{\sigma_{ij}}{(\sigma_i)(\sigma_j)} \tag{16-10}$$

**Example:**

The following statistics were computed in the previous section:

$$\sigma_1 = .0346; \qquad \sigma_2 = .0265; \qquad \sigma_{12} = -.0005$$

Using Equation 16-10:

$$C_{12} = \frac{-.0005}{(.0346)(.0265)}$$

$$= \frac{-.0005}{.00092}$$

$$= -.54$$

**Correlation**, like covariance, measures the extent to which two variables move together through time. These two statistics carry the same algebraic sign. However, the range of a correlation coefficient is from plus one to minus one. This short range simplifies the interpretations of the coefficient. The data sets in Table 16-4 and the corresponding scatter diagrams in Figure 16-2 explain how correlation coefficients are interpreted. Table 16-4 contains the HPY time series for six financial assets. The HPYs of the first two financial assets in this table, $A$ and $B$, are plotted in the first portion of Figure 16-2. Asset $A$'s HPYs are plotted along the vertical axis; $B$'s HYPs are plotted along the horizontal axis. Each point in this graph thus

**Table 16-4.**   HPY Time Series for Six Financial Assets

| End of Year | HPY A | HPY B | HPY C | HPY D | HPY E | HPY F |
|---|---|---|---|---|---|---|
| 1 | .25 | .50 | .10 | −.05 | .30 | .0 |
| 2 | .30 | .60 | −.06 | .03 | .40 | .20 |
| 3 | .10 | .20 | .14 | −.07 | .50 | −.10 |
| 4 | −.15 | −.30 | .20 | −.10 | .40 | −.20 |
| 5 | −.05 | −.10 | .08 | −.04 | .20 | .10 |
| 6 | .20 | .40 | .0 | .0 | .10 | −.30 |

represents a paired set of HPY values. It is possible to draw a straight line—a line with a constant slope—that goes through all six points. This indicates perfect correlation between the HYPs of Assets A and B. The straight line has a positive slope with respect to the horizontal axis; this indicates positive correlation. The HPYs for Assets A and B thus have a correlation coefficient of +1.0; they are said to be perfectly positively correlated.

Perfect positive correlation means two things. First, Asset B's HPYs always change in the same direction as A's, and vice versa. Second, A and B change by a constant and entirely predictable amount *in relation to each other*. In this example, B's HPY is always twice that of A's.

The second portion of Figure 16-2 plots the paired HPY values of Financial Assets C and D contained in Table 16-4. Perfect correlation is once again observed because it is possible to draw a straight line through all six points. In this case, however, the correlation is negative because of the negative slope of the straight line: Financial Assets C and D are said to be perfectly negatively correlated; they have a correlation coefficient of −1.0. This means that the HPY of C and D always change in opposite directions and by a constant amount *in relation to each other*. For this set of financial assets, Asset D's HPY is always equal to −.5 times C's HPY.

The third portion of Figure 16-2 plots the paired HPY's of Financial Assets E and F that are contained in Table 16-4. For these two assets, it is not possible to draw a straight line through all six points; thus, the correlation between these two assets is not perfect. In addition, it is not obvious from this figure whether the correlation is positive or negative. The correlation coefficient is actually +.25. This coefficient means that the HPYs of E and F demonstrate some tendency to change in the same direction, but the relative changes between these two assets are not constant and cannot be predicted with certainty. The dashed line for this scatter diagram approximates the relationship between Assets E and F. The line has a positive slope because of the positive correlation between the two financial

**Figure 16-2.** **Scatter Diagrams for the Table 16-4 Financial Assets**

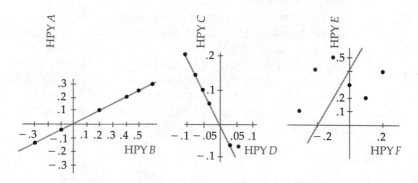

assets. (The end-of-chapter problems ask you to verify these three correlation coefficients by computing their values.)

From the standpoint of minimizing portfolio risk, investors should seek financial assets that are negatively correlated with each other. The closer the correlation is to −1.0, the smaller is the resulting portfolio standard deviation. If two securities have a −1.0 correlation, then one of the portfolios that can be formed using different percentages of these securities will have a standard deviation of zero. This can be looked upon as the ultimate in risk minimization. The portfolio that produces the zero standard deviation will have a constant rate of return. At the opposite extreme, no risk reduction will be possible if two securities have a +1.0 correlation. The smallest portfolio standard deviation obtainable from two securities with a +1.0 correlation occurs when the portfolio consists of only the security with the smaller standard deviation. In actual practice correlations between financial asset HPYs are positive; negative correlations (and thus negative covariances) are seldom found. Minimizing portfolio risk is thus accomplished by combining financial assets having correlations that are positive but low. The chapter appendix explains how to compute portfolio variances using correlations in the place of covariances.

**Diversification and Risk Reduction**

The equation used to measure portfolio variance, Equation 16-9, summarizes the major points concerning the variance (and standard deviation) of a two-security portfolio. First, $\sigma_p^2$ depends on the $X_i$ values. Second, $\sigma_p^2$ can be reduced by finding financial assets with covariances (and therefore with correlations) that are as low as possible. Now consider the following question: What happens to $\sigma_p^2$ if additional securities are added to the portfolio? First, the $\sigma_p^2$ *equation* becomes longer, but no new statistical concepts are introduced (see the appendix to this chapter). Second, the *value* of $\sigma_p^2$ will decrease but only within certain limits. Does doubling the number of securities in the portfolio reduce its variance by 50 percent? In general, the answer is no.

Increasing the number of financial assets in a portfolio is referred to as **diversification**. The impact of diversification on portfolio standard deviation is illustrated by Figure 16-3. This figure assumes that the $X_i$ values are equal within each portfolio. For example, a five-asset portfolio has $X_i$ equal to .2, a ten-asset portfolio has $X_i$ equal to .1, and so on. As additional financial assets are added to the portfolio, Figure 16-3 indicates that $\sigma_p$ decreases until the portfolio contains between 30 and 40 securities. At this point, further diversification leaves $\sigma_p$ essentially unchanged.[1]

**Figure 16-3.**   **Diversification and the Components of Portfolio Risk**

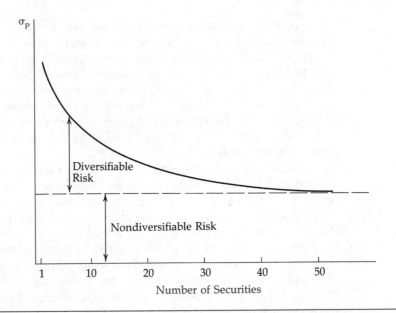

That portion of a portfolio's risk that can be reduced or eliminated by diversification is called **diversifiable risk.** That portion of a portfolio's risk that cannot be eliminated by diversification is called **nondiversifiable risk.** Thus, portfolio risk consists of two components—diversifiable risk and nondiversifiable risk. These components are illustrated in Figure 16-3.

---

[1]Some studies have produced similar results with only 15 securities in the portfolio (see the Archer and Francis article in the Chapter 17 Selected References).

Nondiversifiable risk is often referred to as **systematic risk** and represents that portion of total portfolio risk caused by factors that affect the prices of all securities. National economic and political developments are important sources of systematic risk. Business cycles, inflation, unemployment, fiscal and monetary policies, and expectations about future economic and political developments all combine to produce systematic risk.

Diversifiable risk is often called **unsystematic risk** and represents that portion of total portfolio risk that is unique to a particular firm and/or the industry in which it operates. The goods and services provided by the industry, actions of competitors, the quality of the firm's management, operating leverage, capital structure, financial leverage, and marketing strategies are some of the factors that combine to produce unsystematic risk.

The concept of partitioning portfolio risk into systematic and unsystematic risk provides some important guidelines for portfolio construction and management. A portfolio that contains a large number of securities exhibits only systematic risk because, as illustrated by Figure 16-3, the unsystematic risk components cancel each other out. Once the portfolio contains 30 to 40 securities, portfolio risk consists almost entirely of systematic risk that cannot be reduced through further diversification. However, one or more components of systematic risk can affect the portfolio HPY by reducing or increasing the HPYs of all the securities in the portfolio. An investor's expected rate of return for holding a portfolio of risky financial assets is thus based on the expected rate of return and the systematic risk contained in the portfolio and *not on the risk-return characteristics of individual financial assets*.

# RISK AND RETURN:
# FINANCIAL MARKETS

Important conclusions of the previous section are that the risk of a well-diversified portfolio consists of systematic risk and that this risk is measured by the portfolio variance and standard deviation. These conclusions are frequently stated as follows: a properly diversified portfolio contains only systematic risk. These statements raise two important questions. When is a portfolio properly diversified? Is it possible to measure the systematic risk of individual securities or to measure the impact that individual securities have on a portfolio's systematic risk?

Providing answers to these questions led to the development of an *index* of systematic risk. This index measures the amount of systematic risk contained in individual securities and portfolios relative to financial markets. This index also is used to determine the rate of return that an investor expects from individual securities and portfolios.

**Market Based Index**

The index of systematic risk uses portfolio variance to measure systematic risk and is based on the following ideas. The variance of a portfolio consisting of all the securities that are bought and sold in financial markets measures the systematic risk contained in the overall market. The covariance of any security or portfolio HPY with the market HPY indicates the extent to which systematic risk is also contained in the individual financial assets or financial asset portfolios. This covariance can then be transformed into an index of systematic risk and used as a basis for measuring security and portfolio systematic risk *relative to the market*. As a consequence of this approach, systematic risk is often referred to as **market risk**.

**Market Statistics**

The first step in generating an index of systematic risk for a given security is to measure the risk-return characteristics of the overall financial markets. A good estimate of market characteristics can be obtained by using Standard & Poor's 500 Composite stocks average. The stocks that make up the composite consist of 400 industrial, 20 transportation, 40 public utility, and 40 financial corporations. Table 16-5 lists the S&P 500 HPYs from 1975 through 1982. The mean HPY of this series is an estimate of market returns, $\overline{HPY}_m$. Using Equation 16-4:

$$\overline{HPY}_m = .8003/8$$

$$= .10 \quad \text{or} \quad 10\%$$

The variance of the S&P HPYs provides an estimate of market risk. The intermediate calculations are carried out in Table 16-5. Using Equation 16-5 and letting the variance, $\sigma_m^2$, represent market risk:

**Table 16-5.**   **Estimates of Market Risk and Return Characteristics**

| Year | S&P HPY$_t$ | $(HPY_t - \overline{HPY}_m)$ | $(HPY_t - \overline{HPY}_m)^2$ |
|------|-------------|------------------------------|--------------------------------|
| 1975 | .0830 | −.0170 | .0003 |
| 1976 | .2216 | .1216 | .0148 |
| 1977 | .0089 | −.0911 | .0083 |
| 1978 | .0306 | −.0694 | .0048 |
| 1979 | .1275 | .0275 | .0008 |
| 1980 | .2057 | .1057 | .0112 |
| 1981 | .1300 | .0300 | .0009 |
| 1982 | −.0070 | −.1070 | .0114 |
|  | = .8003 |  | = .0525 |

Sources: S&P HPYs computed from data reported in various issues of the *Economic Report of the President* and the *Federal Reserve Bulletin*.

$$\sigma_m^2 = .0525/8$$

$$= .0066$$

This estimate of market risk along with the S&P HPY time series can be used to compute an index of systematic risk for any security. Other indexes such as the New York Stock Exchange (NYSE) Composite Index or the Dow Jones Industrial Average could be used in place of the S&P data. In addition, estimates of market risk and return change through time as new data are reported, and published estimates are based on more than just eight observations. The important point is to understand how these market estimates are obtained.

**The Beta Coefficient**

The second step in generating a security's index of systematic risk is to compute the covariance between the security's HPYs and market HPYs. This covariance is computed in the same way that Equation 16-8 was used to compute the covariance between two securities. Let:

$HPY_{mt}$ = market HPY for Year $t$

$\sigma_{im}$ = covariance between Security $i$ and the market

Then Equation 16-8 can be written as:

$$\sigma_{im} = \sum_t (HPY_{mt} - \overline{HPY}_m)(HPY_{it} - \overline{HPY}_i)/N \qquad \text{(16-11)}$$

The following example uses the S&P 500 data in illustrating how Equation 16-11 is used to measure $\sigma_{im}$.

---

**Example:**

Column two of Table 16-6 contains the HPY time series for hypothetical Security $i$. Using Equation 16-4:

$$\overline{HPY}_i = .9552/8$$

$$= .1194$$

An index of systematic risk for this security requires that $\sigma_{im}$ be computed. This is accomplished by using the S&P 500 to represent the market. The third column of Table 16-6 lists the S&P HPYs that were given in Table 16-5. The mean HPY for the market was previously calculated to be:

$$\overline{HPY}_m = .10$$

The last three columns of Table 16-6 list the intermediate calculations required to compute $\sigma_{im}$. The values in the Product column are the results of multiplying $(HPY_{it} - \overline{HPY}_i)(HPY_{mt} - \overline{HPY}_m)$ for each year: Take the time to verify the com-

| Table 16-6. | | HPY Data for Computing $\sigma_{im}$ | | | | |
|---|---|---|---|---|---|---|
| | Year | $HPY_{it}$ | $HPY_{mt}$ | $(HPY_{it} - \overline{HPY}_i)$ | $(HPY_{mt} - \overline{HPY}_m)$ | Product |
| | 1975 | .1150 | .0830 | −.0044 | −.0170 | .0001 |
| | 1976 | .2400 | .2216 | .1206 | .1216 | .0147 |
| | 1977 | .0975 | .0089 | −.0219 | −.0911 | .0020 |
| | 1978 | −.0652 | .0306 | −.1846 | −.0694 | .0128 |
| | 1979 | .1123 | .1275 | −.0071 | .0275 | −.0002 |
| | 1980 | .1879 | .2057 | .0685 | .1057 | .0072 |
| | 1981 | .1443 | .1300 | .0249 | .0300 | .0007 |
| | 1982 | .1234 | −.0070 | .0040 | −.1070 | −.0004 |
| | | $\Sigma = .9552$ | | | | $\Sigma = .0369$ |

putations in this Table. The sum of the product column (.0369) is used in Equation 16-11 to arrive at the value of $\sigma_{im}$.

$$\sigma_{im} = .0369/8$$

$$= .0046$$

Having obtained the covariance of Security $i$ with the market, it is now possible to compute a measure of the security's index of market risk. This measure is called the security's **beta** and is computed by dividing the covariance of the security with the market by the market variance. Let:

$$\beta_i = \text{beta of Security } i$$

Then:

$$\beta_i = \sigma_{im}/\sigma_m^2 \tag{16-12}$$

**Example:**   Using the results of the previous example, the beta for Security $i$, using Equation 16-12, is:

$$\beta_i = .0046/.0066$$

$$= .6970$$

A security's beta coefficient measures its systematic risk relative to market risk. A beta of 1.0 means that a security contains the same degree of systematic risk as found in the market. Beta values greater or less than 1.0 indicate that a security contains relatively more or relatively less systematic risk than is contained in the overall market. In actual practice, virtually all corporate beta coefficients have a value that is greater than zero and less than 3.0.

FINANCIAL ASSET BETAS. The theory of finance that led to the development of beta coefficients emerged during the 1950s and 1960s. As a theoretical concept, beta was the subject of numerous articles in journals devoted to financial research. Subsequently a number of firms such as Value Line; Merrill Lynch, Pierce, Fenner and Smith, Inc.; and Wells Fargo Bank began computing corporate betas and publishing the results for use by investors.

Table 16-7 contains beta coefficients for 11 corporations. Two beta coefficients are given for each firm: One was prepared by Foster, the other by Value Line. Both Foster and Value Line used the NYSE price index as a measure of overall market returns. The Foster betas are based on montly observations covering 1971 through 1975. The Value Line betas used five years of weekly data ending in 1981.

According to the data in Table 16-7, General Electric's beta was 1.271 during the time from 1971 to 1975 and .95 from 1977 to 1981. In fact, the betas for all 11 firms differed between time intervals. Three firms saw their betas decrease; the other eight betas increased although the AT&T and the GM betas decreased only slightly. This table thus indicates that a firm's beta coefficient may change over time in response to changes in the firm's degree of systematic risk.

Aside from the fact that Foster and Value Line used slightly different methodologies, what are the reasons that account for changes in a firm's

| Table 16-7. | Beta Coefficients for Selected Companies | | |
|---|---|---|---|
| | Company | Foster Beta | Value Line Beta |
| Aluminum Co. of America | | .662 | 1.20 |
| AT&T | | .589 | .65 |
| Exxon Corporation | | .724 | .85 |
| General Electric Co. | | 1.271 | .95 |
| General Motors Corp. | | .805 | .90 |
| Procter & Gamble Co. | | .871 | .70 |
| Sears, Roebuck and Co. | | 1.023 | .90 |
| Texaco Inc. | | .877 | .95 |
| United States Steel Corp. | | .871 | 1.00 |
| United Technologies Corp. | | .820 | 1.15 |
| Westinghouse Electric Corp. | | .962 | 1.15 |

Sources: George Foster, *Financial Statement Analysis* (Englewood Cliffs, N.J.: Prentice-Hall, Inc., 1978); *Value Line Investment Survey* (Copyright 1983 by Arnold Bernhard & Co., Inc. Reprinted by permission.)

beta? A number of studies indicate that *changes* in a corporation's operating leverage and/or financial leverage affect its beta.[2] Increasing combined leverage tends to increase the firm's beta coefficient. A change in its beta coefficient also is likely to occur when a firm decides to enter new lines of business or to discontinue some of its previously offered products and services.

A number of other factors, such as the growth in a firm's assets, sales, and earnings, have been shown to be positively correlated to a firm's beta. By way of contrast, betas and liquidity, as measured by current ratios, are generally uncorrelated. In addition, negative correlations have been measured between a firm's dividend payout ratio and its beta. It thus appears that numerous factors combine to alter corporate betas over time. However, these same studies indicate that shifts in betas occur gradually; in other words, the firm's degree of systematic risk typically does not shift abruptly but changes gradually from year to year.

**PORTFOLIO BETAS.** The introduction of financial asset betas led quickly to their use in measuring portfolio risk. As explained below, it is relatively easy for investors to use beta based portfolio concepts in deciding on which financial assets to buy and sell. This implies that a firm's market value, as determined by investors trading the firm's securities in resale markets, is not solely a function of its ability to generate earnings and dividends as assumed in the intrinsic value models of Chapter 13, but that it is also a function of how well the firm meets investor portfolio requirements. This being the case, financial managers can use beta concepts in making capital-budgeting and capital structure decisions. The goal that guides these managerial decisions is shareholder wealth maximization in the context of the risk-return characteristics of investor *portfolios*. Because of the importance of the link between investor portfolios and financial management, this section explains how to use beta coefficients in measuring portfolio risk. Chapter 17 explains financial management decision making within the context of investor portfolios.

Portfolio risk is measured by computing its variance ($\sigma_p^2$) and standard deviation ($\sigma_p$) as shown in Equation 16-9. It is also possible to compute $\sigma_p$ by using the beta coefficients of the financial assets held in the portfolio. The first step is to compute $\beta_p$, the **portfolio beta**. Using $\beta_i$ and $X_i$ as previously defined:

$$\beta_p = \sum_i X_i \beta_i \qquad (16\text{-}13)$$

Equation 16-13 states that the beta of a portfolio is simply the weighted

---

[2]A number of these studies are listed in the Chapter 17 Selected References (see especially the texts by Francis and Foster).

average of the financial asset betas contained in the portfolio. This is an explicit way of measuring the portfolio's systematic risk.

---

**Example:**

Four financial assets are purchased with $50,000. The percentage composition of the portfolio and its corresponding betas are:

| Financial Asset | Dollar Investment | $X_i$ | $\beta_i$ |
|---|---|---|---|
| 1 | $20,000 | .40 | 1.3 |
| 2 | 15,000 | .30 | 1.1 |
| 3 | 10,000 | .20 | 1.0 |
| 4 | 5,000 | .10 | .8 |
| | $50,000 | 1.00 | |

Using Equation 16-13:

$$\beta_p = .4(1.3) + .3(1.1) + .2(1.0) + .1(.8)$$

$$= 1.13$$

Now suppose that Asset 1 is sold for $30,000 and the proceeds are invested in Asset 5 with a beta of 1.4. The portfolio composition and its beta change to:

| Financial Asset | Dollar Investment | $X_i$ | $\beta_i$ |
|---|---|---|---|
| 2 | $15,000 | .25 | 1.1 |
| 3 | 10,000 | .17 | 1.0 |
| 4 | 5,000 | .08 | .8 |
| 5 | 30,000 | .50 | 1.4 |
| | $60,000 | 1.00 | |

$$\beta_p = .25(1.1) + .17(1.0) + .08(.8) + .5(1.4)$$

$$= 1.21$$

---

Once $\beta_p$ has been calculated, the standard deviation of the portfolio can be expressed in terms of $\beta_p$, $\sigma_m$ (the standard deviation of the market index) and $C_{pm}$, the correlation between the portfolio and the market index. The equation is:

$$\sigma_p = \frac{(\beta_p)(\sigma_m)}{C_{pm}} \qquad (16\text{-}14)$$

The numerator of Equation 16-14 indicates that portfolio risk is a function of the market risk—that is, the systematic risk—of the individual securities in the portfolio, multiplied by the standard deviation of the market index. Investors have no control over the risk-return characteristics of the market index, but they can still control their portfolio risk by choosing securities that have the desired beta coefficients.

The denominator of Equation 16-14 indicates that portfolio risk is inversely related to the degree of correlation between the portfolio and the market index. This implies that portfolio risk can be reduced by constructing a portfolio having a correlation with the market index that is as close to 1.0 as possible. A portfolio with a $C_{mp}$ that equals 1.0, or is close to 1.0, is said to be *well diversified*. Its risk $(\sigma_p)$ is determined by the individual betas that produce $\beta_p$. In this case, the portfolio contains little unsystematic risk. Conversely, a portfolio having a $C_{mp}$ that is not close to 1.0 is not well diversified and contains unsystematic risk. According to Equation 16-14, its $\sigma_p$ will be larger — other things being equal the portfolio will contain more risk — than that of a well-diversified portfolio.

---

**Example:**  A portfolio of 50 securities has a $\beta_p$ of 1.2. The standard deviation of the market index is calculated to be .07. Using Equation 16-14, the standard deviation of the portfolio equals:

$$\sigma_p = (1.2)(.07)$$

$$= .084$$

In this example, the assumption is made that 50 securities are enough to produce a well-diversified portfolio; thus, $C_{pm}$ equals 1.0.

---

In order to concentrate on the relationship between a portfolio's beta and its standard deviation, the assumption is usually made that the portfolio is well diversified; that is, its $C_{pm}$ is close to 1.0 and contains only systematic risk. As was illustrated in Figure 16-3, it is possible to construct a portfolio with its risk consisting essentially of systematic risk by combining as few as 30 or 40 securities.

## THE FUNDAMENTAL MARKET MODEL

This section develops a general relationship between the risk and return characteristics of financial assets. Return is measured in terms of the rate of return expected from investing in a financial asset. Risk is measured in terms of market or systematic risk, as measured by the financial asset's beta. The resulting risk-return relationship is known as the *market model*, the *capital asset pricing model*, or the *security market line* (SML). This section begins by specifying the assumptions that are needed to develop the SML from a theoretical standpoint. The theoretical SML is then presented. This is followed by some empirical measurements of the SML in order to examine the extent to which the theoretical relationships hold in actual practice. The conclusion is that the theoretical security market line approximates what is observed in the real world and thus can serve as a useful guide in valuing financial asset portfolios.

**Market Model Assumptions**    The set of assumptions used to develop the market model specifies the rules of investor behavior and describes the market in which financial assets are bought and sold. The risk averse investor assumptions used here are the same ones that were specified at the beginning of this chapter. The assumptions concerning financial markets describe a competitive market for financial assets that investors use in adjusting their portfolios. This set of assumptions can be summarized as follows; a detailed list is found in more advanced textbooks.

1.  *Investors are risk averse.* This is one of the investment rules assumed at the beginning of this chapter. It is now extended to include the use of expected rates of return and standard deviations, or betas, of financial assets as measures of risk and return.

2.  *Financial assets trade in perfectly competitive markets.* This means that information concerning expected rates of return and standard deviations of financial assets are known to all investors and used by them in making buy-and-sell decisions. In addition, no costs are incurred in buying and selling securities.

3.  *Investors use the same planning horizon.* The risk and return information on financial assets is received at a specific time, and investors make their investment decisions using this data. At a subsequent time, new information is received and investors react accordingly. The time that elapses between the receipts of information is called the *planning horizon*. It may be useful to think of the planning horizon as being one year in length. Some studies, however, have used planning horizons that are considerably shorter.

4.  *Financial markets are in equilibrium.* This means that at the end of the planning horizon, investors have obtained their *desired* portfolios by buying and selling securities. In the absence of new information, no further buying and selling will be desired.

5.  *There exists a risk-free asset.* One of the financial assets available to investors has a rate of return that is known with certainty for the coming planning horizon. Its standard deviation and beta coefficient are both zero. The rate can, however, be different over different planning horizons. The most frequently used example of a risk-free asset is a Treasury bill.

These assumptions describe a group of risk averse investors who, at a point in time, receive information concerning the risk-return characteristics of financial assets, including a risk-free asset. The investors then buy and sell these securities in order to obtain portfolios that exhibit the desired risk-return characteristics. At a subsequent time, new information becomes available and the process is repeated.

**The Market Model**

The market model or SML that is based on the above assumptions is usually specified in equation form. The first step in generating this equation is to consider the risk-return characteristics of the risk-free asset and of the market index. Let:

$$R_f = \text{rate of return on the risk-free asset}$$

$$R_m = \text{expected rate of return of the market index}$$

$$\beta_m = \text{beta coefficient of the market index}$$

$R_f$ is known with certainty and is constant for the next planning horizon. When 12 months are used as the planning horizon, one-year Treasury bills can be adopted as the empirical estimate of $R_f$.

In the previous section, the S&P 500 Composite stocks average was used as a market index, and its mean holding period yield ($\overline{HPY}_m$) was computed using the historical HPY values listed in Table 16-5. In terms of the market model, $R_m$ is the expected rate of return of the market index, and $HPY_m$ is its empirical estimate for the next planning horizon. The beta coefficient of the market index ($\beta_m$) equals 1.0. This is a consequence of the way beta coefficients are defined.[3]

The relationship between the risk-free security and the risk and return characteristics of the market index is illustrated in Figure 16-4. An investor purchasing only the risk-free security earns a rate of return of $R_f$. On the other hand, a portfolio that replicates the securities contained in the market index has an expected rate of return of $R_m$ and a beta coefficient of 1.0. The difference between these two rates of return is expressed as follows:

$$(R_m - R_f)$$

This is known as the **market risk premium** and is the additional rate of return expected for investing in a risky portfolio having a beta coefficient that is 1.0. In other words, $R_m - R_f$ is the risk premium expected for investing in a portfolio of average systematic risk.

---

[3]Equation 16-12 defines a beta coefficient as follows:
$$\beta_i = \sigma_{im}/\sigma_m^2$$
Let Security $i$ be the market index ($m$); then:
$$\beta_m = \sigma_{mm}/\sigma_m^2$$
The covariance of a security with itself is its own variance:
$$\sigma_{mm} = \sigma_m^2$$
Thus:
$$\beta_m = \sigma_m^2/\sigma_m^2 = 1.0$$

**Figure 16-4.**          **The Security Market Line**

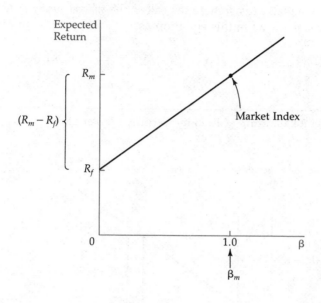

The line that joins $R_f$ and the market index in Figure 16-4 is the security market line. Because $\beta_m$ equals 1.0, the slope of this line is:

$$(R_m - R_f)/\beta_m = (R_m - R_f)$$

Thus, $R_m$ can be written as the following linear equation:

$$R_m = R_f + (R_m - R_f)\beta_m$$

This equation states that the expected rate of return for investing in the risky portfolio that replicates the market portfolio equals the risk-free rate plus a market risk premium equal to $(R_m - R_f)\beta_m$. Since $\beta_m$ equals 1.0, the market risk premium equals $(R_m - R_f)$.

What is the expected rate of return for investing in a risky asset with a beta coefficient that is not equal to 1.0? In general, the SML can be used to calculate the expected rate of return for any risky asset for which a beta coefficient has been estimated. Let Asset $i$ have a beta coefficient of $\beta_i$, and let $R_i$ represent the expected rate of return that is to be estimated. Figure 16-5 indicates how the SML is used to compute $R_i$. Remembering that the slope of SML is $R_m - R_f$, $R_i$ can be written in the following linear equation form:

$$R_i = R_f + (R_m - R_f)\beta_i \qquad \text{(16-15)}$$

Equation 16-15 is the security market line for any financial asset ($i$). This equation is sometimes called the *market model in beta form*. It is also possible to write this equation as:

$$(R_i - R_f) = (R_m - R_f)\beta_i \qquad \text{(16-16)}$$

---

Figure 16-5.    **The Relationship of $R_i$ to the Security Market Line**

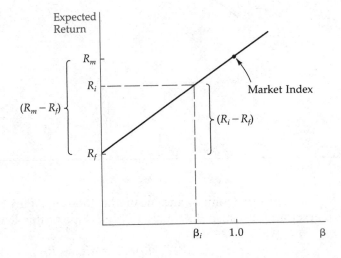

---

Equation 16-16 is the market model or security market line in *risk premium form*. The **risk premium** $(R_i - R_f)$ is the rate of return that an investor expects to earn, over and above the risk-free rate, due to the systematic risk as represented by the asset's beta coefficient. Figure 16-5 illustrates the risk premium $(R_i - R_f)$ that is expected for Asset $i$.

Equations 16-15 and 16-16 are two ways of expressing the basic relationships contained in a SML. In words, *the security market line states that the expected rate of return on a risky asset is the sum of the risk-free rate plus a premium for systematic risk.* The SML further states that the risk premium is proportional to the risky asset's beta coefficient. This implies that a security with a beta coefficient of .5 will have a risk premium only half as large as the market risk premium. Similarly, a security with a beta of 2.0 will have a risk premium twice as large as that of the market risk premium.

**Example:**   Assume that $R_m$ equals .16 and that $R_f$ equals .09. The market risk premium then equals:

$$(R_m - R_f) = (.16 - .09)$$

$$= .07$$

If Asset $i$ has a $\beta_i$ equal to 1.4, its risk premium equals:

$$(R_i - R_f) = (R_m - R_f)\beta_i$$

$$= (.07)(1.4)$$

$$= .098$$

With a beta of 1.4, that is, a beta 40 percent larger than the market index beta of 1.0, Asset $i$'s risk premium of .098 is 40 percent larger than the market risk premium of .07. Asset $i$ thus demonstrates the general relationship that a financial asset's risk premium is proportional to its beta coefficient.

The expected rate of return for Asset $i$ is:

$$R_i = R_f + (R_m - R_f)\beta_i$$

$$= .09 + (.07)1.4$$

$$= .188$$

In general the risk-return coordinates for any risky asset fall along the SML as Asset $i$ does in Figure 16-5. The situations exhibited in Figure 16-6 cannot occur in theory when financial markets are in equilibrium. In that figure, Asset $C$ has an expected rate of return less than the SML indicates it should have for the value of its beta coefficient. As a result, investors operating in competitive markets will decrease the price of this security until its risk-return coordinates fall on the SML. When this happens, the asset's equilibrium expected rate of return is achieved.

In a similar manner, Security $D$ as plotted in Figure 16-6 has an expected rate of return greater than what the SML indicates should obtain for Asset $D$'s beta coefficient. Once again, competitive markets would produce an equilibrium expected rate of return for this security. In this case, however, the price of the security would increase.

The security market line also provides the mechanism for computing the expected rate of return of portfolios. In order to do so, the portfolio beta ($\beta_p$) is computed using Equation 16-13. $\beta_p$ is then used in place of $\beta_i$ in Equation 16-15 in order to compute the portfolio's expected rate of return. The SML can thus be used to compute the equilibrium expected rate of return for individual financial assets as well as for financial asset portfolios. At equilibrium, the risk-return coordinates of individual risky assets and portfolios will all fall along the SML.

**Figure 16-6.**     **Examples of Financial Asset Expected Rates of Return Not in Competitive Equilibrium**

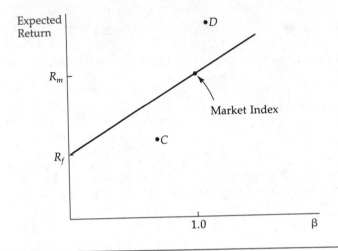

**Market Model Estimates**

Once the theoretical market model in beta form, presented in the previous section, had been developed, a substantial number of research studies sought to generate empirical estimates of the SML.[4] One reason for doing so was to measure how closely the empirical expected rates of return of financial assets approximated the theoretical straight line hypothesized by the SML. If the empirical $R_i$'s corresponded exactly to the theoretical SML, then all the $R_i$ values would fall on the SML shown in Figure 16-5, and the SML would be extremely useful in measuring the risk-return characteristics of financial assets. However, if the $R_i$ values departed greatly from the SML, as C and D do in Figure 16-6, then the SML would have a very limited usefulness.

Some research studies focused on individual securities, but most analyzed portfolio $R_i$ values. In general, SML estimates using individual securities were not satisfactory; however, SML estimates using portfolios produced results that indicated the existence of a positive relationship between return and systematic risk.

SML estimates using historical returns for individual securities produced estimated risk-free rates ($R_f$) that were larger than the actual $R_f$ values. In addition, actual rates of return for individual financial assets appeared to be more closely related to the security's total risk than to its systematic risk. These results have several possible explanations. First, the

---

[4]Some of these are listed in the Chapter 17 Selected References. A good summary appears in Radcliffe.

SML may not be the correct model to use when dealing with the expected rates of return of individual securities. Second, the SML may be the correct model to use, but these results were caused by faulty statistical estimating procedures. Several studies have tried unsuccessfully to resolve this problem. Thus, the theoretical SML may be a correct description of an individual security's $R$ values, but there appears to be no strong and convincing evidence to affirm or deny this hypothesized relationship.

When portfolios of financial assets were used to estimate the SML, the results, while not perfect, were at least consistent with the concept that a portfolio's expected rate of return ($R_p$) is a function of its systematic risk. The research in this area concluded that the relationship between a portfolio's rate of return and its beta coefficient is positive and linear, and that systematic risk is an important determinant of a portfolio's $R_p$. However, these same studies concluded that estimated risk-free rate of return values exceeded the actual $R_f$ values and that the slope of the SML tended to be smaller than that of the theoretical SML. These results mean that the $R_i$ values of portfolios with high betas were generally lower than the rates of return specified by the theoretical SML. Similarly, portfolios with low betas typically had rates of return higher than the $R_i$ values specified in the theoretical SML.

What accounts for this divergence between the theoretical and the empirical SMLs for the case of portfolios? This question is still under study. The fact that individual beta coefficients are not constant through time may account for some of this discrepancy; in addition, some questions have arisen concerning the adequacy of beta coefficients as measurements of systematic risk. There is also the possibility that the introduction of more sophisticated statistical techniques might produce SML estimates that correspond more closely to the theoretical values.

There are two additional reasons why the $R_i$ values of individual securities and portfolios do not plot exactly on the SML. First, the assumptions that were made concerning the markets for financial assets are not entirely realistic. For example, financial markets are not perfectly competitive since brokerage fees and transfer taxes are incurred in buying and selling securities and, in addition, all relevant information may not be known to all investors. It also is likely that investors use different time horizons. Some investors look for short-term profits while others buy securities as long-term investments. Thus, there is some question as to when financial markets are in equilibrium.

The second reason why empirical $R_i$ values do not fall exactly on the SML has to do with the security market line itself. This model is an *expectations model* that specifies the *expected rates of return* from owning risky assets. The data used to estimate the $R_i$ values ($R_m$, $R_f$, and $\beta_i$) are all *actual* or *realized* values. Since it is difficult, if not impossible, to measure expectations directly, actual values are used as surrogates for expected values.

**The SML
Applied**

The Value Line data contained in Table 16-7 can be used to illustrate that rates of return from portfolios tend to be closer to SML forecasts than do rates of return from individual securities because some unsystematic risk can be diversified away. The Value Line beta coefficients were used in conjunction with the SML (Equation 16-15) to compute expected rates of return for six of these firms and for five sample portfolios drawn from the same six firms. The expected and actual rates of return are contained in Table 16-8.

In order to calculate the $R_i$ values using the SML, $R_m$ and $R_f$ coefficients were estimated for the time interval covered by the beta coefficients

| **Table 16-8.** | **Expected and Actual Rates of Return** | | | | |
|---|---|---|---|---|---|
| | | | | Rates of Return | |
| **Company Number** | **Company** | **Beta** | **Expected** | **Actual** |
| 1 | Aluminum Co. of America | 1.20 | 12.17% | 25.66% |
| 2 | AT&T | .65 | 10.93 | 10.25 |
| 3 | Exxon Corporation | .85 | 11.38 | 4.80 |
| 4 | Texaco Inc. | .95 | 11.61 | 3.41 |
| 5 | United States Steel Corp. | 1.00 | 11.72 | −26.36 |
| 6 | Westinghouse Electric Corp. | 1.15 | 12.06 | 57.92 |
| **Portfolio** | **Composition** | | | |
| A | 1, 2, 3 | .90 | 11.49% | 13.57% |
| B | 4, 5, 6 | 1.03 | 11.79 | 11.66 |
| C | 1, 2, 3, 4 | .91 | 11.52 | 11.03 |
| D | 3, 4, 5, 6 | .99 | 11.69 | 9.94 |
| E | 1 through 6 | .97 | 11.65 | 12.61 |

(1977–1981). During this time the average yield on 12-month Treasury bills was 9.45 percent. Similarly, the mean HPY for the NYSE Composite Index was 11.72 percent. Thus:

$$R_m = .1172$$

$$R_f = .0945$$

$$(R_m - R_f) = .0227$$

The resulting SML equation is:

$$R_i = .0945 + (.0227)\beta_i \qquad \text{(16-16)}$$

This equation is plotted in Figure 16-7.

The 12.17 percent expected rate of return for Aluminum Co. of America is computed using its beta coefficient of 1.20 and Equation 16-16:

$$R_i = .0945 + (.0227)(1.20)$$

$$= .1217 \quad \text{or} \quad 12.17\%$$

The expected rates of return for the other companies listed in Table 16-8 were computed in a similar manner.

---

**Figure 16-7.**   **The SML and Portfolio Actual Rates of Return**

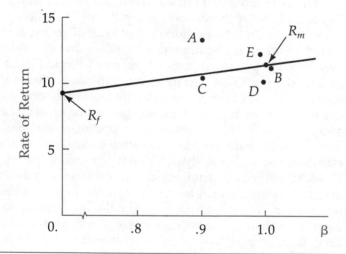

---

The actual rates of return for these six corporations were computed using 1982 price and dividend data and Equation 16-2. The resulting values are listed in Table 16-8. Comparing the expected and actual rates of return for these firms, only AT&T's $R_i$ closely approximates its actual rate of return; the $R_i$ values for the other five firms differ substantially from their actual rates of return.

Portfolios constructed from these same six firms have $R_i$ values that are much closer to their actual rates of return than are the $R_i$ values of the individual firms. This can be seen by looking at the portfolio data in Table 16-8. Portfolio $A$ contains equal percentages of the first three firms listed in the top portion of the table. The beta coefficient for this portfolio is .90 and was computed using Equation 16-13 with $x_i$ equal to .333. The $R_i$ for this portfolio is then obtained by using Equation 16-15:

$$R_i = .0945 + (.0227)(.90)$$

$$= .1149 \quad \text{or} \quad 11.49\%$$

The actual 1982 rate of return for this portfolio was 13.57 percent. Using the same procedure, Portfolio $B$ (as described in Table 16-8) has a beta of 1.03, an $R_i$ of 11.79 percent, and an actual rate of return of 11.66 percent. The rate of return values for Portfolios $C$, $D$, and $E$ are obtained in the same way. Portfolios $C$ and $D$ each contain four securities, and Portfolio $E$ contains all six securities listed in the top portion of Table 16-8. Varying the number of securities in each portfolio was done as a way of illustrating portfolio calculations. In addition, equal $X_i$ values were used in each portfolio in order to simplify the calculations; any set of $X_i$ coefficients can be used in a portfolio as long as they sum to 1.0.

The portfolio actual rates of return are plotted along with the SML in Figure 16-7. With the possible exception of Portfolio $A$, the Figure 16-7 graph shows that the portfolio actual rates of return are fairly consistent with the SML. It is also important to realize that this consistency occurred even though the actual rates of return of the individual securities that go into the portfolios deviate significantly from their SML values. Portfolio actual rates of return are generally more consistent with the SML than are the rates of return of individual securities because the same risk component—systematic risk—is in portfolios and SMLs. The data in Table 16-8 illustrate this idea; however, these data are not presented as a statistical test of the ability of SMLs to forecast future returns.

Beta coefficients of individual financial assets continue to be computed, updated, and published by several organizations that deal with financial information. This allows all investors the opportunity to use beta coefficients in evaluating the systematic risk of individual financial assets and of financial asset portfolios. It is fair to say that beta coefficients are accepted as useful figures in evaluating risky financial alternatives. Thus, the next chapter uses beta and SML concepts in discussing corporate financial decision making under conditions of risk.

## SUMMARY

This chapter is organized around two concepts: the *beta coefficient* as a measure of systematic risk and the *market model in beta form* as a measure of a financial asset's expected rate of return. The topics in this chapter and their order of appearance are intended to systematically develop the financial and statistical concepts that make the SML and beta coefficients understandable.

The early sections of the chapter dealt with investor behavior and how to measure the risk-return characteristics of risky financial assets. Investors are assumed to be risk averse. They evaluate the desirability of risky assets by using HPY means and standard deviations to measure their risk-return characteristics. The historical time series of financial asset HPYs are assumed to provide useful estimates of their HPY probability distributions.

Investors prefer holding portfolios of financial assets as opposed to investing in only one security because portfolios can be constructed to yield risk-return characteristics that are superior to those of individual financial assets. Although measuring portfolio expected rates of return is straightforward, measuring portfolio risk is more involved and requires the use of variances and covariances, in addition to the individual $X_i$ values.

The introduction of the correlation concept leads to partitioning portfolio risk into systematic and unsystematic risk components. A portfolio that contains at least 30 to 40 securities contains only systematic risk because the unsystematic risk components of the individual securities cancel each other out. Thus, portfolio risk is systematic risk.

Measuring the systematic risk of individual financial assets and financial asset portfolios is accomplished by using a market index. The degree of systematic risk that a security exhibits relative to the market index is called the security's beta coefficient. These coefficients are relatively stable but tend to change gradually over time. Studies have identified some of the causal factors in beta changes.

A portfolio beta is the weighted average of the betas of the financial assets contained in the portfolio. A well-diversified portfolio contains only systematic risk. Thus, its standard deviation can be calculated simply by using its beta and the standard deviation of the market index.

Beta coefficients, combined with assumptions concerning investor behavior and financial markets, allow the development of the security market line (SML) — the market model in beta form. This model makes it possible to allow for risk in calculating the expected rate of return of a risky asset. The SML states that the expected rate of return for a risky security is the risk-free rate plus a risk premium for systematic risk. In addition, this risk premium is proportional to the risky asset's beta coefficient. The SML can also be used to calculate the expected rate of return of portfolios.

Empirical estimates of the SML indicate that it is a good but not perfect description of reality. The reasons for this divergence are the somewhat unrealistic assumptions and the use of realized rates of return in a model that measures expected rates of return. In spite of these limitations, beta coefficients are computed and distributed by several organizations and are widely used for evaluating the desirability of risky financial assets.

# QUESTIONS

**16-1.** What are the three rules investors are assumed to use in making investment decisions?

**16-2.** Define, in words and algebra, the holding period yield.

**16-3.** Explain how the risk of owning one financial asset is measured.

**16-4.** Explain how the HPY statistics of two financial assets can be used to rank their relative desirability.

**16-5.** Rank the desirability of the following two financial assets on the basis of their HPY statistics:

|  | A | B |
|---|---|---|
| Mean HPY | .21 | .23 |
| Standard deviation | .18 | .16 |

**16-6.** Rank the desirability of the following two financial assets on the basis of their HPY statistics:

|                    | A    | B    |
|--------------------|------|------|
| Mean HPY           | .11  | .12  |
| Standard deviation | .07  | .09  |

16-7. Explain why investors prefer to own more than one financial asset at any time.

16-8. The covariance between the HPY time series of two particular financial assets is negative. What information does this convey concerning the behavior of the two HPY time series, and what is the impact on the riskiness of a portfolio that contains only these two financial assets?

16-9. The following four portfolios are formed by using various percentages of financial assets $X_1$ and $X_2$. The rate of return ($R_p$) and standard deviation ($\sigma_p$) for each portfolio are computed as follows:

| Portfolio | $X_1$ | $X_2$ | $R_p$ | $\sigma_p$ |
|-----------|-------|-------|-------|------------|
| A         | 1.0   | .0    | .140  | .045       |
| B         | .7    | .3    | .127  | .037       |
| C         | .4    | .6    | .113  | .034       |
| D         | .0    | 1.0   | .095  | .041       |

Rank these portfolios according to their risk-return characteristics.

16-10. The HPY time series of Financial Assets $A$ and $Y$ have a +1.0 correlation coefficient. How do these HPY time series behave in relation to each other?

16-11. How can correlation coefficients be used to select financial assets for inclusion in a portfolio when it is desired to minimize portfolio risk?

16-12. Explain what is meant by (a) diversification, (b) systematic risk, and (c) unsystematic risk.

16-13. Identify some important sources of systematic risk.

16-14. Why does a portfolio that contains 50 securities contain only systematic risk?

16-15. A financial asset's beta is 1.2. Explain the beta concept and interpret this beta coefficient.

16-16. Identify some factors that produce changes in a firm's beta coefficient.

16-17. Explain how a portfolio beta is computed.

16-18. Explain how beta coefficients are used to calculate the standard deviation of a well-diversified portfolio.

16-19. Explain the market model assumption that states that financial markets are in equilibrium.

16-20. Explain the risk-return characteristics of the risk-free asset that is assumed to be available to investors.

16-21. Explain the market risk premium contained in the market model.

16-22. State in words the basic relationships contained in the beta form of the market model.

16-23. State in words the relationships contained in the SML in risk premium form.

16-24. What are the reasons why empirical expected rates of return do not correspond exactly to the theoretical expected rates of return hypothesized in the SML?

# PROBLEMS

**16-1.** The year-end stock prices $(P_t)$ and dividends $(D)$ for Stocks $X$, $Y$, and $Z$ are as follows:

|  | Stock X | | Stock Y | | Stock Z | |
|---|---|---|---|---|---|---|
| Year | $P_t$ | D | $P_t$ | D | $P_t$ | D |
| 1980 | $ 9.00 | 0 | $17.50 | 0 | $38.50 | 0 |
| 1981 | 10.50 | $ .48 | 21.00 | $ .98 | 40.00 | $1.25 |
| 1982 | 15.50 | .73 | 24.50 | 1.21 | 40.00 | 1.46 |
| 1983 | 28.50 | 1.09 | 26.00 | 1.65 | 36.50 | 1.67 |
| 1984 | 36.50 | 1.42 | 24.50 | 1.82 | 34.50 | 1.93 |
| 1985 | 42.50 | 1.65 | 26.50 | 1.92 | 39.50 | 2.18 |

a. Compute the holding period yield for each stock for each year, 1981–1985.

b. Compute the mean, variance, and standard deviation of each stock's HPYs.

c. Compute the expected rate of return of a portfolio consisting of 20% of Stock $X$, 40% of Stock $Y$, and 40% of Stock $Z$.

d. Compute the covariance for each pair of stocks $(\sigma_{XY}, \sigma_{XZ}, \sigma_{ZY})$.

e. Compute the variance and standard deviation of a portfolio $(\sigma_p^2, \sigma_p)$ consisting of 40% of Stock $Y$ and 60% of Stock $Z$.

**16-2.** An investor is considering a portfolio that would contain two common stocks, $J$ and $H$. These stocks have the following historical price $(P_t)$ and dividend $(D)$ data:

|  | Stock J | | Stock H | |
|---|---|---|---|---|
| Year | $P_t$ | D | $P_t$ | D |
| 1980 | $34.00 | | $17.00 | |
| 1981 | 37.00 | $1.10 | 18.00 | $.80 |
| 1982 | 38.40 | 1.10 | 20.20 | .80 |
| 1983 | 36.10 | 1.10 | 18.50 | .95 |
| 1984 | 40.25 | 1.15 | 19.30 | .95 |

a. Compute the mean, variance, and standard deviation for each stock's HPYs and compute the covariance between these two securities.

b. Compute the expected rate of return and standard deviation for each of the following five portfolios:

| Portfolio | Percent Invested in J $(X_1)$ | Percent Invested in H $(X_2)$ |
|---|---|---|
| 1 | 1.00 | 0.0 |
| 2 | 0.0 | 1.00 |
| 3 | .8 | .2 |
| 4 | .4 | .6 |
| 5 | .2 | .8 |

    *c.* Which portfolios, if any, are dominated. Why?
    *d.* Which portfolio is the riskiest?
    *e.* Rank these portfolios on the basis of their risk-return characteristics.

**16-3.** The 1980 through 1985 HPYs for Stocks *A* and *B* are as follows:

| Year | Stock *A*'s HPY | Stock *B*'s HPY |
|---|---|---|
| 1980 | .0783 | .1132 |
| 1981 | .1410 | .1789 |
| 1982 | .1200 | .1620 |
| 1983 | .0934 | .1332 |
| 1984 | −.0244 | −.0100 |
| 1985 | .0638 | .0936 |

    *a.* Compute the coefficient of correlation between Financial Assets *A* and *B*.
    *b.* Evaluate the risk characteristics of a portfolio that contains only Financial Assets *A* and *B*.

**16-4.** Using the data contained in Table 16-4, compute the correlation coefficients for financial assets:

    *a.* *A* and *B*
    *b.* *C* and *D*
    *c.* *E* and *F*

**16-5.** A venture capitalist has invested $200,000 in four financial assets. The dollar amount committed to each asset, the resulting $X_i$ values, and the historical $\overline{HPY}$s are as follows:

| Financial Assets | Dollar Investment | $X_i$ | $\overline{HPY}_i$ |
|---|---|---|---|
| 1 | $80,000 | .4 | .14 |
| 2 | 40,000 | .2 | .09 |
| 3 | 40,000 | .2 | .08 |
| 4 | 40,000 | .2 | .12 |

    *a.* Compute the expected rate of return of this portfolio.
    *b.* This capitalist wishes to invest in a fifth financial asset. Rather than increase the dollar amount invested, he decreases the proportional dollar investment in each financial asset ($X_i$) by .05 and uses the proceeds to invest in the fifth asset ($X_1$ now equals .35, etc.). If he desires a 14% rate of return from the new five-asset portfolio, what must the new financial asset's $\overline{HPY}$ be?

**16-6.** The holding period yields for a particular market index and for Security *A* are given at the top of page 473.

    *a.* Compute the expected value and variance of the market index HPYs.
    *b.* Compute the beta for Security *A*.
    *c.* Interpret the computed beta coefficient.

| Year | Market Index HPY | Security *A* HPY |
|------|------------------|------------------|
| 1980 | .0089 | .1001 |
| 1981 | .0306 | −.0538 |
| 1982 | .1275 | .1112 |
| 1983 | .2075 | .1679 |
| 1984 | .1300 | .1343 |
| 1985 | −.0070 | .1234 |

16-7.  A company has invested the following dollar amounts in four financial assets:

| Financial Asset | Dollar Amounts Invested |
|-----------------|-------------------------|
| 1 | $40,000 |
| 2 | 30,000 |
| 3 | 20,000 |
| 4 | 10,000 |

The covariances of Financial Assets 1, 2, 3, and 4 with the market are .0032, .0056, .0132, and .0092 respectively. The market variance is .0062.

a.  Given this information, compute the beta of this portfolio of financial assets.

b.  Suppose that Asset 3 is sold for $40,000 and that the proceeds are invested in a fifth asset with a market covariance of .0063. Also, a sixth asset with a market covariance of .0023 is bought for $80,000. What is the new portfolio beta?

c.  Assuming that the portfolio in *b* is well diversified and that its correlation with the market index is 1.0, compute the portfolio standard deviation.

16-8.  A portfolio of three securities has a beta of .93. The standard deviation of the market index is .06. Assuming that three securities are *not* enough to produce a well-diversified portfolio and that its correlation with the market index is .82:

a.  Compute the portfolio standard deviation.

b   What can be said of the $\sigma_p$ value computed in *a*?

16-9.  If one-year Treasury bills are currently earning a rate of return of 8% and the expected rate of return on the market index is .12:

a.  What is the market risk premium?

b.  Stock *P* has a beta of .83. What is its risk premium?

c.  What is the expected rate of return for Stock *P*?

# SELECTED REFERENCES

*Note:* See the end of Chapter 17.

# APPENDIX

## COMPUTING PORTFOLIO VARIANCE AND STANDARD DEVIATION

The materials in this appendix explain how to compute the variance and standard deviation of a portfolio that contains two or more financial assets. The portfolio variance equation can be stated using either the covariances or the correlations of the financial assets contained in the portfolio. These two approaches yield the same numerical value and both are explained in this section.

**Portfolio Variance Using Covariances**

The equation for calculating the variance of a portfolio that contains several financial assets when the covariances between each pair of securities are known is expressed as follows:

$$\sigma_p^2 = \sum_i \sum_j X_i X_j \sigma_{ij} \tag{16A-1}$$

Once understood, this double summation expands rather easily. Equation 16-A1 states that the portfolio variance is obtained by computing the value of:

$$X_i X_j \sigma_{ij}$$

for all combinations of securities taken two at a time and adding up the results. However, since:

$$X_i X_j \sigma_{ij} = X_j X_i \sigma_{ji} \tag{16-A2}$$

some of the terms in Equation 16-A1 can be combined. In addition, the notation used in Equation 16-A1 means that:

$$X_i X_i \sigma_{ii} = X_i^2 \sigma_i^2 \tag{16-A3}$$

futher simplifying the needed computations.

The variance of a two-security portfolio using Equation 16-A1 is written as Equation 16-A4. Substituting Equations 16-A2 and 16-A3 into Equation 16-A4 allows the portfolio variance to be written in the more useful form of Equation 16-A5:

$$\sigma_p^2 = \underbrace{X_1 X_1 \sigma_{11}}_{} + \underbrace{X_1 X_2 \sigma_{12} + X_2 X_1 \sigma_{21}}_{} + \underbrace{X_2 X_2 \sigma_{22}}_{} \qquad \text{(16-A4)}$$

$$\sigma_p^2 = \quad X_1^2 \sigma_1^2 \qquad\qquad + 2X_1 X_2 \sigma_{12} \qquad\quad + X_2^2 \sigma_2^2 \qquad \text{(16-A5)}$$

Using this same procedure, the variance of a three-security portfolio can first be written using Equation 16-A1:

$$\sigma_p^2 = X_1 X_1 \sigma_{11} + X_1 X_2 \sigma_{12} + X_1 X_3 \sigma_{13}$$
$$+ X_2 X_1 \sigma_{21} + X_2 X_2 \sigma_{22} + X_2 X_3 \sigma_{23}$$
$$+ X_3 X_1 \sigma_{31} + X_3 X_2 \sigma_{32} + X_3 X_3 \sigma_{33}$$

This equation can be rewritten as follows:

$$\sigma_p^2 = X_1^2 \sigma_1^2 + X_2^2 \sigma_2^2 + X_3^2 \sigma_3^2$$
$$+ 2X_1 X_2 \sigma_{12} + 2X_1 X_3 \sigma_{13} + 2X_2 X_3 \sigma_{23} \qquad \text{(16-A6)}$$

The pattern contained in Equation 16-A6 is simply repeated for portfolios that contain more than three securities. Once computed, the portfolio standard deviation is the square root of the portfolio variance.

---

**Example:**

Three securities of interest to an investor have the following variance and covariance values:

$$\sigma_1^2 = .4 \qquad\qquad \sigma_2^2 = .5 \qquad\qquad \sigma_3^2 = .6$$

$$\sigma_{12} = .3 \qquad\qquad \sigma_{13} = .1 \qquad\qquad \sigma_{23} = .2$$

A portfolio consisting of:

$$X_1 = .2 \qquad\qquad X_2 = .3 \qquad\qquad X_3 = .5$$

is then acquired. The portfolio variance can then be computed using Equation 16-A6:

$$\sigma_p^2 = (.2^2)(.4) + (.3^2)(.5) + (.5^2)(.6)$$
$$+ 2(.2)(.3)(.3) + 2(.2)(.5)(.1)$$
$$+ 2(.3)(.5)(-.2)$$
$$= .207$$

In addition:

$$\sigma_p = \sqrt{.207}$$
$$= .455$$

---

**Portfolio Variance Using Correlations**

One of the important results of Chapter 16 is that the correlation between any two securities ($C_{ij}$) can be computed from:

$$C_{ij} = \sigma_{ij}/\sigma_i\sigma_j \qquad (16\text{-}10)$$

Solving this equation for $\sigma_{ij}$ yields:

$$\sigma_{ij} = C_{ij}\sigma_i\sigma_j \qquad (16\text{-}A7)$$

Substituting the right-hand side of Equation 16-A7 for $\sigma_{ij}$ in Equation 16-A1 produces the equation that is used for calculating the variance of a portfolio that contains several financial assets when the correlations that exist between each pair of securities are known:

$$\sigma_p^2 = \sum_i \sum_j X_i X_j C_{ij}\sigma_i\sigma_j \qquad (16\text{-}A8)$$

This equation can be expanded and simplified in the same way that Equation 16-A1 is. Thus, the variance of a two-security portfolio stated in terms of correlations is:

$$\sigma_p^2 = X_1^2\sigma_1^2 + 2X_1X_2C_{12}\sigma_1\sigma_2 + X_2^2\sigma_2^2 \qquad (16\text{-}A9)$$

Similarly, the portfolio variance for a three-security portfolio is:

$$\sigma_p^2 = X_1^2\sigma_1^2 + X_2^2\sigma_2^2 + X_3^2\sigma_3^2$$
$$+ 2X_1X_2C_{12}\sigma_1\sigma_2 + 2X_1X_3C_{13}\sigma_1\sigma_3 + 2X_2X_3C_{23}\sigma_2\sigma_3 \qquad (16\text{-}A10)$$

The pattern contained in Equation 16-A10 is repeated for portfolios that contain more than three portfolios. The portfolio standard deviation is again computed as the square root of the portfolio variance.

---

**Example:**

In order to demonstrate the equivalence of using either covariances or correlations in calculating portfolio variances, the data from the previous example are used in computing $\sigma_p^2$ using Equation 16-A10.

The first step is to calculate the three $C_{ij}$ values using Equation 16-10. This requires $\sigma_i$ values, computed as follows:

$$\sigma_i = \sqrt{\sigma_i^2}$$

Thus:

$$\sigma_1 = \sqrt{.4} \qquad \sigma_2 = \sqrt{.5} \qquad \sigma_3 = \sqrt{.6}$$
$$= .632 \qquad\quad = .707 \qquad\quad = .775$$

Using Equation 16-10:

$$C_{12} = .3/(.632)(.707)$$
$$= .671$$

$$C_{13} = .1/(.632)(.775)$$
$$= .204$$
$$C_{23} = -.2/(.707)(.775)$$
$$= -.365$$

Using Equation 16-A10 and letting $X_1 = .2$, $X_2 = .3$, and $X_3 = .5$ as in the previous example:

$$\sigma_p^2 = (.2^2)(.4) + (.3^2)(.5) + (.5^2)(.6)$$
$$+ 2(.2)(.3)(.671)(.632)(.707)$$
$$+ 2(.2)(.5)(.204)(.632)(.775)$$
$$+ 2(.3)(.5)(-.365)(.707)(.775)$$
$$= .207$$
$$\sigma_p = \sqrt{.207}$$
$$= .455$$

---

For a given portfolio percentage composition, that is, for a given set of $X_i$ values, the portfolio variance and standard deviation can be calculated using either the covariances in Equation 16-A1 or the correlations in Equation 16-A8.

---

# APPENDIX PROBLEMS

**16A-1.** Write out the variance for a four-security portfolio using covariances.

**16A-2.** Write out the variance for a four-security portfolio using correlations.

**16A-3.** The following information is available concerning Financial Assets $J$, $H$, and $M$:

| Financial Asset | $\sigma_i^2$ | $\overline{HPY}_i$ | $\sigma_{ij}$ |
|---|---|---|---|
| $J$ | .0423 | .0923 | $\sigma_{JH} = .0014$ |
| $H$ | .0394 | .0823 | $\sigma_{JM} = .0324$ |
| $M$ | .1436 | .1232 | $\sigma_{HM} = -.0203$ |

Given this data, compute the expected return and standard deviation for each of the following portfolios using covariances:

| Portfolio | $X_J$ | $X_H$ | $X_M$ |
|---|---|---|---|
| 1 | .2 | .2 | .6 |
| 2 | .3 | .3 | .4 |
| 3 | .6 | .2 | .2 |
| 4 | .2 | .6 | .2 |

**16A-4.** Repeat Problem 16A-3 using correlations rather than covariances.

# CHAPTER 17

# Financial Management within a Capital Asset Pricing Framework

This chapter explains how the capital asset pricing model, developed in the previous chapter, can be used in financial management decision making. Specifically, the concepts of systematic risk, as measured by beta coefficients, and expected rates of return, as measured by security market lines, are applied to several areas of managerial finance, and their impacts on financial decisions are explained.

The first section provides a general framework by summarizing the capital asset pricing model presented in Chapter 16. The second section explains how security market lines can provide estimates for the discount rate used in evaluating capital-budgeting alternatives. Subsequent sections explain how beta coefficients are used to measure the value of a firm. Optimum capital structure and minimum weighted average cost of capital concepts, first introduced in Chapter 14, are reexamined in light of a valuation model that capitalizes firm income on the basis of its systematic risk. In addition, certain complications such as corporate income taxes and bankruptcy costs are introduced, and their impacts on capital structure decisions are explained.

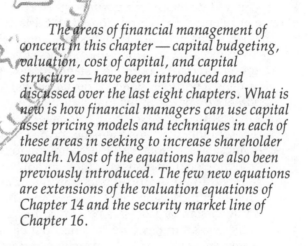

*The areas of financial management of concern in this chapter — capital budgeting, valuation, cost of capital, and capital structure — have been introduced and discussed over the last eight chapters. What is new is how financial managers can use capital asset pricing models and techniques in each of these areas in seeking to increase shareholder wealth. Most of the equations have also been previously introduced. The few new equations are extensions of the valuation equations of Chapter 14 and the security market line of Chapter 16.*

## CAPITAL ASSET PRICING: A SUMMARY

The components of capital asset pricing are based on two sets of assumptions. The first set describes the behavior of risk averse investors in constructing their financial asset portfolios. The second set describes a competitive market for trading financial assets. This section summarizes these assumptions and states their implications in terms of beta coefficients and security market lines.

**Investor Behavior and Portfolio Diversification**

In measuring the desirability of financial assets, investor behavior is characterized by the following assumptions:

1. Investors evaluate financial assets only on the basis of risk and return.

2.  The return from owning a financial asset for a given period of time is measured by the expected value of the financial asset's rate of return; risk is measured by the standard deviation of the financial asset's rate of return. These statistics are computed from a probability distribution of expected rates of return or from a historical time series of rate of return data.

3.  Investors are risk averse: They seek to minimize risk for a given rate of return or to maximize rate of return for a given amount of risk.

These three assumptions, and especially the risk averse assumption, result in investors seeking portfolios of financial assets rather than purchasing only one security. This is because portfolios can be constructed to produce risk-return characteristics that are superior to those of individual financial assets. Portfolio return and risk are measured by using statistical expected values and standard deviations of rates of return. However, the standard deviation of a portfolio must take into account the covariance (or equivalently, the correlation) that exists between each pair of financial assets in the portfolio. Constructing a portfolio that contains securities with covariances or correlations that are negative, or close to zero if positive, will not only reduce a portfolio's standard deviation and thus its risk but may result in a portfolio standard deviation that is less than the standard deviation of any of the individual securities contained in the portfolio.

Portfolio risk can be partitioned into unsystematic and systematic risk components. Unsystematic, or diversifiable, risk is that portion of a financial asset's total risk that is unique to the particular firm; systematic, or nondiversifiable, risk is that portion of a financial asset's total risk common to all securities traded in financial markets. Diversification, the process of increasing the number of securities in a portfolio, decreases the portfolio standard deviation because the unsystematic risks contained in individual securities tend to cancel out against one another, leaving only systematic risk. Once a portfolio contains 40 to 50 securities, further diversification will not reduce portfolio risk appreciably. At this point a portfolio contains only systematic risk.

In order to provide a measure of the degree of systematic risk contained in individual financial assets and in portfolios, an index of systematic risk — called a beta coefficient — is computed. The motivation for this concept is as follows: A portfolio consisting of all the publicly traded financial assets — the market portfolio — contains only systematic risk; this is measured by its variance of returns ($\sigma_m^2$). Dividing the covariance of Security $i$ with the market index ($\sigma_{im}$) by the variance of the market index produces a measure of the degree of systematic risk exhibited by Security $i$ relative to the market portfolio. This ratio is called the beta coefficient of Security $i$ and is written $\beta_i$. This algebraic relationship was originally stated as Equation 16-12 and is repeated as Equation 17-1:

$$\beta_i = \sigma_{im}/\sigma_m^2 \qquad (17\text{-}1)$$

The beta coefficient of a portfolio is a weighted average of the beta coefficients of the securities contained in the portfolio (see Equation 16-13). A beta coefficient of 1.0 indicates that a security or portfolio has the same degree of systematic risk as contained in the market portfolio.

The risk contained in a well-diversified portfolio can thus be expressed in terms of systematic risk as measured by beta coefficients. Consequently, investors choose individual financial assets for their portfolios not on the basis of the assets' total risk but on the basis of systematic risk as measured by their beta coefficients. In addition, the rates of return that investors require from their portfolios are a function of portfolio systematic risk and not simply a function of the riskiness of the individual financial assets contained in the portfolio.

**Financial Markets and the SML**

Investors are assumed to buy and sell financial assets in what are called *perfect capital markets*. The characteristics of these markets can be summarized as follows:

1.  Risk averse investors evaluate the return and risk properties of financial assets and portfolios using expected values, standard deviations, and beta coefficients of rates of return.

2.  Markets for financial assets are perfectly competitive, costless, and all investors have the same information concerning the risk and return characteristics of financial assets.

3.  Investors use the same planning horizon, and financial markets reach competitive equilibrium when investors have obtained their desired portfolios.

4.  There exists a risk-free asset. Its rate of return is known with certainty for the coming planning period and its standard deviation and beta coefficient are both zero.

This set of assumptions, combined with the use of beta coefficients to measure systematic risk, leads to the security market line (SML) in beta form. The SML is stated in terms of the following variables:

$R_i$ = the expected rate of return for risky Asset $i$

$R_f$ = the rate of return of the risk-free asset

$R_m$ = the expected rate of return of the market portfolio

$\beta_i$ = the beta coefficient for risky Asset $i$

The expected rate of return for investing in risky Security $i$ equals the risk-free rate plus an added return, or premium, for risk. Investors who own well-diversified portfolios compute this risk premium ($R_i - R_f$) on the basis of the asset's systematic risk because diversification eliminates the impact of unsystematic risk. The risk premium is estimated as follows: the market risk premium $(R_m - R_f)$ is the additional rate of return expected for investing in a risky asset that has a beta coefficient equal to 1.0. For any risky Asset $i$, the risk premium equals $R_i - R_f$ and is expressed as follows:

$$(R_m - R_f)\beta_i$$

These relationships, illustrated in Figures 16-4 and 16-5, produce two equivalent SML equations (16-5 and 16-6). The one of interest in this chapter is the SML in beta form, written as follows:

$$R_i = R_f + (R_m - R_f)\beta_i \tag{17-2}$$

This equation states that risky Financial Asset $i$, when included as part of a well-diversified portfolio, has an expected rate of return equal to the risk-free rate plus a premium for the asset's systematic risk. As a consequence, the balance of this chapter assumes that corporate financial managers, in seeking to increase shareholder wealth, evaluate the risk and return characteristics of their decisions on the basis of shareholder expected rates of return and the firm's systematic risk as expressed by the security market line.

# CAPITAL BUDGETING AND SYSTEMATIC RISK

The first application of capital asset pricing to corporate financial decision making centers on estimating the discount rate to be used in evaluating capital-budgeting alternatives. In theory this problem is solved by using a security market line to estimate project required rates of return. In practice, a number of complications make this a fairly difficult problem. This section explains the SML approach to measuring an investment alternative's required rate of return, identifies the complications that hinder the direct use of a SML, and presents a number of techniques for approximating the appropriate discount rate.

**Project Betas**

Projects—capital-budgeting alternatives—represent a corporation's investment in real, that is, physical assets. Project rates of return are not known with certainty and are thus risky. This type of risk was labeled *business risk* in Chapter 5: Risky projects cause variability in a corporation's EBIT.

**PROJECT SYSTEMATIC RISK.** The rate of return required by a corporation when it invests in a risky project is a function of the project's return and risk characteristics. The expected value of possible rates of return provides a measure of project return, but the variance, or standard deviation, of possible rates of return is not the relevant measure of project risk. The relevant risk is the systematic risk portion of the project's business risk. Why? Because project risk is ultimately absorbed by the firm's investors and they can diversify away all but systematic risk. Thus, the project rate of return must be sufficient to compensate for its systematic risk if it is to be an attractive investment for the corporation and ultimately for the firm's shareholders.

Each project contains its own degree of systematic risk. This implies that a project's systematic risk is independent of the corporation that is evaluating the project's desirability. This also means that the systematic risk of a project is the same for all firms. A given project, however, may not be equally desirable to all corporations. This is because some of the firms may be able, because of their managerial technical skills or other advantages, to realize larger cash flows and thus higher rates of return than other firms. Thus, the risk adjusted net present value for a particular project may differ from firm to firm.

---

**Example:**     An independent retail food store is put up for sale. Two national convenience food chains evaluate the advisability of purchasing the independent and converting it into a company owned convenience store. Each potential buyer forecasts the cash flows it expects to realize from this project. However, one of the buyers is more experienced at store conversions and can operate the acquisition more efficiently than its competitor. Thus, the more experienced firm's cash flow estimates exceed those of its competitor. In the absence of other factors, the more experienced firm's adjusted net present value will exceed that of its competitor, and the potential acquisition will not be equally desirable to the two firms.

---

USING THE SML. The degree of systematic risk contained in a capital-budgeting alternative is measured by the project's beta coefficient. For any project $(x)$ the associated beta coefficient can be written $\beta_x$. The rate of return $(R_x)$ required by a firm for this project is obtained by using the SML equation:

$$R_x = R_f + (R_m - R_f)\beta_x \qquad \text{(17-3)}$$

Since each project has its own beta coefficient, there is a separate required rate of return, or discount rate, for each project. The appropriate discount rate is obtained by using Equation 17-3.

Suppose that a firm needed to evaluate four projects, A, B, C, and D, on an accept/reject basis. These projects are plotted in Figure 17-1. The coordinates for each project correspond to its beta coefficient and its expected rate of return. Figure 17-1 also plots the firm's required rate of return for capital-budgeting projects using the SML of Equation 17-3.

Which will be accepted? Projects $A$ and $B$ will be accepted while $C$ and $D$ will be rejected. Projects $A$ and $B$ have expected rates of return that plot above the SML: Their expected rates of return exceed their required rates

Figure 17-1.        **Relationship between Systematic Risk and Project Expected Rates of Return**

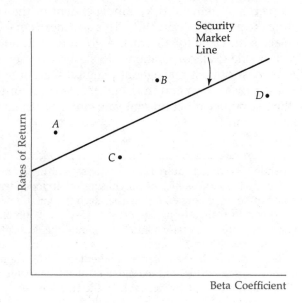

of return when discount rates are based on project systematic risk. Projects $C$ and $D$ will be rejected because their expected rates of return are less than their systematic risk adjusted required rates as specified by the SML. Note in particular that accepting Project $A$ while rejecting Project $D$ means that $D$, which has an expected rate of return in excess of Project $A$'s, will nevertheless be rejected. This occurs because $D$'s expected rate of return is not large enough to compensate for its systematic risk, but Project $A$, with a lower expected rate of return, is acceptable because of its relatively low systematic risk.

**IMPERFECT PROJECT MARKETS.** Figure 17-1 raises two basic questions. First, why don't the projects all plot on the SML? Second, how are project betas measured? There are two reasons why project expected rates of return do not equal the SML rates of return. First, as explained above, the cash flows realized from a particular project may differ from firm to firm because of reasons unique to each firm. Second, markets for capital-budgeting projects are not as perfect or efficient as those for financial assets. The prices of capital-budgeting projects selling in imperfect product markets will not adjust exactly for systematic risk as happens to the prices of financial assets that are traded in financial markets. Since project price is a major component of its net investment, imperfect product markets can produce projects with prices that are low enough to yield expected rates of return in excess of their systematic risk adjusted required rates.

Why are markets for capital-budgeting projects imperfect? One major reason is that these markets deal with physical rather than financial assets. Competing products offered for sale by different manufacturers differ physically in greater or lesser degrees. Competing real assets are often intended by their producers to be different or to be perceived as being different. Consider, for example, the market for small business and personal computers. Each manufacturer strives to offer product lines that are better than those of its competitors. Whether they are better or not, the product lines certainly differ. Purchasers have many options to choose from, such as 8 bit or 16 bit configurations, different memory sizes, different operating systems, and alternative software packages.

A second reason why project markets are imperfect is that the markets themselves may not be as well organized as are financial markets. For example, particular capital goods may be hard to find because they are produced by only a few manufacturers. When manufacturers market their own products, no centralized market offering all the products produced by that industry may exist. Additional reasons can be advanced to further explain the imperfect character of project markets. The important point is to realize that, as a consequence of these imperfect markets, firms purchasing real assets in such markets seek to identify capital-budgeting projects that have expected rates of return in excess of their systematic risk adjusted required rates.

A MEASUREMENT PROBLEM. The second question that arises from Figure 17-1 is how to measure project betas. In general it is not possible to measure project betas directly. Why? Because the covariance between a project's rate of return and the rate of return of a market index of financial assets cannot be measured directly, and it is this covariance that is used in computing a project beta. Projects are offered in imperfect markets that deal in real assets while the market index is composed of financial assets that trade in efficient financial markets. There is no direct way to link the two markets in order to measure the needed covariance. Fortunately a number of techniques have been developed for approximating the beta coefficients of real assets and the remainder of this section explains some of these techniques.

**Constant
Systematic
Business Risk**

A simple way of estimating a project's discount rate is to compute the shareholder expected rate of return, as expressed in the firm's SML, and to equate that rate of return with the discount rate. This is a reasonable approach when certain conditions pertaining to the systematic risk portion of the firm's business risk are met. When the firm uses financial leverage, a modified approach must be used. As described in Chapter 5, financial leverage is present when the firm's capital structure contains bonds or preferred stock. The associated financial risk, like business risk, has a systematic risk component. Thus, there are two components to corporate systematic risk: systematic business risk and systematic financial risk. The firm's beta coefficient reflects both components, and both must be taken into account in arriving at project discount rates.

ALL-EQUITY CAPITAL STRUCTURE. Consider a corporation that operates in only one industry. The firm is not diversified in terms of the goods and services it produces and offers for sale. In this situation the systematic risk component of the firm's business risk is the result of operating only in one area of business and is not a composite, or average risk, resulting from operating in several unrelated industries. Now assume that this corporation is an all-equity firm, that is, a firm with all its long-term financial sources composed of common stock and retained earnings. The risk absorbed by the shareholders of this firm does not contain a financial risk component, and the firm's beta coefficient reflects only the systematic risk contained in the firm's business risk.

In a single industry, all-equity firm, the discount rate used in evaluating capital-budgeting alternatives equals the expected rate of return specified by the firm's SML when the following two conditions are met. First, the project must fall within the scope of the firm's current operations. Second, in financing any new projects, the firm's capital structure must remain 100 percent equity. If these conditions are met, the firm's systematic risk, and thus its beta coefficient, will not change as a result of the capital-budgeting decision, thus allowing the use of the shareholder current expected rate of return as the project discount rate.

---

**Example:**

RPX, Inc., owns a number of fast-food franchises that specialize in fried chicken and do business as the Captain's Turkey. These franchises were originally sold nationwide by the Admiral Bones Company, and they all operate under the Captain Turkey name. RPX has the opportunity to acquire a number of these franchises from other operators. What is the required rate of return to be used in evaluating these potential acquisitions?

The project in this example consists of expanding an existing product line. If RPX has no unrelated operations, if its capital structure is 100 percent equity, and if acquiring the franchises does not require debt or preferred stock financing, the firm's SML can be used as the source of the discount rate to evaluate the proposed acquisitions.

If the beta coefficient for RPX is 1.25, and assuming $R_f$ is equal to 11 percent and $R_m$ is equal to 20 percent, then the discount rate $(k)$ is obtained by using Equation 17-2 as shown below:

$$k = .11 + (.20 - .11)1.25$$
$$= .2225 \quad \text{or} \quad 22.25\%$$

**CONSTANT CAPITAL STRUCTURE.** This example demonstrates the several assumptions that must be met if the SML is to serve as a capital-budgeting discount rate. The easiest assumption to relax pertains to the firm's financing mix. If a corporation's capital structure contains a mix of financing sources, and if the project is to be financed using the same percentage mix currently present in the firm's capital structure, the project's discount rate equals the firm's weighted average cost of capital $(k_w)$ using market value weights for debt $(D)$ and equity $(E)$. Equation 14-9 is used to measure the firm's weighted average cost of capital and is repeated here for purposes of convenience:

$$k_w = k_d\left(\frac{D}{D + E}\right) + k_e\left(\frac{E}{D + E}\right) \qquad (14\text{-}9)$$

The specific cost of debt $(k_d)$ is computed from Equation 14-1:

$$k_d = k_m(1 - t) \qquad (14\text{-}1)$$

Where $k_m$ is the yield on the bonds. The specific cost of common stock and retained earnings is computed using the SML and the firm's beta coefficient. This approach can be used because the expansion that results if the project is accepted does not alter the firm's systematic risk. The firm's increase in asset size is accomplished by investing in a project having a systematic risk equal to the systematic risk of the firm's existing assets. In addition, the project is financed without altering its capital structure composition; thus, its systematic financial risk component also remains constant.

**Example:**    The Sandy Boat Company owns a fleet of fishing trawlers that operate off the coast of New England. This is the firm's only line of business. Sandy Boat is considering expanding its fleet of trawlers. Financing the purchases would be done so as to hold its capital structure percentage composition constant. What is the required rate of return to use in this case? Sandy Boat's capital structure consists of 20 percent debt and 80 percent common equity in market value terms. With a 40 percent tax rate and an assumed 12 percent before-tax yield on new bonds, the specific cost of capital of debt $(k_d)$ is obtained by using Equation 14-1:

$$k_d = (.12)(1 - .4)$$
$$= .072 \quad \text{or} \quad 7.2\%$$

The firm's beta coefficient is reported as 1.05. In addition $R_f$ equals .12 and $R_m$ equals .20.

The rate of return expected by the firm's common shareholders, which is the specific cost of equity capital ($k_e$), is obtained using the SML equation, 17-2:

$$k_e = .12 + (.20 - .12)1.05$$
$$= .204 \quad \text{or} \quad 20.4\%$$

The firm's weighted average cost of capital ($k_w$) using market value weights, is obtained using Equation 14-9:

$$k_w = .072(.2) + .204(.8)$$
$$= .1776 \quad \text{or} \quad 17.76\%$$

Thus, the proposed purchases can be evaluated using a 17.76 percent discount rate.

---

**TARGET CAPITAL STRUCTURE.** A more significant measurement problem occurs when a firm alters its capital structure as a consequence of financing its capital budget. In this situation it is not possible to use the firm's existing weighted average cost of capital because the marginal cost of capital, the cost of financing its capital budget, may differ from its current weighted average cost of capital. The change in its capital structure composition may alter the firm's systematic financial risk component which will change the firm's beta coefficient and thus its specific cost of equity capital.

When accepting a project would change the firm's capital structure, a target capital structure approach can be used to approximate the project discount rate. The assumption in this approach is that corporate management has identified its target capital structure (TCS) and moves toward that target incrementally. This means that the firm changes its capital structure gradually over a period of time — possibly several years — so as to attain its desired capital structure. Associated with this target capital structure is a cost of capital that will have to be earned or exceeded by the firm's investments if shareholder wealth is to increase. This cost of capital is the project discount rate.

The firm's beta coefficient can be expected to change in response to reaching its TCS. However, the beta coefficient contains both systematic business risk and systematic financial risk. A technique is needed that can isolate the values of each systematic risk component and that also can estimate the impact on the firm's beta coefficient resulting from changes in each component. In this section, systematic business risk is held constant while the firm's capital structure and thus its systematic financial risk are allowed to vary. The resulting beta coefficient is used to estimate the discount rate for capital-budgeting projects.

The following procedure can be used to isolate the separate components of systematic risk.[1] Suppose a firm has only common stock and retained earnings in its capital structure. In this all-equity case, the firm's beta coefficient will contain only systematic business risk. Let $\beta_u$ represent the unlevered firm's beta coefficient. If the firm now adds debt to its capital structure *while holding its systematic business risk constant*, the firm's resulting beta coefficient can be written as follows:

$$\beta = \beta_u + \beta_u\left[\frac{D}{E}(1-t)\right] \qquad (17\text{-}4)$$

Where $D$ and $E$ represent the market values of the firm's debt and equity respectively, and $t$ is the corporate tax rate.

Equation 17-4 states that the portion of a firm's beta coefficient attributable to its capital structure is:

$$\beta_u\left[\frac{D}{E}(1-t)\right]$$

This value is added to its $\beta_u$ value to arrive at its beta coefficient.

---

**Example:**    An all-equity firm's capital structure has a $500,000 market value. Its beta coefficient is 1.3; thus:

$$\beta = \beta_u = 1.3$$

The firm then sells $100,000 of bonds and uses the proceeds to retire common stock. If the market value of the common is now $400,000, the resulting beta coefficient for the firm is computed using Equation 17-4. If $t = .4$, then:

$$\beta = 1.3 + 1.3\left[\frac{\$100,000}{\$400,000}(1-.4)\right]$$

$$= 1.495$$

The increase in the firm's beta coefficient from 1.3 to 1.495 (i.e., .195) is due to the change in its capital structure.

---

Now consider the following problem. If a corporation has debt in its capital structure, how can the systematic business risk component be measured? The answer to this problem is obtained by solving Equation 17-4 for $\beta_u$. The resulting equation is:

---

[1]The derivation of Equation 17-4 is based on the article by Hamada listed in the end-of-chapter Selected References. Preferred stock is ignored as a financing instrument.

$$\beta_u = \frac{\beta}{1 + \dfrac{D}{E}(1 - t)} \tag{17-5}$$

**Example:**

A corporation's beta coefficient is 1.5. Its debt has a market value of $400,000, and its common stock has a market value of $1 million. Assuming that $t$ is equal to .4, its systematic business risk component can be measured by using Equation 17-5:

$$\beta_u = \frac{1.5}{1 + \dfrac{\$400,000}{\$1,000,000}(1 - .4)}$$

$$= 1.21$$

The capital structure beta component for this firm is $(1.5 - 1.21) = .29$

In the above example the firm's $\beta_u$ was found to have a value of 1.21. This is an estimate of what the firm's beta coefficient would be in the absence of financial leverage. Because of this interpretation, $\beta_u$ is often referred to as an *unlevered beta coefficient*. Since a firm's beta reflects both components of its systematic risk, care must be taken to remember that $\beta_u$ refers to the systematic risk contained in the firm's assets but not in its capital structure.

Equations 17-4 and 17-5 provide a method for separating a firm's beta coefficients into its two systematic risk components. As a consequence, these equations are used in the procedure for identifying the capital-budgeting discount rate for a firm that is moving toward a target capital structure. This procedure, summarized in the following three steps, assumes that the projects under consideration each have a systematic risk component equal to that present in the firm's existing assets; this implies that the $\beta_u$ coefficient remains constant.

1. Using the existing value of the firm's beta coefficient and the current market values of the firm's debt and equity, solve for $\beta_u$ using Equation 17-5.

2. Compute the beta coefficient that results once the firm attains its TCS. This is accomplished by using the $\beta_u$ value obtained in Step 1 and the debt and equity market values at the TCS. These three values are entered into the right-hand side of Equation 17-4; the resulting value is the TCS beta coefficient.

3. The capital-budgeting discount rate is obtained by computing the weighted average cost of capital (Equation 14-9) using market value weights at the TCS. The specific cost of debt is the after-tax cost of debt using Equation 14-1. The specific cost

of equity is found by using the SML equation (17-2) that contains the beta coefficient computed in Step 2, that is, the beta coefficient at the firm's TCS.

The first step in this procedure identifies that portion of the firm's total systematic risk contained in the firm's assets. The second step estimates the firm's beta coefficient at its TCS. Step 3 explains how to compute the cost of capital for the firm at its TCS.

One additional point needs to be made concerning the firm's TCS. It is not necessary to estimate the actual dollars of financing that will be needed by the firm. Since the firm does not know how many projects will be accepted, it cannot estimate how much additional capital will be required. However, in using Equations 17-4, 17-5, and the weighted average cost of capital equation (14-9), all that is required is that the firm specify its TCS in terms of its debt to equity ratio.

---

**Example:**

OmniVeg is a wholesaler that deals exclusively in vegetable seeds. The firm purchases seeds in bulk from producers and sells them in smaller unit amounts to growers and retailers. The firm is evaluating the desirability of adding additional wholesale outlets in order to serve parts of the country in which it now does not operate.

The OmniVeg capital structure currently contains both debt and equity securities. Its common stock trades actively enough to allow the firm to estimate its beta coefficient at 1.25. The firm's current debt to equity ratio is .2. OmniVeg has identified a TCS of .4 which it expects to reach as the firm's expansion is financed. The firm wants to identify the discount rate to use in evaluating its expansion plans. The before-tax cost of debt is estimated at 14 percent; this is the approximate yield on its existing debt. The risk-free rate is 12 percent, and the rate of return on the market index has been averaging 20 percent. Assume a 40 percent tax rate.

The first step in estimating the firm's project discount rate is to compute its $\beta_u$ coefficient using Equation 17-5:

$$\beta_u = \frac{1.25}{1 + .2(1 - .4)}$$

$$= 1.116$$

The second step is to compute the beta coefficient at the TCS of 40 percent debt to equity. This beta coefficient is obtained by using Equation 17-4:

$$\beta = 1.116 + 1.116[.4(1 - .4)]$$

$$= 1.384$$

Step 3 begins by computing the specific cost of equity capital using a SML and the firm's TCS beta of 1.384. Equation 17-2 is used to obtain the following:

$$k_e = .12 + (.20 - .12)(1.384)$$

$$= .231 \quad \text{or} \quad 23.1\%$$

The weighted average cost of capital that will serve as the project discount rate can now be computed using Equation 14-9:[2]

$$k_w = .14(1 - .4)\left[\frac{4}{4 + 10}\right] + .231\left[\frac{10}{4 + 10}\right]$$

$$= .189 \quad \text{or} \quad 18.9\%$$

**Changes in Systematic Business Risk**

The previous section held systematic business risk constant in order to explain the impact of capital structure composition on a firm's systematic risk. It is quite likely, however, that the various capital-budgeting projects adopted over time will change the degree of the firm's systematic business risk and combine with the firm's systematic financial risk to alter its beta coefficient. Consider the following situation. A corporation, whose only product line consists of manufacturing kitchen appliances for home builders, is evaluating the desirability of opening a chain of retail discount clothing stores. What is the appropriate discount rate to use in evaluating the proposed retail operation? If the project is accepted, the firm will no longer operate exclusively in one business segment. Assuming that the revenues and profits from each segment are not closely related, each segment will contain its own degree of systematic business risk. In addition, if the firm alters its capital structure composition as it expands, the change in its systematic financial risk will further alter the firm's risk-return characteristics. Thus, evaluating the desirability of the retail store project requires that the impact of the firm's two systematic risk components on shareholder expected rates of return be taken into account.

This section explains how to estimate project discount rates and costs of capital when both systematic risk components are subject to change. The procedures to be explained contain some difficult estimation problems, and answers to these problems cannot always be provided. However, since operating in several different industries has increasingly become a basic corporate strategy, it is important that financial managers be able to measure — however imperfectly — the impact on shareholder wealth from diversifying into unrelated product lines while simultaneously moving toward a target capital structure.

USING PROXY COMPANIES. When a corporation seeks to evaluate a project that has a systematic business risk component that is unknown or is expected to differ from the firm's current systematic business risk level a proxy company approach can be used as the first step in estimating the project discount rate. As was explained above, a project's discount rate is a function of its unlevered beta. If the firm does not have an estimate of that

---

[2]The firm's TCS was expressed in terms of a .4 debt to equity ratio: $D/E = .4$. This means that the firm wants to use $4 of debt for every $10 equity. Thus, in computing $k_w$, the value of $D$ was set at four and the value of $E$ was set at ten.

value, it then looks to other companies — referred to as *proxy companies* — that have product lines that are similar to the project under scrutiny. The unlevered betas of the proxy companies are then averaged to produce an estimate of the project's unlevered beta. If the proxy companies have debt in their capital structures, their unlevered betas are estimated by using Equation 17-5.

The kitchen appliance manufacturer example can be used to illustrate the use of proxy companies. Assume that the manufacturer is an all-equity firm and that its beta coefficient is 1.5. The firm's managers expect that the systematic business risk in the retail discount clothing industry, and thus its unlevered beta, is different from 1.5. In order to estimate the project's beta coefficient, they obtain data from two large retailers specializing in discount clothing. Retailer $K$ is an all-equity firm with a beta coefficient of .95. Retailer $W$ has a debt-to-equity ratio of 25 percent and a beta of 1.05.

Retailer $W$'s unlevered beta coefficient is computed by using Equation 17-5 with $t$ equal to .4. Let $\beta_{uw}$ represent the proxy company's unlevered beta:

$$\beta_{uw} = \frac{1.05}{1 + .25(1 - .4)}$$
$$= .91$$

The unlevered beta coefficients for the two proxy companies are then averaged to obtain an estimate $(\beta_{ux})$ of the unlevered beta for that industry. This is computed as follows:

$$\beta_{ux} = \frac{.95 + .91}{2}$$
$$= .93$$

The manufacturer thus uses .93 as the unlevered beta estimate corresponding to the retail store project. Since the manufacturer is an all-equity firm, the project discount rate, the specific cost of equity capital $(k_e)$, is estimated using a SML containing the .93 unlevered beta coefficient. Let $R_f$ equal .12 and $R_m$ equal .20; then:

$$k_e = .12 + (.20 - .12).93$$
$$= .1944 \quad \text{or} \quad 19.44\%$$

Thus the manufacturer would discount the expected cash flow from the retail store operations using a discount rate of 19.44 percent.

**ADJUSTING FOR ASSET AND CAPITAL STRUCTURE CHANGES.** Estimating discount rates and costs of capital when a firm's business risk is changing becomes more difficult when its capital structure contains debt or when the firm's TCS will change the firm's existing capital structure. Separate procedures are used to estimate the project discount rate and the firm's weighted average cost of capital. However, as explained below, these procedures are far from perfect.

*Project Discount Rates.* The following four steps are used to estimate a project's discount rate. Figure 17-2 identifies the variables and equations used in each step and helps to explain the logic of the overall procedure.

1.  Compute the project's unlevered beta ($\beta_{ux}$) using proxy companies.

2.  Compute the beta coefficient needed to measure the project's discount rate. This coefficient ($\beta_j$) contains project systematic risk and the systematic financial risk that occurs at the firm's TCS. To calculate the value of $\beta_j$, substitute the unlevered

Figure 17-2.          **Project Discount Rate-Estimating Procedure**

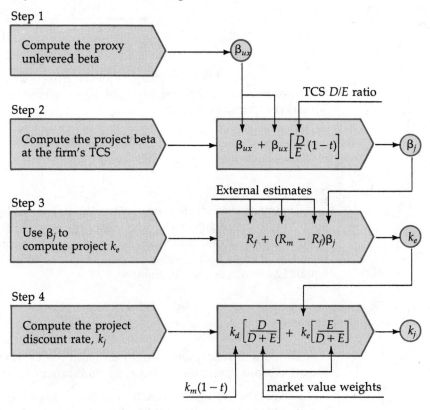

proxy company beta, computed in Step 1, and the firm's TCS debt-to-equity ratio into Equation 17-4.

3. Compute the specific cost of equity capital ($k_e$) for the project. This requires the use of the SML, using project beta at the firm's TCS ($\beta_j$) computed in Step 2.

4. The project's discount rate ($k_j$) is the marginal cost of capital using market value weights at the firm's TCS. The marginal cost of capital represents the weighted costs of debt and equity capital used to finance the project. The specific cost of equity is taken from Step 3. The specific cost of debt is the after-tax cost of debt using Equation 14-1. These specific costs and the market value weights are entered into Equation 14-9.

These four steps estimate the project's discount rate on the basis of project systematic risk and the firm's cost of capital at its TCS. This discount rate is the rate of return the firm needs to earn on the project given the project's systematic risk and the financing mix in the firm's TCS. The unlevered beta coefficient computed in the first step is a measure of the project's systematic business risk. The second and third steps compute the specific cost of equity capital. The fourth step computes the weighted marginal cost of capital at the firm's TCS for the project and equates that cost of capital with the project discount rate.

*Weighted Average Cost of Capital.* The firm's overall risk-return characteristics and thus its weighted average cost of capital are altered as a result of investing in this new project. Not only is the systematic business risk component changed, but its systematic financial risk component also changes as the firm alters its capital structure composition in order to reach its TCS. The following steps are used to estimate the firm's weighted average cost of capital at its TCS. Figure 17-3 identifies the variables and equations for each step and helps explain the logic of the procedure.

1. Compute the *firm's* unlevered beta coefficient prior to investing in the new project.

2. Compute the project's unlevered coefficient using proxy companies.

3. Compute the firm's systematic business risk that emerges once it invests in the new project. This is the firm's new unlevered beta and is estimated by computing the weighted average of the unlevered beta coefficients corresponding to each of the firm's product lines. The weights are the percentages of the firm's market value contained in each product line. In Step 3 of Figure 17-3, $M_p$ is the new project's market value weight, and $M_f$ is the market value weight for the firm's assets excluding the new project.

Figure 17-3        **Estimating Procedure for $k_w$**

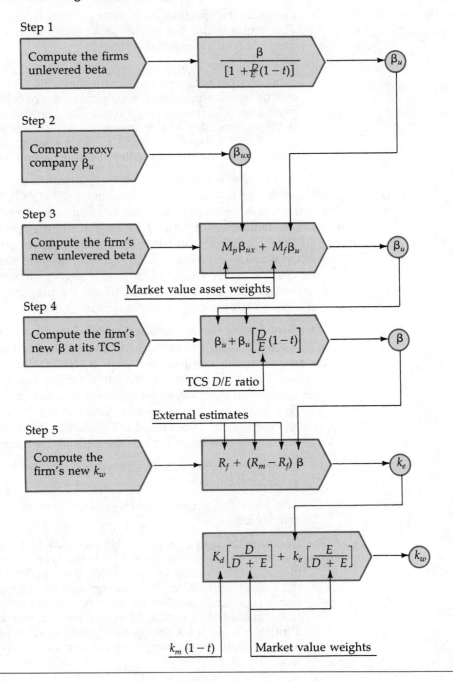

Step 1

Compute the firms
unlevered beta

$$\frac{\beta}{[1 + \frac{D}{E}(1 - t)]}$$

$\beta_u$

Step 2

Compute proxy
company $\beta_u$

$\beta_{ux}$

Step 3

Compute the firm's
new unlevered beta

$$M_p\beta_{ux} + M_f\beta_u$$

$\beta_u$

Market value asset weights

Step 4

Compute the firm's
new $\beta$ at its TCS

$$\beta_u + \beta_u\left[\frac{D}{E}(1 - t)\right]$$

$\beta$

TCS $D/E$ ratio

External estimates

Step 5

Compute the
firm's new $k_w$

$$R_f + (R_m - R_f)\,\beta$$

$k_e$

$$K_d\left[\frac{D}{D + E}\right] + k_e\left[\frac{E}{D + E}\right]$$

$k_w$

$k_m(1 - t)$        Market value weights

4. Compute the *firm's* new beta coefficient at its TCS. This is accomplished by substituting the firm's unlevered beta from Step 3 and its debt to equity TCS ratio into Equation 17-4.

5. The firm's weighted average cost of capital is computed using Equation 14-9 and market value weights at its TCS. The specific cost of capital of debt is the after-tax cost incurred by the firm at its TCS and is computed from Equation 14-1. The specific cost of equity ($k_e$) is computed using a SML and the firm's new beta coefficient which was computed in Step 4.

These five steps provide an estimate of the overall rate of return that the firm will have to earn once it undertakes the capital-budgeting project and attains its TCS. The first two steps compute the firm's unlevered beta prior to expansion and the project's unlevered beta. These two coefficients are used in the third step to compute the firm's new unlevered beta; this provides a measure of the firm's systematic business risk once it has undertaken the project. Since the firm's asset structure now contains investments with different betas, the firm's unlevered beta is computed in this step as a weighted average of the asset betas using asset market values as weights. The fourth step computes the firm's beta that emerges once the project has been accepted and the firm's TCS has been attained. The last step computes the specific costs of capital and uses these values to compute the firm's weighted average cost of capital.

The following example illustrates how these procedures are used to estimate project discount rates and costs of capital when both systematic risk components of a firm are likely to change.

---

**Example:**    DZR & Co. produces and distributes business forms and office supplies and also owns four cable television franchises. The firm is evaluating the desirability of opening a chain of retail paint stores. DZR's management faces the problem of estimating the minimum rate of return that will make this new line of business attractive. Management estimates that the paint stores, once established, will account for 10 percent of the firm's total sales and about 10 percent of its total profits.

The firm also seeks to alter its capital structure to a debt-to-equity ratio of .4 from its current value of .15. Management feels such an increase in financial leverage is desirable because its present lines of business have been very stable and are expected to continue to produce steadily increasing sales and earnings. The firm expects the increased financial leverage to produce further increases in earnings per share. Since this increased leverage will produce higher expected returns on the part of shareholders, the firm must estimate the overall minimum rate of return that will meet shareholder expectations.

DZR's beta coefficient is .95, and its corporate income tax rate is 40 percent. The cost of capital of new debt is estimated to be 14 percent; this figure is based on the yield to maturity of the debt the firm currently has outstanding.

The firm's management obtains the following data on two companies that currently dominate the retail paint store industry:

|  | Company $M$ | Company $G$ |
|---|---|---|
| Beta coefficient | 1.5 | 1.8 |
| Debt/Equity | 0 | .5 |

The firm's financial advisors provide the following data concerning security market rates of return:

$$R_f = .12 \qquad R_m = .20$$

The discount rate for evaluating the paint store project is estimated using the four-step procedure outlined above and illustrated in Figure 17-2.

1. Compute the project's unlevered beta using Proxy Companies $M$ and $G$. Company $M$'s unlevered beta is 1.5 because it is an all-equity firm. Company $G$'s unlevered beta, assuming $t$ equals .4, is found using Equation 17-5:

$$\beta_{ux} = \frac{1.8}{1 + .5(1 - .4)}$$

$$= 1.385$$

The average unlevered beta of these two firms is:

$$(1.5 + 1.385)/2 = 1.443$$

This value is used on DZR's estimate of the paint store project unlevered beta.

2. Compute the project beta ($\beta_j$) at the firm's TCS. This requires the use of Equation 17-4, the average unlevered proxy beta of 1.443, and a TCS of .4:

$$\beta_j = 1.443 + 1.443[.4(1 - .4)]$$

$$= 1.789$$

3. Compute the specific cost of equity ($k_e$) using the firm's beta coefficient at its TCS and Equation 17-2:

$$k_e = .12 + (.20 - .12)1.789$$

$$= .2631 \quad \text{or} \quad 26.31\%$$

4. The project's discount rate is the weighted marginal cost of capital the firm incurs in financing the project with its TCS mix. The specific cost of debt ($k_d$) is obtained using Equation 14-1:

$$k_d = (1 - .4)(.14)$$

$$= .084 \quad \text{or} \quad 8.4\%$$

With $k_e$ equal to .2631, the project's weighted marginal cost of capital ($k_j$) is obtained from Equation 14-9 using TCS market value weights:

$$k_j = .084(.286) + .2631(.714)$$
$$= .2119 \quad \text{or} \quad 21.19\%$$

The firm must expect to earn a rate of return of at least 21.19 percent on the paint store project if it is to be desirable, and this rate of return is used to compute the NPV of the project's cash flows. The weights in the $k_j$ equation are based on the firm's use of $4 of debt for every $10 of equity. The .286 weight, for example, is computed from $4/($4 + $10). The firm's weighted average cost of capital ($k_w$), the rate that it must expect to earn on all its assets if it establishes the paint stores and attains its TCS, is estimated by using the five-step procedure outlined above and illustrated in Figure 17-3.

1. Compute the project's unlevered beta. (This was done in Step 1 above and is 1.385.)

2. Compute the firm's unlevered beta prior to expansion. The firm's current beta is .95, and its existing debt-to-equity ratio is .15. Using Equation 17-5:

$$\beta_u = \frac{.95}{1 + .15(1 - .4)}$$
$$= .872$$

3. Compute the firm's unlevered beta once it establishes the paint store chain. The firm's management decides that its unlevered beta will reflect the relative profit contributions of its product lines: 90 percent from existing operations and 10 percent from the new project. Thus:

$$\beta_u = .9(.872) + .1(1.385)$$
$$= .923$$

4. Compute the firm's beta coefficient at its TCS. The firm's unlevered beta will be .923, and its TCS debt to equity ratio is .4. Using Equation 17-4:

$$\beta = .923 + .923[.4(1 - .4)]$$
$$= 1.145$$

5. Compute the weighted average cost of capital at the firm's TCS. The cost of debt ($k_d$) was previously computed as .084. The cost of equity ($k_e$) is computed using a SML that contains the firm's beta of 1.145:

$$k_e = .12 + (.20 - .12)1.145$$
$$= .2116 \quad \text{or} \quad 21.16\%$$

Using Equation 14-9:

$$k_w = .084(.286) + .2116(.714)$$
$$= .1751 \quad \text{or} \quad 17.51\%$$

The firm must expect to earn an overall 17.51 percent rate of return once the project is established and its TCS is attained in order to meet shareholder expectations.

The changes in DZR & Co.'s beta coefficient and costs of capital as a result of investing in the retail store chain and increasing its degree of financial leverage can be traced as follows. Initially the firm's beta coefficient was .95, consisting of an unlevered beta of .872 and a financial leverage component of .078. The firm's specific cost of debt was 8.4 percent; its specific cost of equity capital was:

$$k_e = .12 + (.20 - .12).95$$
$$= .196 \quad \text{or} \quad 19.6\%$$

With a debt to equity ratio of .15, the firm's weighted average cost of capital was:

$$k_w = .084 \left[ \frac{15}{15 + 100} \right] + .196 \left[ \frac{100}{15 + 100} \right]$$
$$= .1813 \quad \text{or} \quad 18.13\%$$

As a result of accepting the store project and attaining its TCS ratio of 40 percent, the firm's beta coefficient increases to 1.145. This consists of an unlevered beta of .923 and a financial leverage component of .222. The firm's weighted average cost of capital *decreases* to 17.51 percent. These figures are summarized as follows:

| Debt/Equity | Firm Beta | Unlevered Beta | Financial Leverage Component Beta | $k_w$ |
|---|---|---|---|---|
| .15 | .95 | .872 | .078 | 18.13% |
| .40 | 1.145 | .923 | .222 | 17.51% |

What causes the decrease in the firm's overall cost of capital? The shift in the firm's capital structure to the lower cost of capital debt more than offsets the increase in the specific cost of equity. Note that the cost of debt remains constant even though the firm's financial leverage beta component increases from .078 to .222. This example thus implicitly assumed that the additional systematic risk faced by the bondholders would not be sufficient to have them require a higher rate of return.

The increased systematic risk reflected in the firm's increased beta coefficient is absorbed by shareholders, and this produces a higher specific cost of equity capital. Since, however, the increased use of lower cost debt more than offsets — at least in this example — the higher cost of equity, the firm will only have to earn an overall rate of return of 17.51 percent to meet the expectations of both bondholders and shareholders.

In addition to illustrating the procedures for calculating beta coefficients and costs of capital, the above example can also be used to identify some of the difficulties involved in estimating unlevered beta coefficients. One problem occurs with the use of proxy companies. Identifying such companies may not be easy, especially if the proxies operate in more than one industry. In addition, obtaining market value weight debt-to-equity ratios of the proxy companies may pose additional problems unless the firm's financial assets are actively traded in security markets. A sample of several proxy companies may be required to obtain an estimate of the project's unlevered beta.

A second problem occurs in estimating the firm's unlevered beta if it accepts the project. In theory, the firm should use weights for the product lines that reflect their market values. This is a valuation problem that requires further assumptions concerning the value of each product line as a separate company. The above example used product line profits as estimates of their relative market values.

These procedures contain other difficulties as well. Forecasts of specific costs of capital and the weighted average cost of capital at the firm's TCS may turn out to be inaccurate in the light of subsequent developments in security markets. The financial managers must look ahead to a time when the firm realizes its target capital structure and forecast the values of risk-free rates, rates of return on the market index, and the market values of the firm's debt and equity securities. Errors in these forecast values can be substantial if unanticipated occurrences such as recessions, inflation, new federal tax policies, or changes in the firm's competitive environment — to name a few possibilities — impact on the security markets in which these financial assets are traded. For example, the severe inflationary period from 1979-1982 produced historically high and unforeseen rates of return not only for money market securities (see Figure 7-1) but also increased specific costs of capital of long term securities, especially for bonds, to the point where they became prohibitively expensive for many corporations. As a result, many financing and investing plans were altered, delayed, or cancelled. In addition, as discussed earlier, project betas cannot be measured directly as are the beta coefficients of financial assets.

In spite of these limitations, the procedures contained in this section have the advantage of allowing financial managers to recognize the systematic risk components in the firm's asset and capital structures. The costs of capital that emerge are consistent with the requirements of capital asset pricing. Thus, the procedures for estimating project discount rates and costs of capital explained in this section are consistent with the concept that systematic risk is the relevant risk for investors who own well-diversified portfolios.

The flowchart contained in Figure 17-4 integrates the procedures that have been explained in this section and identifies the equation sequences needed to allow for any changes in the firm's systematic risk components that result from its capital-budgeting decision. Thus, the first step in solving a capital-budgeting problem of the type discussed in this section is to use this flowchart to identify the appropriate procedure. This will help reduce or avoid unneeded computation.

**Figure 17-4.**     **Sequences for Estimating $k_j$ and $k_w$**

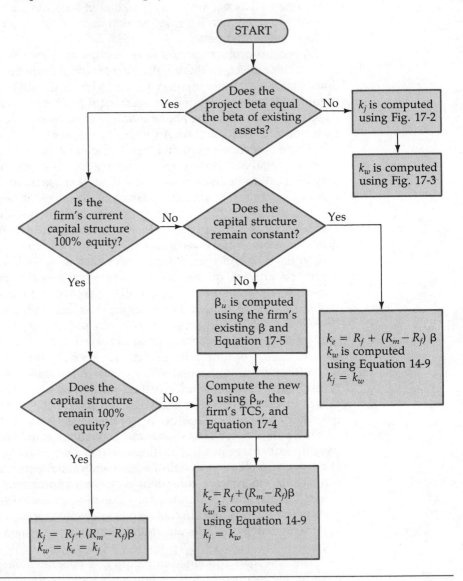

## CAPITAL STRUCTURE AND
## SYSTEMATIC RISK

In presenting techniques for estimating project discount rates the previous section looked at the impact of both components of systematic risk, business and financial, on the firm's cost of capital. However, the impact of capital structure changes on a firm's market value was not discussed. This omission was necessary in order to concentrate on investment decisions. This section explains how the firm's capital structure—or financial— systematic risk component affects its market value and examines the implications of capital asset pricing on the existence of a shareholder wealth-maximizing capital structure. If such an optimal capital structure exists, then the firm should adopt it as its target capital structure in order to increase shareholder wealth. If capital structure has no impact on firm value, then the firm's financing policy is irrelevant, and any capital structure that provides the needed funds will be acceptable.

The impact—or lack of impact—of capital structure on firm value has been one of the most highly discussed and debated topics of finance theory. The conclusions reached in this section are similar to those reached in Chapter 14: capital structure affects firm value, there exists a value-maximizing capital structure, and cost of capital is minimized where firm value is a maximum. What is different here, as compared with Chapter 14, is the use of capital asset pricing and systematic risk as the framework for examining the capital structure question. Chapter 14 used a total risk framework; the intrinsic value model used to measure the market value of the firm's common stock assumed that shareholders absorbed both systematic and unsystematic risk components. In other words, that intrinsic value model did not allow for the existence of investors who own well-diversified portfolios.

The focus of this section can be stated in terms of the following question: Within a capital asset pricing framework, does a firm's capital structure affect shareholder wealth? The answer is a qualified yes. This chapter has already explained how a firm's capital structure affects its beta coefficient and thus its cost of capital. In extending this analysis, however, it is first necessary to hold constant those other variables—many of which were identified in Chapter 2—that affect firm value. This is accomplished by specifying a set of assumptions within which firm value can be expressed in terms of its return and systematic risk characteristics. From this it is possible to measure how the firm's market value changes in response to capital structure decisions. The conclusions that emerge from this analysis are extended by relaxing some of the initial assumptions. The final portion of this section summarizes the conclusions and identifies some of the difficulties faced by financial managers as they attempt to identify and attain corporate value-maximizing capital structures.

**Initial Assumptions**

The assumptions concerning the existence of perfect capital markets and the risk averse behavior of investors who own well-diversified portfolios continue to provide a general analytical framework. The following additional assumptions help focus attention on the financial management problem of measuring the impact of capital structure on firm value.

**CONSTANT TOTAL FINANCING.** The total amount of financing in the firm's capital structure is held constant. This assumption has two implications. First, the firm distributes all earnings as dividends in order to keep its total financing from increasing. Second, capital structure changes are accomplished by selling financial assets, such as bonds, and using the proceeds to purchase common stock from resale markets.

**CONSTANT BUSINESS RISK.** The portion of the firm's total risk contained in its assets is held constant. In particular, the firm's systematic business risk is held constant. This assumption also requires that the firm's probability distribution of EBIT be held constant through time. Assets earn a constant expected value of EBIT, although the actual EBIT earned during each time period can vary.

**RISKLESS DEBT.** When a firm sells bonds, the purchasers of these financial assets consider them riskless in the sense that the firm is not expected to default on interest payments. When bonds mature, their principal is repaid by selling additional securities. This assumption implies that the firm will not become insolvent and face bankruptcy proceedings. As long as the firm's debt is considered riskless, the rate of return expected on these financial assets equals the rate of return available on risk-free assets such as Treasury bills. This very restrictive assumption is relaxed in the latter part of this section.

**OTHER FACTORS HELD CONSTANT.** Other factors that have an impact on the firm's market value and cost of capital are held constant. Investors in the firm's financial assets are assumed to focus on changes in the firm's capital structure. In addition, the firm pays a constant 40 percent tax rate on its taxable income.

**Valuation and Systematic Risk**

The above assumptions make it easy to identify and measure the cash flows that the firm earns and pays to its investors during each time period. The value of the firm to its investors is simply the sum of the present values of the cash flows investors receive over time.

**CASH FLOWS.** The cash flows that a corporation pays its investors consist of the dividends received by shareholders and interest payments received by bondholders. Measuring cash flows is made easier by using the same income statement format and associated variables developed in earlier chapters and by assuming yearly earnings and cash flows. Let:

$$Y = \text{EBIT earned during a given year}$$
$$I = \text{yearly interest payments}$$
$$t = 40\% \text{ tax rate}$$
$$EAT = \text{yearly earnings after taxes}$$

Then:

$$EAT = (Y - I)(1 - t) \qquad \text{(17-6)}$$

When a corporation has no debt outstanding, the value of $I$ in Equation 17-6 is zero. Such a firm was described earlier as an unlevered or all-equity firm. (Remember, unlevered means that the firm's systematic financial risk component is zero. It may have systematic business risk, but that component is being held constant.) Let $CF_u$ represent the unlevered firm's yearly cash flows. Then, using Equation 17-6:

$$CF_u = Y(1 - t) \qquad \text{(17-7)}$$

This equation states that the only cash flows generated are the earnings paid to shareholders.

A levered firm has debt in its capital structure. Thus, bondholders receive interest payments, and shareholders receive the income that remains after the firm has paid its interest and taxes. Let $CF_l$ represent a levered firm's yearly cash flows:

$$CF_l = (Y - I)(1 - t) + I \qquad \text{(17-8)}$$

The first term in this equation is the payment to shareholders; the second term is the bond interest payment. To compute the interest payment, multiply the value of the debt $(D)$ by $k_m$, the interest rate paid on the debt:

$$I = k_m D \qquad \text{(17-9)}$$

Substituting Equation 17-9 into Equation 17-8 produces:

$$CF_l = Y(1 - t) + tk_m D \qquad \text{(17-10)}$$

This can be written as follows:

$$CF_l = CF_u + tk_m D \qquad \text{(17-11)}$$

Equation 17-11 states that the cash flows generated by the levered firm equal the cash flows that would be realized if it were unlevered plus an additional amount based on the amount of debt in its capital structure.

---

**Example:**

An unlevered firm's annual EBIT is $50,000. Its yearly cash flow is obtained using Equation 17-7:

$$CF_u = \$50,000(1 - .4)$$
$$= \$30,000$$

The firm now sells $100,000 of debt that carries a 10 percent interest rate and uses the proceeds to retire a like amount of common stock. Using Equation 17-9, the interest payment is:

$$I = (.1)(\$100,000)$$
$$= \$10,000$$

The total cash flow generated by what is now a levered firm is obtained using Equation 17-8:

$$CF_l = (\$50,000 - \$10,000)(1 - .4) + \$10,000$$
$$= \$24,000 + \$10,000$$
$$= \$34,000$$

Shareholders receive $24,000 in dividends, and bondholders receive $10,000 in interest.

The firm's total cash flow has increased by $4,000 even though its EBIT has remained constant. This increase occurred because the interest on the debt is tax deductible. The firm's after-tax cost of debt is only $6,000. The firm pays $10,000 in interest and has its taxes decrease by $4,000. (For every dollar decrease in taxable income, taxes decrease by $.40). This tax shield on interest payments accounts for the increase in the firm's total cash flow. Equation 17-11 demonstrates the impact of this tax shield. The firm's cash flow, when it was unlevered, was $30,000; then after selling debt:

$$CF_l = \$30,000 + (.4)(.1)(\$100,000)$$
$$= \$30,000 + \$4,000$$
$$= \$34,000$$

---

**FIRM VALUE.** The value of the firm to its investors is simply the sum of the present values of the cash flows received from the firm. The constant business risk assumption implies that for a given capital structure the expected values of the firm's cash flows are constant through time. As a consequence, these cash flows can be treated as perpetuities, and their present values can be obtained by dividing the yearly cash flow amount by the investor expected rate of return.

The value of the unlevered firm is obtained by using Equation 17-7. The annual cash flow received by shareholders is $Y(1 - t)$. Let $k_u$ equal the rate of return expected by shareholders in return for investing in this unlevered firm. Then $V_u$ (the market value of the unlevered firm's cash flows) is:

$$V_u = \frac{Y(1 - t)}{k_u} \tag{17-12}$$

The value of the levered firm $(V_l)$ is obtained from Equation 17-10. The present value of the unlevered portion of the cash flow is obtained by dividing $Y(1 - t)$ by $k_u$. The second term in that equation is the tax shield on the debt. Its present value is obtained by using the market interest rate on the bonds as the discount rate, assuming that the risk of the tax shield is the same as that of the debt. Thus:

$$V_l = \frac{Y(1 - t)}{k_u} + \frac{tk_m D}{k_m}$$

$$= \frac{Y(1 - t)}{k_u} + tD \qquad (17\text{-}13)$$

Equivalently:

$$V_l = V_u + tD \qquad (17\text{-}14)$$

In both these equations, $tD$ is the present value of the tax shield on debt. These two equations state that the value of the levered firm equals its unlevered value plus an added amount based on the dollar value of the debt in its capital structure. The value of the firm is increased by adding debt and retiring stock. Thus, the value of the firm is maximized by maximizing the amount of debt in its capital structure while simultaneously using the proceeds to reduce the amount of stock held by shareholders. This result may be surprising. However, given the set of assumptions that have been made, the firm's value-maximizing capital structure — its optimal capital structure — consists of as much debt and as little common stock as possible.

---

**Example:**

The data from the previous example can be used to illustrate how the value of the firm increases as it alters its capital structure. The firm's cash flow is $30,000. Assuming $k_u$ to be equal to .15, then $V_u$ is computed using Equation 17-12:

$$V_u = \$30,000/.15$$
$$= \$200,000$$

The firm now sells $100,000 of debt at a 10 percent interest rate and retires common stock. The value of the levered firm is found using Equation 17-14:

$$V_l = \$200,000 + .4(\$100,000)$$
$$= \$240,000$$

If the firm sells another $50,000 of debt and retires a similar amount of stock, its value increases to:

$$V_l = \$200,000 + .4(\$150,000)$$

$$= \$260,000$$

These increases in firm value are due to the present value of the tax shield on debt

$tD$ that increases linearly with each added dollar of debt. Figure 17-5 illustrates how the present value of the tax shield contributes to the increase in the value of the levered firm. This figure plots Equation 17-14 with debt on the horizontal axis and the value of the firm on the vertical axis. As long as the cost of debt remains constant, the value of the firm continues to increase as the firm substitutes debt for equity.

**COST OF CAPITAL.** If the value of the levered firm continues to increase as it sells debt and retires stock, can the firm also expect its weighted average cost of capital to decrease as its debt-to-equity ratio increases? The answer is yes, as long as the firm's debt is perceived to be riskless by investors: The capital structure that maximizes firm value also minimizes its weighted average cost of capital. This result is due to the behavior of the specific cost of capital components of the firm's weighted average cost of capital. The specific cost of debt is constant and equal to the risk-free rate. The specific cost of equity capital increases with the firm's debt-to-equity ratio. However, the substitution of cheaper debt more than offsets the increasing cost of equity, thus reducing the firm's weighted average cost of capital.

**Figure 17-5**       **Value of the Firm**

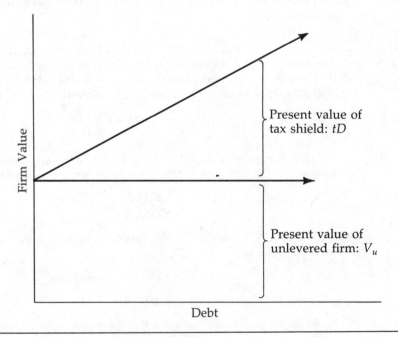

The first step in demonstrating the relationships between cost of capital and capital structure is to state the value of the firm as the sum of the values of its separate financial assets. Let $V_e$ represent the value of the firm's equity; as before, $D$ represents the value of the firm's debt. Then by definition, the value of the levered firm equals:

$$V_l = V_e + D$$

And

$$V_e = V_l - D \qquad \text{(17-15)}$$

Equation 17-15 is needed to compute the specific cost of equity and the resulting weighted average cost of capital.

The specific cost of capital of equity is computed using the firm's SML as shown next:

$$k_e = R_f + (R_m - R_f)\beta$$

The firm's beta coefficient, as explained earlier in this chapter, contains a systematic financial risk component. The beta coefficient and the cost of the equity capital can both be expected to increase as the firm's degree of systematic financial risk increases. The relationship between a firm's beta coefficient and its debt-to-equity ratio is expressed by rewriting Equation 17-4 as follows:

$$\beta = \beta_u \left[ 1 + \frac{D(1-t)}{V_e} \right] \qquad \text{(17-16)}$$

The value of $V_e$ is computed using Equation 17-14 to calculate $V_l$ and then substituting that value into Equation 17-15. For a given capital structure, the firm's beta coefficient is computed using Equation 17-16, and this value is then used in the SML to compute the corresponding $k_e$ value.

The firm's weighted average cost of capital is expressed by rewriting Equation 14-9 as follows:

$$k_w = k_d(1-t)\left(\frac{D}{V_l}\right) + k_e\left(\frac{V_e}{V_l}\right) \qquad \text{(17-17)}$$

This equation uses the same values for $V_l$ and $V_e$ needed to compute the firm's beta coefficient in Equation 17-16.

---

**Example:**   The impacts of capital structure on firm value and its costs of capital can be illustrated as follows. An all-equity firm's beta coefficient ($\beta_u$) is 1.25. Its yearly EBIT is a constant $100,000. The risk-free rate is 10 percent, and the return on the market index is estimated to be 18 percent. With a 40 percent tax rate, the firm's cash flow is computed using Equation 17-7:

$$CF_u = \$100,000(1 - .4)$$
$$= \$60,000$$

The value of this firm, the present value of its cash flow, is computed by capitalizing its $60,000 annual cash flow using the firm's unlevered cost of equity capital. The firm's SML is used to estimate the unlevered discount rate:

$$k_u = .10 + (.18 - .10)1.25$$
$$= .20$$

Using Equation 17-12:

$$V_u = \$100,000(1 - .4)/.2$$
$$= \$300,000$$

Since the firm's capital structure contains only common stock, its weighted average cost of capital equals .20. These values are contained in the first row of Table 17-1.

The firm now sells $50,000 of debt and retires an equal amount of stock. The value of the now levered firm is obtained from Equation 17-14:

$$V_l = \$100,000(1 - .4)/.2 + .4(\$50,000)$$
$$= \$320,000$$

The value of the firm's equity is obtained by using Equation 17-15:

$$V_e = \$320,000 - \$50,000$$
$$= \$270,000$$

The beta coefficient that results from introducing $50,000 of debt into the firm's capital structure is computed using Equation 17-16 as shown next:

$$\beta = 1.25\left[1 + \frac{\$50,000(1 - .4)}{\$270,000}\right]$$
$$= 1.39$$

This value of 1.39 is used in a SML to compute the firm's specific cost of equity capital:

$$k_e = .10 + (.18 - .10)1.39$$
$$= .21$$

The firm's weighted average cost of capital is found by using Equation 17-17:

$$k_w = .1(1 - .4)\left(\frac{\$50,000}{\$320,000}\right) + .21\left(\frac{\$270,000}{\$320,000}\right)$$

$$= .19$$

Adding $50,000 of debt and retiring an equal amount of equity increases the firm value by $20,000, increases its specific cost of equity to 21 percent, and reduces its weighted average cost of capital to 19 percent. These values are listed in the second row of Table 17-1.

The firm now sells another $50,000 of debt and retires an equal amount of equity. The value of levered firm increases to:

$$V_l = \$100,000(1 - .4)/.2 + .4(\$100,000)$$
$$= \$340,000$$

The value of the firm's equity now equals:

$$V_e = \$340,000 - \$100,000$$
$$= \$240,000$$

Its beta coefficient increases to:

$$\beta = 1.25\left[1 + \frac{\$100,000(1 - .4)}{\$240,000}\right]$$
$$= 1.56$$

The firm's specific cost of equity increases to:

$$k_e = .10 + (.18 - .10)1.56$$
$$= .22$$

The firm's weighted average cost of capital decreases to:

$$k_w = .1(1 - .4)\left(\frac{\$100,000}{\$340,000}\right) + .22\left(\frac{\$240,000}{\$340,000}\right)$$
$$= .17$$

These values are listed in the third row of Table 17-1. This table summarizes the impacts on firm value, beta, and costs of capital from adding debt to the capital structure. Additional increases in the firm's debt-to-equity ratio will produce similar results: the firm's value and its beta coefficient will increase, and its weighted average cost of capital will decrease.

**Table 17-1.**   **Firm Value, Beta Coefficients, and Costs of Capital**

| Debt | $V_l$ | $V_e$ | $\beta$ | $k_e$ | $k_w$ |
|---|---|---|---|---|---|
| $    0 | $300,000 | $300,000 | 1.25 | .20 | .20 |
| 50,000 | 320,000 | 270,000 | 1.39 | .21 | .19 |
| 100,000 | 340,000 | 240,000 | 1.56 | .22 | .17 |

Figure 17-6 uses the data in the above example to illustrate the impacts of capital structure on the firm's market value and its costs of capital. The two horizontal axes in this figure plot the firm's debt-to-equity ratio using market value weights. In this figure, $50,000 of debt represents a debt-to-equity ratio of 19 percent and $100,000 of debt corresponds to a debt-to-equity ratio of 42 percent.

The top portion of Figure 17-6 plots firm value as a function of its capital structure; the bottom portion plots costs of capital and its capital structure. Since both graphs have the same horizontal axis, this figure demonstrates the general result that, within a capital asset pricing framework, increasing the amount of debt in a firm's capital structure increases its market value while decreasing its weighted average cost of capital.

**Figure 17-6.**      **The Impact of Capital Structure**

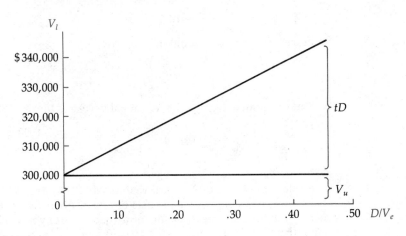

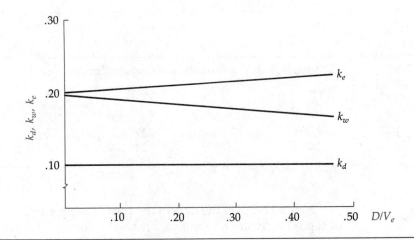

RISKY DEBT. A cursory reading of corporate annual reports will indicate that corporate capital structures do not contain overwhelming amounts of debt. In fact the apparent target capital structures of many firms contain little or no long-term debt. How can this corporate practice be reconciled with the above systematic risk capital structure theory? The answer is found by introducing risky debt into the theory and analyzing the impact on firm value.

One of the assumptions made in order to explain the relationships between capital structure and systematic risk is that the firm can float riskless bonds at a cost of capital equal to the risk-free rate. Investors generally consider bonds to be risky debt when there is some probability or likelihood that the firm will be unable to meet its agreed upon interest payments and principal repayments. In other words, debt is risky when there exists some probability that the firm will default on its bond obligations.

The riskless debt assumption essentially says that the probability of default is so small that the firm's debt is considered to be riskless. This may be a reasonable approach when the firm's capital structure contains relatively small amounts of debt. However, as soon as the firm's debt-to-equity ratio increases to where additional debt is considered risky, then all the bonds in the firm's capital structure become risky. This increased risk causes the specific cost of debt to increase and decrease the market value of the firm's debt. Risky debt thus impacts on the firm's cost of capital and its market value.

When a corporation finances itself by selling bonds, the contract between the issuing corporation and its bondholders gives the bondholders a claim on the firm's cash flows and assets that is superior to shareholder claims. As long as the probability distribution of the firm's EBIT is such that the probability of EBIT being less than the required interest payments is very low, the firm's debt contains a minimum degree of risk. Assume, for example that the expected value of a firm's annual EBIT is $1 million and that the probability of any yearly EBIT value being less than $200,000 is 5 percent. Bondholders may consider the debt to be relatively risk free as long as the total yearly interest payments do not exceed $200,000. However, if required interest payments exceed $200,000 as a consequence of floating additional debt, then all the firm's debt becomes risky because all debt issues have equal claims on the firm's cash flows. Thus, all bondholders share the increased risk that a given yearly EBIT may not be sufficient to cover interest payments.

When a corporation's capital structure contains risky debt, the possibility always exists that the firm may find itself in financial distress. A firm is said to be in *financial distress* when there is a significant probability or likelihood that it will violate the terms of its debt contracts. Not making interest payments to bondholders—defaulting—is an obvious contract violation. The more likely that these payments will not be made as agreed upon, the greater is the firm's degree of financial distress. The situation is made more complicated because of negative covenants in bond contracts. These covenants prohibit or restrict certain actions or practices on the part of the corporation, and violating any negative covenant constitutes an event of default. For example, the firm may have agreed to maintain a current ratio of 1.75 or it may have agreed to maintain a net working capital of $4 million. If its current ratio falls to a value of 1.5 or if its net working capital falls to $3 million, the firm will be in technical default. The bondholders can accelerate the bond maturities and demand almost immediate payment of both principal and interest. Violating bond contracts can also result in bondholders initiating bankruptcy proceedings against the firm. This is most likely to happen when the contract violations involve nonpayment of interest and/or principal.

Firms can find themselves in greater or lesser degrees of financial distress. At one extreme, a minimum degree of financial distress may be incurred when the firm's bond ratings are lowered by rating agencies. This may by taken by bondholders as a sign that the firm's debt has become riskier. At the other extreme, if the firm's management concludes that it will not be able to meet interest payments, the firm suffers a maximum amount of financial distress because of the likelihood that it will find itself in bankruptcy.

It is not possible to say exactly when a firm becomes financially distressed or to measure a firm's exact degree of distress at a specific time. However, there are costs associated with financial distress, and it may be possible to measure some of them. First, there are the costs associated with bankruptcy. If the firm enters these court proceedings, it will need the advice and help of lawyers, accountants, finance specialists, and other consultants. The firm may also have to pay the bankruptcy trustee as it seeks a successful reorganization or undergoes liquidation. If bankruptcy results in liquidation, the firm suffers the added loss from liquidating its assets at prices below their intrinsic values. Second, there is the increased cost of capital of debt that bondholders require in return for investing in increasingly risky financial assets. These costs are referred to as *direct costs* of financial distress because it is possible to associate them with the consequence of floating risky debt.

There are numerous *indirect costs* of financial distress. These costs are difficult to measure; in addition, it may be difficult to link these costs directly to financial distress. When it becomes obvious that a firm's financial condition is deteriorating, it may lose customers who need a reliable source of goods and services. This loss in revenue and EBIT may be accelerated when vendors restrict credit terms or eliminate them completely and sell only on COD terms. The firm's financial distress may be further increased by the resignation of skilled personnel who seek less stressful work environments. The remaining managers may have to spend increasing amounts of time and energy managing the firm's financial crisis in order to prevent involuntary bankruptcy. This will likely result in the firm's delaying or postponing capital-budgeting investments that would have produced positive net present values and would ordinarily be accepted.

Once investors perceive the corporation's debt as being risky, the firm's cost of financial distress increases rapidly as the sale of additional bonds increases its debt-to-equity ratio. The present value of this cost serves to decrease the value of the firm. At the same time, however, the present value of the tax shield increases as bonds are sold, thus increasing the value of the firm.

The combined impact of financial distress and a tax shield on firm value can be expressed in equation form. Let FD represent the sum of the present values of the costs of financial distress. The value of the levered firm can be written by expanding Equation 17-14 to include the costs of financial distress:

$$V_l = V_u + tD - FD \tag{17-18}$$

The behavior of Equation 17-18 is summarized in the top portion of Figure 17-7. In the absence of financial distress the value of the levered firm increases linearly due to the tax shield from added debt. Once the costs of financial distress must be absorbed, the value of the firm increases more slowly and reaches a maximum when the added cost of financial distress equals the added contribution of the tax shield. Beyond this point, adding more debt produces costs of financial distress that exceed the contribution of the tax shield, and the value of the firm begins to fall.

The bottom portion of Figure 17-7 illustrates the behavior of the firm's costs of capital due to adding risky debt. The increase in the specific cost of capital of risky debt causes the firm's weighted average cost of capital to reach a minimum at the same debt-to-equity ratio that produces a maximum firm value. Beyond this point the weighted average cost of capital increases. The firm's optimal capital structure is thus the debt-to-equity ratio that simultaneously maximizes the present value of its cash flows while minimizing its weighted average cost of capital.

Relaxing the riskless debt assumption is thus sufficient, at least in theory, to produce an optimal capital structure for a firm. The idea that debt leads to various degrees of financial distress is sometimes explained in terms of bondholder-shareholder conflicts. For example, if an initial bond issue is perceived as being essentially riskless but a second bond issue makes all bonds risky, the investors who hold the bonds from the initial issue suffer a loss of market value because their bonds fall in price in order to return the higher (and risky) rate offered by the new bonds. At the same time, the second bond sale contributes to the value of shareholder claims because it increases the present value of the tax shield.

These bondholder-shareholder conflicts cannot be resolved completely. Shareholders expect managers to act so as to maximize shareholder wealth. Bondholders do not want increases in shareholder wealth to occur at the expense of bondholders. As a consequence, bond contracts contain any number of covenants that restrict managerial decision making in the

**Figure 17-7.** **The Impact of Risky Debt**

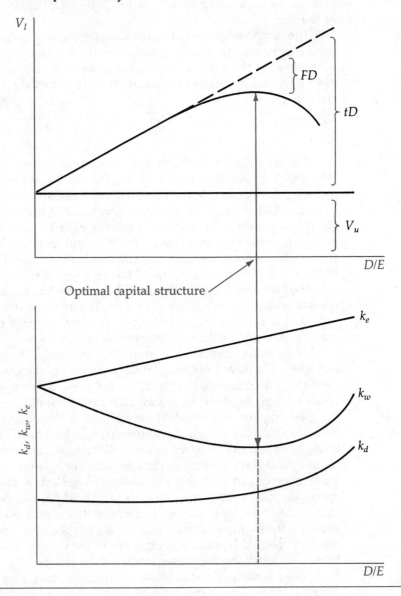

hope of minimizing the degree of risk contained in the firm's bonds. The specific cost of capital of debt reflects the risk that remains in spite of the presence of restrictive covenants. As illustrated earlier, these convenants might focus on maintaining the firm's liquidity. Other covenants may restrict the amount of debt that can be outstanding at any time or prevent the firm from paying all its earnings as dividends. In addition, the firm might be prohibited from selling fixed assets or merging with another firm without the prior approval of bondholders. The costs of managing bondholder-shareholder conflicts must be added to costs of financial distress. This increases the likelihood that firm value will be maximized well before its capital structure contains 99 percent debt. The specific cost of equity capital is also likely to increase because shareholders will have to bear the cost of managing these conflicts, and the bond covenants will reduce the wealth-maximizing strategies available to the firm.

There are no exact procedures available for determining the firm's optimal debt-to-equity ratio (in the presence of risky debt, financial distress, and bondholder-shareholder conflicts). In practice, financial managers can look to other firms in their industry and obtain a range of debt-to-equity ratios associated with those lines of business. In addition, investment bankers, as discussed in Chapter 18, can provide estimates of specific costs of capital for proposed security sales. This allows financial managers to estimate how risky the security markets will perceive additional bond sales. Since investment bankers also help write the bond contracts that contain negative covenants, financial managers can obtain an understanding of the restrictions to be imposed by bondholders before the debt is marketed. The managers can always decide that the costs of capital and/or the restrictive covenants are too high a price for financing the firm. At that point, the financial manager must obtain alternative financing or simply decide not to raise money capital for some period of time.

The conclusions to be drawn from this section are not altogether satisfying although the theory does present some new ways of examining the opportunities and problems of capital structure planning. Given a set of assumptions that includes a constant corporate tax rate and the ability of the firm to sell debt at a constant risk-free rate, capital asset pricing concludes that the firm's value-maximizing capital structure contains almost no equity because of the tax shield that accompanies bonds. However, when the riskless debt assumption is replaced with one that recognizes that corporate debt is risky, can produce financial distress, and that such distress contains costs that can effect the value of the firm, the likelihood emerges that the firm's optimal capital structure will contain only modest or moderate amounts of debt. This corresponds to the observed financing patterns of most corporations. Regardless of which assumption is used with regard to corporate debt, however, this section has described how systematic risk concepts are used to value a firm's cash flow.

# SUMMARY

This chapter has three major parts. First, a summary of capital asset pricing is presented. The idea is to focus on a security market line in beta form. A detailed explanation of the portfolio and financial market concepts that underlie this theory is contained in Chapter 16.

The second portion of this chapter explains how the concept of systematic risk can be used to estimate capital-budgeting discount rates and associated costs of capital. Given that it is possible to estimate an investment alternative's beta coefficient (the project beta), calculating its discount rate and evaluating the impact of the project on the firm's costs of capital depend on whether their firm's systematic business risk component remains constant as a result of adopting the project and whether the firm's capital structure is altered as a result of financing the project. In dealing with these capital-budgeting problems, it is sometimes difficult to decide on the correct sequence of steps and equations. However, Figure 17-4 will help you identify the relevant procedure for solving the types of capital-budgeting problems discussed in this chapter.

The third section examined the impacts of systematic risk and capital structure on firm value and costs of capital. Within a narrow set of assumptions — constant total financing, constant business risk, riskless debt — the value of a levered firm increases as the firm adds debt to its capital structure because of the present value of the resulting tax shield. In this situation, the firm's value-maximizing optimal capital structure essentially contains all debt. Replacing the riskless debt assumption with one that recognizes that bonds can be risky produces a very different set of conclusions. Risky debt can cause financial distress. The direct and indirect costs associated with financial distress, along with bondholder-shareholder conflicts, reduce the value of the levered firm. When these incremental costs equal or exceed the incremental value of the tax shield, the resulting value-maximizing optimal capital structure may contain only modest amounts of debt.

# QUESTIONS

*Note.* Questions 17-1 through 17-8 are a review of capital asset pricing assumptions and theory. (If Chapter 16 was assigned, these eight questions can be omitted or used as a quick review.)

**17-1.** Summarize the assumptions of investor behavior used in capital asset pricing theory.

**17-2.** Identify the types of risk contained in a portfolio.

**17-3.** Explain the impact of diversification on the standard deviation of a portfolio.

**17-4.** What type of risk is found in a well-diversified portfolio? Why?

**17-5.** Explain the significance of a portfolio beta equal to 1.0.

**17-6.** Summarize the characteristics of perfect capital markets.

**17-7.** Explain the SML in words.

**17-8.** When corporate managers use a SML in making financial decisions, what basic assumptions are they making concerning their shareholders?

**17-9.** When evaluating a capital-budgeting alternative, why is the unsystematic risk portion of the project risk not considered?

**17-10.** Why is there a separate discount rate for each capital-budgeting alternative?

**17-11.** Under what conditions would a project with a relatively high expected rate of return be rejected in favor of a project with a lower expected rate of return?

**17-12.** From the standpoint of capital budgeting, why is it important that project markets are imperfect?

**17-13.** Identify some reasons why project markets are imperfect.

**17-14.** What is the basic reason why project betas cannot be measured directly?

**17-15.** In a single industry, all-equity firm, under what condition will a project discount rate equal the expected rate of return computed using a SML?

**17-16.** If both systematic risk components of a firm remain constant as a result of adopting a proposed investment, explain how to compute the project's discount rate.

**17-17.** Explain two equivalent ways of computing the cash flow of a levered firm.

**17-18.** Given riskless debt, explain the components of the value of a levered firm.

**17-19.** Given riskless debt, what is the value-maximizing optimal capital structure for a firm?

**17-20.** Given riskless debt, what is the debt-to-equity ratio value that minimizes the firm's weighted average cost of capital?

**17-21.** Explain the concept of financial distress within the context of risky debt.

**17-22.** Identify some direct costs of financial distress.

**17-23.** Identify some indirect costs of financial distress.

**17-24.** Explain the impact of the costs of financial distress on the value of the firm and optimal capital structure.

**17-25.** Explain the impact of the costs of financial distress on the firm's weighted average cost of capital.

# PROBLEMS

*Note.* Assume a 40% federal corporate income tax rate as needed.

**17-1.** The covariance of a security with the market index equals .015. The variance of the market index equals .01. Compute the beta coefficient of the security.

**17-2.** The covariance of a security with the market index equals .02. The standard deviation of the market index equals .1. Compute the beta coefficient of the security.

**17-3.** A security's beta coefficient is .95. Assuming a risk-free rate of 12%, and a 21% return of the market index, compute the expected rate of return from this security.

**17-4.** A portfolio's beta is 1.2. Assuming a risk-free rate of 11% and a 20% return on the market index, compute the expected rate of return from this portfolio.

**17-5.** A corporation is evaluating three capital-budgeting proposals on an accept/reject basis. (Each project is evaluated on its own merits.) The projects are labeled $K1$, $K2$, and $K3$. The firm computes the expected rate of return and the project beta for each project; the values are as follows:

|      | $R_j$  | $\beta_j$ |
|------|--------|-----------|
| $K1$ | 20.3%  | .9        |
| $K2$ | 21.4%  | 1.2       |
| $K3$ | 23.7%  | 1.4       |

The firm computes a required rate of return for each project by using a SML with a risk-free rate of 9% and an expected rate of return on the market index of 20%. Evaluate each of the three proposals on an accept/reject basis.

**17-6.** A firm's unlevered beta coefficient is 1.05. The firm then sells bonds and retires stock; its resulting debt-to-equity ratio is .25. Compute the firm's new beta coefficient.

**17-7.** A firm's unlevered beta coefficient is .70. The firm restructures its financing sources until the market value of its debt equals $6 million and the market value of its equity equals $20 million. Compute the firm's resulting beta coefficient.

*Note.* For Problems 17-8 through 17-12, use Figure 17-4 to decide the correct sequence needed in computing discount rates and costs of capital.

**17-8.** An all-equity firm has an unlevered beta coefficient of 1.6. The firm finances a new project with a beta of 1.6 by selling $2 million of equity. Assuming a 12% risk-free rate and a 20% rate of return on the market index, compute (*a*) the specific cost of equity capital, (*b*) the weighted average cost of capital, and (*c*) the project discount rate.

**17-9.** Assume that the firm in Problem 17-8 finances the project by selling $2 million of bonds carrying a 14% interest rate. The market value of the firm's equity then becomes $8 million. Assume that the resulting capital structure approximates the firm's TCS. Compute (*a*) the new beta coefficient (*b*) the resulting specific cost of equity capital, (*c*) the weighted average cost of capital, and (*d*) the project discount rate.

**17-10.** A capital-budgeting alternative has a beta of 1.75; the firm's existing assets have the same beta coefficient. The firm's current debt-to-equity ratio is 30% and will remain unchanged if the capital-budgeting alternative is accepted. Assume a risk-free rate of 10%, a 22% rate of return on the market index, and a 12% coupon rate on new bonds. Compute (*a*) the firm's beta coefficient, (b) the specific cost of equity capital, (c) the weighted average cost of capital, and (d) the project discount rate.

**17-11.** Relever, Inc.'s existing assets have a beta coefficient of 1.85. The firm is evaluating product line diversifications that will introduce a new product with a beta of 1.20. When fully marketed, this new product is forecast to account for 25% of the firm's sales and profits. Relever's TCS is its current value of 10%. Assume a risk-free rate of 9% and an 18% rate of return on the market index. New debt will carry an 11% coupon rate, the same rate on bonds currently outstanding. Compute the following:

   a. The new product beta at the firm's TCS
   b. The specific cost of equity capital for the product line
   c. The product discount rate
   d. The unlevered beta if the firm adopts the new product line
   e. The firm's beta if it adopts the new product
   f. The weighted average cost of capital

**17-12.** Roolever & Co. has a beta coefficient of 2.4 and a debt-to-equity ratio of .15. Its target capital structure is a debt-to-equity ratio of .20. A proposed expansion alternative can be used to help attain its TCS. The expansion alternative's unlevered beta is unknown to Roolever; however, a competing firm's beta is 1.9, and that firm has a debt-to-equity ratio of .5. If accepted, the expansion alternative will represent about 15% of the firm's market value. Assume a risk-free rate of 14% and a 23% rate of return on the market index. Bonds will carry the 16% coupon rate paid by bonds currently outstanding. Compute the discount rate for the proposed expansion and the weighted average cost of capital for Roolever once it has accepted the project and attained its TCS.

**17-13.** An all-equity firm's beta coefficient is 1.8. The firm's expected annual EBIT is $400,000. The risk-free rate is 10%, and the rate of return on the market index is 19%. Compute the following:

   a. The specific cost of equity capital and the weighted average cost of capital
   b. The annual cash flow
   c. The value of the unlevered firm

The firm now sells $250,000 of debt and retires an equal amount of stock. Compute:

   d. The present value of the tax shield
   e. The value of the firm
   f. The value of the equity
   g. The new beta coefficient
   h. The specific cost of capital of equity
   i. The weighted average cost of capital

**17-14.** Snoway Company produces gasoline powered implements, such as garden tillers, snowblowers, and lawnmowers, intended for home use. Most sales are made directly to independent hardware stores and to regional wholesalers. Some sales are on a private brand basis and go to a national general merchandise discount chain. Snoway's expected annual EBIT is $12 million. The firm has $4 million of debt outstanding; the market value of its equity is about $24,600,000. Its beta coefficient is 2.0. The risk-free rate is 12% and the rate of return on the market index is 20%. Compute:

a.  The firm's unlevered beta coefficient
b.  The levered firm's specific cost of equity capital
c.  The levered firm's weighted average cost of capital

Snoway sells an additional $3 million of debt and retires an equal amount of equity. Compute the following:

d.  The value of the firm
e.  The new (levered) beta coefficient
f.  The specific cost of equity capital
g.  The weighted average cost of capital

---

# SELECTED REFERENCES

Archer, S., G. Choate, and G. Racette. *Financial Management.* 2d ed. N.Y.: John Wiley & Sons, Inc., 1983.

Barnea, A., R. Haugen, and L. Senbet. "Market Imperfections, Agency Problems, and Capital Structure: A Review." *Financial Management,* Vol. 10, No. 3 (Summer, 1981).

Blume, M. "On the Assessment of Risk." *Journal of Finance,* Vol. 26, No. 1 (March, 1971).

————. "Betas and Their Regression Tendencies." *Journal of Finance,* Vol. 30, No. 3 (June, 1975).

————, and I. Friend. "A New Look at the Capital Asset Pricing Model." *Journal of Finance,* Vol. 28, No. 1 (March, 1973).

Bogue, M., and R. Roll. "Capital Budgeting of Risky Projects with 'Imperfect' Markets for Physical Capital." *Journal of Finance,* Vol. 29, No. 2 (May, 1974).

Boquist, J., and W. Moore. "Estimating the Systematic Risk of an Industry Segment: A Mathematical Programming Approach." *Financial Management,* Vol. 12, No. 4 (Winter, 1983).

Bowman, R. "The Theoretical Relationship between Systematic Risk and Financial (Accounting) Variables." *Journal of Finance,* Vol. 34, No. 3 (June, 1979).

Brealey, R., and S. Myers. *Principles of Corporate Finance.* 2d ed. N.Y.: McGraw-Hill Book Company, 1984.

Carpenter, M., and K. Chew. "The Effects of Default Risk on the Market Model." *Journal of Financial Research,* Vol. 6, No. 3 (Fall, 1983).

Eubank, A., and K. Zumualt. "An Analysis of the Forecast Error Impact of Alternative Beta Adjustment Techniques and Risk Classes." *Journal of Finance,* Vol. 23, No. 5 (December, 1968).

Fabozzi, F., and J. Francis. "Stability Tests for Alphas and Betas over Bull and Bear Market Conditions." *Journal of Finance,* Vol. 32, No. 4 (September, 1977).

———. "Beta as a Random Coefficient." *Journal of Finance and Quantitative Analysis,* Vol. 13, No. 1 (March, 1978).

Fama, E. "Efficient Capital Markets: A Review of Theory and Empirical Work." *Journal of Finance,* Vol. 25, No. 2 (May, 1970).

Foster, G. *Financial Statement Analysis.* Englewood Cliffs, N.J.: Prentice-Hall, Inc., 1978.

Francis, J., and S. Archer. *Portfolio Analysis.* 2d ed. Englewood Cliffs, N.J.: Prentice-Hall, Inc., 1979.

Francis, J. *Investments: Analysis and Management.* 3d ed. N.Y.: McGraw-Hill Book Company, 1980.

Gehr, A. "Financial Structure and Financial Strategy." *Journal of Financial Research,* Vol. 7, No. 1 (Spring, 1984).

Hamada, R. "Portfolio Analysis, Market Equilibrium, and Corporate Finance." *Journal of Finance,* Vol. 24, No. 1 (March, 1969).

Harrington, D. "Stock Prices, Beta, and Strategic Planning." *Harvard Business Review,* Vol. 61, No. 3 (May-June, 1983).

———. *Modern Portfolio Theory and the Capital Asset Pricing Model.* Englewood Cliffs, N.J.: Prentice-Hall, Inc., 1983.

Hill, N., and B. Stone. "Accounting Betas, Systematic Operating Risk, and Financial Leverage: A Risk-Composition Approach to the Determinants of Systematic Risk." *Journal of Financial and Quantitative Analysis,* Vol. 15, No. 3 (September, 1980).

Ibbotson, R., and R. Sinquefield. *Stocks, Bonds, Bills, and Inflation: The Past (1926-1976) and the Future (1977-2000).* Charlottesville, Va.: Financial Analysts Research Federation, 1977.

Jacob, N., and R. Pettit. *Investments.* Homewood, Ill.: Richard D. Irwin, Inc., 1984.

Lintner, J. "The Valuation of Risk Assets and the Selection of Risky Investments in Stock Portfolios and Capital Budgets." *Review of Economics and Statistics,* Vol. 47, No. 1 (February, 1965).

Markowitz, H. "Portfolio Selection." *Journal of Finance,* Vol. 7, No. 1 (March, 1952).

Modigliani, F., and M. Miller. "The Cost of Capital, Corporate Finance, and the Theory of Investment." *American Economic Review,* Vol. 48, No. 3 (June, 1958).

———. "Corporate Income Taxes and the Cost of Capital: A Correction." *American Economic Review,* Vol. 53, No. 3 (June, 1963).

Modigliani, F., and G. Pogue. "An Introduction to Risk and Return." *Financial Analysts Journal,* Vol. 30, No. 3 (May-June, 1974).

Morris, J. "Taxes, Bankruptcy Costs, and the Existence of an Optimal Capital Structure." *Journal of Financial Research,* Vol. 5, No. 3 (Fall, 1982).

Mossin, J. "Equilibrium in a Capital Asset Market." *Econometrica,* Vol. 34, No. 4 (October, 1966).

Mullins, D. "Does the Capital Asset Pricing Model Work?" *Harvard Business Review,* Vol. 60, No. 1 (January-February, 1982).

Myers, S., and S. Turnbull. "Capital Budgeting and the Capital Asset Pricing Model: Good News and Bad News." *Journal of Finance,* Vol. 32, No. 2 (May, 1977).

Radcliffe, R. *Investment: Concepts, Analysis, and Strategy.* Glenview, Ill.: Scott, Foresman and Company, 1982.

Reinganum, M. "A New Empirical Perspective on the CAPM." *Journal of Financial and Quantitative Analysis,* Vol. 16, No. 4 (November, 1981).

Rosenberg, B., and J. Guy, "Prediction of Beta from Investment Fundamentals." *Financial Analysts Journal*, Vol. 32, No. 4 (July-August, 1976).

Rubinstein, M. "A Mean-Variance Synthesis of Corporate Financial Theory." *Journal of Finance*, Vol. 28, No. 1 (March, 1973).

Senbet, L., and R. Taggert. "Capital Structure Equilibrium under Market Imperfections and Incompleteness." *Journal of Finance*, Vol. 39, No. 1 (March, 1984).

Sharpe, W. "Capital Asset Prices: A Theory of Market Equilibrium under Conditions of Risk." *Journal of Finance*, Vol. 19, No. 3 (September, 1964).

Shawky, H., and P. Fischer. "Imperfect Contracts, Me-First Rules, and Firm Value. *Financial Review*, Vol. 18, No. 1 (February, 1983).

Van Horne, J. *Financial Management and Policy.* 6th ed. Englewood Cliffs, N.J.: Prentice-Hall, Inc., 1983.

Welch, J., and T. Kainen. "Risk Adjusted Multiple Hurdle Rates: Better Capital Budgeting." *Financial Executive*, Vol. 51, No. 5 (May, 1983).

# PART 7

# Long-Term Financing

The five chapters that make up Part 7 describe the characteristics of corporate long-term financing instruments and explain the procedures used by corporations in obtaining long-term financing.

Chapter 18 introduces primary securities markets and explains how these markets provide a vehicle for corporate financing. Chapters 19 and 20 present the roles that bonds, preferred stock, and common stock play in corporate financing. Chapter 21 evaluates the roles of term loans and leases as financing instruments. Chapter 22 looks at retained earnings as a source of funds and explains the theory and practice of corporate dividend policy.

# CHAPTER 18

# Capital Markets

*Financial markets, consisting of money markets and capital markets, constitute one of the major elements of a corporation's operating environment. Chapter 2 introduced the concept of financial markets and indicated their importance for financial managers. This chapter explains how corporations use capital markets in raising long-term external funds and explains why capital markets have a continuous impact on shareholder wealth.*

*Capital markets consist of primary securities markets and secondary securities markets. The first section of this chapter explains how corporations use the primary securities market to obtain external financing. The second section describes the impact of the secondary securities market on corporate financing activities and on shareholder wealth. The emphasis is on the primary, rather than the secondary, securities market because actual financing occurs only in the primary securities market.*

## THE PRIMARY SECURITIES MARKET

One of the vital functions of financial markets from the standpoint of our domestic economy is to provide a mechanism for capital formation. Corporations that seek financing exchange their financial assets, such as stocks and bonds, in return for the money capital provided by financial intermediaries or directly by savers. The corporation then converts these funds into real capital such as plant and equipment, and capital formation is said to occur. That portion of the capital market where corporations exchange their financial assets for long-term financing is called the **primary securities market.**

The primary securities market has two distinguishing characteristics. First, it is the only segment of the capital market where capital formation occurs, and second, new issues of corporate stocks and bonds are initially sold in the primary securities market. Subsequent trading in these securities occurs in the secondary securities markets.

The dollar value of stocks and bonds sold in the primary securities market during the last several years is contained in Table 18-1. The table shows that about 63 percent of the $53.2 billion raised in 1982 was in the form of bonds. Preferred stock was the least important of these external sources, accounting for less than 7 percent of the total funds raised in any given year. Common stock accounted for up to one-third of the dollar value of new security issues. The table also indicates that corporations raise very substantial amounts of capital in the primary securities market. It must be pointed out, however, that when *all* long-term sources are considered, corporations raise even larger amounts of funds through retained earnings. The primary securities market, consequently, serves as a major corporate financing mechanism but is second in importance to retained earnings as a source of funds.

## Investment Bankers

The efficient operation of the primary securities market is made possible because of hundreds of **investment bankers,** financial institutions that arrange long-term financial transactions for their clients. Unfortunately the term *investment banker* is a misnomer because such financial institutions are not investors in the sense of making long-term purchases of financial assets, nor are they bankers in the sense of accepting customer deposits. However, the services they provide are so important that corporations that seek long-term external financing invariably turn to these firms in order to take advantage of their knowledge and ability to market security issues in the primary securities market.

**Table 18-1.**    New Security Issues of Corporations (In Millions of Dollars)

|  | 1978 | 1979 | 1980 | 1981 | 1982 |
|---|---|---|---|---|---|
| **Bonds** | | | | | |
| Public offerings | $19,815 | $25,814 | $41,587 | $37,653 | $43,427 |
| Private placements | 17,057 | 14,394 | 11,619 | 6,989 | 9,798 |
| Total bonds | $36,872 | $40,208 | $53,206 | $44,642 | $53,225 |
| **Stocks** | | | | | |
| Preferred stock | $ 2,832 | $ 3,574 | $ 3,631 | $ 1,796 | $ 5,115 |
| Common stock | 7,526 | 7,751 | 16,858 | 23,554 | 25,448 |
| Total stocks | $10,358 | $11,325 | $20,489 | $25,350 | $30,563 |
| **Total bonds and stocks** | $47,230 | $51,533 | $73,695 | $69,992 | $83,787 |

Source: *Federal Reserve Bulletin*

The question often arises as to just who investment bankers are. It turns out that many investment bankers also serve as brokers and dealers in the secondary securities markets. Some of the more well known firms include E. F. Hutton & Company, Inc., Bache Halsey Stuart Shields, Inc., and Blyth Eastman Paine Webber, Inc.

**UNDERWRITING FUNCTION.** There are several different methods of raising capital that involve investment bankers. These methods are classified according to whether or not underwriting is involved. When dealing with new security issues, **underwriting** means that the investment banker guarantees the sale of the securities within a certain amount of time and at a set price. For example, when an investment banker underwrites a bond issue, it guarantees the corporation issuing the bonds that (1) all the bonds will be sold, (2) the corporation will receive a specified amount per bond, and (3) the bonds will be sold and the money received within a specified time. In effect, the investment banker agrees to buy up all the securities that remain unsold at a specified point in time. Unsold securities remain the property of the investment banker and are not returned to the issuing firm. Thus, underwriting transfers the risk associated with raising capital in the primary securities market from the financing corporation to the underwriting investment banker.

**OTHER FUNCTIONS OF INVESTMENT BANKERS.** While underwriting is generally considered to be the single most important function of investment bankers, a number of underwriting related services that they provide help corporations in other financial areas. The other functions of investment bankers can be grouped into three categories:

1. *Advisory*  Before a security issue is underwritten, investment bankers advise the issuing corporation on what financing strategy will best meet the needs of the firm and under what conditions the primary securities market will be responsive to the security issue. Investment bankers also provide considerable advice for marketing security issues that are not underwritten and provide financial analysis in such areas as mergers and capital structure planning.

2. *Administrative*  Investment bankers are given the responsibility for executing the paper work that accompanies the sale of a security issue. This can require a considerable amount of time and effort, especially in meeting the filing and disclosure requirements of the Securities and Exchange Commission (SEC).

3. *Distribution*  When a security issue is to be underwritten, investment bankers have the responsibility of distributing the securities to the investors. In the absence of underwriting, investment bankers provide various types of assistance to the issuing firm in order to help it sell the security issue quickly and at a desirable price.

Later sections of this chapter explain these functions in greater detail.

**Underwriting Techniques**

There are two ways by which investment bankers underwrite a security issue. The first is called *negotiated underwriting,* and the second is referred to as *competitive bidding.* Profit-seeking corporations generally use negotiated underwriting, while state and local governments use competitive bidding in marketing their bond issues. This text concentrates on explaining the mechanics of negotiated underwriting and the implications of this technique for financial managers.

**NEGOTIATED UNDERWRITING.** The essential characteristic of negotiated underwriting is that both the issuing firm and the investment banker negotiate the terms of the security issue and thus work as a team in order to produce a successful underwriting. There are several major steps in this process, some of which go on simultaneously.

*Conducting Early Conferences.* The first major step is for the issuing firm to identify an investment banking house that is willing to negotiate the terms of the underwriting and to draw up a tentative underwriting agreement. This step typically requires a series of meetings sometimes called *pre-underwriting conferences.* The investment banker that attends these meetings is called the *originator.*

The major elements discussed and/or negotiated at these meetings are:

1. How much capital is to be raised.

2. What type of security is to be sold.

3.  Whether the issue can be expected to sell quickly in the primary securities market.

4.  Whether the issuing corporation's financial condition is consistent with the proposed amount and type of financing.

The investment banker also undertakes an extensive financial statement analysis of the issuing company in order to evaluate the firm's current and future prospects. If the investment banker and the issuing corporation are both satisfied with the terms that have been reached, a tentative underwriting agreement is signed. This agreement contains all the major elements of the proposed underwriting except for the price of the security and the date of sale. The agreement also contains a number of escape clauses that can be invoked to stop the underwriting process in the event of significant adverse developments in the securities markets or in the issuing firm.

*Forming the Underwriting Syndicate and the Selling Group.* Once the tentative underwriting agreement has been signed, the originator puts together a group of investment bankers, called the **underwriting syndicate,** to underwrite the proposed issue. The originator becomes the manager of the syndicate. The syndicate in turn puts together a group of up to several hundred companies, called the *selling group,* each of which agrees to buy a specified portion of the issue from the syndicate for resale to the ultimate investors. The selling group consists of other investment bankers, who are not members of that particular syndicate, and securities firms that act as brokers and dealers. Some large firms — such as Merrill Lynch — perform all these functions in a given underwriting. Thus, when Merrill Lynch is a member of an underwriting syndicate, an investor can purchase the securities directly from Merrill Lynch and bypass the selling group.

Figure 18-1 illustrates the relationships among the originator-manager, the underwriting syndicate, the selling group, and the ultimate investors. Note that Investment Banker *A* sells securities to both the selling group and directly to the investing public.

There are three reasons why using a syndicate and a selling group is preferable to having only one investment banker underwrite and distribute the entire issue. First, a single investment banker may not be able to finance the entire issue. Second, a syndicate reduces the risk and degree of loss faced by each of its members. Third, a large number of firms in the selling group assures the rapid distribution of the issue for sale. However, none of these reasons guarantees that the issue will be demanded by the investing public. The combination of the investment banking syndicate and selling group simply makes the supply of the security readily available.

*Registering the Issue.* While the syndicate and the selling group are being formed, and before the security can legally be sold, the proposed security issue must be registered with the SEC and related public disclosure requirements must be met. The registration statement submitted to the SEC must contain all the facts relevant to the proposed issue and to the issuing

**Figure 18-1.**     **Underwriting Syndicate and Selling Group Distribution System**

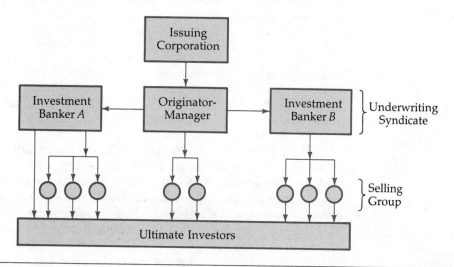

firm that an investor needs in order to make an informed investment decision. The details of the proposed underwriting syndicate must also be disclosed.

A waiting period of 20 days after the required data are submitted to the SEC must be observed before executing the underwriting and selling the security. The SEC has this time to examine the statement for errors or omissions. The SEC does not issue any opinions as to the investment quality of proposed offerings. Its only intent is to see that potential investors have access to correct and relevant information concerning the firm and the security issue.

A portion of the registration statement submitted to the SEC, called the **prospectus,** is the official document that advertises the proposed security. During the 20-day waiting period, copies of the *preliminary prospectus,* sometimes called the *red herring prospectus,* are distributed to potential investors. This is the same document that becomes the prospectus except that the preliminary prospectus omits the selling price and offering date.

*Setting the Price.* When the 20-day waiting period is about to expire, the key members of the issuing firm and the underwriting syndicate meet to set the final price of the securities, as well as the date at which public sale will begin. The final prospectus, containing the price and date, is then printed and distributed.

**Example:**      In February, 1975, PPG Industries, Inc., sold a $75,000,000 bond issue that matures in the year 2000. The prospectus identified the First Boston Corporation as the syndicate manager and listed 98 firms in the underwriting syndicate.

These bonds carry an 8½ percent interest rate. However, when the time came to set the price to the investing public, bond market conditions dictated that this issue return more than 8½ percent. The final price to investors was $990 per $1,000 bond, and the underwriters paid PPG $981.25 per bond. The $8.75 difference was allocated as follows: If a syndicate member sold a bond directly to the investing public, the entire $8.75 became gross profit to that member. The underwriters sold bonds to the selling group for $985.25 each, producing a gross profit of $4 per bond to the underwriter. The sale of bonds by a member of the selling group to the ultimate investors produced a gross profit of $990.00 − $985.25 = $4.75 per bond to the selling group member.

---

*Selling and Market Stabilization.* Although the security issue cannot be sold before the expiration of the 20-day waiting period, members of the underwriting syndicate and the selling group can mail copies of the preliminary prospectus to potential investors and can accept orders for the eventual purchase of the security. Thus, a successful underwriting results in the entire issue being sold to ultimate investors within *hours* of being offered to the public.

Because there is no guarantee that the issue will sell out immediately, the syndicate manager stands ready to stabilize the *resale* price of the security. This is done by entering special types of buy orders in the resale market intended to prevent the resale price of the security from falling below the offering price. Such action is allowed by law as long as full disclosure of the intent to stabilize the market is made in the registration statement.

*Terminating the Syndicate.* The syndicate is terminated as soon as the issue has sold out to the investing public. This may occur within a few hours or within one or two days. If the offering has not sold out within five or six business days, the syndicate will conclude that some errors were made in planning the underwriting and move to cut its losses by selling the unsold securities in the resale markets. In these situations, market stabilization is unable to keep the resale price of the security from falling. Thus, substantial losses can be incurred when the underwriters sell their securities in the resale market.

COMPETITIVE BIDDING. The major distinction between negotiated underwriting and competitive bidding is the way by which the underwriting group is determined. Legal regulations require that firms in the railroad and public utility industries, as well as state and local governments, have their bonds underwritten by competitive bidding. Under this technique the issuing company advertises for sealed competitive bids from underwriting syndicates. The winning syndicate becomes the underwriter. The issuing company or governmental unit has the option of rejecting all bids, however.

This approach to underwriting requires that the issuing firm, usually with the paid assistance of an investment banker, decide on all the provisions of the security issue, except for the price, and submit the issue for SEC registration. This information is then disseminated to the investment banking industry and, hopefully, several syndicates will submit bids. Since all the terms of the issue are already set, the syndicates only have to submit price bids. The winning syndicate then proceeds with underwriting and distribution in the same manner as in negotiated underwriting.

SHELF REGISTRATION. Since March of 1982, some corporations have been allowed by the SEC to use what is called *shelf registration* in selling new security issues. While shelf registration can result in a security issue being underwritten, this approach to the primary securities market differs considerably from negotiated and competitive bidding underwriting techniques. Under **shelf registration** procedures, a corporation files a comprehensive prospectus with the SEC. Once the waiting period has expired, the securities listed in the prospectus can be issued at different points in time. There is no need to prepare additional prospectuses and the security issues are not subject to additional 20-day waiting periods.

---

**Example:**

One of the first security issues that used shelf registration appeared in May of 1982 when AT&T sold 2 million shares of its common stock to Morgan Stanley & Co. The AT&T shelf registration was for 10 million shares. The remaining 8 million shares were sold in August of 1982 to a group of five large securities dealers. These five underwriters then marketed the stock through a selling group of 21 smaller firms.

---

It is important to note that the entire 2 million AT&T shares described above were underwritten by one investment banker and not by a syndicate. Most shelf registrations have been underwritten by syndicates consisting of four underwriters or less. There are two reasons why a single underwriter might want to purchase an entire security issue that is shelf registered. First, only large firms that (1) meet specific SEC requirements and (2) already have securities that are traded in organized exchanges can use shelf registrations. Second, large underwriting firms, such as Salomon Brothers, Merrill Lynch, and Morgan Stanley, can quickly resell the entire issue to a few large institutions. Shelf registrations thus produce situations where one investment banker assumes all the risks usually shared by the members of an underwriting syndicate. In addition, large underwriters have taken to submitting competitive bids for what are seen as the most desirable shelf registered issues. This results in a firm receiving a very favorable price for its securities and decreases the underwriter's per share gross profits.

**Other Techniques of Floating a Security Issue**

There are a number of ways by which a firm can float a security issue in the primary securities market without having the issue underwritten. The two most important non-underwriting techniques, privileged subscriptions and private placements, usually involve the use of investment bankers as selling agents and financial consultants to the issuing corporation.

**PRIVILEGED SUBSCRIPTIONS.** When a corporation decides to finance itself by selling a new issue of common stock, it can extend to its existing shareholders the first opportunity to purchase the new shares before offering them for sale to nonshareholders. This method of issuing common stock in the primary securities market is called a *privileged subscription* and is usually executed through a rights offering.

*Rights Offering.* A **rights offering** is a financing technique that involves selling common stock in the primary securities market by issuing rights to the existing shareholders. Within this context, a **right** is an option to buy a specified number of shares of common stock, at a specified price per share, over a fixed time interval. The firm's shareholders receive one right for each share owned. They have the following three options: (1) to exercise the rights, which means purchasing the new shares directly from the issuing corporation; (2) to sell their rights; and (3) to hold the rights until they expire.

If all the rights are exercised, the offering is fully subscribed and the firm obtains its needed financing. When some rights expire without being exercised, the issuing firm ends up with unsold new shares. The firm uses an investment banker as a selling agent to process the rights as they are exercised and to issue the new common shares. In addition, the investment banker may agree to provide *standby underwriting*. This means that the investment banker agrees to purchase, at a specified price, any shares of common stock that are not bought through the rights offering.

*Characteristics of Rights.* The major characteristics of rights can be summarized as follows:

1. Rights are a form of option. The recipient of the rights is not required to purchase any of the new common shares.

2. The number of rights required to purchase one new share is set by the issuing company and remains constant during the rights offering. For example, 25 rights may be required in order to purchase one new share from the issuing company.

3. The purchase price per share of new common stock, called the *subscription price*, is set by the issuing corporation and remains constant during the rights offering. For example, one new share may require that ten rights plus $50 be sent to the issuing company.

4.  Rights have a fixed life after which they can no longer be used to buy new shares and become worthless. A rights offering typically lasts from 60 to 90 days.

5.  Rights are negotiable. They can be bought and sold in resale markets.

The number of rights needed to purchase one new share of common is a function of the amount of financing that is needed, the subscription price, and the number of common shares outstanding prior to the new issue. The number of new shares to be sold is computed by using Equation 18-1:

$$\text{New shares to be sold} = \frac{\text{desired financing}}{\text{subscription price per share}} \qquad \text{(18-1)}$$

The number of rights needed to purchase one new share is computed by using Equation 18-2:

$$\begin{array}{l}\text{Number of rights to} \\ \text{purchase one new share}\end{array} = \frac{\begin{array}{c}\text{number of common} \\ \text{shares outstanding}\end{array}}{\text{new shares to be sold}} \qquad \text{(18-2)}$$

**Example:**   A corporation wants to raise $20,000,000 of new financing through a rights offering. The subscription price is set at $80 per share, and there are 1,750,000 common shares currently outstanding. The number of new shares that must be sold is computed by using Equation 18-1:

$$\text{New shares to be sold} = \frac{\$20,000,000}{\$80}$$

$$= 250,000 \text{ shares}$$

The number of rights per new share is found by using Equation 18-2:

$$\text{Number of rights per new share} = \frac{1,750,000}{250,000}$$

$$= 7 \text{ rights}$$

*Valuation of Rights.* Rights offerings are structured so as to give rights a resale value. This is accomplished by setting the subscription price below the current market price of the common stock. As a consequence, rights have a theoretical value as well as a market value.

The theoretical value of a right is computed by using the characteristics of rights discussed above along with certain dates that occur during the rights offering. These dates are known as the *date of record* and the **ex-rights date.** In order to receive the rights from the issuing corporation, the investor must be listed as an owner of the stock on the date of record. However, when securities are bought on resale markets, up to four business days are required before the change of ownership is carried out in the corporation's stock transfer books. Thus, the ex-rights date is set four business days before the date of record. In order to receive the rights from the issuing corporation, the stock must be purchased before the ex-rights date. Shares purchased on or after this date will not entitle the buyer to receive the rights from the corporation.

**Example:**  A firm announces a rights offering on June 1 and states that the date of record is June 20. June 16 then becomes the ex-rights date. In order to receive the rights from the corporation, investors must own the stock on June 15.

After the rights offering is announced, and up to but not including the ex-rights date, the common stock that trades in the resale market is described as selling *rights-on*. On the ex-rights date, the price of the common in the resale market should drop by the value of one right. Why? Because the investor no longer receives the valuable right as part of the purchase.

With all these factors in mind, and assuming that the resale price of the common stock falls by the value of one right on the ex-rights date and otherwise remains constant, the theoretical value of one right is computed as follows. Let:

$M$ = market value of the common when it sells rights-on
$S$ = subscription price per new share of common
$N$ = number of rights needed to purchase one new common share
      from the issuing firm
$V$ = theoretical value of one right

Then the theoretical value of one right when the common sells rights-on is:

$$V = \frac{M - S}{N + 1} \qquad (18\text{-}3)$$

On the ex-rights date, the resale price of the common drops to $(M - V)$. Thus, the theoretical value of one right when the common sells ex-rights is computed as:

$$V = \frac{M - V - S}{N} \qquad (18\text{-}4)$$

Solving Equation 18-4 for $V$ produces Equation 18-3. Thus, the theoretical value of one right is the same whether the common is selling rights-on or ex-rights.

---

**Example:**

A rights offering carries a subscription price of $42; 15 rights are required to buy one new share from the issuing corporation. The resale price of the common is $50 per share.

The theoretical value of one right when the common sells rights-on is found by using Equation 18-4.

$$V = \frac{\$50 - \$42}{15 + 1} = \$0.50$$

On the ex-rights date, the market price drops to $(M - V)$, or $50.00 - \$.50 = \$49.50$. The theoretical value of one right is then computed by using Equation 18-4:

$$V = \frac{\$49.50 - \$42}{15} = \$0.50$$

---

*Impact of Rights on Shareholder Wealth.* A rights offering, in and of itself, does not increase shareholder wealth. However, existing shareholders must either exercise their rights or sell them in order to avoid suffering a decrease in market value.

---

**Example:**

An investor owns 100 shares of common stock that have a market value of $31 each. The corporation announces a rights offering with a subscription price of $20; 10 rights are required for each new share. The investor receives 100 rights and can purchase 10 new shares directly from the corporation.

Using Equation 18-3, the theoretical value of one right is $1. Accordingly, the ex-rights price of the common is $30 per share.

Prior to the rights offering, the market value of the 100 shares is ($31)(100) = $3,100. If the shareholder sells the 100 rights rather than exercising them, the decline in market value when the stock goes ex-rights is offset by the proceeds from the rights, as shown below.

| | |
|---|---:|
| Market value of 100 shares ex-rights | $ 3,000 |
| Plus: Proceeds from sale of rights | + 100 |
| Less: Original market value of 100 shares | −3,100 |
| Equals: Change in market value | $ 0 |

If the shareholder decides to exercise the rights and purchase 10 new shares, the market value increases to $3,300 on an ex-rights basis (110 shares) ($30/share). However, the investment cost of the 10 shares, ($20/share)(10 shares) = $200, offsets the increase in market value, as shown below.

| | |
|---|---:|
| Market value of 110 shares ex-rights | $ 3,300 |
| Less: Cost of 10 new shares | − 200 |
| Less: Original market value of 100 shares | −3,100 |
| Equals: Change in market value | $ 0 |

If the shareholder allows the 100 rights to expire, a $100 loss in market value is incurred, as shown below.

| | |
|---|---|
| Market value of 100 shares ex-rights | $ 3,000 |
| Less: Original market value of 100 shares | −3,100 |
| Equals: Change in market value | − $100 |

In actual practice, the resale value of a right decreases as the ex-rights date approaches. When the theoretical value of a right is 50 cents or less, and given the daily changes in the market price of common shares, it can become quite difficult to measure market value losses that arise from neither exercising nor selling the right. Finally, a rights offering does allow shareholders to maintain their ownership and voting percentages in the firm. If, for example, an investor owns 5 percent of a corporation's common stock, a rights offering would allow this investor to purchase 5 percent of the new offering.

PRIVATE PLACEMENTS. A **private placement** is a non-underwriting method of raising funds in the primary securities market by selling an entire security issue to one investor or to a small investing group. Bonds are the most frequent type of security issued in a private placement although preferred or common stock is occasionally issued this way. Table 18-1 illustrates the importance of private placements for bond issues. During the 1978-1982 time period, 27 percent of all the bonds floated were privately placed.

Corporations seeking financing through private placements are helped by investment bankers with two important services. First, investment bankers help locate potential investors, and second, they help the issuing company negotiate the terms of the placement with the potential investor.

Private placements have several important advantages over public sales as a mechanism for corporate financing.

1. Private placements do not require SEC registration. This eliminates a great deal of the time and expense that is required to float a security issue to the investing public.

2. The covenants or restrictions in a bond issue can be negotiated directly between the issuer and the investor. As a result, the issuing firm may be able to avoid some restrictions that would have to be included in a public sale in order to make the issue marketable (see Chapter 19).

3. The investor may allow for renegotiation of the terms of the issue. Renegotiations are allowed in order to change the repayment schedule on a bond issue or to change some restrictive covenants that were included in the original agreement. Renegotiations are difficult or impossible with issues sold to the public.

The most important disadvantage of a private placement is its higher specific cost of capital as compared to an equivalent security issue that is sold to the public. This higher cost of capital is required by the investing firm because it: (1) assumes all the risks of the issue and (2) forgoes the ability to sell the securities in resale markets since the issue is not registered. In addition, the investing firm may insist on a set of very restrictive covenants if the issuer's financial condition is not extremely strong. However, some of these covenants may be renegotiable if and when the issuing firm's profits and liquidity improve significantly.

**BEST EFFORTS.** Security issues are sometimes floated on a best efforts or agency basis. **Best efforts** is a non-underwriting technique in which investment bankers agree to sell the new securities for a specified time at the end of which unsold securities are returned to the issuing corporation. The investment bankers receive a commission on their sales.

A large, profitable corporation, confident that its securities will be demanded by investors, may offer new security issues to investment bankers on a best efforts basis. Most often, however, this technique is used by small firms that are not able to have their securities underwritten. In this latter case, investment bankers will require a commission of between 10 to 20 percent of the securities' selling price, greatly increasing the issuing corporation's cost of capital. Up to 20 percent of all new common stock is sold on a best efforts basis, but only small amounts of bonds and preferred stock reach investors using this technique.

# SECONDARY SECURITIES MARKETS

The **secondary securities markets** consist of that portion of the capital markets where previously issued securities are bought and sold. Corporations do not obtain new financing in these markets. Secondary securities markets consist of the organized exchanges and the over-the-counter (OTC) markets. This section explains the importance of secondary markets from the standpoint of corporate finance. Detailed explanations of the workings of secondary securities markets are found in investments textbooks.

**Functions of Secondary Securities Markets**

Secondary securities markets are vital to the external financing needs of corporations because of the important functions they serve. These functions are:

1. Secondary securities markets allow investors to sell to other investors the securities they buy in the primary securities markets. This provides the liquidity that allows investors to purchase security issues without having to hold them indefinitely or until maturity.

2. Resale markets help corporations price the securities they sell in the primary securities market. For example, the subscription price for a rights offering will be set somewhat below the resale

price of the firm's existing common stock. In addition, rates of return on new bond issues have to be competitive with the rates on equivalent quality bonds currently available in resale markets.

3. Secondary securities markets widen the ownership of a firm's securities when investors make direct purchases in the secondary markets as opposed to depositing their funds with intermediaries. This can serve to generate added demand for subsequent issues that are floated in the primary markets.

4. The price of a firm's securities in secondary securities markets has a direct impact on shareholder wealth. Although security prices are influenced by many variables over which the firm has no control, the firm's ability to generate shareholder returns depends in part on the price of its common stock increasing in response to the firm's profitability.

Many of the same firms that serve as investment bankers in the primary securities market, and other firms that specialize in resale markets, serve as market makers in secondary securities markets. These market makers serve as security brokers and dealers and help create and maintain efficient resale markets. A **broker** buys and sells securities for investors and does not take ownership of the securities. A **dealer** buys and sells securities for his or her own account and takes ownership of the security as part of the transaction. Many firms act as both brokers and dealers in secondary securities markets.

**Organized Exchanges**

There are 13 organized exchanges in the United States. The three biggest and most well known of these are the New York Stock Exchange (NYSE), the American Stock Exchange (AMEX), and the Midwest Stock Exchange. These three account for over 90 percent of the annual dollar volume of the securities transacted in the 13 exchanges.

Each organized exchange is registered with the SEC and has a physical location at which security transactions take place. The brokers and dealers who execute the transactions are employed by firms that have purchased one or more of the limited memberships—called *seats*—in the exchange. The only securities that are traded on an exchange are those that have applied for and have met the exchange's *listing requirements*. Each exchange has its own set of listing requirements. In general, a firm that seeks to list its securities has to meet minimum requirements as to age, size, profitability, and public ownership.

Organized exchanges are described as being centralized markets. This is a consequence of two important characteristics exhibited by organized exchanges. First, all the transactions in each listed security handled by the brokers and dealers who are members of an exchange are carried out at the location on the trading floor designated for that security. Second, prices are determined by an auctionlike process where brokers and dealers bid against each other. These two characteristics, combined with the trading rules and regulations imposed by the exchanges and the SEC, are designed to insure that buyers pay the lowest available prices and that sellers receive the highest available prices for their securities.

**OTC Markets**          The OTC markets are not centralized as are the organized exchanges. Rather, the **over-the-counter market** consists of a large number of broker-dealers who buy and sell for their clients and for themselves. Their offices are linked by telephones, teletypes, and computers. Price setting occurs through a process of negotiations as opposed to the auction system of the organized exchanges. OTC markets are regulated by the National Association of Security Dealers (NASD).

Over 90 percent of corporate bonds and all marketable federal government securities trade in the OTC markets. Historically, insurance and banking stocks traded in OTC markets. However, many of the firms in these two industries are now listed on organized exchanges.

The recent emergence of what are known as third markets and fourth markets provides some indications of how secondary markets can be expected to change in the future. The *third market* is an OTC market for securities that are listed on organized exchanges, primarily the NYSE. The broker-dealers who are the market makers in the third market are not members of the organized exchanges. The third market developed as a result of the fixed commission rates charged by NYSE members. OTC broker-dealers began offering discounts for volume purchases of exchange listed securities that cut transaction costs for investors by 50 percent or more. As a result, the organized exchanges had to modify their commission schedules. The major investors in the third markets are bank trust accounts, mutual funds, and pension funds.

*Fourth markets* are private, unregulated, resale markets for institutions and individuals who trade securities in large blocks. Investors are linked only by electronic communications that are centralized through the market maker firm that provides the particular fourth market. The market maker is not a dealer and may serve only nominally as a broker. Fourth market subscribers can negotiate prices directly by communicating with each other. Alternatively, some fourth markets use the prices quoted in other markets.

Some market makers charge a yearly fee for their services while others charge a fee plus a small commission. As fourth markets have increased in number and in the volume of transactions, they have been perceived as threats to organized exchanges. However, their current impact on secondary markets is to provide financial institutions and other large block investors with a low-cost alternative to the more traditional markets.

# SUMMARY

This chapter has dealt with the capital markets segment of financial markets and focused on the primary securities market. The financing that occurs in this market depends a great deal on the advisory, administrative, underwriting, and distribution functions of investment bankers.

The two major ways of underwriting a security issue are negotiated underwriting and competitive bidding. Most corporate offerings that are underwritten reach the primary market through the negotiated technique. The major differences between these two underwriting techniques revolve around how the terms of the security are set, how the originator-manager is identified, and how the proceeds to the firm are determined. Shelf registration, a recently authorized procedure for registering an issue with the SEC, produces situations where a single investment banker may underwrite the entire issue.

Two of the most important non-underwriting alternatives available to corporations that desire to obtain external financing are privileged subscriptions and private placements. As a third alternative, investment bankers may agree to sell a security issue on a best efforts basis, receiving a commission on what they sell. Privileged subscriptions are usually in the form of a rights offering. Rights have both a theoretical value and a market value. A rights offering does not, in and of itself, increase the wealth of existing shareholders. Moreover, if the rights are not exercised or sold, the shareholders will lose market value per share of their common equal to the value of one right. Private placements are used to float debt securities. This technique has several important advantages over the alternative of a public sale.

The final section of this chapter explained the importance of secondary securities markets for firms that use the primary securities markets as a financing source. Secondary markets consist of organized exchanges and OTC markets. In addition, third and fourth markets have appeared as distinct parts of the OTC markets. The structure of secondary markets will continue to evolve over time, and their importance of financing corporations will continue to increase.

# QUESTIONS

**18-1.** What are the essential characteristics of the primary securities market?

**18-2.** Explain the concept of underwriting in the primary securities market.

**18-3.** Identify the major functions of investment bankers.

**18-4.** What is the essential characteristic of negotiated underwriting?

**18-5.** Why does an originator form an underwriting syndicate and a selling group?

**18-6.** Why would a corporation choose to use shelf registration procedures?

**18-7.** Why is a right described as an option?

**18-8.** In a rights offering, what is the relationship between the subscription price, the market price of the common, and the theoretical value of a right?

**18-9.** What services do investment bankers provide to issuing firms when financing is provided by a private placement?

**18-10.** Explain the role of investment bankers in best efforts financing.

**18-11.** From the standpoint of a firm that uses the primary securities market in order to obtain needed financing, what are the major functions of secondary markets?

**18-12.** Why are organized exchanges called centralized markets?

# PROBLEMS

**18-1.** A corporation has 1 million shares of common stock outstanding. It wishes to raise $50 million of new financing through a rights offering. The subscription price is set at $100 per share.

a. Compute the number of new shares that have to be sold.

b. Compute the number of rights needed to purchase one new share.

c. If the market price of the existing common is $94, compute the theoretical value of a right when the common is selling rights-on.

d. If the market price of the existing common is $94, compute the theoretical value of a right when the common is selling ex-rights.

18-2. A corporation has 2 million shares of common stock outstanding. A rights offering is to be used to raise $25 million of new financing. The subscription price is set at $40 per share.

a. Compute the number of new shares that have to be sold.

b. Compute the number of rights needed to purchase one new share.

c. If the market price of the stock at the beginning of the rights offering is $45, compute the theoretical value of one right when the stock is selling rights-on and when it is selling ex-rights.

d. If a shareholder owns 100 shares, compute the change in market value if the shareholder's rights are sold.

e. If a shareholder owns 100 shares, compute the loss in market value if the rights are allowed to expire.

18-3. Sammarklin, Inc., has announced a rights offering in order to raise $20 million. The firm has 20 million shares of common stock outstanding that currently sell for $14 per share. The subscription price is $10 per share.

a. Compute the number of shares the firm must sell to raise the $20 million.

b. How many rights will existing stockholders receive?

c. Compute the number of rights needed to purchase one new share.

d. Compute the theoretical value of one right when the stock is selling rights-on and when it is selling ex-rights.

18-4. A firm wants to raise $30 million through a rights offering and wants the theoretical value of each right, selling rights-on, to be at least 50 cents. Management has decided to set the subscription price at $50. Assuming that there are 4,200,000 common shares outstanding, what must be the market value of the common stock in order to produce the desired rights value?

---

# SELECTED REFERENCES

Cohen, J., E. Zinbarg, and A. Zeikel. *Investment Analysis and Portfolio Management*. 4th ed. Homewood, Ill.: Richard D. Irwin, Inc., 1982.

Fisher, D., and R. Jordan. *Security Analysis and Portfolio Management*. 2d ed. Englewood Cliffs, N.J.: Prentice-Hall, Inc., 1979.

Francis, J. *Management of Investments*. New York: McGraw-Hill Book Company, 1983.

Robinson, R., and D. Wrightsman. *Financial Markets*. 2d ed. New York: McGraw-Hill Book Company, 1980.

# CHAPTER 19

## Bonds and Preferred Stock

*Bonds and preferred stock are two important instruments of long-term corporate finance. As discussed in Chapter 18, corporations sold $53.2 billion of bonds and $5.1 billion of preferred stock in 1982. Although there are important legal and accounting differences between these two financing instruments, they share one major common denominator: Both provide investors with fixed incomes and are thus forms of trading on the equity to the issuing corporation. Previous chapters have evaluated the impact of corporate trading on the equity from the standpoint of cost of capital, capital structure, and financial leverage. This chapter explains the special characteristics and provisions of bonds and preferred stocks that financial managers consider when evaluating alternative financing strategies.*

## BOND FUNDAMENTALS

A **bond** is a contract in which the issuer promises to make interest payments to the bondholder in specified amounts at specified dates and to repay the principal amount at the stated maturity date. The legal contract that contains all the terms of the lending agreement between the issuer and the bondholders (or their agents) is called the **indenture**.

**Characteristics of Bonds**

Some of the characteristics of a bond are the direct consequence of the definition of a bond. These are:

1. *Credit instrument*   A bondholder is a creditor of the issuing firm. As a creditor, the bondholder is entitled to receive payments of interest and principal and enjoys the other rights contained in the indenture. However, a bond does not represent ownership of the issuing corporation. Thus, bondholders do not share in the dividend payments made to corporate stockholders.

2. *Definite maturity date*   All bond issues sold in this country have a fixed maturity date. Some bond issues mature entirely at one point in time. Other issues mature gradually over time so that most of the bonds are retired before the final maturity date.

3. *Denomination*   Denomination is the bond's face value. Bonds are usually denominated in increments of $1,000, $10,000, or $100,000. Bonds in denominations of $100, such as those sold by AT&T in 1970, are called *baby bonds*.

4. *Priority in liquidation*   In the event that the issuing corporation is liquidated, bondholders' claims are honored ahead of the stockholders' claims. When more than one bond issue must be retired, the priorities among the bond issues are contained in the indenture.

5. *Collateral*   Bond issues may or may not be secured. A **debenture**, for example, is a bond that is not secured by a claim on any specific property. A **mortgage bond** contains a pledge of real property as collateral.

6. *Voting rights*   In general, bondholders do not have the right to vote in corporate decision making. However, the indenture may give bondholders the right to approve or disapprove certain corporate decisions such as selling additional bonds or merging with other firms. In addition, if the corporation violates the terms of the indenture, the bondholders may be able

to exert a substantial amount of control over the corporation's operations.

7. *Provision for a trustee*   When a bond issue is floated as a private placement, the issuing corporation and the buyer(s) are the only parties to the issue. When a bond issue is sold to the investing public, there are three parties to the issue: the issuer, the bondholders, and the trustee.

8. *Interest rates*   Historically, most bond issues promised a rate of interest that was invariant over the life of the bonds. For example, if a bond with a 20-year maturity promised to pay 7 percent interest per year, the investor knew that the bond would carry a constant 7 percent interest rate unless the issuer defaulted. Over the last several years, however, several corporations have issued a new type of bond which has an interest rate that is not constant. These bonds typically are called **floating rate notes,** and their interest rates depend in part on the rate of return available from other marketable securities such as Treasury bills.

The reader may wish to review related bond terminology explained on pages 356-357 in Chapter 13.

---

**Example:**   Floating rate notes of $200 million were sold by Beneficial Corporation on May 31, 1979, through an underwriting syndicate. The various interest rates were as follows:

1. From May 31 through July 1, 1979 — fixed rate of 11.5%
2. From Aug. 1, 1979, through Jan. 31, 1980 — the higher of 11.5% or 1/2% above the rate on 6-month Treasury bills
3. After Jan. 31, 1980, to maturity date — 1/2% above the rate on 6-month Treasury bills, but not less than 6%.

---

**Role of the Trustee**

Before a bond issue is sold to the investing public, the issuer appoints a trustee whose fundamental role is to act in behalf of the bondholders. The issuer pays the trustee's fees. The trustee monitors the bond issuer's actions in adhering to the terms of the indenture. Large commercial banks, such as Manufacturers Hanover Trust and Morgan Guarantee, frequently act as trustees in bond issues.

The trustee's fundamental role is fulfilled by carrying out a number of specific duties such as:

1. Signing all the bonds

2. Collecting interest and principal payments from the bond issuer and distributing the funds to the bondholders

3. Taking title to real property that is pledged as collateral

4. Notifying the bondholders if the bond issuer violates the terms of the indenture (In such an event, the trustee can be empowered by the bondholders to take actions designed to bring the issuer into compliance with the indenture and/or to take legal action to protect bondholder claims.)

**Points and Basis Points**

A *point system* is used to quote changes in bond prices. (Remember that bond prices are quoted in percent of par.) For example, if a bond quotation falls from 98 to 96, the price is said to fall by "two points." Since bonds with large denominations can experience price changes in increments smaller than one point, prices and price changes are quoted in points and fractions of points. For example, if a bond quotation goes from 78½ to 78¾, the bond price has increased by one quarter of a point.

A *basis point system* is used to describe bond interest rates. There are 100 basis points in 1 percent interest. For example, if Bond $A$'s coupon rate is 9½ percent and Bond $B$'s coupon rate is 9¼ percent, Bond $A$'s coupon rate is said to be 25 basis points—one quarter of 1 percent interest—higher than that of Bond $B$. Changes in a bond's current yield or yield to maturity are also quoted in basis points.

**Registered versus Coupon Bonds**

A *registered bond* is one in which the name and address of the bond's owner are recorded on the ownership books of the issuing corporation. Bond payments are mailed directly to the registered owners. A registered bond can be transferred only when properly endorsed by its owner. The new owner is then recognized by the issuing corporation.

A **coupon bond** or **bearer bond** is recognized by possession rather than registration. The owner of a coupon bond is not known to the issuing corporation. Coupon bonds are issued with dated interest coupons attached to them. Each coupon is detached at the date specified on the coupon and presented for payment. The bond itself is surrendered for payment at maturity. A change in ownership is accomplished by a change in possession.

Since January, 1983, all new corporate bond issues sold to the public are registered. This is due to federal tax legislation that was enacted into law in 1982. Bearer bonds that were issued prior to 1983 are still available in secondary bond markets.

**Example:**

Bond issues of Exxon Corporation and United States Steel Corporation illustrate bond terminology.

Exxon sold a bond issue in November, 1967, that matures in November, 1997. Par value of each bond is $1,000 and the bonds are denominated in multiples of $1,000. The coupon rate is 6 percent; interest is payable May 1 and November 1 of each year. The bonds are fully registered and interest checks are mailed to the bondholders.

One of United States Steel Corporation's bond issues has a coupon rate of 4 percent; interest is payable January 15 and July 15. These are coupon bonds. In order to collect the interest, the bondholders detach the coupons and deposit them with their local commercial bank. The bank credits the bondholder with the interest and sends the coupon to Morgan Guarantee Trust in New York City for collection. The bonds are denominated in multiples of $1,000 and $100,000. Bondholders can, at their option, register the bonds in order to establish definite ownership. However, interest payments still require the use of coupons.

**Zero Coupon Bonds**

During 1982, a number of corporations began selling bonds with coupon rates of zero percent—investors received no interest payments on these bonds. These securities quickly became known as *zeros*. Offered at a deep discount from their final maturity or par value, the investor's rate of return depended on the bond's offering price, the par value, and time to maturity.

**Example:**

BankAmerica Corporation sold $500 million of zeros in April, 1982. The maturity dates, prices to investors at the date of issue, and the yields to maturity (YTMs) were as follows:

| Maturity date | Price | YTM |
|---|---|---|
| Aug., 1987 | 50% | 13.479% |
| Sept., 1990 | 33% | 13.544% |
| Nov., 1992 | 25% | 13.582% |

An investor could thus purchase $10,000 of these bonds maturing in November, 1992, for $2,500 (i.e., $10,000 × .25) and earn a rate of return of 13.582 percent before taxes.

Zero coupon bonds were very attractive to both investors and to the issuing corporations. Investors did not need to reinvest their interest payments in order to earn the bond's yield to maturity. Many people thus saw zeros as a way of earning a constant rate of return over the life of the bonds. Investors were, however, required to pay ordinary federal income taxes on the yearly increase in the value of the bonds that represented interest earned but not received. This problem was quickly solved by putting the securities into individual retirement accounts (IRAs) and Keough retirement accounts that allow earnings to accumulate on a tax deferred basis.

Corporations amortized the deep discount of the bonds on a straight-line basis and expensed the discount yearly against their taxable income, even though no interest had actually been paid. This tax treatment greatly reduced the specific cost of capital of zeros. One estimate was given as follows: a traditional interest-paying coupon bond with a cost of capital of

8.1 percent would have a cost of capital of only 4.61 percent if the bond were instead issued as a zero coupon bond maturing in 30 years.

General Electric Credit Corporation, General Motors, J. C. Penney, and Associated Dry Goods Corporation were only a few of the firms that together sold several billion dollars of zeros during the early months of 1982. Congress then passed legislation severely limiting the issuing corporation's tax break on amortizing the discount, thus raising the cost of capital of these bonds. Since then, only limited amounts of zero coupon bonds have appeared on the primary markets.

**Bond Ratings**          Investors measure the desirability of a bond issue on the basis of its risk-return characteristics. Although yield to maturity provides a useful measure of a bond's rate of return, no comparable equation exists for measuring its investment risk. This type of risk is the probability or likelihood that the issuer will fail to make interest and/or principal payments as required. Standard & Poor's Corporation (S&P) and Moody Investors Service, Inc. (Moody's) have established rating systems that are widely used as a way of measuring the relative investment risks of bond issues.

PUBLISHED RATINGS. Most publicly traded bond issues are rated by S&P and Moody's. S&P uses the 10 categories of bond ratings from AAA (triple A) to D (single D) that are explained in Table 19-1. Moody's uses the nine categories ranging from Aaa to C that are explained in Table 19-2.

A bond issue rated AAA or AA by S&P and Aaa or Aa by Moody's is considered to have the least amount of investment risk. S&P's A and BBB ratings are comparable to Moody's A and Baa ratings. These ratings characterize bonds as medium-grade obligations, which means that they are riskier than double A and triple A but are suitable for investors who are willing to accept the higher level of risk. The remaining ratings describe bonds as being speculative and/or identify those that are currently in default.

Within a rating category the yields to maturity of bonds are quite similar except when they differ greatly in years to maturity. The highest rated bonds (AAA, Aaa) typically return the lowest YTM; yields increase as ratings decrease. Thus, an investor who accepts the added risk of a medium-grade bond also expects to realize a YTM commensurate with the higher level of risk.

IMPACTS OF RATINGS ON BOND ISSUERS. A corporation will minimize its specific cost of capital of bonds when they are rated double A or triple A. Bonds rated BBB or higher will also have the widest possible market because many institutional investors have adopted the policy of not investing in bonds that have ratings below BBB.

Changes in bond ratings also can have important impacts on bond issuers. If a bond rating is upgraded from BBB to A, the issuer may be able to float additional debt at a favorable cost of capital and may find a ready

**Table 19-1**            Standard and Poor's Corporate and Municipal Bond Rating Definitions

**AAA**   Debt rated AAA has the highest rating assigned by Standard & Poor's. Capacity to pay interest and repay principal is extremely strong.

**AA**   Debt rated AA has a very strong capacity to pay interest and repay principal and differs from the highest rated issues only in small degree.

**A**   Debt rated A has a strong capacity to pay interest and repay principal although it is somewhat more susceptible to the adverse effects of changes in circumstances and economic conditions than debt in higher rated categories.

**BBB**   Debt rated BBB is regarded as having an adequate capacity to pay interest and repay principal. Whereas it normally exhibits adequate protection parameters, adverse economic conditions or changing circumstances are more likely to lead to a weakened capacity to pay interest and repay principal for debt in this category than in higher rated categories.

**BB**
**B**
**CCC**
**CC**   Debt rated BB, B, CCC and CC is regarded, on balance, as predominantly speculative with respect to capacity to pay interest and repay principal in accordance with the terms of the obligation. BB indicates the lowest degree of speculation and CC the highest degree of speculation. While such debt will likely have some quality and protective characteristics, these are outweighed by large uncertainties or major risk exposures to adverse conditions.

**C**   The rating C is reserved for income bonds on which no interest is being paid.

**D**   Debt rated D is in default, and payment of interest and/or repayment of principal is in arrears.

**Plus (+) or Minus (−):** The ratings from *AA* to *B* may be modified by the addition of a plus or minus sign to show relative standing within the major rating categories.

**Provisional Ratings:** The letter *p* indicates that the rating is provisional. A provisional rating assumes the successful completion of the project being financed by the debt being rated and indicates that payment of debt service requirements is largely or entirely dependent upon the successful and timely completion of the project. This rating, however, while addressing credit quality subsequent to completion of the project, makes no comment on the likelihood of, or the risk of default upon failure of, such completion. The investor should exercise his own judgment with respect to such likelihood and risk.

**NR**   Indicates that no rating has been requested, that there is insufficient information on which to base a rating or that S&P does not rate a particular type of obligation as a matter of policy.

**Debt Obligations of issuers outside the United States and its territories** are rated on the same basis as domestic corporate and municipal issues. The ratings measure the creditworthiness of the obligor but do not take into account currency exchange and related uncertainties.

**Bond Investment Quality Standards:** Under present commercial bank regulations issued by the Comptroller of the Currency, bonds rated in the top four categories (AAA, AA, A, BBB, commonly known as "Investment Grade" ratings) are generally regarded as eligible for bank investment. In addition, the Legal Investment Laws of various states impose certain rating or other standards for obligations eligible for investment by savings banks, trust companies, insurance companies and fiduciaries generally.

Source: Standard and Poor's *Corporation Credit Directory.* Reproduced with permission.

---

**Table 19-2.**        **Moody's Bond Ratings**

---

Moody's Ratings represent the mature opinion of Moody's Investors Service, Inc. as to the relative investment classification of bonds. As such, they should be used in conjunction with the description and statistics appearing in Moody's Manuals. Reference should be made to these statements for information regarding the issuer. Moody's Ratings are not commercial credit ratings. In no case is default or receivership to be imputed unless expressly so stated in the Manual.

### Aaa

Bonds which are rated **Aaa** are judged to be of the best quality. They carry the smallest degree of investment risk and are generally referred to as "gilt edge." Interest payments are protected by a large or by an exceptionally stable margin, and principal is secure. While the various protective elements are likely to change, such changes as can be visualized are most unlikely to impair the fundamentally strong position of such issues.

### Aa

Bonds which are rated **Aa** are judged to be of high quality by all standards. Together with the **Aaa** group they comprise what are generally known as high grade bonds. They are rated lower than the best bonds because margins of protection may not be as large as in **Aaa** securities or fluctuation of protective elements may be of greater amplitude or there may be other elements present which make the long term risks appear somewhat larger than in **Aaa** securities.

### A

Bonds which are rated **A** possess many favorable investment attributes and are to be considered as upper medium grade obligations. Factors giving security to principal and interest are considered adequate but elements may be present which suggest a susceptibility to impairment sometime in the future.

### Baa

Bonds which are rated **Baa** are considered as medium grade obligations, i.e., they are neither highly protected nor poorly secured. Interest payments and principal security appear adequate for the present but certain protective elements may be lacking or may be characteristically unreliable over any great length of time. Such bonds lack outstanding investment characteristics and in fact have speculative characteristics as well.

### Ba

Bonds which are rated **Ba** are judged to have speculative elements; their future cannot be considered as well assured. Often the protection of interest and principal payments may be very moderate and thereby not well safeguarded during both good and bad times over

the future. Uncertainty of position characterizes bonds in this class.

### B

Bonds which are rated **B** generally lack characteristics of the desirable investment. Assurance of interest and principal payments or of maintenance of other terms of the contract over any long period of time may be small.

### Caa

Bonds which are rated **Caa** are of poor standing. Such issues may be in default or there may be present elements of danger with respect to principal or interest.

### Ca

Bonds which are rated **Ca** represent obligations which are speculative in a high degree. Such issues are often in default or have other marked shortcomings.

### C

Bonds which are rated **C** are the lowest rated class of bonds and issues so rated can be regarded as having extremely poor prospects of ever attaining any real investment standing.

*Note:* Moody's applies numerical modifiers, **1**, **2** and **3** in each generic rating classification from **Aa** through **B** in its corporate bond rating system. The modifier **1** indicates that the security ranks in the higher end of its generic rating category; the modifier **2** indicates a mid-range ranking; and the modifier **3** indicates that the issue ranks in the lower end of its generic rating category.

**Absence of Rating:** Where no rating has been assigned or where a rating has been suspended or withdrawn, it may be for reasons unrelated to the quality of the issue.

Should no rating be assigned, the reason may be one of the following:

1. An application for rating was not received or accepted.
2. The issue or issuer belongs to a group of securities or companies that are not rated as a matter of policy.
3. There is a lack of essential data pertaining to the issue or issuer.
4. The issue was privately placed, in which case the rating is not published in Moody's publication.

Suspension or withdrawal may occur if new and material circumstances arise, the effects of which preclude satisfactory analysis; if there is no longer available reasonable up-do-date data to permit a judgment to be formed; if a bond is called for redemption; or for other reasons.

Source: *Moody's Bond Guide.* Reproduced with permission.

market for the bonds. However, a decrease in the bond rating, especially if the new rating is BB or lower, can result in a situation where the issuing corporation is unable to finance itself by selling additional bonds unless it agrees to some very restrictive covenants and incurs a high cost of capital.

**Trading on the Equity (TOTE)**

A corporation trades on its equity when it finances itself by selling bonds. A major consequence of TOTE is the resulting impact on the risk-return characteristics of the corporation. The rate of return generated by the bond proceeds must exceed the bond's specific cost of capital if the firm's EPS is not to decrease. Because of the financial leverage generated by TOTE, the decision to float bonds can affect the ability of the firm to increase shareholder wealth. The probability that the firm will be unable to earn at least the cost of capital of the bonds is the financial risk faced by investors.

The financial ratios in Chapters 3 and 5 are often used to measure a corporation's financial risk. The debt to total assets ratio measures the capital structure composition of the firm. The times interest earned ratio measures the ability of the firm to meet interest payments. The financial leverage ratio, $Y/(Y - I)$, measures the extent to which changes in EBIT produce magnified percentage changes in EPS. The impact on the firm's market value and subsequent cost of capital resulting from changes in financial risk was illustrated in Chapter 14. When financial ratios indicate that the corporation's financial risk has not changed significantly, the market value of the corporation may increase, thus adding to shareholder wealth. However, if financial ratios indicate that TOTE has increased the firm's financial risk, the market value of the firm may decrease and subsequent financing may carry with it a higher specific cost of capital.

## THE BOND INDENTURE

Indentures tend to be long and complicated documents. However, the agreements in the indenture can be classified into four major types of provisions: general, collateral, protective, and retirement or repayment provisions.

**General Provisions**

The general provisions of the indenture specify the size of the bond issue, the interest rate, the maturity date, and the dates at which principal and interest payments will be made. If the bonds are registered, a registrar is appointed to mail payments to the registered bondholders. When the issue is in the form of coupon bonds, the corporation appoints a commercial bank to make necessary payments. The general provisions also appoint the trustee and list the trustee's duties and responsibilities. The indenture may also allow the bondholders to replace the trustee if they are not satisfied with the incumbent's performance.

**Collateral**
**Provisions**

Any collateral pledged against a bond issue is specifically identified in the indenture. Collateralizing a bond is designed to decrease the investment risk of the bondholder and to increase the marketability of the issue. In the event that the corporation defaults on the terms of the indenture, bonds that are collateralized with specific corporate assets have a prior claim on those assets in seeking to recover unpaid interest and/or principal.

DEBENTURES. As defined earlier, a bond that is not secured with any specific collateral is called a debenture. Debenture holders are general creditors of the corporation. In the event of default, debenture owners join the other general creditors as claimants against those assets of the firm not collateralized in other lending agreements. **Subordinated debentures** have secondary claims against the firm's assets — their claims are subordinated to other specified debenture issues. For example, if a corporation sells an issue of debentures and later sells subordinated debentures, the debenture holders will have a prior claim on unsecured assets ahead of subordinated debenture holders in the event that the corporation defaults on its bonds.

MORTGAGE BONDS. The mortgage bond was also defined earlier as one that is secured with a claim on real property. In the event of default, the trustee has the power to sell the secured property and to use the proceeds to settle the claims of the mortgage bondholders. Should the proceeds from the sale be insufficient to settle their claims, the mortgage bondholders become general creditors of the corporation to the extent of their unsatisfied claims. A **first mortgage bond** gives the bondholders first claim on the secured property. A **second mortgage bond** gives the bondholders a secondary claim on real property already secured by a first mortgage. In the event of default, the claims of second mortgage bondholders are not met until the claims of the first mortgage bondholders are satisfied.

When a bond issue is to be secured by a mortgage, the collateral provisions in the indenture may limit the ability of the firm to issue additional mortgage bonds. A **closed end mortgage** prohibits the corporation from using the secured property as collateral in another mortgage bond of the same priority. In addition, an indenture containing an **after acquired clause** requires that all real property subsequently acquired by the corporation be added to the property already pledged and become additional mortgage collateral.

A **limited open end mortgage bond** allows the corporation, within specified limits, to use the secured property as collateral in selling another issue of mortgage bonds of the same priority. An **open mortgage** does not prevent the corporation from using the same real property as collateral in subsequent bond issues. In an open mortgage, all the mortgage bond issues have equal claim on the mortgaged property in the event of default.

**Protective**
**Provisions**

Every bond indenture contains protective provisions that may include negative covenants. This portion of the indenture describes the events of default on the part of the issuing corporation and states what actions the trustee and/or the bondholders can take in the event of default or if the covenants are violated. Protective provisions are intended to minimize the investment risk the bondholders incur by purchasing the bonds.

EVENTS OF DEFAULT. The indenture lists a set of events any one of which constitutes default of the bond contract on the part of the corporation. For example, the firm defaults if it fails to pay bond principal when due, or fails to pay interest when due, or enters voluntary or involuntary bankruptcy proceedings.

ACCELERATION CLAUSE. Given that one or more events of default occur, the indenture allows the **acceleration clause** to be invoked. This clause declares all unpaid principal and interest to be due and payable within a very short period of time such as 60 days. The indenture spells out the mechanism for invoking the acceleration clause. For example, the trustee may be able to invoke the clause without prior approval of the bondholders. Alternatively, the trustee may have to invoke the acceleration clause when directed to do so by a stated percentage of the bondholders. In addition, a stated percentage of the bondholders may be able to invoke the acceleration clause directly and not have to work through the trustee.

NEGATIVE COVENANTS. The indenture may contain a set of negative covenants similar to those found in term loan agreements. Violating any of these covenants and failing to take remedial action within a stated time may be specified as an event of default. Examples of negative covenants are:

1. The issuing corporation must maintain a minimum amount of net working capital.

2. Total yearly dividends must not exceed a specified dollar amount.

3. The corporation must not enter into a merger unless it obtains the prior approval of a majority of the bondholders.

4. The corporation must not engage in additional long-term debt financing unless the proposal is approved by a majority of the bondholders.

**Repayment and Retirement Provisions**

Besides specifying when and how the bond issue will be repaid, the indenture may also contain some options that allow the bond issue to be retired prior to its maturity date.

CALLABLE BONDS. The issuer of a **callable** or **redeemable bond** can, at its option, retire the bonds prior to their stated maturity dates. This option typically cannot be exercised during the early years of the bond's life. For example, a bond issue sold in 1982 and maturing in 1997 may not be callable before 1987. Most new bond issues contain a call provision.

When a bond issue is redeemable, the bondholders face the possibility that they will have to surrender their bonds early and seek a new investment vehicle. In return for accepting this option, the issuer establishes a set of **call prices** that are above the par values of the bonds. The call prices decrease over the life of the bonds. For example, in 1967 Exxon Corporation floated a bond issue that matures in 1997. The bond was callable beginning in 1977 at a call price of 103¾. The call price decreases by one-quarter of a point each year until it reaches par value.

**CONVERTIBLE BONDS.** Holders of a **convertible bond** can, at their option, exchange it for another security. Convertible bonds are usually exchanged for shares of common stock although some bonds are convertible into preferred stock. The indenture specifies the terms of conversion. These terms include:

1. The time span over which the bond can be converted

2. The security to be received by the bondholders if they choose to convert

3. The number of common or preferred shares that are issued in exchange for each bond (The exchange rate is fixed and is adjusted for stock splits and stock dividends.)

Most convertible bonds are also callable. If the firm calls the bonds while they are still convertible, the bondholders have the choice of accepting the call price or exercising their conversion option. Under favorable market conditions, the firm essentially can force conversion by calling the bonds.

---

**Example:**    A $1,000 bond is callable and convertible into 25 shares of common stock. The firm calls the bonds at a price of 102 at a time when its common stock is selling at $50 per share. The bondholders can accept the call price and receive $1,020. Alternatively, they can convert each bond into 25 shares of common stock having a total market value of ($50) (25) = $1,250. Given this choice, most bondholders will convert into common stock.

---

The possibility of realizing a large increase in market value by converting, as in the above example, can make convertible bonds very attractive to investors. The indenture terms are set so that conversion becomes profitable to the bondholders if the resale price of the corporation's common stock increases by 10 to 15 percent after the bonds are floated. The market demand for convertible bonds allows the corporation to offer a low coupon rate and thus incur a cost of capital that is lower than equivalent risk bonds that are not convertible. However, conversion means that a corporation's capital structure is altered by replacing relatively low-cost bonds with equity that carries a higher cost of capital. Conversion also results in a corporation's creditors becoming its owners. As a consequence, the existing equity holders may have to approve any plans on the part of the corporation to issue convertible securities.

SINKING FUNDS. A **sinking fund** provision requires the issuing corporation to retire specified dollar amounts of bonds at specified times. The effect of a sinking fund requirement is to retire most of the bond issue before its maturity date. Sinking fund retirements are not usually required during the early years of a bond issue.

Sinking fund requirements specify the minimum dollar amounts of bonds to be retired each year. Unless the indenture specifies to the contrary, the corporation can retire bonds in years where no sinking fund payments are required and/or retire bonds in excess of sinking fund amounts.

---

**Example:**

PPG Industries, Inc., has the following issues of sinking fund debentures outstanding: One issue due in 1995 carries a 9 percent coupon rate and requires sinking fund payments of $8 million from 1980 to 1994. Another issue due in 2000 carries an 8½ percent coupon rate and requires annual sinking fund payments of $4.5 million from 1985 to 1999.

The corporation has other issues of long-term debt outstanding. The total amounts of maturing debt and sinking fund payments required from 1980 through 1983 are as follows:

$61,000,000 in 1980
$16,500,000 in 1981
$16,800,000 in 1982
$41,900,000 in 1983

---

A corporation may be able to retire the required amount of debt by purchasing bonds in secondary markets. Alternatively, it can give the trustee an amount of money equal to the sinking fund requirement. The trustee then pays out the sinking fund amount by calling randomly selected bonds. If the bonds are registered, the bondholders are notified directly. Coupon bondholders are notified by having the serial numbers of the called bonds published in newspapers and business periodicals.

REFUNDING. When a bond issue matures, the corporation faces the problem of generating sufficient cash to make the final interest payment and to repay the par value of the maturing principal. One way of generating the needed funds is to refund the debt. **Refunding** occurs when a corporation floats a new bond issue and uses the proceeds to retire an existing or maturing bond issue. Refunding can occur at the final maturity date of the existing bond issue or before maturity by calling the outstanding bonds and using the proceeds from a new bond issue to retire the called bonds.

## REFUNDING A BOND ISSUE

Given a corporation's ability to refund a bond issue before its scheduled retirement, the problem then becomes one of identifying the conditions under which refunding is a desirable strategy. There are at least three major reasons for refunding before maturity:

1. Falling interest rates can make refunding a profitable strategy. If rates on newly issued bonds are as little as 50 to 75 basis points below the coupon rate on previously floated debt, the corporation might decide to refund the existing bond issue in order to decrease its financing costs and thus increase its earnings.

2. The corporation might refund a bond issue to eliminate collateral provisions, negative covenants, and/or to delay or eliminate sinking fund requirements.

3. The corporation might want to reduce its TOTE by calling the entire bond issue, using internally generated funds to pay off a portion of the issue and refunding the remaining bonds.

To evaluate the bond-refunding decision from a profitability stand-point, tax aspects are considered first since they are part of the profitability calculations. Then the mechanics of evaluating the desirability of refunding are explained in terms of an accept/reject, capital-budgeting decision. This section assumes that the life of the new bond issue equals the remaining lifetime of the called bonds.

**Bond Refunding and Taxes**

Refunding a bond issue gives rise to cash inflows and outflows that would not occur in the absence of the decision to refund. Some of these cash flows affect the corporation's federal income tax liability. Other tax considerations are involved in the accounting treatment of refunding. Changes in the coupon rate as a result of refunding alter the amounts of the tax deductible interest expense. Bond premium and discount, call premium, and flotation costs also have tax related effects.

BOND PREMIUM AND DISCOUNT. If a corporation nets a price per bond above par value, the difference is called **bond premium.** If a bond nets a price less than its par value, the difference is called **bond discount.** Bond premium and bond discount are capitalized over the life of the bond and amortized as ordinary income or expense by using a straight-line method. If a bond is retired before maturity, all unamortized bond premium or bond discount is treated as ordinary income or expense in the year of retirement.

CALL PREMIUM. The difference between a bond's par value and its call price is the **call premium.** When a bond is called and the corporation pays a bond premium, the call premium is treated as an ordinary expense in the year of the call.

**FLOTATION COSTS.** Expenses incurred by a corporation in selling a bond issue are referred to as *flotation*, or *issue*, costs. These costs are amortized by using a straight-line method over the life of the bond and are treated as ordinary expenses. If a bond is retired before maturity, the unamortized portion of flotation costs is treated as an ordinary expense in the year of retirement.

**Steps in the Refunding Decision**

The capital-budgeting decision to refund a bond issue prior to maturity is reached by executing three steps:

1. Compute the net cash flow that occurs at Time zero, the point at which refunding would occur.

2. Compute the net cash flows that occur during the life of the new bond.

3. Compute the net present value (NPV) of the net cash flows attained in Steps 1 and 2.

These steps are explained by using the data in the following example.

**Example:**

A corporation floated a $25 million bond issue five years ago, carrying a 12 percent coupon rate and having an original maturity of 25 years. Flotation costs were $300,000. It netted a price of 99 per bond, and the issue can be called now at 102.

The existing issue can be refunded by selling a $25 million bond with a life of 20 years. The coupon rate would be 10 percent, and the corporation expects to net a price of 100 per bond. Flotation costs are estimated at $500,000. From the standpoint of NPV, should the corporation refund the existing issue? Assume a 40 percent corporate income tax rate.

**NET CASH FLOW AT TIME ZERO.** At the time of refunding, the corporation incurs cash outflows in order to retire the called bonds and to pay the flotation costs. Tax shields are provided by the unamortized bond discount and the flotation costs of the called issue. The call premium is a tax deductible expense.

In the example, the net cash flow at Time zero is calculated as follows:

*Cash flows*

| | |
|---|---:|
| Proceeds from new issue | $25,000,000 |
| Flotation costs of new issue | −    500,000 |
| Payment of called bonds at 102 | −25,500,000 |
| | −$1,000,000 |

*Tax shields*

| | | |
|---|---|---:|
| Unamortized discount of called bonds: (20/25) ($250,000) | | $200,000 |
| Unamortized flotation costs of called bonds: (20/25) ($300,000) | + | 240,000 |
| Call premium: $25,500,000 − $25,000,000 | + | 500,000 |
| | | $940,000 |
| | | |
| Tax shield: ($940,000) (.4) | | $376,000 |

*Net cash flow*

| | | |
|---|---|---:|
| Cash flow | | −$1,000,000 |
| Tax shield | + | 376,000 |
| Net cash flow | − | $624,000 |

**NET CASH FLOWS DURING THE LIFE OF THE NEW BONDS.** Once the corporation refunds the bond issue, yearly tax deductible interest payments are required on the new bonds. Flotation costs of the new bonds are amortized yearly and provide a tax shield. On the called issue, the corporation no longer pays interest nor amortizes flotation costs and bond discount.

When all the cash flows and tax shields are combined, the resulting values are the yearly *incremental* net cash flows that occur as a result of refunding. In arriving at these incremental values, the interest on the new bonds produces cash outflows. The interest on the called bonds is treated as if it were a set of cash inflows, and the corresponding tax shields are treated as cash outflows.

The incremental yearly net cash flows of the new $25,000,000 bond issue are computed as follows:

*New bond issue*

| | | |
|---|---:|---:|
| Yearly interest: (.10) ($25,000,000) | | −$2,500,000 |
| Yearly amortization of flotation costs: (1/20) ($500,000) | $ 25,000 | |
| Interest | 2,500,000 | |
| Yearly expense | $2,525,000 | |
| Yearly tax savings: ($2,525,000) (.4) | | 1,010,000 |
| Yearly net cash flow | | −$1,490,000 |

*Called bond issue*

| | | |
|---|---:|---:|
| Yearly interest: (.12) ($25,000,000) | | $3,000,000 |
| Yearly amortization of flotation costs: (1/25) ($300,000) | $ 12,000 | |
| Yearly amortization of bond discount: (1/25) ($250,000) | 10,000 | |
| Interest | 3,000,000 | |
| Yearly expense | $3,022,000 | |

|  |  |
|---|---|
| Yearly tax savings: ($3,022,000) (.4) | − 1,208,800 |
| Yearly net cash flow | $1,791,200 |

*Yearly incremental net cash flows*
| | |
|---|---|
| Yearly net cash flow of the new bond issue: | −$1,490,000 |
| Yearly net cash flow of the old bond issue: | + 1,791,200 |
| Yearly incremental net cash flows | $  301,200 |

**NPV OF THE NET CASH FLOWS.** The NPV of the refunding alternative is computed by using the specific cost of capital of the new debt as the discount rate. Refunding is desirable if the computed NPV is zero or positive. If the NPV is negative, refunding is not a profitable strategy although it may be desirable for other reasons.

The NPV of the net cash flows in the example is computed as follows:

Specific cost of capital of the new debt: $(.1)(1 − .4) = .06$ or 6%
Interest factor (from Appendix Table A-4) of 6% for 20 years = 11.470

$$NPV = (11.47)($301,200) − $624,000 = $2,830,764$$

Since the NPV is positive, refunding is desirable from the standpoint of profitability.

## BONDS AS A FINANCING INSTRUMENT

The advantages and limitations of bonds help determine the circumstances under which they are the most desirable type of instrument to meet a given financing requirement. However, events that occur subsequent to a bond issue can turn what was initially a good decision into one that is regretted by the corporation's financial managers. This can happen because some bond characteristics, increased financial leverage, and certain bond indenture provisions are desirable or undesirable only within the context of the firm's current financial condition.

**Advantages of Bond Financing**

The advantages of using bonds as a financing instrument can be grouped into five categories:

1.  The specific cost of capital of bonds is less than that of preferred or common stock. Two factors account for this advantage of debt over equity financing. First, the tax deductibility of interest payments reduces the effective cost of bonds to the issuing corporation. Second, indenture provisions and the bondholders' status as creditors make a corporation's bonds a less

risky investment than its equity. Thus, investors require a lower rate of return on the firm's debt.

2. Long-term borrowing in the form of a bond issue is often preferable to repeated short-term borrowing. For example, bonds avoid the extra costs of commitment fees and/or compensating balance requirements found in revolving credit loans. Bonds also avoid the fixed repayment schedules contained in term loans. In addition, short-term borrowing rates fluctuate constantly, and the availability of short-term loans is not guaranteed after the end of the lending agreement. For these reasons, corporations frequently sell bond issues for the explicit purpose of repaying short-term borrowings.

3. The call option allows the corporation to refund and/or retire bonds when it is advantageous to do so. Making bonds both convertible and callable creates the possibility of exchanging the bonds for stock, thus eliminating fixed interest payments as well as repayment or refunding problems. A corporation may also be able to lower its cost of capital of debt financing by making its bonds convertible.

4. Bonds do not carry voting rights as do stock issues. Thus, bondholders do not pose control or ownership problems to the managers or stockholders.

5. The financial leverage that is created by selling bonds makes these a desirable financing instrument when the corporation can earn more than the bonds' cost of capital. A related advantage is that bonds are a hedge against inflation from the standpoint of the issuing corporation. This means that fixed interest payments become a decreasing burden when inflation increases the firm's revenue.

**Limitations of Bond Financing**

The limitations or disadvantages of bond financing fall into five categories:

1. If the corporation does not earn at least the cost of capital of the debt, the financial leverage created by TOTE will produce magnified decreases in corporate EPS.

2. The corporation must meet the payments of fixed interest and principal. Required sinking fund payments are additional fixed obligations. The corporation may have to make these payments during times when its cash flow is inadequate to meet both short-term and long-term obligations as they come due. Under these conditions the corporation may be faced with the possibility of defaulting on its debt obligations.

3. From the standpoint of capital structure planning, a corporation can expect to be able to sell only a limited amount of debt before its financial risk and cost of capital increase significantly.

Floating debt at the present time may reduce its financing options or flexibility for the next several years. If a corporation has established a desired capital structure composition, bond financing will be desirable only to the extent that total long-term debt does not exceed its target percentage composition in the capital structure.

4. Conditions in the bond market may make debt financing an undesirable source of funds. This happens primarily when the YTM required on new bonds is so high that the corporation becomes uncertain of its ability to consistently earn the bond's cost of capital over the life of the issue. This may cause the corporation to delay its long-term financing, to rely instead on short-term sources, to defer any debt financing indefinitely, and/or to attempt equity financing.

5. The negative covenants contained in the bond indenture may restrict the corporation's operations. For example, liquidity requirements may prevent the firm from making desirable long-term investments, and dividend restrictions may reduce returns to owners.

## PREFERRED STOCK FUNDAMENTALS

**Preferred stock** is a type of equity security that provides its owners with limited or fixed claims on the corporation's income and assets. Of the four major types of long-term corporate financing—debt, preferred stock, common stock, and retained earnings—preferred stock provides the smallest dollar amount of new financing. Preferred stock is an important financing instrument in arranging mergers that involve the exchange of securities between the two merging corporations rather than the outright cash purchase of one corporation's common stock. Newer forms of preferred stock, called *preference shares*, now appear in the balance sheets of a number of corporations. However, the characteristics of preference shares vary so widely among issuing corporations that little in the way of useful comparisons can be provided. Consequently, preference shares are not discussed in this chapter.

**Characteristics of Preferred Stock**

Preferred stock is frequently called a *hybrid security* because it contains characteristics of both debt and equity. These characteristics are:

1. Preferred stock represents ownership in the issuing corporation.

2. It has no maturity date because it is an equity security.

3. No collateral is pledged because it is an equity security.

4. Income is paid as dividends. These represent a distribution of corporate profits but are not guaranteed to be paid. The distinguishing characteristic of preferred stock dividends is that the per share dividends are fixed. This implies that preferred stock is a form of trading on the equity. Dividends are not a deductible expense in computing federal corporate income taxes.

5. Preferred stock has priority as to dividends. If the preferred stock dividends are not paid in a given year, the corporation cannot pay dividends to common stockholders.

6. It has priority in liquidation. Claims of preferred stockholders must be satisfied before any liquidating payments can be made to common stockholders.

7. It has limited voting rights. If the corporation fails to pay preferred dividends for a stated time interval, preferred stockholders may be given the right to elect a stated number of members of the board of directors. In addition, they may have to approve the sale of additional issues of preferred stock or of bonds that would be convertible into preferred stock.

**Special Provisions of Preferred Stock Issues**

Preferred stock issues sometimes carry special provisions relating to dividend payments and/or retirement options. These provisions are primarily intended to make the securities more marketable although the conversion feature, as in the case of convertible bonds, also can be a way of deferred common stock financing.

CUMULATIVE PREFERRED. One way a corporation can conserve its cash flow during a period of financial stress is to "pass" or "omit" dividends. If the stock is **cumulative as to dividends,** all previously omitted preferred dividends must be paid before the corporation is allowed to pay common stock dividends. Since there is no legal requirement to pay preferred dividends, the cumulative feature is the strongest statement that the corporation can make to preferred shareholders about its determination to pay the stated dividends. Most new issues of preferred stock are cumulative as to dividends.

PARTICIPATING PREFERRED. With a **participating preferred stock** the shareholders can receive dividends in excess of the stated amount by sharing — or participating — with common shareholders in dividend distributions. The participating feature generates extra dividends for preferred owners *only after* the common shareholders have received a stated amount of per share dividends. Preferred and common shareholders participate in any additional dividends according to a preset formula. For example, Kollmorgen Corporation had a participating preferred stock issue up through September, 1978. Its per share dividend was 67 cents per year plus twice the amount by which the annual common stock dividend exceeded 20 cents per share.

**CONVERTIBLE PREFERRED.** Owners of **convertible preferred stock,** at their option, can exchange their securities for common stock. The exchange rate, or conversion rate, is predetermined. Converting preferred into common stock results in the reduction of corporate TOTE and the elimination of the preferred dividend requirement. Since both types of stocks are equity securities, conversion does not change the corporation's debt-to-equity ratio in its capital structure.

**CALLABLE PREFERRED.** At the option of the issuing corporation, **callable** or **redeemable preferred stock** can be retired. Call prices are initially set somewhat above the share's par value or liquidating value. Call prices tend to decline over time to the par/liquidating value. Most preferred stock issues are callable, and virtually all convertible preferreds are callable. The intent behind issuing callable and convertible preferreds is to eliminate the corporation's TOTE and allow it to engage in deferred common stock financing.

---

**Example:**   The participating preferred stock issue of Kollmorgen Corporation mentioned earlier was also callable and convertible. The entire issue was converted as follows:

1. The call price was $35 per share ($10 higher than its liquidating value).
2. The conversion rate was two common shares for one preferred share.
3. The number of common shares issued in 1977 due to voluntary conversion was 178,000.
4. The shares unconverted by September, 1978, were called at $35.
5. The number of common shares issued in exchange for the entire preferred was 258,500 through 1978.

**Example:**   Another example is provided by the Federal Express Corporation which has two preferred stock issues outstanding. One issue is cumulative, convertible, and has a mandatory call provision. Its features are:

1. The cumulative dividend is $8 per share.
2. The par value is $1 per share.
3. The issue became callable at the firm's option beginning in 1981.
4. The mandatory redemption value is $100 per share beginning in 1985, and the entire issue must be retired by 1989.

The other preferred stock issue outstanding is cumulative and callable but not convertible. Its features are:

1. The cumulative dividend is $9.50 per share.
2. The par value is $1 per share.
3. The issue is callable at any time.
4. The mandatory redemption value is $100 per share, and the entire issue must be retired by 1988.

---

**ADJUSTABLE RATE PREFERRED.** In 1982, the Chase Manhattan Bank sold a $250 million issue of preferred stock. Its dividend per share was not to be constant but would instead vary with the rate of return on U.S. Treasury securities. Preferred stocks having dividends per share that are not constant but are tied to interest rates are called *adjustable rate, variable rate,* or *floating rate* preferred.

Dividend rates on adjustable rate preferred are generally fixed for a brief period following the date of issue. In addition, the issuing corporation specifies the minimum and maximum dividend rates that will be paid on the securities. In the Chase Manhattan example, the dividend was set initially at 14.1 percent; the annualized rate, although tied to Treasury rates, will not be less than 7.5 percent nor more than 16.25 percent.

Adjustable rate preferred are generally cumulative and callable. Corporations have purchased the greatest portions of these securities; this is because 85 percent of preferred stock dividends received as income by a corporation are excluded from the firm's federal corporate taxable income.

**Trading on the Equity**

When a corporation floats preferred stock, it is trading on its equity because of the stock's fixed dividend characteristic. The corporation's degree of financial leverage increases even though preferred stock is a form of equity rather than debt.

Floating preferred stock can change the risk-return characteristics of the corporation. When computing the firm's capital structure composition, financial statement analysis usually combines preferred and common stock. Thus, measures of financial risk that reflect the presence of preferred stock in a corporation's balance sheet take the form of a fixed charge coverage ratio and the coefficient of financial leverage. Let:

$$Y = \text{EBIT}$$
$$I = \text{dollars of bond interest}$$
$$E = \text{dollars of preferred stock dividends}$$
$$t = \text{corporate tax rate of } 40\%$$

Then a simple fixed charge coverage ratio can be given as:

$$\frac{Y}{I + \dfrac{E}{1 - t}} \tag{19-1}$$

The coefficient of financial leverage is computed by using Equation 5-10:

$$(FL \mid Y) = \frac{Y}{Y - I - \dfrac{E}{1 - t}}$$

These equations imply that a given amount of preferred stock dividends increases financial risk by a larger degree than does the same amount of bond interest.

---

**Example:**  A corporation is considering the floating of $1,000,000 of 10 percent bonds. As an alternative, it could sell 10,000 shares of preferred stock for $100 each and paying a $10 per share dividend. If the corporation's EBIT is $500,000, the fixed charge coverage and financial leverage ratios for each alternative are computed as follows:

**Fixed Charge Coverage**          **Financial Leverage**

$$\text{Debt:} \quad \frac{\$500,000}{\$100,000} = 5 \qquad\qquad \frac{\$500,000}{\$500,000 - \$100,000} = 1.25$$

$$\text{Preferred:} \quad \frac{\$500,000}{\$100,000/(1 - .4)} = 3.0 \qquad\qquad \frac{\$500,000}{\$500,000 \times \dfrac{\$100,000}{1 - .4}} = 1.5$$

In this example, both ratios identify preferred stock as the alternative containing the greater amount of financial risk. In general, financial risk increases with a decreasing fixed coverage and with an increasing coefficient of financial leverage.

---

## PREFERRED STOCK AS A
## FINANCING INSTRUMENT

Preferred stock, you will recall, is frequently called a *hybrid security* because it contains characteristics of both debt and equity. Financial managers consider preferred stock a close substitute for debt, and corporations have sold preferred stock when debt financing did not appear to be desirable. Whether investors perceive preferred stock primarily as debt or equity is an open question. However, some mergers have been executed by exchanging preferred stock of the surviving corporation for the common stock of the corporation being acquired.

**Advantages of Preferred Stock Financing**

The advantages of preferred stock as a financing instrument can be grouped into five categories:

1. A major advantage occurs when the corporation is able to earn a rate of return that exceeds the stock's specific cost of capital. Under these conditions the financial leverage generated by the preferred stock produces magnified percentage increases in EPS. Thus, preferred stock can serve as a substitute for debt financing when the corporation seeks to increase returns to owners by trading on the equity. Preferred stock financing also provides a hedge against inflation because the fixed dividend

payments become less of a burden as inflation increases the firm's EBIT.

2. As an instrument of equity financing, the specific cost of capital of preferred is less than that of common stock. This occurs because preferred stock has priority over common as to dividends and as to repayment in the event of liquidation.

3. Most preferred stock issues carry limited voting rights even though they are a form of equity security. Thus, preferred stockholders do not present major control or ownership problems as long as the dividends are paid regularly.

4. Preferred stock does not mature although it may contain a mandatory redemption provision. In the absence of such a requirement, repayment of the security is not required. A preferred stock issue can be tailored for eventual redemption by including callable and convertible provisions. This allows the preferred to serve as a means of deferred common stock financing. The corporation may be able to reduce the cost of capital of preferred stock by making the issue convertible.

5. There is no legal requirement to pay preferred dividends. This means that a corporation does not face bankruptcy or legal proceedings if it passes a preferred dividend. This ability to delay or omit dividends is an advantage when the corporation's liquidity position is impaired and cash is not readily available for dividend payments.

**Limitations of Preferred Stock Financing**

The limitations of preferred stock as a financing instrument can be grouped into six categories:

1. If the corporation should be unable to earn at least the cost of capital of the preferred stock, the resulting decrease in EPS will more than offset any advantages of this type of financing.

2. The cost of capital of preferred stock is higher than that of debt. This reflects both the lack of a tax shield for preferred dividends and the larger amount of investment risk assumed by preferred stockholders as opposed to bondholders.

3. Although there is no legal requirement to pay dividends, omitting them can have adverse effects on both common and preferred shareholder wealth. Passing preferred dividends decreases or eliminates entirely the current return to both classes of owners. When the security is cumulative as to dividends, passing the dividends for several quarters will substantially reduce the market value of both preferred and common shares if investors perceive that the corporation will be unable to pay the accumulated dividends in the near future. In addition, the continued failure to pay preferred dividends

may result in the preferred shareholders being given the right to elect a substantial proportion of the board of directors.

4. Mandatory redemptions, required in some issues, can cause the corporation to suffer a substantial and prolonged cash drain. Even in the absence of redemption requirements, the dividend represents a regular use of corporate funds that may not always be readily available.

5. Preferred stock can cause some control and/or ownership problems. Existing preferred shareholders may have to approve the sale of debt that is convertible into preferred and/or approve the sale of additional issues of preferred stock. The common stockholders may have to approve the sale of convertible preferred. The conversion of preferred into common may change the ownership composition of the common shares, and thus new owners may object to some of the policies adopted by the corporate management.

6. If investors consider preferred stock to be a close substitute for debt, then the corporation can reduce its subsequent financing options by floating preferred stock. The corporation may be unable to float substantial amounts of either debt or preferred stock until additional financing is obtained from common stock and/or retained earnings.

# SUMMARY

Although bonds and preferred stock are different in many important respects, they are both forms of trading on the equity and it is for this reason that both types of securities are included in the same chapter.

The major characteristics of bonds are due to the creditor status of bondholders vis-à-vis the issuing corporation. Changes in various bond yield measurements are quoted in points and basis points. The widespread use of bond ratings as an aid in bond selection on the part of investors is due to the desire on their part to identify bonds with desirable risk-return characteristics. At the same time, ratings can affect a bond's marketability. Bond ratings are one determinant of the specific cost of capital and yield to maturity of bonds.

The indenture contains all the provisions of a bond issue. Indenture provisions are classified as general, collateral, protective, and repayment or retirement. When the indenture allows the corporation to call a bond issue, the decision to execute the option requires that refunding be considered partly as an accept/reject, capital-budgeting alternative.

Preferred stock is a hybrid security containing debt and equity characteristics. Its debtlike characteristics are the fixed dividend payments, priority over common stock, and limited voting rights. Its equity characteristics are its ownership status and the absence of legally mandated dividends. From the standpoint of financial management, preferred stock is regarded primarily as a close substitute for debt.

The special provisions that are most often attached to preferred stock issues are cumulative dividends, convertibility, and callability. Passing preferred dividends in the presence of a cumulative provision can result in all of the corporation's equity securities decreasing substantially in value. Preferred issues that are both convertible and callable can be used as a way of deferred common stock financing. However, calling a preferred issue will not result in conversion unless the market value of the common received in exchange for the preferred exceeds the preferred stock's call price.

# QUESTIONS

**19-1.** Are floating rate notes a form of TOTE? Explain.

**19-2.** What is the fundamental role of a trustee as a party to a bond issue? What are the duties of a trustee in fulfilling this role?

**19-3.** How do S&P and Moody bond ratings affect the financing strategies of issuing corporations?

**19-4.** What is the purpose of collateralizing a bond issue?

**19-5.** What is the purpose of an acceleration clause in a bond indenture?

**19-6.** What are the disadvantages of having bondholders convert their bonds to common stock when the bonds are called?

**19-7.** What are the major reasons for refunding a bond issue before maturity?

**19-8.** In the absence of refunding, what are the tax treatments for bond premium, bond discount, and flotation costs?

**19-9.** Summarize the advantages and limitations of using long-term bonds as a financing alternative.

**19-10.** In what sense is preferred stock preferred?

**19-11.** Why is preferred stock called a hybrid security?

**19-12.** Why is preferred stock considered to be a form of TOTE?

**19-13.** Summarize the advantages and limitations of using preferred stock as an instrument of long-term finance.

# PROBLEMS

**19-1.** A bond issue is floated at Time zero and has a 20-year maturity. The call option becomes effective at the end of Year 5, and the call price at that time is 102½. The call price decreases by one-quarter point at the end of each year until it reaches par. What is the call price at the end of Year 7? Year 10? Year 16?

**19-2.** A $10 million bond issue carrying an 11% coupon rate and having an original maturity of 30 years was floated 10 years ago. Flotation costs were $150,000. The corporation netted a price of 99 per bond, and it can now be called for 103.

The existing bond can be refunded by selling a $10 million issue with a life of 20 years. The coupon rate would be 10%, and the corporation expects to net a price of 100 per bond. Flotation costs are estimated to be $200,000. From the standpoint of NPV, should the corporation refund the existing bond issue? Assume a 40% tax rate.

**19-3.** A $50 million bond issue was floated 10 years ago and has 10 years remaining before maturity. The bonds carry an 11% coupon rate and are currently callable at 102. The corporation netted a price of 101 when the bonds were sold and incurred $1 million in flotation costs.

The bond issue can be refunded with a $50 million issue carrying a 10% coupon and maturing in 10 years. The corporation would net par on the issue, and flotation costs are estimated at $1,500,000. From the standpoint of NPV, should the corporation refund the existing bond issue? Assume a 40% tax rate.

**19-4.** A $25 million, 20-year bond issue was floated 10 years ago. The bonds carry a 10.5% coupon rate and are currently callable at 105. The firm netted a price of 102 when the bonds were sold and incurred $750,000 in flotation costs.

The bond issue can be refunded with a $25 million issue carrying a 10% coupon rate and maturing in 10 years. The corporation would net par on the issue, and flotation costs are estimated at $1,250,000. Assuming a tax rate of 40%, is refunding desirable from a NPV standpoint?

**19-5.** Bert Corporation floated a $10 million bond issue 10 years ago. The debt carries a 17% coupon rate and had an original maturity of 20 years. Flotation costs were $100,000. It netted a price of 98 per bond, and the issue is now callable at 104.

The existing issue can be refunded by selling a $10 million bond issue with a life of 10 years. The coupon rate would be 15%, and the corporation expects to net par per bond. Flotation costs are estimated at $150,000. From the standpoint of NPV, and assuming a 40% tax rate, should the corporation refund the issue?

**19-6.** A corporation is considering selling 15,000 shares of preferred stock for $50 each and paying a $5 per share dividend. As an alternative, it could float a $750,000 bond issue carrying a 10% coupon rate.

a. Assuming that the firm's EBIT is $450,000, compute the fixed charge coverage and financial leverage ratios for each alternative.

b. In terms of these ratios, which alternative contains the greater financial risk?

**19-7.** A corporation's existing balance sheet includes $20 million of 10% bonds and 400,000 shares of $8 preferred. The firm is going to raise $10 million of additional capital and will float either 12% debt or 100,000 shares of $12 preferred stock. Assume a 40% tax rate and an EBIT of $18,000,000.

a. Compute the fixed charge coverage and the coefficient of financial leverage of the existing capital structure.

b. Compute the fixed charge coverage and the coefficient of financial leverage for each financing alternative.

c. Which alternative increases financial risk by the greater degree? Why?

## SELECTED REFERENCES

See the end of Chapter 20.

# CHAPTER 20

# Common Stock
# and
# Warrants

*Common stock is second in importance only to bonds as a source of corporate external financing. Common stock is also vital to the existence of a corporation since ownership is vested in its common shares. This chapter explains the characteristics and terminology of common stock, denotes the rights of common stockholders, and discusses the advantages and limitations of common stock as a financing instrument. This chapter also summarizes the role of warrants in a corporation's financing plan.*

## CHARACTERISTICS OF COMMON STOCK

**Common stock** is a financial asset that represents the ownership in a corporation. The characteristics of common stock are a direct consequence of its equity position in the corporation.

**Corporate Ownership**

Both preferred and common stock constitute corporate ownership. However, since preferred stock has a prior claim on corporate profits and assets, common stock is sometimes described as a form of residual ownership. This ownership status means that common shareholders bear the ultimate investment risks. If business and/or financial risks produce greatly reduced levels of earnings per share (EPS), or if the corporation operates at a deficit, the resale price and intrinsic value of the corporation's common equity will decrease accordingly. If the corporation is liquidated, common stockholders will share only those liquidating proceeds that remain after all creditor and preferred stockholder claims have been settled.

**Limited
Liability**

One of the most important characteristics of common stock is that it carries limited liability. This means that the liability of common shareholders for the acts of the corporation is limited to the amount of their common stock investment. Assume, for example, that the corporation is liquidated under bankruptcy proceedings and that the cash from the sale of the firm's assets is insufficient to satisfy creditor claims. Limited liability prevents the creditors from seeking additional payments from the common shareholders' personal wealth.

**Corporate
Control**

A distinguishing characteristic of a large corporation is that the ownership of its common stock is widely dispersed, and no single stockholder controls the corporation. As a result, the firm's managers control the operations of the corporation, and common shareholders are limited to voting on specific issues and exercising their preemptive rights.

VOTING RIGHTS. With the possible exception of electing the board of directors, common shareholders indicate their approval or disapproval of proposed managerial actions on the basis of majority voting. Each shareholder votes on an issue by casting one vote for each share owned. For example, majority voting is used to vote on proposed mergers and on proposed changes in the corporation's charter.

Some corporations use *cumulative voting* when electing candidates to their board of directors. The number of votes that a shareholder can cast equals the number of shares owned multiplied by the number of positions to be filled. If, for example, a person owns 80 shares and five positions are to be filled the shareholder can cast a total of 400 votes. In addition, the 400 votes can be distributed across candidates as the shareholder sees fit. This means that all 400 votes can be cast for one candidate. Cumulative voting is thus designed to make it possible for a minority of shareholders to band together and elect their candidate to the board of directors.

**PREEMPTIVE RIGHTS.** A corporation that extends preemptive rights to its common shareholders allows them to maintain their percentage of ownership of the corporation when additional shares of common stock are to be sold. In addition, preemptive rights allow common shareholders to purchase a sufficient amount of new securities that are convertible into common stock so as to maintain their percentage of ownership after all the securities have been converted. When common stock does not carry preemptive rights, the firm sells new shares by using the techniques described in Chapter 18, including the option of treating the shareholders as if they had preemptive rights and issuing rights to them.

**Right to Receive Dividend Income**

Once a corporation has deducted its federal corporate income tax liability from its taxable income and has paid any required preferred stock dividends, the earnings that remain are referred to as *earnings available to common*. Paying these earnings to common stockholders as dividends represents a distribution of profits. Although common shareholders are entitled to receive these profits, there is no legal requirement that they be paid. Earnings available to common and not paid as dividends become *retained earnings* and are the single most important source of long-term financing to corporations.

Corporations cannot include dividends paid as tax deductible expenses in their income statements. Thus, dividends paid do not reduce the corporation's taxable income. Corporate dividends can be increased, decreased, or omitted entirely. As a result, a corporation does not trade on its equity when it sells common stock.

**Other Rights**

Common shareholders have the right to sell or transfer their common shares to other parties. The corporation cannot prevent such sales or transfers, and these actions have no impact on the legal existence of the corporation. Further, common shareholders have the right to inspect the books of the corporation. In practice, however, this right is severely limited and is restricted to information that is publicly available.

**Maturity**

Common stock does not mature, is not callable, and is not convertible. Voluntary liquidation may produce sizeable liquidating dividends to common shareholders. However, as discussed in Chapter 25, an involuntary liquidation in bankruptcy may produce little or no final payments to common shareholders.

## COMMON STOCK TERMINOLOGY

Common stock terminology is used primarily to explain the equity portion of a corporation's balance sheet. These balance sheet accounts state the amount of dollars raised by the sale of common stock, the number of shares held by common stockholders, and the amount of earnings available to common shareholders that have been retained by the corporation.

**Authorized and Issued Shares**

The total number of shares of common stock that a corporation can issue without amending its charter is referred to as *authorized shares*. The number of shares that are held by shareholders is known as *issued*, or *outstanding shares*. For various reasons a corporation may repurchase some of the stock it had previously issued. Stock that has been repurchased and is now held by the corporation is called **treasury stock.** The corporation's balance sheet lists the number of authorized shares, the number of shares issued, and the amount of treasury stock currently held.

---

**Example:**

A corporation has 100,000 authorized shares of common, sells 80,000 shares, and later repurchases 4,000 shares through the secondary market. These figures can appear in the balance sheet in either of the following forms:

Common stock: 100,000 shares authorized; 80,000 shares issued less 4,000 shares in treasury.

Common stock: 100,000 shares authorized; 76,000 shares outstanding after deducting 4,000 shares in treasury.

---

The computation of per share figures, such as EPS and dividends per share, excludes treasury stock. In the above example, per share computations would be based on 76,000 shares.

**Par Value and Paid-in Surplus**

The par value of common stock is its nominal dollar value, or face value. Unlike bonds and preferred stock, the par value of common has little practical significance. Some corporations list a very low par value for their common, while others list no par value whatsoever.

A corporation's paid-in surplus (also known as capital surplus or additional paid-in capital) represents the proceeds in excess of par value from the sale of common stock. The par value and the paid-in surplus are recorded separately in the equity section of the balance sheet.

---

**Example:**

The par value of a corporation's 100,000 authorized shares is $1. The corporation sells 60,000 shares at $15. The proceeds of $15 per share are broken into two components: $1 reflects the par value, and the remaining $14 represents paid-in surplus. The balance sheet accounts then appear as follows:

| | |
|---|---:|
| Common stock ($1 par value): 100,000 shares authorized; 60,000 shares issued | $ 60,000 |
| Paid-in surplus | 840,000 |
| Total stockholders' equity | $900,000 |

---

**Book Value**     The book value of a firm's common stock is the sum of the proceeds from the sale of common plus retained earnings, less the acquisition cost of any treasury stock. The book value per share of common equals the book value of the common divided by the number of common shares that are outstanding.

---

**Example:**     A corporation's balance sheet contains the following information:

Common stock ($0.10 par value): 500,000 shares authorized;
| | |
|---|---:|
| 400,000 shares issued less 15,000 shares in treasury | $ 38,500 |
| Paid-in surplus | 3,811,500 |
| Retained earnings | 7,450,000 |
| Total stockholders' equity | $11,300,000 |

The book value per share of common equals $11,300,000/385,000 shares = $29.35 per share.

---

On the basis of the valuation concepts discussed in Chapter 13, the book value per share of common would seem to have little relationship to its per share market value or intrinsic value. However, a corporation's per share book value of common stock can be expected to increase as long as the firm operates profitably and pays out less than 100 percent of its earnings as dividends.

## COMMON STOCK AS A FINANCING INSTRUMENT

Common stock is an important corporate financing instrument. The advantages of raising long-term funds by selling common stock generally outweigh the disadvantages, although each situation must be evaluated on its own merits.

**Advantages of Common Stock Financing**     The advantages of common stock financing can be summarized as follows:

1. Since common stock does not mature, it is a permanent source of funds. The firm can, if it so desires, retire shares by purchasing them in resale markets or by offering to buy them from shareholders at a stated price.

2. Since common stock is not a form of trading on the equity, selling a new issue increases corporate flexibility from the standpoint of capital structure planning. A typical strategy is to use the proceeds from a stock issue to retire short-term debt.

Another strategy is to decrease the firm's debt to equity ratio by floating an issue of common and to subsequently take advantage of this increased equity base by selling a bond issue.

3. Common stock does not involve making mandatory payments to shareholders.

4. It may be possible to market an issue of common stock quickly and inexpensively by using a rights offering coupled with standby underwriting. This technique is also used by corporations whose common does not carry preemptive rights. The corporation simply mails the rights to the date-of-record shareholders and prices its new shares so as to insure that the rights have a cash value on secondary markets.

5. For most large corporations, selling additional shares of common involves no change in the relationship between ownership and control. Existing shareholders can maintain their percentage of ownership by exercising their preemptive rights. Alternatively, they can purchase common shares in resale markets.

**Limitations of Common Stock Financing**

The limitations of common stock financing can be summarized as follows:

1. Common stock has the highest specific cost of capital of all financing instruments. This requires that investment alternatives have equally high rates of return for the given level of overall corporate risk.

2. Common stock dividends are paid from after-tax earnings. Dividends, unlike bond interest, are not deductible for corporate federal income tax purposes.

3. The payment of dividends may be restricted by covenants in bond issues. The presence of these restrictions may make it difficult to market a new issue of common. At a minimum, these covenants can be expected to increase the common's cost of capital.

4. In closely held corporations, floating an issue of common stock can produce substantial problems in ownership and control. In such situations shareholders who are also corporate managers may have their ownership percentage diluted because they are unable to meet the large cash outlay required to exercise their rights or to make equivalent open market purchases.

5. A new issue of common stock can reduce EPS at least temporarily. In turn, such a drop in per share earnings can have an adverse impact on the resale price of the common.

## WARRANTS

A **warrant** is an option to purchase a specified number of shares of common stock at a specified price. The owner of a warrant is not required to purchase the shares. The warrants can be sold in secondary markets or held as an investment.

The investor who chooses to exercise the warrant sends the required amount of cash and the warrants to the issuing corporation. In return, the corporation issues the common shares. Although warrants are not a major source of capital to corporations, their characteristics can help the corporation to attain its desired capital structure.

**Characteristics of Warrants**

Warrants have a number of unique characteristics which are summarized below. These characteristics allow investors to use warrants as speculative instruments in both the primary and secondary markets. A corporation also can take advantage of these characteristics in floating some of its security issues.

1. Warrants are most frequently issued by attaching them to securities, primarily bonds. When issued in this fashion, warrants are often called *sweeteners* or *equity kickers* because they make the bond purchase more attractive. They can be detached from the bonds and treated as separate securities. Warrants are sometimes given to underwriters as compensation for their services. In addition, a new corporation might issue warrants to the investors who provide the firm's initial capital.

2. The number of common shares that can be bought with a warrant is fixed and is stated on the warrants.

3. The **exercise price**—the price paid for a share of common stock upon exchange of the warrant—is stated on the warrant. This price can be fixed over the life of the issue. Alternatively, the corporation can specify a schedule of exercise prices spread over the life of the issue. The exercise price is adjusted in the event of a stock split (see Chapter 22).

4. Many warrant issues have a specified lifetime after which they cannot be exercised and thus become worthless, but some issues do not expire and have a perpetual life.

5. Warrants are not callable, carry no voting rights, and are not entitled to receive dividend or interest payments.

**Valuation of Warrants**

One of the most important consequences of a warrant's characteristics is that it has a *theoretical value* in addition to its resale value. For any given value of the underlying stock, this theoretical value seeks to measure the lowest price that the warrant will sell for in the securities markets. The theoretical value, also called the *minimum value*, is expressed as follows. Let:

$M$ = market price of the underlying common stock

$X$ = exercise price of the warrant

$N$ = the number of common shares that can be purchased with one warrant.

Then $V$, the theoretical value of a warrant, is given as:

$$V = (M - X)(N) \qquad \text{(20-1)}$$

**Example:** An issue of warrants has an exercise price of $40 per common share, and each warrant can be used to purchase two shares. When the underlying stock's market price is $50 per share, the warrant's theoretical value is:

$$V = (\$50 - \$40)(2) = \$20$$

If the market price of the common increases to $60 per share, the warrant's theoretical value increases to ($60 − $40)(2) = $40.

When the market price of the common falls below its exercise price, the warrant's theoretical value is negative when computed by using Equation 20-1. However, since one function of the theoretical value is to identify the price below which a warrant is not likely to sell, its theoretical value is said to be zero whenever the underlying stock's price is equal to or less than the exercise price.

**Example:** A warrant issue has a perpetual lifetime and an exercise price of $10. Each warrant can be used to purchase one common share. The theoretical values for selected stock prices are:

| Market Price of Common | Theoretical Value of Warrant |
|:---:|:---:|
| $ 5 | $ 0 |
| 10 | 0 |
| 15 | 5 |
| 20 | 10 |
| 25 | 15 |

**RELATIONSHIP BETWEEN THEORETICAL VALUE AND STOCK PRICE.** The general relationship between a warrant's theoretical value and the price of its associated common stock is illustrated by the solid line in Figure 20-1. The warrant is shown to have a zero dollar value for stock prices that are equal to or less than the exercise price. The warrant's theoretical value is positive and linearly related to the stock price for all stock prices greater than the exercise price.

**Figure 20-1.**    **Theoretical and Market Values of a Warrant as Functions of Its Stock Price**

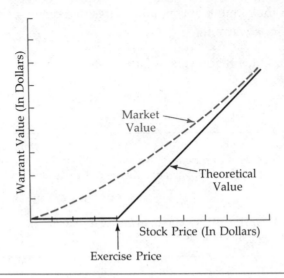

**RELATIONSHIP AMONG THEORETICAL VALUE, MARKET VALUE, AND STOCK PRICE.** The general relationship among a warrant's theoretical value, its market value, and the price of the underlying stock is shown by the broken line in Figure 20-1. This line shows that the warrant's market value is greater than zero and is above its theoretical value for all stock prices greater than zero. The difference between the warrant's market value and theoretical value is called the *premium* over the theoretical value. Figure 20-1 shows that the premium is largest when the stock price is at or close to its exercise price and that the premium decreases as the stock price increases beyond the exercise price.

**BEHAVIOR OF A WARRANT'S MARKET VALUE.** When a warrant being sold is not close to its expiration date and when there are no erratic movements in the price of its underlying stock, Figure 20-1 provides a fairly adequate representation of the behavior of a warrant's market value. There are several reasons that account for the location and slope of this market value line. *First,* the market value of a warrant will tend to stay at or above its theoretical value when it is traded in active secondary markets.

**Example:**    A warrant's exercise price is $30. It can be used to purchase one share of common stock. When the common stock sells for $35 per share, the warrant's theoretical value is $5. If the stock price remains at $35 but the price of the warrant falls to $4, investors will buy up all the warrants available at that price, exercise them immediately, and sell the common stock. Aside from brokerage commissions, the investors will make a profit of $1 on each warrant:

| | |
|---|---:|
| Selling price of common | $35 |
| Less: Exercise price per share | −30 |
| Less: Warrant purchase price | − 4 |
| Equals: Profit per warrant | $ 1 |

The demand for warrants will drive the price up to its theoretical value. In addition, there are more sophisticated trading techniques that will accelerate the increase of the warrant price.

*Second*, the market value of the warrant will remain positive even when its theoretical value is zero because a positive price is required in order for buying and selling to take place.

*Third*, the warrant's premium reaches its largest value at about the exercise price of its associated common stock because of leverage effects and expectations of subsequent increases in the stock price.

**Example:**

A warrant has an exercise price of $30 and can be used to purchase one share of common. When the common is selling for $32 per share, the theoretical value of the warrant is $2. When the stock price increases to $40, the theoretical value of the warrant increases to $10. Thus, the stock price increases by 25 percent ($8/$32), but the theoretical value of the warrant increases by 400 percent ($8/$2).

Now assume that the same stock sells for $80 per share and the theoretical value of the associated warrant is $50. If the stock price increases by 10 percent to $88, the theoretical value of the warrant increases by only 16 percent to $58.

This example demonstrates that the leverage effect—the ability of changes in stock prices to magnify the percentage changes in the theoretical value of associated warrants—is greatest when the stock price is close to its exercise price. Investors who anticipate that the associated common stock will increase in price will be willing to pay the premium in order to benefit from any subsequent leverage effects. Since the leverage effect is greatest in the vicinity of the stock's exercise price, this is where investors will be willing to pay the largest premium. However, the process is self-limiting because the leverage effect decreases as the premium increases.

**Warrants as a Financing Instrument**

Warrants are not sold as separate instruments of external financing as is the case with stocks and bonds. Warrants do provide financing, however, and the corporation's capital structure is altered when warrant options are exercised. Thus, a corporation that is evaluating the desirability of attaching warrants to a forthcoming security issue must consider certain factors and the eventual consequences for the firm if investors exercise their options. These factors can be summarized as follows:

1. Warrants are intended to increase the demand for the security to which they are attached. This demand arises because warrants have a separate market value. The anticipated result is the ability to market the security issue quickly and to lower the cost of capital of the security to which the warrant is attached.

2. The corporation is never sure when, if ever, the warrant options will be exercised. However, warrants that are exchanged for common stock provide the corporation with a permanent amount of financing.

3. The number of outstanding shares of common stock increases when warrants are exercised. This reduces both the firm's debt to equity ratio and the extent to which it trades on its equity.

4. Exchanging warrants for common stock dilutes EPS at least temporarily, increases the cash dividend requirement, and increases the number of votes that can be cast by common shareholders. In a closely held corporation, this can dilute the voting control held by a small group of shareholders.

# SUMMARY

Common stock is a major source of external financing and represents residual ownership in the corporation. Common shareholders bear the ultimate investment risks in the firm, are subject only to limited liability, exercise voting control over major corporate decisions, and may have preemptive rights. Shareholders are entitled to receive the corporation's profits in the form of dividends, have a residual claim on the firm's assets in the event of liquidation, and have the right to sell or transfer their shares to other parties.

Common stock does not mature, is not a form of trading on the equity, and has the highest specific cost of capital of all corporate financing instruments. Dividend payments are not mandatory. They are paid from after-tax earnings and may be restricted by covenants in bond issues. A new issue of common stock can reduce corporate EPS at least temporarily.

Warrants are a form of option and are frequently used to increase the marketability of a stock or bond issue. When the warrant option is exercised, the corporation obtains permanent financing and issues additional shares of common stock. This affects the corporation's capital structure, EPS, cash dividend requirements, and may alter the voting control among the shareholders.

# QUESTIONS

**20-1.** In what ways does common stock represent residual ownership in a corporation?

**20-2.** Explain what is meant by a common stock's limited liability.

**20-3.** What is the major reason why common shareholders have little practical impact on corporate control and dividend policy?

**20-4.** Does selling an issue of common stock constitute a form of trading on the equity? Explain.

**20-5.** How does treasury stock affect the computation of a corporation's EPS?

**20-6.** Summarize the major advantages of common stock as a financing instrument.

**20-7.** What are some of the limitations of common stock as a financing instrument?

**20-8.** In what way is a warrant an option?

**20-9.** What does the theoretical value of a warrant seek to measure?

**20-10.** Why is a warrant's premium likely to be the largest when the underlying stock price is close to the exercise price?

# PROBLEMS

**20-1.** A corporation has 1,000,000 common shares authorized with par value of 10 cents per share. The firm sells 500,000 shares at $20 each. Prepare the balance sheet accounts under stockholders' equity.

**20-2.** A corporation balance sheet contains the following information:

|  |  |
|---|---|
| Common stock ($1 par value): | |
| 400,000 shares authorized; | |
| 300,000 shares outstanding | |
| less 10,000 shares in treasury | $  290,000 |
| Paid-in surplus | 5,700,000 |
| Retained earnings | 3,450,000 |
| Total | $9,440,000 |

Compute the book value per share of common.

**20-3.** An issue of warrants has an exercise price of $50. Each warrant can be used to purchase three common shares. Compute the theoretical value of a warrant when the common stock price is: $35, $50, $62, and $75.

**20-4.** A warrant issue has an exercise price of $23. Each warrant can be used to purchase one share of common.

   a. Calculate the warrant's theoretical value when the common stock price equals: $25 and $30.
   b. What is the percentage increase in the warrant's theoretical value when the stock price increases from $25 to $30?
   c. Assume that the warrant's market price is $4 when the stock price is $25 and increases to $9 when the stock price increases to $30. What is the percentage increase in the warrant's market price?
   d. Why is the percentage increase in the warrant price less than the percentage increase in its theoretical value?

**20-5.** Bert Company's warrants currently sell for $3 each. One common share can be purchased with each warrant at a cost of $17 per share.

   a. Assuming that Bert's common shares sell for $16 each, what is the minimum price that each warrant can fall to?
   b. What is the minimum price (assuming Bert's common shares sell for $18)?
   c. What is the warrant premium (assuming a common share value of $18 per share)?

**20-6.** Mull Corporation's warrant issue carries an exercise price of $40 per warrant. One common share can be purchased with each warrant. During last year, the following market values of Mull's common stock were observed: $20, $40, $50, $55, $60.

   a. Compute the theoretical value of one warrant for each of the five common stock values observed last year.
   b. Assuming that the market value per warrant held steady at $20 last year, compute the warrant premium at each of the five common share values.
   c. What conclusions can be drawn concerning the warrant's premium as the common share value increases?

# SELECTED REFERENCES

Agmon, T., A. Ofer, and A. Tamir. "Variable Rate Debt Instruments and Corporate Debt Policy." *Journal of Finance*, Vol. 36, No. 1 (March, 1981).

Clemente, H. "Innovative Financing." *Financial Executive*, Vol. 50, No. 4 (April, 1982).

Cordes, J., and S. Sheffrin. "Estimating the Tax Advantage of Corporate Debt." *Journal of Finance*, Vol. 38, No. 1 (March, 1983).

Dyl, E., and M. Joehnk, "Sinking Funds and the Cost of Corporate Debt." *Journal of Finance*, Vol. 34, No. 4 (September, 1979).

Federal Reserve Bank of New York. "The Characteristics of Corporate Bonds." *Quarterly Review*, Vol. 2, No. 2 (Autumn, 1977).

———. "Original Issue Deep Discount Bonds." *Quarterly Review*, Vol. 6, No. 4 (Winter, 1981-82).

Franks, J., and J. Pringle. "Debt Financing, Corporate Financial Intermediaries and Firm Valuation." *Journal of Finance*, Vol. 37, No. 3 (June, 1982).

Galai, D., and M. Schellner. "Pricing of Warrants and the Value of the Firm." *Journal of Finance*, Vol. 33, No. 5 (December, 1978).

Marshall, W., and J. Yawitz. "Optimal Terms of the Call Provision on a Corporate Bond." *Journal of Financial Research*, Vol. 3, No. 2 (Summer, 1980).

Ofer, A., and R. Taggert. "Bond Refunding: A Clarifying Analysis." *Journal of Finance*, Vol. 32, No. 1 (March, 1977).

Osteryoung, J. *Capital Budgeting*. 2d ed. Columbus, Ohio: Grid Publishing, Inc., 1978.

Shelton, J. "The Relation of the Price of a Warrant to the Price of Its Associated Stock." *Financial Analysts Journal*, Vol. 23, No. 3 (May–June, 1967) and No. 4 (July–August, 1967).

Yawitz, J., and J. Anderson. "The Effect of Bond Refunding on Shareholder Wealth." *Journal of Finance*, Vol. 32, No. 5 (December, 1977).

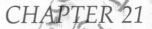

# CHAPTER 21

# Term Loans and Leases

*Although term loans and leases differ markedly in their basic characteristics, they are explained in the same chapter because they provide intermediate term financing to corporations. This means that the financing agreements last longer than one year but generally less than ten years. In addition, some lease contracts now last as long as 20 years; leasing can thus provide both intermediate and long-term financing. The first section of this chapter explains the use of term loans as financing instruments. The second section explains some characteristics of leases from both accounting and finance standpoints and provides a net present value (NPV) criterion for making lease/purchase decisions. Term loans and leases are becoming increasingly important financing strategies. Long-term leases in particular now provide an alternative to selling bonds or stock as a way of obtaining long-term corporate financing.*

## TERM LOANS

A **term loan** is a debt instrument that has an original maturity longer than one year, provides a specified amount of financing, and contains a repayment schedule that requires the borrower to make regular principal and interest payments. The repayment schedule typically is in annuity form. Term loans are a type of trading on the equity (TOTE) and thus increase the borrower's financial leverage.

**Characteristics of Term Loans**

Term loans are negotiated directly between borrower and lender. As a result, the provisions contained in the loan agreements can differ widely. Because the loan is obtained directly from the lender, term loans can be viewed as a form of private placement exempt from registration requirements of the Securities and Exchange Commission (SEC). The general characteristics that term loans have in common are origination, payment schedule, costs, collateral, covenants, and defaults.

**ORIGINATION.** The term *origination* refers to the type of lenders that offer term loans. Commercial banks, life insurance companies, and finance companies are the most important sources of term loans. The maturities provided by these lenders are generally as follows: finance companies, less than five years; commerical banks, up to five or six years; life insurance companies, up to ten years.

Term loans are used frequently to repay borrowings obtained under commercial bank revolving credit agreements. Many agreements specifically give the borrower the option of repaying such borrowings by the end of the credit period or of converting unpaid borrowings into a term loan. When this option is included in a lending agreement that provides revolving credits, the provisions of the term loan are also included in the initial lending agreement. Thus, the borrower knows what to expect if the term loan option is exercised.

**Example:**

Electronics Corporation of America executed a $6,000,000 revolving credit and term loan agreement with two banks during 1978. The revolving credit was convertible into a four-year term loan on June 30, 1981. The lending agreement specifies floating interest rates, and the nominal interest rate increases by ¼ percent if unpaid borrowings are converted into a term loan. In addition, the revolving credit carries a ¼ percent of 1 percent commitment fee, a 10 percent compensating balance requirement against the line, and a 10 percent compensating balance requirement against borrowings.

PAYMENT SCHEDULE. Term loans generally specify that a repayment schedule be in annuity form. Balloon payments are sometimes included. In addition, the loan agreement may allow the borrower to "take down" (or borrow) the money as needed during the first portion of the lending period with repayments starting at a specified future date.

| | |
|---|---|
| **Example:** | A revolving credit agreement is converted into a term loan. Unpaid revolving credit borrowings are $1,000,000. The repayment schedule requires four equal annual payments, and the interest rate is set at 13 percent.<br>The annual payment is found by using the present value annuity factor for four payments and 13 percent:<br><br>Annual payments = $1,000,000/2.974 = $336,247.48 |

A balloon payment occurs when the last payment is larger than the other payments. When the loan agreement specifies the portion of the principal to be repaid by the balloon payment, interest on such portion must be paid each year. This interest is paid along with the annual payments and the balloon payment.

| | |
|---|---|
| **Example:** | A $500,000 term loan with 10 percent interest is to be repaid in four equal annual installments plus a balloon payment at the end of Year 5. The balloon payment is to repay $200,000 of principal.<br>The annual payments are computed by dividing the loan into two parts. One part consists of $200,000 borrowed at Time zero that requires only interest payments during the first four years and a principal-and-interest payment at the end of Year 5. The other part consists of $300,000 borrowed at Time zero and repaid in four equal installments.<br>The annual interest payment on the $200,000 principal is $(.1)(\$200,000) =$ $20,000. Thus, the size of the balloon payment is $200,000 + $20,000 = $220,000.<br>The size of each annuity payment for the $300,000 portion of the principal is found by using the present value annuity factor for four payments and 10 percent:<br><br>Annual payment = $300,000/3.17 = $94,637<br><br>The repayment schedule of the term loan is:<br><br>Payments 1 through 4 = $20,000 + $94,637 = $114,637<br>Payment 5            = $220,000 |

COSTS. The costs involved in term loans depend to some extent on the type of lender. Lenders have gradually shifted from charging a fixed interest rate to charging a floating rate tied to the prime rate. Commercial banks do not require compensating balances on term loans, but approximately half of these loans now contain commitment fees. For example, if a borrower seeks a $100,000 term loan but does not want the money until six months from now, the bank may impose a fee for committing the funds six months before they are needed. In addition, if the borrower intends to borrow the $100,000 only as it is needed, the bank may impose a commitment fee on unused borrowing during the take-down period.

Lenders also may require so-called equity kickers. For example, a commercial bank lender may require the borrower to pay an agreed upon percentage of any profits generated from the loan. An insurance company may use an equity kicker in the form of options, such as warrants, that allow the insurance company to purchase a specified number of common shares directly from the borrower at a price that is set below the borrower's current market share price.

**COLLATERAL.** Over half the term loans made by commercial banks are fully collateralized. When a revolving credit agreement that does not require collateral is converted into a term loan, the borrower may then have to secure the loan according to the conditions of the loan agreement. Working capital assets, as well as fixed assets, can serve as collateral. When borrowings are used to purchase specific assets, such as assembly line machinery, the bank may require that these assets be pledged as loan collateral. Fully collateralized term loans advanced by commercial banks have higher interest rates than uncollateralized term loans from the same lenders. This reflects the risk-return characterstics of the borrower as perceived by the lending banks. A higher risk loan requires not only a higher rate of return but also collateral to protect the lender in the event of default. Longer maturity loans obtained from insurance companies may require the borrower to pledge real estate as collateral.

**COVENANTS.** Term loans contain both affirmative and negative covenants. Affirmative convenants require the borrowing corporation to keep the lender informed of its financial position. The borrower thus submits quarterly and annual financial statements and cash and working capital forecasts. The borrower also notifies the lender of any events that have or could have a significant impact on the borrower's financial condition.

Negative covenants restrict or prohibit the borrower from specified actions, require the borrower to maintain minimum liquidity, and impose limits on capital structure changes. Examples of negative covenants are:

1.  Restricting or prohibiting the borrower from specified actions, such as increasing its dividend payments, making loans to its officers and/or directors, and purchasing or leasing fixed assets.

2.  Requiring the borrower to maintain minimum liquidity, such as maintaining a minimum current or quick ratio. The most common negative covenant requires the borrower to maintain a specified minimum amount of working capital.

3.  Imposing limits on long-term borrowings that increase the borrower's debt ratios.

A term loan obtained by a major motion picture corporation, for example, requires the firm to maintain a minimum current ratio of 1.7. Its ratio of total liabilities to net worth cannot exceed a value of 2.0. Its cash dividends in any year cannot exceed 50 percent of earnings for that year.

**DEFAULTS.** If the borrower fails to make interest or principal payments on a term loan, or if the borrower becomes insolvent or bankrupt, the lender can invoke the acceleration clause that is always contained in lending agreements. The acceleration clause makes all term loan borrowings and accrued interest payable on demand. In actual practice, the lender will allow brief grace periods (a few days) with respect to interest payments.

If the borrower violates certain negative covenants, the lender will notify the borrower of the covenant violation(s). The lender has the option of allowing a specified grace period for the borrower to correct the violation(s) or it can notify the borrower that the maturity of the term loan is being partially or completely accelerated.

**Term Loans as a Financing Instrument**

The characteristics that describe term loans contain both advantages and limitations for the potential borrower. The large and growing volume of this type of financing indicates that, on balance, the advantages of term loans outweight their limitations.

**ADVANTAGES OF TERM LOANS.** The advantages of term loans may be summarized as follows:

1.  Since term loans are a form of trading on the equity, the borrowing corporation obtains the greatest benefits from them when profits on the borrowed funds exceed the cost of borrowing. Otherwise this type of financing is hard to justify.

2.  The borrowing corporation can negotiate the provisions of the initial lending agreement directly with the lender(s) when the term loan involves only one or two lenders This allows the borrower to tailor a lending agreement that is consistent with its financial status and meets its financing needs. And as long as loan covenants have not been violated, the borrower can request modifications in the original lending agreement.

3.  The borrowing corporation can expect to qualify for term loans with commercial bank lenders as the customer relationship develops over time. A revolving credit agreement that is convertible into a term loan allows the borrower to extend the maturity of the loan beyond the revolving credit period. In addition, the conversion lowers the effective cost of capital of the term loan when compensating balances and commitment fees are eliminated.

4. Corporations that have or can qualify for commercial paper ratings can negotiate term loans that require no collateral and have interest rates that are at or close to the prime rate. This is because commercial banks consider commercial paper to be a substitute for term loans.

**LIMITATIONS OF TERM LOANS.** The limitations of term loans may be summarized as follows:

1. The financial leverage created by this form of TOTE decreases the firm's earnings when it is unable to earn at least the financing costs of a term loan.

2. The negative covenants of the term loan can restrict the borrower's investment and financing strategies in several important and undesirable ways.

3. Requirements to collateralize term loans can be disadvantageous because assets that are pledged as collateral cannot be used to secure other financing unless the lenders are willing to accept second mortgages.

4. The annuity payments required may represent a large cash drain because each payment requires a payment to principal as well as to interest.

# LEASES

Leasing emerged as a major industry after World War II. The value of equipment owned by leasing companies is currently estimated to be in excess of $150 billion, and 20 percent of all equipment is now leased. During the 1980s, leasing revenues have exceeded $60 billion per year. Leasing is currently most dominant in the transportation industry where over one-third of all cars, trucks, railroad cars, and aircraft are leased. Almost any asset that can be purchased can also be leased. This includes computers, word processors, general office equipment, nuclear fuel cores, dairy cattle, entire manufacturing plants, and medical, dental, and hospital equipment. This very rapid growth of the leasing industry and its increasingly frequent use as a corporate financing alternative make leasing an important topic in both intermediate and long-term financing.

**Characteristics of Leases**

A **lease** is a contract by which the owner of an asset allows another party the use of that asset in return for specified payments. The owner is called the **lessor**, and the person or business obtaining the use of the asset is called the **lessee**. The amounts and frequency of the lease payments are negotiated as part of the lease contract, with the payment schedule frequently being in annuity form. Thus, the lessee views a lease as a form of trading on the equity. Like other forms of TOTE, leases increase the lessee's degree of financial leverage.

**Types of Leases**

Historically, leases have been classified as either **operating** or **financial** based on the following criteria:

1. The life of the lease as compared with the economic life of the asset

2. Whether the lessor or the lessee maintains and services the asset

3. Whether the lease payments allow the lessor to recover the full cost of the asset

4. Whether the lease can be cancelled before its expiration

Recent accounting pronouncements have differentiated further between operating and financial leases and have prescribed how each type is to be reflected in financial statements. Because of their importance to financial management, these accounting standards are discussed later in this chapter. Table 21-1 lists the characteristics of financial leases and operating leases.

**Table 21-1.**      Characteristics of Operating and Financial Leases

|  | **Operating Leases** | **Financial Leases** |
|---|---|---|
| Life of contract | Shorter than the economic life of the asset | Approximates economic life of the asset |
| Maintenance and service | Provided by and costs borne by lessor, and included in lease payments | Covered by a separate agreement if provided by the lessor |
| Lease payments | Not sufficient to recover cost of asset | Return cost of asset and allow for profit |
| Lease cancellation | May be cancelled before expiration date | May be cancelled only if lessee pays substantial cancellation payments |

**OPERATING LEASES.** Other names for operating leases are *service leases, maintenance leases, non-full-payout leases,* or *non-fully amortized leases.* Because IBM was a pioneer of operating leases for its computer systems, such leases are often called *IBM leases.* Operating leases are used to acquire a wide variety of assets — from office equipment to car and truck fleets and telephone communications equipment.

**FINANCIAL LEASES.** Most financial leases involve real estate. However, they have been used also to acquire ships, planes, and railroad rolling stock.

## Leasing Arrangements

There are three types of leasing arrangements available when operating or financial leases are executed. These are direct leasing, sale and leaseback, and leveraged leasing.

**DIRECT LEASING.** A corporation executes a **direct lease** when it leases an asset directly from its manufacturer or distributor, or through a specialized leasing company. For example, manufacturers of computer and office equipment make direct leasing available to their customers. A specialized leasing company makes a direct lease by purchasing the asset from the manufacturer and leasing the asset to its customer. When a leasing company executes a direct leasing arrangement, the manufacturer of the asset is not a party to the lease.

**SALE AND LEASEBACK.** A **sale-and-leaseback** arrangement is made when a company sells an asset it currently owns to a purchaser and simultaneously executes a lease agreement with the same firm, which now becomes a purchaser-lessor. The selling company receives cash for the asset sold, retains the use of the asset for the duration of the lease, and makes periodic lease payments to the purchaser-lessor. The sale and leaseback of real estate is arranged most often with a life insurance company serving as purchaser-lessor. The sale and leaseback of machinery and equipment can be executed with most types of leasing companies.

**LEVERAGED LEASING.** A **leveraged leasing** arrangement is one in which the lessor borrows part of the purchase price of the assets to be leased. There are three parties to this type of leasing arrangement: the lessor, the lessee, and the lender. The lessor may borrow as much as 80 percent of the purchase price of the leased asset. The lessee may not view this arrangement as being any different from a direct lease. However, some specialized leveraged leasing arrangements are more complicated. These involve the lessor selling bonds in order to raise the funds to purchase the leased asset. The bonds may provide as much as 75 percent of the cost of the asset, with the remainder being provided by the lessor. Thus, the bondholder(s) become the lender(s), and the bonds are guaranteed by the lessee. The lease payments must be large enough to meet the principal and interest payments on the bonds, as well as provide a return to the lessor.

## Lease Accounting and Financial Management

During the 1960s the dollar value of leased assets gradually increased as more corporations financed their capital budgets by leasing as opposed to using more traditional capital sources. However, before 1965 there did not exist a set of accounting standards for including lease obligations as part of a company's financial statements. This meant that long-lived financial leases, which from a managerial finance standpoint are a form of trading on the equity, were not always disclosed by corporations or were described only in footnotes to the financial statements. The lack of an accounting standard for leases made it difficult if not impossible to judge the amount and duration of the long-term liabilities a corporation had incurred by executing financial leases. The phrase *off the balance sheet financing* was used to describe how financial leases could be executed without reflecting either the value of the leased asset or the corresponding long-term liability in a corporation's balance sheet.[1]

From 1965 to 1973, a series of *Opinions* issued by the Accounting Principles Board (APB) of the American Institute of Certified Public Accountants (AICPA) established lease-accounting requirements and procedures. In 1976, the Financial Accounting Standards Board (FASB) issued *Standard Number 13 — Accounting for Leases*. This standard, referred to as *FASB-13*, is the most comprehensive and detailed treatment of lease accounting yet established.

**IMPORTANCE OF FASB-13.** There are several reasons why FASB-13 is important to financial managers and financial analysis:

1. It contains specific definitions of operating and financial leases that provide a classification system for leases that is useful to both accountants and financial managers.

2. It prescribes uniform accounting treatments and disclosure requirements. This makes it much easier to evaluate the extent to which corporations have incurred long-term lease liabilities. It also simplifies the problem of comparing capital structures between corporations.

3. It requires that certain types of leases be capitalized and included in the balance sheet. The capitalized value of a lease is essentially the sum of the present values of the future lease payments. It also specifies the appropriate discount rate — the cost of capital — to be used in computing the capitalized value.

**LEASE DEFINITIONS IN FASB-13.** Two types of leases are defined in FASB-13: capital leases and operating leases. If a lease does not meet the requirements of a capital lease, it becomes an operating lease. Capital leases must be capitalized and accounted for by including appropriate asset and liability accounts on the lessee's balance sheet. Operating leases are not capitalized and need not appear on the lessee's balance sheet.

---

[1]The remainder of this chapter can be omitted without loss of continuity. A number of simplifications have been made in order to present a concise treatment of this subject. The suggestions made by D. Bradlee Hodson, Associate Professor of Accounting at the University of Southern Maine are gratefully acknowledged.

A lease for *new* assets is a **capital lease** if it meets one or more of the following criteria:

1.  The lease includes a provision transferring ownership of the asset to the lessee at the end of the lease.

2.  The lease provides the lessee with a bargain purchase option.

3.  The lease term extends for at least 75 percent of the leased asset's estimated economic life.

4.  The sum of the present values of the minimum lease payments is at least 90 percent of the fair value of the leased asset, excluding executory costs and any investment tax credit retained by the lessor.

The criteria for capital leases on *used* assets are only slightly different. If 75 percent or more of the asset's estimated economic life has elapsed at the beginning of the lease, the lease is a capital lease if it meets either of the first two criteria. If less than 75 percent of the asset's estimated economic life has elapsed, the lease is treated as a capital lease if it meets *any* of the four criteria.

**LEASE TERMINOLOGY.** The four criteria for capital leases contain a number of special terms that are used in classifying leases. These terms are listed and explained below.

1.  *Bargain purchase option*   If the lease does not transfer ownership of the asset to the lessee at the end of the lease, the lessee may be given the option of purchasing the asset at a price called the *bargain purchase price*. This price is far enough below the expected fair value of the asset when the option is exercised so as to make the purchase reasonably certain.

2.  *Lease term*   The lease term equals the length of time during which the lease is noncancellable plus the number of years that can be added to the life of the lease if options to extend the lease are exercised. However, the lease term does *not* extend beyond the date a bargain purchase option becomes exercisable.

3.  *Estimated economic lifetime*   This represents the estimated number of years during which the asset will be useful economically. This estimate is independent of the lease term and of the number of different users who might lease or buy the asset.

4.  *Estimated residual value*   This constitutes the estimated market value of the asset at the end of the lease term.

5.  *Minimum lease payment*   This represents the lease payments made to the lessor which exclude costs of insurance, maintenance, or property taxes. These excluded costs are called *executory costs*.

6. *Discount rate*   The discount rate, or capitalization rate, to be used in computing the sum of the present values of the minimum lease payments. The discount rate is the lower of the interest rate implicit in the lease or the lessee's incremental borrowing rate. The lessee's incremental borrowing rate is the before-tax specific cost of debt that the lessee would incur if the asset were purchased rather than leased and if the purchase were financed by issuing debt securities. Since the borrowing rate may depend in part on the amount borrowed, the lessee must also estimate the fair value of the leased asset.

7. *Lease asset fair value*   The selling price of the asset is equal to the lease asset fair value. In certain cases the lessee may have to estimate the asset's fair value by obtaining price quotations from the open market.

8. *Guaranteed residual value*   If the contract requires the lessee to purchase the asset at the end of the lease term, the guaranteed residual value is the lessee's purchase price. Alternatively, the lessee, although not required to buy the asset, may have to guarantee that the lessor will realize a minimum amount when the asset is sold. If the sale fails to generate this guaranteed residual value, the lessee must pay the difference to the lessor.

9. *Investment tax credit*   This represents specified reductions in federal income tax liability for investing in certain types of business property. Real estate investments do not qualify for this tax credit.

**COMPUTING THE NPV OF A LEASE.** In this chapter it is assumed that leased assets do not qualify for the investment tax credit or that its impact on the desirability of the lease is negligible.

---

**Example:**    A new asset has a lease term of five years. The lease has a bargain purchase option of $2,000 at the end of Year 5. The minimum yearly lease payment is $5,000. The lessee's cost of capital is 10 percent.

Assuming that the lease payments are made at the end of each year, the payments consist of a five-year annuity and the purchase price in Year 5. The present value of the lease obligation is as follows:

$$\$5,000 \,(3.791) + \$2,000 \,(.621) = \$20,197$$

Typically, however, the lease payments begin at Year zero. Thus, the present value of the lease equals $5,000 at Year zero, plus the present value of the four remaining lease payments made at the end of Years 1 through 4, plus the present value of the purchase option of $2,000 in Year 5. The present value of the lease obligation then becomes:

$$\$5,000 + \$5,000 \,(3.17) + \$2,000 \,(.621) = \$22,092$$

---

ACCOUNTING PROCEDURES. The accounting procedures used for capital and operating leases are summarized below.

*For a Capital Lease.* The lease is entered on the balance sheet as both an asset and a liability. The asset account is titled *Leased property under capital lease.* The initial value for both accounts is the sum of the present values of the minimum lease payments.

The asset account is amortized by using a method such as straight-line depreciation. However, as explained below, only a portion of the lease payment is used to reduce the balance sheet liability. Because of this, the values of the asset account and the liability account are likely to differ after the first lease payment.

*For an Operating Lease.* Since operating leases are not capitalized, lease payments are charged to income statement expenses on a straight-line basis. The following example illustrates the comparative balance sheets that result from using an operating lease and a capital lease.

---

**Example:**

Assume a corporation is about to sign a $100,000 lease. The impact on the lessee's balance sheet depends on whether or not the lease is capitalized. If the lessee's total assets are $150,000, an operating.lease does not change the balance sheet values. On the other hand, a capital lease increases total assets and total liabilities by $100,000.

**Balance Sheet**

| | Operating Lease | Capital Lease |
|---|---|---|
| **Assets** | | |
| Leased property under capital lease, less accumulated amortization | $    0 | $100,000 |
| All other assets | 150,000 | 150,000 |
| Total assets | $150,000 | $250,000 |
| **Liabilities and Equity** | | |
| Obligations under capital leases | $    0 | $100,000 |
| Long-term debt | 50,000 | 50,000 |
| Stockholders' equity | 100,000 | 100,000 |
| Total liabilities and equity | $150,000 | $250,000 |

The capital lease increases not only total assets but also the amount of TOTE contained in the balance sheet. The debt to total assets ratio is $50,000/$150,000 = 33 percent for the operating lease balance sheet, but increases to $150,000/$250,000 = 60 percent for the capital lease.

---

DISCLOSURE OF LEASES. In addition to entering capitalized leases on the corporation's balance sheet, certain other lease information must be included in the footnotes to the financial statements. For example, the footnotes for capital leases must state the total future minimum lease payments. This value must be broken down so as to identify the amounts of the minimum lease payments that will become payable during the lease term, as well as the present value of subsequent payments. Similar footnote disclosure requirements must be met for operating leases if the remaining noncancellable portion of their lease terms exceeds one year.

HOW TO CLASSIFY A LEASE. In addition to the four criteria for a capital lease, the present value computations must allow for the fact that most leases require that payments be made at the beginning rather than at the end of a lease year. The data set in the following example is used to show how to classify a lease when there is no bargain purchase option and when transfer of ownership is not specified. The same data set is used for other examples in the remainder of this chapter.

**Example:**

A corporation has to classify a lease on the basis of the following information:

| | | |
|---|---|---|
| 1. | Expected economic life of asset: | 10 years |
| 2. | Fair value of asset: | $385,000 |
| 3. | Lease term: | 10 years, noncancellable |
| 4. | Annual lease payments: | $63,000, of which $3,000 represents property taxes, maintenance, and insurance. Lease payments are to be made at the beginning of each year. |
| 5. | Guaranteed residual value: | $5,000 |
| 6. | Discount rate: | 12% |
| 7. | Bargain purchase price: | None stipulated |
| 8. | Ultimate ownership of asset: | Not specified |

From the data given, the minimum lease payment is $63,000 − $3,000 = $60,000. The present value of the minimum lease payments is computed as follows:

| | |
|---|---|
| Payment at Year zero | $ 60,000 |
| Present value of 9 payments beginning at the end of Year 1 is ($60,000) (5.328) | 319,680 |
| Present value of residual payment at end of Year 10 is ($5,000) (.322) | 1,610 |
| Total present values | $381,290 |

The fair value of the asset at Year zero is $385,000, and 90 percent of that value is $346,500. Since the sum of the present values of the minimum lease payments ($381,290) exceeds the 90 percent fair value of $346,500, the lease must be capitalized.

Another reason why the lease must be capitalized is the ten years of the lease term that extends over 100 percent of the asset's expected economic life. Since the lease term exceeds 75 percent of the asset's economic life, the lease must be capitalized.

| Cash Flow Analysis for Leases | The accounting requirements of FASB-13 can be used to measure the cash flows generated by leases. Capital-budgeting techniques use these cash flows to evaluate the desirability of leases as investment alternatives. Since operating leases are not capitalized, their cash flows consist of the lease payments and the tax reduction created by including the payments as income statement expenses. The cash flows associated with capital leases consist of the cash lease payments and the tax shields generated from amortizing the balance sheet asset. Measuring these cash flows is explained by using the capital-lease data contained in the previous example. |
|---|---|

**CASH PAYMENTS.** The actual cash lease payments are the easiest portion of the cash flows to identify. These consist of the minimum lease payments plus any related payments for insurance, maintenance, and taxes.

| Example: | The annual lease payment is $63,000. Each payment is composed of a $60,000 minimum lease payment and $3,000 for maintenance, insurance, and taxes. |
|---|---|

**AMORTIZATION OF BALANCE SHEET ASSET ACCOUNT.** A capital lease is entered as an asset on the balance sheet at its capitalized value and is amortized over the lease term on a straight-line basis for financial reporting purposes.

| Example: | The capitalized value of the lease is $381,290. This is the balance sheet value of the lease at Year zero. With a ten-year lease term, annual straight-line amortization is $381,290/10 years = $38,129 per year. |
|---|---|

**REDUCTION OF LONG-TERM LIABILITY ACCOUNT.** The capitalized value of the lease is also entered on the balance sheet as a long-term liability at Year zero. The lease payments reduce the balance sheet liability account in the same way that term-loan payments reduce loan principal. The lease payment made at the beginning of each year reduces the end-of-year lease liability by an amount equal to the payment to principal on an equivalent term loan. At the end of the lease term, the balance sheet lease liability equals any residual amount specified in the lease.

**Example:**    At Time zero the long-term lease liability entered on the balance sheet is $381,290. The first minimum lease payment of $60,000 is also made at that time. At the end of Year 1, the lease is treated *as if it were* a $381,290 term loan obtained at Time zero. After subtracting the first $60,000 minimum lease payment, the amount of $321,290 incurs interest at a 12 percent rate during the year.

The computations for Year 1 are summarized as follows:

| | |
|---|---:|
| Long-term lease liability at Year zero | $381,290 |
| Payment made at Year zero | −60,000 |
| Interest is incurred on | $321,290 |
| | |
| Payment on an equivalent term loan | $ 60,000 |
| Payment to interest (.12) ($321,290) | −38,555 |
| Payment to principal | $ 21,445 |
| | |
| Long-term lease liability at Year zero | $381,290 |
| Payment to principal | −21,445 |
| Long-term lease liability at end of Year 1 | $359,845 |

The complete set of values is contained in Table 21-2. At the end of Year 10, the value of the long term lease liability should equal the $5,000 guaranteed residual value. The computed value is $4,953, and the $47 error is due to rounding.

**Table 21-2.    Payments to Meet Lease Liability**

| Year | Lease Liability at Beginning of Year | Minimum Lease Payment | Interest Incurred on | Payment to Interest | Payment to Principal | Lease Liability at End of Year |
|---|---|---|---|---|---|---|
| 1 | $381,290 | $60,000 | $321,290 | $38,555 | $21,445 | $359,845 |
| 2 | 359,845 | 60,000 | 299,845 | 35,981 | 24,019 | 335,826 |
| 3 | 335,826 | 60,000 | 275,826 | 33,099 | 26,901 | 308,925 |
| 4 | 308,925 | 60,000 | 248,925 | 29,871 | 30,129 | 278,796 |
| 5 | 278,796 | 60,000 | 218,796 | 26,256 | 33,744 | 245,052 |
| 6 | 245,052 | 60,000 | 185,052 | 22,206 | 37,794 | 207,258 |
| 7 | 207,258 | 60,000 | 147,258 | 17,671 | 42,329 | 164,929 |
| 8 | 164,929 | 60,000 | 104,929 | 12,591 | 47,409 | 117,520 |
| 9 | 117,520 | 60,000 | 57,520 | 6,902 | 53,098 | 64,422 |
| 10 | 64,422 | 60,000 | 4,422 | 531 | 59,469 | 4,953 |

**TIMING OF CASH FLOWS.** It is important to recognize the timing of the cash flows generated by the lease payments and expense items that provide tax shields. The initial lease payment is made at Time zero, but the tax shield expenses do not occur until the end of Year 1.

**Example:**   The accounts that are used to generate the cash flows are contained in Table 21-3. The values in the *Interest* column are taken from Table 21-2. The *Total* column is the yearly tax shield that appears in the income statement. The maintenance, insurance, and property tax expenses are also charged to the income statement but do not generate a tax shield because the company incurs a cash outflow for these items at the beginning of the year.

**Table 21-3.**   **Cash Flow Accounts of the Capital Lease**

| End of Year | Interest | Amortization | Total | Other* Expenses | Cash Lease Payment |
|---|---|---|---|---|---|
| 0 | 0 | 0 | 0 | 0 | $63,000 |
| 1 | $38,555 | $38,129 | $76,684 | $3,000 | 63,000 |
| 2 | 35,981 | 38,129 | 74,110 | 3,000 | 63,000 |
| 3 | 33,099 | 38,129 | 71,228 | 3,000 | 63,000 |
| 4 | 29,871 | 38,129 | 68,000 | 3,000 | 63,000 |
| 5 | 26,256 | 38,129 | 64,385 | 3,000 | 63,000 |
| 6 | 22,206 | 38,129 | 60,335 | 3,000 | 63,000 |
| 7 | 17,671 | 38,129 | 55,800 | 3,000 | 63,000 |
| 8 | 12,591 | 38,129 | 50,720 | 3,000 | 63,000 |
| 9 | 6,902 | 38,129 | 45,031 | 3,000 | 63,000 |
| 10 | 531 | 38,129 | 38,660 | 3,000 | 5,000 |

*Other expenses are for insurance, taxes, and maintenance.

## LEASE/PURCHASE DECISIONS

The growth of the leasing industry effectively allows a corporation to lease rather than purchase many of its long-term assets. This gives rise to a mutually exclusive capital-budgeting problem. The simplest approach to solving this problem is to compute the NPV of each alternative and to use the mutually exclusive decision rule developed in Chapter 11.

**Cash Flows for Lease/Purchase Alternatives**   The lease/purchase problem is explained by extending the same capital-lease example developed earlier. The corporation is assumed to have the alternative of purchasing the asset from the manufacturer for $385,000 instead of signing a capital lease.

**Example:**   Purchasing the asset generates a straight-line depreciation of $38,500 per year, and the purchaser will incur the $3,000 per year cost of maintenance, insurance, and property taxes (MITS). The asset is assumed to generate $110,000 of profits before expenses, depreciation, and federal corporate income taxes. Salvage value at the end of Year 10 is negligible.

The cash outflow at Time zero is also the net investment and equals $385,000 regardless of how the purchase is financed. Any loan obtained for this purchase will generate interest expenses, but these are excluded from the cash flow computations because they are reflected in the cost of capital used as the discount rate.

The yearly cash flows for this purchase alternative are computed in the following format:

| | |
|---|---:|
| Profits before MITS and depreciation | $110,000 |
| Less: MITS | − 3,000 |
| Less: Depreciation | −38,500 |
| Taxable profit | $ 68,500 |
| Less: Federal income taxes (40%) | −27,400 |
| Profit after taxes | $ 41,100 |
| Plus: Depreciation | +38,500 |
| Cash flow | $ 79,600 |

When an asset is leased, there is no initial investment although a lease payment typically is required at Time zero. The yearly cash flows must recognize both the tax shield provided by amortization and "interest" expenses and the actual lease payments.

**Example:**   The cash flows for the capital lease are computed in the format shown in Table 21-4. At Time zero the cash flow is −$63,000. The yearly interest and amortization expenses are taken from Table 21-3. At the end of Year 10, the $5,000 residual value is paid to the lessor and is a cash outflow.

**NPV Computations for Lease/Purchase Alternatives**

The net present value of each alternative is computed by using capital-budgeting discounting techniques. The relevant cost of capital is taken to be 12 percent.

**Example:**   The NPV of the purchase alternative is computed by treating the yearly cash flows as a ten-year annuity. The present value factor from Appendix Table A-4 is 5.65.

$$NPV = (5.65)(\$79,600) - \$385,000 = \$64,740$$

The NPV of the capital lease is computed in Table 21-5 to be $107,665. Because the cash flows are not in annuity form, the present value factors are taken from Appendix Table A-3 — the present value, single payment table.

**Table 21-4.**   Computations for the Capital Lease Cash Flows

| | | | End of Year | | | |
|---|---|---|---|---|---|---|
| | 0 | 1 | 2 | 3 | 4 | 5 |
| Profit before MITS, tax shields, and federal taxes | $0 | $110,000 | $110,000 | $110,000 | $110,000 | $110,000 |
| Less: MITS | | – 3,000 | – 3,000 | – 3,000 | – 3,000 | – 3,000 |
| Less: "Interest" and amortization tax shields | | –76,684 | –74,110 | –71,228 | –68,000 | –64,385 |
| Taxable income | | $ 30,316 | $ 32,890 | $ 35,772 | $ 39,000 | $ 42,615 |
| Less: Federal income taxes (40%) | | –12,126 | –13,156 | –14,309 | –15,600 | –17,046 |
| Profit after taxes | | $ 18,190 | $ 19,734 | $ 21,463 | $ 23,400 | $ 25,569 |
| Plus: "Interest" and amortization | | +76,684 | +74,110 | +71,228 | +68,000 | +64,385 |
| Profit after taxes and tax shields | | $ 94,874 | $ 93,844 | $ 92,691 | $ 91,400 | $ 89,954 |
| Less: Cash lease payment | –63,000 | –63,000 | –63,000 | –63,000 | –63,000 | –63,000 |
| Cash flow | –$63,000 | $ 31,874 | $ 30,844 | $ 29,691 | $ 28,400 | $ 26,954 |

| | | | End of Year | | |
|---|---|---|---|---|---|
| | 6 | 7 | 8 | 9 | 10 |
| Profit before MITS, tax shields, and federal taxes | $110,000 | $110,000 | $110,000 | $110,000 | $110,000 |
| Less: MITS | – 3,000 | – 3,000 | – 3,000 | – 3,000 | – 3,000 |
| Less: "Interest" and amortization tax shields | –60,335 | –55,800 | –50,720 | –45,031 | –38,660 |
| Taxable income | $ 46,665 | $ 51,200 | $ 56,280 | $ 61,969 | $ 68,340 |
| Less: Federal income taxes (40%) | –18,666 | –20,480 | –22,512 | –24,788 | –27,336 |
| Profit after taxes | $ 27,999 | $ 30,720 | $ 33,768 | $ 37,181 | $ 41,004 |
| Plus: "Interest" and amortization | +60,335 | +55,800 | +50,720 | +45,031 | +38,660 |
| Profit after taxes and tax shields | $ 88,334 | $ 86,520 | $ 84,488 | $ 82,212 | $ 79,664 |
| Less: Cash lease payment | –63,000 | –63,000 | –63,000 | –63,000 | – 5,000 |
| Cash flow | $ 25,334 | $ 23,520 | $ 21,488 | $ 19,212 | $ 74,664 |

**Use of the Mutually Exclusive Decision Rule**

Once the NPV of each alternative has been obtained, the mutually exclusive decision rule identifies which alternative is preferable or recommends that both alternatives be rejected as investment opportunities.

**Table 21-5.**  NPV Calculations for the Capital Lease Alternative

| End of Year | Cash Flow | Present Value Factor | Present Value |
|---|---|---|---|
| 0 | −$63,000 | 1.000 | −$63,000 |
| 1 | 31,874 | .893 | 28,463 |
| 2 | 30,844 | .797 | 24,583 |
| 3 | 29,691 | .712 | 21,140 |
| 4 | 28,400 | .636 | 18,062 |
| 5 | 26,954 | .567 | 15,283 |
| 6 | 25,334 | .507 | 12,844 |
| 7 | 23,520 | .452 | 10,631 |
| 8 | 21,488 | .404 | 8,681 |
| 9 | 19,212 | .361 | 6,936 |
| 10 | 74,664 | .322 | 24,042 |
| | | Total | $107,665 |

**Example:**

The NPV of the purchase alternative is $64,740, and the NPV of the capital lease alternative is $107,665. Both alternatives are desirable since both have a positive NPV. However, leasing is the preferred alternative because it has the higher (and positive) NPV.

**Leasing as an Investment-Financing Instrument**

The decision to lease or buy involves considerations that go beyond capital-budgeting analysis. Some of these considerations are technological, while others are primarily financial.

**OBSOLESCENCE AND PROFITABILITY RISKS.** An asset can become obsolete for two reasons:

1. It can simply wear out before the end of its forecast economic life and become unprofitable to the firm.

2. It can become obsolete when a new line of replacement assets becomes available.

These two risks of obsolescence can be minimized by (1) entering into operating leases with lease terms that are short in relation to the expected economic lifetime of the leased assets or (2) negotiating cancellable leases that contain acceptable termination penalties.

The profitability risk is partially contained in the first type of obsolescence. In addition, even usable assets will not be profitable in the absence of effective demand. Since the fixed payments in a capital lease are a form of TOTE, the lessee has the opportunity to magnify earnings per share if the leased asset is used profitably in return for assuming the added risk of increased financial leverage.

The second type of obsolescence may be more apparent than real. The price of a replacement asset is almost always higher than the original fair value of the asset that is currently owned or leased, even though the replacement asset may appear to be more profitable because of such features as increased capacity.

When replacement assets become substitutes for items currently leased, and if the lessee is required to make substantial payments to the lessor for terminating the lease before the end of its term, the lessee has the following two general alternatives:

1. If the leased asset is meeting the lessee's required rate of return, the lessee can simply decide not to evaluate the replacement. This is a fairly typical response within high-technology industries that produce new and/or improved product lines almost continuously.

2. Undertake a replacement type of capital budgeting that was explained in Chapter 11. The data set in such an analysis must include lease termination payment penalties. However, it may be possible to negotiate a new lease that (1) allows the lessee to acquire the replacement assets by having the lessor purchase the assets, (2) returns the obsolete leased assets to the lessor, and (3) requires little or no lease termination penalties. These types of leasing arrangements occur with some frequency in the computer, data processing, and office equipment industries.

**FINANCING STRATEGIES.** The desirability of leasing over purchasing of assets also depends on leasing as a financing strategy. In the presence of capital rationing, leasing may be the only financing alternative available or may be the only desirable alternative when depressed security prices in capital markets would impose unusually high costs of capital. A corporation may also consider a sale-and-leaseback strategy in order to generate cash for other business needs. In the extreme, this approach may be used to meet a serious but temporary shortage of working capital.

Leasing is often seen as a way of maintaining a corporation's financing flexibility in that other financing sources are not utilized. However, disclosure and capitalization requirements for financial leases effectively inform potential lenders and investors that some portion of the lessee's borrowing capacity has been absorbed by these leases. Operating leases that do not have to be capitalized can maintain the firm's financing flexibility, but the effective cost of operating leases may make financial leases or purchase-borrow alternatives much more desirable. In general, the accounting requirements of FASB-13 serve to eliminate off-the-balance-sheet financing because the added financial risk from trading on the equity through leasing is identified in the resulting financial statements.

Leasing does allow the corporation to avoid the expense and effort of financing through the primary security markets. Flotation costs, registration requirements, and underwriting arrangements can be avoided. In this sense, leasing can be seen as a form of private placement. In addition, lease contracts do not generally contain negative covenants that are contained in publicly sold debt securities and in most term loans, such as restrictions on dividend policy, the sale of fixed assets, and the flotation of senior debt.

# SUMMARY

Term loans and leases provide intermediate-term financing. When these financing instruments provide maturities that extend beyond ten years, long-term financing is provided.

Term loans are characterized by the type of lender, annuity payments that may or may not include a balloon payment, fixed or floating interest rates, collateral requirements, affirmative and negative covenants, and default provisions. Commercial banks are the major source of term loans, and many term loans begin as revolving credit conversion options.

The advantages of term loans include magnifying earnings per share when the rate of return on borrowings exceeds borrowing costs, the advantages of private placement negotiations, and the flexibility that results when revolving credits and term loans are combined into lending agreements. The limitations of term loans include the risk of unfavorable financial leverage, affirmative and negative covenants, the cash drain from annuity payments to principal and interest, and the consequences of not meeting the payment schedule and/or violating loan covenants.

Leases have historically been recognized as being either operating or financial. FASB-13 classifies leases as either capital or operating, and this terminology has become generally accepted. The accounting requirements for capital leases have implications for financial statement analysis and have major impacts on lease/purchase decisions. When evaluating leasing as a combined investment-financing instrument, other factors must be considered beyond capital-budgeting analysis. These factors include obsolescence and profitability risks, as well as the advantages and limitations of leasing as a financing instrument.

# QUESTIONS

**21-1.** Explain what is meant by a term loan.

**21-2.** What is the purpose of affirmative covenants?

**21-3.** In what sense are negative covenants negative?

**21-4.** What are the advantages to a borrowing firm of negotiating a revolving credit agreement that is convertible into a term loan?

**21-5.** Why are term loans a form of trading on the equity?

**21-6.** Why are leases a form of trading on the equity?

**21-7.** According to FASB-13, when is a lease for a new asset a capital lease?

**21-8.** A lease is noncancellable for four years and has three renewal years. A bargain purchase option becomes exercisable at the end of Year 5. What is the length of the lease term?

**21-9.** How is the capitalized value of a lease computed?

**21-10.** What are the profitability risks in leasing?

**21-11.** In what sense can leasing be considered a private placement type of financing?

# PROBLEMS

**21-1.** A term loan with an original principal of $750,000 is to be repaid in 11 equal annual installments beginning one year from now. The interest rate is 14%. What is the size of each annual payment?

**21-2.** A $1,400,000 term loan is to be repaid in six equal annual payments plus a balloon payment at the end of Year 7. The balloon payment is to repay $400,000 of principal. If the interest rate is 11%, compute the size of the annuity payment and the size of the balloon payment.

**21-3.** A corporation is preparing to apply for a term loan. As a first step, a forecast is prepared of the firm's ability to repay the loan. The firm estimates that it can make annual principal and interest payments of $600,000 in each of the next five years. The corporation's lead lender is currently charging 12% on equivalent risk loans. Based on these figures, what is the maximum term loan principal the corporation should obtain?

**21-4.** A five-year lease requires the following lease payments.

| End of Year | Minimum Lease Payment |
|:-----------:|:---------------------:|
| 1 | $2,500 |
| 2 | 2,500 |
| 3 | 2,500 |
| 4 | 1,500 |
| 5 | 1,500 |

There is no bargain purchase option or guaranteed residual value. Assuming an incremental borrowing rate of 10%, compute the capitalized value of the lease.

**21-5.** Compute the capitalized value of the lease described in Problem 21-4 if the minimum lease payments are as follows:

| End of Year | Minimum Lease Payment |
|---|---|
| 0 | $2,500 |
| 1 | 2,500 |
| 2 | 2,500 |
| 3 | 1,500 |
| 4 | 1,500 |

**21-6.** A corporation is interested in acquiring the use of or owning a new metal-cutting machine. The purchase price is $40,000 and the machine's expected economic lifetime is ten years.

A leasing company is willing to purchase the machine and lease it to the firm. The proposed lease runs for five years and is renewable for two more years. At the end of Year 5, the lessee has a $5,000 bargain purchase option. Minimum lease payments are $10,000 per year payable at the beginning of each year. The lessee is responsible for maintenance, insurance, and property taxes. The lessee's incremental borrowing rate is estimated to be 12%.

a. Is this lease a capital or an operating lease? Why?
b. What is the length of the lease term? Why?
c. Compute the capitalized value of the lease.
d. Compute the annual amortization of the asset on a straight-line basis.
e. Compute the balance sheet liability for each year.

**21-7.** A corporation is faced with the following lease or purchase decision: it can purchase the machinery and equipment needed for a new automated production process for $1,800,000. The estimated economic lifetime is eight years and the expected salvage value is negligible. Straight-line depreciation is to be used. Yearly maintenance, insurance, and property taxes (MITS) are estimated to be $20,000. Profits before MITS, depreciation, and federal corporate income taxes are forecast at $700,000 per year. A 40% corporate federal income tax rate is assumed. The cost of capital is 15%.

Under the lease alternative, the lease runs eight years. The lessee receives title to the asset at the end of Year 8. MITS expenses are paid by the lessee. No bargain purchase option is included. Annual lease payments are $320,000. The incremental borrowing rate is 12%.

a. How many of the four criteria of FASB-13 make this a capital lease? Explain.
b. Compute the NPV of the purchase alternative.
c. Compute the NPV of the lease alternative.
d. From an NPV standpoint, what is the best strategy for the purchaser-lessee?

# SELECTED REFERENCES

American Bankers Association. *Term Lending by Commercial Banks*. New York: American Bankers Association, 1964.

————. *A Banker's Guide to Commercial Loan Analysis*. Washington, D.C.: American Bankers Association, 1977.

Fabozzi, F. *Equipment Leasing: A Comprehensive Guide for Executives*. Homewood, Ill.: Dow Jones-Irwin, 1981.

Financial Accounting Standards Board. *Statement of Financial Accounting Standards No. 13 — Accounting for Leases*. High Ridge Park, Stamford, Conn.: Financial Accounting Standards Board, November, 1976.

Johnson, R. W., and W. G. Lewellen. "Analysis of the Lease-or-Buy Decision." *Journal of Finance*, Vol. 27, No. 4 (September, 1972).

Schall, L. D. "The Lease-or-Buy and Asset Acquisition Decisions." *Journal of Finance*, Vol. 29, No. 4 (September, 1974).

Stephens, W. "The Lease or Buy Decision: Make the Right Choice." *Financial Executive*, Vol. 51, No. 5 (May, 1983).

# CHAPTER 22

# Dividend Policy
## and
## Retained Earnings

*Retained earnings are the single most important source of long-term corporate financing. From 1980 through 1982, for example, $232.4 billion of the $425.8 billion in profits that corporations earned after taxes were transferred to retained earnings. The remaining $193.4 billion were paid as dividends. During these same three years, corporations raised $153.4 billion in long-term funds externally. Thus, retained earnings provided 60.2 percent of total long-term financing.*

*Since earnings available to shareholders are the source of both common stock dividends and retained earnings, corporations have developed dividend policies intended to help corporate boards of directors decide how best to allocate earnings between dividends and retained earnings. This chapter identifies the major components of a dividend policy and gives some examples of how common dividend policies are carried out. It also explains the mechanics of paying dividends on common stock. Finally, this chapter considers the role of stock splits and stock dividends in corporate dividend policies.*

## COMPONENTS OF A DIVIDEND POLICY

Paying dividends to shareholders is one of the few ways that a corporation can directly affect the wealth of its owners. Thus, the goal of a dividend policy is to maximize its contribution toward increasing shareholder wealth. However, because a dividend policy is influenced by a large number of factors, increasing shareholder wealth is not equivalent to paying all earnings as dividends. For example, if a corporation expresses its dividend policy in the form of a target payout ratio, some factors will favor a high payout, others will favor a lower payout, and still others will constrain the range of dividend payout that the firm can adopt.

The factors that impact on a dividend policy can be grouped into four components: retained earnings as a financing instrument, capital structure requirements, shareholder requirements, and legal constraints. These components are not mutually exclusive.

**Retained Earnings as a Financing Instrument**

The first component of a dividend policy evaluates retained earnings as a financing instrument. For the most part, the factors that make up this component favor the retention of profits as retained earnings and thus argue for low dividend payments.

**COST OF CAPITAL.** As explained in Chapter 14, the specific cost of capital of retained earnings is higher than that of bonds and preferred stock. Retained earnings, however, do not carry interest or dividend payments and thus are not a drain on corporate cash. In the absence of external financing costs, the specific cost of capital of retained earnings is slightly lower than that of common stock.

**ALTERNATIVE TO COMMON STOCK.** Retained earnings can serve as a substitute for common stock in that both of these financing sources are neither a form of trading on the equity nor sources that mature. However, in closely held corporations where a new issue of common stock can create problems of ownership and control, retained earnings are preferred over common stock because these problems can be avoided.

**ABSENCE OF OTHER ALTERNATIVES.** New corporations that are relatively small may find that external capital is difficult to obtain and/or carries a very high cost of capital, especially if their common stock is not actively traded in secondary markets. In this situation retained earnings become a vital financing source, and dividends are not paid.

Rapidly growing corporations typically finance their asset expansion by raising external capital and retaining all their earnings. In this situation a second rationale for omitting dividends occurs when the firm's rate of return exceeds the rate available on other shareholder investments of comparable risk.

**MARKET TIMING.** External influences on security prices and yields can cause a corporation to delay marketing new security issues. Inflation, for example, can push bond prices down and yields up to levels that result in unacceptably high costs of capital of bonds. When the firm's financial managers forecast that a lower cost of capital for new external financing can be obtained by delaying the sale of the issue for perhaps a year or longer, the problem of interim financing can be solved at least in part by cutting dividends. When such an action is contrary to established dividend policy, interim financing may be obtainable through commercial bank revolving credit agreements and term loans.

**Capital Structure Requirements**

As a component of dividend policy, capital structure requirements are a consequence of capital structure planning. The factors that make up this component can be grouped into two categories: financing flexibility and residual dividend policy.

**FINANCING FLEXIBILITY.** The decision to raise capital through debt or equity financing is based in part on the desire to maintain financing flexibility over time. In this context, flexibility means that only a limited amount of funds can be raised by trading on the equity before the resulting financial risk changes the risk-return characteristics of the corporation. However, selling common stock and retaining earnings builds a base of common equity that allows subsequent financing through various combinations of stocks and bonds. The decision to attain or maintain this financing flexibility can result in a dividend policy that pays only a small percentage of corporate earnings as dividends.

**RESIDUAL DIVIDEND POLICY.** When a corporation identifies a set of investment alternatives, the eventual capital budget is a function of the corporation's marginal cost of capital and the profitability of the investment alternatives. If the firm has identified a capital structure that is believed to be optimal from the standpoint of maximizing its market value, it will adopt the set of investment alternatives that promises the largest total net present value when the marginal cost of capital is used as the discount rate. The fixed financing percentages in the firm's capital structure require that current earnings provide a specified amount of equity financing. Any remaining earnings are paid as dividends. The dividend policy contained in this approach is simply to pay any residual earnings that are not needed to meet the required financing mix. This is a passive dividend policy and can result in a series of dividend payments that appear random to common shareholders.

This residual dividend policy implies that the dividends are irrelevant to both investors and to the firm. In the absence of personal taxes, and given perfect capital markets as described in Chapters 16 and 17, investors are indifferent between receiving dividends and having the corporation retain earnings as a financing source so long as the firm pursues value-maximizing capital-budgeting and capital structure policies. Earnings not needed for this purpose will be paid as dividends. At the same time, Chapter 13 described the intrinsic value of a share of common stock as the sum of the present value of future dividends. Irrelevance is consistent with this intrinsic value concept and argues that the present value of future dividends remains constant or increases even though the timing of the receipt of dividends by shareholders changes as a function of the firm's investment opportunities. Current earnings not paid as dividends are reinvested by the firm so as to produce future dividends having present values that maintain or increase the intrinsic value of the investors' common stock. Thus, postponing current dividends for future dividends is a matter of indifference to shareholders when the intent is to increase shareholder wealth.

**Shareholder Requirements**

The factors of the third component look at dividend policy from the standpoint of common shareholders. On balance, these factors do not argue for high or low dividend payouts; rather, these factors argue for a dividend policy that is consistent over time.

**RETURNS TO OWNERS.** Common shareholders, as the firm's residual owners, are entitled to receive as dividends the corporate earnings that would otherwise be added to retained earnings. At the same time, the corporation's board of directors is under no obligation to declare and pay common dividends.

Inflation has added another complication to this component of dividend policy. If a corporation pays a constant dollar amount of dividends each year, shareholders receive an annuity of payments the real value or purchasing power of which declines steadily because of inflation.

Some corporations have adopted dividend policies designed to counteract the impact of inflation on shareholder returns. This type of dividend policy seeks to increase yearly per share dividends by an amount at least equal to the increase in the cost of living. For example, in discussing its dividend policy the Ball Corporation stated:

> We must achieve a consistent growth in earnings allowing us to increase dividends at a rate in excess of inflation.[1]

---

[1]Ball Corporation, *Annual Report* (1982).

The American Telephone & Telegraph Company (AT&T) is another corporation that seeks to allow for inflation in structuring its dividend policy. It stated:

> As improved earnings have permitted us to do so, it has been our practice to raise the dividend in step with the increasing book value of our shareowners' equity and to maintain the integrity of the dividend against inflation.[2]

**CLIENTELE EFFECT.** Some investors purchase common stock primarily to realize steady income through dividend payments while others primarily seek capital gains. Some investors seek out investments that promise a combination of current income and capital gains. These shareholder preferences are affected in part by the desire for current income and in part by the different treatments accorded dividends and capital gains for federal income tax purposes.

As a consequence of shareholder preferences and the different tax treatments, some investors prefer to invest in corporations with high payouts in order to receive a steady dividend income, while other investors prefer low-payout corporations in seeking possible capital gains. This preference of income versus capital gains on the part of shareholders implies that a corporation with a consistent dividend policy will attract a shareholder clientele whose investment goals are consistent with corporate policies.

**INFORMATIONAL CONTENT.** A corporation's dividend policy and changes in that policy can contain what is called *informational content*. This can be especially important in those cases where a clientele effect has been established. The information being conveyed to the common shareholders is management's expectations about future earnings and dividends. For example, if a firm's dividend policy is to maintain a 40 percent payout ratio, an increase in the dividend conveys management's forecast of higher EPS.

The management of Tenneco, Inc., made the informational content of their dividends explicit when they included the following statement in their 1982 annual report:

> We increased our common stock dividend from 65 cents to 68 cents per share for the fourth quarter of 1982. This translates into a new annual rate of $2.72 per share, an indication of the confidence we have in our ability to continue to produce future earnings.

Researchers have suggested that unanticipated changes in dividends carry the greatest amount of informational content, especially when dividends are unexpectedly reduced or omitted. Such actions are generally taken to signify that management expects lower EPS in the future. When

---

[2]American Telephone & Telegraph Company, *Annual Report* (1977).

a corporation whose dividend policy has attracted a shareholder clientele that seeks current income decreases the per share dividend or fails to increase the dividend as expected, the resale price of the firm's common stock may fall as shareholders sell their stock and seek a new source of dividend income. AT&T's dividend policy that was cited earlier, for example, resulted in the quarterly per share dividend being increased each February. However, in February, 1980, company directors did not increase the dividend above the $1.25 that had been established in 1979. The informational content of this unexpected decision immediately caused the resale price of the company's common stock to fall by $1 per share.

**Legal Constraints**

The fourth component of dividend policy, legal constraints, contains a set of factors that constrains the dividends paid by corporations. These factors can force a corporation to deviate from its historical dividend policies or prevent it from implementing desired policies.

NEGATIVE COVENANTS. Negative covenants contained in bond indentures can prevent corporations from increasing their per share dividends. Alternatively, these covenants may limit the total amount of dividends that can be paid during any given year or force reductions in dividends when specified liquidity requirements are not met. Similar restrictions may be contained in revolving credit agreements that are convertible into term loans when the lending agreement is to be in effect for two years or more.

PREFERRED STOCK REQUIREMENTS. As explained in Chapter 19, preferred stock issues impose two constraints on payments of common stock dividends. First, common dividends cannot be paid in any year where the preferred dividends are omitted. Second, unpaid dividends on cumulative preferred stock prevent dividend payments to common shareholders until the accumulated, unpaid preferred stock dividends are paid.

OTHER CONSTRAINTS. Corporations engaged in bankruptcy proceedings cannot pay dividends when they are declared legally insolvent (see Chapter 25). In addition, some states have established *legal lists* for fiduciaries such as insurance companies and pension funds incorporated in those states. Institutional investors have established comparable lists. The affected investors can purchase only the securities of those corporations contained in these lists. One requirement for inclusion in these lists is that the corporations not reduce their per share common dividends.

## COMMONLY HELD DIVIDEND POLICIES

Corporations that elect to pay common stock dividends on a continuing basis must establish a dividend policy that takes into account the often conflicting dividend components discussed above. Other factors, such as industry dividend policies and the average dividend payout of competitive firms, are often considered. Although hundreds of distinct dividend policies can be formulated, most policies fall into one of the following three general categories: constant dividend payout ratio, stable per share dividends, and regular dividends plus extras.

**Constant Dividend Payout Ratio**

There are several ways by which a constant dividend payout ratio can be used to structure a dividend policy. A corporation can decide to:

1. Pay a fixed percentage of each year's earnings.

2. Set the dividend in a given year equal to a fixed percentage of the previous year's earnings.

3. Adopt a target payout ratio in the form of a long-run average payout. The actual payout ratio for any given year may be larger or smaller than the targeted value, but the intent is to keep each payout ratio close to the desired value.

The Dun & Bradstreet Corporation's payout ratio, for example, has been essentially constant for the last several years. Its payout ratios have been:

| Year | Payout Ratio |
|------|--------------|
| 1978 | 54% |
| 1979 | 52% |
| 1980 | 54% |
| 1981 | 53% |
| 1982 | 53% |

Kollmorgen Corporation's stated dividend policy is to pay out 25 percent of the previous year's earnings as dividends. The corporation adopted this policy in 1973 and has met its target since 1976. The dividend policy of U.S. Leasing International, Inc., is to pay an annual dividend that equals approximately 20 percent of its previous year's net income.

**Stable Per Share Dividends**

Many corporations that pay dividends on a regular basis adopt a stable dividend policy. The most common practice under this policy is to establish a per share dividend amount and to increase the size of the payments when they are supported by higher earnings. A stable dividend policy contains substantial informational content for common shareholders, especially when corporations with cyclical earnings maintain their dividend payments during periods of reduced earnings. Since dividends are paid from cash and not from accounting earnings, a stable dividend policy indicates the ability of the firm to maintain high levels of profitability and liquidity.

Table 22-1 contains examples of stable dividend policies of the Adolph Coors, General Electric, IC Industries, and Goodyear Tire & Rubber companies for 1976 through 1982, by listing their EPS and dividends per share (DPS) values. An interpretation of this table is as follows:

1. Adolph Coors Company's DPS have been increased four times and have not decreased even though EPS have generally fallen since 1976. This can be taken as an indication that management expects to reverse the downward trend in earnings.

2. General Electric and IC Industries have increased their DPS each year, corresponding to their steady growth in EPS. These trends in DPS can be taken as a signal that management expects continued growth in EPS.

3. Goodyear is an example of a firm that maintains a stable dividend policy in spite of cyclical EPS. Corporate EPS fell in 1979 and again in 1982. However, DPS were never decreased; rather, DPS were increased three times in these seven years.

The informational content in Goodyear's dividend policy is illustrated in Figure 22-1. Goodyear maintained the $1.30 DPS in 1979 that was established in 1978, even though EPS fell by $1.10 (from $3.12 to $2.02). Dividends per share were increased in 1982 even though EPS fell 44 cents per share to $2.92. This dividend policy indicates that management expects the positive overall trend in EPS to continue.

**Table 22-1.**  Examples of Stable Dividend Policies

| | Adolph Coors Co. | | General Electric Co. | | IC Industries, Inc. | | Goodyear Tire & Rubber Co. | |
|------|------|------|------|------|------|------|------|------|
| | EPS | DPS | EPS | DPS | EPS | DPS | EPS | DPS |
| 1976 | $2.16 | $0.08½ | $4.12 | $1.70 | $3.58 | $1.35 | $1.69 | $1.10 |
| 1977 | 1.92 | 0.15 | 4.79 | 2.10 | 4.55 | 1.49 | 2.85 | 1.20 |
| 1978 | 1.56 | 0.25 | 5.39 | 2.50 | 4.82 | 1.64 | 3.12 | 1.30 |
| 1979 | 1.95 | 0.25 | 6.20 | 2.70 | 5.31 | 1.80 | 2.02 | 1.30 |
| 1980 | 1.86 | 0.27½ | 6.65 | 2.95 | 6.02 | 1.96 | 2.85 | 1.30 |
| 1981 | 1.48 | 0.30 | 7.26 | 3.15 | 6.65 | 2.15 | 3.36 | 1.30 |
| 1982 | 1.32 | 0.30 | 8.00 | 3.30 | 3.52 | 2.24 | 2.92 | 1.37½ |

**Regular Dividends Plus Extras**

The regular-dividends-plus-extras policy consists of establishing a regular dollar dividend and paying additional amounts in those years where earnings increase substantially. The regular dollar dividend may also be increased over time. The advantage in paying the extra dividends is that they can be omitted without decreasing the regular dividend. A possible disadvantage of this policy is that shareholders may come to expect extra dividends. If these extras are not paid as expected, the resale price of the common stock may fall.

**Figure 22-1.**     **EPS and DPS Data for the Goodyear Tire & Rubber Company**

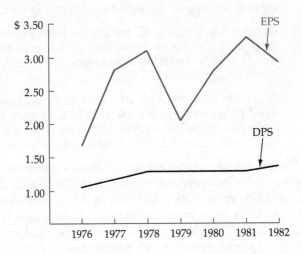

**Example:**     General Motors Corporation is the best known example of a company with a dividend policy that consists of a regular dividend coupled with extras. The quarterly dividends paid by GM from 1977 through 1979 were as follows:

|      | Q1     | Q2     | Q3     | Q4     |
|------|--------|--------|--------|--------|
| 1977 | $0.85  | $1.85  | $0.85  | $3.25  |
| 1978 | 1.00   | 1.50   | 1.00   | 2.50   |
| 1979 | 1.00   | 1.65   | 1.15   | 1.50   |

In 1977, the regular quarterly dividend was 85 cents, and extras were paid in the second and fourth quarters. In 1978, the regular quarterly dividend was increased to $1 per share, and extras were again paid in the second and fourth quarters. In 1979, the regular dividend was increased to $1.15 in the second quarter; a 50-cent extra was paid in that quarter, and a 35-cent extra was paid in the fourth quarter.

By way of contrast, GM's quarterly DPS for 1980 through 1982 were as follows:

|      | Q1     | Q2     | Q3     | Q4     |
|------|--------|--------|--------|--------|
| 1980 | $1.15  | $0.60  | $0.60  | $0.60  |
| 1981 | 0.60   | 0.60   | 0.60   | 0.60   |
| 1982 | 0.60   | 0.60   | 0.60   | 0.60   |

What caused this dramatic change in dividend policy? The recession that began in 1980 adversely affected domestic automobile production and sales to the point that GM reported negative EPS in 1980. The yearly GM EPS and DPS are as follows:

|      | EPS     | DPS    |
|------|---------|--------|
| 1977 | $11.62  | $6.80  |
| 1978 | 12.24   | 6.00   |
| 1979 | 10.04   | 5.30   |
| 1980 | −2.65   | 2.95   |
| 1981 | 1.07    | 2.40   |
| 1982 | 3.09    | 2.40   |

The fact that the firm maintained a 60-cent quarterly DPS in 1980 in spite of negative EPS and allowed its payout ratio to exceed 100 percent in 1981 can be seen as management's forecast that EPS would quickly recover.

## DIVIDEND PAYMENT PROCEDURES

Most corporate dividend policies are tailored to pay cash dividends on a quarterly basis. As an alternative to receiving cash dividends, dividend reinvestment plans are offered to common shareholders.

**Paying Cash Dividends**

The procedures for declaring and paying cash dividends use four important dates. These dates are known as the declaration date, the date of record, the ex-dividend date, and the payment date.

**DECLARATION DATE.** The declaration date is the day on which the corporate directors meet, decide to pay dividends, and announce the specifics of their decision. For example, assume that the directors of D. Z. Ray, Inc., meet on September 28, 1984, and decide to pay a quarterly dividend of 40 cents per share. September 28 becomes the declaration date. The board of directors then issues the following statement:

The board of directors of D. Z. Ray, Inc., met on September 28, 1984, and declared a regular quarterly dividend of 40 cents per common share, payable to holders of record as of October 26. The payment is to be made November 9, 1984.

**DATE OF RECORD.** In order to receive the cash dividend that is declared by a corporation, investors must be listed as owners of the stock on the date of record. This date is also known as the holder-of-record date. In the above example, investors who are listed in D. Z. Ray's stock transfer books as owners on October 26 receive the 40 cents per share dividend.

**EX-DIVIDEND DATE.** When an investor buys or sells corporate securities on resale markets, up to four business days are required before the change of ownership is executed in the corporation's stock transfer books. As a consequence, when dividends are declared, an ex-dividend date is set four business days prior to the date of record. Investors who wish to receive dividends on stock they do not own must purchase the shares *before* the ex-dividend date. If the stock is purchased on or after the ex-dividend date, the purchaser will not appear as the holder of record on the corporation's books and the seller will receive the dividend.

The date of record for D. Z. Ray, Inc., is October 26. Since this is a Friday, the ex-dividend date is set as Monday, October 22. Investors who purchase the common shares of this firm on or after October 22 will not receive the dividend that was declared on September 28.

**PAYMENT DATE.** Once the date of record has passed, the corporation prints the checks and makes them payable to the investors who owned the stock as of the date of record. The dividend checks are mailed on the payment date. The payment date for D. Z. Ray, Inc., is November 9, 1984.

**Dividend Reinvestment Plans**

Many large corporations have established automatic dividend reinvestment plans that allow the shareholders to purchase additional common stock as an alternative to receiving cash dividends. In most cases the shareholder receives newly issued stock. Corporations view such plans as a source of equity capital. Shareholders do not pay transaction costs of acquiring these new shares, but they must pay ordinary income taxes on the cash dividend they would otherwise receive. The market price of the stock on the payment date is used as the purchase cost to the shareholder.

**Example:**

A corporation declares a $1 per share dividend on its common stock. An investor who owns 100 shares should receive $100 in dividends. If the corporation has an automatic dividend reinvestment plan, the shareholder can receive either the cash dividend or additional shares of common. If the investor elects to receive the additional shares, and if the market price of the stock is $20 per share on the payment date, the shareholder will receive five additional shares in place of the cash dividend.

## STOCK DIVIDENDS AND STOCK SPLITS

Some corporations use a dividend policy that involves distributing additional shares of stock in place of, or in conjunction with, cash dividends. Shareholders receive the additional shares at no cost to themselves. Distributing these additional common shares is accomplished by declaring stock dividends or stock splits. Although the accounting treatment of these two approaches differs, there are no meaningful differences from the standpoint of managerial finance.

**Stock Dividends**

A **stock dividend** is a distribution of additional shares of common stock to existing shareholders on a pro rata basis. For example, in a 10 percent stock dividend, shareholders receive one additional share for every ten shares owned.

The accounting treatment of stock dividends consists of transferring an amount equal to the market value of the stock dividends from the retained earnings account to the common stock and paid-in surplus accounts and increasing the number of shares outstanding. The par value or stated value of the common is not changed.

**Example:**

The middle portion of Table 22-2 illustrates the accounting treatment of a 20 percent stock dividend that is declared and paid by D. Z. Ray, Inc. The top portion of the table lists the common and the equity accounts before the stock dividends are declared.

**Table 22-2.**

**Effect of a Stock Dividend and a Stock Split for D. Z. Ray, Inc.**

**Equity Accounts**

| | |
|---|---:|
| Common stock ($1 par value): | |
| 2,500,000 shares authorized | |
| 500,000 shares outstanding | $ 500,000 |
| Paid-in surplus | 4,500,000 |
| Retained earnings | 7,000,000 |
| Total | $12,000,000 |

**Equity Accounts after a 20% Stock Dividend**

| | |
|---|---:|
| Common stock ($1 par value): | |
| 2,500,000 shares authorized | |
| 600,000 shares outstanding | $ 600,000 |
| Paid-in surplus | 6,900,000 |
| Retained earnings | 4,500,000 |
| Total | $12,000,000 |

**Equity Accounts after a 2 for 1 Stock Split**

| | |
|---|---:|
| Common stock ($0.50 par value): | |
| 2,500,000 shares authorized | |
| 1,000,000 shares outstanding | $ 500,000 |
| Paid-in surplus | 4,500,000 |
| Retained earnings | 7,000,000 |
| Total | $12,000,000 |

Since there are 500,000 shares of common outstanding, the corporation issues a total of (.2)(500,000) = 100,000 additional shares. If the market price of the stock is $25, then a total of ($25) (100,000) = $2,500,000 is transferred from the retained earnings account as follows:

$$
\begin{array}{lr}
\text{To common stock account: (\$1) (100,000)} & = \$ \ \ 100,000 \\
\text{To paid-in surplus account:} & = \underline{\ \ 2,400,000} \\
\text{Total transferred from retained earnings} & = \underline{\underline{\$2,500,000}}
\end{array}
$$

**Stock Splits**

A **stock split** is similar to a stock dividend in that additional shares are distributed to existing shareholders except that the pro rata distribution is much higher. A 2 for 1 stock split, for example, means that shareholders receive one additional share for each share owned.

In accounting for a stock split, the par value or stated value is divided by the size of the split, but no transfers are made from retained earnings.

**Example:**

The bottom portion of Table 22-2 illustrates the accounting treatment of a 2 for 1 stock split for D. Z. Ray, Inc.

Since there are 500,000 shares of $1 par value stock outstanding, a 2 for 1 split means that the corporation issues a total of (1) (500,000) = 500,000 additional shares and reduces the par value from $1 to 50 cents. None of the dollar amounts in the equity section are affected.

**Implications of Stock Dividends and Stock Splits**

The use of stock dividends and stock splits as part of a corporation's dividend policy has a number of important implications for the firm's shareholders. These implications can be summarized as follows:

1. A stock dividend alters the firm's individual equity accounts. Total assets, total liabilities, and total equity are not changed, however. A stock split has no impact on balance sheet accounts other than reducing the par value or stated value of the common.

2. By themselves, stock splits and stock dividends do not alter shareholder wealth. EPS and the market price of the common decrease in proportion to the amount of shares distributed, and each shareholder's proportional ownership remains unchanged.

   Assume, for example, that a corporation's EPS is $6 and its stock sells for $30. The firm declares a 3 for 1 stock split. The earnings are restated as $2 per share, and the stock's market price is reduced to $10 per share. The shareholders end up with three times as much stock, but each share now represents one-third as much value.

3.  Shares received in the form of stock dividends and stock splits are not taxable to shareholders. This is consistent with the fact that stock dividends and splits do not change shareholder wealth. For example, an investor who owns 100 shares of common stock with a per share price of $80 and who receives 100 added shares when the stock splits 2 for 1, pays no taxes as a result of receiving the additional 100 shares. The stock split reduces the share price to $40, leaving the investor's wealth unchanged.

4.  Stock splits and large stock dividends can have informational content in those cases where a corporation's EPS is growing rapidly. When the price of a growth company's stock increases along with its per share earnings, a stock split may indicate management's expectation of continued growth in the firm's earnings.

5.  Some firms have adopted a dividend policy of paying both cash and stock dividends on a regular basis. Duro-Test Corporation, for example, has paid cash and stock dividends since 1952. Investors who purchased this company's shares in 1951 have received a steadily increasing cash dividend income and have more than doubled their number of shares owned as a result of stock dividends.

# SUMMARY

A firm's current earnings can be retained or paid as dividends. The dividend policy that puts that decision into practice reflects the importance of: retained earnings as a financing instrument, the firm's capital structure requirements, shareholder requirements, and legal constraints. Some of the factors that make up these four components of a dividend policy argue for high payouts, while others favor the retention of earnings. The dividend policies adopted by firms that seek to pay dividends on a regular basis can be grouped into three general categories: a constant dividend payout ratio, a stable dollar dividend policy, and regular dividends plus extras.

The dividend payment procedure uses a declaration date, a date of record, an ex-dividend date, and a payment date. Stock dividends and stock splits are ways of distributing shares of common stock to existing shareholders. Stock dividends and stock splits do not by themselves increase shareholder wealth, but they can contain informational content to shareholders.

# QUESTIONS

**22-1.** What is the goal of a corporate dividend policy?

**22-2.** Identify the four major components of dividend policy.

**22-3.** To what extent are retained earnings a substitute for common stock?

**22-4.** Does the desire on the part of a corporation to maintain financing flexibility argue for larger or smaller payouts? Explain.

**22-5.** Explain what is meant by a residual dividend policy.

**22-6.** Explain what is meant by the clientele effect in dividend policy.

**22-7.** What are the three general types of dividend policies used by corporations?

**22-8.** Explain the characteristics of a stable per share dividend policy.

**22-9.** What types of informational content can be found in a dividend policy that pays regular dividends plus extras?

**22-10.** What is the relationship between the date of record and the ex-dividend date? What is the importance of the ex-dividend date?

**22-11.** From the standpoint of managerial finance, what are the differences between stock splits and stock dividends?

# PROBLEMS

*Note:* Problems 22-1 through 22-4 use the data contained in Table 22-3 covering the years 1980 through 1987.

**22-1.** The EPS and DPS time series for Firm *A* are contained in Table 22-3. What type of dividend policy do these figures exhibit? Why? On the basis of your answers, forecast the 1987 DPS for Firm *A*.

**22-2.** What type of dividend policy does Firm *B* follow? What is your forecast of 1987 DPS for this firm?

**22-3.** Forecast the 1987 DPS for Firm *C* and explain the reasons for your forecast.

**22-4.** Firm $D$'s dividend policy is to establish a regular dividend and to pay extras. The regular dividend was set at $2 per share in 1980 and increased to $2.50 per share in 1982. The DPS contained in Table 22-3 for this firm shows that extra dividends were paid almost every year. On the basis of these data, forecast the 1987 DPS for Firm $D$.

Table 22-3.     EPS and DPS for Four Hypothetical Firms

|      | Firm $A$ | | Firm $B$ | | Firm $C$ | | Firm $D$ | |
|------|------|------|------|------|------|------|------|------|
|      | EPS | DPS | EPS | DPS | EPS | DPS | EPS | DPS |
| 1980 | $2.40 | $0.88 | $1.00 | $0.10 | $8.40 | $2.10 | $10.00 | $2.50 |
| 1981 | 2.70 | 0.96 | 1.10 | 0.10 | 9.00 | 2.20 | 10.50 | 3.00 |
| 1982 | 3.10 | 1.08 | 1.25 | 0.10 | 9.75 | 2.30 | 12.00 | 4.00 |
| 1983 | 2.90 | 1.24 | 1.40 | 0.10 | 9.60 | 2.40 | 9.75 | 3.25 |
| 1984 | 3.00 | 1.16 | 1.60 | 0.15 | 9.20 | 2.40 | 8.00 | 2.50 |
| 1985 | 3.20 | 1.20 | 1.75 | 0.15 | 8.70 | 2.40 | 9.10 | 2.75 |
| 1986 | 3.60 | 1.28 | 2.00 | 0.20 | 8.60 | 2.40 | 9.90 | 3.00 |
| 1987 | 3.75 | — | 2.15 | — | 8.60 | — | 10.00 | — |

**22-5.** A firm's equity accounts are as follows:

Equity Accounts

| | |
|---|---|
| Common stock ($5 par value): | |
| 1,000,000 shares authorized | |
| 100,000 shares outstanding | $ 500,000 |
| Paid-in surplus | 1,500,000 |
| Retained earnings | 5,000,000 |
| Total | $7,000,000 |

The firm's common stock sells for $20 per share in resale markets. The corporation declares a 4% stock dividend. Prepare the resulting equity accounts section of the firm's balance sheet.

**22-6.** Assume that the firm in Problem 22-5 decides not to declare the stock dividend but declares a 4 for 1 stock split. Prepare the resulting equity accounts.

**22-7.** An investor owns 100 shares of stock in a corporation as of 1981. The firm declares the following set of stock and cash dividends:

1982 — 20% stock dividend
1983 — 10% stock dividend
1984 — $0.50 per share cash dividend

How much cash does the investor receive from the 1984 cash dividend?

# SELECTED REFERENCES

Aharony, J., and I. Swary. "Quarterly Dividend and Earnings Announcements and Stockholders' Returns: An Empirical Analysis." *Journal of Finance*, Vol. 35, No. 1 (March, 1980).

Feldstein, M., and J. Green. "Why Do Companies Pay Dividends?" *American Economic Review*, Vol. 73, No. 1 (March, 1983).

Kalay, A. "Signaling, Information Content, and the Reluctance to Cut Dividends." *Journal of Financial and Quantitative Analysis*, Vol. 15, No. 4 (November, 1980).

Modigliani, F., and M. Miller. "The Cost of Capital, Corporate Finance, and the Theory of Investment." *American Economic Review*, Vol. 48, No. 3 (June, 1958).

Van Horne, J. *Financial Management and Policy.* 6th ed. Englewood Cliffs, N.J.: Prentice-Hall, Inc., 1983.

Walter, J. "Dividend Policy: Its Influence on the Value of the Firm." *Journal of Finance*, Vol. 18, No. 2 (May, 1963).

Woolridge, J. "Stock Dividends as Signals." *Journal of Financial Research*, Vol. 6, No. 1 (Spring, 1983).

# PART 8

# Special Topics in Managerial Finance

The three chapters that make up the final portion of this text cover special topics. Chapter 23 is a survey of international finance, an area of managerial finance that is becoming increasingly important. Chapter 24 explains why mergers are so common and provides a set of techniques for evaluating their desirability. Chapter 25 considers the problems of failure and bankruptcy, an area of managerial finance on which recent federal legislation is having a major impact.

# CHAPTER 23

# International
# Financial Management

Increasing involvement of a U.S.
corporation in world trade and investment
complicates the task of its financial manager.[1]
In the past, many managers have lacked the
expertise to guide their companies in international financial matters because the domestic
orientation of their firms provided no experience
in foreign money markets or in controlling
foreign subsidiary operations. Only when such
companies elected to expand into foreign markets
by exporting, licensing foreign manufacturers,
forming joint ventures with overseas investors,
or establishing wholly owned subsidiaries did
their managers become aware of the additional
uncertainties and risks that accompanied the
quest for profits. The foreign legal and tax
environment, floating exchange rates, balance of
payments deficits, and political events suddenly
became vital concerns for them. To cope with the
problems of financing overseas operations,
financial managers found it necessary to become
acquainted with the foreign business customs,

---

[1]The materials in this chapter were prepared by Ruel C. Kahler, Professor of Marketing and
Director of International Business Programs at the University of Cincinnati.

*practices, and institutions that impacted on their firms. In some instances, such as simultaneously dealing in several currencies, the problems were new. In others, the challenges were similar to domestic ones, but traditional practices needed modification in the new environment.*

*This chapter surveys the difficulties and opportunities of international corporate finance. Particular attention is paid to specific aspects of business and financial risk that a U.S. corporation faces only when it is engaged in international operations.*

*Some concept of the international involvement of U.S. companies may be gleaned from the following data. In 1982, the U.S. exported goods and services valued at $350 billion. Imports for the same period were approximately equal since a merchandise deficit of $36.3 billion was almost offset by net service receipts of $36.1 billion. Included in the service receipts were $23.7 billion in income from direct investments abroad and $7.1 billion in fees and royalty income. Sales of U.S. affiliates abroad were greater than exports. Some large U.S. multinationals have reported that foreign* *operations contribute 50 percent or more to their after-tax profits. Also, international sources for raw materials, components, equipment, and finished goods have become significant in the global competitive environment.*

*In general it can be seen that global opportunities for trade and investment are present. As a result, corporate financial officers increasingly find it necessary to evaluate projects and funding in a multinational context. While each corporation must decide for itself whether it is willing to accept the unique opportunities and risks that accompany international operations, the firm, nonetheless, may not be able to avoid international competition. This is evidenced by the recent penetration of the U.S. market by foreign banks and manufacturing and service establishments.*

## RISKS IN INTERNATIONAL OPERATIONS

A firm establishes or expands international operations on the basis of desirable risk-return characteristics. The opportunity cost of foreign investment must be evaluated against alternatives such as further expansion in the home market or diversification into other product lines, as well as other international projects. Implicit in this evaluation is a consideration of the risks involved in each alternative. Generally, higher profits abroad are associated with higher risks. However, the multinational firm with operations in several countries achieves a geographical dispersion of these risks. Thus, the question of whether total risk is increased can be determined only after careful analysis. In any case, the financial manager needs to determine which risks will be incurred and which risk management strategies can be employed.

The risks involved in overseas operations are of several kinds. Some have direct counterparts in the domestic scene and appear strange only because of the foreign environment. Others, such as exchange risk, are unique to companies operating across national borders. The major risks faced by corporations when dealing in international trade and/or international investments are described as political, cultural, and exchange risks.

**Political Risk**  **Political risk** refers to the probability that a political event will impact adversely on the domestic firm. This risk is always present since any firm doing business in foreign sovereign nations does so only at the pleasure of the governments of those nations. Each sovereign nation reserves the right to establish the rules and regulations to which the businesses within its jurisdiction must conform. The nation establishes its own tax laws, antitrust policies, and fiscal and monetary policies that impact directly on both foreign and local businesses. For example, regulations may restrict the repatriation of profits. National policy may prohibit reductions in the work force during periods of reduced sales or because of improved technology. Exchange controls may be implemented to block the transfer of funds outside the country. Laws may be enforced in a manner that discriminates between local and foreign firms. Any of these actions, plus numerous others, hampers the ability of the company to earn profits and to utilize them efficiently on a worldwide basis.

**Expropriation** is probably the most extreme form of political risk. When a nation expropriates, it formally takes over the property of the firm, with or without making payment. Although any firm faces the possibility of expropriation, the risk is increased under certain circumstances. There are some industries that are more sensitive to expropriation because of their importance to the country. Extractive and natural resource based industries have been frequent targets in the less developed countries. A company producing national defense materials or providing communication service may also be susceptible.

There is general agreement regarding a country's right to expropriate if adequate compensation is made. However, there is little agreement on what constitutes adequate compensation. The company often believes that the appropriate level of compensation should be determined by the going concern value, while the expropriating authorities prefer a lower value, perhaps based on book value. The resulting wide gap in perceptions often leads to a less than satisfactory resolution from the company's viewpoint.

Although expropriation is initiated by the host government, the chances of expropriation occurring may be lessened by company policy and the manner in which the investment is structured in the host country. Local pressures for expropriation are reduced when the company can show that it makes a continuing contribution to the local economy through the injection of new technology or by increasing the country's exports. The need, however, is to show a *continuing contribution*. While the company may originally have been welcomed because of its contribution of a simple technology, the mastery of that technology by locals may lead the government to question the value of the firm's current contribution. Measures that have been suggested to reduce political risk include (1) joint ventures with local firms, (2) selling securities in the local market, (3) inclusion of the World Bank in the financing plan, and (4) the use of debt financing. U.S. companies may obtain guarantees against losses from expropriation or from inconvertibility of profits or principal in approved investments from the Overseas Private Investment Corporation (OPIC).

Less obvious than expropriation is the risk associated with changes in government policy that affect the firm's continued operations. Shifts in tax policy, antitrust legislation, price controls, and a myriad of other policy measures affect the firm's risk and profit position. Political risk varies widely not only by country but also by product and by company. Financial managers need to constantly monitor conditions within a country to evaluate the political risk and to develop a strategy for coping.

**Cultural Risk**

The management of normal business functions may be very frustrating when the manager is faced with a variety of business customs and institutions. Business people tend to think and act according to the norms of the culture in which they have been raised. When conducting business in a different culture, they frequently find themselves at a disadvantage. Negotiations may be frustrating or may even break down because of cultural differences in the negotiation process.

Financial institutions and practices likewise differ among countries. Debt to equity ratios in Japan and many other countries are higher than in the U.S. Lending policies and interest rates vary among countries. Institutions may carry similar names but perform different functions. For example, banks in Europe may perform both investment banking and commercial banking functions. Some of them are permitted to take equity positions in their client firms. Commercial banks in the U.S., on the other hand, are not allowed to operate as investment bankers and are prohibited from owning common stocks of other corporations for their own accounts. (An exception is the recent legislation allowing banks to take equity positions in export trading companies. Edge Act corporations, which are subsidiaries of U.S. banks set up to carry out international business, may also operate as investment and commercial banks in overseas operations.)

**Exchange Risk**

One of the most critical problems in international finance results from the need to deal with more than one currency. **Exchange risk** results from possible changes in the value of these currencies relative to each other. Changes in the **exchange rate**, which is the price of one currency in terms of another, are of major concern to the financial manager responsible for raising funds and controlling overseas finances.

An advantage of the multinational firm is its ability to raise funds in any of several financial markets and to transfer them where most needed. Figure 23-1 shows that funds may be transferred from the parent company to foreign subsidiaries, from the subsidiaries to the parent, or between subsidiaries. Each of these transfers may involve converting funds from one currency to another. Furthermore, there is no necessary relationship between the country where the proceeds of a loan are to be employed and the currency in which the loan is denominated. An American company may negotiate a loan for Swiss francs but intend to convert the francs into U.S.

dollars for use in the U.S. Examples may help to clarify the nature of exchange risk.

Figure 23-1.    **Flow of Funds in the Multinational Corporation**

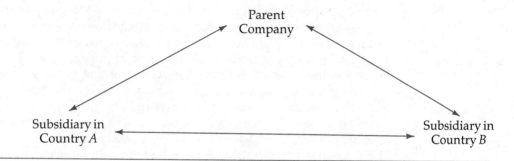

**Example:**    A firm needs funds for one year. The financial officer is confronted with two alternatives: one is a loan denominated in U.S. dollars and bearing an interest rate of 10 percent; the other is a loan denominated in West German deutsche marks carrying a rate of 8 percent. A comparison of the interest rates clearly indicates the deutsche mark loan to be less costly. *But* the effective cost of the loan is affected by any movement that occurs in exchange rates, as well as in the interest rate. If the deutsche mark appreciates more than 2 percent against the dollar during the period of the loan, borrowing in dollars would be cheaper. Obviously, however, if exchange rates do not change or if the dollar appreciates relative to the deutsche mark, the dollar loan would be more costly.

**Example:**    Assume that an American exporter has sold a machine tool to a British manufacturer for £100,000 (100,000 pounds sterling) and that payment is due in 90 days. At the time of the sale, the British pound was worth $2 (i.e., the exchange rate was £1 = $2). But by the time of payment, the exchange rate had changed to £1 = $1.80. Although the American exporter originally expected to receive the pound equivalent of $200,000, the decline in the value of the pound meant that he actually received only $180,000 (i.e., £100,000 × 1.80). Of course, if the exchange rate had changed to £1 = $3, the exporter would have received $300,000. Because the sale was denominated in pounds sterling, the exchange risk was borne by the exporter. If the British manufacturer had agreed to purchase the tool for $200,000 instead of £100,000, the importer would have borne the risk. The gains and losses in this example result entirely from fluctuations in the rate of exchange. Since exchange rates change constantly, it is fortunate that corporations can manage exchange risks by executing transactions in the foreign exchange market.

## FOREIGN EXCHANGE MARKET

Under the Bretton Woods Agreement following World War II, most of the major trading nations agreed to establish a par value for their currencies in terms of gold or the U.S. dollar. The countries agreed to maintain these fixed rates within 1 percent of the par and were permitted to change the par only to meet fundamental disequilibria in their balance of payments, and then only after consultation with the International Monetary Fund. Despite these agreements and restrictions, over 150 changes in par occurred, often with changes of 10 to 40 percent. This system of fixed rates collapsed in the early 1970s and was replaced by a system of floating rates. Theoretically such floating rates are permitted to vary according to the supply and demand for the currencies. In most instances, however, the currencies do not float freely as they are subject to intervention by governments. In addition, many of the smaller nations continue to peg their monetary unit to one of the major currencies. To further complicate matters, in 1979, several European Community countries formed the European Monetary System to establish fixed exchange rates within the group and to float rates against outside currencies.

Thus, in the early 1980s there existed a mixed system dominated by the floating of major currencies. International financing was subject to widely fluctuating exchange rates, and financial managers became acutely aware of the need to protect their investments against adverse movements. The foreign exchange market is one mechanism of protection.

**Organization of the Market**

The **foreign exchange market** is the mechanism by which buyers and sellers of currencies are able to meet their foreign currency requirements. Although foreign exchange markets operate in centers of international trade activity, such as London, New York, and Hong Kong, in most instances these markets do not have a central meeting place for transactions. Rather, the transactions are negotiated and finalized by an over-the-counter system of telephone and cables. The major participants in the market include commercial banks, exchange brokers and dealers, and central banks.

The New York market, for example, has been described as three-tiered as follows:

1.  First-tier operations include transactions between commercial banks and their customers.

2.  Second-tier operations include banks dealing with other domestic banks. These operations normally are conducted through foreign exchange brokers. The brokers also may act for the U.S. Treasury or the Federal Reserve System.

3.  Third-tier operations connect the New York transactions with the rest of the world as the domestic banks trade with banks in London, Paris, or other centers.

The ultimate customers represent a wide diversity of interests. Multi-national companies need foreign exchange for transferring funds and making payments. Tourists need foreign exchange for travel expenses. Speculators seek profits from exchange rate movements. Finally, central banks seek to stabilize the value of their currencies. From the interaction of those who supply and demand currencies, exchange rates are established for two types of transactions — spot exchange transactions and forward transactions.

SPOT EXCHANGE. **Spot exchange transactions** occur when currencies are traded for delivery within one or two days. For example, an American importer may need French francs now to pay for a shipment of perfume that has been received. The importer exchanges dollars for francs at the *spot rate*, i.e., the rate for immediate delivery.

FORWARD EXCHANGE. **Forward exchange transactions** occur when purchasers and sellers contract to buy and sell currencies for delivery at a future date. They contract for a specific amount of the currency, at a specific rate of exchange, and at a specific future delivery date. The *forward rate* is set at the time the parties enter into the contract and remains fixed for the contract regardless of future exchange rate shifts.

Table 23-1 shows both spot exchange and forward exchange U.S. dollar rates for selected currencies in 1979 and 1983. Forward rates are given for 30- and 90-day periods. Notice that in 1979, the 90-day rate for the Japanese yen and the West German deutsche mark were trading at slight premiums over the spot rate. Apparently the market expected those currencies to appreciate in value against the U.S. dollar. However, the forward rate for the British pound was at a discount from the spot rate.

The change in rates between 1979 and 1983 reflects the strengthening of the dollar in the early eighties. The very substantial changes illustrate the financial officer's problem in evaluating the exchange risk. Forecasting exchange rate movements is difficult at any time but especially under a mixed system of floating and fixed rates. Because the international firm may have large exposures in several currencies, we turn now to a description of the various kinds of foreign exchange exposure and some possible approaches to managing the firm's position.

Note that in Table 23-1 the exchange rates are expressed in terms of U.S. dollars. Thus, in 1983, a British pound was worth approximately $1.52. The rate could also be expressed to show the value of one U.S. dollar in pounds. That rate would be the reciprocal (1/1.52) of the dollar rate or £.66 (i.e., $1 = £.66).

**Management of Foreign Exchange Exposure**

*Foreign exchange exposure* is present whenever some of a company's assets and/or liabilities are not denominated in the currency of its home country. The process of managing financial affairs so as to minimize the possible detrimental effects of fluctuating exchange rates is known as **expo-**

**sure management.** There are three different types of foreign exchange exposure: transaction (or conversion) exposure, translation exposure, and economic exposure.

**TRANSACTION EXPOSURE.** A **transaction (or conversion) exposure** occurs when the value of a future cash flow is known with certainty and

| Table 23-1. | Selected Foreign Exchange Rates in 1979 and 1983 | | | |
|---|---|---|---|---|
| **Currency** | **Transaction** | **7/25/83** | **8/24/79** |
| British pound sterling | Spot | $1.5230 | $2.2340 |
|  | 30-day | 1.5234 | 2.2311 |
|  | 90-day | 1.5245 | 2.2242 |
| Canadian dollar | Spot | .8107 | .8574 |
| Italian lira | Spot | .000649 | .001225 |
| Japanese yen | Spot | .004158 | .004563 |
|  | 30-day | .004172 | .004584 |
|  | 90-day | .004196 | .004622 |
| West German deutsche mark | Spot | .3839 | .5476 |
|  | 30-day | .3857 | .5483 |
|  | 90-day | .3889 | .5526 |

requires a foreign exchange transaction. For example, an American exporter who will receive Mexican pesos in 90 days as payment for a sale made today faces transaction exposure.

Financial managers can lessen their transaction exposure by anticipating the currency conversion that will take place at a future date. They can take action to eliminate uncertainty regarding the exchange rate at which the conversion will be consummated in either the foreign exchange market or the financial (or money) market.

*Using the Foreign Exchange Market to Lessen Transaction Exposure.* The following example illustrates the use of the foreign exchange market to minimize transaction exposure.

**Example:**  An American exporter sells equipment to a British importer for £10,000 with payment due in 60 days. To shift the exchange risk, the exporter sells £10,000 for future delivery in the foreign exchange market. The sequence of events is:

June 10 — Exporter delivers the equipment with payment due on August 10.
  — Exporter sells £10,000 in a 60-day forward exchange contract.
  — The 60-day price for pounds is $2.

Aug. 10 — Importer makes payment of £10,000.
  — Exporter delivers the £10,000 against the forward exchange contract and receives $20,000.

The exporter's sale of pounds for future delivery determined, or "locked in," the number of dollars to be received. If the forward exchange transaction had not been entered into, the exporter would have converted the pounds on August 10 at whatever spot rate existed. If the spot rate on August 10 was $1.95, the exporter would have received only $19,500.

*Using the Financial Market to Lessen Transaction Exposure.* Using the same sale of equipment as in the previous example, the following illustrates how the exchange risk can be minimized by entering the financial (or money) market rather than the foreign exchange market.

**Example:**   The American exporter borrows pounds sterling from a British bank, and the sequence of events is:

June 10 — Exporter delivers the equipment with payment due on August 10.
  — Exporter borrows £10,000 from a British bank. The bank discounts the loan, and the exporter receives £9,756.
  — Exporter converts the pounds into dollars at an assumed $2 spot rate and receives (£9,756) ($2) = $19,512.
  — Exporter invests the $19,512 in a U.S. bank at 8 percent interest for 60 days. The interest earned is ($19,512) (.08)/6 = $260.

Aug. 10 — Importer makes payment of £10,000.
  — Exporter pays £10,000 to the British bank.
  — Exporter nets $19,512 + $260 from the transaction.

Again assuming that the spot rate on August 10 was $1.95, the exporter would have received only $19,500.

**TRANSLATION EXPOSURE.** The probability that a multinational company may suffer a decrease in asset values due to devaluation of a foreign currency even if no foreign exchange transactions occur is called **translation (or accounting) exposure**. Accountants generally agree that translation exposure should be measured so that the balance sheets and income statements reflect changes in value.

The multinational corporation with extensive overseas operations chooses a single currency for measuring its resources and consolidating its financial statements. Usually the currency chosen is that of the parent company's home country. Translation exposure occurs when the company's foreign balances are expressed in terms of the single selected currency. Changes in exchange rates can alter the values placed on assets, liabilities, expenses, and profits of foreign subsidiaries. Although accountants agree that a firm's net translation exposure is determined by its exposed assets minus its exposed liabilities (i.e., assets and liabilities exposed to translation at current rates), there has been little agreement on the meaning of these terms.

*FASB-8.* The Financial Accounting Standards Board attempted to resolve differences in measuring and reporting exchange gains and losses through its Statement 8 (FASB-8). This statement determined when historical or current rates were to be used for translation. It also required that exchange gains and losses be reported in the period in which they occur. The latter provision eliminated the use of reserve accounts to defer unrealized gains or losses. In the income statement, revenues and most operating expenses are presented at current rates (average rate for the period), while cost of goods sold and depreciation appear at historical rates. Essentially FASB-8 required that assets (including inventory) carried at cost on foreign statements be translated at rates at which they were acquired. Assets carried at current values are translated at the current exchange rate.

FASB-8 caused many companies to change their accounting system for exchange gains and losses. Often the new system resulted in more widely fluctuating earnings in the short term, and executives became concerned about the effect of these fluctuations on earnings and share prices. This, in turn, increased awareness of exposure measurement and management.

*FASB-52.* In order to deal with some of the problems under FASB-8, FASB-52 was issued. Under Statement 52, a company must select a functional currency to measure performance for each of its foreign entities. Normally, the functional currency will be that of the environment in which the entity generates or spends cash (for example, the deutsche mark for a West German subsidiary). In some instances (in highly inflationary countries or where the foreign entity is merely a sales branch, for example) the functional currency will be the U.S. dollar. When the foreign entity's local currency is the functional currency, the financial statements are translated at current exchange rates, and the resulting adjustments for exchange rate variation are made directly to a separate stockholders' equity account instead of current income as under FASB-8. If the U.S. dollar is the functional currency, the financial statements are translated as under FASB-8, and the translational adjustments are made to current income.

*Decision Areas in Translation Exposure Management.* Two related decision areas are involved in translation exposure management:

1. Managing balance sheet items to minimize net exposure

2. Deciding whether to use the foreign exchange market or money market to hedge any remaining exposure

Financial managers often attempt to keep a rough balance between exposed assets and liabilities. Maintaining such a balance should bring about offsetting changes in values when the balance sheet is translated. If the value of the currency declines relative to the home country's currency, the translated asset values will be lower, but the translated liabilities also should be lower.

When the financial manager of a multinational company expects a currency devaluation in a foreign country, subsidiaries in that country may be asked to borrow needed funds in local currency or to make early payment of accounts payable to the parent or subsidiaries in other countries with appreciating currencies. The subsidiary in the devaluating country may reduce cash by making dividend or royalty payments, or it may delay in collecting receivables from other foreign subsidiaries of the company. These actions, taken before the devaluation occurs, tend to reduce assets held in the devaluating country, thereby reducing net exposure. However, effective exposure management by these methods requires that the financial manager forecast changes in the exchange rate. It also requires that the financial control system provide the manager with information on the extent of the foreign exchange exposure of the subsidiaries in each of the foreign countries.

ECONOMIC EXPOSURE. The probability that changes in foreign exchange rates will decrease the intrinsic (or capitalized) value of the firm is referred to as **economic exposure**. Since the intrinsic value of the firm equals the sum of the present values of future cash flows discounted at the investor's required rate of return, the risks contained in economic exposure require a determination of the effect of changes in the exchange rate on each of the expected cash flows.

The identification and measurement of translation exposure is not, however, an adequate measurement of economic exposure. The firm's economic exposure may be greater or less than its translation exposure since the net present value of future cash flows can either be increased or decreased by a devaluation or a revaluation of a currency. Devaluation of a currency may reduce prices in the subsidiary's foreign markets. If the demand for the product is elastic, sales and profits may increase despite a net increase in translation exposure. However, if the product contains many imported components, cost will increase and prices and profits may decline. The measurement of economic exposure requires a detailed analysis of the effect of the exchange rate change on each of the *future* cash flows rather than on the present asset-and-liability structure.

## FINANCING EXPORTS

Financing exports is a complex process involving coordination between financial, marketing, and production managers. The financial manager must be knowledgeable about the variety of financing methods available and the banks, factors, and finance companies that provide the funds and may also carry out some of the document transfers to facilitate the collection process.

When a sale is negotiated, certain basic decisions must be reached concerning the currency and financing methods to be employed. Denominating the sale in the exporter's currency shifts the exchange risk to the importer. The importer, however, may not be willing to accept the risk and may have alternative suppliers who will be willing to quote in the importer's currency. Competitive conditions may dictate that the exporter do likewise, thereby increasing the exporter's transaction exposure. Other terms to be negotiated include the amount of credit, if any, to be granted and the payment mechanism to be used.

**Cash Payment**

While exporters would prefer to receive cash in advance or cash on delivery, such terms naturally are resisted by importers who would bear the entire financing burden. Sellers may request cash in advance when an order requires special treatment or product modification. The use of cash terms, however, is less prominent than in the past for several reasons:

1.  Increased competition in the world market and the ready availability of substitute products have meant that importers have alternative sources that may be willing to grant credit.

2.  The use of letters of credit and the development of international credit information and credit insurance have reduced the risk of credit extension.

3.  Credit terms are frequently one of the most important factors in negotiating a sale.

Thus, cash terms are used mainly when there is a substantial risk that cannot be covered by insurance or when economic and political conditions are likely to result in delayed payment or blocked funds.

**Open Account**

When a sale is made on open account, the goods are shipped without documents that call for payment. The exporter's commercial invoice indicates the amount of the liability. The burden of export financing under open account rests with the exporter unless the exporter shifts the risk by factoring the accounts without recourse.

In the international market, sales on open account often are predicated on a previously satisfactory relationship with the buyer. Initial sales to a buyer may be based on letters of credit or other instruments providing more security than open account. Later transactions may be on open account as the buyer establishes a record of satisfactory payment.

A disadvantage of open account financing is the absence of documentary evidence of the debt which can make collection by legal action difficult in some countries. Another problem lies in the importer's ability to defer payment due to the absence of a specific maturity date.

Export credit insurance in the U.S. is offered by the Foreign Credit Insurance Association (FCIA) in collaboration with the Export-Import Bank of the United States. The Export-Import Bank assumes responsibility for political risk coverage and shares responsibility with FCIA member companies for commercial risks. Political risk, *as defined for insurance purposes,* consists of inconvertibility of foreign currency into U.S. dollars, expropriation, confiscation, war, civil commotion or like disturbances, and cancellation of export or import licenses. (Note that the insurance does *not* cover risks of fluctuating exchange rates.) *Commercial credit risks* are defined as insolvency of the buyer or the buyer's protracted default.

## Drafts, or Bills of Exchange

A **draft** is a document drawn by the seller ordering the buyer or the buyer's agent to pay a specific sum of money at a specified time. If the buyer agrees to the terms of the draft, acknowledgement of the agreement is indicated by writing an acceptance on the face of the draft and signing it. A **sight draft** calls for immediate payment upon presentation of the draft. An **arrival draft** calls for payment upon arrival of the merchandise. The **date draft** calls for payment on a specified date or at a specified number of days after the specified date. A draft drawn without collateral documents is a **clean draft**. One with certain stipulated documents, such as a bill of lading or insurance certificate, is known as a **documentary draft**. Documentary drafts are commonly employed in international trade.

In an export transaction involving a sight draft, the seller forwards the draft and supporting documents at the time of shipment to a bank in the importer's city. When the importer accepts the draft by making payment, the documents of title are delivered and the importer takes possession of the merchandise. The bank then remits the funds by cable to the exporter's bank where they are credited to the exporter's account.

A **banker's acceptance** is a date draft accepted by a bank. The bank guarantees that payment will be made upon maturity. Such acceptance may be readily discounted to furnish immediate funds for the exporter.

## Letter of Credit

A **letter of credit** is a bank's promise, made at the request of an importer, to honor drafts drawn upon it by the exporter. Thus, the letter of credit provides the exporter with more security than open account financing or bills of exchange. Before the seller can receive payment, however, the bank assures itself that all the requirements specified in the letter of credit including delivery dates, documents, etc., have been met. The slightest deviation from the requirements set forth in the letter of credit may result in nonpayment. Because of the degree of protection it offers, the letter of credit is widely used in international trade.

Letters of credit are of various types. They may be *revocable* or *irrevocable*, and *confirmed* or *unconfirmed*. An irrevocable letter of credit provides more protection for the seller because the issuing bank agrees not to cancel or modify the credit without the seller's permission. With a confirmed letter of credit, the obligation of the issuing bank is guaranteed by a bank in the seller's country. Thus, the letter is guaranteed by both the issuing and the confirming banks, giving the seller double protection.

---

**Example:**

Figure 23-2 shows how a letter of credit and a banker's acceptance are used to finance an export transaction. The sequence of events (numbered in the flow chart) is described as follows:[2]

1. A Brussels firm sends a purchase order to a Rockford firm.
2. The Brussels firm also applies to its local bank for a letter of credit, stipulating that the draft is to be drawn at 90 days sight and that it agrees to bear the charges for discounting of the draft in the U.S. by the Rockford firm.
3. A Brussels bank issues and mails the 90-day sight draft to its correspondent in Chicago for delivery to the Rockford firm.
4. A Chicago bank verifies the authenticity of the signatures on the letter of credit and mails it to the Rockford firm.
5. The Rockford firm inspects the terms of the letter of credit and, being satisfied with them, makes the shipment. It then collects the bill of lading and other documents called for under the letter of credit, draws a draft at 90 days sight on the Chicago bank, and presents them to the bank along with the letter of credit.
6. The Chicago bank satisfies itself that the documents are in compliance with the terms of the credit. It then accepts the draft, thereby creating a banker's acceptance (9). The bank discounts the draft, charging the discount and other charges to the account of the Brussels bank, and pays the face amount of the draft to the Rockford firm.
7. The Chicago bank mails shipping documents, advice of debit covering the acceptance fee and other charges, and notification of due date of the acceptance to the Brussels bank, which makes appropriate entries on its books.
8. The Brussels bank forwards the documents to the Brussels firm, which will use them to clear the merchandise when it arrives.
9. The Chicago bank sells the acceptance to an acceptance dealer.

---

[2]Adapted from *Business Conditions* (Federal Reserve Bank of Chicago, May, 1976).

**Figure 23-2.**      **A Banker's Acceptance Is Created, Discounted, Sold, and Paid at Maturity**

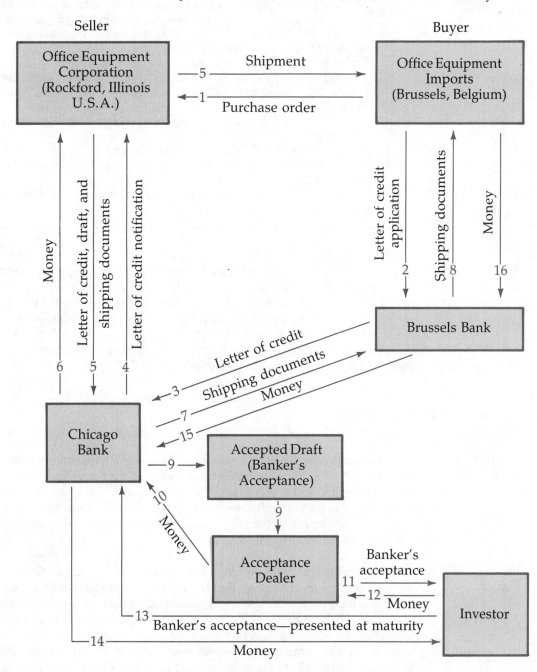

10. The Chicago bank receives the face amount of the acceptance less discount at the going bankers' acceptance rate for the number of days remaining to maturity. Thus, the Chicago bank has been able to (*a*) earn some income arising from the difference in the rates at which it discounted the draft and sold it to the dealer, and (*b*) earn interest for the period during which it held the draft.
11. The dealer in turn sells the acceptance to an investor.
12. The dealer receives the net proceeds, after deduction of a discount, which should be slightly less than what the dealer charged to the bank.
13. At maturity of the acceptance, the investor presents it for payment to the Chicago bank.
14. The investor receives the face amount of the draft.
15. In the meantime the Chicago bank will have received payment from the Brussels bank.
16. The Brussels bank in turn has received payment from the Brussels firm.

---

Bankers' acceptances arise out of the financing of a U.S. import in a similar manner. The major difference is that, if the foreign exporter submits the draft for acceptance, it does so to a U.S. bank that is a correspondent to its home bank. The reason the acceptance is not created by its home bank is that the U.S. acceptance market is the only one of consequence among the various national financial markets. The procedure for a third country acceptance may follow a similar procedure, with the major difference being that the trading participants are outside the U.S.

## SOURCES OF FUNDS FOR FINANCING INTERNATIONAL OPERATIONS

The multinational firm constantly seeks funds to support its worldwide operations. Large amounts of capital are required for both fixed capital and working capital since the establishing of manufacturing or processing plants can involve expenditures of a billion dollars or more. Meeting such massive needs requires that the financial officer tap a variety of sources internal and external to the enterprise.

**Internal Sources**

The parent corporation provides capital to its foreign subsidiaries through several mechanisms. Equity may be provided through a cash inflow, dividend postponement, or by providing equipment or other valuable assets. The parent also may borrow money in the home or third country markets at an advantageous rate and lend it to the subsidiary. One advantage of the intracompany loans over equity financing is the reduction of taxes when interest expenses reduce the tax base. Deferring payment for materials and services supplied by the parent or other company units is an additional source of working capital.

**External Sources**

Seldom is the parent company of a multinational organization capable or willing to finance its entire foreign operations from internal sources. Many rely on a number of external sources to furnish either debt or equity capital. These sources may be either public (governmental) or private institutions and may be located in the foreign market of operations, the home country, or a third country.

Some multinationals seek outside equity capital in order to diversify their ownership base. Many of them have sought local investors in countries where they maintain operations in order to achieve a mutuality of interests between the firm and the host nation. In some countries a joint venture with local investors may be a necessary condition for permission to establish operations. These joint ventures may lessen the risk of expropriation, as mentioned earlier. In the Andean countries, substantial local ownership is a condition for participating in the trade advantages of the Andean Common Market.

Debt financing, however, is commonly employed to gain both tax and leverage advantages. In countries such as Japan, West Germany, and Sweden where debt to equity ratios typically exceed those in the United States, multinational firms may also rely more heavily on debt financing.

**EUROCURRENCY MARKETS. Eurocurrencies** are monies deposited outside the country of origin. Thus, U.S. dollars deposited in England or France are known as Eurodollars, and deutsche marks deposited in England or France would be called Euromarks. These deposits are largely outside the control of national banking activities. Thus, they are not subject to reserve requirements and interest rate restrictions that apply to domestic banking. Freedom from these restrictions enables Eurobanks to offer better terms to both lenders and borrowers. Treasurers of multinational firms may earn a higher interest on Euro deposits or may pay a lower interest on loans.

**EUROBOND MARKETS.** Like the Eurocurrency market, the Eurobond market has emerged as another significant source of capital in the post–World War II period. A distinction may be drawn between the two types of bonds floated in the international bond market. **Foreign bonds** are denominated in the currency of the country where they are largely sold. **Eurobonds** are denominated in a currency (often U.S. dollars) different from that of the country where they are sold. Thus, the bonds of a West German manufacturer sold in the U.S. and denominated in dollars would be foreign bonds. Those bonds of the same manufacturer denominated in dollars but sold in France, Britain, and Sweden are known as Eurobonds.

**INTERNATIONAL AGENCIES.** A number of international agencies exist to aid the financing of specific projects. For example, the International Finance Corporation assists developing countries by helping to finance private sector projects. Regional development banks, such as the European Investment Bank, the Asian Development Bank, and the International Development Bank, help secure both private and public financing for high-priority development projects. Multinationally owned private investment companies, such as the Atlantic Development Group for Latin America (ADELA), make equity investments in private business.

**NATIONAL AGENCIES.** Many agencies at the national level offer incentives for firms to invest within their country or to finance exports. In the U.S., the Export-Import Bank of the United States makes direct loans to buyers outside the U.S. for purchase of U.S. made goods, guarantees repayment of credit extended by private lenders to outside purchasers of U.S. goods, and lends funds to commercial banks to assist in financing exports. Other countries have similar or expanded programs which the multinational firm may use through its foreign subsidiaries.

**COMMERCIAL BANKS.** The primary source of short-term funds for the multinational firm is commercial banks. The firm may elect to work through local banks in the host country or through domestic banks. Many large U.S. banks maintain branches in major financial centers, and a growing number of foreign banks have established branches in the U.S. Even a bank with no foreign branches is able to conduct international financing through its correspondent banks abroad. American banks have established subsidiaries that engage solely in international banking. These subsidiaries are known as Edge Act or Agreement Corporations. They provide capital for financing outside of the U.S. and are allowed to make equity investments in foreign firms.

# SUMMARY

The large amount of international trade and foreign investments by domestic corporations makes it necessary for a financial manager to have a basic understanding of international financial management. While profit motivates international operations, political, cultural, and exchange risks provide international operations with a unique set of risk-return characteristics. Political risk, for example, may not be constant over time. The probability of expropriation may be negligible at the time a U.S. firm builds a subsidiary in a foreign country. However, subsequent unanticipated political developments may make expropriation likely or even inevitable.

Exchange risks can be managed by executing transactions in the foreign exchange market. This does not eliminate exchange risk completely since spot and forward exchange rates are seldom equal to each other. An as alternative to foreign exchange markets, exchange risk can be managed by executing transactions in the international money markets.

Financing international operations can be accomplished with a variety of mechanisms. Exports can be financed by making sales on open account or using drafts, bills of exchange, or letters of credit.

A combination of sources that are internal or external to the corporation may be used to fi-

nance international investments. Local investors in the host country can provide either debt or equity capital. Joint ventures with local firms may lessen the risk of expropriation. Eurocurrency and Eurobond markets can be used to obtain long-term capital. International agencies provide financing for specific projects, and national agencies help in financing exports. Commercial banks, including foreign subsidiaries of U.S. banks, are a major source of working capital to foreign subsidiaries and affiliates of U.S. domestic corporations.

# QUESTIONS

**23-1.** What adverse actions are contained in the concept of political risk?

**23-2.** An American importer buys some equipment from a French exporter. The purchase price is stated in dollars and is to be paid in 90 days. Who bears the exchange risk? Why?

**23-3.** An American exporter sells some farm equipment to an Italian importer. The purchase price is stated in dollars and is to be paid in 60 days. Who bears the exchange risk? Why?

**23-4.** Who are the major buyers and sellers of currency in the foreign exchange market?

**23-5.** What is the purpose of foreign exchange exposure management?

**23-6.** The financial manager of a firm expects that the country in which the firm has a sizable operation is about to devalue its currency. What strategies can the financial manager use in order to reduce the impact of this type of translation exposure?

# PROBLEMS

**23-1.** Using the 1983 data in Table 23-1, answer each of the following questions:

   *a.* How many U.S. dollars are needed to purchase 5,000 pounds sterling in the spot market?

   *b.* How many U.S. dollars can be purchased by converting 6 million lira in the spot market?

   *c.* How many marks can be purchased for 30-day delivery in exchange for $10,000?

   *d.* How many U.S. dollars can be purchased for 90-day delivery in exchange for 2 million yen?

**23-2.** Using the 1983 data in Table 23-1, compute the amounts of the following foreign currencies that can be purchased in exchange for $1,000:

    *a*. Canadian dollars, spot market
    *b*. Japanese yen, 90-day delivery
    *c*. West German deutsche marks, 30-day delivery
    *d*. British pounds, 90-day delivery

**23-3.** An American exporter sells some machinery to a Japanese importer for 60 million yen. The goods are delivered on September 28 and payment is due on November 28. On September 28 the spot rate for yen is $0.0051 and the 60-day forward rate is $0.0050. If the exporter uses the foreign exchange market to minimize transaction exposure, how many U.S. dollars does the exporter realize on November 28?

**23-4.** Assume that the exporter in Problem 23-3 minimizes transaction exposure by using international money markets. The exporter borrows yen from a Japanese bank on September 28. In return for a 60-day maturity, the exporter receives loan proceeds equal to 95% of the amount to be repaid at maturity. The exporter then converts the loan immediately to U.S. dollars and invests the proceeds for 60 days. On November 28, the exporter's investment matures and returns 102% of the invested principal. How many U.S. dollars does the U.S. exporter realize on November 28?

**23-5.** On July 25, 1983 the Italian lira was quoted as being worth $.000649. Assume that a friend offered to give you 200,000 lira in exchange for $100. Should you accept the offer?

**23-6.** Using the spot rates for July 25, 1983, in Table 23-1 determine the value of one U.S. dollar in terms of:
    *a*. West German deutsche marks
    *b*. Japanese yen
    *c*. Canadian dollars

**23-7.** What is the current value of the West German deutsche mark, the Japanese yen, the Canadian dollar, and the Italian lira?

# SELECTED REFERENCES

Arnold, J. "Banker's Acceptance: A Low-Cost Financing Choice." *Financial Executive,* Vol. 48, No. 7 (July, 1980).

Barone, R. "Risk and International Diversification: Another Look," *Financial Review,* Vol. 18, No. 2 (May, 1983).

Henning, C., W. Pigott, and R. Scott. *International Financial Management.* New York: McGraw-Hill Book Company, 1978.

Kahler, R. *International Marketing.* 5th ed. Cincinnati: South-Western Publishing Co., 1983.

Melton, W., and J. Mahr. "Banker's Acceptances." *Quarterly Review,* Vol. 6, No. 2 (Summer, 1981).

Militello, F. "Statement No. 52: Changes in Financial Management Practices." *Financial Executive,* Vol. 51, No. 8 (August, 1983).

Riehl, H., and R. Rodriquez. *Foreign Exchange Markets.* New York: McGraw-Hill Book Company, 1977.

Rodriquez, R., and E. Carter. *International Financial Management.* 2d ed. Englewood-Cliffs, N.J.: Prentice-Hall, Inc., 1979.

Srinivasula, S. "Classifying Foreign Exchange Exposure." *Financial Executive,* Vol. 51, No. 2 (February, 1983).

# CHAPTER 24

## Mergers and Acquisitions

A **merger** occurs when a company acquires one or more firms and retains its identity. For example, the acquisition of the Green Giant Company by the Pillsbury Company was a merger because the resulting firm continued to be known as the Pillsbury Company. When a corporation acquires a relatively small firm, the transaction may be described as an acquisition rather than a merger. However, acquisitions and mergers are synonymous from the standpoint of managerial finance.

An average of over 2,000 mergers a year have occurred since 1980. By the end of 1982, the annual merger rate had increased to 2,300. Some of these mergers, as measured by the market value of the acquired company, are very large. The acquisition value of Marathon Oil by U.S. Steel in 1982, for example, was $6.6 billion. Most mergers, however, involve target companies that have a market value less than $500 million. Mergers that involve relatively small target companies are also important. Some commercial banks, for example, have increased their geographic markets by repeated acquisitions of small banks with total assets that frequently are below $10 million.

This chapter explains why firms merge and classifies mergers according to their economic characteristics. The techniques for evaluating the *desirability of a proposed merger are then presented, followed by a discussion of tender offers. Finally, the implications to managerial finance of the accounting treatment of mergers are discussed.*

## SYNERGY AND SHAREHOLDER WEALTH

The fundamental reason why a corporation seeks to acquire another firm through a merger is the desire to increase the wealth of its own shareholders. However, the shareholders of the acquiring firm may be able to realize the same increase in their wealth by investing directly in both corporations. Thus, for a merger to be desirable, the resulting increase in shareholder wealth has to exceed that available from simply purchasing the common shares of both corporations. A proposed merger that meets this test of increased shareholder wealth is said to contain *synergistic properties*.

Synergy in a merger results in a change in the risk-return characteristics of the acquiring firm. The merger may increase shareholder returns and/or decrease business and financial risks. These beneficial synergistic effects can occur as a result of operating economies, financial economies, or increased market penetration.

**Operating Economies**

A merger may be judged advantageous from the standpoint of operating economies if the level of EBIT of the acquiring firm is increased, if a reduction in the variability of its EBIT reduces its business risk, or if both occur.

There are several ways of generating operating economies. The merged firms might be able to lower their combined costs of production, or they might be able to significantly increase their combined production capacities. Management might be able to eliminate some fixed costs. Duplicate programs, such as research and development efforts, may be eliminated or substantially reduced. The accounting, credit, and purchasing departments might be centralized. Separate sales and advertising departments might be combined and streamlined, and the quality of the marketing program may be improved as a result of integrating the marketing skills of the two firms. Finally, a corporate reorganization might reduce management costs if certain positions become unnecessary and are eliminated.

**Financial Economies**

A merger can produce financial economies by improving the working capital and capital structure composition of the acquiring firm. This can reduce the firm's financial risk, magnify the growth in its EPS, or both.

Many firms become target companies — candidates for acquisition — because their net working capital positions indicate excess liquidity. Their excess working capital becomes a long-term financing source to the acquiring company. Acquisition minded firms also seek out companies with balance sheets that have little or no long-term debt. The resulting merger reduces the extent to which the acquiring company trades on its equity, thus reducing its degree of financial leverage and its debt to equity ratio. As a result, its financial risk is lessened, and it may realize a decrease in its weighted average cost of capital.

Given that operating economies produce an increased level of EBIT, financial economies that reduce trading on the equity (TOTE) can reduce the variability of the acquiring firm's EPS. The overall financial result is a higher return with little or no additional financial risk. Another alternative is to use the equity base of the target company to trade on the equity in order to increase the level and growth rate of the acquiring firm's EPS. This alternative seeks to increase shareholder returns by an amount that more than compensates for the accompanying increase in financial risk.

**Market Penetration**

Market penetration is a major factor in evaluating the desirability of a proposed merger. When a firm acquires a target company having product lines that are competitive, complementary, or unrelated, the acquiring firm can expand its markets into geographic locations not reached prior to the merger. A firm can achieve market penetration through horizontal, vertical, or conglomerate mergers.

HORIZONTAL MERGERS. A **horizontal merger** is a merger of two or more companies that compete in the same industry and operate at the same level of production or distribution. A merger between two retailers who sell the same product lines is an example of a horizontal merger. Horizontal mergers are designed to produce substantial operating economies.

Because horizontal mergers result in a decrease in the number of competitors in a given industry, these types of mergers are sometimes objected to by the federal government on the basis of antitrust considerations. Mergers in the banking, railroad, and newspaper industries typically must be approved by federal regulatory agencies before they can be carried out.

VERTICAL MERGERS. A **vertical merger** involves two or more firms that compete in the same industry but operate at different stages of the production-distribution system. For example, a manufacturer might purchase some of the wholesalers that distribute its product lines. Alternatively, a manufacturer might purchase some of its raw materials suppliers. In addition to the operating and financial economies that may result, vertical mergers can allow the acquiring firm to market its existing product lines in new geographic areas by using the marketing channels owned by the acquired firm. This may be preferable to the alternative of investing in a set of new distribution channels.

CONGLOMERATE AND CONGENERIC MERGERS. A **pure conglomerate** is a merger of two or more firms that operate in different, unrelated industries. A merger between firms with product lines that are complementary but not directly competitive is sometimes referred to as a **congeneric merger**. Current usage, however, refers to pure conglomerates and congenerics simply as conglomerates.

An example of a pure conglomerate involves the acquisition of soft drink producers by tobacco companies. The acquisition of leasing companies, consumer loan companies, and factors by commercial banks are examples of congeneric mergers. Conglomerates do not reduce the number of competitors in a given industry. Rather, the acquiring firm becomes a competitor in a new industry. Conglomerates can produce both operating and financial economies. In addition, vertical congeneric mergers can be used to increase the geographic market penetration of the acquiring firm's product lines.

# FINANCIAL ANALYSIS OF MERGERS

Merger alternatives must be analyzed from a number of different perspectives. If, for example, a horizontal merger is proposed on the basis of operating economies, an engineering analysis may have to be done to estimate the extent of the economies of scale in production. If a vertical merger is proposed on the basis of expanding distribution channels, a marketing analysis may be required in order to estimate the desirability of the resulting distribution system. Pure conglomerates typically are evaluated on the basis of financial economies.

When these types of analyses suggest that a merger is advisable, the acquiring firm then undertakes a financial analysis to estimate the purchase price it will offer to the shareholders of the target corporation. The purchase price may be quoted in dollars per share. Or the acquiring firm may offer its own securities, usually common stock, in exchange for the common stock of the target firm. In either case, the acquiring firm must estimate the maximum purchase price it is willing to pay for the target firm's equity shares. If the merger is expected to produce operating and/or financial economies, the acquiring firm may offer a price that is sufficiently above the market price of the target firm's common stock so as to elicit a favorable response from the stockholders. However, in the absence of synergy, the maximum purchase price may equal the current market price of the target firm's common, thus increasing the possibility that the shareholders will reject the offer.

**Determining the Purchase Price**

There are three general approaches that an acquiring firm can use to determine the purchase price of a target firm. These are (1) a cash purchase, (2) an exchange of stock based on each firm's EPS, and (3) an exchange of stock based on the market price of each firm's common stock.

CASH PURCHASE. A cash offer can be made on the basis of the target firm's net cash flows. If the merger is approved on this basis, the shareholders of the target firm receive cash for their shares and are subject to federal income taxes on this transaction.

The cash purchase price of a target firm can be estimated by the following capital-budgeting procedure:

1. Compute the sum of the present values of the target firm's forecast net cash flows (profit after taxes plus depreciation). The discount rate is the acquiring firm's cost of capital.

2. Because the acquiring firm becomes responsible for paying the target firm's liabilities, the market value of these liabilities is treated as a cash outflow at Time zero.

3. Subtract the target firm's liabilities from the present value of its net cash flows to yield the maximum purchase price that the acquiring firm can offer.

This procedure can be summarized in the following equation. Let:

$$F_t = \text{net cash flow in Year } t$$

$$L = \text{market value of the liabilities}$$

$$k = \text{discount rate}$$

$$\text{MPP} = \text{maximum purchase price}$$

Then:

$$\text{MPP} = \sum_t \frac{F_t}{(1 + k)^t} - L \qquad (24\text{-}1)$$

The biggest problem of the acquiring firm in determining its MPP is to estimate the future net cash flows of the target firm. The valuation models contained in Chapter 13 provide several ways of generating the needed forecasts.

**Example:** The Runner Company is considering the acquisition of Settlevision, Inc., through a merger. Table 24-1 contains the financial data for both firms. Runner would like to acquire Settlevision for cash. There is some uncertainty concerning the net cash flows of the target firm, although Runner's management estimates that Settlevision's future net cash flows will at least equal their current value.

A first estimate of the MPP can be obtained by assuming that (1) Settlevision's net cash flows will remain at their current level indefinitely and (2) the merger will produce no synergistic effects. The net cash flows can then be considered as a perpetuity. Using Equation 24-1:

$$MPP = \frac{\$210,000}{.15} - \$300,000 = \$1,100,000$$

Dividing the MPP by the 80,000 outstanding shares of Settlevision produces a cash offer of $13.75 per share. This offer most likely will be rejected, given that Settlevision's stock sells for $26 per share.

**Table 24-1.** **Financial Data for the Runner-Settlevision Merger**

| | Settlevision, Inc. | Runner Company |
|---|---|---|
| Current EPS | $1.50 | $4.00 |
| Current market price of common stock | $26.00 | $52.00 |
| Number of shares outstanding | 80,000 | 600,000 |
| Cost of capital | — | 15% |
| Current earnings after taxes | $120,000 | $2,400,000 |
| Net cash flow, current year | $210,000 | |
| Total liabilities | $300,000 | |

A second estimate can be obtained by forecasting the growth rate ($g$) of Settlevision's net cash flow. Assuming that $g = .05$ and that no synergistic effects will occur, the MPP is computed by substituting Equation 13-7 into Equation 24-1

$$MPP = \frac{(\$210,000)(1.05)}{(.15 - .05)} - \$300,000 = \$1,905,000$$

This produces a per share offer of $1,905,000/80,000 = $23.81. Once again, the shareholders can be expected to reject this offer.

A third estimate assumes that the synergistic effects of the merger will increase Settlevision's growth rate to 7 percent. Thus:

$$MPP = \frac{(\$210,000)\,(1.07)}{(.15 - .07)} - \$300,000 = \$2,508,750$$

The cash offer then becomes $2,508,750/80,000 = \$31.36$ per share. Since this price if $5.36 higher than the $26 market price, Settlevision's shareholders may be willing to accept the offer.

---

**EXCHANGE OF STOCK BASED ON EPS.** In the second approach to determining the purchase price of a target firm, the acquiring firm may offer its common shares in exchange for the target firm's shares based on each firm's EPS. The offer is stated in the form of an **exchange ratio (ER),** which is defined as the number of shares that the acquiring firm is willing to give for each of the target firm's shares. For example, if the target firm's current EPS is $3 and that of the acquiring firm is $4, the EPS based ER is $3/$4 = .75. Thus, the acquiring firm offers .75 share of its common for each share of the target firm's stock. A merger that is accomplished through an exchange of shares is a tax-free transaction to the target firm's shareholders.

An EPS based exchange ratio that reflects only current EPS may not be high enough to win approval of the target firm's shareholders. This is because the use of current EPS to compute an ER assumes that no synergistic effects are anticipated and that the two firms have identical EPS growth rates. A proposed merger may be of interest to the target firm's shareholders if the ER takes into account the following:

1.  The future EPS of each firm in the absence of a merger

2.  The impact of merger caused synergistic effects of the acquiring firm's EPS

3.  The change in market value that the target firm's shareholders will realize as a result of exchanging their shares for those of the acquiring firm

---

**Example:**   As an alternative to acquiring Settlevision, Inc., for cash, Runner Company is considering an exchange of common shares based on EPS. A first approximation to an EPS based ER can be obtained by using current EPS:

$$ER = \$1.50/\$4 = .375$$

Runner would offer .375 common shares for each common share of Settlevision. The 80,000 shares of Settlevision would be exchanged for $(.375)\,(80,000) = 30,000$ shares of Runner. The postmerger EPS for Runner would then be:

$$EPS = \frac{\$120,000 + \$2,400,000}{30,000 + 600,000} = \$4$$

Thus, a .375 ER leaves Runner's EPS unchanged. The earnings accruing to Settlevision's shareholders are also unchanged. The 80,000 shares of Settlevision would represent (80,000) ($1.50) = $120,000 in earnings. On this basis, Settlevision's shareholders would be indifferent to the merger.

Although the .375 EPS based ER provides no incentive for Settlevision's shareholders to exchange their shares, the market value of the shares received in the exchange would almost certainly stop the merger. For example, the market value of 100 shares of Settlevision prior to the merger is (100) ($26) = $2,600. These shares would be exchanged for 37.5 shares of Runner, with a market value of (37.5) ($52) = $1,950. Thus, Settlevision's shareholders would lose $2,600 − $1,950 = $650 in market value for every 100 shares exchanged.

The loss in market value is due to the following three reasons: (1) the price/earnings (P/E) multiple, or the ratio of current market price to current EPS, is different for the two firms; (2) Settlevision's P/E multiple is $26/$1.50 = 17.33, which is higher than Runner's P/E multiple of $52/$4 = 13; and (3) the implicit assumption has been made that Runner's P/E will not change as a result of the merger. As long as these three conditions are unchanged, Settlevision's shareholders will lose market value in a merger that is based on an exchange ratio using only current EPS.

---

An alternative approach is to estimate the EPS growth rates that will occur as a result of the merger and to compute the ER on the basis of the EPS that will occur at a specific time in the future. The growth rates should reflect any synergistic effects. This technique can increase the ER and cause a temporary drop in the EPS of the acquiring firm. Consequently, there is no guarantee that the shareholders of the target firm will approve the merger.

---

**Example:** Runner Company's EPS growth rate is forecast to be 2 percent indefinitely. Settlevision's EPS growth rate is currently 5 percent but is estimated to increase to 7 percent if the merger takes place. The ER based on the EPS that will occur five years from now is:

$$ER = (1 + .07)^5 ($1.50)/(1 + .02)^5 ($4) = .477$$

This means that (.477) (80,000) = 38,160 shares of Runner are offered immediately in exchange for Settlevision's 80,000 shares.

As a result of the merger, Runner Company's current EPS will decrease to:

$$EPS = \frac{$120,000 + $2,400,000}{38,160 + 600,000} = $3.95$$

The earnings accruing to Settlevision shareholders would increase slightly. In the absence of a merger, 100 Settlevision shares represent $150 of earnings. After the merger, the 47.7 shares of Runner received under the merger terms would represent (47.7) ($3.95) = $188.42 of earnings. Thus, Settlevision's shareholders would realize $188.42 − $150 = $38.42 in increased earnings per 100 shares.

Offsetting this increase in their earnings, however, would be a decrease in market value. The current value of 100 shares of Settlevision is $2,600. When exchanged for 47.7 shares of Runner Company, these shares would have a market value of $(47.7)($52) = $2,480.40$. Thus, Settlevision shareholders would suffer a loss in market value of $2,600 - $2,480.40 = $119.60$ for each 100 shares exchanged. The reasons for this decrease in market value are the same as those for the previous example.

**EXCHANGE OF STOCK BASED ON MARKET PRICE.** The third approach to determine a purchase price is for the acquiring firm to offer its common stock in exchange for the target firm's common on the basis of the market price of each firm's common stock. The offer is also stated in the form of an ER. For example, if the target firm's common sells for $30 a share and that of the acquiring firm sells for $60 a share, the market price based ER is $30/$60 = .5$. Thus, the acquiring firm offers one-half share of its common for each share of the target firm's common. This transaction is tax free to the target firm's shareholders.

Most merger offers that involve an exchange of common stock are quoted on exchange ratios based on market price. In order to secure a quick acceptance by the shareholders of the target company, the acquiring firm typically offers an ER that is higher than the market price ER. This yields an immediate increase in the price of the target firm's common shares. The acquiring firm makes these high offers when it concludes that the target firm's shares are undervalued in the market or when it estimates that synergistic effects resulting from the merger justify the ER.

One problem posed by exchange ratios that exceed the ratio of the current market prices is the possibility of reducing, at least temporarily, the EPS of the acquiring firm. A second problem is that of estimating the P/E multiple that will result after the merger. A reduced P/E multiple, even when EPS increases, can result in a lower market price of the acquiring firm's common stock. In this situation the merger fails to increase the wealth of both firms' shareholders. A merger that uses a market price ER must therefore consider the same factors that are used in evaluating EPS based ER mergers.

**Example:**    Assume that Runner Company seeks to merge with Settlevision through an exchange of common stock based on a market price ER. The ER is computed as follows:

$$ER = $26/$52 = .5$$

This means that Runner offers one-half common share for each share of Settlevision. Thus, Runner would issue $(.5)(80,000) = 40,000$ shares, and Runner's resulting EPS would decrease from $4 to $3.94.

$$EPS = \frac{$120,000 + $2,400,000}{40,000 + 600,000} = $3.94$$

This ER assumes that no synergy will result from the merger. If the P/E multiple for Runner remains at 13, its market price will fall from $52 to (13)($3.94) = $51.22.

Prior to the merger, 100 common shares of Settlevision have a market value of (100)(17.33)($1.50) = $2,600. If Settlevision's shareholders exchange 100 shares for 50 Runner shares, they will then own shares that sell at a P/E multiple of 13 which return an EPS of $3.94. Thus, the market value of these 50 shares is (50)(13) ($3.94) = $2,561. For each 100 shares exchanged, the Settlevision shareholders face a decrease in market value of $2,600 − $2,561 = $39. Consequently, Settlevision's owners would have little reason to favor the merger.

If synergistic effects are forecast as a result of the merger, the shareholders of either or both firms may favor the merger on the basis of the subsequent growth in the acquiring firm's EPS and in the market price of its common.

**Example:**

As a result of the merger, assume that the earnings provided by Settlevision will, because of synergy, grow by 7 percent per year as compared with its premerger 5 percent. As computed earlier, Runner Company's EPS falls to $3.94 at the time of the merger. How many years will it take for Runner's EPS to exceed what it would have been without the merger?

The EPS growth rate for Runner Company is 2 percent if the merger does not occur. Current EPS is $4. Thus, EPS for any year ($t$) equals

$$EPS = \$4(1 + .02)^t \qquad 4.77(1+.02)^t$$

For example, one year from now:

$$EPS = \$4(1.02) = \$4.08$$

The EPS values for subsequent years, without a merger, are contained in Runner's *No Merger* column of Table 24-2.

If the merger occurs, Settlevision's current earnings of $120,000 will be owned by Runner; these earnings will grow at the rate of 7 percent per year. Runner's premerger earnings of $2,400,000 will grow at 2 percent. In addition, 640,000 common shares of Runner Company will be outstanding. Using these values, Runner's EPS for any year is computed as follows:

$$EPS = \frac{(1 + .02)^t(\$2,400,000) + (1 + .07)^t(\$120,000)}{640,000}$$

For example, when $t = 1$:

$$EPS = \frac{(1.02)(\$2,400,000) + (1.07)(\$120,000)}{640,000} = \$4.03$$

The EPS values for subsequent years are contained in Runner's *Merger* column of Table 24-2.

The second and third columns of Table 24-2 indicate that, for five years after the merger, Runner's EPS remains below what it would have been if the merger had not

**Table 24-2.**  **EPS Projections with or without Merger**

$$4.77(1+.02)^t$$

| | Runner Company EPS | | | Settlevision, Inc., EPS* | |
| Years | No Merger | Merger | Gain (+) Loss (−) | No Merger | Gain (+) Loss (−) |
|---|---|---|---|---|---|
| 0 | $4.00  4.77 | $3.94  5.20 | −$.06 | $3.00 | +$.94 |
| 1 | 4.08  4.87 | 4.03 | − .05 | 3.15 | + .88 |
| 2 | 4.16  4.96 | 4.11 | − .05 | 3.31 | + .80 |
| 3 | 4.24  5.06 | 4.21 | − .03 | 3.47 | + .74 |
| 4 | 4.33  5.16 | 4.30 | − .03 | 3.65 | + .65 |
| 5 | 4.42  5.27 | 4.40 | − .02 | 3.83 | + .57 |
| 6 | 4.50  5.37 | 4.50 | .00 | 4.02 | + .48 |
| 7 | 4.60  5.48 | 4.61 | + .01 | 4.22 | + .39 |
| 8 | 4.69  5.59 | 4.72 | + .03 | 4.43 | + .29 |

*Based on an ER of .5.

taken place. The year-by-year differences are contained in the fourth column of that table. At the end of Year 6, the same EPS occurs for either alternative. In subsequent years the merger alternative produces the higher EPS level.

Figure 24-1 summarizes the impact of the merger on the EPS of the Runner Company. It shows the EPS dilution that occurs at the time of the merger. It also illustrates that, while the firm's EPS grows under either alternative, the merger alternative does not become more profitable, in terms of EPS, until seven years after the merger.

What is the impact of the merger on the shareholders of Settlevision? The shares of Runner that they receive earn the EPS shown in Runner's *No Merger* column of Table 24-2. The EPS on their Settlevision stock *that is equivalent* in any given year to the EPS they realize from the merger is computed by dividing the Settlevision EPS by the ER:

$$EPS = (\$1.50)(1 + .05)^t/.5$$

For Year 1:

$$EPS = (\$1.50)(1.05)/.5 = \$3.15$$

The EPS values for subsequent years are contained in Settlevision's *No Merger* column of Table 24-2. These values are subtracted from the EPS that Runner earns if the merger takes place; the results are listed in the last column of Table 24-2. This last set of numbers indicates that the Settlevision shareholders will realize a higher EPS if they exchange their shares for those of Runner. However, this advantage decreases gradually over time.

The results of this market price based ER merger, summarized in Table 24-2, assume that the merger produces synergy by increasing Settlevision's EPS growth rate. On the basis of these figures, it appears that the shareholders of Runner

Company would have no incentive to favor the merger. However, the shareholders of Settlevision would realize a substantial gain in their EPS and might accept the exchange offer.

One important generalization can be made about merger offers that use a market price based ER. *If the acquiring firm's P/E multiple is higher than that of the target firm, the acquiring firm's EPS will immediately increase. If the acquiring firm's P/E multiple is lower than that of the target firm, the acquiring firm's EPS will suffer immediate dilution.* In the previous example, Runner

**Figure 24-1.**        **EPS Projections for the Runner Company**

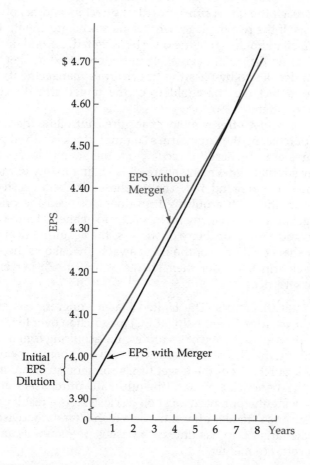

Company's P/E of 13 was lower than Settlevision's P/E of 17.33. The merger would thus cause Runner's EPS to decrease from $4 to $3.94.

When a firm with a high P/E acquires a firm with a low P/E, there is always the possibility that the acquiring firm's P/E multiple will fall. For example, this might happen if subsequent to the merger the acquiring firm's EPS turns out to be less than its forecast value. The resale price of the acquiring firm's common stock would decrease if its P/E multiple remained constant. However, if both the firm's EPS and its P/E multiple decrease, its shareholders would suffer a substantial decrease in their wealth. This is apparently what happened during the 1970s to a number of corporations that used conglomerate mergers as a way of generating a rapid EPS growth rate.

**Making Tender Offers**

There are two general approaches by which an acquiring firm makes a merger offer to a target firm's shareholders. First, the acquiring firm can approach the target firm's board of directors and negotiate a set of merger terms. If the two management teams reach agreement, they recommend to their shareholders that the offer be accepted. Second, if the management of the target firm is not agreeable to the proposed merger, or if the acquiring firm decides to by-pass the target firm's management, the acquiring firm can contact the shareholders of the target firm directly by means of a tender offer.

A **tender offer** is a bid to acquire controlling interest in a corporation by purchasing the target firm's common stock at a fixed price per share. The shares are purchased directly from the shareholders. The acquiring firm may stipulate how many shares it is willing to buy or may purchase all the shares that are tendered. The purchase may be for cash or for an exchange of securities. An acquiring firm does not need the prior approval of the target firm's management in order to make a tender offer. In order to maximize the probability of success, the acquiring firm frequently sets the per share cash price or the ER at a value that allows the shareholders of the target firm to tender their shares at a 20 to 30 percent premium above market prices.

**REGULATIONS.** The United States Congress has given the Securities and Exchange Commission (SEC) jurisdiction over tender offers. If an offer involves an exchange of securities, the acquiring firm must notify the target firm and the SEC of its intent at least 30 days before the offer is made. When block purchases of the target firm's common stock are made, the identities of the beneficial owner (the ultimate purchaser) and those who are financing the purchase must be disclosed. As a result of these regulations, a "surprise" tender offer must be a cash offer. Otherwise, the management of the target firm has time, if it wishes, to mount a campaign designed to prevent the merger.

**DEFENSIVE TACTICS.** When the management of a target firm decides that a particular tender offer is not in the best interests of its shareholders, it can employ a number of defensive tactics to thwart the tender. The firm can mount a media campaign in business publications explaining why its shareholders should not tender their shares. The firm can also send letters and other literature directly to its shareholders indicating why the tender offer is not in their best interests. Lawsuits can be initiated aimed at blocking or at least delaying the tender offer until other actions can be taken. Finally, the target firm can encourage other firms to make competitive — and more lucrative — offers. This last strategy has, on occasion, resulted in a winning tender offer that allows the shareholders to exchange their shares for cash or securities as much as 50 percent above the market value of their shares.

## Accounting for Mergers

After a merger offer is accepted, the balance sheet of the acquiring firm must be adjusted to reflect the facts that it has (1) paid cash and/or issued securities in accordance with the merger agreement and (2) acquired the target firm's balance sheet accounts. The two accounting methods used to make these balance sheet adjustments are called the *purchase method* and the *pooling-of-interest (POI) method*. The choice of which accounting method to use in a given merger is dictated by SEC regulations and statements issued by the American Institute of Certified Public Accountants (AICPA). The specific rules governing these procedures are explained in advanced accounting courses. This text discusses the implications of these two approaches for financial analysis and management.

**Purchase Method**

When a merger is treated as a purchase, the acquiring firm's total assets (as well as its total liabilities and equity) increase by an amount equal to the purchase price plus the liabilities of the target firm. The total liabilities contained in the postmerger balance sheet are the sum of the two firms' liabilities. The total common equity equals the acquiring firm's common equity plus the purchase price. On the asset side, the acquiring firm is allowed to replace the book value of the target firm's assets with their fair market values. These assets are then combined into the acquiring firm's balance sheet. If the resulting total assets are less than the resulting total of liabilities and equity, the difference is accounted for by creating an intangible asset called *goodwill*. The goodwill account is entered on the balance sheet.

**Example:**

Assume that an acquiring firm called Buyer makes an offer to a target firm called Seller. Buyer acquires Seller for $125,000,000, and the resulting merger is treated as a purchase. The balance sheets for each firm before the merger are contained in the first two columns of Table 24-3.

The adjusted total assets are:

$400,000,000 (Buyer's total assets before the merger)
+   20,000,000 (Seller's total liabilities)
+ 125,000,000 (value of the merger offer)
$545,000,000

The adjusted current liabilities are $50,000,000 + $20,000,000 = $70,000,000. Long-term debt is unchanged. Common equity equals $200,000,000 + $125,000,000 = $325,000,000.

The adjusted current assets are $140,000,000 + $30,000,000 = $170,000,000. Assume that Buyer revalues Seller's net fixed assets up to $90,000,000. Thus, Buyer's net fixed assets are increased to $260,000,000 + $90,000,000 = $350,000,000. The amount that is entered as goodwill is the total asset-balancing figure which is computed as follows:

$545,000,000
−  170,000,000
−  350,000,000
$  25,000,000 (goodwill)

**Table 24-3.**    **Balance Sheets for Purchase and Pooling-of-Interests Methods in Merger Accounting**

Thousands of Dollars

| ASSETS | Buyer | Seller | Merged Purchase | Merged POI |
|---|---|---|---|---|
| Current assets | $140,000 | $ 30,000 | $170,000 | $170,000 |
| Net fixed assets | 260,000 | 70,000 | 350,000 | 330,000 |
| Goodwill | 0 | 0 | 25,000 | 0 |
| Total assets | $400,000 | $100,000 | $545,000 | $500,000 |
| **LIABILITIES AND EQUITY** | | | | |
| Current liabilities | $ 50,000 | $ 20,000 | $ 70,000 | $ 70,000 |
| Long-term debt | 150,000 | 0 | 150,000 | 150,000 |
| Common equity | 200,000 | 80,000 | 325,000 | 280,000 |
| Total liabilities and equity | $400,000 | $100,000 | $545,000 | $500,000 |

This example demonstrates the following important ways by which an acquiring firm's postmerger balance sheet is affected by the purchase method:

1. The total assets of the merged firm can exceed the sum of the two firms' premerger total assets.

2. The acquiring firm's postmerger common equity exceeds the

sum of the two firms' premerger common equity when the purchase price exceeds the target firm's common equity.

3.  If the book value of the target firm's net fixed assets is increased, the acquiring firm realizes an income statement taxshield benefit from the added depreciation expense, but its profit after taxes is reduced.

Standard accounting practice requires that goodwill be amortized over a period not to exceed 40 years. However, the yearly expense is not deductible for federal corporate income tax purposes. Thus, goodwill expense is subtracted from profit after taxes and has the effect of lowering reported earnings.

The implications for financial management of using the purchase method in accounting for mergers are:

1.  In the absence of a synergistic increase in profits after taxes, amortization of goodwill decreases profits per dollar of assets of the acquiring firm. This is because earnings are decreased and total assets are increased.

2.  When the purchase price exceeds the value of the target firm's common equity, the difference lowers the debt to equity ratio of the acquiring firm below what it otherwise would have been. In the absence of a synergistic increase in profit after taxes, the rate of return on common equity is also reduced.

3.  If the net fixed assets of the target firm are revalued upward, the resulting increased depreciation expense decreases the acquiring firm's profit after taxes but increases its net cash flow.

**Pooling-of-Interests Method**

The AICPA has established a set of conditions that must be satisfied in order to account for a merger by using the pooling-of-interests method. For our purposes, the two most important conditions are (1) that the target firm's shareholders must retain an ownership position in the acquiring firm and (2) that in exchange for at least 90 percent of the target firm's voting stock, the acquiring firm must issue only common stock that is identical to its outstanding voting common stock. When all the specified conditions are met, the POI method must be used.

In treating a merger as a pooling of interests, the two firms' balance sheets are combined by adding the values of their corresponding balance sheet items. The purchase price does not affect the acquiring firm's balance sheet, and goodwill is not created.

---

**Example:**

Using the data from the previous example, assume that Buyer acquires Seller and that the merger is to be accounted for by the POI method. The first two columns in Table 24-3 contain the premerger balance sheets. The fourth column in that table represents the balance sheet of the merged companies. Each value in that balance sheet is obtained by adding the corresponding accounts of the premerger balance sheets.

The above example demonstrates the following effects of the POI method on the acquiring firm's balance sheet:

1. The total assets of the merged firm equal the sum of the two firms' premerger total assets.

2. The purchase price of the merger does not affect the acquiring firm's balance sheet. Thus, any portion of the purchase price that exceeds the target firm's common equity is not recognized as a cost in the firm's financial statements.

3. There is neither goodwill nor asset revaluation to alter the acquiring firm's profits after taxes or net cash flow.

Thus, the implications for financial management of using the POI method in accounting for a merger are:

1. In the absence of synergistic effects on profits, the POI method implies that the merger does nothing more than increase the acquiring firm's assets. By itself, this does nothing to advance shareholder wealth.

2. If the purchase price of the target firm is expected to exceed the value of its common equity, pooling of interests is preferred to the purchase method because the POI method results in higher reported earnings, higher profits per dollar of assets, and higher rates of return on common equity.

# SUMMARY

The goal of a merger is to increase the wealth of the acquiring firm's shareholders. In order for a merger to be desirable, the increase in shareholder wealth must exceed the amount that these shareholders can realize by purchasing the shares of the target firm. Mergers that meet this test of shareholder wealth are said to contain synergistic properties.

Merger caused synergy can occur as a result of operating economies, financial economies, or increased market penetration. Depending on the complementary or competitive relationships between the produce lines of the merging firms, mergers are characterized as being horizontal, vertical, and conglomerate or congeneric.

One of the most important financial aspects of analyzing the desirability of a proposed merger is for the acquiring firm to determine the purchase price of the target company. This can be done by (1) treating the target firm as a capital-budgeting investment alternative and computing the purchase price on the basis of the target firm's net cash flows, (2) computing an EPS based ER, or (3) computing an ER based on market price. When exchange ratios are used to price a merger, the shareholders of the target firm must usually be offered an ER that exceeds its current value if they are to accept the acquiring firm's offer.

An acquiring firm can ask for the help and approval of the target firm's board of directors in making a merger offer to its shareholders. Alternatively, the target firm's management can be bypassed in order to extend a tender offer directly to its shareholders. When the offer involves an exchange of securities, the acquiring firm must follow the relevant SEC regulations. This gives the target firm's management time to execute defensive tactics if management opposes the merger or hopes to secure more favorable merger terms.

Accounting for mergers is accomplished through the purchase method or by a pooling of interests. The choice of method is determined by SEC regulations and AICPA guidelines. From the standpoint of managerial finance pooling of interests is the preferred method.

# QUESTIONS

24-1. What fundamental requirement must be met if a proposed merger is to be attractive?

24-2. Explain how merger caused operating economies contribute to increasing shareholder wealth.

24-3. Explain how merger caused financial economies contribute to increasing shareholder wealth.

24-4. Explain how a vertical merger can increase a firm's market penetration.

24-5. What is the difference between conglomerate and congeneric mergers?

24-6. Explain how an acquiring firm can estimate the purchase price of a target firm on the basis of net cash flows.

24-7. If an acquiring firm's P/E multiple is lower than that of the target firm, and if the ER is based on market prices, what is the impact on the acquiring firm's EPS?

24-8. Summarize the implications for financial management of using the purchase method in accounting for mergers.

**24-9.** From the standpoint of managerial finance, why is pooling of interests preferable to the purchase method in accounting for mergers?

# PROBLEMS

*Note:* Problems 24-1, 24-2, and 24-3 use the data contained in Table 24-4.

**24-1.** Assume that Beyer Company seeks to acquire Soller Company through a merger. Beyer wants to calculate its maximum purchase price based on Soller's net cash flows.

    *a.* Compute the maximum purchase price assuming a constant net cash flow and no synergy. What is the maximum purchase price per share?

    *b.* Compute the maximum purchase price and the price per share assuming no synergy and a growth rate of 10% for Soller's net cash flow. (Use Equations 13-7 and 24-1.)

    *c.* Compute the maximum purchase price and the price per share if synergy increases the growth rate of Soller's net cash flow to 13%. (Use Equations 13-7 and 24-1.)

    *d.* Of the prices computed in *a*, *b*, and *c*, which, if any, are Soller's shareholders likely to accept?

**24-2.** Assume that Beyer wishes to make a merger offer to Soller on an exchange ratio based on EPS.

    *a.* Compute the ER based on current EPS. How many shares does Beyer have to issue? Compute Beyer's EPS immediately after the merger.

    *b.* Assume that Soller's EPS growth rate increases to 13% if the merger occurs and that Beyer's EPS growth rate is 5%. Compute the ER on the EPS that will occur four years after the merger. How many shares does Beyer issue? Compute Beyer's EPS immediately after the merger.

**24-3.** Assume that Beyer wishes to make a merger offer to Soller using an exchange ratio based on market price.

    *a.* Compute the ER using current market prices. How many shares does Beyer issue?

    *b.* Compute Beyer's EPS immediately after the merger.

    *c.* Assume that Beyer's EPS growth rate will be 5% and, as a result of the merger, Soller's EPS growth rate will be 13%. Compute the EPS that Beyer will realize in one, two, and three years after the merger.

**Table 24-4.**  **Financial Data for the Beyer-Soller Merger**

|  | Soller Company | Beyer Company |
|---|---|---|
| Current EPS | $1.80 | $6.00 |
| Current market price of common stock | $18.00 | $120.00 |
| Number of shares outstanding | 200,000 | 1,000,000 |
| Current earnings after taxes | $360,000 | $6,000,000 |
| Cost of capital | — | 20% |
| Net cash flow, current year | $550,000 | |
| Total liabilities | $1,000,000 | |

*Note:* Problems 24-4, 24-5, and 24-6 use the data contained in Table 24-5.

24-4. Giant Company wants to acquire Small Company by way of a merger. The purchase price is to be based on Small's net cash flow.

 a. Compute the maximum purchase price (MPP) assuming a constant net cash flow for Small. What is the purchase price stated in dollars per share?

**Table 24-5.**  **Financial Data for the Giant-Small Merger**

|  | Small Company | Giant Company |
|---|---|---|
| Current EPS | $1.00 | $10.00 |
| Current market price | $35.00 | $100.00 |
| Number of common shares outstanding | 500,000 | 2,000,000 |
| Current earnings after taxes | $500,000 | $20,000,000 |
| Cost of capital | — | 20% |
| Current net cash flow | $700,000 | |
| Total liabilities | $2,000,000 | |

 b. Compute the MPP on the assumption that Small's net cash flow grows at a 15% annual rate indefinitely. What is the purchase price in dollars per share?

24-5. Assume that Giant wants to acquire Small on the basis of an EPS based ER.

 a. Compute the ER on the basis of current EPS. How many shares does Giant have to issue? Compute Giant's EPS immediately after the merger.
 b. Assume that Giant's EPS growth rate is 8% and Small's is 15%. Compute

the EPS-based ER on the EPS that will occur five years from now. How many shares does Giant issue, and what is its EPS immediately after the merger?

c.  Assume that the merger would increase Small's EPS growth rate to 20% and leave Giant's at 8%. Compute the EPS based ER on the EPS that will occur five years from now. How many shares does Giant issue, and what is its EPS immediately after the merger?

**24-6.**  Assume that Giant wants to acquire Small on an ER based on market price.

a.  Compute the ER using current market prices. How many shares does Giant issue? Compute Giant's EPS immediately after the merger.

b.  Giant's EPS growth rate is estimated at 8% per year. In the absence of the merger, compute Giant's EPS in 5, 8, 10, 12, and 15 years from now.

c.  If the merger occurs, Giant's EPS growth rate will remain at 8%, but Small's will grow at 20% due to synergy. Compute Giant's postmerger EPS immediately after the merger and in 5, 8, 10, 12, and 15 years from now.

d.  On the basis of b and c, approximately how many years will it take for Giant's postmerger EPS to exceed its no merger EPS?

**24-7.**  Table 24-6 contains the premerger balance sheets for Giant Company and Small Company.

a.  Prepare the Giant Company's postmerger balance sheet using the purchase method if Small Company is acquired for $12,000,000. Assume no revaluation of Small Company's assets.

**Table 24-6.**   **Premerger Balance Sheets for Small Company and Giant Company**

|  | Small Company | Giant Company |
|---|---|---|
| **ASSETS** | | |
| Current assets | $4,000,000 | $35,000,000 |
| Net fixed assets | 3,000,000 | 22,000,000 |
| Total assets | $7,000,000 | $57,000,000 |
| **LIABILITIES AND COMMON EQUITY** | | |
| Current liabilities | $1,000,000 | $10,000,000 |
| Long-term debt | 1,000,000 | 7,000,000 |
| Common equity | 5,000,000 | 40,000,000 |
| Total liabilities and common equity | $7,000,000 | $57,000,000 |

b.  Prepare the Giant Company's postmerger balance sheet using the POI method if Small Company is acquired for $12,000,000.

# SELECTED REFERENCES

Asquith, P., and E. Kim. "The Impact of Merger Bids on the Participating Firms' Security Holders." *Journal of Finance*, Vol. 37, No. 5 (December, 1982).

Choi, D., and G. Philippatos. "An Examination of Merger Synergism." *Journal of Financial Research*, Vol. 6, No. 3 (Fall, 1983).

Halpern, P. "Corporate Acquisitions: A Theory of Special Cases? A Review of Event Studies Applied to Acquisitions." *Journal of Finance*, Vol. 38, No. 2 (May, 1983).

Mueller, D. "The Effects of Conglomerate Mergers: A Survey of the Empirical Evidence." *Journal of Banking and Finance*, Vol. 1 (June, 1977).

Salter, M., and W. Weinhold. "Diversification via Acquisition: Creating Value." *Harvard Business Review*, Vol. 56 (July-August, 1978).

Sharp, J. "Find the Right Partner for Your Company." *Financial Executive*, Vol. 51, No. 6 (June 1983).

# CHAPTER 25

## *Business Failure and Corporate Bankruptcy*

*Throughout this text the impact of corporate decisions on the firm's risk-return characteristics and the resulting ability of the firm to increase shareholder wealth have been emphasized. Unfortunately there is always the possibility that a set of corporate decisions, possibly coupled with external factors, will cause the firm to fail and impose losses on its owners and creditors. This chapter begins with the basic definitions of the major legal terms involved in corporate bankruptcy situations, followed by an example illustrating how basic bankruptcy law works. The next section presents a brief overview of the failure record for American corporations. The third section of this chapter examines alternatives to bankruptcy. The final section discusses reasons why solvent firms often file voluntary petitions of bankruptcy.[1]*

## BASIC DEFINITIONS UNDER FEDERAL BANKRUPTCY LAW

This section contains some definitions and explains some of the terminology that is used when dealing with business failures and/or bankruptcies.

---

[1]The materials in this chapter were prepared by Professors John Houlihan of the University of Southern Maine and George Hartman of the University of Cincinnati.

Congress has passed a series of laws designed to provide a nationwide, uniform standard governing all forms of bankruptcy law. This federal standard means that corporations generally need not worry about state laws when considering liquidation or reorganization, the two major alternatives presented by the bankruptcy laws.

**Liquidation or Straight Bankruptcy**

Liquidation is utilized when either the debtor corporation voluntarily decides to cease existence or some creditors of the debtor corporation petition the Federal Bankruptcy Court to terminate the debtor corporation. In both voluntary and involuntary liquidations there is a definite legal finality to the bankruptcy proceedings. The goal is to assemble all the debtor corporation's assets, pay off all claims of the creditors, and distribute the remaining assets, if any, to the shareholders of the corporation.

**Reorganization**

Reorganization is utilized when the debtor corporation and most of its creditors believe that the corporation can become a profitable entity in the future provided certain changes are made. These changes may be as minor as a court ordered moratorium on debt repayment which allows a debtor corporation with temporary cash flow or liquidity problems the opportunity to survive the temporary cash scarcity. Such temporary problems are usually due to unanticipated extra costs or to an unanticipated revenue shortfall. However, the changes provided by reorganization are often major in nature and involve changes in management, sale of corporate assets or divisions, and the development of a plan that recapitalizes the corporation by giving creditors equity shares in exchange for all or part of the debt owed to them by the debtor corporation.

**Involuntary Bankruptcy**

The legal standards that allow creditors to file an involuntary petition of bankruptcy requesting either liquidation or reorganization of the debtor corporation are straightforward.

**LESS THAN TWELVE CREDITORS.** When the debtor has less than twelve creditors, any single creditor may file a petition as long as that creditor is owed $5,000 or more. Two or more creditors may combine their claims to satisfy the $5,000 requirement.

**TWELVE OR MORE CREDITORS.** If the debtor firm has twelve or more creditors, at least three must file. Even if one creditor is owed $5,000 or more, he or she must persuade other creditors to join in the petition in order to satisfy the three-or-more requirement. The three creditors who file must have total claims amounting to $5,000 or more.

In both cases, the $5,000 requirement must be satisfied by actual claims that are presently owed to the creditors by the corporation. A *contingent claim* (any claim that a debtor corporation has a potentially valid legal reason for disputing) or a future claim may not be used to satisfy the $5,000 requirement. However, the debtor corporation can defeat the bankruptcy petition and continue to operate without interference by showing that the corporation is *not* insolvent in the equity sense.

## Insolvency in the Equity Sense

Major changes were made in the bankruptcy laws in 1978. One of these significant changes involved the definition of insolvency. Insolvency in the equity sense is what a creditor or creditors must prove if the debtor corporation challenges an involuntary petition. A corporation is *insolvent in the equity* sense if (1) it generally is not paying its debts as they become due (for example, all recent checks have been returned due to insufficient funds in the corporation's bank accounts) or (2) a custodian for the corporation's assets has been appointed at any time in the 120 days prior to the filing of the involuntary petition by the creditor or creditors. Insolvency in the equity sense is far easier to prove than the old *insolvency in the bankruptcy sense* test which used a balance sheet approach that required the sum of the debtor corporation's liabilities to be greater than the sum of the debtor corporation's assets.

## Custodian

A *custodian* is an assignee under a general assignment for the benefit of creditors, or any trustee, receiver, or agent authorized by contract or through court proceedings (other than a bankruptcy petition). The appointment of a custodian is a signal to other creditors that the debtor corporation is in serious financial difficulties and that they should file quickly an involuntary petition in bankruptcy court to protect their own interests. A custodian may be called a *trustee* or *receiver* but is not the same as a trustee in bankruptcy which is a special term defined below.

## Trustee in Bankruptcy

A person appointed as representative of the estate of the debtor corporation (*estate* is a particularly apt word in a liquidation situation) by a majority of creditors at the first creditors' meeting is a *trustee in bankruptcy*. A majority of creditors is not a numerical majority (e.g., 51 out of 100 creditors) but a majority of the aggregate amount of actual claims. Thus, a creditor who is owed $100,000 has 100,000 votes, and a creditor who is owed $20,000 has 20,000 votes. The trustee's primary duty is to collect all the assets of the debtor corporation and to use these assets to pay off all debtors, both secured and unsecured. The trustee has the power to recover for the debtor corporation's estate all assets that were transferred illegally to third parties or creditors through preferences (see page 674) or fraudulent transactions (see page 675). The trustee also has numerous legal powers that allow him or her to defeat secured creditors who did not immediately and effectively perfect, or legally establish, their security interest.

**Secured Creditor**

A *secured creditor* is a person who has a priority claim on a certain asset or assets of the debtor corporation. The claim may be a special one, called a *purchase money security interest,* which arises when the creditor lends the corporation money specifically designated for the purchase of particular assets, when the creditor finances the purchase of particular assets, or when the creditor finances the purchase of particular items on credit. For example, if a bank lends the Boyle Corporation money to purchase specific raw materials, a purchase money security interest is usually created. The bank usually has the highest and best legal right (the first priority) to recover those particular raw materials if the debtor corporation becomes insolvent in the equity sense. A purchase money security interest usually is created if the Boyle Corporation purchases machinery on credit from, say, the Giant Machinery Corporation. Then the Giant Machinery Corporation usually has the highest and best legal right (the first priority) to recover that machinery if the Boyle Corporation becomes insolvent in the equity sense.

The claim of a secured creditor may often be a general one covering all assets of a particular type; for example, all inventory or all accounts receivable. Some creditors even demand as security *after-acquired property,* that is, any and all assets presently held and to be acquired in the future by the debtor corporation. An after-acquired property clause is also called an *octopus* clause. In a normal bankruptcy proceeding, general secured claims are more vulnerable to legal attack by the trustee in bankruptcy than are specific purchase money security interests. In either case, a security interest is less vulnerable if it was *perfected* at the time the credit was extended. This normally requires that the creditor either retain possession of the collateral or file a valid financing statement with the appropriate state office.

**Unsecured Creditors**

*Unsecured creditors* are those creditors who have no special legal protection in a bankruptcy case. Unsecured creditors are entitled only to the assets of the debtor corporation that remain (1) after all valid secured creditors are paid; (2) after administrative expenses (lawyers', accountants', and the trustee's fees) are paid; and (3) after special priority interests (employees owed back wages or benefits and taxes owed to federal, state, or local government entities) are paid. In a normal corporate bankruptcy, there usually are few assets, if any, left to pay off unsecured creditors. These unsecured creditors often receive only 1 to 10 cents for each dollar owed them by the debtor corporation.

**Preferences**

A *preferential transfer* is a payment made by an insolvent debtor corporation within 90 days of the filing of the bankruptcy petition, which is designed to pay off the preexisting (antecedent) debt owed to one or more general creditors. The problem is that a preferential transfer is unfair to the debtor corporation's other creditors—the debtor is paying one of its creditors in full while usually paying most other creditors nothing. Preferential transfers usually are made because the debtor corporation likes one special creditor or because a certain creditor threatens to make public the shaky financial situation of the debtor corporation unless he or she is paid in full. The trustee in bankruptcy has the right to recover automatically all preferential transfers and return them to the debtor corporation's estate for pro rata distribution to all creditors.

Preferential transfers include preferential liens which are also subject to the foregoing rules. In addition, if the special or favored creditor is an *insider*—an officer, director, or relative of an officer or director—the trustee in bankruptcy can recover preferential transfers made up to one year (rather than 90 days) prior to the date that the bankruptcy petition is filed.

One caveat is necessary. Bankruptcy law does not consider all transactions made within 90 days of the date of the bankruptcy petition to be preferential transfers. Only those transactions that pay off the preexisting debt of a particular creditor are considered preferences. Suppose that the Cutwright Lawnmower Corporation is having significant difficulties and wishes to purchase for cash $10,000 worth of new lawnmowers from the Walnut Warehouse Corporation. When Cutwright purchases the lawnmowers, the cash payment is not a preference because it is not payment for a preexisting or past debt but merely a current purchase. Cutwright now has $10,000 worth of lawnmowers and all its creditors still have $10,000 worth of assest to claim against. In fact, bankruptcy law permits payment to any creditor in the ordinary course of business if the payment is made within 45 days of the date the debt was incurred. This allows a corporation in financial difficulty to continue to order raw materials, supplies, and inventory and to pay for these goods within 45 days of purchase.

The intent of the debtor corporation or of the creditor does not matter. A preference automatically occurs if the debtor corporation makes payments, transfers assets, or allows liens to be established to the benefit of one creditor in payment of a preexisting debt. If Chatter Industries pays $60,000 to a supplier, Ferrous Fabrication, Inc., on March 3 (because the $60,000 is Chatter Industries' longest past due debt), and then Chatter

Industries has a involuntary bankruptcy petition filed against it by other disgruntled creditors on April 23, the $60,000 payment is a preferential transfer because it occured within 90 days of April 23, the date of the bankruptcy petition. Intent is only important when a transfer to an insider is made by the debtor corporation within one year before the date of the bankruptcy petition but *not* within 90 days prior to the bankruptcy petition. In insider transfers that occur more than 90 days but less than one year prior to the bankruptcy filing, the trustee in bankruptcy must prove that the insider knew or should have known that the debtor corporation was insolvent at the time the transfer occurred. The transfer is then treated as a preference.

**Fraudulent Transactions**

Corporations faced with a very gloomy financial future often try to hide assets from creditors. Many times this concealment is accomplished by selling assets to corporate insiders at much less than fair market value or by transferring title to property to related corporations that probably will not be involved in any bankruptcy proceedings. In a fraudulent transaction the debtor corporation intends to cheat or defraud its creditors, and the trustee in bankruptcy has the power to void all transactions made for insufficient or no consideration within one year of the date on which the bankruptcy petition is filed.[2] Suppose the All-Purpose Sportswear Corporation is in very shaky financial shape. Its president, Mary Mayfield, decides to sell the All-Purpose factory in Jackson, New Jersey, to Formula Fashions Corporation, a competitor. Alvin Quincy, president of Formula Fashions, is a good friend of Mary going back to their college days. Both know that the fair market value of the All-Purpose factory is between $1,500,000 and $2,500,000. Formula Fashions purchases the factory for $250,000 on July 1, 1982. On June 7, 1983, an involuntary petition in bankruptcy is filed against All-Purpose Sportswear Corporation by seven of its creditors. The trustee in bankruptcy can recover the All-Purpose factory from Formula Fashion because it was a transfer for less than a reasonably equivalent value and occurred within one year of June 7, 1983.

A fraudulent transaction also occurs when an owner or company officer hires a spouse or other close relative as a consultant at, say, a $50,000-a-year salary and the so-called consultant provides little or no actual service for the company.

**Example:**

Metaphor Metals, Inc., was engaged in the production of zinc, copper, and iron products for industrial use. As of March, 1985, Metaphor had seen sales decrease 50 percent in zinc products and 15 percent in copper products over the past two

---

[2]*Consideration* is a legal term that means value.

years. Its iron products continued to be profitable, and sales had increased 12 percent in the past two years. Total sales for the past two years came 25 percent from zinc products, 25 percent from copper products, and 50 percent from iron products. The total volume of sales for the past two years was $40 million. Metaphor lost $300,000 on its zinc business and $100,000 on its copper business. It earned a profit of $200,000 from its iron business. Metaphor's losses on zinc and copper produced a negative cash flow situation which had led the company to delay paying most of its suppliers for 180 days. Metaphor also had not made the last six payments on a machinery loan of $1 million owed to the Northwest National Bank. Each monthly payment was $25,000. Northwest National Bank made this loan in 1983 but only perfected its secured interest in January, 1985. Metaphor's balance sheet for March 15, 1985, is given in Table 25-1.

---

**Table 25-1.**     **Metaphor Metals, Inc., Balance Sheet (as of March 15, 1985)**

**Assets**

| | |
|---|---|
| Inventory of zinc products | $  500,000 |
| Inventory of copper products | 600,000 |
| Inventory of iron products | 100,000 |
| Factory in Perth, North Carolina | 1,000,000 |
| Factory in Prussia, Georgia | 800,000 |
| Machinery | 200,000 |
| All other assets | 300,000 |
| Total Assets | $3,500,000 |

**Liabilities and Equity**
Current Liabilities

| | |
|---|---|
| Northwest National Bank | $  150,000 |
| Statewide Copper Company | 600,000 |
| York Zinc Corporation | 400,000 |
| Industrial Iron Corporation | 800,000 |
| Other bank loans | 50,000 |
| Other raw materials suppliers | 200,000 |
| All other creditors | 300,000 |
| Total Current Liabilities | $2,500,000 |
| Long-term Liabilities | 1,500,000 |
| Owners' Equity (Deficit) | (500,000) |
| Total Liabilities and Equity | $3,500,000 |

---

Metaphor paid $150,000 to the York Zinc Company on April 1, 1985, to reduce its balance due York to $250,000. Metaphor also paid all its small suppliers $100,000 on May 1, 1985, because the small suppliers had threatened to file an involuntary bankruptcy petition against Metaphor unless they were paid what was due. Metaphor sold its factory in Prussia, Georgia, on June 1, 1985, for $400,000 to Industrial Iron Corporation. Metaphor then transferred title of its factory in Perth, North Carolina, to a sister corporation, Dynamic Metals, Inc. On July 21, 1985, Metaphor had an involuntary bankruptcy petition filed against it by six creditors with aggregate claims of $1,500,000.

There are two criteria that must be met for the petition to have been valid. First of all, a petition must be filed by three or more creditors (assuming the total number of creditors is twelve or more) who have aggregate claims of $5,000. Six creditors with aggregate claims of $1,500,000 filed, and this requirement was met. Second, the firm must be insolvent in the equity sense. Since Metaphor had not paid its suppliers or the Northwest National Bank for six months because of cash flow problems, Metaphor was insolvent in the equity sense.

The creditors then appointed a trustee in bankruptcy. The trustee must see if any preferences or fraudulent transactions have been made by Metaphor and ascertain whether any creditors have superior claims. The trustee's main tasks will include determining the following:

1. Metaphor's payment of $100,000 to its small suppliers on May 1, 1985, will likely be considered a preference because it was within 90 days prior to the date of the bankruptcy petition, and it was a payment of antecedent debt.

2. Metaphor's sale of its factory in Prussia, Georgia, on June 1, 1985, may have been for less than reasonably equivalent value and may be void as a fraudulent transaction. The factory's balance sheet value was $800,000, and it was sold for $400,000. However, Metaphor may be able to prove that $400,000 was indeed a reasonably equivalent value for that factory and avoid the fraudulent transaction rule. Then Metaphor will face a second hurdle since the trustee will ask whether Metaphor actually received $400,000 in cash or whether Industrial Iron Corporation wrote off all or some of the $800,000 debt which Metaphor already owed it. If Metaphor did not receive and keep the $400,000 in cash, the transaction will be judged a preference since it occurred within 90 days of the date of the bankruptcy petition and was for an antecedent debt. Many creditors try to hide preferences by designing the transaction as a purchase, but, unless the debtor corporation actually receives sufficient value, the transaction is a preference and can be voided by the trustee in bankruptcy.

3. Metaphor's transfer of its factory in Perth, North Carolina, to Dynamic Metals, Inc., probably was a fraudulent transaction. No payment was received, the transfer was to a sister corporation, and the transaction occurred within one year of the date of the bankruptcy petition.

4. Metaphor's $150,000 payment to York Zinc Company was not a regular preference because it occurred more than 90 days before the date of the bankruptcy petition. The trustee in bankruptcy may try to prove that York was an insider and knew that Metaphor was insolvent on April 1, 1985, when the $150,000 payment was made. It is unlikely, however, that York Zinc Company was an insider and, therefore, York Zinc will be able to keep the $150,000 Metaphor paid it on April 1, 1985.

5. The trustee in bankruptcy may be able to reduce Northwest National Bank's rights from those of a secured creditor holding a purchase money interest in machinery to those of an unsecured creditor. This is because Northwest National made this loan two years ago but only perfected its security interest this year, and this time gap may make Northwest National Bank an unsecured creditor.

Should Metaphor be liquidated or reorganized? This is a tough question. Metaphor has two losing metal divisions, zinc and copper. Each has substantial inventories that may not be salable at the value listed on Metaphor's balance sheet. Zinc and copper have lost money for two years and may continue to lose money in both the short and long run. Metaphor has substantial past due debts and a definite cash flow problem. Metaphor has total liabilities of $4,000,000 and total assets of $3,500,000. Metaphor seems to have a quite profitable iron division, however, with a business future that looks bright. Reorganization may give Metaphor the opportunity to close down and sell off the unprofitable zinc and copper operations, reschedule and restructure its remaining debts, and emerge as a small but profitable company making iron products. This is a case where a detailed financial analysis of Metaphor's present financial situation and future financial potential should be made using the tools treated in the preceding chapters of this book.

## THE FAILURE RECORD

Dun & Bradstreet defines business failures as follows:

Business failures include those businesses that ceased operations following assignment or bankruptcy; ceased with loss to creditors after such actions as execution, foreclosure, or attachement; voluntarily withdrew leaving unpaid obligations; were involved in court actions such as receivership, reorganization, or arrangement; or voluntarily compromised with creditors.[3]

Business failure, as defined by Dun & Bradstreet, occurs most often among small firms. Approximately 70 percent of all failed firms have current liabilities under $100,000 when they fail. In addition, one-half of all firms that failed were in business for five years or less. What are the causes of business failure? Subjective estimates are that over 90 percent of all business failures, regardless of size and age, are caused by managerial inexperience and/or managerial incompetence. Fraud, disasters, and all other causes account for less than 10 percent of business failures.

In the past the number of large corporate bankruptcies has been relatively small: Penn Central in 1970, W. T. Grant in 1974, and a few others.

---

[3]*The Business Failure Record* (New York: Dun & Bradstreet, Inc., 1978), p. 15. Reprinted with permission.

In 1982, however, the pace of bankruptcy filings by large companies greatly accelerated, partly because of the new law and partly because of a depressed economy. These included such companies as Braniff International, an airline; AM International, an office equipment maker; Wickes Companies, a furniture retailer and diversified manufacturer; Saxon Industries, a photocopier manufacturer; Lionel Corporation, a manufacturer of toys and electronics; and Brentano's Inc., a chain of bookstores. In addition, many other companies — International Harvester, Nucorp Energy, Inc., Texas Air Corporation — were on the verge of filing for bankruptcy. Indeed, it has been suggested that over two hundred of the two thousand largest concerns in the United States have been potential bankruptcy candidates in this decade.

Table 25-2 contains the number and distribution of business failures (using Dun & Bradstreet's definition) since 1970. Total failures are listed as are the percentage distributions across major industries. The time series of total business failures has no trend; the large values that occurred in 1980 and 1981 can be interpreted as a cyclical high caused by the combination of historically high interest rates coupled with a relatively severe recession. In terms of percentages of the whole, mining and manufacturing failures show a slow and steady decline while construction failures show a slow and steady increase. The largest number of business failures occurs in the retail trade industry.

**Table 25-2.**       Distribution of Commercial and Industrial Failures since 1970

| Year | Total Number of Failures | Mining and Manufacturing | Wholesale Trade | Retail Trade | Construction | Commercial Service |
|------|------|------|------|------|------|------|
| 1970 | 10,748 | 18.9% | 9.2% | 43.3% | 15.7% | 12.9% |
| 1971 | 10,326 | 18.7 | 9.3 | 42.9 | 14.9 | 14.2 |
| 1972 | 9,566 | 16.5 | 10.1 | 45.9 | 14.4 | 13.1 |
| 1973 | 9,345 | 15.7 | 10.1 | 46.4 | 15.2 | 12.6 |
| 1974 | 9,915 | 15.7 | 9.7 | 42.7 | 18.6 | 13.3 |
| 1975 | 11,432 | 14.4 | 9.5 | 42.0 | 19.8 | 14.3 |
| 1976 | 9,628 | 14.1 | 10.7 | 43.0 | 18.4 | 13.8 |
| 1977 | 7,919 | 14.2 | 11.2 | 43.0 | 18.5 | 13.1 |
| 1978 | 6,619 | 15.3 | 11.2 | 43.6 | 18.2 | 11.7 |
| 1979 | 7,564 | 15.4 | 12.0 | 42.1 | 18.2 | 12.3 |
| 1980 | 11,742 | 13.6 | 10.9 | 41.8 | 20.1 | 13.6 |
| 1981 | 16,794 | 13.2 | 10.2 | 41.0 | 21.5 | 14.1 |
| 1982 | 25,346 | 14.8 | 11.1 | 38.8 | 19.6 | 15.7 |
| 1983 | 31,334 | 14.8 | 11.2 | 35.4 | 16.8 | 21.8 |

Source: *Survey of Current Business* (various issues); and Dun & Bradstreet, Inc.

## NONBANKRUPTCY REMEDIES

Contrary to popular opinion, creditors of business enterprises are not interested in destroying a firm by throwing it into bankruptcy at the first sign of financial distress. Rather, many creditors will cooperate with debtors and seek to preserve the firm's viability during a period of financial distress. Several nonbankruptcy remedies are available to the parties, five of which are (1) composition, (2) extension, (3) general assignment for the benefit of creditors, (4) creditors' committee, and (5) receivership. These nonbankruptcy remedies are all based on the voluntary actions of creditors, while bankruptcy proceedings (outside involuntary bankruptcy) are based on debtors' plans to protect themselves from creditors.

**Composition**

*Composition* is a multiparty agreement between the debtor and the firm's creditors and among the creditors themselves, voluntarily entered into by the financially distressed debtor and two or more secured and/or unsecured creditors. This remedy is a rehabilitation device for the debtor. In the agreement the debtor offers and the creditors accept, individually and for one another, one of the following terms:

1.  A lesser amount than is actually due the creditors can be paid. All creditors must be treated alike, and no secret preferences shall be extended by the debtor. The actual cash settlement — 25 cents on the dollar, for example — is negotiated and accepted by the creditors as full payment and satisfaction of their respective debts.

2.  An extension of the time within which the full amount will be paid can be negotiated.

3.  A combination of the prior two possibilities can also be negotiated. In other words, it is possible to agree to a scaled down partial cash payment to be made over an extended period of time.

The crucial part of the first and third composition agreements is the reduced cash payment made to the creditors in full settlement of the debt. In all the agreements all creditors must be treated alike, and no secret preferences shall be extended by the debtor.

The advantages of the composition agreement are as follows:

1.  Substantial losses can be minimized through its use, because creditors receive more than they would if they initiated formal bankruptcy proceeding.

2.  The debtor often can remain in business as a viable enterprise, thus remaining a customer for the creditors.

The disadvantages of composition are as follows:

1.  Small creditors may demand full payment of their claims rather than sign the composition agreement. This is not a serious disadvantage since small claims — $100 or less — usually can be paid to *all* creditors, and all claims over $100 will receive the agreed upon percentage settlement. For example, if the composition agreement specifies 50 cents on the dollar, all claims of $100 or less are paid in full. On the other hand, a creditor having a $1,000 claim will receive $500.

2.  One of the problems causing the financial distress still remains; namely, the same debtor is still running the business. This may or may not lead to further deterioration of the firm.

**Extension**

*Extension* like composition, is a voluntary agreement and requires the consent of the individual parties. It intends full payment of the creditors' claims but extends payments beyond the original due dates.

An extension will be successful only if the debtor is ultimately a good risk; that is, if the debtor has the character and the ability to make the business prosper, provided general business conditions are conducive to the firm's recovery. As part of the extension agreement, the debtor firm typically must discontinue dividend payments, provide special security (mortgages on the firm's assets or personal notes from the owners), and pay cash for all merchandise purchased.

Extension, like composition, is designed to keep the business alive so that it can avoid bankruptcy and court proceedings. The basic difference is that extension is a means of settling *in full* the debtor's debts over a period of time while composition is an actual reduction in the debtor's debts with each creditor receiving a prorated amount.

**General Assignment**

In *general assignment*, the debtor corporation voluntarily transfer its property to assignees so that they can liquidate the property for the benefit of the creditors. Sometimes the assignees are the debtor's creditors. The general assignment remedy is designed to protect the debtor's assets from levies by creditors. This remedy is directed towards eventual liquidation of the business firm. However, with the recent developments in bankruptcy law, the general assignment remedy does not appear to be very important as a voluntary remedy.

**Creditors' Committee**

There are times when the control and management of a debtor corporation will be turned over to a committee of its creditors. The creditors' committee operates the firm until its debts are paid and then returns control to the firm's owners.

This remedy is stronger than extension but not as harsh as the actual liquidation of the debtor's business. The underlying problem is frequently one of management, and it is questionable whether this remedy can prevent the firm from becoming an economic failure.

**Receivership**    Receivership involves a court action but still does not require bankruptcy. Under *receivership* a court administers the property of the debtor. This receivership can be for all creditors or for particular creditors. Receivership can be superseded easily by bankruptcy and has been narrowly restricted by the bankruptcy remedy.

## SOME RECENT DEVELOPMENTS

The Bankruptcy Reform Act of 1978 attempted to simplify both the rules and the terminology employed in bankruptcy cases. The area of corporate reorganizations was modified in order to encourage viable businesses that were suffering significant short-term losses to reorganize rather than to liquidate. One result of these changes is that reorganization now provides a harbor for solvent and profitable corporations burdened with long-term contractual liabilities (either in the form of collective bargaining agreements or long-term purchase commitments to suppliers) or with significant potential long-term liabilities. An example of the latter is the Manville Corporation and other corporations that manufacture asbestos for industrial and residential uses. They have filed for protection under the reorganization section of the bankruptcy law. Manville and the other corporations are asking the bankruptcy court to shelter them from the cloud of contingent liability that has arisen and may in the future arise due to asbestosis, a chronic and often fatal disease which is caused by inhalation of asbestos fibers. These are profitable corporations that are using bankruptcy reorganization law to protect themselves from potential long-term liabilities. On the other hand, many people allegedly injured by exposure to asbestos fibers have charged that these corporations are using the bankruptcy law to thwart legitimate personal injury claims for which the companies and their insurers are responsible.

Many meat-packing firms, processed foods companies, and other corporations burdened with collective bargaining agreements which set higher wages than these corporations could pay during the 1981–82 recession filed bankruptcy reorganization petitions, so that they could reopen wage discussions and possibly cancel existing agreements. Thus, the present bankruptcy reorganization laws often provide corporations with a way to maneuver around existing or potential legal obligations. How the bankruptcy courts handle these reorganization petitions will set precedents for future bankruptcy filings by corporations in times of downturn or uncertainty.

# SUMMARY

Major changes were made by the federal Bankruptcy Reform Act of 1978. A corporation may now file for either liquidation or reorganization under the bankruptcy laws. In liquidation proceedings the corporation's assets will be collected and distributed to creditors, and the corporation will go out of business. In reorganization proceedings the court will try to restructure the financial position of the corporation so that it can continue as a viable company.

A corporation may be dragged into involuntary bankruptcy by one or more of its creditors if the corporation is believed to be insolvent in the equity sense. A corporation is insolvent in the equity sense if it is generally not paying its debts as they become due or if a custodian has recently been appointed for the corporation's assets.

The trustee in bankruptcy is a person selected by the creditors of a corporation. The trustee's primary duty is to collect all the assets of the corporation. The trustee has the legal power to recover all assets if their transfer by the corporation is considered by the trustee to be a preference or a fraudulent transaction. The trustee then pays off valid claims of secured creditors and distributes any remaining assets on a pro rata basis to all unsecured creditors.

Bankruptcy occurs most often among small firms, but recently some Fortune 500 corporations have filed for protection under the bankruptcy laws. Most bankruptcies are caused by mismanagement which produces or exacerbates already existing financial problems for the corporation.

A variety of nonbankruptcy remedies also exist. The nonbankruptcy remedies of composition and extension seek to accomplish voluntarily and outside the courts what would otherwise require a complex, lengthy, and expensive case if a bankruptcy petition were filed. Assignment, creditors' committees, and receivership are other nonbankruptcy remedies which can be used by creditors.

Recently many large corporations have filed voluntary petitions for bankruptcy reorganization. Some corporations hope that bankruptcy law will shield them from claims arising from asbestos injuries, for example. Other corporations hope that bankruptcy law will allow them to renegotiate burdensome collective bargaining agreements. At the present time the jury is still out on whether the bankruptcy laws can be used by financially solvent corporations to avoid certain legal liabilities.

# QUESTIONS

**25-1.** The Felicia Corporation recently has suffered a series of financial reverses. A fire totally destroyed one large warehouse, and the economic recession throughout the world has produced a sales drop of 20% and a loss of $500,000 for this fiscal year. The company has not paid most of its suppliers in the last four months and barely has enough cash on hand to meet its payroll and other necessary expenditures. In addition, the Felicia Corporation has received significant unfavorable publicity in the past year because at least seven children were seriously injured when their supposedly fire-retardant pajamas caught fire and burned. Is the Felicia Corporation a candiate for either liquidation or reorganization under the bankruptcy laws?

**25-2.** How does a preference differ from a fraudulent transfer?

# SELECTED REFERENCES

Anderson, R., I. Fox, and D. Twomey. *Business Law: Principles, Cases, Environment.* 8th ed. Cincinnati, Ohio: South-Western Publishing Company, 1983.

Collier, W. *Collier on Bankruptcy.* 15th ed. New York: Matthew Bender & Co., Inc., 1979.

Commerce Clearing House. *Bankruptcy Law Reporter.* Chicago, Ill.: Commerce Clearing House, Inc., 1979.

Herzog, A. *Bankruptcy Code.* New York: Matthew Bender & Co., Inc., 1983.

Murphy, P. *Creditors' Rights in Bankruptcy.* New York: McGraw-Hill Book Company, 1980.

West Publishing Company. *Bankruptcy Code, Rules, and Forms.* St. Paul, Minn.: West Publishing Company, 1983.

# APPENDIX TABLES

**Appendix Table A-1.**   **Compound Amount of $1**

| Year | 1% | 2% | 3% | 4% | 5% | 6% | 7% | 8% | 9% | 10% | 11% | 12% | 13% | 14% | 15% |
|---|---|---|---|---|---|---|---|---|---|---|---|---|---|---|---|
| 1 | 1.010 | 1.020 | 1.030 | 1.040 | 1.050 | 1.060 | 1.070 | 1.080 | 1.090 | 1.100 | 1.110 | 1.120 | 1.130 | 1.140 | 1.150 |
| 2 | 1.020 | 1.040 | 1.061 | 1.082 | 1.102 | 1.124 | 1.145 | 1.166 | 1.188 | 1.210 | 1.232 | 1.254 | 1.277 | 1.300 | 1.322 |
| 3 | 1.030 | 1.061 | 1.093 | 1.125 | 1.158 | 1.191 | 1.225 | 1.260 | 1.295 | 1.331 | 1.368 | 1.405 | 1.443 | 1.482 | 1.521 |
| 4 | 1.041 | 1.082 | 1.126 | 1.170 | 1.216 | 1.262 | 1.311 | 1.360 | 1.412 | 1.464 | 1.518 | 1.574 | 1.630 | 1.689 | 1.749 |
| 5 | 1.051 | 1.104 | 1.159 | 1.217 | 1.276 | 1.338 | 1.403 | 1.469 | 1.539 | 1.611 | 1.685 | 1.762 | 1.842 | 1.925 | 2.011 |
| 6 | 1.062 | 1.126 | 1.194 | 1.265 | 1.340 | 1.419 | 1.501 | 1.587 | 1.677 | 1.772 | 1.870 | 1.974 | 2.082 | 2.195 | 2.313 |
| 7 | 1.072 | 1.149 | 1.230 | 1.316 | 1.407 | 1.504 | 1.606 | 1.714 | 1.828 | 1.949 | 2.076 | 2.211 | 2.353 | 2.502 | 2.660 |
| 8 | 1.083 | 1.172 | 1.267 | 1.369 | 1.477 | 1.594 | 1.718 | 1.851 | 1.993 | 2.144 | 2.305 | 2.476 | 2.658 | 2.853 | 3.059 |
| 9 | 1.094 | 1.195 | 1.305 | 1.423 | 1.551 | 1.689 | 1.838 | 1.999 | 2.172 | 2.358 | 2.558 | 2.773 | 3.004 | 3.252 | 3.518 |
| 10 | 1.105 | 1.219 | 1.344 | 1.480 | 1.629 | 1.791 | 1.967 | 2.159 | 2.367 | 2.594 | 2.839 | 3.106 | 3.395 | 3.707 | 4.046 |
| 11 | 1.116 | 1.243 | 1.384 | 1.539 | 1.710 | 1.898 | 2.105 | 2.332 | 2.580 | 2.853 | 3.152 | 3.479 | 3.836 | 4.226 | 4.652 |
| 12 | 1.127 | 1.268 | 1.426 | 1.601 | 1.796 | 2.012 | 2.252 | 2.518 | 2.813 | 3.138 | 3.498 | 3.896 | 4.335 | 4.818 | 5.350 |
| 13 | 1.138 | 1.294 | 1.469 | 1.665 | 1.886 | 2.133 | 2.410 | 2.720 | 3.066 | 3.452 | 3.883 | 4.363 | 4.898 | 5.492 | 6.153 |
| 14 | 1.149 | 1.319 | 1.513 | 1.732 | 1.980 | 2.261 | 2.579 | 2.937 | 3.342 | 3.797 | 4.310 | 4.887 | 5.535 | 6.261 | 7.076 |
| 15 | 1.161 | 1.346 | 1.558 | 1.801 | 2.079 | 2.397 | 2.759 | 3.172 | 3.642 | 4.177 | 4.785 | 5.474 | 6.254 | 7.138 | 8.137 |
| 16 | 1.173 | 1.373 | 1.605 | 1.873 | 2.183 | 2.540 | 2.952 | 3.426 | 3.970 | 4.595 | 5.311 | 6.130 | 7.067 | 8.137 | 9.358 |
| 17 | 1.184 | 1.400 | 1.653 | 1.948 | 2.292 | 2.693 | 3.159 | 3.700 | 4.328 | 5.054 | 5.895 | 6.866 | 7.986 | 9.276 | 10.761 |
| 18 | 1.196 | 1.428 | 1.702 | 2.026 | 2.407 | 2.854 | 3.380 | 3.996 | 4.717 | 5.560 | 6.544 | 7.690 | 9.024 | 10.575 | 12.375 |
| 19 | 1.208 | 1.457 | 1.754 | 2.107 | 2.527 | 3.026 | 3.617 | 4.316 | 5.142 | 6.116 | 7.263 | 8.613 | 10.197 | 12.056 | 14.232 |
| 20 | 1.220 | 1.486 | 1.806 | 2.191 | 2.653 | 3.207 | 3.870 | 4.661 | 5.604 | 6.728 | 8.062 | 9.646 | 11.523 | 13.743 | 16.367 |
| 21 | 1.232 | 1.516 | 1.860 | 2.279 | 2.786 | 3.400 | 4.141 | 5.034 | 6.109 | 7.400 | 8.949 | 10.804 | 13.021 | 15.668 | 18.822 |
| 22 | 1.245 | 1.546 | 1.916 | 2.370 | 2.925 | 3.604 | 4.430 | 5.437 | 6.659 | 8.140 | 9.934 | 12.100 | 14.714 | 17.861 | 21.645 |
| 23 | 1.257 | 1.577 | 1.974 | 2.465 | 3.072 | 3.820 | 4.741 | 5.871 | 7.258 | 8.954 | 11.026 | 13.552 | 16.627 | 20.362 | 24.891 |
| 24 | 1.270 | 1.608 | 2.033 | 2.563 | 3.225 | 4.049 | 5.072 | 6.341 | 7.911 | 9.850 | 12.239 | 15.179 | 18.788 | 23.212 | 28.625 |
| 25 | 1.282 | 1.641 | 2.094 | 2.666 | 3.386 | 4.292 | 5.427 | 6.848 | 8.623 | 10.835 | 13.585 | 17.000 | 21.231 | 26.462 | 32.919 |
| 26 | 1.295 | 1.673 | 2.157 | 2.772 | 3.556 | 4.549 | 5.807 | 7.396 | 9.399 | 11.918 | 15.080 | 19.040 | 23.990 | 30.167 | 37.857 |
| 27 | 1.308 | 1.707 | 2.221 | 2.883 | 3.733 | 4.822 | 6.214 | 7.988 | 10.245 | 13.110 | 16.739 | 21.325 | 27.109 | 34.390 | 43.535 |
| 28 | 1.321 | 1.741 | 2.288 | 2.999 | 3.920 | 5.112 | 6.649 | 8.627 | 11.167 | 14.421 | 18.580 | 23.884 | 30.633 | 39.204 | 50.066 |
| 29 | 1.335 | 1.776 | 2.357 | 3.119 | 4.116 | 5.418 | 7.114 | 9.317 | 12.172 | 15.863 | 20.624 | 26.750 | 34.616 | 44.693 | 57.575 |
| 30 | 1.348 | 1.811 | 2.427 | 3.243 | 4.322 | 5.743 | 7.612 | 10.063 | 13.268 | 17.449 | 22.892 | 29.960 | 39.116 | 50.950 | 66.212 |

| Year | 16% | 17% | 18% | 19% | 20% | 21% | 22% | 23% | 24% | 25% | 26% | 27% | 28% | 29% | 30% |
|---|---|---|---|---|---|---|---|---|---|---|---|---|---|---|---|
| 1 | 1.160 | 1.170 | 1.180 | 1.190 | 1.200 | 1.210 | 1.220 | 1.230 | 1.240 | 1.250 | 1.260 | 1.270 | 1.280 | 1.290 | 1.300 |
| 2 | 1.346 | 1.369 | 1.392 | 1.416 | 1.440 | 1.464 | 1.488 | 1.513 | 1.538 | 1.563 | 1.588 | 1.613 | 1.638 | 1.664 | 1.690 |
| 3 | 1.561 | 1.602 | 1.643 | 1.685 | 1.728 | 1.772 | 1.816 | 1.861 | 1.907 | 1.953 | 2.000 | 2.048 | 2.097 | 2.147 | 2.197 |
| 4 | 1.811 | 1.874 | 1.939 | 2.005 | 2.074 | 2.144 | 2.215 | 2.289 | 2.364 | 2.441 | 2.520 | 2.601 | 2.684 | 2.769 | 2.856 |
| 5 | 2.100 | 2.192 | 2.288 | 2.386 | 2.488 | 2.594 | 2.703 | 2.815 | 2.932 | 3.052 | 3.176 | 3.304 | 3.436 | 3.572 | 3.713 |
| 6 | 2.436 | 2.565 | 2.700 | 2.840 | 2.986 | 3.138 | 3.297 | 3.463 | 3.635 | 3.815 | 4.002 | 4.196 | 4.398 | 4.608 | 4.827 |
| 7 | 2.826 | 3.001 | 3.185 | 3.379 | 3.583 | 3.797 | 4.023 | 4.259 | 4.508 | 4.768 | 5.042 | 5.329 | 5.629 | 5.945 | 6.275 |
| 8 | 3.278 | 3.511 | 3.759 | 4.021 | 4.300 | 4.595 | 4.908 | 5.239 | 5.590 | 5.960 | 6.353 | 6.768 | 7.206 | 7.669 | 8.157 |
| 9 | 3.803 | 4.108 | 4.435 | 4.785 | 5.160 | 5.560 | 5.987 | 6.444 | 6.931 | 7.451 | 8.005 | 8.595 | 9.223 | 9.893 | 10.604 |
| 10 | 4.411 | 4.807 | 5.234 | 5.695 | 6.192 | 6.728 | 7.305 | 7.926 | 8.594 | 9.313 | 10.086 | 10.915 | 11.806 | 12.761 | 13.786 |
| 11 | 5.117 | 5.624 | 6.176 | 6.777 | 7.430 | 8.140 | 8.912 | 9.749 | 10.657 | 11.642 | 12.708 | 13.862 | 15.112 | 16.462 | 17.922 |
| 12 | 5.936 | 6.580 | 7.288 | 8.064 | 8.916 | 9.850 | 10.872 | 11.991 | 13.215 | 14.552 | 16.012 | 17.605 | 19.343 | 21.236 | 23.298 |
| 13 | 6.886 | 7.699 | 8.599 | 9.596 | 10.699 | 11.918 | 13.264 | 14.749 | 16.386 | 18.190 | 20.175 | 22.359 | 24.759 | 27.395 | 30.287 |
| 14 | 7.988 | 9.007 | 10.147 | 11.420 | 12.839 | 14.421 | 16.182 | 18.141 | 20.319 | 22.737 | 25.421 | 28.396 | 31.691 | 35.339 | 39.374 |
| 15 | 9.266 | 10.539 | 11.974 | 13.590 | 15.407 | 17.449 | 19.742 | 22.314 | 25.196 | 28.422 | 32.030 | 36.062 | 40.565 | 45.587 | 51.186 |
| 16 | 10.748 | 12.330 | 14.129 | 16.172 | 18.488 | 21.114 | 24.086 | 27.446 | 31.243 | 35.527 | 40.358 | 45.799 | 51.923 | 58.808 | 66.542 |
| 17 | 12.468 | 14.426 | 16.672 | 19.244 | 22.186 | 25.548 | 29.384 | 33.759 | 38.741 | 44.409 | 50.851 | 58.165 | 66.461 | 75.862 | 86.504 |
| 18 | 14.463 | 16.879 | 19.673 | 22.901 | 26.623 | 30.913 | 35.849 | 41.523 | 48.039 | 55.511 | 64.072 | 73.870 | 85.071 | 97.862 | 112.46 |
| 19 | 16.777 | 19.748 | 23.214 | 27.252 | 31.948 | 37.404 | 43.736 | 51.074 | 59.568 | 69.389 | 80.731 | 93.815 | 108.89 | 126.24 | 146.19 |
| 20 | 19.461 | 23.106 | 27.393 | 32.429 | 38.338 | 45.259 | 53.358 | 62.821 | 73.864 | 86.736 | 101.72 | 119.14 | 139.38 | 162.85 | 190.05 |
| 21 | 22.574 | 27.034 | 32.324 | 38.591 | 46.005 | 54.764 | 65.096 | 77.269 | 91.592 | 108.42 | 128.17 | 151.31 | 178.41 | 210.08 | 247.06 |
| 22 | 26.186 | 31.629 | 38.142 | 45.923 | 55.206 | 66.264 | 79.418 | 95.041 | 113.57 | 135.53 | 161.49 | 192.17 | 228.36 | 271.00 | 321.18 |
| 23 | 30.376 | 37.006 | 45.008 | 54.649 | 66.247 | 80.180 | 96.889 | 116.90 | 140.83 | 169.41 | 203.48 | 244.05 | 292.30 | 349.59 | 417.54 |
| 24 | 35.236 | 43.297 | 53.109 | 65.032 | 79.497 | 97.017 | 118.21 | 143.79 | 174.63 | 211.76 | 256.39 | 309.95 | 374.14 | 450.98 | 542.80 |
| 25 | 40.874 | 50.658 | 62.669 | 77.388 | 95.396 | 117.39 | 144.21 | 176.86 | 216.54 | 264.70 | 323.05 | 393.63 | 478.90 | 581.76 | 705.64 |
| 26 | 47.414 | 59.270 | 73.949 | 92.092 | 114.48 | 142.04 | 175.94 | 217.54 | 268.51 | 330.87 | 407.04 | 499.92 | 613.00 | 750.47 | 917.33 |
| 27 | 55.000 | 69.345 | 87.260 | 109.59 | 137.37 | 171.87 | 214.64 | 267.57 | 332.96 | 413.59 | 512.87 | 634.89 | 784.64 | 968.10 | 1192.5 |
| 28 | 63.800 | 81.134 | 102.97 | 130.41 | 164.84 | 207.97 | 261.86 | 329.11 | 412.86 | 516.99 | 646.21 | 806.31 | 1004.3 | 1248.9 | 1550.3 |
| 29 | 74.008 | 94.927 | 121.50 | 155.19 | 197.81 | 251.64 | 319.47 | 404.81 | 511.95 | 646.23 | 814.23 | 1024.0 | 1285.5 | 1611.0 | 2015.4 |
| 30 | 85.850 | 111.06 | 143.37 | 184.68 | 237.38 | 304.48 | 389.76 | 497.91 | 634.82 | 807.79 | 1025.9 | 1300.5 | 1645.5 | 2078.2 | 2620.0 |

## Appendix Table A-2.　Compound Amount of an Annuity of $1

| n | 1% | 2% | 3% | 4% | 5% | 6% | 7% | 8% | 9% | 10% | 11% | 12% | 13% | 14% | 15% |
|---|---|---|---|---|---|---|---|---|---|---|---|---|---|---|---|
| 1 | 1.000 | 1.000 | 1.000 | 1.000 | 1.000 | 1.000 | 1.000 | 1.000 | 1.000 | 1.000 | 1.000 | 1.000 | 1.000 | 1.000 | 1.000 |
| 2 | 2.010 | 2.020 | 2.030 | 2.040 | 2.050 | 2.060 | 2.070 | 2.080 | 2.090 | 2.100 | 2.110 | 2.120 | 2.130 | 2.140 | 2.150 |
| 3 | 3.030 | 3.060 | 3.091 | 3.122 | 3.152 | 3.184 | 3.215 | 3.246 | 3.278 | 3.310 | 3.342 | 3.374 | 3.407 | 3.440 | 3.472 |
| 4 | 4.060 | 4.122 | 4.184 | 4.246 | 4.310 | 4.375 | 4.440 | 4.506 | 4.573 | 4.641 | 4.710 | 4.779 | 4.850 | 4.921 | 4.993 |
| 5 | 5.101 | 5.204 | 5.309 | 5.416 | 5.526 | 5.637 | 5.751 | 5.867 | 5.985 | 6.105 | 6.228 | 6.353 | 6.480 | 6.610 | 6.742 |
| 6 | 6.152 | 6.308 | 6.468 | 6.633 | 6.802 | 6.975 | 7.153 | 7.336 | 7.523 | 7.716 | 7.913 | 8.115 | 8.323 | 8.536 | 8.754 |
| 7 | 7.214 | 7.434 | 7.662 | 7.898 | 8.142 | 8.394 | 8.654 | 8.923 | 9.200 | 9.487 | 9.783 | 10.089 | 10.405 | 10.730 | 11.067 |
| 8 | 8.286 | 8.583 | 8.892 | 9.214 | 9.549 | 9.897 | 10.260 | 10.637 | 11.028 | 11.436 | 11.859 | 12.300 | 12.757 | 13.233 | 13.727 |
| 9 | 9.369 | 9.755 | 10.159 | 10.583 | 11.027 | 11.491 | 11.978 | 12.488 | 13.021 | 13.579 | 14.164 | 14.776 | 15.416 | 16.085 | 16.786 |
| 10 | 10.462 | 10.950 | 11.464 | 12.006 | 12.578 | 13.181 | 13.816 | 14.487 | 15.193 | 15.937 | 16.722 | 17.549 | 18.420 | 19.337 | 20.304 |
| 11 | 11.567 | 12.169 | 12.808 | 13.486 | 14.207 | 14.972 | 15.784 | 16.645 | 17.560 | 18.531 | 19.561 | 20.655 | 21.814 | 23.045 | 24.349 |
| 12 | 12.682 | 13.412 | 14.192 | 15.026 | 15.917 | 16.870 | 17.888 | 18.977 | 20.141 | 21.384 | 22.713 | 24.133 | 25.650 | 27.271 | 29.002 |
| 13 | 13.809 | 14.680 | 15.618 | 16.627 | 17.713 | 18.882 | 20.141 | 21.495 | 22.953 | 24.523 | 26.212 | 28.029 | 29.985 | 32.089 | 34.352 |
| 14 | 14.947 | 15.974 | 17.086 | 18.292 | 19.599 | 21.015 | 22.551 | 24.215 | 26.019 | 27.975 | 30.095 | 32.393 | 34.883 | 37.581 | 40.505 |
| 15 | 16.097 | 17.293 | 18.599 | 20.024 | 21.579 | 23.276 | 25.129 | 27.152 | 29.361 | 31.772 | 34.405 | 37.280 | 40.417 | 43.842 | 47.580 |
| 16 | 17.258 | 18.639 | 20.157 | 21.825 | 23.657 | 25.672 | 27.888 | 30.324 | 33.003 | 35.950 | 39.190 | 42.753 | 46.672 | 50.980 | 55.717 |
| 17 | 18.430 | 20.012 | 21.762 | 23.697 | 25.840 | 28.213 | 30.840 | 33.750 | 36.974 | 40.545 | 44.501 | 48.884 | 53.739 | 59.118 | 65.075 |
| 18 | 19.615 | 21.412 | 23.414 | 25.645 | 28.132 | 30.906 | 33.999 | 37.450 | 41.301 | 45.599 | 50.396 | 55.750 | 61.725 | 68.394 | 75.836 |
| 19 | 20.811 | 22.840 | 25.117 | 27.671 | 30.539 | 33.760 | 37.379 | 41.446 | 46.019 | 51.159 | 56.939 | 63.440 | 70.749 | 78.969 | 88.212 |
| 20 | 22.019 | 24.297 | 26.870 | 29.778 | 33.066 | 36.786 | 40.996 | 45.762 | 51.160 | 57.275 | 64.203 | 72.052 | 80.947 | 91.025 | 102.44 |
| 21 | 23.239 | 25.783 | 28.676 | 31.969 | 35.719 | 39.993 | 44.865 | 50.423 | 56.765 | 64.003 | 72.265 | 81.699 | 92.470 | 104.77 | 118.81 |
| 22 | 24.472 | 27.299 | 30.537 | 34.248 | 38.505 | 43.392 | 49.006 | 55.457 | 62.873 | 71.403 | 81.214 | 92.503 | 105.49 | 120.44 | 137.63 |
| 23 | 25.716 | 28.845 | 32.453 | 36.618 | 41.430 | 46.996 | 53.436 | 60.893 | 69.532 | 79.543 | 91.148 | 104.60 | 120.20 | 138.30 | 159.28 |
| 24 | 26.973 | 30.422 | 34.426 | 39.083 | 44.502 | 50.815 | 58.177 | 66.765 | 76.790 | 88.497 | 102.17 | 118.16 | 136.83 | 158.66 | 184.17 |
| 25 | 28.243 | 32.030 | 36.459 | 41.646 | 47.727 | 54.864 | 63.249 | 73.106 | 84.701 | 98.347 | 114.41 | 133.33 | 155.62 | 181.87 | 212.79 |
| 26 | 29.526 | 33.671 | 38.553 | 44.312 | 51.113 | 59.156 | 68.677 | 79.954 | 93.324 | 109.18 | 128.00 | 150.33 | 176.85 | 208.33 | 245.71 |
| 27 | 30.821 | 35.344 | 40.710 | 47.084 | 54.669 | 63.706 | 74.484 | 87.351 | 102.72 | 121.10 | 143.08 | 169.37 | 200.84 | 238.50 | 283.57 |
| 28 | 32.129 | 37.051 | 42.931 | 49.968 | 58.402 | 68.528 | 80.698 | 95.339 | 112.97 | 134.21 | 159.82 | 190.70 | 227.95 | 272.89 | 327.10 |
| 29 | 33.450 | 38.792 | 45.219 | 52.966 | 62.323 | 73.640 | 87.347 | 103.97 | 124.14 | 148.63 | 178.40 | 214.58 | 258.58 | 312.09 | 377.17 |
| 30 | 34.785 | 40.568 | 47.575 | 56.085 | 66.439 | 79.058 | 94.461 | 113.28 | 136.31 | 164.49 | 199.02 | 241.33 | 293.20 | 356.79 | 434.75 |

| n | 16% | 17% | 18% | 19% | 20% | 21% | 22% | 23% | 24% | 25% | 26% | 27% | 28% | 29% | 30% |
|---|-----|-----|-----|-----|-----|-----|-----|-----|-----|-----|-----|-----|-----|-----|-----|
| 1 | 1.000 | 1.000 | 1.000 | 1.000 | 1.000 | 1.000 | 1.000 | 1.000 | 1.000 | 1.000 | 1.000 | 1.000 | 1.000 | 1.000 | 1.000 |
| 2 | 2.160 | 2.170 | 2.180 | 2.190 | 2.200 | 2.210 | 2.220 | 2.230 | 2.240 | 2.250 | 2.260 | 2.270 | 2.280 | 2.290 | 2.300 |
| 3 | 3.506 | 3.539 | 3.572 | 3.606 | 3.640 | 3.674 | 3.708 | 3.743 | 3.778 | 3.813 | 3.848 | 3.883 | 3.918 | 3.954 | 3.990 |
| 4 | 5.066 | 5.141 | 5.215 | 5.291 | 5.368 | 5.446 | 5.524 | 5.604 | 5.684 | 5.766 | 5.848 | 5.931 | 6.016 | 6.101 | 6.187 |
| 5 | 6.877 | 7.014 | 7.154 | 7.297 | 7.442 | 7.589 | 7.740 | 7.893 | 8.048 | 8.207 | 8.368 | 8.533 | 8.700 | 8.870 | 9.043 |
| 6 | 8.977 | 9.207 | 9.442 | 9.683 | 9.930 | 10.183 | 10.442 | 10.708 | 10.980 | 11.259 | 11.544 | 11.837 | 12.136 | 12.442 | 12.756 |
| 7 | 11.414 | 11.772 | 12.142 | 12.523 | 12.916 | 13.321 | 13.740 | 14.171 | 14.615 | 15.073 | 15.546 | 16.032 | 16.534 | 17.051 | 17.583 |
| 8 | 14.240 | 14.773 | 15.327 | 15.902 | 16.499 | 17.119 | 17.762 | 18.430 | 19.123 | 19.842 | 20.588 | 21.361 | 22.163 | 22.995 | 23.858 |
| 9 | 17.518 | 18.285 | 19.086 | 19.923 | 20.799 | 21.714 | 22.670 | 23.669 | 24.712 | 25.802 | 26.940 | 28.129 | 29.369 | 30.664 | 32.015 |
| 10 | 21.321 | 22.393 | 23.521 | 24.709 | 25.959 | 27.274 | 28.657 | 30.113 | 31.643 | 33.253 | 34.945 | 36.723 | 38.593 | 40.556 | 42.619 |
| 11 | 25.733 | 27.200 | 28.755 | 30.404 | 32.150 | 34.001 | 35.962 | 38.039 | 40.238 | 42.566 | 45.031 | 47.639 | 50.398 | 53.318 | 56.405 |
| 12 | 30.850 | 32.824 | 34.931 | 37.180 | 39.581 | 42.142 | 44.874 | 47.788 | 50.895 | 54.208 | 57.739 | 61.501 | 65.510 | 69.780 | 74.327 |
| 13 | 36.786 | 39.404 | 42.219 | 45.244 | 48.497 | 51.991 | 55.746 | 59.779 | 64.110 | 68.760 | 73.751 | 79.107 | 84.853 | 91.016 | 97.625 |
| 14 | 43.672 | 47.103 | 50.818 | 54.841 | 59.196 | 63.910 | 69.010 | 74.528 | 80.496 | 86.949 | 93.926 | 101.47 | 109.61 | 118.41 | 127.91 |
| 15 | 51.659 | 56.110 | 60.965 | 66.261 | 72.035 | 78.331 | 85.192 | 92.669 | 100.82 | 109.69 | 119.35 | 129.86 | 141.30 | 153.75 | 167.29 |
| 16 | 60.925 | 66.649 | 72.939 | 79.850 | 87.442 | 95.780 | 104.93 | 114.98 | 126.01 | 138.11 | 151.38 | 165.92 | 181.87 | 199.34 | 218.47 |
| 17 | 71.673 | 78.979 | 87.068 | 96.022 | 105.93 | 116.89 | 129.02 | 142.43 | 157.25 | 173.64 | 191.73 | 211.72 | 233.79 | 258.15 | 285.01 |
| 18 | 84.141 | 93.406 | 103.74 | 115.27 | 128.12 | 142.44 | 158.40 | 176.19 | 195.99 | 218.04 | 242.59 | 269.89 | 300.25 | 334.01 | 371.52 |
| 19 | 98.603 | 110.28 | 123.41 | 138.17 | 154.74 | 173.35 | 194.25 | 217.71 | 244.03 | 273.56 | 306.66 | 343.76 | 385.32 | 431.87 | 483.97 |
| 20 | 115.38 | 130.03 | 146.63 | 165.42 | 186.69 | 210.76 | 237.99 | 268.79 | 303.60 | 342.94 | 387.39 | 437.57 | 494.21 | 558.11 | 630.16 |
| 21 | 134.84 | 153.14 | 174.02 | 197.85 | 225.03 | 256.02 | 291.35 | 331.61 | 377.46 | 429.68 | 489.11 | 556.72 | 633.59 | 720.96 | 820.21 |
| 22 | 157.41 | 180.17 | 206.35 | 236.44 | 271.03 | 310.78 | 356.44 | 408.88 | 469.06 | 538.10 | 617.28 | 708.03 | 812.00 | 931.04 | 1067.3 |
| 23 | 183.60 | 211.80 | 244.49 | 282.36 | 326.24 | 377.05 | 435.86 | 503.92 | 582.63 | 673.63 | 778.77 | 900.20 | 1040.4 | 1202.0 | 1388.5 |
| 24 | 213.98 | 248.81 | 289.49 | 337.01 | 392.48 | 457.23 | 532.75 | 620.82 | 723.46 | 843.03 | 982.25 | 1144.3 | 1332.7 | 1551.6 | 1806.0 |
| 25 | 249.21 | 292.10 | 342.60 | 402.04 | 471.98 | 554.24 | 650.96 | 764.61 | 898.09 | 1054.8 | 1238.6 | 1454.2 | 1706.8 | 2002.6 | 2348.8 |
| 26 | 290.09 | 342.76 | 405.27 | 479.43 | 567.38 | 671.63 | 795.17 | 941.46 | 1114.6 | 1319.5 | 1561.7 | 1847.8 | 2185.7 | 2584.4 | 3054.4 |
| 27 | 337.50 | 402.03 | 479.22 | 571.52 | 681.85 | 813.68 | 971.10 | 1159.0 | 1383.1 | 1650.4 | 1968.7 | 2347.7 | 2798.7 | 3334.8 | 3971.8 |
| 28 | 392.50 | 471.38 | 566.48 | 681.11 | 819.22 | 985.55 | 1185.7 | 1426.6 | 1716.1 | 2064.0 | 2481.6 | 2982.6 | 3583.3 | 4302.9 | 5164.3 |
| 29 | 456.30 | 552.51 | 669.45 | 811.52 | 984.07 | 1193.5 | 1447.6 | 1755.7 | 2129.0 | 2580.9 | 3127.8 | 3789.0 | 4587.7 | 5551.8 | 6714.6 |
| 30 | 530.31 | 647.44 | 790.95 | 966.71 | 1181.9 | 1445.2 | 1767.1 | 2160.5 | 2640.9 | 3227.2 | 3942.0 | 4813.0 | 5873.2 | 7162.8 | 8730.0 |

# Appendix Table A-3.  Present Value of $1

| Year | 1% | 2% | 3% | 4% | 5% | 6% | 7% | 8% | 9% | 10% | 11% | 12% | 13% | 14% | 15% |
|---|---|---|---|---|---|---|---|---|---|---|---|---|---|---|---|
| 1 | 0.990 | 0.980 | 0.971 | 0.962 | 0.952 | 0.943 | 0.935 | 0.926 | 0.917 | 0.909 | 0.901 | 0.893 | 0.885 | 0.877 | 0.870 |
| 2 | 0.980 | 0.961 | 0.943 | 0.925 | 0.907 | 0.890 | 0.873 | 0.857 | 0.842 | 0.826 | 0.812 | 0.797 | 0.783 | 0.769 | 0.756 |
| 3 | 0.971 | 0.942 | 0.915 | 0.889 | 0.864 | 0.840 | 0.816 | 0.794 | 0.772 | 0.751 | 0.731 | 0.712 | 0.693 | 0.675 | 0.658 |
| 4 | 0.961 | 0.924 | 0.888 | 0.855 | 0.823 | 0.792 | 0.763 | 0.735 | 0.708 | 0.683 | 0.659 | 0.636 | 0.613 | 0.592 | 0.572 |
| 5 | 0.951 | 0.906 | 0.863 | 0.822 | 0.784 | 0.747 | 0.713 | 0.681 | 0.650 | 0.621 | 0.593 | 0.567 | 0.543 | 0.519 | 0.497 |
| 6 | 0.942 | 0.888 | 0.837 | 0.790 | 0.746 | 0.705 | 0.666 | 0.630 | 0.596 | 0.564 | 0.535 | 0.507 | 0.480 | 0.456 | 0.432 |
| 7 | 0.933 | 0.871 | 0.813 | 0.760 | 0.711 | 0.665 | 0.623 | 0.583 | 0.547 | 0.513 | 0.482 | 0.452 | 0.425 | 0.400 | 0.376 |
| 8 | 0.923 | 0.853 | 0.789 | 0.731 | 0.677 | 0.627 | 0.582 | 0.540 | 0.502 | 0.467 | 0.434 | 0.404 | 0.376 | 0.351 | 0.327 |
| 9 | 0.914 | 0.837 | 0.766 | 0.703 | 0.645 | 0.592 | 0.544 | 0.500 | 0.460 | 0.424 | 0.391 | 0.361 | 0.333 | 0.308 | 0.284 |
| 10 | 0.905 | 0.820 | 0.744 | 0.676 | 0.614 | 0.558 | 0.508 | 0.463 | 0.422 | 0.386 | 0.352 | 0.322 | 0.295 | 0.270 | 0.247 |
| 11 | 0.896 | 0.804 | 0.722 | 0.650 | 0.585 | 0.527 | 0.475 | 0.429 | 0.388 | 0.350 | 0.317 | 0.287 | 0.261 | 0.237 | 0.215 |
| 12 | 0.887 | 0.788 | 0.701 | 0.625 | 0.557 | 0.497 | 0.444 | 0.397 | 0.356 | 0.319 | 0.286 | 0.257 | 0.231 | 0.208 | 0.187 |
| 13 | 0.879 | 0.773 | 0.681 | 0.601 | 0.530 | 0.469 | 0.415 | 0.368 | 0.326 | 0.290 | 0.258 | 0.229 | 0.204 | 0.182 | 0.163 |
| 14 | 0.870 | 0.758 | 0.661 | 0.577 | 0.505 | 0.442 | 0.388 | 0.340 | 0.299 | 0.263 | 0.232 | 0.205 | 0.181 | 0.160 | 0.141 |
| 15 | 0.861 | 0.743 | 0.642 | 0.555 | 0.481 | 0.417 | 0.362 | 0.315 | 0.275 | 0.239 | 0.209 | 0.183 | 0.160 | 0.140 | 0.123 |
| 16 | 0.853 | 0.728 | 0.623 | 0.534 | 0.458 | 0.394 | 0.339 | 0.292 | 0.252 | 0.218 | 0.188 | 0.163 | 0.141 | 0.123 | 0.107 |
| 17 | 0.844 | 0.714 | 0.605 | 0.513 | 0.436 | 0.371 | 0.317 | 0.270 | 0.231 | 0.198 | 0.170 | 0.146 | 0.125 | 0.108 | 0.093 |
| 18 | 0.836 | 0.700 | 0.587 | 0.494 | 0.416 | 0.350 | 0.296 | 0.250 | 0.212 | 0.180 | 0.153 | 0.130 | 0.111 | 0.095 | 0.081 |
| 19 | 0.828 | 0.686 | 0.570 | 0.475 | 0.396 | 0.331 | 0.277 | 0.232 | 0.194 | 0.164 | 0.138 | 0.116 | 0.098 | 0.083 | 0.070 |
| 20 | 0.820 | 0.673 | 0.554 | 0.456 | 0.377 | 0.312 | 0.258 | 0.215 | 0.178 | 0.149 | 0.124 | 0.104 | 0.087 | 0.073 | 0.061 |
| 21 | 0.811 | 0.660 | 0.538 | 0.439 | 0.359 | 0.294 | 0.242 | 0.199 | 0.164 | 0.135 | 0.112 | 0.093 | 0.077 | 0.064 | 0.053 |
| 22 | 0.803 | 0.647 | 0.522 | 0.422 | 0.342 | 0.278 | 0.226 | 0.184 | 0.150 | 0.123 | 0.101 | 0.083 | 0.068 | 0.056 | 0.046 |
| 23 | 0.795 | 0.634 | 0.507 | 0.406 | 0.326 | 0.262 | 0.211 | 0.170 | 0.138 | 0.112 | 0.091 | 0.074 | 0.060 | 0.049 | 0.040 |
| 24 | 0.788 | 0.622 | 0.492 | 0.390 | 0.310 | 0.247 | 0.197 | 0.158 | 0.126 | 0.102 | 0.082 | 0.066 | 0.053 | 0.043 | 0.035 |
| 25 | 0.780 | 0.610 | 0.478 | 0.375 | 0.295 | 0.233 | 0.184 | 0.146 | 0.116 | 0.092 | 0.074 | 0.059 | 0.047 | 0.038 | 0.030 |
| 26 | 0.772 | 0.598 | 0.464 | 0.361 | 0.281 | 0.220 | 0.172 | 0.135 | 0.106 | 0.084 | 0.066 | 0.053 | 0.042 | 0.033 | 0.026 |
| 27 | 0.764 | 0.586 | 0.450 | 0.347 | 0.268 | 0.207 | 0.161 | 0.125 | 0.098 | 0.076 | 0.060 | 0.047 | 0.037 | 0.029 | 0.023 |
| 28 | 0.757 | 0.574 | 0.437 | 0.333 | 0.255 | 0.196 | 0.150 | 0.116 | 0.090 | 0.069 | 0.054 | 0.042 | 0.033 | 0.026 | 0.020 |
| 29 | 0.749 | 0.563 | 0.424 | 0.321 | 0.243 | 0.185 | 0.141 | 0.107 | 0.082 | 0.063 | 0.048 | 0.037 | 0.029 | 0.022 | 0.017 |
| 30 | 0.742 | 0.552 | 0.412 | 0.308 | 0.231 | 0.174 | 0.131 | 0.099 | 0.075 | 0.057 | 0.044 | 0.033 | 0.026 | 0.020 | 0.015 |

| Year | 16% | 17% | 18% | 19% | 20% | 21% | 22% | 23% | 24% | 25% | 26% | 27% | 28% | 29% | 30% |
|------|-----|-----|-----|-----|-----|-----|-----|-----|-----|-----|-----|-----|-----|-----|-----|
| 1 | 0.862 | 0.855 | 0.847 | 0.840 | 0.833 | 0.826 | 0.820 | 0.813 | 0.806 | 0.800 | 0.794 | 0.787 | 0.781 | 0.775 | 0.769 |
| 2 | 0.743 | 0.731 | 0.718 | 0.706 | 0.694 | 0.683 | 0.672 | 0.661 | 0.650 | 0.640 | 0.630 | 0.620 | 0.610 | 0.601 | 0.592 |
| 3 | 0.641 | 0.624 | 0.609 | 0.593 | 0.579 | 0.564 | 0.551 | 0.537 | 0.524 | 0.512 | 0.500 | 0.488 | 0.477 | 0.466 | 0.455 |
| 4 | 0.552 | 0.534 | 0.516 | 0.499 | 0.482 | 0.467 | 0.451 | 0.437 | 0.423 | 0.410 | 0.397 | 0.384 | 0.373 | 0.361 | 0.350 |
| 5 | 0.476 | 0.456 | 0.437 | 0.419 | 0.402 | 0.386 | 0.370 | 0.355 | 0.341 | 0.328 | 0.315 | 0.303 | 0.291 | 0.280 | 0.269 |
| 6 | 0.410 | 0.390 | 0.370 | 0.352 | 0.335 | 0.319 | 0.303 | 0.289 | 0.275 | 0.262 | 0.250 | 0.238 | 0.227 | 0.217 | 0.207 |
| 7 | 0.354 | 0.333 | 0.314 | 0.296 | 0.279 | 0.263 | 0.249 | 0.235 | 0.222 | 0.210 | 0.198 | 0.188 | 0.178 | 0.168 | 0.159 |
| 8 | 0.305 | 0.285 | 0.266 | 0.249 | 0.233 | 0.218 | 0.204 | 0.191 | 0.179 | 0.168 | 0.157 | 0.148 | 0.139 | 0.130 | 0.123 |
| 9 | 0.263 | 0.243 | 0.225 | 0.209 | 0.194 | 0.180 | 0.167 | 0.155 | 0.144 | 0.134 | 0.125 | 0.116 | 0.108 | 0.101 | 0.094 |
| 10 | 0.227 | 0.208 | 0.191 | 0.176 | 0.162 | 0.149 | 0.137 | 0.126 | 0.116 | 0.107 | 0.099 | 0.092 | 0.085 | 0.078 | 0.073 |
| 11 | 0.195 | 0.178 | 0.162 | 0.148 | 0.135 | 0.123 | 0.112 | 0.103 | 0.094 | 0.086 | 0.079 | 0.072 | 0.066 | 0.061 | 0.056 |
| 12 | 0.168 | 0.152 | 0.137 | 0.124 | 0.112 | 0.102 | 0.092 | 0.083 | 0.076 | 0.069 | 0.062 | 0.057 | 0.052 | 0.047 | 0.043 |
| 13 | 0.145 | 0.130 | 0.116 | 0.104 | 0.093 | 0.084 | 0.075 | 0.068 | 0.061 | 0.055 | 0.050 | 0.045 | 0.040 | 0.037 | 0.033 |
| 14 | 0.125 | 0.111 | 0.099 | 0.088 | 0.078 | 0.069 | 0.062 | 0.055 | 0.049 | 0.044 | 0.039 | 0.035 | 0.032 | 0.028 | 0.025 |
| 15 | 0.108 | 0.095 | 0.084 | 0.074 | 0.065 | 0.057 | 0.051 | 0.045 | 0.040 | 0.035 | 0.031 | 0.028 | 0.025 | 0.022 | 0.020 |
| 16 | 0.093 | 0.081 | 0.071 | 0.062 | 0.054 | 0.047 | 0.042 | 0.036 | 0.032 | 0.028 | 0.025 | 0.022 | 0.019 | 0.017 | 0.015 |
| 17 | 0.080 | 0.069 | 0.060 | 0.052 | 0.045 | 0.039 | 0.034 | 0.030 | 0.026 | 0.023 | 0.020 | 0.017 | 0.015 | 0.013 | 0.012 |
| 18 | 0.069 | 0.059 | 0.051 | 0.044 | 0.038 | 0.032 | 0.028 | 0.024 | 0.021 | 0.018 | 0.016 | 0.014 | 0.012 | 0.010 | 0.009 |
| 19 | 0.060 | 0.051 | 0.043 | 0.037 | 0.031 | 0.027 | 0.023 | 0.020 | 0.017 | 0.014 | 0.012 | 0.011 | 0.009 | 0.008 | 0.007 |
| 20 | 0.051 | 0.043 | 0.037 | 0.031 | 0.026 | 0.022 | 0.019 | 0.016 | 0.014 | 0.012 | 0.010 | 0.008 | 0.007 | 0.006 | 0.005 |
| 21 | 0.044 | 0.037 | 0.031 | 0.026 | 0.022 | 0.018 | 0.015 | 0.013 | 0.011 | 0.009 | 0.008 | 0.007 | 0.006 | 0.005 | 0.004 |
| 22 | 0.038 | 0.032 | 0.026 | 0.022 | 0.018 | 0.015 | 0.013 | 0.011 | 0.009 | 0.007 | 0.006 | 0.005 | 0.004 | 0.004 | 0.003 |
| 23 | 0.033 | 0.027 | 0.022 | 0.018 | 0.015 | 0.012 | 0.010 | 0.009 | 0.007 | 0.006 | 0.005 | 0.004 | 0.003 | 0.003 | 0.002 |
| 24 | 0.028 | 0.023 | 0.019 | 0.015 | 0.013 | 0.010 | 0.008 | 0.007 | 0.006 | 0.005 | 0.004 | 0.003 | 0.003 | 0.002 | 0.002 |
| 25 | 0.024 | 0.020 | 0.016 | 0.013 | 0.010 | 0.009 | 0.007 | 0.006 | 0.005 | 0.004 | 0.003 | 0.003 | 0.002 | 0.002 | 0.001 |
| 26 | 0.021 | 0.017 | 0.014 | 0.011 | 0.009 | 0.007 | 0.006 | 0.005 | 0.004 | 0.003 | 0.002 | 0.002 | 0.002 | 0.001 | 0.001 |
| 27 | 0.018 | 0.014 | 0.011 | 0.009 | 0.007 | 0.006 | 0.005 | 0.004 | 0.003 | 0.002 | 0.002 | 0.002 | 0.001 | 0.001 | 0.001 |
| 28 | 0.016 | 0.012 | 0.010 | 0.008 | 0.006 | 0.005 | 0.004 | 0.003 | 0.002 | 0.002 | 0.001 | 0.001 | 0.001 | 0.001 | 0.001 |
| 29 | 0.014 | 0.011 | 0.008 | 0.006 | 0.005 | 0.004 | 0.003 | 0.002 | 0.002 | 0.002 | 0.001 | 0.001 | 0.001 | 0.001 | 0.000 |
| 30 | 0.012 | 0.009 | 0.007 | 0.005 | 0.004 | 0.003 | 0.003 | 0.002 | 0.002 | 0.001 | 0.001 | 0.001 | 0.001 | 0.000 | 0.000 |

## Appendix Table A-4.

### Present Value of an Annuity of $1

| n | 1% | 2% | 3% | 4% | 5% | 6% | 7% | 8% | 9% | 10% | 11% | 12% | 13% | 14% | 15% |
|---|------|------|------|------|------|------|------|------|------|------|------|------|------|------|------|
| 1 | 0.990 | 0.980 | 0.971 | 0.962 | 0.952 | 0.943 | 0.935 | 0.926 | 0.917 | 0.909 | 0.901 | 0.893 | 0.885 | 0.877 | 0.870 |
| 2 | 1.970 | 1.942 | 1.913 | 1.886 | 1.859 | 1.833 | 1.808 | 1.783 | 1.759 | 1.736 | 1.713 | 1.690 | 1.668 | 1.647 | 1.626 |
| 3 | 2.941 | 2.884 | 2.829 | 2.775 | 2.723 | 2.673 | 2.624 | 2.577 | 2.531 | 2.487 | 2.444 | 2.402 | 2.361 | 2.322 | 2.283 |
| 4 | 3.902 | 3.808 | 3.717 | 3.630 | 3.546 | 3.465 | 3.387 | 3.312 | 3.240 | 3.170 | 3.102 | 3.037 | 2.974 | 2.914 | 2.855 |
| 5 | 4.853 | 4.713 | 4.580 | 4.452 | 4.329 | 4.212 | 4.100 | 3.993 | 3.890 | 3.791 | 3.696 | 3.605 | 3.517 | 3.433 | 3.352 |
| 6 | 5.795 | 5.601 | 5.417 | 5.242 | 5.076 | 4.917 | 4.767 | 4.623 | 4.486 | 4.355 | 4.231 | 4.111 | 3.998 | 3.889 | 3.784 |
| 7 | 6.728 | 6.472 | 6.230 | 6.002 | 5.786 | 5.582 | 5.389 | 5.206 | 5.033 | 4.868 | 4.712 | 4.564 | 4.423 | 4.288 | 4.160 |
| 8 | 7.652 | 7.325 | 7.020 | 6.733 | 6.463 | 6.210 | 5.971 | 5.747 | 5.535 | 5.335 | 5.146 | 4.968 | 4.799 | 4.639 | 4.487 |
| 9 | 8.566 | 8.162 | 7.786 | 7.435 | 7.108 | 6.802 | 6.515 | 6.247 | 5.995 | 5.759 | 5.537 | 5.328 | 5.132 | 4.946 | 4.772 |
| 10 | 9.471 | 8.983 | 8.530 | 8.111 | 7.722 | 7.360 | 7.024 | 6.710 | 6.418 | 6.145 | 5.889 | 5.650 | 5.426 | 5.216 | 5.019 |
| 11 | 10.368 | 9.787 | 9.253 | 8.760 | 8.306 | 7.887 | 7.499 | 7.139 | 6.805 | 6.495 | 6.207 | 5.938 | 5.687 | 5.453 | 5.234 |
| 12 | 11.255 | 10.575 | 9.954 | 9.385 | 8.863 | 8.384 | 7.943 | 7.536 | 7.161 | 6.814 | 6.492 | 6.194 | 5.918 | 5.660 | 5.421 |
| 13 | 12.134 | 11.348 | 10.635 | 9.986 | 9.394 | 8.853 | 8.358 | 7.904 | 7.487 | 7.103 | 6.750 | 6.424 | 6.122 | 5.842 | 5.583 |
| 14 | 13.004 | 12.106 | 11.296 | 10.563 | 9.899 | 9.295 | 8.745 | 8.244 | 7.786 | 7.367 | 6.982 | 6.628 | 6.302 | 6.002 | 5.724 |
| 15 | 13.865 | 12.849 | 11.938 | 11.118 | 10.380 | 9.712 | 9.108 | 8.559 | 8.061 | 7.606 | 7.191 | 6.811 | 6.462 | 6.142 | 5.847 |
| 16 | 14.718 | 13.578 | 12.561 | 11.652 | 10.838 | 10.106 | 9.447 | 8.851 | 8.313 | 7.824 | 7.379 | 6.974 | 6.604 | 6.265 | 5.954 |
| 17 | 15.562 | 14.292 | 13.166 | 12.166 | 11.274 | 10.477 | 9.763 | 9.122 | 8.544 | 8.022 | 7.549 | 7.120 | 6.729 | 6.373 | 6.047 |
| 18 | 16.398 | 14.992 | 13.754 | 12.659 | 11.690 | 10.828 | 10.059 | 9.372 | 8.756 | 8.201 | 7.702 | 7.250 | 6.840 | 6.467 | 6.128 |
| 19 | 17.226 | 15.678 | 14.324 | 13.134 | 12.085 | 11.158 | 10.336 | 9.604 | 8.950 | 8.365 | 7.839 | 7.366 | 6.938 | 6.550 | 6.198 |
| 20 | 18.046 | 16.351 | 14.877 | 13.590 | 12.462 | 11.470 | 10.594 | 9.818 | 9.129 | 8.514 | 7.963 | 7.469 | 7.025 | 6.623 | 6.259 |
| 21 | 18.857 | 17.011 | 15.415 | 14.029 | 12.821 | 11.764 | 10.836 | 10.017 | 9.292 | 8.649 | 8.075 | 7.562 | 7.102 | 6.687 | 6.312 |
| 22 | 19.660 | 17.658 | 15.937 | 14.451 | 13.163 | 12.042 | 11.061 | 10.201 | 9.442 | 8.772 | 8.176 | 7.645 | 7.170 | 6.743 | 6.359 |
| 23 | 20.456 | 18.292 | 16.444 | 14.857 | 13.489 | 12.303 | 11.272 | 10.371 | 9.580 | 8.883 | 8.266 | 7.718 | 7.230 | 6.792 | 6.399 |
| 24 | 21.243 | 18.914 | 16.936 | 15.247 | 13.799 | 12.550 | 11.469 | 10.529 | 9.707 | 8.985 | 8.348 | 7.784 | 7.283 | 6.835 | 6.434 |
| 25 | 22.023 | 19.523 | 17.413 | 15.622 | 14.094 | 12.783 | 11.654 | 10.675 | 9.823 | 9.077 | 8.422 | 7.843 | 7.330 | 6.873 | 6.464 |
| 26 | 22.795 | 20.121 | 17.877 | 15.983 | 14.375 | 13.003 | 11.826 | 10.810 | 9.929 | 9.161 | 8.488 | 7.896 | 7.372 | 6.906 | 6.491 |
| 27 | 23.560 | 20.707 | 18.327 | 16.330 | 14.643 | 13.211 | 11.987 | 10.935 | 10.027 | 9.237 | 8.548 | 7.943 | 7.409 | 6.935 | 6.514 |
| 28 | 24.316 | 21.281 | 18.764 | 16.663 | 14.898 | 13.406 | 12.137 | 11.051 | 10.116 | 9.307 | 8.602 | 7.984 | 7.441 | 6.961 | 6.534 |
| 29 | 25.066 | 21.844 | 19.188 | 16.984 | 15.141 | 13.591 | 12.278 | 11.158 | 10.198 | 9.370 | 8.650 | 8.022 | 7.470 | 6.983 | 6.551 |
| 30 | 25.808 | 22.396 | 19.600 | 17.292 | 15.372 | 13.765 | 12.409 | 11.258 | 10.274 | 9.427 | 8.694 | 8.055 | 7.496 | 7.003 | 6.566 |

| n | 16% | 17% | 18% | 19% | 20% | 21% | 22% | 23% | 24% | 25% | 26% | 27% | 28% | 29% | 30% |
|---|-----|-----|-----|-----|-----|-----|-----|-----|-----|-----|-----|-----|-----|-----|-----|
| 1 | 0.862 | 0.855 | 0.847 | 0.840 | 0.833 | 0.826 | 0.820 | 0.813 | 0.806 | 0.800 | 0.794 | 0.787 | 0.781 | 0.775 | 0.769 |
| 2 | 1.605 | 1.585 | 1.566 | 1.547 | 1.528 | 1.509 | 1.492 | 1.474 | 1.457 | 1.440 | 1.424 | 1.407 | 1.392 | 1.376 | 1.361 |
| 3 | 2.246 | 2.210 | 2.174 | 2.140 | 2.106 | 2.074 | 2.042 | 2.011 | 1.981 | 1.952 | 1.923 | 1.896 | 1.868 | 1.842 | 1.816 |
| 4 | 2.798 | 2.743 | 2.690 | 2.639 | 2.589 | 2.540 | 2.494 | 2.448 | 2.404 | 2.362 | 2.320 | 2.280 | 2.241 | 2.203 | 2.166 |
| 5 | 3.274 | 3.199 | 3.127 | 3.058 | 2.991 | 2.926 | 2.864 | 2.803 | 2.745 | 2.689 | 2.635 | 2.583 | 2.532 | 2.483 | 2.436 |
| 6 | 3.685 | 3.589 | 3.498 | 3.410 | 3.326 | 3.245 | 3.167 | 3.092 | 3.020 | 2.951 | 2.885 | 2.821 | 2.759 | 2.700 | 2.643 |
| 7 | 4.039 | 3.922 | 3.812 | 3.706 | 3.605 | 3.508 | 3.416 | 3.327 | 3.242 | 3.161 | 3.083 | 3.009 | 2.937 | 2.868 | 2.802 |
| 8 | 4.344 | 4.207 | 4.078 | 3.954 | 3.837 | 3.726 | 3.619 | 3.518 | 3.421 | 3.329 | 3.241 | 3.156 | 3.076 | 2.999 | 2.925 |
| 9 | 4.607 | 4.451 | 4.303 | 4.163 | 4.031 | 3.905 | 3.786 | 3.673 | 3.566 | 3.463 | 3.366 | 3.273 | 3.184 | 3.100 | 3.019 |
| 10 | 4.833 | 4.659 | 4.494 | 4.339 | 4.192 | 4.054 | 3.923 | 3.799 | 3.682 | 3.571 | 3.465 | 3.364 | 3.269 | 3.178 | 3.092 |
| 11 | 5.029 | 4.836 | 4.656 | 4.487 | 4.327 | 4.177 | 4.035 | 3.902 | 3.776 | 3.656 | 3.543 | 3.437 | 3.335 | 3.239 | 3.147 |
| 12 | 5.197 | 4.988 | 4.793 | 4.611 | 4.439 | 4.278 | 4.127 | 3.985 | 3.851 | 3.725 | 3.606 | 3.493 | 3.387 | 3.286 | 3.190 |
| 13 | 5.342 | 5.118 | 4.910 | 4.715 | 4.533 | 4.362 | 4.203 | 4.053 | 3.912 | 3.780 | 3.656 | 3.538 | 3.427 | 3.322 | 3.223 |
| 14 | 5.468 | 5.229 | 5.008 | 4.802 | 4.611 | 4.432 | 4.265 | 4.108 | 3.962 | 3.824 | 3.695 | 3.573 | 3.459 | 3.351 | 3.249 |
| 15 | 5.575 | 5.324 | 5.092 | 4.876 | 4.675 | 4.489 | 4.315 | 4.153 | 4.001 | 3.859 | 3.726 | 3.601 | 3.483 | 3.373 | 3.268 |
| 16 | 5.668 | 5.405 | 5.162 | 4.938 | 4.730 | 4.536 | 4.357 | 4.189 | 4.033 | 3.887 | 3.751 | 3.623 | 3.503 | 3.390 | 3.283 |
| 17 | 5.749 | 5.475 | 5.222 | 4.990 | 4.775 | 4.576 | 4.391 | 4.219 | 4.059 | 3.910 | 3.771 | 3.640 | 3.518 | 3.403 | 3.295 |
| 18 | 5.818 | 5.534 | 5.273 | 5.033 | 4.812 | 4.608 | 4.419 | 4.243 | 4.080 | 3.928 | 3.786 | 3.654 | 3.529 | 3.413 | 3.304 |
| 19 | 5.877 | 5.584 | 5.316 | 5.070 | 4.843 | 4.635 | 4.442 | 4.263 | 4.097 | 3.942 | 3.799 | 3.664 | 3.539 | 3.421 | 3.311 |
| 20 | 5.929 | 5.628 | 5.353 | 5.101 | 4.870 | 4.657 | 4.460 | 4.279 | 4.110 | 3.954 | 3.808 | 3.673 | 3.546 | 3.427 | 3.316 |
| 21 | 5.973 | 5.665 | 5.384 | 5.127 | 4.891 | 4.675 | 4.476 | 4.292 | 4.121 | 3.963 | 3.816 | 3.679 | 3.551 | 3.432 | 3.320 |
| 22 | 6.011 | 5.696 | 5.410 | 5.149 | 4.909 | 4.690 | 4.488 | 4.302 | 4.130 | 3.970 | 3.822 | 3.684 | 3.556 | 3.436 | 3.323 |
| 23 | 6.044 | 5.723 | 5.432 | 5.167 | 4.925 | 4.703 | 4.499 | 4.311 | 4.137 | 3.976 | 3.827 | 3.689 | 3.559 | 3.438 | 3.325 |
| 24 | 6.073 | 5.746 | 5.451 | 5.182 | 4.937 | 4.713 | 4.507 | 4.318 | 4.143 | 3.981 | 3.831 | 3.692 | 3.562 | 3.441 | 3.327 |
| 25 | 6.097 | 5.766 | 5.467 | 5.195 | 4.948 | 4.721 | 4.514 | 4.323 | 4.147 | 3.985 | 3.834 | 3.694 | 3.564 | 3.442 | 3.329 |
| 26 | 6.118 | 5.783 | 5.480 | 5.206 | 4.956 | 4.728 | 4.520 | 4.328 | 4.151 | 3.988 | 3.837 | 3.696 | 3.566 | 3.444 | 3.330 |
| 27 | 6.136 | 5.798 | 5.492 | 5.215 | 4.964 | 4.734 | 4.524 | 4.332 | 4.154 | 3.990 | 3.839 | 3.698 | 3.567 | 3.445 | 3.331 |
| 28 | 6.152 | 5.810 | 5.502 | 5.223 | 4.970 | 4.739 | 4.528 | 4.335 | 4.157 | 3.992 | 3.840 | 3.699 | 3.568 | 3.446 | 3.331 |
| 29 | 6.166 | 5.820 | 5.510 | 5.229 | 4.975 | 4.743 | 4.531 | 4.337 | 4.159 | 3.994 | 3.841 | 3.700 | 3.569 | 3.446 | 3.332 |
| 30 | 6.177 | 5.829 | 5.517 | 5.235 | 4.979 | 4.746 | 4.534 | 4.339 | 4.160 | 3.995 | 3.842 | 3.701 | 3.569 | 3.447 | 3.332 |

# ANSWERS TO SELECTED PROBLEMS

**2-7.** Accumulated depreciation and book value after three years, $22,500 and $67,500

**2-8.** Loss on disposal, $5,000; tax reduction, $2,000

**2-10.** $2,000,000

**2-11.** $30,000; $45,600; $44,400

**3-1.** 1979: 2.70 and 1.38; 1978: 2.93 and 1.86

**3-2.** 1979: 2.79, 1.42 and 83.63; 1978: 3.69, 1.46 and 75.25

**3-3.** 1978: 43%, 51%, 13.0 times

**3-4.** 1979: $3.42, $0.37, 10.8%, 5.54%, 7.87%, 15.6%

**3-6.** Change in net plant and equipment, 1979: $855,000; total sources, $2,365,000

**3-9.** 1984: 2.57, 1.31

**3-10.** 1984: 3.51, 1.78, 60 days

**3-11.** 1984: .30, .47, 10.56

**3-12.** 1984: $4.41, $1.60, 36.3%, 4.50%, 8.01%, 15.2%

**3-14.** Total uses: $488,924

**4-1.** $6,000; $17,400; $17,800; $19,500

**4-2.** $11,000; $21,500; $22,700; $38,760

**4-3.** Expected cash inflow for October: $22,550

**4-4.** Expected cash outflow for October: $21,300

**4-5.** End-of-month loan for November: $1,530

**4-6.** Expected cash inflows, July through September: $30,000, $25,000, $35,000; expected cash outflows, July through September: $28,000, $26,000, $26,000

**4-7.** End-of-month loan, January through March: $1,350; $1,363; $876

**4-10.** 1985 accounts receivable, $186,667; accounts payable, $194,400; additional financing needed, $515,767; total assets, $2,356,267

**4-11.** 1985 additional financing needed, $1,215

**4-12.** 1985 cost of goods sold, $16,128,000; operating expenses, $6,144,000; addition to retained earnings, $454,000

**5-1.** (a) $5,000

**5-2.** (a) 15,000 units; (b) $(Y|T = 20,000) = \$30,000$; $(OL|T = 20,000) = 4.0$

**5-3.** 36.8%

**5-4.** 35%; $108,000

**5-8.** $215,888 to $296,584

**5-11.** (a) $0.48

**5-12.** (a) \$175,000; (b) when EBIT = \$200,000, EPS = \$1.50, $FL$ = 8.0

**5-15.** For Data Set 2: (a) \$16,000; (b) \$0.96; (c) 769 units; (d) 0; (e) 769 units; (f) 1.625; (g) 1.0; (h) 1.625; (i) 1.625

**6-1.** 1974: \$57 million, 2.43, .31, .27, .65; 1977: \$87 million, 2.58, .32, .25, .66, .68

**6-6.** Company 1: current liabilities to total assets, .44; $(1 - LR_1)$, .63

**7-1.** \$162,500

**7-3.** \$18,750

**7-5.** Incremental investment in accounts receivable, \$315,000; incremental loss due to bad debts, \$81,000

**7-7.** (a) 40 times per year, \$400, \$25, \$425; (c) $Q^*$ = 400

**8-1.** 48.98%

**8-3.** April 1 loan size, \$90,000; interest payment, \$1,125

**8-4.** \$42,500

**8-5.** July, \$625

**8-6.** \$141,644

**9-2.** \$8,995; \$5,012.40; \$1.126

**9-3.** \$25,180; $3 < i < 4$; \$3,371.87; 3

**9-4.** $11 < i < 12$

**9-5.** \$3,246; \$67,152; 20%; \$4,343.34

**9-7.** \$11,070; \$8,745; \$24,730; 0%; \$9,483.88; 10

**9-10.** \$24,944.43

**9-13.** \$953.97; \$5,000; \$9,348

**9-14.** Loan 1: 5 payments (5th payment is a balloon payment of \$4,303.86)

**9-16.** $A$: \$18,025

**9-17.** \$12,500

**10-1.** \$2,850,000; \$820,000 for three years, \$870,000 fourth year

**10-2.** \$914,000

**10-4.** \$5,390,000; \$1,210,400 for four years, \$1,685,400 fifth year

**10-5.** $A$: four years

**10-6.** $A$: \$54,850; $B$: \$36,430

**10-7.** 20.95%

**10-8.** $A$: 14.39%

**10-9.** $A$: 15.66%

**11-1.** (a) Reject all three; (b) $A$ and $C$; (c) $A$ and $C$

**11-3.** (a) \$1,280,000; (c) Years 1–4; \$100,000; Years 5–6, \$160,000; Year 7, \$560,000

**11-5.** (a) Project $A$, NPV = \$5,100; (b) Project $B$, IRR = 14.95%

**11-7.** (a) NPV for Project $NLX$: \$7,334; (b) IRR for Project $NLX$: 29.6%

**12-1.** \$330; 44,100; \$210; .636

**12-3.** $E_{NPV}$ = \$327; $V_{NPV}$ = 3.25

**12-4.** RANPV = −\$1,156

**13-1.** (a) 7.69%; (b) 8.22%; (c) \$8,572 and −\$528

**13-2.** 11.54%

**13-3.** 4.62%, 8.29%
**13-6.** (a) $43.18; (b) $75.00
**13-7.** (a) 9%; (b) 16.1%
**13-8.** 8%
**13-9.** (b) $76.50; (c) 10.16%; (d) $82.80
**13-11.** $51.64

**14-1.** 6.6%; 4.818%
**14-2.** 9.8%; 11.7%
**14-3.** 7.47%; 10%
**14-4.** 7.12%; 9.62%
**14-5.** 9.7%
**14-6.** 10.1%
**14-7.** At $50,000 debt, $k_w = 11.70\%$
**14-8.** At $50,000 debt, $k_w = 11.88\%$
**14-9.** Up to $2.5 million, weighted MCC is 9.8%

**15-2.** $1,340,000
**15-3.** (a) $Y_b = 0$; (c) $1,200,000; (e) $4,200,000
**15-4.** $5,970,000
**15-5.** (a) Alternative $A$: $800,000; (b) $4,400,000

**16-1.** (a) Stock $X$: 1981, 22.0%; 1982, 54.6%; 1983, 90.9%; (b) Stock $X$: .4430, .0689, .2625; (c) 17.26%; (d) $\sigma_{XY} = -.0026$; (e) .005, .071
**16-2.** (a) Stock $J$: .0759, .0046, .0682; $\sigma_{JH} = .0035$; (b) Portfolio 3: .0772, .0657
**16-3.** (a) 1.0
**16-6.** (a) .0829, .006; (b) .47
**16-7.** (a) 1.05; (c) .0523
**16-8.** (a) .68
**16A-3.** Portfolio 1: .1088, .2408; Portfolio 2: .1017, .1830

**17-1.** 1.5
**17-3.** .2055
**17-6.** 1.2075
**17-8.** (a) .2480
**17-9.** (a) 1.84; (b) .2672
**17-11.** (a) 1.272; (c) .1919; (e) 1.789; (f) .2342
**17-12.** .2554, .3081
**17-13.** (c) $916,031; (d) $100,000; (f) $766,031; (h) .2937

**18-1.** (a) $500,000; (b) 2; (c) $2.00; (d) $2.00
**18-4.** $54.00

**19-2.** Yes, NPV = $371,140
**19-4.** NPV = -$976,680
**19-6.** (a) Bond alternative: 6, 1.20
**19-7.** (a) Bond alternative: 2.11, 1.90

**20.2.** $32.55
**20-3.** 0, 0, $36, $75
**20-4.** (b) 250%

**20-5.** (*a*) 0; (*c*) $2

**21-1.** $137,539
**21-3.** $2,163,000
**21-4.** $8,174
**21-6.** (*d*) $8,641
**21-7.** (*b*) $434,526

**22-7.** $66.00

**23-1.** (*a*) $7,625; (*b*) $3,894; (*c*) 25,926.88
**23-2.** (*a*) 1,233.50
**23-3.** $300,000
**23-4.** $296,514
**23-6.** (*a*) 2.60 marks

**24-1.** (*a*) $1,750,000 or $8.75 per share; (*b*) $5,050,000 or $25.25 per share
**24-2.** (*a*) .3, 60,000 shares, $6.00; (*b*) .402, 80,400 shares, $5.89
**24-3.** (*a*) .15, 30,000 shares; (*b*) $6.17; (*c*) $6.51, $6.87, $7.25
**24-6.** (*d*) 12 years

# GLOSSARY

## A

**acceleration clause** A provision of a bond indenture that declares all unpaid principal and interest due and payable within a very short time period if an event of default occurs.

**accept/reject decision** Occurs when an individual project is accepted or rejected without regard to any other investment alternative.

**acid-test ratio** *See* quick ratio.

**activity ratio** Measures the degree of efficiency a firm displays in using its resources.

**administered pricing** The practice whereby a company sets its price schedules and offers its product lines at the stated prices rather than letting prices fluctuate according to supply and demand.

**after acquired clause** A clause in a mortgage bond indenture requiring that all real property subsequently acquired by the corporation become part of the mortgage collateral.

**agency basis** *See* best efforts.

**aggressive current asset strategy** A working capital strategy that seeks to minimize the amount of funds invested in cash and marketable securities.

**aggressive current liability strategy** A working capital strategy designed to maximize the amount of short-term debt that is used to finance current assets.

**aggressive working capital strategy** A working capital strategy that seeks to minimize excess liquidity while meeting short-term requirements.

**annuity** A series of cash flows that are equal in size and occur at equally spaced points in time.

**arrival draft** A draft that calls for payment upon arrival of the merchandise.

**assets** The investments that a firm makes in its profit-seeking activities.

**assignment** A nonbankruptcy voluntary remedy where the debtor firm transfers its assets to assignees who liquidate the assets for the benefit of the creditors.

**average collection period** An activity ratio that measures the average number of days it takes for a firm to collect its accounts receivable.

## B

**balance sheet** Summarizes a corporation's financial position at a particular time and lists the firm's assets, liabilities, and equity accounts.

**balance sheet leverage** *See* financial leverage.

**balloon payment** The final payment in a loan contract; larger than the other payments. A balloon payment contains all remaining principal and interest due, and is used to close out a loan after a specified number of payments.

**banker's acceptance** A date draft accepted by a bank.

**bankruptcy** A law for the benefit and relief of creditors and their debtors when debtors are unable or unwilling to pay their debts.

**bargain purchase option** An option that allows the lessee to purchase the leased asset far enough below its expected fair value so as to make the purchase reasonably certain.

**bearer bonds** *See* coupon bond.

**best efforts** A non-underwriting technique where investment bankers sell a security issue on a commission basis, with unsold securities remaining the property of the issuing corporation.

**beta coefficient** A measure of the systematic risk contained in a financial asset or a financial asset portfolio relative to market risk.

**bond** A contract by which the issuer promises to make interest payments in specified amounts at specified points in time and to repay the principal amount at the stated maturity date.

**bond discount** When the selling price of a bond is less than its par value, the difference is bond discount.

**bond premium** When the selling price of a bond is in excess of its par value, the difference is bond premium.

**book value** The dollar value of an asset as listed in the firm's balance sheet.

**breakeven** *See* operating breakeven and financial breakeven.

**broker** An agent who buys and sells securities for investors and who does not take ownership of the securities.

**business cycle indicators** A measure of the overall business cycle or some component of the business cycle.

**business cycles** The recurring patterns of expansion and contraction experienced by the general economy.

**business failure** A business firm that ceases operations with a loss to creditors.

**business risk** That part of overall corporate risk contained in asset composition and operating decisions.

# C

**callable bond** A bond that can be retired by the corporation prior to the maturity date of the issue.

**callable preferred stock** Preferred stock that can be retired at the option of the issuing corporation.

**call premium** The difference between a bond's call price and its par value.

**call price** The price to be paid to bondholders when a corporation exercises a call option and retires the bond issue.

**capital** Items of value that are owned and used and items of value that are used but not owned.

**capital asset pricing model** *See* security market line.

**capital budget** A set of investment alternatives having cash flows that occur over two or more years.

**capital budgeting** The set of procedures that generates the capital budget that is adopted at a particular point in time.

**capital lease** A lease that meets the requirements of FASB-13.

**capital markets** The primary and secondary markets for financial assets having maturities that are longer than one year or that have no maturity date.

**capital rationing** A situation where a corporation is unable to finance its entire capital budget because of a constraint on the size of the net investment funds available.

**capital structure** The corporation's mix of long-term liabilities and equity capital.

**capital structure leverage** *See* financial leverage.

**cash budget** A forecast of a firm's cash inflows and outflows over a designated planning period.

**cash flow** Profit after taxes plus depreciation.

**cash-to-cash cycle** The amount of time that cash is tied up in the corporation's operating process for each unit of output.

**clean draft** A draft drawn without collateral documents, such as a bill of lading or an insurance certificate.

**closed end mortgage** A mortgage under which the corporation is prohibited from using the property secured by the mortgage as collateral in another mortgage of the same priority.

**coefficient of variation** The standard deviation divided by the expected value; this measures risk per dollar of return.

**combined leverage** The ratio of the resulting percentage change in EPS divided by a given percentage change in output.

**commercial credit** Credit sales made between corporations.

**commitment fee** A charge as part of a revolving credit agreement that requires the borrower to pay a stated monthly rate on the unused portion of the line.

**common size income statement** An income statement where all the dollar values are expressed as a percentage of net sales.

**common stock** A financial asset that represents the ownership of a corporation.

**compensating balance requirements** The amount(s) of cash that must be deposited in a noninterest-bearing account at a lending bank as a condition for obtaining certain types of business loans or services from the bank.

**composition** A nonbankruptcy voluntary agreement between a firm and two or more of its creditors that reduces the amount of the creditors' claims and/or extends the term of the debt.

**compound amount**   The sum of the payment or payments that includes the associated compound interest.

**compounding**   The process of adding interest and determining the resulting compound amount.

**compounding frequency**   The number of times per year that interest is added to a deposit account.

**compound interest**   Interest earned on interest.

**congeneric merger**   A merger between two or more firms that have product lines that are complementary but not directly competitive.

**conglomerate merger**   Any merger that involves firms that have product lines that are unrelated. The term also applies to congeneric mergers.

**conservative current asset strategy**   A working capital strategy that seeks to maintain substantial amounts of liquid assets in the form of cash and marketable securities.

**conservative current liability strategy**   A working capital strategy that seeks to minimize the amount of short-term debt in the corporation's capital structure.

**conservative working capital strategy**   A working capital strategy that provides liquidity in excess of expected needs.

**conventional cash flow**   A time series of cash flows that contains only one change in sign.

**conversion exposure**   *See* transaction exposure.

**convertible bond**   A bond that can be exchanged at the owner's option for another security.

**convertible preferred stock**   Preferred stock that can be exchanged at the owner's option for shares of common stock.

**corporation**   A state chartered legal entity that has a legal existence apart from its owners and that issues common stock as evidence of ownership.

**correlation**   A measure of the extent to which the time series of two variables increase and decrease together.

**cost of capital**   The minimum rate of return a corporation must earn in order to satisfy the rate of return required by investors.

**cost-push inflation**   Price increases caused by increases in the cost of production.

**coupon bond**   A bond that contains detachable interest coupons that are presented for payment at specified dates.

**coupon rate**   The interest rate paid on a bond's par value.

**covariance**   The basic statistical measure of the degree to which two variables move together.

**credit management**   The management of accounts receivable.

**cross-sectional analysis**   The evaluation of the financial condition of a corporation at a specific time.

**cumulative as to dividends**   A provision of preferred stock that prohibits the payment of dividends on common stock as long as current or past preferred dividends remain unpaid.

**current assets**   The firm's most liquid assets; they can be converted into cash, sold, or consumed within one year.

**current liabilities**   Liabilities that are payable in one year or less.

**current ratio**   A measure of a firm's liquidity, computed by dividing current assets by current liabilities.

**current yield**   A measure of a bond's rate of return equal to the yearly interest payment divided by the current price in dollars.

# D

**data outlier**   Any value that deviates substantially from the other data points.

**date draft**   A draft that calls for payment on a specified date or at a specified number of days after the specified date.

**dealer**   A firm that buys and sells securities for its own account and takes ownership of the securities as part of the transaction.

**debenture**   An unsecured bond.

**debt ratios**   Measure the extent to which a corporation finances itself with debt as opposed to equity.

**default risk**   The probability or likelihood that the issuer of a security will not pay off the security at maturity.

**demand-pull inflation**   Price increases caused by a large demand relative to the supply of a product.

**depreciation**   The process that allocates the original cost of fixed assets to the time periods during which such assets provide useful services.

**depression**   A severe and sustained recession.

**desired minimum cash balance**   The minimum amount of cash, after meeting transactions requirements, needed to satisfy precautionary and compensating balance requirements.

**direct lease**   A lease that is executed with an asset's manufacturer or distributor, or with a leasing company.

**discounting**   The process of obtaining present values of cash flows.

**disintermediation**   Withdrawing funds from financial intermediaries in order to purchase financial assets directly from issuers.

**dividends per share**   A profitability ratio computed by dividing common stock cash dividends by the number of shares of common stock outstanding.

**diversifiable risk**   *See* unsystematic risk.

**diversification**   Adding additional financial assets to a portfolio.

**documentary draft**   A draft that has collateral documents such as a bill of lading and an insurance certificate.

**double taxation**   A term used to describe federal government taxation of both corporate profits and dividends.

**draft**   A document drawn by the seller ordering the buyer or his agent to pay a specified sum of money at a specified time.

# E

**earnings per share (EPS)**   A profitability ratio computed by dividing earnings after taxes less preferred dividends by the number of common shares outstanding.

**economic exposure**   The probability that changes in foreign exchange rates will decrease the intrinsic value or capitalized value of the firm.

**economic failure**   The inability of a business

firm to cover all costs and to operate at a profit.

**economic independence**   An investment proposal is economically independent when the proposal's net investment and cash flows do not affect and are unaffected by the net investments of other projects and when accepting or rejecting the proposal has no impact on the desirability of other projects.

**economic wealth**   Consists of a person's stocks of money and material economic goods.

**eurobonds**   Bonds sold in a foreign country and denominated in the currency of a different country.

**eurocurrencies**   Money deposited outside the country of origin.

**exchange rate**   The price of one currency in terms of another currency.

**exchange ratio**   The number of shares that an acquiring firm is willing to give for each of the target firm's shares.

**exchange risk**   The probability of loss due to the change in the value of currencies relative to each other.

**ex-dividend date**   Occurs four business days before the date of record. Investors who purchase the security on or after the ex-dividend date do not receive the dividend.

**exercise price**   The price paid for a share of common stock upon exchange for a warrant.

**exogenous variables**   Variables that are beyond the control of the decision maker, such as environmental factors.

**expansion**   That portion of the business cycle characterized by vigorous business activity and low unemployment.

**expected rate of return**   The holding period yield that is expected from owning a financial asset or a financial asset portfolio for one year.

**expected value (of a probability distribution)**   The sum of the products of each possible outcome multiplied by its associated probability.

**exposure management**   The management of financial affairs so as to minimize the detrimental effects of changing exchange rates.

**expropriation** The process by which a domestic company's foreign affiliate or subsidiary is taken over by the foreign country in which it is located.

**ex-rights date** Occurs four business days before the date of record. Investors who purchase the security on or after the ex-rights date do not receive the rights from the issuing company.

**extension** A nonbankruptcy voluntary agreement between a firm and its creditors that requires full payment of creditor claims but extends the payments beyond the original due dates.

## F

**factoring** The sale of accounts receivable without recourse.

**feasible set** As used in capital budgeting, the set of investment alternatives that contains no mutually exclusive alternatives and meets all the capital-rationing constraints.

**financial asset** A claim against the income or the assets of the issuer.

**financial breakeven** The value of EBIT that makes EPS equal to zero.

**financial institutions** The set of organizations that performs intermediary and/or marketing functions in the financial markets.

**financial intermediaries** Firms that provide money capital to corporations by purchasing their financial assets with funds obtained from the intermediaries' own investors or depositors.

**financial lease** A fully amortized noncancellable lease that does not include maintenance; its term equals the expected economic life of the asset.

**financial leverage** The ratio of the resulting percentage change in EPS divided by a given percentage change in EBIT. Financial leverage is increased by trading on the equity.

**financial markets** Any market where financial assets are bought, sold, or exchanged.

**financial risk** That part of overall corporate risk contained in capital structure decisions.

**financial statement analysis** A set of techniques used to evaluate corporate performance as reflected in its income statements, balance sheets, and funds statements.

**financing** The management of capital sources.

**first mortgage bond** A bond secured with real property that gives the bondholder first claim on the collateral in the event of default.

**fixed assets** A firm's long-term (more than one year) financial claims and investments in physical capital.

**floating lien** A claim on all the items that fall in a specified category.

**floating prime rate** A prime rate with a value that is set primarily by conditions in the money markets.

**floating rate notes** Bonds with an interest rate that is tied at least in part to yields available on other marketable securities, such as Treasury bills.

**foreign bonds** Bonds sold largely in a foreign country and denominated in the currency of that country.

**foreign exchange exposure management** *See* exposure management.

**foreign exchange market** The market in which buyers and sellers of foreign currencies meet their foreign currency requirements.

**forward exchange transactions** Trading of currencies for delivery at a future date.

**funds** As a general concept, synonymous with capital. More narrowly, *funds* means net working capital or simply cash.

**funds statement** *See* sources and use of funds statement.

## G

**going concern value** The dollar value of a business as an operating entity.

**gross national product** The dollar value of the economy's output of final goods and services. Nominal GNP is the GNP in current dollars. Real GNP represents the GNP adjusted for price changes.

**guaranteed residual value** The lessee's purchase price at the end of the lease term. Alternatively, this is the lessor's sale price of the asset that is guaranteed by the lessee.

# H

**holding period yield (HPY)** The rate of return realized from owning a financial asset or a financial asset portfolio for one year.

**horizontal merger** A merger of two or more firms that compete in the same industry and operate at the same level of production or distribution.

# I

**imperfect competition** Competitive conditions in an industry with outputs and prices that are determined by a few dominant firms.

**indifference point analysis** The use of financial break-even and return measurement equations to compare the profitability of alternative capital structures.

**income statement** Summarizes a corporation's revenue, expenses, and profits over a period of time.

**incremental borrowing rate** In leasing, one of two discount rates used in computing the sum of the present values of the minimum lease payments. It is the before-tax specific cost of debt that would be incurred in financing the purchase of an asset rather than leasing it.

**incremental cash flow** In replacement decisions, the cash flow of the present asset subtracted from the cash flow of the replacement asset.

**indenture** The contract executed between a corporation that issues bonds and the bondholder(s) or the trustee acting for the bondholders.

**indifference point** (EBIT-EPS indifference point) the value of EBIT that produces the same EPS value for mutually exclusive capital structures.

**industrial concentration** The historical tendency of the competitive economy to concentrate in a relatively small number of very large corporations.

**inflation** The rate of increase in the price level over time.

**insolvency** A firm is technically insolvent when it is unable to pay its debts as they mature. Legal insolvency is the insufficiency of a business firm's assets at fair valuation to pay its debts.

**installment credit** A form of retail credit that makes available extended, secured credit.

**interest** The price paid for the use of money over time.

**interest rate risk** The probability or likelihood that an investor will incur a loss on the sale of a marketable security that is sold before maturity due to an increase in the level of interest rates.

**intermediate cash flows** In capital budgeting, these consist of all the cash flows earned by an investment other than the final one.

**intermediation** The process of transferring funds from savers to ultimate users through the use of a third party.

**internal rate of return** (The IRR of an investment proposal.) The discount rate that produces a zero NPV and is the project's actual rate of return.

**intrinsic value** The sum of the present values of the cash flows returned by an asset when discounted at the required rate of return.

**inventory turnover** An activity ratio computed by dividing cost of goods sold by inventory.

**investing** The management of capital uses.

**investment banker** A financial institution that arranges long-term financial transactions for its clients.

# L

**lease** A contract by which the owner of an asset (the lessor) allows another party (the lessee) the use of the asset in return for specified periodic payments.

**lease term** The length of time a lease is noncancellable plus the number of years added if renewal options are exercised. However, the lease term does not extend beyond the date a bargain purchase option becomes exercisable.

**lessee** In leasing, the party that leases an asset and makes the lease payments.

**lessor** In leasing, the party that owns the asset that is leased.

**letter of credit** A bank's promise, made at

the request of an importer, to honor drafts drawn upon it by the exporter.

**leverage**   The percentage change in a dependent variable divided by the percentage change in the independent variable.

**leveraged lease**   A lease that involves the lessor borrowing a portion of the purchase price of the leased asset.

**leverage ratios**   *See* debt ratios and the specific leverage ratios.

**liabilities**   A firm's liabilities are amounts owed to creditors.

**limited open end mortgage bond**   A mortgage bond that allows the corporation, within specified limits, to use the secured property as collateral in selling another issue of mortgage bonds of the same priority.

**line of credit**   An informal arrangement by which a commercial bank states its willing-ness to extend credit up to a specific limit to a business firm.

**liquidating value**   The amount of cash that would remain after a firm's assets were sold and its liabilities paid off.

**liquidity ratios**   Ratios that indicate a firm's ability to pay its current liabilities as they come due.

**long-term debt to equity**   A debt ratio that measures the extent to which long-term financing sources are provided by creditors.

**long-term liabilities**   Liabilities that will not become payable until more than one year has elapsed.

## M

**managerial finance**   The management of capital sources and uses so as to attain a desired goal.

**marginal cost of capital**   The cost of capital of additional or incremental financing.

**market model**   *See* security market line.

**market risk**   The probability or likelihood that an active resale market will not exist for a marketable security when an investor desires to sell the security. *See also* systematic risk.

**market risk premium**   The additional rate

of return expected by an investor who purchases a risky portfolio with a beta of 1.0.

**market value**   The price that can be obtained from the sale of an asset.

**merger**   A business combination where a company acquires one or more firms and retains its identity.

**minimum lease payment**   The amount of a lease payment less any portion of the payment made to cover maintenance, property taxes, and insurance.

**money market loans**   Business loans advanced by commercial banks that have very short maturities and have fixed interest rates based on negotiable certificate of deposit rates.

**money markets**   The primary and secondary markets for financial assets with a maturity of one year or less.

**mortgage bond**   A bond that is collateralized with a pledge of specified real property.

**mutually exclusive alternatives**   Two or more investment alternatives are said to be mutually exlcusive when accepting one of the alternatives excludes the other from being adopted.

## N

**negative externality**   An occurrence when a producer acts in such a way as to harm some part of the economy without having to pay the costs of that harm.

**net investment**   The net cash outflow that occurs when an investment project is accepted and funds are invested.

**net present value**   The sum of the present value of the inflows less the sum of the present values of the outflows.

**net profit margin**   *See* profit margin.

**net working capital**   Current assets minus current liabilities.

**nondiversifiable risk**   *See* systematic risk.

## O

**oligopoly**   A market structure that occurs when (1) a few sellers dominate the market, (2) the firms are interdependent or at least perceive that they are, and (3) the firms have some control over their product prices and output.

**open account sales**   *See* trade credit sales.

**open charge credit**   A type of retail credit offering unsecured interest-free terms and a stated amount of time to remit payment.

**open mortgage bond**   A mortgage bond that does not prohibit the corporation from issuing other mortgage bonds of equal priority and using the same real property as collateral.

**operating breakeven**   The value of output that makes EBIT equal to zero.

**operating lease**   A non-full payout lease that is shorter than the expected economic life of the leased asset, includes maintenance, etc., and is cancellable. FASB-13 defines an operating lease as one that does not meet the requirements of a capital lease.

**operating leverage**   The ratio of the resulting percentage change in EBIT divided by a given percentage change in output.

**operating risk**   *See* business risk.

**optimal capital structure**   The capital structure that minimizes the firm's weighted average cost of capital and maximizes the value of the firm to its investors.

**overall breakeven**   The level of output that makes EPS equal to zero.

**overall risk**   The probability or likelihood that a corporation's share prices will fall to zero.

**overstock**   An unintended accumulation of inventory caused by actual sales being less than forecast sales.

**over-the-counter market**   A network of brokers and dealers who buy and sell securities for their clients and for themselves.

## P

**participating preferred stock**   A type of preferred stock that allows the shareholders, under certain conditions, to receive dividends in excess of the stated amounts.

**partnership**   A business owned by two or more persons (partners).

**par value**   The stated value, or face value, of a security.

**payback**   The number of years required for an investment's cumulative cash flows to equal its net investment.

**payout ratio**   A profitability ratio computed by dividing dividends per share by earnings per share.

**perpetuity**   An annuity that has an indefinitely long life.

**pledging accounts receivable**   Using accounts receivable as loan collateral.

**political risk**   In international finance, the probability that a political event will impact adversely on the firm.

**portfolio**   Any set of investments owned by an individual or a firm.

**portfolio beta**   The weighted average of the financial asset betas contained in the portfolio. *See* beta coefficient.

**precautionary requirement**   The amount of cash needed to meet unanticipated cash outflows.

**preferred stock**   A type of equity security with claims that rank ahead of those of common stock and that provides its owners with fixed or limited claims on the corporation's income and assets.

**present value**   The dollar value at Year zero of a future payment or payments adjusted for the time value of money.

**primary securities market**   That portion of financial markets where a financial asset appears for the first time.

**prime rate**   The minimum interest rate commercial banks charge their most creditworthy business customers for commercial and industrial loans.

**principal**   An original deposit. The original amount borrowed or lent.

**private placement**   A non-underwriting method of raising funds in the primary securities market by selling an entire security issue to one investor or to a small investing group.

**probability distribution**   A set of possible outcomes coupled with the corresponding probabilities of occurrence.

**profit margin**   A profitability ratio computed by dividing earnings after taxes by net sales.

**profitability ratios**   Measurement of the ability of a corporation to earn a positive rate of return for its shareholders.

**pro forma balance sheet**   A forecast in balance

sheet form of the corporation's capital at the end of a planning period.

**pro forma income statement** A forecast in income statement form of the corporation's revenues, expenses, and profits over a planning period.

**project cost** The amount of funds needed to acquire or begin an investment proposal.

**prospectus** The official document that advertises a new security issue.

**pure conglomerate** A merger or the resulting firm that comprises two or more companies that have unrelated product lines.

## Q

**quick assets** Current assets minus inventories.

**quick ratio** A measure of liquidity computed as current assets, minus inventories, and divided by current liabilities.

## R

**receivership** The court administers the property of the debtor.

**recession** Occurs when the real GNP declines for at least two consecutive calendar quarters.

**recovery** The upturn in business and decrease in unemployment that occurs subsequent to a recession or depression.

**redeemable bond** *See* callable bond.

**redeemable preferred stock** *See* callable preferred stock.

**refunding** The process whereby a corporation floats a bond issue and uses the proceeds to retire an existing or maturing bond issue.

**replacement decision** The decision to replace one productive asset with another.

**retail credit** Credit sales made by retailers to consumers.

**retained earnings** The profits that a corporation earns, does not pay out as dividends, and reinvests in itself.

**return on investment** A profitability ratio computed by dividing earnings after taxes by total assets. Alternatively, profit margin multiplied by total asset turnover.

**return on net worth** *See* return on stockholder equity.

**return on stockholder equity** A profitability ratio computed by dividing earnings after taxes by stockholder equity.

**return on total assets** *See* return on investment.

**revolving credit** A form of retail credit most commonly exemplified by credit card purchases and allowing the purchaser to make repeated unsecured purchases against a maximum line of credit.

**revolving credit agreement** A legal commitment on the part of a commercial bank to extend credit up to a specified limit to a business firm.

**right** An option to buy a specified number of shares of common stock at a specified price per share over a fixed time interval.

**rights offering** A financing technique that involves selling common stock in the primary securities market by issuing rights to the existing shareholders.

**risk** The probability or likelihood that the value of a variable will deviate from its expected or required value.

**risk adjusted net present value** The net present value of a risky capital-budgeting alternative. Each expected value of future cash flows is discounted using an appropriate risk adjusted discount rate.

**risk premium** The expected rate of return, over and above the risk-free rate, due to an asset's systematic risk.

## S

**safety stock** An amount of inventory that exceeds forecast sales and that is deliberately acquired to protect against unforeseen demand.

**sale and leaseback** The sale of an owned asset to a lessor while simultaneously executing a lease agreement for the asset with the purchasor-lessor.

**secondary securities markets** That portion of the financial markets where previously issued securities are offered for resale.

**second mortgage bond** A bond secured by real property that gives bondholders second claim on the property because it is already secured by a first mortgage.

**security market line**   A way of expressing the risk and return characteristics of a risky asset which states that the expected rate of return is the sum of the risk-free rate plus a premium for the asset's systematic risk.

**shelf registration**   The filing of a comprehensive prospectus with the SEC that allows the issuing firm to subsequently sell the registered securities without the need of additional prospectuses or waiting periods.

**sight draft**   A draft that calls for immediate payment upon presentation of the draft.

**sinking fund**   A provision in a bond indenture requiring the corporation to retire specified amounts of bonds at specified points in time.

**sole proprietorship**   An unincorporated business firm owned by one person.

**sources and uses of funds statement**   Lists the firm's sources and uses of funds over a designated time interval.

**specific cost of capital**   The cost of capital for each source of capital.

**spot exchange transaction**   Trading of currencies for delivery in one or two days.

**standard deviation**   The square root of the variance.

**statement of changes in financial position**   *See* sources and uses of funds statement.

**statement of retained earnings**   A financial statement that lists the distribution of net income between dividends and retained earnings.

**stock dividend**   A distribution of additional shares of common stock on a pro rata basis.

**stockout**   A situation that occurs when an item is demanded and its inventory level has fallen to zero.

**stock split**   A distribution of additional shares of common stock on a pro rata basis. The par value or stated value is reduced, but no transfers are made from retained earnings.

**subordinated debenture**   A debenture with claims against a firm's assets that are secondary to specified other debentures.

**systematic risk**   That portion of total portfolio risk caused by factors affecting the prices of all securities.

## T

**tender offer**   An offer to purchase the common shares of a corporation at a fixed price per share.

**term loan**   A loan with an original maturity longer than one year that provides a specified amount of financing over a given time period and that contains an annuity repayment schedule.

**time series analysis**   The evaluation of the financial condition of a corporation by examining its performance over several periods of time.

**times interest earned**   A debt ratio that measures the firm's ability to pay the interest on its debt.

**total asset turnover**   An activity ratio computed by dividing net sales by total assets.

**total debt to total assets**   A debt ratio that measures the percentage of total funds provided by debt.

**trade credit sales**   Short-term unsecured, noninterest-bearing commercial credit.

**trading on the equity (TOTE)**   Obtaining funds on which a fixed or limited return is paid.

**transaction exposure**   The probability of exchange loss when a future cash flow is known with certainty and requires a foreign exchange transaction.

**transaction requirement**   The amount of cash needed to meet the forecast outflows contained in a firm's cash budget.

**translation exposure**   The probability that a multinational company will suffer a decrease in asset values due to the devaluation of a foreign currency.

**treasury stock**   Shares of stock that have been repurchased by the issuing corporation.

## U

**underwriting**   The guarantee by an investment banker that the issuing corporation will receive a specified price for its security issue within a specified period of time.

**underwriting syndicate**   A group of investment bankers who jointly agree to underwrite a security issue.

**unsystematic risk**   That portion of total portfolio risk that is unique to a particular firm and/or the industry in which it operates.

## V

**valuation**   The process of estimating the value or utility of real or financial assets.

**variance (of a probability distribution)**   The sum of the products obtained by multiplying each squared deviation from the expected value by its associated probability of occurrence.

**vertical merger**   A merger involving two or more firms in the same industry that operate at different stages of the production-distribution system.

## W

**warrant**   An option to purchase a specified number of shares of common stock at a specified price.

**wealth**   Refers to economic wealth and consists of a person's stocks of money and material economic goods.

**weighted average cost of capital**   A measure of a corporation's overall cost of capital computed by multiplying each specific cost of capital by its percentage in the capital structure and adding the products.

**working capital**   A corporation's investment in current assets.

**working capital management**   The management of a corporation's sources and uses of working capital so as to advance the financial welfare of the shareholders.

## Y

**yield to maturity (YTM)**   The internal rate of return on a bond. The discount rate that produces a zero NPV.

# INDEX

# Table A-1.  Compound Amount of $1

| Year | 1% | 3% | 5% | 6% | 7% | 8% | 9% | 10% | 11% | 12% | 13% | 14% | 15% | 16% | 17% | 18% | 19% | 20% | 22% | 24% | 26% | 28% | 30% |
|---|---|---|---|---|---|---|---|---|---|---|---|---|---|---|---|---|---|---|---|---|---|---|---|
| 1 | 1.010 | 1.030 | 1.050 | 1.060 | 1.070 | 1.080 | 1.090 | 1.100 | 1.110 | 1.120 | 1.130 | 1.140 | 1.150 | 1.160 | 1.170 | 1.180 | 1.190 | 1.200 | 1.220 | 1.240 | 1.260 | 1.280 | 1.300 |
| 2 | 1.020 | 1.061 | 1.102 | 1.124 | 1.145 | 1.166 | 1.188 | 1.210 | 1.232 | 1.254 | 1.277 | 1.300 | 1.322 | 1.346 | 1.369 | 1.392 | 1.416 | 1.440 | 1.488 | 1.538 | 1.588 | 1.638 | 1.690 |
| 3 | 1.030 | 1.093 | 1.158 | 1.191 | 1.225 | 1.260 | 1.295 | 1.331 | 1.368 | 1.405 | 1.443 | 1.482 | 1.521 | 1.561 | 1.602 | 1.643 | 1.685 | 1.728 | 1.816 | 1.907 | 2.000 | 2.097 | 2.197 |
| 4 | 1.041 | 1.126 | 1.216 | 1.262 | 1.311 | 1.360 | 1.412 | 1.464 | 1.518 | 1.574 | 1.630 | 1.689 | 1.749 | 1.811 | 1.874 | 1.939 | 2.005 | 2.074 | 2.215 | 2.364 | 2.520 | 2.684 | 2.856 |
| 5 | 1.051 | 1.159 | 1.276 | 1.338 | 1.403 | 1.469 | 1.539 | 1.611 | 1.685 | 1.762 | 1.842 | 1.925 | 2.011 | 2.100 | 2.192 | 2.288 | 2.386 | 2.488 | 2.703 | 2.932 | 3.176 | 3.436 | 3.713 |
| 6 | 1.062 | 1.194 | 1.340 | 1.419 | 1.501 | 1.587 | 1.677 | 1.772 | 1.870 | 1.974 | 2.082 | 2.195 | 2.313 | 2.436 | 2.565 | 2.700 | 2.840 | 2.986 | 3.297 | 3.635 | 4.002 | 4.398 | 4.827 |
| 7 | 1.072 | 1.230 | 1.407 | 1.504 | 1.606 | 1.714 | 1.828 | 1.949 | 2.076 | 2.211 | 2.353 | 2.502 | 2.660 | 2.826 | 3.001 | 3.185 | 3.379 | 3.583 | 4.023 | 4.508 | 5.042 | 5.629 | 6.275 |
| 8 | 1.083 | 1.267 | 1.477 | 1.594 | 1.718 | 1.851 | 1.993 | 2.144 | 2.305 | 2.476 | 2.658 | 2.853 | 3.059 | 3.278 | 3.511 | 3.759 | 4.021 | 4.300 | 4.908 | 5.590 | 6.353 | 7.206 | 8.157 |
| 9 | 1.094 | 1.305 | 1.551 | 1.689 | 1.838 | 1.999 | 2.172 | 2.358 | 2.558 | 2.773 | 3.004 | 3.252 | 3.518 | 3.803 | 4.108 | 4.435 | 4.785 | 5.160 | 5.987 | 6.931 | 8.005 | 9.223 | 10.604 |
| 10 | 1.105 | 1.344 | 1.629 | 1.791 | 1.967 | 2.159 | 2.367 | 2.594 | 2.839 | 3.106 | 3.395 | 3.707 | 4.046 | 4.411 | 4.807 | 5.234 | 5.695 | 6.192 | 7.305 | 8.594 | 10.086 | 11.806 | 13.786 |
| 11 | 1.116 | 1.384 | 1.710 | 1.898 | 2.105 | 2.332 | 2.580 | 2.853 | 3.152 | 3.479 | 3.836 | 4.226 | 4.652 | 5.117 | 5.624 | 6.176 | 6.777 | 7.430 | 8.912 | 10.657 | 12.708 | 15.112 | 17.922 |
| 12 | 1.127 | 1.426 | 1.796 | 2.012 | 2.252 | 2.518 | 2.813 | 3.138 | 3.498 | 3.896 | 4.335 | 4.818 | 5.350 | 5.936 | 6.580 | 7.288 | 8.064 | 8.916 | 10.872 | 13.215 | 16.012 | 19.343 | 23.298 |
| 13 | 1.138 | 1.469 | 1.886 | 2.133 | 2.410 | 2.720 | 3.066 | 3.452 | 3.883 | 4.363 | 4.898 | 5.492 | 6.153 | 6.886 | 7.699 | 8.599 | 9.596 | 10.699 | 13.264 | 16.386 | 20.175 | 24.759 | 30.287 |
| 14 | 1.149 | 1.513 | 1.980 | 2.261 | 2.579 | 2.937 | 3.342 | 3.797 | 4.310 | 4.887 | 5.535 | 6.261 | 7.076 | 7.988 | 9.007 | 10.147 | 11.420 | 12.839 | 16.182 | 20.319 | 25.421 | 31.691 | 39.374 |
| 15 | 1.161 | 1.558 | 2.079 | 2.397 | 2.759 | 3.172 | 3.642 | 4.177 | 4.785 | 5.474 | 6.254 | 7.138 | 8.137 | 9.266 | 10.539 | 11.974 | 13.590 | 15.407 | 19.742 | 25.196 | 32.030 | 40.565 | 51.186 |
| 16 | 1.173 | 1.605 | 2.183 | 2.540 | 2.952 | 3.426 | 3.970 | 4.595 | 5.311 | 6.130 | 7.067 | 8.137 | 9.358 | 10.748 | 12.330 | 14.129 | 16.172 | 18.488 | 24.086 | 31.243 | 40.358 | 51.923 | 66.542 |
| 17 | 1.184 | 1.653 | 2.292 | 2.693 | 3.159 | 3.700 | 4.328 | 5.054 | 5.895 | 6.866 | 7.986 | 9.276 | 10.761 | 12.468 | 14.426 | 16.672 | 19.244 | 22.186 | 29.384 | 38.741 | 50.851 | 66.461 | 86.504 |
| 18 | 1.196 | 1.702 | 2.407 | 2.854 | 3.380 | 3.996 | 4.717 | 5.560 | 6.544 | 7.690 | 9.024 | 10.575 | 12.375 | 14.463 | 16.879 | 19.673 | 22.901 | 26.623 | 35.849 | 48.039 | 64.072 | 85.071 | 112.46 |
| 19 | 1.208 | 1.754 | 2.527 | 3.026 | 3.617 | 4.316 | 5.142 | 6.116 | 7.263 | 8.613 | 10.197 | 12.056 | 14.232 | 16.777 | 19.748 | 23.214 | 27.252 | 31.948 | 43.736 | 59.568 | 80.731 | 108.89 | 146.19 |
| 20 | 1.220 | 1.806 | 2.653 | 3.207 | 3.870 | 4.661 | 5.604 | 6.728 | 8.062 | 9.646 | 11.523 | 13.743 | 16.367 | 19.461 | 23.106 | 27.393 | 32.429 | 38.338 | 53.358 | 73.864 | 101.72 | 139.38 | 190.05 |
| 21 | 1.232 | 1.860 | 2.786 | 3.400 | 4.141 | 5.034 | 6.109 | 7.400 | 8.949 | 10.804 | 13.021 | 15.668 | 18.822 | 22.574 | 27.034 | 32.324 | 38.591 | 46.005 | 65.096 | 91.592 | 128.17 | 178.41 | 247.06 |
| 22 | 1.245 | 1.916 | 2.925 | 3.604 | 4.430 | 5.437 | 6.659 | 8.140 | 9.934 | 12.100 | 14.714 | 17.861 | 21.645 | 26.186 | 31.629 | 38.142 | 45.923 | 55.206 | 79.418 | 113.57 | 161.49 | 228.36 | 321.18 |
| 23 | 1.257 | 1.974 | 3.072 | 3.820 | 4.741 | 5.871 | 7.258 | 8.954 | 11.026 | 13.552 | 16.627 | 20.362 | 24.891 | 30.376 | 37.006 | 45.008 | 54.649 | 66.247 | 96.889 | 140.83 | 203.48 | 292.30 | 417.54 |
| 24 | 1.270 | 2.033 | 3.225 | 4.049 | 5.072 | 6.341 | 7.911 | 9.850 | 12.239 | 15.179 | 18.788 | 23.212 | 28.625 | 35.236 | 43.297 | 53.109 | 65.032 | 79.497 | 118.21 | 174.63 | 256.39 | 374.14 | 542.80 |
| 25 | 1.282 | 2.094 | 3.386 | 4.292 | 5.427 | 6.848 | 8.623 | 10.835 | 13.585 | 17.000 | 21.231 | 26.462 | 32.919 | 40.874 | 50.658 | 62.669 | 77.388 | 95.396 | 144.21 | 216.54 | 323.05 | 478.90 | 705.64 |
| 26 | 1.295 | 2.157 | 3.556 | 4.549 | 5.807 | 7.396 | 9.399 | 11.918 | 15.080 | 19.040 | 23.990 | 30.167 | 37.857 | 47.414 | 59.270 | 73.949 | 92.092 | 114.48 | 175.94 | 268.51 | 407.04 | 613.00 | 917.33 |
| 27 | 1.308 | 2.221 | 3.733 | 4.822 | 6.214 | 7.988 | 10.245 | 13.110 | 16.739 | 21.325 | 27.109 | 34.390 | 43.535 | 55.000 | 69.345 | 87.260 | 109.59 | 137.37 | 214.64 | 332.96 | 512.87 | 784.64 | 1192.5 |
| 28 | 1.321 | 2.288 | 3.920 | 5.112 | 6.649 | 8.627 | 11.167 | 14.421 | 18.580 | 23.884 | 30.633 | 39.204 | 50.066 | 63.800 | 81.134 | 102.97 | 130.41 | 164.84 | 261.86 | 412.86 | 646.21 | 1004.3 | 1550.3 |
| 29 | 1.335 | 2.357 | 4.116 | 5.418 | 7.114 | 9.317 | 12.172 | 15.863 | 20.624 | 26.750 | 34.616 | 44.693 | 57.575 | 74.008 | 94.927 | 121.50 | 155.19 | 197.81 | 319.47 | 511.95 | 814.23 | 1285.5 | 2015.4 |
| 30 | 1.348 | 2.427 | 4.322 | 5.743 | 7.612 | 10.063 | 13.268 | 17.449 | 22.892 | 29.960 | 39.116 | 50.950 | 66.212 | 85.850 | 111.06 | 143.37 | 184.68 | 237.38 | 389.76 | 634.82 | 1025.9 | 1645.5 | 2620 |

# Table A-4.    Present Value of an Annuity of $1

| n | 1% | 3% | 5% | 6% | 7% | 8% | 9% | 10% | 11% | 12% | 13% | 14% | 15% | 16% | 17% | 18% | 19% | 20% | 22% | 24% | 26% | 28% | 30% |
|---|----|----|----|----|----|----|----|-----|-----|-----|-----|-----|-----|-----|-----|-----|-----|-----|-----|-----|-----|-----|-----|
| 1 | 0.990 | 0.971 | 0.952 | 0.943 | 0.935 | 0.926 | 0.917 | 0.909 | 0.901 | 0.893 | 0.885 | 0.877 | 0.870 | 0.862 | 0.855 | 0.847 | 0.840 | 0.833 | 0.820 | 0.806 | 0.794 | 0.781 | 0.769 |
| 2 | 1.970 | 1.913 | 1.859 | 1.833 | 1.808 | 1.783 | 1.759 | 1.736 | 1.713 | 1.690 | 1.668 | 1.647 | 1.626 | 1.605 | 1.585 | 1.566 | 1.547 | 1.528 | 1.492 | 1.457 | 1.424 | 1.392 | 1.361 |
| 3 | 2.941 | 2.829 | 2.723 | 2.673 | 2.624 | 2.577 | 2.531 | 2.487 | 2.444 | 2.402 | 2.361 | 2.322 | 2.283 | 2.246 | 2.210 | 2.174 | 2.140 | 2.106 | 2.042 | 1.981 | 1.923 | 1.868 | 1.816 |
| 4 | 3.902 | 3.717 | 3.546 | 3.465 | 3.387 | 3.312 | 3.240 | 3.170 | 3.102 | 3.037 | 2.974 | 2.914 | 2.855 | 2.798 | 2.743 | 2.690 | 2.639 | 2.589 | 2.494 | 2.404 | 2.320 | 2.241 | 2.166 |
| 5 | 4.853 | 4.580 | 4.329 | 4.212 | 4.100 | 3.993 | 3.890 | 3.791 | 3.696 | 3.605 | 3.517 | 3.433 | 3.352 | 3.274 | 3.199 | 3.127 | 3.058 | 2.991 | 2.864 | 2.745 | 2.635 | 2.532 | 2.436 |
| 6 | 5.795 | 5.417 | 5.076 | 4.917 | 4.767 | 4.623 | 4.486 | 4.355 | 4.231 | 4.111 | 3.998 | 3.889 | 3.784 | 3.685 | 3.589 | 3.498 | 3.410 | 3.326 | 3.167 | 3.020 | 2.885 | 2.759 | 2.643 |
| 7 | 6.728 | 6.230 | 5.786 | 5.582 | 5.389 | 5.206 | 5.033 | 4.868 | 4.712 | 4.564 | 4.423 | 4.288 | 4.160 | 4.039 | 3.922 | 3.812 | 3.706 | 3.605 | 3.416 | 3.242 | 3.083 | 2.937 | 2.802 |
| 8 | 7.652 | 7.020 | 6.463 | 6.210 | 5.971 | 5.747 | 5.535 | 5.335 | 5.146 | 4.968 | 4.799 | 4.639 | 4.487 | 4.344 | 4.207 | 4.078 | 3.954 | 3.837 | 3.619 | 3.421 | 3.241 | 3.076 | 2.925 |
| 9 | 8.566 | 7.786 | 7.108 | 6.802 | 6.515 | 6.247 | 5.995 | 5.759 | 5.537 | 5.328 | 5.132 | 4.946 | 4.772 | 4.607 | 4.451 | 4.303 | 4.163 | 4.031 | 3.786 | 3.566 | 3.366 | 3.184 | 3.019 |
| 10 | 9.471 | 8.530 | 7.722 | 7.360 | 7.024 | 6.710 | 6.418 | 6.145 | 5.889 | 5.650 | 5.426 | 5.216 | 5.019 | 4.833 | 4.659 | 4.494 | 4.339 | 4.192 | 3.923 | 3.682 | 3.465 | 3.269 | 3.092 |
| 11 | 10.368 | 9.253 | 8.306 | 7.887 | 7.499 | 7.139 | 6.805 | 6.495 | 6.207 | 5.938 | 5.687 | 5.453 | 5.234 | 5.029 | 4.836 | 4.656 | 4.487 | 4.327 | 4.035 | 3.776 | 3.543 | 3.335 | 3.147 |
| 12 | 11.255 | 9.954 | 8.863 | 8.384 | 7.943 | 7.536 | 7.161 | 6.814 | 6.492 | 6.194 | 5.918 | 5.660 | 5.421 | 5.197 | 4.988 | 4.793 | 4.611 | 4.439 | 4.127 | 3.851 | 3.606 | 3.387 | 3.190 |
| 13 | 12.134 | 10.635 | 9.394 | 8.853 | 8.358 | 7.904 | 7.487 | 7.103 | 6.750 | 6.424 | 6.122 | 5.842 | 5.583 | 5.342 | 5.118 | 4.910 | 4.715 | 4.533 | 4.203 | 3.912 | 3.656 | 3.427 | 3.223 |
| 14 | 13.004 | 11.296 | 9.899 | 9.295 | 8.745 | 8.244 | 7.786 | 7.367 | 6.982 | 6.628 | 6.302 | 6.002 | 5.724 | 5.468 | 5.229 | 5.008 | 4.802 | 4.611 | 4.265 | 3.962 | 3.695 | 3.459 | 3.249 |
| 15 | 13.865 | 11.938 | 10.380 | 9.712 | 9.108 | 8.559 | 8.061 | 7.606 | 7.191 | 6.811 | 6.462 | 6.142 | 5.847 | 5.575 | 5.324 | 5.092 | 4.876 | 4.675 | 4.315 | 4.001 | 3.726 | 3.483 | 3.268 |
| 16 | 14.718 | 12.561 | 10.838 | 10.106 | 9.447 | 8.851 | 8.313 | 7.824 | 7.379 | 6.974 | 6.604 | 6.265 | 5.954 | 5.668 | 5.405 | 5.162 | 4.938 | 4.730 | 4.357 | 4.033 | 3.751 | 3.503 | 3.283 |
| 17 | 15.562 | 13.166 | 11.274 | 10.477 | 9.763 | 9.122 | 8.544 | 8.022 | 7.549 | 7.120 | 6.729 | 6.373 | 6.047 | 5.749 | 5.475 | 5.222 | 4.990 | 4.775 | 4.391 | 4.059 | 3.771 | 3.518 | 3.295 |
| 18 | 16.398 | 13.754 | 11.690 | 10.828 | 10.059 | 9.372 | 8.756 | 8.201 | 7.702 | 7.250 | 6.840 | 6.467 | 6.128 | 5.818 | 5.534 | 5.273 | 5.033 | 4.812 | 4.419 | 4.080 | 3.786 | 3.529 | 3.304 |
| 19 | 17.226 | 14.324 | 12.085 | 11.158 | 10.336 | 9.604 | 8.950 | 8.365 | 7.839 | 7.366 | 6.938 | 6.550 | 6.198 | 5.877 | 5.584 | 5.316 | 5.070 | 4.843 | 4.442 | 4.097 | 3.799 | 3.539 | 3.311 |
| 20 | 18.046 | 14.877 | 12.462 | 11.470 | 10.594 | 9.818 | 9.129 | 8.514 | 7.963 | 7.469 | 7.025 | 6.623 | 6.259 | 5.929 | 5.628 | 5.353 | 5.101 | 4.870 | 4.460 | 4.110 | 3.808 | 3.546 | 3.316 |
| 21 | 18.857 | 15.415 | 12.821 | 11.764 | 10.836 | 10.017 | 9.292 | 8.649 | 8.075 | 7.562 | 7.102 | 6.687 | 6.312 | 5.973 | 5.665 | 5.384 | 5.127 | 4.891 | 4.476 | 4.121 | 3.816 | 3.551 | 3.320 |
| 22 | 19.660 | 15.937 | 13.163 | 12.042 | 11.061 | 10.201 | 9.442 | 8.772 | 8.176 | 7.645 | 7.170 | 6.743 | 6.359 | 6.011 | 5.696 | 5.410 | 5.149 | 4.909 | 4.488 | 4.130 | 3.822 | 3.556 | 3.323 |
| 23 | 20.456 | 16.444 | 13.489 | 12.303 | 11.272 | 10.371 | 9.580 | 8.883 | 8.266 | 7.718 | 7.230 | 6.792 | 6.399 | 6.044 | 5.723 | 5.432 | 5.167 | 4.925 | 4.499 | 4.137 | 3.827 | 3.559 | 3.325 |
| 24 | 21.243 | 16.936 | 13.799 | 12.550 | 11.469 | 10.529 | 9.707 | 8.985 | 8.348 | 7.784 | 7.283 | 6.835 | 6.434 | 6.073 | 5.746 | 5.451 | 5.182 | 4.937 | 4.507 | 4.143 | 3.831 | 3.562 | 3.327 |
| 25 | 22.023 | 17.413 | 14.094 | 12.783 | 11.654 | 10.675 | 9.823 | 9.077 | 8.422 | 7.843 | 7.330 | 6.873 | 6.464 | 6.097 | 5.766 | 5.467 | 5.195 | 4.948 | 4.514 | 4.147 | 3.834 | 3.564 | 3.329 |
| 26 | 22.795 | 17.877 | 14.375 | 13.003 | 11.826 | 10.810 | 9.929 | 9.161 | 8.488 | 7.896 | 7.372 | 6.906 | 6.491 | 6.118 | 5.783 | 5.480 | 5.206 | 4.956 | 4.520 | 4.151 | 3.837 | 3.566 | 3.330 |
| 27 | 23.560 | 18.327 | 14.643 | 13.211 | 11.987 | 10.935 | 10.027 | 9.237 | 8.548 | 7.943 | 7.409 | 6.935 | 6.514 | 6.136 | 5.798 | 5.492 | 5.215 | 4.964 | 4.524 | 4.154 | 3.839 | 3.567 | 3.331 |
| 28 | 24.316 | 18.764 | 14.898 | 13.406 | 12.137 | 11.051 | 10.116 | 9.307 | 8.602 | 7.984 | 7.441 | 6.961 | 6.534 | 6.152 | 5.810 | 5.502 | 5.223 | 4.970 | 4.528 | 4.157 | 3.840 | 3.568 | 3.331 |
| 29 | 25.066 | 19.188 | 15.141 | 13.591 | 12.278 | 11.158 | 10.198 | 9.370 | 8.650 | 8.022 | 7.470 | 6.983 | 6.551 | 6.166 | 5.820 | 5.510 | 5.229 | 4.975 | 4.531 | 4.159 | 3.841 | 3.569 | 3.332 |
| 30 | 25.808 | 19.600 | 15.372 | 13.765 | 12.409 | 11.258 | 10.274 | 9.427 | 8.694 | 8.055 | 7.496 | 7.003 | 6.566 | 6.177 | 5.829 | 5.517 | 5.235 | 4.979 | 4.534 | 4.160 | 3.842 | 3.569 | 3.332 |

# Table A-3. Present Value of $1

| Year | 1% | 3% | 5% | 6% | 7% | 8% | 9% | 10% | 11% | 12% | 13% | 14% | 15% | 16% | 17% | 18% | 19% | 20% | 22% | 24% | 26% | 28% | 30% |
|---|---|---|---|---|---|---|---|---|---|---|---|---|---|---|---|---|---|---|---|---|---|---|---|
| 1 | 0.990 | 0.971 | 0.952 | 0.943 | 0.935 | 0.926 | 0.917 | 0.909 | 0.901 | 0.893 | 0.885 | 0.877 | 0.870 | 0.862 | 0.855 | 0.847 | 0.840 | 0.833 | 0.820 | 0.806 | 0.794 | 0.781 | 0.769 |
| 2 | 0.980 | 0.943 | 0.907 | 0.890 | 0.873 | 0.857 | 0.842 | 0.826 | 0.812 | 0.797 | 0.783 | 0.769 | 0.756 | 0.743 | 0.731 | 0.718 | 0.706 | 0.694 | 0.672 | 0.650 | 0.630 | 0.610 | 0.592 |
| 3 | 0.971 | 0.915 | 0.864 | 0.840 | 0.816 | 0.794 | 0.772 | 0.751 | 0.731 | 0.712 | 0.693 | 0.675 | 0.658 | 0.641 | 0.624 | 0.609 | 0.593 | 0.579 | 0.551 | 0.524 | 0.500 | 0.477 | 0.455 |
| 4 | 0.961 | 0.888 | 0.823 | 0.792 | 0.763 | 0.735 | 0.708 | 0.683 | 0.659 | 0.636 | 0.613 | 0.592 | 0.572 | 0.552 | 0.534 | 0.516 | 0.499 | 0.482 | 0.451 | 0.423 | 0.397 | 0.373 | 0.350 |
| 5 | 0.951 | 0.863 | 0.784 | 0.747 | 0.713 | 0.681 | 0.650 | 0.621 | 0.593 | 0.567 | 0.543 | 0.519 | 0.497 | 0.476 | 0.456 | 0.437 | 0.419 | 0.402 | 0.370 | 0.341 | 0.315 | 0.291 | 0.269 |
| 6 | 0.942 | 0.837 | 0.746 | 0.705 | 0.666 | 0.630 | 0.596 | 0.564 | 0.535 | 0.507 | 0.480 | 0.456 | 0.432 | 0.410 | 0.390 | 0.370 | 0.352 | 0.335 | 0.303 | 0.275 | 0.250 | 0.227 | 0.207 |
| 7 | 0.933 | 0.813 | 0.711 | 0.665 | 0.623 | 0.583 | 0.547 | 0.513 | 0.482 | 0.452 | 0.425 | 0.400 | 0.376 | 0.354 | 0.333 | 0.314 | 0.296 | 0.279 | 0.249 | 0.222 | 0.198 | 0.178 | 0.159 |
| 8 | 0.923 | 0.789 | 0.677 | 0.627 | 0.582 | 0.540 | 0.502 | 0.467 | 0.434 | 0.404 | 0.376 | 0.351 | 0.327 | 0.305 | 0.285 | 0.266 | 0.249 | 0.233 | 0.204 | 0.179 | 0.157 | 0.139 | 0.123 |
| 9 | 0.914 | 0.766 | 0.645 | 0.592 | 0.544 | 0.500 | 0.460 | 0.424 | 0.391 | 0.361 | 0.333 | 0.308 | 0.284 | 0.263 | 0.243 | 0.225 | 0.209 | 0.194 | 0.167 | 0.144 | 0.125 | 0.108 | 0.094 |
| 10 | 0.905 | 0.744 | 0.614 | 0.558 | 0.508 | 0.463 | 0.422 | 0.386 | 0.352 | 0.322 | 0.295 | 0.270 | 0.247 | 0.227 | 0.208 | 0.191 | 0.176 | 0.162 | 0.137 | 0.116 | 0.099 | 0.085 | 0.073 |
| 11 | 0.896 | 0.722 | 0.585 | 0.527 | 0.475 | 0.429 | 0.388 | 0.350 | 0.317 | 0.287 | 0.261 | 0.237 | 0.215 | 0.195 | 0.178 | 0.162 | 0.148 | 0.135 | 0.112 | 0.094 | 0.079 | 0.066 | 0.056 |
| 12 | 0.887 | 0.701 | 0.557 | 0.497 | 0.444 | 0.397 | 0.356 | 0.319 | 0.286 | 0.257 | 0.231 | 0.208 | 0.187 | 0.168 | 0.152 | 0.137 | 0.124 | 0.112 | 0.092 | 0.076 | 0.062 | 0.052 | 0.043 |
| 13 | 0.879 | 0.681 | 0.530 | 0.469 | 0.415 | 0.368 | 0.326 | 0.290 | 0.258 | 0.229 | 0.204 | 0.182 | 0.163 | 0.145 | 0.130 | 0.116 | 0.104 | 0.093 | 0.075 | 0.061 | 0.050 | 0.040 | 0.033 |
| 14 | 0.870 | 0.661 | 0.505 | 0.442 | 0.388 | 0.340 | 0.299 | 0.263 | 0.232 | 0.205 | 0.181 | 0.160 | 0.141 | 0.125 | 0.111 | 0.099 | 0.088 | 0.078 | 0.062 | 0.049 | 0.039 | 0.032 | 0.025 |
| 15 | 0.861 | 0.642 | 0.481 | 0.417 | 0.362 | 0.315 | 0.275 | 0.239 | 0.209 | 0.183 | 0.160 | 0.140 | 0.123 | 0.108 | 0.095 | 0.084 | 0.074 | 0.065 | 0.051 | 0.040 | 0.031 | 0.025 | 0.020 |
| 16 | 0.853 | 0.623 | 0.458 | 0.394 | 0.339 | 0.292 | 0.252 | 0.218 | 0.188 | 0.163 | 0.141 | 0.123 | 0.107 | 0.093 | 0.081 | 0.071 | 0.062 | 0.054 | 0.042 | 0.032 | 0.025 | 0.019 | 0.015 |
| 17 | 0.844 | 0.605 | 0.436 | 0.371 | 0.317 | 0.270 | 0.231 | 0.198 | 0.170 | 0.146 | 0.125 | 0.108 | 0.093 | 0.080 | 0.069 | 0.060 | 0.052 | 0.045 | 0.034 | 0.026 | 0.020 | 0.015 | 0.012 |
| 18 | 0.836 | 0.587 | 0.416 | 0.350 | 0.296 | 0.250 | 0.212 | 0.180 | 0.153 | 0.130 | 0.111 | 0.095 | 0.081 | 0.069 | 0.059 | 0.051 | 0.044 | 0.038 | 0.028 | 0.021 | 0.016 | 0.012 | 0.009 |
| 19 | 0.828 | 0.570 | 0.396 | 0.331 | 0.277 | 0.232 | 0.194 | 0.164 | 0.138 | 0.116 | 0.098 | 0.083 | 0.070 | 0.060 | 0.051 | 0.043 | 0.037 | 0.031 | 0.023 | 0.017 | 0.012 | 0.009 | 0.007 |
| 20 | 0.820 | 0.554 | 0.377 | 0.312 | 0.258 | 0.215 | 0.178 | 0.149 | 0.124 | 0.104 | 0.087 | 0.073 | 0.061 | 0.051 | 0.043 | 0.037 | 0.031 | 0.026 | 0.019 | 0.014 | 0.010 | 0.007 | 0.005 |
| 21 | 0.811 | 0.538 | 0.359 | 0.294 | 0.242 | 0.199 | 0.164 | 0.135 | 0.112 | 0.093 | 0.077 | 0.064 | 0.053 | 0.044 | 0.037 | 0.031 | 0.026 | 0.022 | 0.015 | 0.011 | 0.008 | 0.006 | 0.004 |
| 22 | 0.803 | 0.522 | 0.342 | 0.278 | 0.226 | 0.184 | 0.150 | 0.123 | 0.101 | 0.083 | 0.068 | 0.056 | 0.046 | 0.038 | 0.032 | 0.026 | 0.022 | 0.018 | 0.013 | 0.009 | 0.006 | 0.004 | 0.003 |
| 23 | 0.795 | 0.507 | 0.326 | 0.262 | 0.211 | 0.170 | 0.138 | 0.112 | 0.091 | 0.074 | 0.060 | 0.049 | 0.040 | 0.033 | 0.027 | 0.022 | 0.018 | 0.015 | 0.010 | 0.007 | 0.005 | 0.003 | 0.002 |
| 24 | 0.788 | 0.492 | 0.310 | 0.247 | 0.197 | 0.158 | 0.126 | 0.102 | 0.082 | 0.066 | 0.053 | 0.043 | 0.035 | 0.028 | 0.023 | 0.019 | 0.015 | 0.013 | 0.008 | 0.006 | 0.004 | 0.003 | 0.002 |
| 25 | 0.780 | 0.478 | 0.295 | 0.233 | 0.184 | 0.146 | 0.116 | 0.092 | 0.074 | 0.059 | 0.047 | 0.038 | 0.030 | 0.024 | 0.020 | 0.016 | 0.013 | 0.010 | 0.007 | 0.005 | 0.003 | 0.002 | 0.001 |
| 26 | 0.772 | 0.464 | 0.281 | 0.220 | 0.172 | 0.135 | 0.106 | 0.084 | 0.066 | 0.053 | 0.042 | 0.033 | 0.026 | 0.021 | 0.017 | 0.014 | 0.011 | 0.009 | 0.006 | 0.004 | 0.002 | 0.002 | 0.001 |
| 27 | 0.764 | 0.450 | 0.268 | 0.207 | 0.161 | 0.125 | 0.098 | 0.076 | 0.060 | 0.047 | 0.037 | 0.029 | 0.023 | 0.018 | 0.014 | 0.011 | 0.009 | 0.007 | 0.005 | 0.003 | 0.002 | 0.001 | 0.001 |
| 28 | 0.757 | 0.437 | 0.255 | 0.196 | 0.150 | 0.116 | 0.090 | 0.069 | 0.054 | 0.042 | 0.033 | 0.026 | 0.020 | 0.016 | 0.012 | 0.010 | 0.008 | 0.006 | 0.004 | 0.002 | 0.002 | 0.001 | 0.001 |
| 29 | 0.749 | 0.424 | 0.243 | 0.185 | 0.141 | 0.107 | 0.082 | 0.063 | 0.048 | 0.037 | 0.029 | 0.022 | 0.017 | 0.014 | 0.011 | 0.008 | 0.006 | 0.005 | 0.003 | 0.002 | 0.001 | 0.001 | 0.000 |
| 30 | 0.742 | 0.412 | 0.231 | 0.174 | 0.131 | 0.099 | 0.075 | 0.057 | 0.044 | 0.033 | 0.026 | 0.020 | 0.015 | 0.012 | 0.009 | 0.007 | 0.005 | 0.004 | 0.003 | 0.002 | 0.001 | 0.001 | 0.000 |

## Table A-2. Compound Amount of an Annuity of $1

| n | 1% | 3% | 5% | 6% | 7% | 8% | 9% | 10% | 11% | 12% | 13% | 14% | 15% | 16% | 17% | 18% | 19% | 20% | 22% | 24% | 26% | 28% | 30% |
|---|---|---|---|---|---|---|---|---|---|---|---|---|---|---|---|---|---|---|---|---|---|---|---|
| 1 | 1.000 | 1.000 | 1.000 | 1.000 | 1.000 | 1.000 | 1.000 | 1.000 | 1.000 | 1.000 | 1.000 | 1.000 | 1.000 | 1.000 | 1.000 | 1.000 | 1.000 | 1.000 | 1.000 | 1.000 | 1.000 | 1.000 | 1.000 |
| 2 | 2.010 | 2.030 | 2.050 | 2.060 | 2.070 | 2.080 | 2.090 | 2.100 | 2.110 | 2.120 | 2.130 | 2.140 | 2.150 | 2.160 | 2.170 | 2.180 | 2.190 | 2.200 | 2.220 | 2.240 | 2.260 | 2.280 | 2.300 |
| 3 | 3.030 | 3.091 | 3.152 | 3.184 | 3.215 | 3.246 | 3.278 | 3.310 | 3.342 | 3.374 | 3.407 | 3.440 | 3.472 | 3.506 | 3.539 | 3.572 | 3.606 | 3.640 | 3.708 | 3.778 | 3.848 | 3.918 | 3.990 |
| 4 | 4.060 | 4.184 | 4.310 | 4.375 | 4.440 | 4.506 | 4.573 | 4.641 | 4.710 | 4.779 | 4.850 | 4.921 | 4.993 | 5.066 | 5.141 | 5.215 | 5.291 | 5.368 | 5.524 | 5.684 | 5.848 | 6.016 | 6.187 |
| 5 | 5.101 | 5.309 | 5.526 | 5.637 | 5.751 | 5.867 | 5.985 | 6.105 | 6.228 | 6.353 | 6.480 | 6.610 | 6.742 | 6.877 | 7.014 | 7.154 | 7.297 | 7.442 | 7.740 | 8.048 | 8.368 | 8.700 | 9.043 |
| 6 | 6.152 | 6.468 | 6.802 | 6.975 | 7.153 | 7.336 | 7.523 | 7.716 | 7.913 | 8.115 | 8.323 | 8.536 | 8.754 | 8.977 | 9.207 | 9.442 | 9.683 | 9.930 | 10.442 | 10.980 | 11.544 | 12.136 | 12.756 |
| 7 | 7.214 | 7.662 | 8.142 | 8.394 | 8.654 | 8.923 | 9.200 | 9.487 | 9.783 | 10.089 | 10.405 | 10.730 | 11.067 | 11.414 | 11.772 | 12.142 | 12.523 | 12.916 | 13.740 | 14.615 | 15.546 | 16.534 | 17.583 |
| 8 | 8.286 | 8.892 | 9.549 | 9.897 | 10.260 | 10.637 | 11.028 | 11.436 | 11.859 | 12.300 | 12.757 | 13.233 | 13.727 | 14.240 | 14.773 | 15.327 | 15.902 | 16.499 | 17.762 | 19.123 | 20.588 | 22.163 | 23.858 |
| 9 | 9.369 | 10.159 | 11.027 | 11.491 | 11.978 | 12.488 | 13.021 | 13.579 | 14.164 | 14.776 | 15.416 | 16.085 | 16.786 | 17.518 | 18.285 | 19.086 | 19.923 | 20.799 | 22.670 | 24.712 | 26.940 | 29.369 | 32.015 |
| 10 | 10.462 | 11.464 | 12.578 | 13.181 | 13.816 | 14.487 | 15.193 | 15.937 | 16.722 | 17.549 | 18.420 | 19.337 | 20.304 | 21.321 | 22.393 | 23.521 | 24.709 | 25.959 | 28.657 | 31.643 | 34.945 | 38.593 | 42.619 |
| 11 | 11.567 | 12.808 | 14.207 | 14.972 | 15.784 | 16.645 | 17.560 | 18.531 | 19.561 | 20.655 | 21.814 | 23.045 | 24.349 | 25.733 | 27.200 | 28.755 | 30.404 | 32.150 | 35.962 | 40.238 | 45.031 | 50.398 | 56.405 |
| 12 | 12.682 | 14.192 | 15.917 | 16.870 | 17.888 | 18.977 | 20.141 | 21.384 | 22.713 | 24.133 | 25.650 | 27.271 | 29.002 | 30.850 | 32.824 | 34.931 | 37.180 | 39.581 | 44.874 | 50.895 | 57.739 | 65.510 | 74.327 |
| 13 | 13.809 | 15.618 | 17.713 | 18.882 | 20.141 | 21.495 | 22.953 | 24.523 | 26.212 | 28.029 | 29.985 | 32.089 | 34.352 | 36.786 | 39.404 | 42.219 | 45.244 | 48.497 | 55.746 | 64.110 | 73.751 | 84.853 | 97.625 |
| 14 | 14.947 | 17.086 | 19.599 | 21.015 | 22.551 | 24.215 | 26.019 | 27.975 | 30.095 | 32.393 | 34.883 | 37.581 | 40.505 | 43.672 | 47.103 | 50.818 | 54.841 | 59.196 | 69.010 | 80.496 | 93.926 | 109.61 | 127.91 |
| 15 | 16.097 | 18.599 | 21.579 | 23.276 | 25.129 | 27.152 | 29.361 | 31.772 | 34.405 | 37.280 | 40.417 | 43.842 | 47.580 | 51.659 | 56.110 | 60.965 | 66.261 | 72.035 | 85.192 | 100.82 | 119.35 | 141.30 | 167.29 |
| 16 | 17.258 | 20.157 | 23.657 | 25.672 | 27.888 | 30.324 | 33.003 | 35.950 | 39.190 | 42.753 | 46.672 | 50.980 | 55.717 | 60.925 | 66.649 | 72.939 | 79.850 | 87.442 | 104.93 | 126.01 | 151.38 | 181.87 | 218.47 |
| 17 | 18.430 | 21.762 | 25.840 | 28.213 | 30.840 | 33.750 | 36.974 | 40.545 | 44.501 | 48.884 | 53.739 | 59.118 | 65.075 | 71.673 | 78.979 | 87.068 | 96.022 | 105.93 | 129.02 | 157.25 | 191.73 | 233.79 | 285.01 |
| 18 | 19.615 | 23.414 | 28.132 | 30.906 | 33.999 | 37.450 | 41.301 | 45.599 | 50.396 | 55.750 | 61.725 | 68.394 | 75.836 | 84.141 | 93.406 | 103.74 | 115.27 | 128.12 | 158.40 | 195.99 | 242.59 | 300.25 | 371.52 |
| 19 | 20.811 | 25.117 | 30.539 | 33.760 | 37.379 | 41.446 | 46.019 | 51.159 | 56.939 | 63.440 | 70.749 | 78.969 | 88.212 | 98.603 | 110.28 | 123.41 | 138.17 | 154.74 | 194.25 | 244.03 | 306.66 | 385.32 | 483.97 |
| 20 | 22.019 | 26.870 | 33.066 | 36.786 | 40.996 | 45.762 | 51.160 | 57.275 | 64.203 | 72.052 | 80.947 | 91.025 | 102.44 | 115.38 | 130.03 | 146.63 | 165.42 | 186.69 | 237.99 | 303.60 | 387.39 | 494.21 | 630.16 |
| 21 | 23.239 | 28.676 | 35.719 | 39.993 | 44.865 | 50.423 | 56.765 | 64.003 | 72.265 | 81.699 | 92.470 | 104.77 | 118.81 | 134.84 | 153.14 | 174.02 | 197.85 | 225.03 | 291.35 | 377.46 | 489.11 | 633.59 | 820.21 |
| 22 | 24.472 | 30.537 | 38.505 | 43.392 | 49.006 | 55.457 | 62.873 | 71.403 | 81.214 | 92.503 | 105.49 | 120.44 | 137.63 | 157.41 | 180.17 | 206.35 | 236.44 | 271.03 | 356.44 | 469.06 | 617.28 | 812.00 | 1067.3 |
| 23 | 25.716 | 32.453 | 41.430 | 46.996 | 53.436 | 60.893 | 69.532 | 79.543 | 91.148 | 104.60 | 120.20 | 138.30 | 159.28 | 183.60 | 211.80 | 244.49 | 282.36 | 326.24 | 435.86 | 582.63 | 778.77 | 1040.4 | 1388.5 |
| 24 | 26.973 | 34.426 | 44.502 | 50.815 | 58.177 | 66.765 | 76.790 | 88.497 | 102.17 | 118.16 | 136.83 | 158.66 | 184.17 | 213.98 | 248.81 | 289.49 | 337.01 | 392.48 | 532.75 | 723.46 | 982.25 | 1332.7 | 1806.0 |
| 25 | 28.243 | 36.459 | 47.727 | 54.864 | 63.249 | 73.106 | 84.701 | 98.347 | 114.41 | 133.33 | 155.62 | 181.87 | 212.79 | 249.21 | 292.10 | 342.60 | 402.04 | 471.98 | 650.96 | 898.09 | 1238.6 | 1706.8 | 2348.8 |
| 26 | 29.526 | 38.553 | 51.113 | 59.156 | 68.677 | 79.954 | 93.324 | 109.18 | 128.00 | 150.33 | 176.85 | 208.33 | 245.71 | 290.09 | 342.76 | 405.27 | 479.43 | 567.38 | 795.17 | 1114.6 | 1561.7 | 2185.7 | 3054.4 |
| 27 | 30.821 | 40.710 | 54.669 | 63.706 | 74.484 | 87.351 | 102.72 | 121.10 | 143.08 | 169.37 | 200.84 | 238.50 | 283.57 | 337.50 | 402.03 | 479.22 | 571.52 | 681.85 | 971.10 | 1383.1 | 1968.7 | 2798.7 | 3971.8 |
| 28 | 32.129 | 42.931 | 58.402 | 68.528 | 80.698 | 95.339 | 112.97 | 134.21 | 159.82 | 190.70 | 227.95 | 272.89 | 327.10 | 392.50 | 471.38 | 566.48 | 681.11 | 819.22 | 1185.7 | 1716.1 | 2481.6 | 3583.3 | 5164.3 |
| 29 | 33.450 | 45.219 | 62.323 | 73.640 | 87.347 | 103.97 | 124.14 | 148.63 | 178.40 | 214.58 | 258.58 | 312.09 | 377.17 | 456.30 | 552.51 | 669.45 | 811.52 | 984.07 | 1447.6 | 2129.0 | 3127.8 | 4587.7 | 6714.6 |
| 30 | 34.785 | 47.575 | 66.439 | 79.058 | 94.461 | 113.28 | 136.31 | 164.49 | 199.02 | 241.33 | 293.20 | 356.79 | 434.75 | 530.31 | 647.44 | 790.95 | 966.71 | 1181.9 | 1767.1 | 2640.9 | 3942.0 | 5873.2 | 8730.0 |